English Interpretation of the Meaning of

Qur'an

Final Revelation

Presented to:

_____

finalrevelation.net
Houston, Texas

Qur'an

Published by:
finalrevelation.net
a6h@yahoo.com
P.O. Box – 890071
Houston, TX 77289
281-488-3191

Interpretation of Meaning by: Abdul Hye, PhD

1st Print: July / 2006
2nd Print: December / 2006
3rd Print: December / 2007

Printed in the United States of America

Library of Congress Catalog Card Number: 2006906270

ISBN 9780966819090

Qur'an

Introduction

The Qur'an is the final revelation for the Guidance of mankind from the same Almighty God who sent Abraham, Moses, and Jesus. This Qur'an is translated / interpreted word-for-word from Arabic to English in a simple way so that it can be understood easily by everyone. Any word needed to complete a meaning or to make the interpretation clear is added in parenthesis. It should help the reader to understand clearly. All 25 names of the prophets mentioned in the Qur'an are listed as English names so the reader can find the same name mentioned in previously revealed scriptures. A Prophet tree is provided at the beginning with a list of places, nations, landmarks, etc. for each prophet as references. A map is provided to show the location of each of these places and nations. A brief list of the life events of Prophet Muhammad is given to understand the goals and objectives of his mission. Since he has been sent as the **final Messenger for the entire universe** until the last Day of this world, all of his efforts focused on reaching out to all nations through delegations and letters towards peace for all mankind in this world and the hereafter. He personally traveled 27 expeditions and wrote letters to different kings and rulers of different nations. A list of those places and nations are listed. Besides the Qur'an, all of his sayings with events (Hadith) narrated by his companions during his lifetime and afterwards were preserved and recorded in systematic order so a reader can find the detailed reference / reason in Hadith for any particular revelation in the Qur'an which was revealed during 23 years. Two copies of the originally compiled Qur'an are still preserved in Tashkent, Uzbekistan and Istanbul, Turkey. Today's Arabic Qur'an is the same as the one originally compiled.

All this information will help the reader understand the continuation of the religion of Abraham through Moses, Jesus and finally through Muhammad, who has been sent with this **Qur'an** to deliver the final version of the religion of Allah to mankind, **Islam**.

Abdul Hye, PhD
finalrevelation.net
December 1, 2007

Table of Contents

#	Chapter Name	Chapter Name Meaning	# Verses	Revealed @	Page #
1	Al-Fatihah	The Opening	7	Makkah	31
2	Al-Baqarah	The Cow	286	Madinah	31
3	Al-'Imran	The family of Imran	200	Madinah	53
4	An-Nisa'	The Woman	176	Madinah	65
5	Al-Ma'idah	The Table Spread	120	Madinah	79
6	Al-An'am	The Cattle	165	Makkah	89
7	Al-A'raf	The Heights	206	Makkah	100
8	Al-Anfal	The Spoils of War	75	Madinah	113
9	At-Taubah	The Repentance	129	Madinah	118
10	Yunus	Jonah	109	Makkah	127
11	Hud	Hud	123	Makkah	134
12	Yusuf	Joseph	111	Madinah	141
13	Ar-Ra'd	The Thunder	43	Madinah	148
14	Ibrahim	Abraham	52	Makkah	151
15	Al-Hijr	The Rock Tract	99	Makkah	155
16	An-Nahl	The Bee	128	Makkah	158
17	Al-Isra'	The Night Journey	111	Makkah	165
18	Al-Kahf	The Cave	110	Makkah	171
19	Maryam	Mary	98	Makkah	178
20	Ta-Ha	Ta-Ha	135	Makkah	182
21	Al-Anbiya'	The Prophets	112	Makkah	188
22	Al-Hajj	The Pilgrimage	78	Madinah	193
23	Al-Muminun	The Believers	118	Makkah	198
24	An-Nur	The Light	64	Madinah	203
25	Al-Furqan	The Criterion	77	Makkah	207
26	Ash-Shuara'	The Poets	227	Makkah	211
27	An-Naml	The Ant	93	Makkah	218
28	Al-Qasas	The Narration	88	Makkah	222
29	Al-Ankabut	The Spider	69	Makkah	228
30	Ar-Rum	The Romans	60	Makkah	232
31	Luqman	Luqman	34	Makkah	235

32	As-Sajdah	The Prostration	30	Makkah	237
33	Al-Ahzab	The Confederates	73	Madinah	239
34	Saba'	Sheba	54	Makkah	244
35	Fatir	The Originator of Creation	45	Makkah	247
36	Ya-Seen	Ya-Seen	83	Makkah	250
37	As-Saffat	Those who set the Ranks	182	Makkah	254
38	Sad	Sad	88	Makkah	258
39	Az-Zumar	The Groups	75	Makkah	262
40	Ghafir	The Forgiver	85	Makkah	266
41	Fussilat	The Detailed Explanation	54	Makkah	271
42	Ash-Shura	The Consultation	53	Makkah	274
43	Az-Zukhruf	The Gold Adornments	89	Makkah	278
44	Ad-Dukhan	The Smoke	59	Makkah	282
45	Al-Jathiyah	The Kneeling	37	Makkah	284
46	Al-Ahqaf	The Curved Sand-Hills	35	Makkah	286
47	Muhammad	Muhammad	38	Madinah	288
48	Al-Fath	The Victory	29	Madinah	291
49	Al-Hujurat	The Private Apartments	18	Madinah	293
50	Qaf	Qaf	45	Makkah	294
51	Adh-Dhariyat	The Winds that Scatter	60	Makkah	296
52	At-Tur	The Mount Tur	49	Makkah	298
53	An-Najm	The Star	62	Makkah	300
54	Al-Qamar	The Moon	55	Makkah	302
55	Ar-Rahman	The Gracious	78	Madinah	304
56	Al-Waqi'ah	The Event	96	Makkah	306
57	Al-Hadid	The Iron	29	Madinah	308
58	Al-Mujadilah	The Woman who Disputes	22	Madinah	310
59	Al-Hashr	The Gathering	24	Madinah	312
60	Al-Mumtahanah	The Woman to be Examined	13	Madinah	314
61	As-Saff	The Rank	14	Madinah	315
62	Al-Jumu'ah	The Congregation	11	Madinah	316
63	Al-Munafiqun	The Hypocrites	11	Madinah	317
64	At-Taghabun	The Mutual Loss and Gain	18	Madinah	318
65	At-Talaq	The Divorce	12	Madinah	319
66	At-Tahrim	The Prohibition	12	Madinah	320
67	Al-Mulk	The Sovereignty	30	Makkah	321
68	Al-Qalam	The Pen	52	Makkah	323
69	Al-Haqqah	The Inevitable	52	Makkah	324
70	Al-Ma'arij	The Ways of Ascent	44	Makkah	326
71	Nuh	Noah	28	Makkah	327
72	Al-Jinn	The Jinn	28	Makkah	328
73	Al-Muzzammil	The one wrapped in Garments	20	Makkah	329
74	Al-Muddaththir	The one Enveloped	56	Makkah	330
75	Al-Qiyamah	The Resurrection	40	Makkah	332
76	Ad-Dahr	The Time	31	Madinah	333
77	Al-Mursalat	Those sent forth	50	Makkah	334

78	An-Naba'	The Great News	40	Makkah	335
79	An-Nazi'at	Those who Pull Out	46	Makkah	336
80	'Abasa	He Frowned	42	Makkah	337
81	At-Takwir	The Overthroughing	29	Makkah	338
82	Al-Infitar	The Cleaving	19	Makkah	339
83	Al-Mutaffifin	Those who deal in Fraud	36	Makkah	339
84	Al-Inshiqaq	The Splitting Asunder	25	Makkah	340
85	Al-Buruj	The Big Stars 'Buruj'	22	Makkah	341
86	At-Tariq	The Night-Comer	17	Makkah	342
87	Al-A'la	The High	19	Makkah	342
88	Al-Ghashiyah	The Overwhelming	26	Makkah	343
89	Al-Fajr	The Dawn	30	Makkah	343
90	Al-Balad	The City	20	Makkah	344
91	Ash-Shams	The Sun	15	Makkah	344
92	Al-Lail	The Night	21	Makkah	345
93	Ad-Duha	The Forenoon	11	Makkah	345
94	Ash-Sharh	The Opening Forth	8	Makkah	346
95	At-Tin	The Fig	8	Makkah	346
96	Al-'Alaq	The Clot	19	Makkah	346
97	Al-Qadr	The Night of Decree	5	Makkah	347
98	Al-Bayyinah	The Clear Evidence	8	Madinah	347
99	Az-Zalzalah	The Earthquake	8	Madinah	347
100	Al-'Adiyat	Those that Run	11	Makkah	348
101	Al-Qari'ah	The Striking Hour	11	Makkah	348
102	At-Takathur	The Piling Up	8	Makkah	348
103	Al-'Asr	The Time	3	Makkah	348
104	Al-Humazah	The Slanderer	9	Makkah	349
105	Al-Fil	The Elephant	5	Makkah	349
106	Quraish	Quraish	4	Makkah	349
107	Al-Ma'un	The Small Kindness	7	Makkah	349
108	Al-Kauther	A River in Paradise	3	Makkah	349
109	Al-Kafirun	The Disbelievers	6	Makkah	350
110	An-Nasr	The Help	3	Madinah	350
111	Al-Masad	The Palm Fiber	5	Makkah	350
112	Al-Ikhlas	The Purity	4	Makkah	350
113	Al-Falaq	The Daybreak	5	Makkah	350
114	An-Nas	The Mankind	6	Makkah	350
	Total		6,236		

Foreword

Dr. Zakir Naik

President, Islamic Research Foundation

Islam is an Arabic word. It comes from the word 'Salm' which means peace and from the word 'Silm', which means submitting your will to Allah – the Almighty God. Thus, Islam means peace acquired by submitting your will to Allah. A Muslim is a person who submits his/her will to Allah -the Almighty God.

Many people have a misconception that Islam is a new religion that was formulated about 1400 years ago, and that Prophet Muhammad was the founder of Islam. However, Islam is not the name of some unique religion presented for the first time by Prophet Muhammad. Prophet Muhammad was not the founder of Islam but he was the last and final messenger of Allah sent to earth. Almighty God revived through him the same genuine faith, which had been conveyed by all His previous Prophets.

The Qur'an states that Islam - the complete submission of man before his only Unique Creator - is the only faith and way of life consistently revealed by God to humankind from the very beginning. Noah, Abraham, Isaac, David, Solomon, Moses, and Jesus - prophets who appeared at different times and places - all propagated the same faith and conveyed the same message of *Tawheed* (Oneness of Allah), *Risalat* (prophet hood) and *Aakhirah* (the Hereafter). These prophets of God were not founders of different religions to be named after them. They were each repeating the message and faith of their predecessors.

Islam thus makes it an article of faith to believe in all the earlier prophets, starting with Adam, and continuing with Noah, Abraham, Ishmael, Isaac, Jacob, Moses, David and Jesus amongst many others. However, Muhammad was the last Prophet of God conveying the same message as all earlier prophets. This original message had been corrupted and it split into various religions' by people of different ages, who indulged in interpolations and admixture. God eliminated these alien elements, and Islam - in its pure and original form - was transmitted to humankind through Prophet Muhammad. Hence, Islam is the culmination of the same Divine religion of God to humankind since the advent of humanity, purged and purified, from all human adulterations and restored to its original purity.

Since there was to be no messenger after Prophet Muhammad, the Book revealed to him (i.e. the Qur'an) was preserved word for word so that it should be the same source of guidance for all times. Thus the religion of all the prophets was 'total submission to Allah's will' and one word for that in the Arabic language is 'Islam'. Abraham and Jesus too were Muslims, as Allah testifies in the Qur'an 3:67 and 3:52 respectively. "Surely, We have sent you with the truth, as a bearer of happy news, and as a Warner: And there were never any people, without a Warner who did not live among them (in the past)" [35.24]. "And the messengers We have already told you before, and others We have not (told you)." [4.164]

It means that some of the Prophets have been mentioned by name in the Qur'an while of the others there is no mention. 25 messengers are specifically mentioned in the Qur'an. One of the followers of the Prophet Muhammad named Abu Dhar asked: 'O Messenger of Allah, altogether how many messengers were sent?' The Prophet said, '124,000'." [Mishkat-Ul-Masabih, authenticated by Shaikh Nasiruddun Albani, vol. 3, pg. No. 1599, Hadith no. 5737] [Hadith: recorded traditions, sayings and actions of the Prophet]. However, all the messengers that came before the last and final messenger Prophet Muhammad came with a message that was meant only for a particular period of time. For example, the Qur'an says, "And (We appointed Jesus) a messenger to the Children of Israel:" [3.49]

Jesus came as a messenger only to the children of Israel. A similar message is given in the Bible where Jesus says, "I am not sent but unto the lost sheep of the house of Israel." [Gospel of Matthew 15:24]. Jesus further says in the Bible, "Go not into the way of the Gentiles, and into any city of the Samaritans enter ye not: but go rather to the lost sheep of the house of Israel." [Gospel of Matthew 10:5-6]. So Jesus was sent only for the Jews and not for the whole of humanity.

However, Prophet Muhammad was not sent only for the Muslims or only for the Arabs, but for the entire humankind. The Qur'an says, "And We did not send you (O Prophet), except as a mercy to all worlds." [21.107]. "And We have not sent you (O Muhammad) except as one to give them good news, and to warn them (of the punishment; As a messenger and a guide to mankind), but most men do not understand." [34.28]. The religion of all the prophets was 'total submission to Creator's Will' and the one word for that in the Arabic language is 'Islam'; and the person who does that is a 'Muslim'.

Allah says in the Qur'an that Abraham was a Muslim. "Ibrahim (Abraham) was neither a Jew nor even a Christian; but he was true in Faith, and surrendered his will to Allah's, (like a Muslim) and he did not join gods with Allah." [3.67]. It is mentioned in the Qur'an that Jesus was a Muslim [3.52]. Jesus also says in the Bible. "I seek not my own will, but the will of the Father which hath sent me." [Gospel of John 5:30]. And anybody who seeks the Will of Allah is referred to as a Muslim.

Islam is the first religion and the only religion, which is acceptable in the sight of God. Therefore Allah says: "If anyone desires a religion other than Islam (submission to Allah), it will never be accepted from him; in the Hereafter, he will be with those who have lost (all spiritual reward)." [3.85]. Allah has sent a revelation in every age. Allah says in the Qur'an, "Allah permitted (or ordered, for) each period is a Book (revealed)." [13.38]

There are several revelations sent by Allah in different ages for the guidance of human beings of the respective ages. Only 4 revelations are mentioned by name in the Qur'an. These are the Torah, Zabur, Injeel and the Qur'an. Torah is the revelation that was revealed to Prophet Moses. Zabur is the revelation that was revealed to Prophet David. Injeel is the revelation which was revealed to Prophet Jesus and the Qur'an is the last and the final revelation, that was revealed to the Last and Final Messenger Prophet Muhammad.

The Arabic word 'Qur'an' comes from the root word 'qara'a' or 'qa-ra-a', which means to read, to recite, and to proclaim. The Qur'an is a collection to be read or to be recited. Since there was to be no messenger after Muhammad, the book revealed to him (i.e., the Qur'an) was preserved word for word so that it should be a source of Divine Guidance for all times. Each of the revelations, prior to the revelation of the Qur'an, was meant only for a particular period and for a particular group of people.

As the Qur'an was the last and final revelation of Almighty Allah, it was revealed not just for Muslims or Arabs but it was revealed for the whole of humankind. Further, the Qur'an was not revealed only for the era of the Prophet but it was revealed for all of humankind until the Last Day. Allah says in the Qur'an,

"...A Book (the Qur'an) which We have revealed to you, (O Prophet!) so that you may lead mankind from the depths of darkness into Light- by the permission of their Lord- to the Path (towards Him), the Exalted in Power, the (One) Worthy of all Praise" [14.1]. "The month of Ramadan is the (month) in which was sent down the Qur'an as a guide to mankind, also Clear (Signs for) guidance and judgment (between right and wrong)" [2.185]

Islam and Universal Brotherhood

There are various types of brotherhoods - brotherhood based on blood relations, brotherhood based on regional affiliations, or brotherhood on the basis of race, caste, creed, ideology, etc. But all these types of brotherhood are limited in their scope, coverage and benefits.

Islam, on the other hand, prescribes Universal Brotherhood. It rejects the thought that human beings have been created in castes or in different levels. In chapter The Inner Apartments (of the Prophet) - Al-Hujurat [49:13], Allah describes the Islamic concept of Universal Brotherhood. "O mankind! We have created you from a single (pair) of male and female, and made you into nations and tribes so that you may know one another (not that you may hate each other). Surely, the most honorable of you, in the Sight of Allah is (he, who is) the most righteous of you. Verily, Allah is All Knowing and is Well-Aware (of all things)." This verse of the Qur'an indicates that the entire human race originated from a single pair of male and female. All humans have common great-grandparents and ancestors.

Allah says that he has made nations and tribes, so that humans can recognize each other, and not so that they may despise each other and fight amongst themselves. This verse also clarifies that the criteria for judgment in the sight of Allah does not depend on caste, color, creed, gender or wealth, but on Taqwa i.e. Allah's consciousness, piety and righteousness. Anyone who is righteous, pious and God-conscious is honored in the sight of Allah.

Further it is stated in chapter The Romans - Ar-Rum [30.22], that, "And among His Signs is the creation of the heavens and the earth, and the difference in your languages, and your colors. Surely, there are signs in this for those who know." These variations in color and language are not for the purpose of creating animosity or differences between groups of humans. Every language on earth has its own beauty and significance. A foreign language may sound strange and funny to you, but it sounds sweet to those who speak it. Allah says in chapter The Night Journey - Al-Isra [17.70], "We have honored the children of Adam." Allah has not honored only Arabs or Americans or any particular race uniquely. He states that He has honored all the children of Adam, irrespective of race, caste, color, creed or gender.

While there are some religions that believe that humankind originated from a single pair - Adam and Eve, there are some faiths that say that it is because of the sin of the woman (Eve) that the humans are born in sin. They blame only the woman, who is Eve, for the downfall of human beings. The Qur'an speaks about the story of Adam and Eve in several chapters, but in all the places, the blame is placed equally on both - Adam and Eve. According to chapter The Heights - Al-A'raf [7.19-27], both of them disobeyed Allah, both of them repented, and both were forgiven. Both are equally blamed for the mistake. There is not a single verse in the Qur'an which puts the blame only on Eve. In chapter Ta Ha (Qur'anic letters) - Taha [20.121], it is stated that Adam disobeyed Allah. Certain faiths on the other hand state that because Eve disobeyed God, she is responsible for the 'sin of humankind'. Hence, God cursed the woman, and said that she will bear labor pains. This implies that pregnancy is a curse.

Islam of course does not support this unjust perspective. In chapter The Women *An-Nisa* [4.1], Allah states, "And revere (and respect) the wombs (that bore you):" In Islam, pregnancy does not degrade a woman. On the contrary, it elevates the status of a woman. In chapter The Wise (or the person Luqman) *Luqman* [31.14], it is stated that, "And We have commanded man (to be good) to his parents: In weakness and hardship his mother bore him, and in two years (after) was his weaning:" The Qur'an says in chapter The Winding Sand Tracts - *Al-Ahqaf* [46.15], " And We have commanded that it is essential for man to be kind to his parents: In pain did his mother bear him, and in pain did she give him birth."

Islam states that men and women are created equal. The foundation of an Islamic society is justice and equity. Allah has created men and women as equal, but with different capabilities and different responsibilities. Men and women are different, physiologically and psychologically. Their roles and responsibilities are different. Men and women are equal in Islam, but not identical.

According to a Hadith mentioned in Sahih Bukhari, vol. no. 8, in the Book of Adab, chapter 2, Hadith no.2. "A person came to Prophet Mohammed, and asked him, 'Who is the person who deserves the maximum love and companionship in this world?' The Prophet replied, 'Your mother.' The man asked, 'Who next?' The Prophet said, 'Your mother.' The man asked, 'After that who?' The Prophet repeated for the 3rd time, 'Your mother.' The man asked, 'After that who?' Then the Prophet said, 'Your father.'"

So, 75% or 3/4 of the love and companionship of the children are due to the mother and only 25% or 1/4 of the love and companionship goes to the father. In other words, the mother gets the gold medal; she gets the silver medal, as well as the bronze medal. The father has to be satisfied with a mere consolation prize.

Amongst the teachings of Islam, it is stated that men and women are equal - but being equal does not mean that both are identical. There are many misconceptions about the status of women in Islam. Such misconceptions can be removed if one studies the authentic sources of knowledge of Islam and their teachings - the Qur'an and the Sahih Hadith. Let's take an example. In a class, two students – student A and B get the highest marks in a subject, say 80 out of 100. The question paper consisted of 10 questions, each of 10 marks. In the first answer student A gets 9 out of 10, student B gets 7 out of 10. So in question 1, student A has a degree of advantage than student B. In question 2, student B gets 9 out of 10, and student A gets 7 out of 10. So in question 2, student B has a degree of advantage than student A. In the remaining 8 questions, both get 8 out of 10, and if you total the marks of both students, both get 80 out of 100. So if you analyze, both student A and B have got over all equal marks. But in answers to some questions, student A has a degree of advantage and in answers to some other questions, student B has a degree of advantage - but in terms of overall marks, both are equal. Similarly, in Islam, men and women are equal.

As another example, if a robber enters my house, I will not say, 'I believe in women's rights, and I believe in women's liberation and therefore my sister, my wife or my mother should go and fight the robber.' Allah says in chapter The Women - *An-Nisa* [4.34], "Allah has given the one more (strength) than the other." Normally, men have more strength than the women. So where strength is concerned, men have a degree of advantage. Since they have been given more strength, it is their duty to protect women. Where love and companionship from children is concerned, the mother gets 3 times more love and companionship than the father. Here women have a degree of advantage.

Brotherhood in Islam does not only mean that the same sexes are equal. 'Universal Brotherhood' in Islam means that besides race, caste, and creed, even the sexes are overall equal. Men and women are equal in Islam, but in some aspects, men have a degree of advantage while in some other aspects, women have a degree of advantage - but overall both are equal.

The Miracle of Prophet Muhammad: Qur'an, for all Times

The miracles performed by the previous prophets such as parting of sea by Prophet Moses, giving life to the dead by Prophet Jesus, etc. convinced the people of that time but these miracles cannot be analyzed and verified by us today. Prophet Muhammad is the last and final Messenger of God, sent for the whole of humankind and the message he delivered is for eternity. Therefore, the miracle of the last and final Messenger should also be everlasting, examinable and verifiable by people of all ages. While Prophet Muhammad performed several miracles as are mentioned in the Hadith, he never emphasized them. Though we Muslims believe in these miracles we only boast of the ultimate miracle given to him by Almighty God, which is the Qur'an. The Qur'an is the miracle of all times which proved itself to be a miracle 1400 years ago and which can be reconfirmed today and forever. In short, it is the Miracle of Miracles.

Logical Concept of God

The first question to the atheist is: "What is the definition of God?" For a person to say there is no God, he should know what the meaning of God is. Suppose I hold a book and say 'this is a pen'. The opposite person should know the definition of a pen for him to refute and say that it is not a pen. In a similar manner, for an atheist to say 'there is no god', he should at least know the concept of God. His concept of God is derived from the surroundings in which he lives or has been brought up. The deity that people worship has human qualities and hence he does not believe in such a god. Similarly, a Muslim too does not believe in such false gods.

Concept of God according to Chapter: The Purity of Faith - Al-Ikhlas

The best definition, of Almighty God, that you can find in the Qur'an is in the 4 verses of chapter The Purity of Faith - *Al-Ikhlas* [112]

112.1. Say (O Muhammad): "He is Allah, The One (Ahad; and Only One).
112.2. Allah the Eternal (Samad, the Ever Enduring), The Absolute (and Alone);
112.3. He begets not (has no descendents, no children, none), Nor was He (ever) begotten;
112.4. And there is none like (or comparable) unto Him."

This is a 4-line statement about Almighty Allah according to Qur'an. If any candidate claims to be God and satisfies this definition, Muslims have no objection in accepting such a candidate as god. This chapter The purity of Faith - *Al-Ikhlas* is the acid test - it is the '*Furqan*' or the criteria to judge between the One True God and the false claimants to divinity. Whichever deity that any human being on the face of this earth worships - if that deity fulfils these 4 criteria then such a deity is none else than the one true God.

a. It is the Touchstone of Theology

The chapter The Purity of Faith - *Al-Ikhlas* [112] is the touchstone of Theology. 'Theo' in Greek means God and 'logy' means study. Thus 'Theology' means 'study of God' and chapter The Purity of Faith - *Al-Ikhlas* is the touchstone of the study of God.

If you want to purchase or sell your gold jewelry, you would first evaluate it. A goldsmith with the help of a touchstone does such an evaluation of gold jewelry. He rubs the gold jewelry on the touchstone and compares its color with rubbing samples of gold. If it matches with 24 Karat gold, he will say that your jewelry is 24 Karat pure gold. If it is not high quality pure gold, he will tell you its value -whether it is 22 Karats, 18 Karats or it may not be gold at all. It may be fake because everything that glitters is not gold.

Similarly chapter The Purity of Faith - *Al-Ikhlas* [112] is the touchstone of theology, which can verify whether the deity that you worship is a true God or a false God. If anyone claims to be, or is believed to be Almighty God, and satisfies this 4-line definition, then not only will Muslims readily accept that deity as God but this deity is worthy of all worship and is the One True God. For example, if some one says that Bhagwan Rajneesh or 'Osho' is Almighty God, lets apply the test.

b. Is Rajneesh God?

Let us put this candidate Rajneesh to the test of Divinity as prescribed by chapter The Purity of Faith - *Al-Ikhlas* [112], the touchstone of Divinity.

(i) The 1st criterion is "Say, 'He is Allah One and Only'". Is Rajneesh One and Only? We know several such fake god-men and claimants of divinity amongst humans. Rajneesh is surely not the one and only. However, some disciples of Rajneesh may still state that Rajneesh is unique and that he is the one and only.

(ii) Let us analyze the 2nd criterion "Allah the Absolute and Eternal." Is Rajneesh absolute and eternal? We know from his biography that he suffered from diabetes, asthma, and chronic backache. He alleged that the US government gave him slow poison while he was in their jail. Imagine! Almighty God being poisoned! Moreover, all are aware that Rajneesh died and was cremated / buried. So Rajneesh was neither eternal, nor absolute.

(iii) The 3rd criteria is "He begets not, nor is begotten". However, Rajneesh was begotten. He was born in Jabalpur in India. Like all humans, he too had a mother and a father. Later on they chose to become his disciples. Rajneesh was a very intelligent person. In May 1981 he went to USA. He established a town in Oregon and named it 'Rajneeshpuram'. It seems that he took America for a ride since the US government arrested him and later deported him out of America in 1985. So Rajneesh returned to India and started a 'Raineesh Neosanyas commune in Pune in India which was later renamed the 'Osho commune'. If you visit this 'Osho commune' in Pune, you will find it written on his tombstone, "Osho - never born, never died, only visited the planet earth between 11 December 1931 to 19 January 1990". They conveniently forget to mention on this tombstone that Rajneesh was not given a visa for 21 different countries of the world. Imagine Almighty God visiting the earth and requiring a visa! The Arch Bishop of Greece had said that if Rajneesh was not deported they would burn his house and those of his disciples.

(iv) The 4th test is so stringent that none besides the One True God, Allah can pass it. "There is none like Him." The moment you can imagine or compare the candidate or claimant to godhood to anything, this candidate is not god. Neither can you have a mental picture of God. We know that Rajneesh was a human being. He had one head, 2 hands, 2 feet, and a white flowing beard. The moment you can think or imagine what the claimant to godhood is, he or she is not god.

The Name Allah preferred to the word 'God'

The Muslims prefer calling Allah with His Name Allah, instead of the English word 'God'. The Arabic word Allah is pure and unique, unlike the English word God that can be manipulated. If you add 's' to God, it becomes 'gods' that is plural of God. Allah is one and singular, there is no plural of Allah. If you add 'dess' to God, it becomes 'goddess' that is a female God. There is nothing like male Allah or female Allah. Allah has no gender. If you add father to God, it becomes 'godfather'. "He is my Godfather," means, "he is my guardian". There is nothing like' Allah Abba' or 'Allah father' in Islam. If you add mother to God it becomes 'godmother', there is nothing like 'Allah Ammi' or 'Allah Mother' in Islam. If you put tin before God, it becomes tin-god i.e. a fake God, there is nothing like 'tin Allah' or 'fake Allah' in Islam. Allah is a unique word, which does not conjure up any mental picture nor can it be played around with. Hence, the Muslims prefer the name Allah when referring to the Almighty Creator. However, sometimes while speaking to non-Muslims we may have to use the inappropriate word God for Allah as has been used in these pages.

Qur'an and Modern Science

These methods of proving the existence of God to an atheist may satisfy some but not all. Many atheists demand a scientific proof for the existence of God. We agree that today is the age of science and technology. Let us use scientific knowledge to prove the existence of God and simultaneously also prove that the Qur'an is a revelation of God.

Some Scientific Facts Mentioned in the Qur'an

1. Creation of the Universe. 'The Big Bang'

Astrophysicists in a widely accepted phenomenon, popularly known as the 'Big Bang', explain the creation of the universe. It is supported by observational and experimental data gathered by astronomers and astrophysicists for decades. According to the 'Big Bang', the whole universe was initially one big mass (primary Nebula). Then there was a 'Big Bang' (secondary separation), which resulted in the formation of Galaxies. These then divided to form stars, planets, the sun, the moon, etc. The origin of the universe was unique and the probability of it occurring by 'chance' is zero. The Qur'an contains the following verse, regarding the origin of the universe. "Do the disbelievers not see that the heavens and the earth were joined together (as one), before We tore them apart?" [21.30]. The striking congruence between the Qur'anic verse and the 'Big Bang' is inescapable! How could a book, which first appeared in the deserts of Arabia 1400 years ago, contain this profound scientific truth?

2. Shape of the Earth

In early times, people believed that the earth is flat. For centuries, men were afraid to venture out too far, lest they should falloff the edge. Sir Francis Drake was the first person who proved that the earth is spherical when he sailed around it in 1577.

Consider the following Qur'anic verse regarding the alternation of day and night. "Do you not see that Allah blends the night into day and He blends the day into night?" [31.29]. Merging here means that the night slowly and gradually changes to day and vice versa. This phenomenon can only take place if the earth is spherical. If the earth were flat, there would have been a sudden change from night to day and from day to night. The earth is not exactly round like a ball, but geospherical i.e. it is flattened at the poles. The following verse contains a description of the earth's shape. "And more, He has extended the earth (far and wide or also in the shape of an egg)" [79.30]. The Arabic word for egg here is 'dahaha', which means an ostrich-egg. The shape of an ostrich-egg resembles the geo-spherical shape of the earth. Thus, the Qur'an correctly describes the shape of the earth, though the prevalent notion when the Qur'an was revealed was that the earth is flat.

3. The light of the moon is reflected light

It was believed by earlier civilizations that the moon emanates its own light. Science now tells us that the light of the moon is reflected light. However, this fact was mentioned in the Qur'an, 1400 years ago in this verse: "He is the blessed (One) Who made groups of stars in the skies, and placed a Lamp in there and a Moon giving light;" [25.61]. The Arabic word for the sun in the Qur'an is 'shams'. It is referred to as 'siraj', which means a 'torch', or as 'wahhaj', which means a 'blazing lamp', or as 'diya', which means a 'shining glory'. All 3 descriptions are appropriate to the sun, since it generates intense heat and light by its internal combustion. The Arabic word for the moon is 'qamar' and it is described in the Qur'an as 'muneer', which is a body that gives 'nur' i.e. light. Again, the Qur'anic description matches perfectly with the true nature of the moon, which does not give off light itself and is an inert body that reflects the light of the sun. Not once in the Qur'an, is the moon mentioned as 'siraj', 'wahhaj' or 'diya' or the sun as 'nur' or 'muneer'. This implies that the Qur'an recognizes the difference between the nature of sunlight and moonlight.

4. The sun rotates

In 1609, the German scientist Yohannus Keppler published the 'Astronomia Nova'. In this he concluded that not only do the planets move in elliptical orbits around the sun, they also rotate upon their axes at irregular speeds. With this knowledge, it became possible for European scientists to explain correctly many of the mechanisms of the solar system including the sequence of night and day. After these discoveries, it was thought that the sun was stationary and did not rotate about its axis like the earth.

Consider the following Qur'anic verse: "And it is He Who created the night and the day, and the sun and the moon: All (the heavenly bodies) go along, each in its rounded path." [21.33]

The Arabic word used in the above verse is 'yasbahun'. The word 'yasbahun' is derived from the word 'sabaha'. It carries with it the idea of motion that comes from any moving body. If you use the word for a man on the ground, it would not mean that he is rolling but would mean he is walking or running. If you use the word for a man in water, it would not mean that he is floating but would mean that he is swimming. Similarly, if you use the word 'yasbah' for a celestial body such as the sun, it would not mean that it is only flying through space but would mean that it is also rotating as it goes through space. Most of the school textbooks have incorporated the fact that the sun rotates about its axis. The rotation of the sun about its own axis can be proved with the help of an equipment that projects the image of the sun on the table top so that one can examine the image of the sun without being blinded. It is noticed that the sun has spots, which complete a circular motion once every 25 days i.e. the sun takes approximately 25 days to rotate around its axis. In fact, the sun travels through space at roughly 150 miles per second, and takes about 200 million years to complete one revolution around the center of our Milky Way Galaxy. One cannot help but be amazed at the scientific accuracy of the Qur'anic verses. Should we not ponder over the question, "What was the source of knowledge contained in the Qur'an?"

5. Every living thing is made of water

Consider the following Qur'anic verse. "We made every living thing from water. Then, will they not believe?" [21.30]. Only after the advancement of science, do we now know that cytoplasm, the basic substance of the cell is made up of 80% water. Modem research has also revealed that most organisms consist of 50% to 90% water and that every living entity requires water for its existence.

Was it possible 14 centuries ago for any human being to guess that every living being was made of water? Moreover, would such a guess be conceivable by a human being in the deserts of Arabia where there has always been a scarcity of water?

6. Everything made in pairs

Allah says in the Qur'an, "Glory to Allah, Who created all the things in pairs that the earth produces, and also their own kind (also created in pairs) and (other) things about whom they do not know." [36.36]. The Qur'an here says that everything is created in pairs, including things that the humans do not know at present and may discover later.

7. Man is created from Alaq - A leech-like substance

A few years ago a group of Arabs collected all information concerning embryology from the Qur'an, and presented to Professor Keith Moore, PhD, who was the Professor of Embryology and Chairman of the Department of Anatomy at the University of Toronto, in Canada. At present, he is one of the highest authorities in the field of Embryology.

Dr. Moore said that most of the information concerning embryology mentioned in the Qur'an is in perfect conformity with modem discoveries in the field of embryology and does not conflict with them in any way. He added that there were however a few verses, on whose scientific accuracy he could not comment. He could not say whether the statements were true or false, since he himself was not aware of the information contained therein. There was also no mention of this information in modem writings and studies on embryology.

One such verse is: "Proclaim! (And read aloud!) In the Name of the Lord and Cherisher, Who created. Created man, out of a (mere) clot of thickened blood" [96.1-2]. The word 'alaq' besides meaning a congealed clot of blood also means something that clings, a leech-like substance. Dr. Keith Moore had no knowledge whether an embryo in the initial stages appears like a leech. To check this out he studied the initial stage of the embryo under a very powerful microscope in his laboratory and compared what he observed with a diagram of a leech and he was astonished at the striking resemblance between the two!

Dr. Keith Moore had earlier authored the book, 'The Developing Human'. After acquiring new knowledge from the Qur'an, he wrote in 1982, the 3rd edition of the same book, 'The Developing Human'. The book was the recipient of an award for the best medical book written by a single author. This book has been translated into several major languages of the world and is used as a textbook of embryology in the first year of medical studies.

In 1981, during the 7th Medical Conference in Dammam, Saudi Arabia, Dr. Moore said, "It has been a great pleasure for me to help clarify statements in the Qur'an about human development. It is clear to me that these statements must have come to Muhammad from God or Allah, because almost all of this knowledge was not discovered until many centuries later. This proves to me that Muhammad must have been a messenger of God or Allah."

8. Fingerprints

"Does man think that We cannot assemble his bones together? Yes! We are able to put together the very tips of his fingers perfectly." [75.3-4]. The disbelievers argue regarding resurrection taking place after bones of dead people have disintegrated in the earth and how each individual would be identified on the Day of Judgment. Almighty Allah answers that He can not only assemble our bones but can also reconstruct perfectly our very fingertips.

Why does the Qur'an, while speaking about determination of the identity of the individual, speak specifically about fingertips? In 1880, fingerprinting became the scientific method of identification, after research done by Sir Francis Golt. No two persons in the world can ever have exactly the same fingerprint pattern. That is the reason why police forces worldwide use fingerprints to identify the criminal. 1400 years ago, who could have known the uniqueness of each human's fingerprint? Surely it could have been none other than the Creator Himself!

9. Pain receptors present in the skin

It was thought that the sense of feeling and pain was only dependent on the brain. Recent discoveries prove that there are pain receptors present in the skin without which a person would not be able to feel pain. When a doctor examines a patient suffering from bum injuries, he verifies the degree of bums by a pinprick. If the patient feels pain, the doctor is happy, because it indicates that the bums are superficial and the pain receptors are intact. On the other hand if the patient does not feel any pain, it indicates that it is a deep bum and the pain receptors have been destroyed.

The Qur'an gives an indication of the existence of pain receptors in this verse. "Surely, those who reject Our Signs, We shall soon throw (them) into the Fire: As often as their skins are roasted through, We shall change them for fresh skins, that they may taste the penalty: Truly, Allah is Almighty, All-Wise." [4.56]

Prof. Tagatat Tejasen, Chairman of the Department of Anatomy at Chiang Mai University in Thailand, has spent a great amount of time on research of pain receptors. Initially he could not believe that the Qur'an mentioned this scientific fact 1,400 years ago. He later verified the translation of this particular Qur'anic verse. Prof. Tejasen was so impressed by the scientific accuracy of the Qur'anic verse that at the 8th Saudi Medical Conference held in Riyadh on the Scientific Signs of Qur'an and Sunnah, he proclaimed in public. "There is no God but Allah and Muhammad is His Messenger."

Theory of Mathematical Probability

In mathematics, there is a theory known as 'Theory of Probability'. If you have 2 options out of which one is right and one is wrong, the chances that you will choose the right one is half i.e. one out of the 2 will be correct. You have 50% chances of being correct, similarly if you toss a coin, the chances that your guess will be correct is 50% (1 out of 2) i.e. 1/2. If you toss a coin the second time, the chances that you will be correct in the 2nd toss is again 50% i.e. 1/2. But the chances that you will be correct in both the tosses are half x half (1/2 x 1/2), which is equal to 1/4. i.e. 50% of 50% i.e. equal to 25%. If you toss a coin the 3rd time, chances that you will be correct all 3 times is (1/2 x 1/2 x 1/2) that is 1/8 or 50% of 50% of 50% that is 12.5%.

A dice has got 6 sides. If you throw a dice and guess any number between 1 and 6, the chances that your guess will be correct are 1/6. If you throw the dice the 2nd time, the chances that your guess will be correct in both the throws is (1/6 x 1/6) which is equal to 1/36. If you throw the dice the 3rd time, the chances that all your 3 guesses are correct is (1/6 x 1/6 x 1/6) is equal to 1/216 that is less than 1/2 a percent.

Let us apply this theory of probability to the Qur'an and assume that a person has guessed all the information that is mentioned in the Qur'an, which was unknown at that time. Let us discuss the probability of all the guesses being correct. At the time when the Qur'an was revealed, people thought the world was flat. There are several other options for the shape of the earth. It could be triangular; it could be quadrangular, pentagonal, hexagonal, heptagonal, octagonal, spherical, etc. Let's assume there are about 30 different options for the shape of the earth. The Qur'an rightly says it is spherical, if it was a guess the chances of the guess being correct is 1/30.

The light of the moon can be its own light or a reflected light. The Qur'an rightly says it is a reflected light. If it was a guess, the chances that it will be correct is 1/2 and the probability that both the guesses i.e. the earth is spherical and the light of the moon is reflected light is 1/30 x 1/2 = 1/60.

Further, the Qur'an also mentions every living thing is made up of water. The options are say about 10,000. Every living thing can be made up of wood, stone, copper, aluminum, steel, silver, gold, oxygen, nitrogen, hydrogen, oil, water, cement, concrete etc. The Qur'an rightly says that every living thing is made up of water. Therefore if it's a guess, the chances that it will be correct is 1/10,000 and the probability of all the 3 guesses i.e. earth is spherical, light of moon is reflected, every living thing is created from water being correct is 1/30 x 1/2 x 1/10,000 = 1/600,000 which is equal to about 0.00017%.

The Qur'an speaks about hundreds of things that were not known at that time. Only in 3 options, the result is 0.00017%. We leave it up to you the intellectual readers to work out the probability if all the hundreds of the unknown facts were guesses, the chances of all the guesses being correct and not a single wrong. It is beyond human capacity to have all the guesses correct without a single mistake, which in itself is sufficient to prove to a logical person that the origin of the Qur'an is divine.

Qur'an is a Book of Signs and not Science

Let us be reminded that Qur'an is not a book of Science, but a book of 'signs' i.e. a book of verses. The Qur'an contains more than 6000 verses that is 'signs' out of which more than a thousand speak about science. For Muslims, the Qur'an is the 'Furqan' i.e. the criteria to judge right from wrong and it is the ultimate yard stick which is more superior to scientific knowledge. But for an educated man who is an atheist, scientific knowledge is the ultimate test, which he believes in. Using the ultimate yardstick of the atheist, we try to prove to him that the Qur'an is the word of God and while it was revealed 1400 ago, it contains the scientific knowledge that was discovered recently. Therefore, at the end of the discussion, we both come to the same conclusion that God, though superior to science, does not conflict with it.

The Creator is the Source of the Qur'an

The only logical answer to the question, who could have mentioned all these scientific facts 1400 years ago before they were discovered, is exactly the same answer that would be given by the atheist or any person, to the question "who is the first person who will be able to tell the mechanism of the unknown object?" It is the 'CREATOR,' the Producer, the Manufacturer of that object. Another name in the English Language for this Creator, Producer, Manufacturer of the whole universe and its contents, is 'God' or more appropriately in the Arabic Language is ' Allah'.

Science is eliminating Models of God but not God

Francis Bacon, the famous philosopher has rightly said that a little knowledge of science makes you an atheist, but an in-depth study of science makes you a believer in God. Scientists today are eliminating models of god, but they are not eliminating God.

If you translate this act - of rejecting false models and wrong notions of God - into Arabic, it is 'La ilaha illallah' which means "there is no god, but God". "There is no god (god with a small 'g' that is fake deities), but God (with a capital 'G'). Prof. Tejasen accepted Islam on the strength of just one scientific 'sign' mentioned in the Qur'an. Some people may require 10 signs while some may require 100 signs to be convinced about the Divine Origin of the Qur'an. Some would be unwilling to accept the Truth even after being shown 1,000 signs. The Qur'an condemns such a closed mentality in the verse, "They are deaf, dumb, and blind, so they will not return (to the right path)." [2.18]

The Qur'an contains a complete code of life for the individual and society. Alhamdulillah (Praise be to Allah), the Qur'anic way of life is far superior to the 'isms' that modem man has invented out of sheer ignorance. Who can give better guidance than the Creator Himself? In chapter The Detailed Explanation - Al-Fussilat [41] Allah says: "Soon We will show them Our Signs in the (very far) regions (of the earth, and also deep) in their own souls, till it becomes clear to them that this is the Truth. Is it not enough that your Lord Who Witnesses all things?" [41.53]

And Our Final Call is - All praises are for the One and Only God and Creator Allah, Who Alone is worthy of devotion, complete submission and worship. I declare that there is no other deity or god besides Allah. I also declare that Prophet Muhammad is the Last and Final Messenger of Allah.

Dr. Zakir Naik
Islamic Research Foundation
Mumbai, India.

Prophets mentioned in the Qur'an

(Links between prophets may or may not indicate direct descendants)

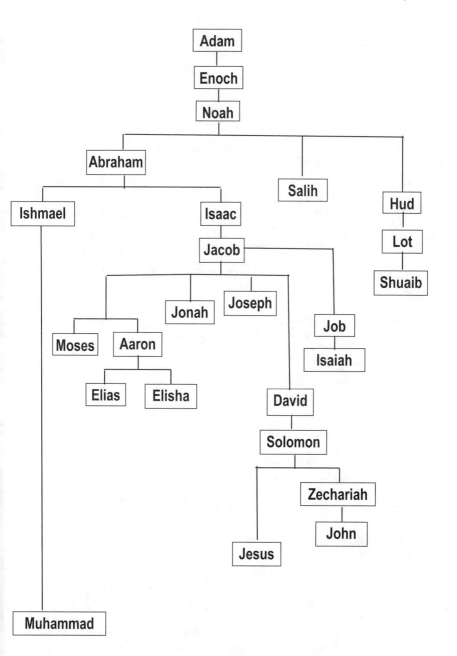

#	Prophet	Places, Nations, Landmarks	Map Locations
1	Adam	Makkah, Jedda, India, Sri Lanka, Syria	1, 3, 75, 76, 74
2	Enoch(Idris)	Babylon, Hebron, Manf	64, 35, 30
3	Noah (Nuh)	People of Noah (Kufah), Mt. Judi	65, 72
4	Hud	Al-Ahqaf, People of 'Ad	19, 21
5	Salih	Hadramawt, Madain Saleh, People of Thamud	24, 23, 22
6	Abraham (Ibrahim)	Ur, Babylon, Harran, Aleppo, Jerusalem, Hebron, Makkah, Al-Gizah	66, 64, 52, 57, 33, 35, 1, 31
7	Isaac (Ishaq)	Ur, Babylon, Urfa, Jerusalem, Hebron	66, 64, 67, 33, 35
8	Ishmael (Ismail)	Makkah, Mina, Muzdalefa, Arafat	1, 4, 5, 6
9	Lot (Lut)	Sodom & Gomorrah, Dead Sea, Sughar	54, 39, 55
10	Jacob (Yaqub)	Hebron, Jerusalem, Harran, Faddan, Manf, Heliopolis	35, 33, 52, 41, 30, 29
11	Joseph (Yusuf)	Jerusalem, Hebron, San Al-Hajar	33, 35, 32
12	Shuaib (Shu'aib)	Midian, Al-Aikah (Tabuk)	18, 16
13	Moses (Musa)	Manf, Midian, Al-Aqabah, Mt. Tur, Heliopolis, Red Sea, Sinai, Jordan River, Mt. Nibu	30, 18, 60, 17, 29, 47, 73, 51, 62
14	Aaron(Harun)	Sinai, Mt. Haur	73, 61
15	Elias (Ilyus)	Balabak, Jal'ad, B'ir Sheva, Sinai	45, 53, 42, 73
16	Elisha (Al-Yasa)	Balabak, Jal'ad, B'ir Sheva, Sinai	45, 53, 42, 73
17	David (Dawud)	Ashdod, Bait Dajan, Ramlah, Abu Ghush, Jerusalem	48, 44, 37, 59, 33
18	Solomon (Solaiman)	Jerusalem, Ashdod, Asqalan (Valley of Ants), Marib (Yemen), Queen Bilqis	33, 48, 49, 26, 27
19	Job (Ayub)	Bathaniyyah, Damascus, Adoum	46, 38, 58
20	Isaiah (Dhul-Kifl)	Mt. Qasiyun (Damascus)	56
21	Jonah (Yunus)	Jaffa, Aleppo, Nasibain, Minawa (Mosul)	50, 57, 63, 68
22	Zachariah (Zakariyya)	Jerusalem, Aleppo	33, 57
23	John(Yahya)	Jerusalem, Damascus	33, 38
24	Jesus ('Isa)	Bethlehem, Nazareth, Gaza, Farma, Heliopolis, Jordan River, Jerusalem	34, 36, 40, 43, 29, 51, 33
25	Muhammad	Makkah, Syria, Taif, Jerusalem, Al-Aqabah, Madinah, Badr, Uhud, Hudaibiyah, Khaibar, Hunayun, Tabuk, Mina, Muzdalefa, Arafat	1, 74, 11, 33, 60, 2, 9, 8, 10, 13, 12, 15, 4, 5, 6

Location of Places, Nations, Landmarks

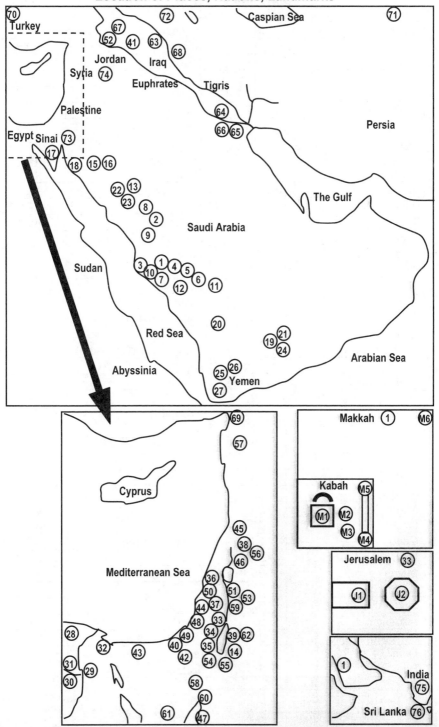

Place	Location	Place	Location
Makkah	1	Hebron	35
Kabah	M1	Nazareth	36
Station of Abraham	M2	Ramlah	37
ZamZam	M3	Damascus	38
Safa	M4	Dead Sea	39
Marwa	M5	Gaza	40
Cave Hira	M6	Faddan	41
Madinah	2	B'ir Sheva	42
Jeddah	3	Farma	43
Mina	4	Bait Dajan	44
Muzdalefa	5	Balabak	45
Arafat	6	Bathaniyyah	46
Mt. Thawr	7	Red Sea	47
Uhud	8	Ashdod	48
Badr	9	Asqalan (Valley of Ants)	49
Hudaibiyah	10	Jaffa	50
Taif	11	Jordan River	51
Hunayan	12	Harran	52
Khaibar	13	Jal'ad	53
Mutah	14	Sodom and Gomorrah	54
Tabuk	15	Sughar	55
Al-Aikah (Tabuk)	16	Mt. Qasiyun (Damascus)	56
Mt. Tur	17	Aleppo	57
Midian	18	Adoum	58
Al-Ahqaf	19	Abu Ghush	59
Najran	20	Al-Aqabah	60
People of Ad	21	Mt. Haur	61
People of Thamud	22	Mt. Nibu	62
Madain Saleh	23	Nasibain	63
Hadramawt	24	Babylon	64
Sana	25	People of Noah (Kufah)	65
Marib (Yemen)	26	Ur	66
Queen Bilqis	27	Urfa	67
Cairo	28	Minawa (Mosul)	68
Heliopolis	29	Antakiya	69
Manf (Egypt)	30	Istanbul	70
Al-Gizah	31	Tashkent	71
San Al-Hajar	32	Mt. Judi	72
Jerusalem	33	Sinai	73
Al-Aqsa Mosque	J1	Syria	74
Dome of the Rock	J2	India	75
Bethlehem	34	Sri Lanka	76

Life of Prophet Muhammad

Year	Event *	Age
570	Birth of Prophet Muhammad at Makkah (March / April). His father Abdullah died several months before he was born. He was raised by Halimah as wet-mother according to Makkah's tradition.	0
576	Death of Aminah (Prophet's mother). Muhammad was taken care by his grandfather Abd Al-Muttalib.	6
578	Death of Abd Al-Muttalib. Then Muhammad grew up under the protective care of his uncle Abu Talib.	8
582	Journey to Syria with uncle Abu Talib.	12
582-94	Worked as a shepherd for his uncle and later as a merchant. He lived a simple life. He was compassionate to the poor, widow, and orphans. He volunteered in many community activities. People of Makkah named him '**Al-Siddiq** (the Truthful)' and '**Al-Ameen** (the Trustworthy)' due to his honesty and good character. Acted as a business agent for Khadijah, a business woman of Makkah. Muhammad carried goods to the north and returned with a profit.	12-24
595	Impressed by Muhammad's honesty and character, Khadijah (who was a widow) proposed for marriage and eventually they got married. He was 25, she was 40.	25
609	Kabah was rebuilt by the people of Quraish. Muhammad helped to resolve disputes between the tribes.	39
610	First revelation came (August) to Muhammad at Cave Hira with a message (verses 96:1-5) from Allah by the Angel Gabriel.	40
610-13	Received several verses during this period and later they were compiled to become part of the Qur'an. He was belittled, ridiculed, then persecuted and physically attacked by the people of Makkah for his message of 'Oneness' of Allah, departing from the traditional tribal ways, including idol worshipping at the Kabah.	40-43
615	Muslims emigrated to Abyssinia to avoid sufferings / persecution from the people of Makkah. The king Negus offered asylum.	45
617-20	Embargo and boycott of Prophet's family by the people of Quraish.	47-50
620	Death of Abu Talib, Prophet's uncle. Death of Khadijah, Prophet's wife. The Quraish tried to assassinate him. **Journey to Taif**. Talked with the community leaders and people to convey his message. They rejected and stoned him to injury.	50
621	Ascension of Prophet Muhammad on the night of Meraj with angel Gabriel. The journey took him from Makkah to Jerusalem and then through the 7 heavens. Allah showed him all the activities, features of heaven and hell. He was then returned to Makkah with full knowledge, so he was able to describe everything. First Pledge of Al-Aqabah (between the prophet and 12 people from Madinah). They swore allegiance to him.	51

622	Second Pledge of Al-Aqabah (between the prophet and 75 people from Madinah). They swore to defend him. **Emigration to Madinah** (July). Established Quba Mosque as the first mosque of Islam. Treaty with Jews and non-Muslims in Madinah with equal rights of citizenship and full religious liberty. Expedition of Hamza (December).	52
623	Expedition of Ubaidah (February); Al-Kharrar Expedition (March); Marriage to Aisha (April); **Al-Abwa'** Expedition (June); **Buwat** Expedition (July); **Safawan** Expedition (First Badr) (July); **Ushairah** Expedition (October).	53
624	Change of Qiblah from Jerusalem to Makkah (January) when he received the commandment of Allah while he was praying at the mosque known as the Masjid Al-Qiblatain. **Batn Nakhlah** Expedition (January); **Badr** Expedition (March). Salim bin Umair Expedition (April); Banu Qainuqa' Expedition (April); Marriage of Prophet's daughter Fatimah to Ali (June); **Sawiq** Expedition (June); **Bani Sulaim** (Al-Kudr) Expedition (July); An-Nadir Expedition (September); **Dhi Amar** Expedition (September); Buhran Expedition (November); Al-Qaradah Expedition (December)	54
625	**Uhud** Expedition (March); **Hamra' Al-Asad** Expedition (April)	55
626	Abu Salamah Expedition (July); Abdullah bin Unais Expedition (July); **Dhatur-Riqa'** Expedition (July); Al-Mundhir bin Amr (August); Raji Expedition (August); **Daumatul-Jandal** Expedition (August); Banu An-Nadir Expedition (September).	56
627	**Banu Mustaliq** Expedition (January); **Ahzab** Expedition (Trench around Madinah to defend the city) (February - March); **Banu Quraizah** Expedition (April); **Second Badr** Expedition (May); Al-Qurata Expedition (June); **Banu Lihyan** Expedition (August); **Dhu Qarad** Expedition (August); Ghamr Expedition (August); Dhul-Qassah Expedition (September); Dhul Qassah (Abu Ubaidah) Expedition (September); Zaid bin Harith 5 Expeditions (August / 627 - February / 628).	57
628	Daumatul-Jandal (Abdul Rahman bin Awf) Expedition (January); Fadak Expedition (January); Khaibar: (Abdullah bin Atik) Expedition (February), (Abdullah bin Rawaha) Expedition (March); 'Urainah Expedition (March); Ad-Damri Expedition; **Treaty of Hudaibiyah** between the Quraish of Makkah and Muslims (April). The Prophet Muhammad and Muslims returned to Madinah without Umrah as a part of the treaty with a provision to return to Makkah next year for Umrah. Makkans breached the treaty a year later. Invitation letters to Kings and world leaders (April - May) of Abyssinia, Bahrain, Persia, Jerusalem (Roman King), Alexandria, Oman, Yamamah, Damascus. *See attached map later.* **Khaibar** Expedition (May - June).	58

629	Turabah (Umar bin Khattab) Expedition (January); Najd Expedition (Abu Bakr) (January); Fadak Expedition (Bashir bin Sa'd) (January); Mayf'ah Expedition (January); Yamn and Jabar Expedition (January). **Performance of missed Umrah** (Umratul-Qada') (April). Banu Sulaim Expedition (May); Kadid and Fadak Expedition (July); Al-Asadi Expedition (August); Dhat Atla Expedition (August); Mutah Expedition (October); Dhatus-Salasil Expedition (November); Al-Khabt Expedition (December)	59
630	Abu Qatadah Expedition (January); **Victory of Makkah** (January); The Prophet entered Makkah with 10,000 Muslims without any bloodshed. The Makkans joined the Muslims after they saw no revenge or retaliation rather he announced general amnesty to all the enemies and treated the citizens of the city with generosity. Nakhlah (Khalid bin Al-Walid) Expedition (January); Suwa-Banu Hudhail (Amr bin Al-'Aas) Expedition (January); Al-Mushallal (Sa'd bin Zaid) Expedition (January); Banu Jadhimah (Khalid bin Al-Walid) Expedition (February). **Hunain** Expedition (February); **At-Taif** Expedition (February). Birth of Ibrahim (Prophet's son) (March); Banu Tamim Expedition (May); Tabalah Expedition (June); Dahhak Al-Kilabi Expedition (July); Jeddah Expedition (August); Ali bin Abi Talib (August); Al-Asadi Expedition (August). Death of Negus, King of Abyssinia (October). **Tabuk** Expedition (October - December).	60
631	Death of Ibrahim (Prophet's son) (January). Hajj Pilgrimage led by Abu Bakr (March). Najran Expedition by Khalid (July).	61
632	Yemen Expedition by Ali (January); Last Revelation (February - March). **Farewell Pilgrimage** to Makkah and thousands of Muslims joined (February - March). Last Sermon at Arafat (March); Usamah Expedition (June).	62
632	Death of Prophet Muhammad (June). He was buried in the mosque in Madinah. During the last 10 years of his life, ➤ he destroyed idolatry in Arabia; ➤ raised the status of women to legal equality with men; ➤ stopped drunkenness and immorality in the society; ➤ made people live with faith, sincerity and honesty; transformed the nation from the ignorance of darkness into fully knowledgeable societies. ➤ His mission transformed a society from all forms of injustice into universal human brotherhood as servants of Allah. Within 100 years, Islam and his way of life had spread from the remote corners of Arabia to as far east as Indo-China and as far west as Morocco, France, and Spain. He is the LAST messenger for the entire world from the SAME Allah of Abraham, Moses, and Jesus. The Qur'an is the FINAL REVELATION.	62+

* Prophet Muhammad participated in expeditions in Bold.

Prophet's letters to Rulers and Leaders

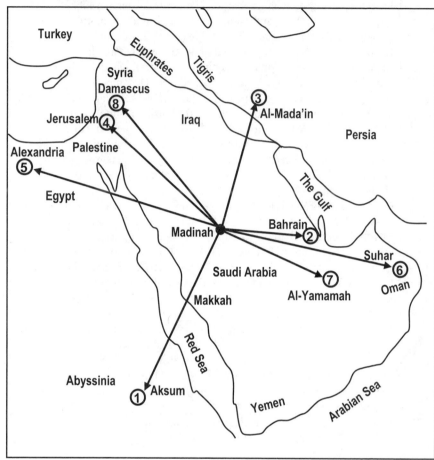

#	City	Ruler / Country
1	**Aksum**	King Negus / Abyssinia
2	**Bahrain**	Al-Mundhir bin Sawa / Bahrain
3	**Al-Mada'in**	Chosroes / Persia
4	**Jerusalem**	Hercules, Caesar / Rome
5	**Alexandria**	Al-Muqawqis / Egypt
6	**Suhar**	Jayfar, 'Abd, sons of Al-Julandi / Oman
7	**Yamamah**	Hawdhah bin Ali / Al-Yamamah
8	**Damascus**	Al-Harith bin Abi Shamr Al-Gassani / Syria

Prophet's Letter

Seal of the Prophet

The Last Sermon of the Prophet Muhammad

(This Sermon was delivered at Arafat in March, 632 CE)

After praising and thanking Allah, he said:

O People, lend me an attentive ear, for I know not whether after this year, I shall ever be amongst you again. Therefore listen to what I am saying to you very carefully and take these words to those who could not be present here today.

O People, just as you regard this month, this day, and this city as sacred; so regard the life and property of every Muslim as a sacred trust. Return the goods entrusted to you to their rightful owners. Hurt no one so that no one may hurt you. Remember that you will indeed meet your Lord, and He will indeed reckon your deeds. Allah has forbidden you to take usury (interest); therefore all interest obligations shall henceforth be waived. Your capital, however, is yours to keep. You will neither inflict nor suffer inequity. Allah has judged that there shall be no interest and that all the interest due to Abbas ibn 'Abd'al Muttalib shall henceforth be waived. Every right arising out of homicide in pre-Islamic days is henceforth waived and the first such right that I waive is that arising from the murder of Rabiah ibn al Harith.

O People, the unbelievers indulge in tampering with the calendar in order to make permissible that which Allah forbade, and to forbid that which Allah has made permissible. With Allah, the months are twelve in number. Four of them are holy, three of these are successive and one occurs singly between the months of Jumada and Sha'ban. Beware of Satan, for the safety of your religion. He has lost all hope that he will ever be able to lead you astray in big things, so beware of following him in small things.

O People, it is true that you have certain rights with regard to your women, but they also have rights over you. Remember that you have taken them as your wives only under Allah's trust and with His permission. If they abide by your right then they have the right to be fed and clothed in kindness. Do treat your women well and be kind to them for they are your partners and committed helpers. And it is your right that they do not make friends with any one of whom you do not approve, as well as never to be unchaste.

O People, listen to me in earnest, worship Allah, say your five daily prayers (Salah), fast during the month of Ramadan, and give your wealth in Zakat. Perform Hajj if you can afford it. You know that every Muslim is the brother of another Muslim. You are all equal. Nobody has superiority over another except by piety and good action. Remember, one day you will appear before Allah and answer for your deeds. So beware, do not astray from the path of righteousness after I am gone.

O People, no prophet or apostle will come after me and no new faith will be born. Reason well, therefore, O People, and understand my words which I convey to you. I leave behind me two things, the Qur'an and my example, the Sunnah and if you follow these you will never go astray.

All those who listen to me shall pass on my words to others and those to others again; and may the last ones understand my words better than those who listen to me directly. Be my witness O Allah that I have conveyed Your message to Your people.

The History of Compilation of the Qur'an**

During the life of the Prophet Muhammad (570 - 632 CE)

• The Prophet used to recite the Qur'an before angel Gabriel once every Ramadan, and he recited it twice (in the same order as we have today) in the last Ramadan before his death.

• Each verse received was recited by the Prophet, and its location relative to other verses and chapters was identified by him.

• The verses were written by scribes, selected by the Prophet, on any suitable object - the leaves of trees, pieces of wood, parchment or leather, flat stones, and shoulder blades. Scribes included Ali Ibn Abi Talib, Mu'awiyah Ibn Abi Sufyan, Ubey Ibn Ka'ab, and Zayed Ibn Thabit. Some of the companions wrote the Qur'an for their own use. Several hundred companions memorized the Qur'an by heart.

During the caliphate of Abu Bakr (632 - 634 CE)

• Umar Ibn Al-Khattab urged Abu Bakr to preserve and compile the Qur'an. This was prompted after the battle of Yamamah, where heavy casualties were suffered among those who memorized the Qur'an.

• Abu Bakr entrusted Zayed with the task of collecting the Qur'an. Zayed had been present during the last recitation of the Qur'an by the Prophet to Angel Gabriel.

• Zayed, with the help of the companions who memorized and wrote verses of the Qur'an, accomplished the task and handed Abu Bakr the first authenticated copy of the Qur'an. The copy was kept in the residence of Hafsah, daughter of Umar and wife of the Prophet.

During the caliphate of Uthman (644 - 656 CE)

• Uthman ordered Zayed Ibn Thabit, Abdullah Ibn Al Zubayr, Saeed Ibn Al-Aas, and Abdur-Rahman Ibn Harith to make perfect copies of the authenticated copy kept with Hafsa due to the rapid expansion of the Islamic state and concern about differences in recitation.

• Copies were sent to various places in the Muslim world. The original copy was returned to Hafsa, and a copy was kept in Madinah.

Three stages of dotting and diacritization

• Dots were put as syntactical marks by Abu Al-Aswad Al Doaly, during the time of Mu'awiya Ibn Abi Sufian (661-680 CE).

• The letters were marked with different dotting by Nasr Ibn Asem and Hayy ibn Ya'mor, during the time of Abd Al-Malek Ibn Marawan (685-705 CE).

• A complete system of diacritical marks (damma, fataha, kasra) was invented by Al Khaleel Ibn Ahmad Al Faraheedy (d. 786 CE).

**University of Southern California - MSA

Original copies of the Qur'an still exist: (1) Tashkent, Uzbekistan, (2) Istanbul, Turkey.

4 Caliphs after the Prophet Muhammad		
Name	Period	Years
Abu Bakr Siddique	632 - 634 CE	2
Omar Ibn Khattab	634 - 644 CE	10
Uthman Ibn Affan	644 - 656 CE	12
Ali ibn Abi Talib	656 - 661 CE	5

Alphabetic	#	Alphabetic	#	Alphabetic	#
'Abasa	80	Al-Isra'	17	Ar-Rahman	55
Ad-Dahr	76	Al-Jathiyah	45	Ar-Rum	30
Ad-Duha	93	Al-Jinn	72	Ash-Shams	91
Ad-Dukhan	44	Al-Jumu'ah	62	Ash-Sharh	94
Adh-Dhariyat	51	Al-Kafirun	109	Ash-Shuara'	26
Al-'Adiyat	100	Al-Kahf	18	Ash-Shura	42
Al-Ahqaf	46	Al-Kauther	108	As-Saff	61
Al-Ahzab	33	Al-Lail	92	As-Saffat	37
Al-A'la	87	Al-Ma'arij	70	As-Sajdah	32
Al-'Alaq	96	Al-Ma'idah	5	At-Taghabun	64
Al-An'am	6	Al-Masad	111	At-Tahrim	66
Al-Anbiya'	21	Al-Ma'un	107	At-Takathur	102
Al-Anfal	8	Al-Muddaththir	74	At-Takwir	81
Al-Ankabut	29	Al-Mujadilah	58	At-Talaq	65
Al-A'raf	7	Al-Mulk	67	At-Tariq	86
Al-'Asr	103	Al-Muminun	23	At-Taubah	9
Al-Balad	90	Al-Mumtahanah	60	At-Tin	95
Al-Baqarah	2	Al-Munafiqun	63	At-Tur	52
Al-Bayyinah	98	Al-Mursalat	77	Az-Zalzalah	99
Al-Buruj	85	Al-Mutaffifin	83	Az-Zukhruf	43
Al-Fajr	89	Al-Muzzammil	73	Az-Zumar	39
Al-Falaq	113	Al-Qadr	97	Fatir	35
Al-Fath	48	Al-Qalam	68	Fussilat	41
Al-Fatihah	1	Al-Qamar	54	Ghafir	40
Al-Fil	105	Al-Qari'ah	101	Hud	11
Al-Furqan	25	Al-Qasas	28	Ibrahim	14
Al-Ghashiyah	88	Al-Qiyamah	75	Luqman	31
Al-Hadid	57	Al-Waqi'ah	56	Maryam	19
Al-Hajj	22	An-Naba'	78	Muhammad	47
Al-Haqqah	69	An-Nahl	16	Nuh	71
Al-Hashr	59	An-Najm	53	Qaf	50
Al-Hijr	15	An-Naml	27	Quraish	106
Al-Hujurat	49	An-Nas	114	Saba'	34
Al-Humazah	104	An-Nasr	110	Sad	38
Al-Ikhlas	112	An-Nazi'at	79	Ta-Ha	20
Al-'Imran	3	An-Nisa'	4	Ya-Seen	36
Al-Infitar	82	An-Nur	24	Yunus	10
Al-Inshiqaq	84	Ar-Ra'd	13	Yusuf	12

Prayer Direction

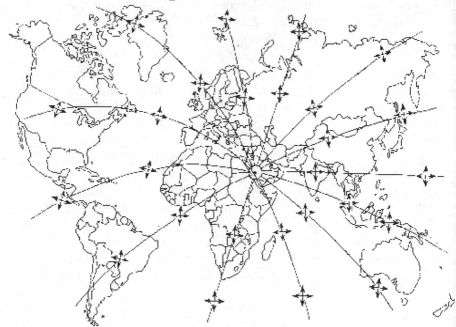

1. Al-Fatihah : The Opening

1:1 In the name of Allah, the Gracious, the Merciful.

1:2 All the praises be for Allah, the Rabb (few meanings are: Master, Owner, Sustainer, Guardian) of the worlds.

1:3 The Gracious, the Merciful.

1:4 Owner of the Day of Judgment.

1:5 You (Allah) alone we worship and you (Allah) alone we seek help.

1:6 Guide us to the right way.

1:7 The way of those whom you (Allah) have favored; not of those who have earned your (Allah's) wrath, nor of those who have lost the way.

2. Al-Baqarah : The Cow

In the name of Allah, the Gracious, the Merciful

2:1 Alif-Lam-Mim. ?

2:2 This is the book (the Qur'an) in which there is no doubt. It is a guidance for those who fear Allah,

2:3 who believe in the unseen, establish prayers, and spend in charity of what Allah has provided for them,

2:4 who believe in this revelation (the Qur'an) sent to you (O Muhammad), which was revealed before you (like Torah, Psalms, Gospel), and firmly believe in the hereafter.   ⌐ Lord ?

2:5 They are on true guidance from their Rabb. They are those who are the successful.

2:6 Surely, those who disbelieve, it is the same, whether you (Muhammad) warn them or do not warn them, they will not believe.

2:7 Allah has sealed on their hearts, on their hearings, and on their eyes there is a covering. For them there is a severe punishment.

2:8 There are some people who say: "We believe in Allah and the last day," while they do not believe.

2:9 They (think to) deceive Allah and those who believe, while they deceive only themselves, and they do not realize it.

2:10 In their hearts there is a disease (of doubt and hypocrisy), and Allah increases their disease. For them there is a painful punishment because they used to tell lies.

2:11 When it is said to them: "Do not make mischief on earth," they say: "We are only peace-makers."

2:12 Surely! They are the ones who make mischief but they do not realize it.

2:13 When it is said to them: "Believe as the other people believe," they say: "Shall we believe as the fools believe?" Surely, they themselves are the fools, but they do not know.

2:14 When they meet those who believe, they say: "We believe," but when they are alone with their Satans, they say: "Truly, we are with you, we were only mocking."

2:15 Allah mocks at them and gives them (increase) in their wrong-doings to wander blindly.

2:16 These are they who have purchased error for guidance, so their business is profitless and they are not guided.

2:17 Their example is like the one who kindled a fire; then when it lighted all around them, Allah took away their light and left them in darkness, so they could not see.

2:18 (They are) deaf, dumb, and blind, so they will not return (to the right way).

2:19 Or like a rainstorm from the sky with darkness, thunder, and lightning. They press their fingers in their ears from (the sound of) thunderclaps for fear of death. But Allah surrounds the disbelievers.

2:20 The lightning almost snatches away their sight; whenever it flashes for them, they walk in it; and when it darkens against them, they stand still. If Allah willed, Allah could have taken away their hearing and their sight. Certainly, Allah has power over all things.

2:21 O mankind! Worship your Rabb, who created you and those who were before you so that you may become pious.

2:22 It is Allah who has made for you the earth a resting place, the sky as a canopy, sends down rain from the sky, and brings out with it fruits as a provision for you. So do not set up rivals to Allah while you know.

2:23 If you are in doubt about what Allah has sent down to the messenger Muhammad, then produce a chapter like this, and call your witnesses besides Allah, if you are truthful.

2:24 But if you can not do it, and you are not able do it, then fear the hellfire, whose fuel is human and stones, prepared for the disbelievers.

2:25 Give glad tidings to those who believe and do good deeds, for them will be gardens under which rivers flow (paradise). Whenever they will be given from there with fruit as a provision, they will say: "This is what we were provided with before," and they will be given from there things having resemblance (of earth). For them therein will be chaste spouses, and they will reside therein forever.

2:26 Surely, Allah is not reluctant to set forth an example even of a mosquito and even something more (insignificant) than it. As for those who believe, they know that it is the truth from their Rabb. For those who disbelieve, they say: "What does Allah mean by this example?" Allah misleads many by it and guides many by it. Allah does not mislead by it except the disobedient ones:

2:27 those who break the covenant of Allah after its approval, sever what Allah has ordered to be joined, and do mischief in the earth. It is they, who are the losers.

2:28 How can you disbelieve in Allah? While you were lifeless and Allah gave you life. Then Allah will give you death, then again will bring you to life (on the day of Resurrection), and then you will return to Allah.

2:29 It is Allah, who has created for you all that is in the earth. Then Allah turned towards the heaven and made them 7 heavens. Allah has knowledge of everything.

2:30 (Remember) when your Rabb said to the angels: "Surely, I (Allah) am going to place a vicegerent in the earth." They said: "Will you (Allah) place in it those who will make mischief in it and shed blood, while we glorify you (Allah) with praises and thank you (Allah)?" Allah said: "Indeed I (Allah) know what you do not know."

2:31 Allah taught Adam the names of all things, then showed them before the angels and said: "Say the names of these to me (Allah) if you are truthful."

2:32 They (angels) replied: "Glory is to you (Allah); we have no knowledge except what you (Allah) have taught us. Surely, it is you (Allah), the All-Knower, the All-Wise."

2:33 Allah said: "O Adam! Inform them their names." When he informed them their names, Allah said: "Did I (Allah) not tell you that I (Allah) know the unseen of the heavens and the earth, and I (Allah) know what you reveal and what you conceal?"

2:34 (Remember) when Allah ordered the angels: "Prostrate to Adam," they all prostrated except Satan; he refused, was proud, and was one of the disbelievers.

2:35 Allah said: "O Adam! You and your wife reside in the paradise, both of you eat from it freely with pleasure from wherever you wish, but do not come near this tree, or you both will be of the wrongdoers."

2:36 Then Satan made both of them (disobey Allah's commandment) slip from (paradise), and got them out from where they were in it. Allah said: "Get down from here, some of you as enemy to others. There is for you in the earth a residing place and a livelihood for a specific time."

2:37 Then Adam received words (after his repentance) from his Rabb and Allah pardoned him. Surely, Allah is the Acceptor of repentance, the Merciful.

2:38 Allah said: "You all of you get down from it (paradise). Whenever guidance comes to you from me (Allah), whoever follows the guidance, then there is no fear on them, and they shall not grieve."

2:39 But those who disbelieve and deny my (Allah's) verses, they are the inmates of the hellfire. They shall reside in it forever."

2:40 O children of Israel! Remember my (Allah's) favor which I (Allah) bestowed upon you, fulfill your covenant with me (Allah) and I (Allah) will fulfill my (Allah's) covenant, and fear me (Allah) alone.

2:41 Believe in what I (Allah) has sent down (this Qur'an) confirming that which is with your (scriptures); do not be first disbeliever in it, and do not buy a small price (by selling) my (Allah's) verses, and fear me (Allah) alone.

2:42 Do not mix the truth with the falsehood, or conceal the truth while you know (the truth).

2:43 Establish prayers, give obligatory charity (Zakat), and bow down with those who bow down (in worship).

2:44 Do you enjoin piety and righteousness on the people, and forget to practice yourselves while you recite the scripture? Don't you understand?

2:45 Seek the help (of Allah) in patience and prayer. Truly it is very hard except on the humble minded,

2:46 who realize that surely they are going to meet their Rabb and that they are going to return to Allah (for Judgment).

2:47 O children of Israel! Remember my (Allah's) favor which I (Allah) bestowed upon you, and that I (Allah) preferred you over all the nations.

2:48 Fear a day (of Judgment) when a person will not avail another: no intercession will be accepted, no compensation will be taken, and no help will be given.

2:49 (Remember) when Allah delivered you (people of Moses) from the people of Pharaoh, who were afflicting you with a horrible punishment, killing your sons, sparing your women, and that was a mighty trial from your Rabb.

2:50 (Remember) when Allah separated the sea for you, saved you, and Allah drowned the people of Pharaoh while you were looking (at them covered by water).

2:51 (Remember) when Allah appointed for Moses 40 nights, and during his absence, you took the calf for worship, and you were wrongdoers.

2:52 Then Allah forgave you after that, so that you might be grateful.

2:53 (Remember) when Allah gave Moses the book (Torah) and the criterion (of right and wrong) so that you may be (rightly) guided.

2:54 (Remember) when Moses said to his people: "O my people! Surely, you have wronged yourselves by your taking (for worship) the calf. So turn in repentance to your creator (Allah) and kill (the wrongdoers among you), that is better for you with your Rabb." Then Allah accepted your repentance. Truly, Allah is the one who accepts repentance, the Merciful.

2:55 (Remember) when you said: "O Moses! We shall never believe in you till we see Allah plainly (with our own eyes)," you were seized with a thunderbolt (lightening) while you were looking.

2:56 Then Allah raised you after your death so that you might be grateful.

2:57 Allah even shaded over you with the clouds, sent down on you Manna (sweet dish) and Salva (quail's meat) (saying): "Eat from good things which Allah has provided for you." They did not wrong Allah but they wronged themselves.

2:58 (Remember) when Allah said: "Enter this town, eat there wherever you wish with pleasure, enter the gate in prostration (with humility), and say: 'Forgive us', Allah will forgive you your sins, and Allah will increase provision for the righteous."

2:59 But they did wrong who changed the word other than that which was told to them. So Allah sent upon those wrongdoers a punishment from the heaven because they disobeyed Allah.

2:60 Remember, when Moses asked for water for his people, Allah said: "Strike the stone with your stick." Then 12 springs gushed out from it. Each tribe knew its drinking place. (They were commanded): "Eat, drink from the provision of Allah, and do not act corruptly making mischief in the earth."

2:61 Remember, when you (people of Moses) said: "O Moses! We cannot endure on one kind of food. So invoke your Rabb for us to bring out for us which the earth grows: its herbs, cucumbers, garlic, lentils, and onions." Allah said: "Would you exchange that which is better for that which is worse? You go down to any town and indeed for you is what you have asked for!" They were stuck upon them with humiliation, misery, and they drew the wrath from Allah. That was because they used to disbelieve in the verses of Allah and killed the prophets without just cause. That was because they disobeyed and used to transgress.

2:62 Surely! Those who believe (Muslims) and those who are Jews, Christians, and Sabians; whoever believes in Allah, the last day, and do good deeds; they will have their reward with their Rabb, there will be no fear on them, nor they will grieve.

2:63 Remember, (O children of Israel) when Allah took your covenant and Allah raised above you the (mount) Tur (saying): "Hold with strength (firmly) to what Allah has given you (Torah), and remember what is therein so that you may become pious."

2:64 Then after that you turned away. Had it not been for the grace of Allah upon you and Allah's Mercy, indeed you would have been among the losers.

2:65 Indeed you know those who transgressed amongst you in the matter of the Sabbath (Saturday). Allah ordered them: "You be monkeys, and rejected."

2:66 Allah made this an example of punishment in front of them (own people) and to those after them (succeeding generations), and a lesson for the pious.

2:67 (Remember) when Moses said to his people: "Surely, Allah commands you that you slaughter a cow," they said: "Do you make fun of us?" Moses said: "I take refuge with Allah from being among the ignorant."

2:68 They said: "Call upon your Rabb for us so that Allah will make clear to us what it is!" Moses said: "Allah says, surely, it should be a cow neither old nor young but between that (2 conditions), so do what you are commanded."

2:69 They said: "Call upon your Rabb for us to make clear to us what its color is." Moses said: "Surely, Allah says, it is a cow yellow bright in its color that pleases the beholders (who look at)."

2:70 They said: "Call upon your Rabb for us to make clear to us what it is. Surely, the cows are all alike to us. Surely, if Allah wills, we will be guided."

2:71 Moses said: "Allah indeed says, it is neither a cow trained to till the soil nor waters the fields; a healthy one with no mark in it." They said: "Now you have brought the truth." So they slaughtered it and they were near to not doing it.

2:72 (Remember) when you (Moses) killed a man and then you disputed it, but Allah brought out what you were concealing.

2:73 So Allah said: "Strike him (dead body) with a piece of it (slaughtered cow)." Thus Allah brought the dead to life and showed you Allah's signs so that you may understand.

2:74 After (seeing) that, your hearts were hardened so that they were as stones or even worse in hardness. Indeed, there are some stones from which rivers gush out, and indeed, there are of them (stones) which split apart so that the water flows from them, and indeed, there are of them (stones) which fall down for fear of Allah. Allah is not unaware of what you do.

2:75 Do you (believers) desire that they (people of the book) will believe in you (religion) while indeed a group of them used to hear the word of Allah, then they used to change it knowingly after what they understood it?

2:76 When they (people of the book) meet those who believe (Muslims), they say: "We (also) believe," but when they meet privately some of them with some others, they say: "Will you tell those (Muslims) what Allah has revealed to you so that they (Muslims) may argue with you about it before your Rabb? Don't you understand?"

2:77 Do they not know that Allah knows what they conceal and what they reveal?

2:78 Among them, there are unlettered people who do not know the book, but they trust false desires and they do not but guess.

2:79 So woe to those who write the book with their own hands and then they say: "This is from Allah," so that they may purchase it with a little price! So woe to them for what their hands have written and woe to them for what they have earned.

2:80 They (Jews) say: "The hellfire shall never touch us but for a few numbered days." Say (Muhammad to them): "Have you taken a covenant from Allah which Allah will not break? Or do you say against Allah what you do not know?"

2:81 Yes! Those who earn evil and their sins surround them, they are inmates of the hellfire; they shall reside therein forever.

2:82 Those who believe and do good deeds, they are residents of paradise; they will reside in it forever.

2:83 (Remember) when Allah took a covenant from the children of Israel, saying: "You shall worship none but Allah; be good to parents, relatives, orphans, poor, speak fair to the people, establish the prayer, and give obligatory charity." Then you turned back, except a few of you, while you were opposed.

2:84 (Remember) when Allah took your covenant (saying): You shall not shed your people's blood and you shall not turn out yourself (expel own people) from your homes. You ratified this and you bore witness (to this).

2:85 Yet, you are those who kill yourselves, drive out a group of you from their homes, and assist one another against them in sin and transgression. If they come to you as captives, you ransom them, though their expulsion was forbidden to you. Do you believe in part of the scripture and reject some of it? Then what is the punishment of those who do so among you, except disgrace in the life of this world, and they would be consigned to the most grievous punishment on the day of Resurrection? Allah is not unaware of what you do.

2:86 Those are they who have bought the life of this world for the price of the hereafter. The punishment on them neither shall be lightened nor shall they be helped.

2:87 Indeed, Allah gave Moses the book (Torah) and followed him up after him by prophets. Allah gave Jesus, son of Mary, clear signs and supported him with the Holy Spirit (Gabriel). Then whenever a messenger came to you with what you yourselves did not desire, you grew arrogant, some you disbelieved, and some you killed.

2:88 They said: "Our hearts are wrapped (do not hear or understand Allah's word)." Nay, Allah has cursed them for their disbelief, so little is that which they believe.

2:89 When there has come to them a book (this Qur'an) from Allah confirming what is with the previous scriptures, even though previously they were invoking Allah for victory over those who disbelieved, and when what came to them which they recognized, they disbelieved in it. So the curse of Allah is on the disbelievers.

2:90 How bad is that (for which) they have sold their own selves, that they should disbelieve in which Allah has revealed (the Qur'an), grudging that Allah should reveal graces of Allah on whom Allah wills of Allah's servants! They have drawn (on themselves) wrath upon wrath. For the disbelievers, there is a disgraceful punishment.

2:91 When it is said to them: "Believe in what Allah has sent down," they say: "We believe in what was sent down to us (Torah)." They disbelieve in that what came after it; while it is the truth confirming what is with them. Ask (O Muhammad): "Then why did you kill the prophets of Allah previously, if you were true believers?"

2:92 Indeed Moses came to you with clear proofs, yet you took (for worship) the calf after him, and you were wrongdoers.

2:93 (Remember) when Allah took your covenant and raised above you the (Mount) Tur (saying): "Hold firmly to what Allah has given you and hear (Allah's word)." They said: "We have heard and disobeyed." They were loved in their hearts (the worship of) the calf because of their disbelief. Say: "Evil is what commands you by your faith, if you are believers."

2:94 Say (O Muhammad): "If the home of the hereafter with Allah is indeed exclusively for you and not for other people, then wish for death if you are truthful."

2:95 But they will never ever wish for the death because of what their hands have sent ahead (their deeds). Allah is aware of the wrong-doers.

2:96 Surely, you will find them the greediest of mankind for life and of those who ascribed partners to Allah. Each one of them wishes that if a life of 1,000 years could be given. But this will not remove anyone away from the punishment though that life is given. Allah is watching what they do.

2:97 Say (O Muhammad): "Whoever is an enemy to Gabriel should know that indeed Gabriel has brought it (this Qur'an) down to your heart by the permission of Allah, confirming what came before it, and is a guidance and glad tidings for the believers.

2:98 Whoever is enemy to Allah, Allah's angels, Allah's messengers, Gabriel, and Michael; then surely, Allah is the enemy to the disbelievers."

2:99 Indeed Allah has sent down to you clear verses (of the Qur'an) and none disbelieve in them but disobedient ones.

2:100 Is it not the case that whenever they contract a covenant, a group of them threw it away? Nay! Most of them do not believe.

2:101 Whenever a messenger from Allah came to them confirming what was with them, a group of those who were given the scripture threw away the book of Allah behind their backs as if they did not know,

2:102 and they followed what the devils (falsely) recited in the kingdom of Solomon. Solomon did not disbelieve, but the devils disbelieved, teaching people magic and what was revealed at (the city of) Babylon to the 2 angels, Harut and Marut. Neither of these 2 angels taught (magic) anyone till they had said: "We are only for trial, so do not disbelieve." (In spite of this warning) people did learn from these 2 angels by which they could separate between husband and wife, but they could not harm anyone with it except by the permission of Allah. They learned what harms them and not profits them. Indeed they knew that whoever buys it (magic), there is no share in the hereafter. How bad indeed was what they sold it for their own selves, if they would know that!

2:103 If they would have believed and became pious, indeed for them reward from Allah would be better if they did know!

2:104 O you who believe! Do not say (to the prophet): "Raina" (pay attention to us) but say "Unzurna" (please look upon us) and listen. For the disbelievers there is a painful punishment.

2:105 Those who disbelieved among the people of the scripture or polytheists do not like that there should be sent down upon you (O Muhammad) any good from your Rabb. But Allah chooses for Allah's Mercy whom Allah wills. Allah is the owner of great bounty.

2:106 Whatever of a verse Allah repeals or causes it to be forgotten, Allah brings better than it or similar to it. Do you not know that Allah has power over every thing?

2:107 Don't you know that to Allah belongs the dominion of the heavens and the earth? Besides Allah you have neither any guardian nor any helper!

2:108 Or do you want to ask your messenger (Muhammad) as Moses was asked before? Whoever changes faith for disbelief, surely went astray from the right way.

2:109 Many of the people of the scripture wish that if they could turn you back as disbeliever after you have believed, (out of) envy from their own selves what has become clear to them after the truth. So forgive and overlook, till Allah brings Allah's command. Surely, Allah has power over every thing.

2:110 Establish prayers, give obligatory charity, and whatever good deeds you send ahead for yourselves; you shall find it with Allah. Certainly, Allah is All-Seer of what you do.

2:111 They say: "None shall enter paradise except who is a Jew or a Christian." These are their vain desires. Say (O Muhammad): "Bring your proof if you are truthful."

2:112 Yes, whoever submits itself to Allah and is a righteous, then its reward is with the Rabb, and will have nothing to fear or to grieve.

2:113 The Jews say: "The Christians are not on anything right" and the Christians say: "The Jews are not on anything (right)," though they both recite the scripture (Torah or Gospel). Similarly those who have no knowledge (the pagan Arabs) say: they like (both) their words. So Allah will judge between them on the day of Resurrection about that in which they have been differing.

2:114 Who is more unjust than those who forbids mentioning Allah's name in Allah's mosques and strives in their ruin? It is not proper for them to enter them (mosques) except in fear. For them there is disgrace in the world and for them there is great punishment in the hereafter.

2:115 To Allah belongs the east and the west, so wherever you turn (face) there will be the face (presence) of Allah. Surely! Allah is All-Embracing, All-Knower.

2:116 They say: "Allah has taken a son." Glory is to Allah! But to Allah belongs what is in the heavens and the earth, and all are obedient to Allah.

2:117 Allah is the Originator of the heavens and the earth. When Allah decrees a matter, Allah only says to it: "Be" and it becomes.

2:118 Those who do not know say: "Why does not Allah speak to us (face to face) or a sign come to us?" Those people who were before them have said like their words. Their hearts are alike. Allah has indeed made clear the signs for people who believe firmly.

2:119 Surely, Allah has sent you (O Muhammad) with the truth (Islam), a bearer of glad tidings and a warner. You will not be asked about the residents of the blazing fire.

2:120 The Jews or the Christians will never be pleased with you (O Muhammad) until you follow their religion. Say: "Surely, the guidance of Allah is the only guidance." If you (Muhammad) follow their desires after what came to you of the knowledge (the Qur'an), there shall be no protector or any helper for you from the wrath of Allah.

2:121 Those whom Allah gave the book, recite it as it has right to be recited, are those who believe in it. Whoever disbelieves in it, then they are those who are the losers.

2:122 O children of Israel! Remember my (Allah's) favor which I (Allah) bestowed upon you, and that I (Allah) preferred you over all the nations.

2:123 Fear the day (of Judgment) when neither one shall avail another, nor any ransom (compensation) shall be accepted from anyone, nor intercession shall benefit anyone, nor any help will be given.

2:124 (Remember) when the Rabb of Abraham tried him with commands, he fulfilled them. Allah said (to him): "Surely, I (Allah) will make you a leader for mankind." Abraham asked: "And of my offspring?" Allah said: "My (Allah's) covenant will not include wrongdoers."

2:125 (Remember) when Allah made the House (the Ka'bah) a resort for mankind and safety, and took the station of Abraham as a place of prayer. Allah commanded Abraham and Ishmael that they purify Allah's House (the Ka'bah) for those who walk around it, those who stay (in I'tikaf), and those who bow down and prostrate (in prayers).

2:126 (Remember) when Abraham said: "My Rabb, make this Makkah a city of security and provide its people with fruits, those of them who believe in Allah and the last day." Allah said: "Those who disbelieve, I (Allah) would let them enjoy in contentment for a while, then I (Allah) will compel them to the punishment of the hellfire, and that is worst destination!"

2:127 (Remember) when Abraham and Ishmael raised the foundations of the House (the Ka'bah) (saying): "Our Rabb! Accept from us. Surely! You (Allah) are the All-Hearer, the All-Knower.

2:128 Our Rabb! Make us submissive to you (Allah) and our offspring a nation submissive to you (Allah). Show us our rites of worship, and accept our repentance. Surely, you (Allah) are the Accepter of repentance, the Merciful.

2:129 Our Rabb! Send amongst them a messenger out of them, who shall recite to them your (Allah's) verses and teach them the book and the wisdom, and purify them. Surely! Allah is the All-Mighty, the All-Wise."

2:130 Who turns away from the religion of Abraham except the one who is foolish? Surely, Allah chose Abraham in the world and surely, in the hereafter he will be among the righteous.

2:131 When Abraham's Rabb said: "Submit (be a Muslim)!" Abraham said: "I have submitted myself (as a Muslim) to the Rabb of the worlds."

2:132 This submission to Allah was enjoined by Abraham to his sons and by Jacob, (saying): "O my sons! Surely Allah has chosen for you the true religion, then you do not die unless you are Muslims."

2:133 Or were you witnesses when the death approached to Jacob? When he said to his sons: "What will you worship after me?" They said: "We will worship your Rabb, and the Rabb of your fathers, Abraham and Ishmael, and Isaac, one Rabb, and to whom (Allah) we submit (as Muslims)."

2:134 That was a nation which has passed away. For them what they earned and for you what you earn. You will not be asked of what they used to do.

2:135 They said: "Be Jews or Christians, you will be guided." Say (O Muhammad): "Nay, (we follow) the religion of Abraham, the upright one, and he was not of the polytheists."

2:136 Say (Muslims): "We believe in Allah and what has been sent down to us; and what was sent down to Abraham, Ishmael, Isaac, Jacob, and their descendents, and what was given to Moses, Jesus, and what was given to the prophets from their Rabb. We make no distinction between any of them and to Allah we have submitted (in Islam)."

2:137 So, if they believe (accept Islam) like what you have believed, then they will be guided in what they have received guidance. But if they turn away, then they will only be in opposition. So Allah will be sufficient for you against them. Allah is the All-Hearer, the All-Knower.

2:138 (Our religion) takes its hue from Allah, and who can give a better hue than Allah? We are worshippers to Allah.

2:139 Say (O Muhammad): "Do you dispute with us about Allah while Allah is our Rabb and your Rabb? For us are our deeds and for you are your deeds. We are sincere to Allah.

2:140 Or do you say that Abraham, Ishmael, Isaac, Jacob, and their descendants were all Jews or Christians? Say: Do you know better or Allah? Who is more unjust than the one who conceals testimony from Allah? Allah is not unaware of what you do."

2:141 That was a nation which has passed away. For them what they earned (rewarded) and for you what you earn. You will not be asked what they used to do.

2:142 The fools among the people would say: "What has turned those (Muslims) from their Qiblah (prayer direction) which they used to face in prayer?" Say (O Muhammad): "To Allah belongs the east and the west. Allah guides whom Allah wills to the right way."

2:143 Thus Allah has made you a just nation so that you are witnesses over mankind and the messenger over you a witness. Allah has made the Qiblah (towards Jerusalem) that you used to face, except that Allah tests those who follow the messenger from those who would turn on their heels (disobey). Indeed it was hard test except for those whom Allah has guided. Allah does not let lose your faith. Truly, Allah is full of Kindness, the Merciful to mankind.

2:144 Surely! Allah has seen the turning of your (Muhammad's) face towards the heaven. Surely, Allah will turn you to a Qiblah that you will be pleased with it. So turn your face towards the Sacred Mosque (at Makkah). Wherever you people are, turn your faces in prayer towards it. Certainly, those who were given the scriptures know well that the truth is from their Rabb. Allah is not unaware of what they do.

2:145 Even if you were to bring all proofs to those who were given the scripture, they would neither follow your Qiblah, nor would you be a follower of their Qiblah. Some of them are not followers of the Qiblah of others. If you follow their desires after what came to you of the knowledge (from Allah), then indeed you will be of the wrongdoers.

2:146 Those whom Allah has given the scripture recognize it as they recognize their children. But surely, a group of them conceal the truth while they know it.

2:147 The truth is from your Rabb. So do not be of those who doubt.

2:148 For every nation there is a direction to which they turn (for prayers). So try to excel (one another) in good deeds. Wherever you may be, Allah will bring you all together (on the day of Resurrection). Truly, Allah has power over every thing.

2:149 From wherever you come forth, turn your face in prayer towards the Sacred Mosque (at Makkah), and indeed this is the truth from your Rabb. Allah is not unaware of what you do.

2:150 From wherever you come forth (for prayers), turn your face towards the Sacred Mosque (at Makkah). Wherever you may be, turn your faces towards it so that people may not have an argument against you except those of them who do injustice. Do not fear them but fear me (Allah), so that I (Allah) may complete my (Allah's) favors upon you and that you may be guided,

2:151 as Allah has sent among you a messenger (Muhammad) from among you who recites to you Allah's verses (the Qur'an), purifies you, teaches you the book (the Qur'an) and wisdom, and teaches you what you did not know.

2:152 Therefore remember me (Allah), I (Allah) will remember you, be grateful to me (Allah), and do not be ungrateful to me (Allah).

2:153 O you who believe! Seek help (from Allah) with patience and prayer. Surely! Allah is with the patient ones.

2:154 You do not say of those who are killed (martyrs) in the way of Allah: "They are dead." Nay, they are alive, but you do not perceive it.

2:155 Surely, Allah will test you with something of the fear, the hunger, and loss of wealth, lives, and fruits (crops). But give glad tidings to the patient ones;

2:156 when those who are afflicted with calamity, say: "Truly! We belong to Allah and indeed to Allah we shall return."

2:157 They are those on whom are the blessings and Mercy from their Rabb, and they are those who are the guided ones.

2:158 Surely! Safa and Marwah (2 mountains in Makkah) are of the symbols of Allah. So whoever performs Hajj (obligatory pilgrimage to Makkah) of the House (the Ka'bah at Makkah) or performs Umrah (optional visit to Makkah), there is no sin if one walks between the two. Whoever does good voluntarily, then surely, Allah is All-Recognizer, the All-Knower.

2:159 Surely, those who conceal what Allah has sent down of the clear proofs and the guidance, after that Allah has made it clear for the mankind in the book; such are those Allah curses them and the cursers curse them;

2:160 except those who repent, reform (their ways), and declare (the truth). For those, I (Allah) will accept repentance for them, and I (Allah) am the Receiver of repentance, the Merciful.

2:161 Surely, those who disbelieve, and die while they are disbelievers; it is they on them is the curse of Allah, of the angels, and of mankind combined;

2:162 they will abide in it (hell), neither the punishment will be lightened, nor will they be reprieved.

2:163 Your deity is one Allah; there is no one worthy of worship but Allah, the Beneficent, the Merciful.

2:164 Surely! In the creation of the heavens and the earth, in the alternation of the night and the day, in the ships which sail through the sea which benefit the mankind, in the sky of rain what Allah sends down, in the making of earth alive after its death and scatters in it (all kinds) of moving creatures, in turning of the winds and the clouds which are controlled between the sky and the earth; are indeed proofs for people who understand.

2:165 Yet, there are some people who take (for worship) others besides Allah as rivals (with Allah). They love them like the love of Allah. But those who believe are strong in their love for Allah. If only those who do wrong could see (the Day of Judgment) when they will see the punishment that all power belongs to Allah wholly and that Allah is severe in punishment.

2:166 (On that day) those (leaders) who were followed will disown (declare innocent of) those who followed them when they will see the punishment, and then all relations will be cut off between them.

2:167 Those who have followed will say: "If we could have a (chance to) return (to the worldly life again), then we would disown (declare innocent from) them (leaders) as they have disowned (declare innocent from) us (today)." Thus Allah will show them their deeds as regrets for them. They will never get out of the hellfire.

2:168 O mankind! Eat of that which is lawful and good in the earth, and do not follow the footsteps of Satan. Surely, Satan is for you an open enemy.

2:169 Only he (Satan) commands you of the evil, the obscenity, and that you say against Allah what you do not know.

2:170 When it is said to them: "Follow what Allah has sent down." They say: "Nay! We will follow what we found our fathers on it (practiced)." (Would they follow) even if their fathers did not understand anything nor they did find right guidance?

2:171 The example of those who disbelieve is like the one who shouts to a group of sheep that does not hear except shouts and cries. (They are) deaf, dumb, and blind. So they do not understand.

2:172 O you who believe! Eat of the lawful things that Allah has provided you, and be grateful to Allah if you worship Allah only.

2:173 Surely! Allah has forbidden on you the dead (flesh), blood, flesh of swine, and that which is slaughtered in any other name than Allah. But if one is forced by necessity without willful disobedience or transgression, then there is no sin. Surely, Allah is Forgiving, Merciful.

2:174 Surely, those who conceal what Allah has sent down of the book (the Qur'an), and purchase therewith a small gain (worldly things), they do not eat into their bellies but fire. Allah will neither speak to them on the day of Resurrection nor will purify them, and for them will be a painful punishment.

2:175 Those are they who have purchased error at the price of guidance, and punishment at the price of forgiveness. So how bold are they to face the hellfire!

2:176 That is because Allah has sent down the book (the Qur'an) with the truth. Surely, those who differed in the book (the Qur'an) are far in a divergence.

2:177 It is not piety that you turn your faces towards the east and (or) the west (in prayers); but piety is to believe in Allah, the last day, the angels, the books, the prophets; give wealth in spite of love for it to relatives, orphans, poor, travelers, and to those who ask (for help); in ransom (to set free) of captives, establish prayer, pay obligatory charity, fulfill their promises when they promise, remain patient in adversity, affliction (disease), and at the time of fighting (war). Such are they who have proved true and those are they who are pious.

2:178 O you who believe! Retribution is prescribed for you in cases of murder: the free for the free, and the captive for the captive, and the female for the female. But if the killer is forgiven by (victim's) brother (or relatives), then something (of blood money for killing should be decided) according to usage (with fairness) and payment be made to the heir (of the victim) in a good manner. This is less painful and a Mercy from your Rabb. Whoever transgresses after this shall have a painful punishment.

2:179 There is (saving of) life for you in retribution, O people of understanding, so that you may become pious.

2:180 It is prescribed for you when death approaches any of you, if you leave wealth, that you make a bequest (the will) for parents and next of kin according to reasonable manners. It is an obligation on the pious.

2:181 Whoever changes it (the will) after hearing it, then only its sin will be upon those who change it. Truly, Allah is All-Hearer, All-Knower.

2:182 But whoever fears from a testator (who legally make will valid before death) partiality (some unjust act) or wrongdoing, and makes peace between the parties, there is no sin. Surely, Allah is Forgiving, Merciful.

2:183 O you who believe! The fasting is prescribed for you as it was prescribed for those before you, so that you may become pious.

2:184 Fasting days are numbered. If any of you are sick or on a journey, the same number of days (should be made up from) other days. For those who can fast with difficulty (such as old man), (can either fast or) ransom by feeding a poor (for every missed day). But whoever does good voluntarily, it is better. Your fasting is better for you if you know.

2:185 It is the month of Ramadan in which the Qur'an was revealed, guidance for mankind with clear proofs, and the criterion (between right and wrong). So whoever of you witnesses the crescent on the first night of the month, should fast therein. Whoever is sick or on a journey, fast the same number of days (make up from) other (later days). Allah wants for you ease, and does not want hardship for you so that you complete the (same) number (of days), and that you should glorify Allah as Allah has guided you, so that you may give thanks.

2:186 When my (Allah's) servants ask you (Muhammad) about me (Allah), then (answer them), indeed I (Allah) am near (to them). I (Allah) respond to the call of the caller when calls on me (Allah) (without any mediator). So let them respond to me (Allah) and believe in me (Allah) so that they may walk in the right way.

2:187 It is allowed for you on the night of the fasts to approach your wives. They are garments for you, and you are garment for them. Allah knows that you were deceiving yourselves, so Allah accepted your repentance and forgave you. So now you can approach your wives and seek what Allah has ordained for you (offspring). Eat and drink until the white thread (light of dawn) becomes distinct to you from the black thread (darkness of night), then complete fasts till the nightfall. Do not approach them (your wives) while you are confining yourselves in the mosques (I'tikaf during the last 10 days of Ramadan). These are the limits of Allah, so do not approach them. Allah makes clear Allah's verses to mankind so that they may become pious.

2:188 Do not seize one another's property by unjust means, nor present it to the authorities (or bribe the judges) so that you seize a portion of property of others sinfully while you know.

2:189 They ask you (Muhammad) of new moons. Say: They are (to determine) times for mankind and for pilgrimage. It is not piety that you enter the houses from their back doors, but the pious is the one who fears (Allah). So enter the houses through their (proper) doors and fear Allah so that you may attain success.

2:190 Fight in the way of Allah (against) those who fight you, but do not exceed (limit). Surely, Allah does not like the transgressors.

2:191 Kill them wherever you find them, and turn them out from where they have turned you out. (Though killing is bad) creating mischief is worse than killing. Do not fight them at the sacred mosque (at Makkah), unless they (first) fight you there. But if they fight you there, then kill them. Such is the reward of the disbelievers.

2:192 But if they cease, then surely Allah is Forgiving, Merciful.

2:193 Fight them until no oppression exists and worship becomes for Allah (alone). But if they cease, (there should be) no hostility except against the wrongdoers.

2:194 The sacred month is for the prohibited month, and for the prohibited things, (there is) the law of equality (subject to retaliation). Whoever transgresses against you, you transgress likewise. Fear Allah, and know that Allah is with the pious.

2:195 Spend in the cause of Allah and do not throw yourselves into destruction, and do good. Surely, Allah loves the righteous.

2:196 Complete the Hajj (obligatory pilgrimage to Makkah) and Umrah (optional visit to Makkah) for Allah. But if you are prevented from completing them, then send sacrifice whatever is easy to obtain from the offering, and do not shave your head until the offering has reached its appointed place. Whoever is sick among you or has an ailment in the scalp (needs shaving), then (that person must pay) ransom by fasting (for 3 days) or feed the poor (6 people) or sacrifice (one sheep). If you are safe and whoever performs Umrah till Hajj, then sacrifice whatever you can afford with ease of offering. Whoever cannot afford, then fast for 3 days during the pilgrimage and 7 days after return (to home), that is 10 days in all. That is for those whose family is not present at the Sacred Mosque. Fear Allah and know that Allah is severe in punishment.

2:197 The pilgrimage is in the well-known months. Whoever intends to perform Hajj in these months, then (there should be) no obscenity (sexual relations), nor wickedness (obscene language), nor wrangling (dispute unjustly) during the Hajj. Whatever good you do, Allah knows it. Take provision with you for the journey, but surely the best provision is piety. So fear Allah, O people of understanding.

2:198 There is no sin on you if you seek bounty of your Rabb during pilgrimage. When you return from Arafat, then remember Allah at the Mash'ar-al-Haram (at Muzdalifah). Remember Allah as Allah has guided you, and indeed before this you were with those who had lost the right way.

2:199 Then return from where the people return and ask forgiveness of Allah. Surely, Allah is Forgiving, Merciful.

2:200 So when you have accomplished your Hajj rites, then remember Allah as you used to remember your forefathers or with far more remembrance. But there are people who say: "Our Rabb! Give us (Allah's bounties) in this world!" Such people will have nothing in the hereafter.

2:201 Of them there are those who say: "Our Rabb! Give us good in the world and good in the hereafter, and save us from punishment of the fire!"

2:202 Such people will have a portion from (both worlds) what they earned. Allah is Swift in reckoning.

2:203 Remember Allah during the appointed days. But whoever hastens (to leave Mina) in 2 days, there is no sin and whoever delays, there is no sin, if the aim is to obey. Fear Allah, and know that you will be gathered to Allah.

2:204 Among the mankind, there is one whose speech fascinates you in the worldly life, and even calls Allah to witness on what is in its heart, yet that person is most quarrelsome of the opponents.

2:205 When one turns away (from you O Muhammad); strives in the land to spread mischief, destroy the crops, and the living being (cattle). Allah does not like the mischief.

2:206 When it is said to the one: "Fear Allah", arrogance takes it to sin. So hell is enough for such person, and worst indeed is the resting place!

2:207 Of mankind there is one who would sell (give away) life seeking the pleasure of Allah. Allah is full of Kindness to (Allah's) devotees.

2:208 O you who believe! Enter into Islam completely and do not follow footsteps of Satan. Indeed Satan is for you open enemy.

2:209 Then if you slide back after what came to you the clear signs, then know indeed that Allah is All-Mighty, All-Wise.

2:210 Do they wait for (anything else) except that Allah should come to them in shadows of the clouds along with the angels and the matter will be decided? To Allah all matters are returned (for decision).

2:211 Ask the children of Israel, how many clear signs Allah gave them. Whoever changes the favor (revelations) of Allah after that has come, then indeed Allah is Severe in punishment.

2:212 The worldly life is beautified for those who disbelieve, and they mock at those who believe. But those who are pious will be above them on the day of Resurrection. Allah grants (bounty) to whom Allah wills without limit.

2:213 Mankind was one community (with one religion). Allah sent the prophets with glad tidings and warnings, and sent with them the scripture with the truth to judge between people in what they differed in it. They did not differ in it except those who were given the book, after the clear proofs came to them, through hatred of one to another. Then Allah guided those who believed to what they differed in it of the truth by Allah's will. Allah guides whom Allah wills to right way.

2:214 Or do you think that you will enter paradise while trials have not yet come to you like those who passed away before you? Adversity and affliction befall them and were so shaken that even the messenger and those who believed with the messenger said: "When will help of Allah come?" (They were told) Yes! Certainly, the help of Allah is near!

2:215 They ask you (Muhammad) what they should spend (in charity). Say: "Whatever you spend of good wealth is for parents, kindred, the orphans, the poor, the travelers, and whatever good you do. Indeed Allah is Well-informed of it."

2:216 Fighting (in Allah's cause) is ordained for you (Muslims) though you dislike it. It may be that you dislike a thing and it is good for you, and it may be that you like a thing and it is bad for you. Allah knows but you do not know.

2:217 They ask you (Muhammad) about fighting in the sacred month (1st, 7th, 11th, and 12th months of Islamic calendar). Say: "Fighting in it is a great (offence). But preventing from the way of Allah, disbelieving in Allah, and expelling its inhabitants from the Sacred Mosque (at Makkah) are greater (offences) in the sight of Allah. Persecution is (more terrible) than killing. They (disbelievers) will not cease fighting you till they turn you back from your religion, if they can. Whoever of you turns away from its religion and dies as a disbeliever, such are those as their (deeds are) rendered void in this world and in the hereafter, and are the inmates of the fire. They will abide in it forever.

2:218 Surely, those who have believed, those who have emigrated (for Allah) and have striven hard in the way of Allah, all these hope for the Mercy of Allah. Allah is Forgiving, Merciful."

2:219 They ask you (Muhammad) about intoxicants and games of chance. Say: "There is great evil in both and (some) benefits for mankind, and their evil is greater than their benefit." They ask you how much they should spend. Say: "The surplus (beyond your needs)." Thus Allah makes clear to you Allah's revelations so that you may think

2:220 in this world and the hereafter. They ask you about orphans. Say: "Seeking good for them is best and if you intermix (your affairs) with theirs, then they are your brothers. Allah knows the mischievous (misuse property) from the well-wisher (protect property). If Allah wished, Allah could have put you into difficulties. Indeed Allah is All-Mighty, All-Wise."

2:221 Do not marry idolatresses (women worship idol) until they believe (in Allah alone). Indeed a believing captive woman is better than a free idolatress even though she pleases you. Do not give (your daughters) in marriage to idolaters (men worship idol) until they believe in (Allah alone) and indeed a believing captive (man) is better than a free idolater even though he pleases you. Those (idolaters) invite you to the fire, and Allah invites you to paradise and to forgiveness by Allah's grace. Allah makes Allah's verses clear for mankind so that they may remember.

2:222 They ask you about menstruation. Say: It is a harmful (illness), so keep away from women during menses and do not approach (sexual intercourse) them till they are cleansed. When they are cleansed, then go to them as Allah has commanded you. Surely, Allah loves those who repent and loves those who purify themselves.

2:223 Your wives are as a tilth (place of cultivation) for you, so go to your tilth as you wish. Send (good deeds) before you (leave the world) for yourselves. Fear Allah, and know that you will meet Allah (in the hereafter), and (O Muhammad) give good news to the believers.

2:224 Do not make (Allah's name) as an excuse in your oaths that you do good, act piously, and reconcile among people. Allah is All-Hearer, All-Knower.

2:225 Allah will not blame you for your vain utterances (unintentional) in your oaths, but Allah will call you to account for what your hearts have earned. Allah is Forgiving, Forbearing.

2:226 For those who swear for abstinence (sexual relation) from their wives, wait 4 months. Then if they reconcile, surely, Allah is Forgiving, Merciful.

2:227 If they decide upon divorce, then surely, Allah is All-Hearer, All-Knower.

2:228 Divorced women shall wait concerning themselves for 3 menstrual periods. It is not allowed for them that they conceal what Allah has created in their wombs, if they believe in Allah and the last day. Their husbands have right to take them back in that period, if they wish reconciliation. They (women) have rights similar to those (of men) over them in a just manner, but men have a degree (of responsibility) over them. Allah is All-Mighty, All-Wise.

2:229 (If) the divorce is (pronounced) twice, then either retain her with honor or release her with kindness (after 3rd pronouncement). It is not lawful for you (men) to take back what you have given them (wives) anything, except that both fear that you will not be able to keep the limits of Allah. Then if you fear that you will not be able to keep the limits of Allah, then there is no sin on both of you if she gives back as ransom for that (divorce). These are the limits of Allah, so do not transgress them. Whoever transgresses the limits of Allah, those are the wrongdoers.

2:230 If he divorces her (after 3rd pronouncement), then she is not lawful for him thereafter until she marries a husband other than him. Then, if he (new husband) divorces her, there is no sin on both of them that they return (marry again) to one another if both of them think that they will be able to keep the limits of Allah. These are the limits of Allah; Allah makes them clear to people who know.

2:231 When you divorce women and they reach their prescribed (waiting) period, then retain them with honor or let them go with kindness. But do not retain them to hurt, if you transgress and whoever does that, surely, he wrongs himself. You do not take the verses of Allah as a joke. But remember the favors of Allah upon you, and that Allah has sent down upon you of the book (the Qur'an) and of the wisdom (by which) Allah instructs you. With it fear Allah, and know that Allah is All-Aware of everything.

2:232 When you divorce women and they reach their prescribed (waiting) period, and then do not prevent them that they get married to their (former) husbands, when they mutually agree in a just manner. This is enjoyed on every one of you who believes in Allah and the last day. That is more virtuous and purer for you. Allah knows and you do not know.

2:233 The mothers shall breast-feed their children for 2 whole years for those (parents) who desire to complete the breast-feeding. But on him (father) to whom the child is born (shall bear the cost of) their mother's food and their clothing in a fair manner. No one should be charged except to its capacity. Neither mother should be made to suffer for her child, nor father to whom the child is born for his child. On the (father's) heir is incumbent the like of that (on the father). If both decide on weaning (withhold mother's milk and use other nourishment) by mutual consent and after due consultation, then there is no sin on them. If you decide to give out to nurse (foster mother) for your children, then there is no sin on you when you pay (the mother) what is due from you in an honorable manner. Fear Allah and know well that Allah is All-Seer of what you do.

2:234 Those who die and leave wives behind them, they (wives) shall wait (to marry again) with regard to themselves for 4 months and 10 days. When they reach their waiting term, then there is no sin on you what they (wives) do concerning themselves in a just manner. Allah is Well-acquainted with what you do.

2:235 There is no sin on you if you offer marriage proposal to (such) woman (during their waiting period) or you conceal it in yourselves. Allah knows that you will remember them (in your hearts), but do not make a promise with them secretly except that you say (if you wish to marry) in an honorable manner. Do not confirm on the tie of marriage till the prescribed term reaches its end. Know that Allah knows what is in your minds, so beware of Allah. Know that Allah is Forgiving, Forbearing.

2:236 There is no sin on you, if you divorce women while you have not yet touched (sexual relation) them, or fixed for them a settled portion (dower). Provide for them, the wealth according to its (person's) means and the poor according to its means, a reasonable provision, and a duty upon the righteous people.

2:237 If you divorce them before you touch (sexual relation with) them, and indeed you have fixed for them a settled portion (dower), then pay ½ of what you have fixed unless that they (women) agree to give up, or he (the husband) agrees to give up (pay full dowry) in whose hand is the knot of marriage. If you agree to give up (full dowry) that is closer to piety. You do not forget to show kindness among yourselves. Surely, Allah is All-Seer of what you do.

2:238 Be watchful over the (obligatory) prayers and the middle prayer. Stand before Allah with true devotion.

2:239 If you fear (an enemy), then pray on foot or riding. When you feel secure, then remember Allah as Allah has taught you that which you did not know.

2:240 Those of you who die and leave behind wives (should make) a bequest (will) for their wives for maintenance for one year without turning them out. But if they leave, then there is no sin on you in what they do for themselves in an honorable manner. Allah is All-Mighty, All-Wise.

2:241 For divorced women, a reasonable provision is a duty on the pious.

2:242 Thus Allah makes clear for you Allah's verse so that you may understand.

2:243 Have you (O Muhammad) not looked at those (people of Israel) who went from their homes in thousands for fear of death? Allah said to them: "Die". Then Allah revived them (to life). Surely, Allah is Bountiful to mankind, but most people do not give thanks.

2:244 Fight in the way of Allah and know that Allah is All-Hearer, All-Knower.

2:245 Who will lend Allah a beautiful loan so that Allah will multiply it many times? Allah decreases and increases (your provisions), and to Allah you will be returned.

2:246 Have you not thought about the chiefs of the children of Israel after Moses? When they said to a prophet of theirs: "Appoint for us a king and we will fight in the way of Allah." The prophet said: "Would you refrain from fighting, if fighting is prescribed for you?" They said: "Why should we not fight in the way of Allah when we along with our children have been driven out from our homes?" But when fighting was prescribed for them, they turned back except a few of them. Allah is All-Aware of the wrongdoers.

2:247 Their Prophet (Samuel) said to them: "Indeed Allah has appointed Saul a king for you." They said: "How can he be a king over us when we are more deserving for the kingdom than he, and he has not been given plenty of wealth?" He said: "Surely, Allah has chosen him over you and has increased him abundantly in knowledge and stature. Allah grants kingdom to whom Allah wills. Allah is All-Knower."

2:248 Their Prophet (Samuel) said to them: "Surely! A sign of his kingdom is that there shall come to you the ark (a wooden box), in which there is peace from your Rabb and a remnant of what is left by the family of Moses and family of Aaron, it will be carried by the angels. Surely, in that is a sign for you if you are believers."

2:249 When Saul set out with the army, he said: "Surely! Allah will test you with a river. Whoever drinks from it, he is not of me, and whoever not taste it, indeed he is of me, except him who takes in the hollow of his hand." Yet, they all drank from it, except a few of them. So when he had crossed the river and those who believed with him, they said: "There is no strength for us today against Goliath and his forces." But those who knew that they were to meet Allah, said: "How often a small group overcame a large group by the Grace of Allah? Allah is with the patient ones."

2:250 When they went forth for Goliath and his forces, they said: "Our Rabb! Pour on us patience, make our steps firm, and grant us victory over the disbelievers."

2:251 They routed those (disbelievers) by the permission of Allah, David killed Goliath, Allah gave David the kingdom and wisdom, and taught him what Allah willed. If Allah had not been repelling some people of them by some others, the earth surely would be filled with mischief. But Allah is Gracious to the worlds.

2:252 These are the verses of Allah; Allah recites them to you (O Muhammad) with truth. Surely, you are one of the messengers (of Allah).

2:253 Those messengers! Allah preferred some of them over some others. To some of them, Allah spoke directly, and Allah raised some of them in degrees of honor. Allah gave Jesus, the son of Mary, clear signs and supported him with Holy Spirit (angel Gabriel). If Allah willed, the people who received the clear verses (of Allah) would not have fought against each other. But they differed, some of them believed, and some of them disbelieved. If Allah willed, they would not have fought one another, but Allah does what Allah likes.

2:254 O you who believe! Spend of that which Allah has provided for you before a day comes when there will be no bargaining, no friendship, and no intercession. The disbelievers are they indeed who are the wrongdoers.

2:255 Allah! There is no one worthy of worship except Allah, the Ever-Living, the Sustainer and Protector. Neither slumber, nor sleep overtakes Allah. To Allah belongs what is in the heavens and what is on the earth. Who can intercede with Allah except with Allah's permission? Allah knows what happens to them (creations) in this world, and what will happen to them in the hereafter. They cannot gain access to anything out of Allah's knowledge except what Allah wills. Allah's Chair (Throne) extends over the heavens and the earth, and Allah does not feel fatigue in guarding them. Allah is the Exalted, the Great.

2:256 There is no compulsion in the religion. Surely, the right way has become distinct from the wrong (way). So whoever disbelieves in false deities and believes in Allah, indeed has grasped the firm handle that will never break. Allah is All-Hearer, All-Knower.

2:257 Allah is the Guardian of those who believe. Allah brings them out from darkness into light. Those who disbelieve, their supporters are false deities; they bring them out from light to darkness. They are the inmates of the fire; they will abide in it forever.

2:258 Have you not looked at him (Namrud) who disputed with Abraham about his Allah, because Allah had given him the kingdom? When Abraham said to him: "My Allah gives life and causes death." He said: "I give life and cause death." Abraham said, "Surely! Allah brings out the sun from the east; you bring it from the west." So he who disbelieved was completely defeated. Allah does not guide the wrongdoers.

2:259 Or like the one (Ezra) who passed by a town and it had tumbled upon its roofs. He said: "How will Allah ever bring life to this town after its death?" So Allah caused him to die for 100 years, and then Allah raised him to life. Allah asked: "How long did you remain dead?" Ezra said: "I remained dead for a day or part of a day." Allah said: "Nay, you have remained dead for 100 years: look at your food and your drink, they did not show change (not rotten); and look at your donkey (even its bones decayed)! Thus Allah has made you a sign for mankind. Look at the bones (of the donkey), how Allah will put them together and then will clothe them with flesh (and bring back to life)?" When it became clear to him, he said, "I know now that Allah has power over every thing."

2:260 (Remember) when Abraham said: "My Rabb! Show me how Allah gives life to the dead." Allah said: "Do you not believe?" Abraham said: "Yes! But to satisfy my heart (faith)." Allah said: "Then take 4 birds, and tame them to incline to yourself (slaughter them, cut them into pieces), and then put a portion on every hill of them, then call them, they will come to you in haste (flying). Know that Allah is All-Mighty, All-Wise."

2:261 The example of those who spend their wealth in the way of Allah is like that of a grain, it sprouts into 7 ears, and in every ear has 100 grains. Allah multiplies for whom Allah wills. Allah is All-Knower.

2:262 Those who spend their wealth in the way of Allah, then they do not follow up what they spent with reminder of generosity or injure them (feeling of the recipients), they will have their reward with their Rabb. There is no fear on them, nor shall they grieve.

2:263 A kind word and forgiving of faults are better than charity which is followed by injury. Allah is Rich (free from all needs), Forbearing.

2:264 O you who believe! Do not render in vain your charity by reminder of generosity or by injury (feelings of recipients), like those who spend their wealth to be seen by people, and do not believe in Allah, and the last day. Their example is like a smooth rock with dust over it; and when heavy rain falls on it, leaves it bare. They have no control over anything (reward) for what they have earned. Allah does not guide the disbelievers.

2:265 The example of those who spend their wealth seeking the pleasure of Allah and to strengthen their souls is like the example of a garden on a hill. When heavy rain falls on it and it yields double its harvest. If heavy rain does not fall on it, then even light rain is sufficient. Allah is All-Seer of what you do.

2:266 Would any of you wish to have a garden of date-palms and grapes with rivers flowing underneath it, and all kinds of fruits are in it for him; and while old age has taken over him, and he has weak children (can not look after themselves); be struck and burnt down by a fiery whirlwind? Thus Allah makes clear for you (Allah's) verses so that you may give thought.

2:267 O you who believe! Spend good things which you have legally earned, and what Allah has produced for you from the earth. Do not aim at bad (or worthless) things to spend (in charity) though you would not take it for yourself except you overlook (defects) in it. Know that Allah is Self-Sufficient, Praiseworthy.

2:268 Satan promises you of poverty and orders you of indecency; whereas Allah promises you forgiveness from Allah and bounty. Allah is Self-Sufficient, All-Knower.

2:269 Allah grants wisdom to whom Allah wills, and whoever is granted wisdom, is indeed granted good abundantly. But none remembers except people of understanding.

2:270 Whatever you spend out of your spending or you vow to spend out of your vows, indeed Allah knows that. The wrongdoers shall have no helpers.

2:271 If you declare your charity, it is well, and if you conceal it and give it to the poor, that is better for you. Allah will remove some of your bad deeds. Allah is All-Aware of what you do.

2:272 Not upon you (O Muhammad) is their guidance, but Allah guides whom Allah wills. Whatever good you spend, it is for yourselves, provided you do not spend but seek the pleasure of Allah. Whatever good you spend, it will be repaid back to you in full, and you will not be wronged.

2:273 Charity is for the poor who are wrapped up in the cause of Allah so that they are not able to move about to work in the earth. The ignorant people think them of wealthy because of modesty. You know them by their mark; they do not beg people with repeated demands. Whatever good you spend, surely Allah knows about that well.

2:274 Those who spend their wealth in Allah's cause by night, by day, secretly, and openly, their rewards are with their Rabb. There is no fear on them, nor shall they grieve.

2:275 Those who devour interest (usury), they will not stand (before Allah) except like those who are confused (insane) by the touch of Satan. That is because they say: "Indeed trade is like usury," while Allah has made the trade lawful and the usury unlawful. So those who receive admonition from their Rabb and they refrain, stop eating usury, shall not be punished for the past. Their case is left to Allah (to judge). But those who repeats (to usury), they are inmates of the fire; they will abide in it forever.

2:276 The usury deprives the blessings of Allah and increases by the charity. Allah does not like all ungrateful sinners.

2:277 Indeed those who believe, do righteous deeds, establish prayer, and give obligatory charity; for them their rewards are with their Rabb. There is no fear on them, nor shall they grieve.

2:278 O you who believe! Fear Allah and give up what remains due to you of usury if you are believers.

2:279 But if you do not do it, then be warned of war from Allah and Allah's messenger. If you repent, you may retain your capital sums. You do not wrong (by asking more than your capital), you will not be wronged (by receiving less than your capital).

2:280 If the debtor is in difficulty to pay (has no money), then delay until it is easy to repay. If you remit it by way of charity that is better for you if you know.

2:281 Fear the day when you shall be brought back to Allah. Then one will be paid what was earned and none shall be dealt unjustly.

2:282 O you who believe! When you contract a debt from one another for a fixed period, write it down. Let a scribe write it down between you in justice. A scribe shall not refuse to write it down as Allah has taught, so let the scribe write. Let the one (debtor) dictate on whom is the liability fearing Allah, the Rabb, and not diminish anything of what the person owes. But if the debtor is of poor understanding, or weak, or is not capable to dictate for itself, then let its guardian dictate in justice. Call for 2 witnesses out of your own men. If 2 men are not available, then a man and 2 women, such as you agree as witnesses, so that if one of the 2 women errs, one of them (2 women) reminds other. The witnesses should not refuse when they are called. Do not become weary to write down your contract, small or large for its period. That is more just with Allah, more reliable for evidence, and more convenient to prevent doubts among yourselves, except when it is a present trade which you carry out among yourselves, and then there is no sin on you if you do not write it down. But take witnesses when you trade with one another. Let neither scribe nor witness suffer harm and if you do (such harm), then it is wickedness on your part. So fear Allah and Allah teaches you. Allah is All-Knower of every thing.

2:283 If you are on a journey and you cannot find a scribe, then take a pledge in hand. But if any of you trusts another, then let one who is trusted fulfill its trust (faithfully), and let him fear Allah, his Rabb. You do not conceal the evidence, and whoever conceals it, surely its heart is sinful. Allah is All-Knower of what you do.

2:284 To Allah belongs what is in the heavens and what is in the earth. If you declare what is in your own selves or you conceal it, Allah will call you to account for it. Allah will forgive whom Allah wills and will punish whom Allah wills. Allah has power over everything.

2:285 The messenger (Muhammad) believes in what has been sent down to him from his Rabb and so do the believers. All believe in Allah, Allah's angels, Allah's books, and Allah's messengers. (They say): "We do not make distinction between any one of Allah's messengers." (They say): "We hear, and we obey. We seek Allah's forgiveness, our Rabb, and to Allah is the return (of all)."

2:286 Allah does not burden any one but beyond its capacity. Every person will get reward for what they have earned (good) and against them what they earned (evil). (The believers say): "Our Rabb! Punish us not if we forget or fall into error. Our Rabb! Do not lay on us a burden like that which Allah laid on those who were before us. Our Rabb! Do not lay on us burdens of which we do not have power (to bear). Pardon us. Forgive us. Have mercy on us. Allah is our Protector, so grant us victory over the disbelievers."

3. Al-'Imran : The Family of Imran

In the name of Allah, the Gracious, the Merciful

3:1 Alif-Lam-Mim.

3:2 Allah! There is no one worthy of worship but Allah, the Living, the Sustainer.

3:3 Allah has sent down to you (Muhammad) the book (the Qur'an) with truth confirming what came before it. Allah sent down the Torah and the Gospel,

3:4 before as a guidance for mankind. Allah sent down Al-Furqan (the criterion to judge between right and wrong). Surely, those who disbelieve in the verses of Allah, for them are severe punishment; and Allah is All-Mighty, All-Able of retribution.

3:5 Surely, nothing is hidden from Allah in the earth or in the heaven.

3:6 It is Allah who shapes you in the wombs as Allah wills. There is no one worthy of worship but Allah, the All-Mighty, the All-Wise.

3:7 It is Allah who has sent down to you (Muhammad) the book (this Qur'an). In it are verses absolutely clear, which are the basis of the book; and others are not clear. But those in whose hearts there is deviation (from the truth), they follow what is unclear thereof, seeking mischief, and seeking for its hidden meanings, but no one knows its hidden meanings except Allah. Those who are firmly rooted in knowledge they say: "We believe in it all from our Rabb." But none will heed except the people of understanding.

3:8 (They say): "Our Rabb! Do not deviate our hearts (from the truth) after when Allah has guided us, and grant us from Allah's Mercy. Surely Allah is the Bestower of bounties.

3:9 Our Rabb! Allah surely will gather mankind on a day, there is no doubt in it. Surely, Allah does not break Allah's promise."

3:10 Surely, those who disbelieve, neither their wealth nor their offspring will avail them anything from Allah and those are they who will be fuel of the fire.

3:11 (This will be) like the behavior of people of Pharaoh and those before them. They misrepresented Allah's verses, so Allah destroyed them for their sins. Allah is Severe in punishment.

3:12 Say (O Muhammad) to those who disbelieve: "You will be overpowered and gathered together to hell, and that is an evil resting place."

3:13 Indeed there was a sign for you in 2 groups which met in combat (in the battle of Badr): One group was fighting in the cause of Allah and the other was of disbelievers. They (the believers) were seeing them (the disbelievers) twice (in number) of them with their own eyes. Allah supports with victory whom Allah wills. Surely, in that is a lesson for those who have eyes to see.

3:14 Beautified is for men with love of things they desire from women and children, store up heaps of gold and silver, branded (beautiful) horses and cattle, and land. Those are possessions of the life of this world; but with Allah is an excellent abode (paradise) to return.

3:15 Say (O Muhammad): "Shall I inform you of better things than that? For those who fear, with their Rabb there are gardens in paradise beneath which rivers flow. They will abide forever in it, with pure spouses, and the pleasure of Allah. Allah is All-Seer of the servants."

3:16 Those who say: "Our Rabb! We have indeed believed, so forgive us for our sins and save us from punishment of the fire."

3:17 They are the patient, truthful, obedient, those who spend (in the way of Allah), and who pray for forgiveness in the early morning.

3:18 Allah bears witness that there is no one worthy of worship but Allah, (so do) the angels and people of knowledge, standing firm on justice. There is no one worthy of worship but Allah, the All-Mighty, the All-Wise.

3:19 Surely, the religion with Allah is Islam. Those who were given the scripture did not differ except after what the knowledge had come to them through transgression among themselves. Those who disbelieve in the verses of Allah, then surely, Allah is Swift in reckoning.

3:20 If they argue with you (Muhammad) say: "I have submitted my face to Allah (in Islam), and (so are) those who follow me." Say to those who were given the scripture and the illiterates (Arab pagans): "Do you submit yourselves (to Allah)?" If they submit, then indeed they are rightly guided. But if they turn away, then (do not worry) only upon you is to convey. Allah is All-Seer of all servants.

3:21 Surely! Those who disbelieve in the verses of Allah, kill the prophets without right, and kill those who command with justice of the people; give them tidings of a painful punishment.

3:22 They are those whose works will be lost in this world and in the hereafter, and they will have no helpers.

3:23 Have you not seen those who have been given a portion of the scripture? When they are invited to the book of Allah to settle their disputes, a party from them turns away, and they are averse.

3:24 This is because they say: "The fire shall not touch us but for few days." They deceive them in their religion by what they used to invent.

3:25 What will it be when Allah will gather them together on a day (there is) no doubt in it, every one will be paid (for) what they have earned, and none will be dealt unjustly?

3:26 Say (O Muhammad): "O Allah! Rabb of the kingdom, you (Allah) give the kingdom to whom you (Allah) please, take away the kingdom from whom you (Allah) please; you (Allah) give honor whom you (Allah) please, you (Allah) humiliate whom you (Allah) please; all the good is in your (Allah's) authority. Surely, you (Allah) have power over every thing.

3:27 You (Allah) make the night into the day and you (Allah) make the day into the night. You (Allah) bring out the living from the dead and you (Allah) bring out the dead from the living. You (Allah) give sustenance to whom you (Allah) please without measure."

3:28 Let not the believers take the disbelievers as allies instead of the believers. Whoever does that, there will not (be help) from Allah in anything, except that you fear of them for protection. Allah warns you of Allah's punishment and to Allah is the final return.

3:29 Say (O Muhammad): "Whether you conceal what is in your hearts or you reveal it, Allah knows it. Allah knows what is in the heavens and what is in the earth. Allah has power over every thing."

3:30 On the day when every one will be confronted with what they have done of good and what they have done of evil. (Wrongdoers) will wish if (there were) indeed a great distance between them and their evil deeds. Allah warns you of Allah's punishment and Allah is very kind to Allah's devotees.

3:31 Say (O Muhammad): "If you love Allah then follow me (the Qur'an and your way of life), Allah will love you and forgive your sins. Allah is Forgiving, Merciful."

3:32 Say (O Muhammad): "Obey Allah and the messenger (Muhammad)." If they turn away, then indeed Allah does not like the disbelievers.

3:33 Surely Allah chose Adam, Noah, the family of Abraham, and the family of Imran above mankind.

3:34 They were offspring of one another. Allah is All-Hearer, All-Knower.

3:35 (Allah heard) when the wife of Imran said: "O my Rabb! I have vowed to you (Allah) what is in my womb to be dedicated (for Allah's services). So accept this from me. Surely, you (Allah) are All-Hearer, All-Knower."

3:36 When she delivered her (Mary), she said: "My Rabb! I have delivered a female (instead of male)." Allah knew better what she delivered: "The male is not like the female, and I have named her Mary, and I seek refuge for her with you (Allah) and her offspring from Satan, the rejected."

3:37 Her Rabb accepted her with right acceptance. Allah made her grow in good manner and put her in the care of Zachariah. Whenever Zachariah entered to see her at her praying place, he found her with food. He said: "O Mary! From where you got this?" She said: "This is from Allah. Surely, Allah provides sustenance to whom Allah wills, without measure."

3:38 Thereupon, Zachariah invoked his Rabb, saying: "My Rabb! Grant me a good offspring. You (Allah) indeed the All-Hearer of invocation."

3:39 Then the angels called out to him while he was standing in prayer in the prayer place saying that: "Allah gives you glad tidings of John, (he will) confirm the word from Allah, noble, chaste, and a prophet from among the righteous."

3:40 He said: "My Rabb! How is it that I will have a son when old age has overtaken me and my wife is barren?" Allah said: "Allah does what Allah wills."

3:41 He said: "My Rabb! Make for me a sign." Allah said: "Your sign is that you will not speak to people for 3 days except by gesture. Remember your Rabb much, and glorify Allah in the evening and in the morning."

3:42 When the angels said: "O Mary! Surely, Allah has chosen you and purified you, and chosen you above all the women of the world.

3:43 O Mary! Remain obedient to your Rabb and prostrate, and bow down with those who bow down."

3:44 This is from the news of unseen which Allah inspires to you (O Muhammad). You were not with them when they (priests of the temple) threw their pens as to which of them should take care of Mary; and you were not with them when they disputed.

3:45 When the angels said: "O Mary! Surely, Allah gives you the glad tidings of a word (that you will have a son) from Allah; his name will be Messiah Isa (Jesus Christ), the son of Mary. He will be honored in this world and the hereafter, and will be one of those who are near (to Allah).

3:46 He will speak to the people in the cradle, in maturity, and will be of the righteous."

3:47 She said: "My Rabb! How is it that I shall have a son when no man has touched me?" Allah said: "Even so, Allah creates whatever Allah wills. When Allah decided a thing, Allah just says to it: 'Be!' and it is.

3:48 Allah will teach him (Jesus) the book and the wisdom, and the Torah and the Gospel

3:49 and (will make Jesus) a messenger to the children of Israel (saying) that: 'I have come to you with a sign from your Rabb. I will make for you from clay like a figure of a bird, breathe into it, and it will become a bird by the permission of Allah. I will heal the born blind, leper, and will bring life to the dead by the permission of Allah. I will inform you of what you eat, and what you store in your houses. Surely, in these are signs for you, if you are believers.

3:50 (I have come) to confirm that which is before me of the Torah, and to make lawful to you part of what was forbidden to you. I have come to you with a sign from your Rabb. So fear Allah and obey me.

3:51 Surely! Allah is my Rabb and your Rabb, so worship Allah. This is the right way.'"

3:52 When Jesus came to know of their disbelief, he said: "Who will be my helpers in the cause of Allah?" The disciples said: "We are helpers of the cause of Allah; we believe in Allah, and bear witness that we are Muslims."

3:53 (Then they said): "Our Rabb! We believe in what you (Allah) have sent down, and we follow the messenger (Jesus); so write us with those who bear witness."

3:54 They (disbelievers) plotted (to kill Jesus) and Allah also planned, and Allah is the best of planners.

3:55 (Remember) when Allah said: "O Jesus! I (Allah) will take you, will raise you to me (Allah), will purify you (of the statement that Jesus is Allah's son) of those who disbelieve, and I (Allah) will make those who follow you superior to those who disbelieve till the day of Resurrection. Then you will return to me (Allah) and I (Allah) will judge between you in which you used to dispute in it.

3:56 As to those who disbelieve, I (Allah) will punish them with severe punishment in this world and in the hereafter, and they will have no helpers.

3:57 As to those who believe (in the oneness of Allah) and do righteous deeds, Allah will grant them their reward in full. Allah does not love the wrongdoers."

3:58 Allah recites this to you (O Muhammad) of the verses and the wise reminder (the Qur'an).

3:59 Surely, the example of Jesus (born without father) to Allah is like the example of Adam (born without father and mother). Allah created him from dust, then Allah said to him: "Be!" and he was.

3:60 This is the truth from your Rabb, so do not be of those who doubt it.

3:61 Whoever disputes with you in it (concerning birth of Jesus) after what has come to you of knowledge, say (O Muhammad): "Come, let us call our sons and your sons, our women and your women, ourselves and yourselves: then we pray humbly and we invoke the curse of Allah on the liars."

3:62 Surely! This is the true story (about Jesus), and there is no one worthy of worship but Allah. Indeed, Allah is the All-Mighty, the All-Wise.

3:63 If they turn away (do not accept these proofs), then surely, Allah is All-Aware of mischief-makers.

3:64 Say (O Muhammad): "O people of the scripture! Come to a word common between us and between you: that we do not worship but Allah, that we do not associate with Allah anything, and that we shall not take others as Rabb besides Allah." If they turn away, then tell them: "Bear witness that we are Muslims."

3:65 O people of the scripture! Why do you dispute about Abraham (whether he was a Jew or Christian?), while the Torah and the Gospel were not sent down but long after him? Don't you understand?

3:66 You are those who have disputed about which you have knowledge. Why then you dispute about which you do not have any knowledge? Allah knows, and you do not know.

3:67 Abraham was neither a Jew and nor a Christian, but was a wholly devoted Muslim and he was not of the polytheists.

3:68 Surely, best of people (to claim near relationship) with Abraham are those who followed him, this prophet (Muhammad), and those who have believed in him. Allah is the Guardian of the believers.

3:69 A party of people of the scripture wishes to lead you astray, but they shall not lead astray anyone but themselves, and they do not realize it.

3:70 O people of the scripture! Why do you reject the verse of Allah while you bear witness (to the truth)?

3:71 O people of the scripture! Why do you mix truth with falsehood and conceal the truth while you know?

3:72 A party of people of the scripture says: "Believe in what is sent down on those who believe (Muslims) in early part of the day, and reject it at the end of the day, so that they (Muslims) may turn back (abandon truth).

3:73 You do not believe anyone but the one who follows your religion." Say (O Muhammad): "Surely! The true guidance is the guidance of Allah." (These people of the book do not believe) that someone (besides them) could be given revelation like what you have been given, or they will argue with you before your Rabb. Say (O Muhammad): "Surely! The bounty is in the hand of Allah; Allah gives it to whom Allah wills. Allah is Generous, All-knower."

3:74 Allah selects Mercy for whom Allah wills and Allah is the Owner of great bounty.

3:75 Among the people of the scripture (there are some) who, if you entrust them with a heap of wealth, will pay it back to you; and among them there are others who, if you entrust them with one dinar coin, will not pay it back to you unless you keep on demanding, that is because they say: "There is no blame on us (to betray and take the properties of) the unlettered people (who are not Jews or Christians)." But they tell a lie against Allah while they know it.

3:76 Yes, those who fulfill their covenant and fear Allah; surely Allah loves those who fear Allah.

3:77 Surely, those who sell the covenants of Allah and their oaths, they have a small price (gain), shall have no share for them in the hereafter. Neither Allah will speak to them, nor look at them on the day of Resurrection, nor Allah will purify them, and for them will be a painful punishment.

3:78 Surely, there is a party among them, they twist their tongues in reciting the book, so that you think it is from the book, but it is not from the book. They say: "It is from Allah," but it is not from Allah. They speak against Allah a lie while they know it.

3:79 It is not possible for a person whom Allah has given the book, the wisdom, and the Prophethood; then that person will say to people: "Worship me instead of

Allah." But (the person would say): "Be people of Allah according to the book you have been teaching and studying."

3:80 Nor that person will command you to take the angels and the prophets as your deity. Would that person command you to disbelieve after when you have become Muslims?

3:81 Allah took the covenant of the prophets, saying: "Whatever I (Allah) gave you of the book and wisdom, there will come to you a messenger (Muhammad) confirming what is with you; you must then believe in him and you must help him." Allah said: "Do you agree and do you take on my (Allah's) covenant?" They said: "we agree." Allah said: "Then bear witness; and I (Allah) am with you among the witnesses."

3:82 Whoever turns away after this, then they will be the transgressors.

3:83 Do they seek other than the religion of Allah, while all submitted to Allah who are in the heavens and the earth, willingly or unwillingly? To Allah they will be returned.

3:84 Say (O Muhammad): "We believe in Allah, what has been sent down to us, what was sent down to Abraham, Ishmael, Isaac, Jacob, and the tribes, and what was given to Moses, Jesus, and the prophets from their Rabb. We do not make distinction between any one of them and to Allah we surrender (in Islam)."

3:85 Whoever is seeking a religion other than Islam, it will never be accepted from that person, and will be among the losers in the hereafter.

3:86 How shall Allah guide those people who disbelieved after their belief, bore witness that the messenger (Muhammad) is true, and after the clear proofs had come to them? Allah does not guide the wrongdoers.

3:87 They are those whose recompense is that on them is the curse of Allah, and of the angels, and all of mankind.

3:88 They will abide forever in it (hell). Neither the punishment for them will be lightened, nor will they be reprieved,

3:89 except those who repent after that and mend their ways (do righteous deeds). Surely, Allah is Forgiving, Merciful.

3:90 Surely, those who disbelieve after their belief, then grow in disbelief, their repentance will never be accepted. They are those who are astray.

3:91 Surely, those who disbelieve, and die while they are disbelievers, will not be accepted from any one of them even if they offer earth of gold as ransom by it. Those are for them (there will be) a painful punishment and for them no helpers.

3:92 You never attain piety unless you spend (in Allah's cause) of what you love; and whatever you spend of a thing, surely, Allah knows all about that.

3:93 All food (which are lawful in Islam) was also lawful to the children of Israel, except what Israel (Yaqoob) made unlawful for himself before the Torah was revealed (to Moses). Say (O Muhammad): "Bring the Torah and recite it, if you are truthful."

3:94 Then, whoever invents the lie against Allah after that, those are they who are wrongdoers.

3:95 Say (O Muhammad): "Allah has spoken the truth; so follow the creed of Abraham upright, and he was not of the polytheists."

3:96 Surely, the first House (of worship) was set up for mankind which is at Bakka (Makkah), full of blessing, and guidance for the worlds.

3:97 In it are clear signs like station of Abraham (where he used to pray). Whoever enters it becomes secure. Allah has a right on the mankind to perform pilgrimage to the House (Ka'bah) who can afford the journey to it; and the one who denies (the Hajj), then surely Allah is not in need of the worlds.

3:98 Say: "O people of the scripture! Why do you reject the signs of Allah when Allah is Witness to what you do?"

3:99 Say: "O people of the scripture! Why do you stop from the way of Allah those who have believed, seek to make (the way) crooked, when you are witnesses? Allah is not unaware of what you do."

3:100 O you who believe! If you obey a group of those who were given the scripture, they would make you disbelievers after your belief!

3:101 How would you disbelieve, when the verses of Allah are recited to you, and among you is Allah's messenger (Muhammad)? Whoever holds fast to Allah, will indeed be guided to a right way.

3:102 O you who believe! Fear Allah as the right that Allah should be feared, and you do not die except when you are Muslims.

3:103 Hold fast the rope (Islam) of Allah all together, and you be not divided. Remember the favor of Allah on you when you were enemies, Allah made friendship between your hearts, you became brothers by Allah's Grace, you were on the brink of pit of the fire, and Allah saved you from it. Thus Allah makes clear to you Allah's verses, so that you may be guided.

3:104 There must be out of you a group of people who invite to the good, command the right, and forbid from the wrong. Those are they who will be the successful.

3:105 You do not be like those who are divided and disputed after the clear signs have come to them. For them is a terrible punishment.

3:106 On the day (of Resurrection) some faces will be brightened and some faces will be blackened. As for those blackened, their faces (will be said): "Did you disbelieve after your faith? Then taste the punishment (in hell) for your disbelief."

3:107 As for those brightened their faces, are in the Mercy of Allah, they will abide in paradise forever.

3:108 These are the verses of Allah, Allah recites them to you (O Muhammad) in truth, and Allah does not desire injustice to the worlds.

3:109 For Allah is what is in the heavens and what is in the earth, and all the matters go back (for decision) to Allah.

3:110 You are the best people raised for mankind. You command the good, forbid from the evil, and you believe in Allah. Had people of the scripture believed, it would have been better for them; some of them are believers, but most of them are transgressors.

3:111 They can never harm you except a little (annoyance); if they fight you, they will turn to you the backs, and they will not be helped.

3:112 Disgrace will be stamped upon them wherever they are found, except with a covenant (protection) from Allah, a covenant from people; and they have incurred wrath from Allah. The humiliation is stamped upon them because they used to reject the verses of Allah and they used to kill the prophets without right. That is because they disobeyed and used to transgress.

3:113 They are not all alike: a group of people of the scripture stand upright, they recite the verses of Allah during hours of the night, and they prostrate.

3:114 They believe in Allah and the last day, they command the good and forbid from the wrong, they hasten in doing good deeds, and they are of the righteous.

3:115 Whatever good they do, they will never be denied (its rewards) of good; and Allah knows the pious well.

3:116 Surely, those who disbelieved, neither their wealth will avail them nor their offspring from (the wrath of) Allah anything. They are companions of the fire; they will abide in it forever.

3:117 Example of what they spend in this life of the world is like the example of a wind with severe cold; it strikes harvest of people who have wronged themselves and destroy it. Allah has not wronged them, but they have wronged themselves.

3:118 O you who believe! Do not take as friends except from out of you (your religion); they (disbelievers) do not spare any effort to make you corrupt. They desire whatever distresses you. Indeed their hatred is apparent from their (sayings), and what their hearts conceal is even greater. Surely, Allah has made plain to you the verses if you understand.

3:119 You are those who love them but they do not love you, and you believe in all the scripture (Torah, Gospel, while they disbelieve in Qur'an). When they meet you, they say: "We believe." But when they go apart, they bite (tips of their) fingers at you in rage. Say (to them): "Perish in your rage." Certainly, Allah knows all what are in their hearts.

3:120 If a good befalls you, it grieves them; and if a misfortune overtakes you, they rejoice at it. But if you remain steadfast and become pious, their design would not harm you at all. Surely, Allah encompasses of what they do.

3:121 (Remember) when you (Muhammad) left from your household early morning to post the believers at their stations for the battle (of Uhud); Allah is All-Hearer, All-Knower.

3:122 (Remember) when 2 groups of you were about to show weakness and Allah was their protector (by strengthening hearts). In Allah the believers should trust.

3:123 Certainly Allah helped you at Badr when you were completely weak. So fear Allah that you may be grateful.

3:124 (Remember) when you (Muhammad) said to the believers: "Is it not sufficient for you that your Rabb helps you by sending down 3,000 angels?"

3:125 Yes, if you are steadfast and fear Allah, when they (enemy) come to you rushing; your Rabb will help you with 5,000 of marked angels.

3:126 Allah has not but made glad tidings for you and assures your hearts with it. There is no help except from Allah, the All-Mighty, the All-Wise.

3:127 (Allah might) cut off a group of those who disbelieve, or subdue them, and they (withdraw) frustrated.

3:128 The decision is not for you (Muhammad) whether Allah turns in Mercy to them or Allah punishes them; surely, they are wrongdoers.

3:129 To Allah belongs what is in the heavens and what is in the earth. Allah forgives whom Allah wills, and Allah punishes whom Allah wills. Allah is Forgiving, Merciful.

3:130 O you who believe! Do not devour usury which is doubled and redoubled, but fear Allah so that you may achieve success.

3:131 Fear the fire, which is prepared for the disbelievers.

3:132 Obey Allah and the messenger (Muhammad) so that you may be shown mercy.

3:133 Rush to forgiveness from your Rabb, and for paradise whose width (is like that of) the heavens and the earth, which is prepared for the pious,

3:134 those who spend (in the way of Allah) in prosperity and in adversity, who control their anger, who forgive the people; Allah loves such righteous people,

3:135 and those who, when they do indecent or wrong themselves, they remember Allah and ask forgiveness for their sins. No one can forgive the sins but Allah. They do not persist on what wrong they have done, while they know.

3:136 For such people, their reward is forgiveness from their Rabb, gardens with the rivers flow underneath (paradise), and they will abide forever in it. How excellent is the reward for those who do (good deeds)!

3:137 Passed before you (many such) situations. So travel in the earth and see how the ending of the deniers (of truth) was.

3:138 This (the Qur'an) is a declaration for mankind, a guidance and admonition for the pious.

3:139 Do not be weak (against your enemy), nor be grieved, and you will be upper handed if you are true believers.

3:140 If a wound has touched you, so have (disbelieving) people touched a wound similar to that. These days, Allah turns them among people so that Allah knows those who believe, and Allah may take martyrs from among you. Allah does not like the wrongdoers,

3:141 so that Allah may purse those who believed and destroy the disbelievers.

3:142 Do you think that you will enter paradise before Allah tests those of you who strove hard (in Allah's cause) and tests those who were the steadfast?

3:143 Indeed you used to wish for death before you met it. Surely, you have faced it now and you are observing it.

3:144 Muhammad is not but a messenger; indeed messengers have passed away before him. Then if he dies or is killed, will you turn back on your heels (become disbelievers)? Whoever turns back on its heels, will not harm Allah at all, and Allah will give reward to the grateful.

3:145 No one can die without the permission of Allah at an appointed term. Whoever desires a reward of the world, Allah will give it here; and whoever desires a reward of the hereafter, Allah will give it there. Allah will reward the grateful.

3:146 (In the past) many prophets have fought with large religious people. Neither had they lost heart for what they suffered in the way of Allah, nor did they weaken, nor did they degrade themselves. Allah loves the steadfast.

3:147 Their saying was not except what they said: "Our Rabb! Forgive our sins and our excesses (transgressions) in our affairs, set firmly our feet, and help us against the disbelievers."

3:148 So Allah gave them reward of this world, and excellent reward will be given in the hereafter. Allah loves the righteous people.

3:149 O you who believe! If you obey those who disbelieve, they will drive you back on your heels, and you will turn back (from faith to disbelief) as losers.

3:150 But Allah is your protector, and Allah is the best of the helpers.

3:151 Allah will cast terror into the hearts of those who disbelieve, because they associated (others in worship) with Allah whom Allah has not sent any authority with it. Their abode is the fire and evil is the abode of the wrongdoers.

3:152 Indeed Allah was truthful to you in Allah's promise when you were destroying (your enemy in the battle of Uhud) with Allah's permission, until when you showed weakness and fell into dispute about the order, and you disobeyed (the prophet) after what Allah showed you (the booty) which you loved. There were some among you who desired this world and some of you who desired the hereafter. Then Allah made you flee from them (your enemy) so that Allah may test you. Surely, Allah forgave you, and Allah is Gracious to the believers.

3:153 (Remember) when you were climbing (the hill to flee), and you were not paying a heed to anyone, and the messenger (Muhammad) was calling you in your rear. Then Allah rewarded you grief for grief (to teach lesson) so that you may neither grief over what you escaped, nor on (any misfortune) which befalls you. Allah is Well-Aware of what you do.

3:154 Then after this grief, Allah sent down upon you an inner peace. Slumber overtook a group of you. Another group was concerned about themselves (on how to save themselves, ignoring the others and the prophet) and thought wrongly of Allah, thought of the (days of) ignorance. They said: "Is there for us anything in the affair?" Say (O Muhammad): "Indeed all the affairs are for Allah." They hide within themselves (in mind) what they did not reveal to you. They said: "If there was anything for us in the affair, none of us would have been killed here." Say (to them): "Even if you had remained in your houses, those for whom death were destined would have gone forth to the place of their death. But it was the test of Allah what was in your hearts so that Allah may purge what was in your hearts. Allah is All-Knower of what is in the hearts."

3:155 Surely, those of you who turned their backs on the day when the 2 armies met (the battle of Uhud); only Satan made them slip (run away from the battle) for some sins of what they had earned. But indeed, Allah has forgiven them. Surely, Allah is Forgiving, Forbearing.

3:156 O you who believe! You do not be like those disbelievers who say to their brethren when they travel through the earth or are fighting: "If they had stayed with us, neither would they have died nor they would have been killed." Allah may make it a cause of regret in their hearts. Allah gives life and causes death. Allah is All-Seer of what you do.

3:157 If indeed you are killed in the way of Allah or die, surely forgiveness and Mercy from Allah are better than what you could gather (of worldly wealth).

3:158 If indeed you die, or are killed; surely to Allah you all will be gathered.

3:159 By the Mercy of Allah, you (Muhammad) deal with them gently. Had you been rough and hard-hearted, surely they would have broken away from you.

So pardon them, ask (Allah's) forgiveness for them; and consult them in the affairs. But when you have taken a decision, then put your trust in Allah. Surely, Allah loves those who put their trust in Allah.

3:160 If Allah helps you, then none can overcome you. If Allah forsakes you, then who is there who can help you after Allah? In Allah alone the believers should put their trust.

3:161 It is not (conceivable) for a prophet that he defrauds (take booty illegally) and he who defrauds will bring forth what he has defrauded on the day of Resurrection. Then every person shall be fully compensated what it has earned, and they shall not be wronged (unjustly).

3:162 Can a person who follows the good pleasure of Allah, be like the one who is laden with the wrath of Allah (by taking booty illegally)? Its abode is hell and the worst destination.

3:163 They have different grades with Allah, and Allah is All-Seer of what they do.

3:164 Indeed Allah has done a great favor on the believers when Allah has sent to them a messenger (Muhammad) from among themselves, who recites to them Allah's verses (the Qur'an), purifies them, teaches them the book (the Qur'an) and the wisdom, and indeed they were before in clear error.

3:165 Or when a calamity indeed falls on you, you have already inflicted (enemies at the battle of Badr) twice to that you say: "From where does this come to us?" Say: "It is from yourselves (for your evil deeds)." Indeed Allah has power over every thing.

3:166 What befall you on the day (the battle of Uhud) when 2 armies met, was by the permission of Allah in order that Allah might test the true believers,

3:167 and that Allah might know those who were tainted with hypocrisy. It was said to them: "Come, fight in the way of Allah or at least defend (yourselves)." They said: "Had we known that fighting, we would have certainly followed you." On that day, they were nearer to disbelief than to faith. They said with their mouths what was not in their hearts. Allah has full knowledge of what they were concealing.

3:168 Those who said to their brethren while they sat at home: "Had they followed us, they would not have been killed." Say: "Avert the death from your own selves, if you are truthful."

3:169 You do not think about those who are killed in the way of Allah as dead. But they are alive with their Rabb, they are well-provided.

3:170 They are pleased for what Allah has bestowed upon them out of Allah's bounty, rejoice for those who have not yet joined them (in their happiness) but are left behind so that no fear shall come on them and they will not grieve.

3:171 They rejoice at the favor of Allah's bounty, and that Allah does not waste reward of the believers.

3:172 Those who after their injury (in the battle of Uhud) responded to the call of Allah and the messenger (Muhammad); there will be a great reward for such of those who do good and fear Allah,

3:173 those believers to them the people (hypocrites) said: "Surely, the people (pagans) have gathered against you a great army, so fear them." But it increased them in faith, and they said: "Allah alone is sufficient for us, and Allah is the excellent Guardian."

3:174 So they returned (home) with favor and bounty of Allah, and no harm touched them. They followed the good pleasure of Allah. Allah is the Owner of great bounty.

3:175 It is only Satan that suggests fear to you of its supporters. So you do not fear them, but fear Allah, if you are true believers.

3:176 (O Muhammad) let not those who rush in towards disbelief, grieve you. Surely, they can never harm Allah the least. It is Allah's will that Allah will not give them any portion in the hereafter. For them there is a great punishment.

3:177 Surely, those who purchase disbelief at the price of faith, they will never harm Allah the least. For them, there is a painful punishment.

3:178 Let not those who disbelieve think that Allah gives respite to them (by postponing punishment) is good for them. Only Allah gives respite to them so that they may add more sins. For them there is a humiliating punishment.

3:179 Allah will not leave the believers on what they are now, until Allah separates the evil from the good. Allah will not inform you about the unseen, but Allah chooses messengers whom Allah wills. So believe in Allah and Allah's messengers. If you believe and fear Allah, then for you there is a great reward.

3:180 Do not think those who greedily withhold (charity) of what Allah has granted them of Allah's bounty (wealth), it is good for them, but it is bad for them. They will be hung around their necks with what they greedily withheld of their wealth on the day of Resurrection. For Allah is the heritage of the heavens and the earth. Allah is Well-Acquainted with what you do.

3:181 Indeed, Allah has heard the saying of those who say: "Truly, Allah is poor and we are rich!" Allah will record what they have said, their killing of the prophets in defiance of right, and Allah will say: "Taste the punishment of the burning fire!

3:182 That is for what evil your hands have sent. Allah is never unjust to (Allah's) servants."

3:183 They (disbelievers) say: "Surely, Allah has taken our promise that we shall not believe a messenger until he brings to us an offering that it will consume the fire (from heaven)." Say: "Surely, messengers have come to you before me with clear signs and even with what you are asking for. Then why did you kill them if you are truthful?"

3:184 If they reject you (O Muhammad), so were messengers rejected before you, who came with clear signs and the scripture, and the book of enlightenment.

3:185 Everyone shall taste death. Only you shall be paid your reward on the day of Resurrection. Whoever is drawn away from the fire and is admitted to paradise, will indeed be successful. The life of this world is nothing except enjoyment of illusion (deception).

3:186 You shall certainly be put to test in your wealth and your lives. You shall certainly hear from those who have been given the book before you, and from those who practiced polytheism with many hurtful things. If you remain patient and become pious, then surely, that will be a proof of your firm determination.

3:187 (Remember) when Allah took a covenant of those who were given the scripture so that they explain it to people and not hide it. But they threw it away behind their backs, and bought with it a little gain. Worst is what they buy!

3:188 Those who rejoice for what they have done, and love that they are praised for what they have not done, should not think that they will escape from the punishment, but for them there is a painful punishment,

3:189 for Allah belongs the dominion of the heavens and the earth, and Allah has power over every thing.

3:190 Surely! In the creation of the heavens and the earth, and in the alternation of night and day, surely are signs for people of understanding.

3:191 Those who remember Allah while standing, sitting, and lying on their sides, and they think deeply on the creation of the heavens and the earth, (say): "Our Rabb! You (Allah) have not created all this in vain. Glory is to you (Allah)! Save us from the punishment of the fire.

3:192 Our Rabb! Surely, those whom you (Allah) admit to the fire, you (Allah) have disgraced them, and there will be no helpers for the wrongdoers.

3:193 Our Rabb! Surely, we have heard a crier calling for the faith (saying): 'Believe in your Rabb,' so we have believed. Our Rabb! Forgive us our sins, remove from us our evil deeds, and make us die with the truly righteous.

3:194 Our Rabb! Grant us what you (Allah) promised us through your (Allah's) messengers and do not disgrace us on the day of Resurrection. Indeed you (Allah) never violate promise."

3:195 Their Rabb answered to them: "I (Allah) do not let the good deed of any worker among you go to waste, whether male or female. Each of you is from the other (offspring). So those who emigrated, or were driven out from their homes, and those who were persecuted in my (Allah's) cause, and who fought, and were killed (in Allah's cause); surely, I (Allah) will remit from them their evil deeds and will certainly admit them to gardens under them rivers flow (in paradise), a reward from Allah. Allah holds best of rewards."

3:196 Let not deceive you by free movement and wealth of those who disbelieved in the land.

3:197 Their enjoyment is brief. Their destination is hell; the worst resting place.

3:198 But those who fear their Rabb, for them are gardens under which rivers flow (in paradise). They will reside in it forever, hospitality from the presence of Allah. With Allah is best for the truly righteous.

3:199 Certainly, among people of the scripture, there are those who believe in Allah and what has been revealed to you (Muhammad) and what has been revealed to them (before you). They bow in humility to Allah; they do not sell the verses of Allah at a little price. For them, their reward is with their Rabb. Surely, Allah is Swift to take account.

3:200 O you who believe! Be steadfast, be more patient than enemy, stand firm as guards against enemy, and fear Allah; so that you may be successful.

4. An-Nisa' : The Woman

In the name of Allah, the Gracious, the Merciful

4:1 O mankind! Fear your Rabb, who created you from a single person (Adam), created from him his mate (Eve), and spread from both of them many men and women. Fear Allah whom you demand (your rights) through Allah, and (do not cut relations of) the wombs (kinship). Surely, Allah is All-Watcher over you.

4:2 Give orphans their wealth (when they are able to handle), you do not exchange your bad things for their good ones, and you do not devour their wealth by adding it to your wealth. Surely, this is a great sin.

4:3 If you fear that you will not be able to do justice among the orphans, then marry women (without orphan child) of your choice: 2, 3, or 4. But if you fear that you will not be able to do justice (between wives), then marry only one or what your right hands possess (your captives). That is nearer to prevent you from doing injustice.

4:4 Give women (whom you marry) their dower (as obligation) willingly. But if they willingly give up to you any part of it on their own, then you may enjoy it without fear of any harm.

4:5 You do not give your wealth (for business) to foolish people whom Allah has made a means of support for you (your family); but feed them from it, clothe them, and speak to them with good words.

4:6 Test the orphans (their abilities) until they reach the age of marriage. Then if you perceive of them mature minded, then deliver to them their wealth. You do not eat it wastefully and hastily (fearing) that they would grow up (and demand it). Whoever (amongst guardians) is rich, should abstain entirely (from taking wages for taking care of their wealth), and whoever is poor, let him take what is just and reasonable. When you deliver their wealth to them, take witness in their presence. Allah is All-Sufficient in taking account.

4:7 There is a share for men from what is left by parents and near relatives and a share for women from what is left by parents and near relatives: whether the property is small or large, a legal share.

4:8 If the relatives, orphans, and the poor come (at the time of) division of an inheritance, then give them something out of it, and speak to them kind words.

4:9 Let those (executors and guardians) have the same fear in their minds as they would have for their own if they were to leave weak offspring behind. So fear Allah and speak right and fair words.

4:10 Surely, those who eat up (misuse) wealth of orphans wrongfully, they eat up only fire in their bellies, and they will soon be burnt in the blazing fire.

4:11 Allah enjoins you in your children (inheritance): share of one male (son) shall be equal to share of 2 females (daughters). If there are more than 2 daughters, then for them is $2/3^{rd}$ of what was left (inheritance); and if there is only one daughter, then her share is ½. For parents, each one of them will get $1/6^{th}$ of what was left if the deceased left children behind, and if the deceased left no children and the parents are only heirs, then the mother shall get $1/3^{rd}$ and if the deceased left brothers or (sisters), then the mother will get $1/6^{th}$. (This distribution in all cases shall be) after fulfilling the terms of the (last) will and the payment of debts. With respect to parents and children, you do not know who is more beneficial to you; therefore Allah has issued this ordnance. Indeed Allah is All-Knower, All-Wise.

4:12 For you is ½ of what left of your wives if they did not leave a child. If they had a child, then for you a $1/4^{th}$ of what they left after fulfilling the term of their (last) will and the payment of debt. For your wives a $1/4^{th}$ of what you have left if you did not leave a child. If you leave a child, then for them is $1/8^{th}$ of what you have left behind, after fulfilling the terms of your (last) will and the payment of debt. If man or woman is testator having no parents and children or women but has a brother or a sister, then for each one of the 2 is a 1/6th. But if they are more than 2, then they shall share in a 1/3rd after fulfilling the terms of the (last) will and the payment of debt, without being harmful (no loss to anyone). This is the commandment from Allah. Allah is All-Knowing, Forbearing.

4:13 These are limits (set by) Allah and whoever obeys Allah and Allah's messenger (Muhammad), will be admitted to gardens under them the rivers flow (in paradise) to abide forever therein, and that will be the great success.

4:14 Whoever disobeys Allah and Allah's messenger (Muhammad), and transgresses Allah's limits, Allah will admit them to fire, they will abide in it forever; and they will have a disgraceful punishment.

4:15 Those who commit lewdness (illegal sexual intercourse) of your women, call to witness against them 4 of you; and if they bear witness, then confine them (i.e. women) in their houses until the death comes to them or Allah makes for them a way.

4:16 Those 2 (man and woman) who commit (illegal sexual intercourse) among you (married or unmarried), punish them both. Then if they repent and mend their ways (do good deeds), then leave them alone. Surely, Allah is Acceptor of the repentance, Merciful.

4:17 Surely, (acceptance of) repentance by Allah is for those who do evil in ignorance, then they repent soon; and for those Allah accepts their repentance. Allah is All-Knower, All-Wise.

4:18 The repentance is not for those who do evil deeds until when one of them faces death and says: "Surely I repent now;" or those who die while they are disbelievers. Allah has prepared for them a painful punishment.

4:19 O you who believe! It is not lawful for you that you inherit the women by force and you do not put constrains upon them, so that you take away a part of (dowry) what you have given them, except that they commit open lewdness (illegal sexual intercourse). Reside with them in a good manner. If you dislike them, it may be that you dislike a thing and Allah has placed in it much good.

4:20 But if you intend to replace your wife by another and you have given one of them a heap of gold (as dowry), do not take away anything from her. Would you take it by slander and with clear sin (accuse her unjustly)?

4:21 How you could take it back when one of you has gone in to another (with happiness), and they have taken from you a firm pledge (of marriage)?

4:22 You do not marry woman whom your fathers married, except what has happened before. Indeed it was lewdness and admonition, and an evil way.

4:23 Forbidden to you (for marriage) are: your mothers, your daughters, your sisters, your father's sisters, your mother's sisters, your brother's daughters, your sister's daughters, your (foster) mothers who gave you suck, your (foster) milk suckling sisters, your wife's mothers, your step daughters who are under your guardianship; born from your wives you had conjugal relations with them, but if you did not have conjugal relations with them then there is no sin on you (to marry their daughters), the wives of your sons who are from your own side, and 2 sisters in wedlock at the same time, except what happened before. Surely, Allah is Forgiving, Merciful.

4:24 (Also forbidden are) married women, except those (captives) whom your right hands possess. This is a decree of Allah upon you. Allah has made lawful for you those who are beyond these limits that you seek (them in marriage) by your wealth (with bridal gift) desiring chastity, not sin (commit illegal sexual intercourse). You benefit of it from them (enjoy sexual relations), you give them their bridal-due as a duty; and there is no sin on you for what you mutually agree of it after its prescription. Surely, Allah is All-Knower, All-Wise.

4:25 Whoever of you is not able to afford that he marries free believing women, (they may wed) believing girls from among those (captives) whom your right hands possess, and Allah knows all about your faith, you are one from another. Then marry them with permission of their guardians and give them their bridal-due in a fair manner; they (the above said captive girls) should be chaste (in wedlock), not adulterous, nor give secret love affairs. When they are married, if they commit lewdness (illegal sexual intercourse), then upon them (punishment is) half of what is upon the free (unmarried) women. This is for those who fear (falling into) sin but that of you whose self-restraint is better for you. Allah is Forgiving, Merciful.

4:26 Allah wishes to make clear to you, and to guide you to ways of those who were before you, and to accept repentance of you, and Allah is All-Knower, All-Wise.

4:27 Allah wishes to accept repentance of you, and wishes those who follow their lusts that you (believers) deviate far away (from the right way).

4:28 Allah wishes to lighten (burden) for you; and human was created weak (by nature).

4:29 O you who believe! You do not eat up your wealth between you unjustly except that it is trading by mutual consent among you. You do not kill yourselves. Surely, Allah is Merciful to you.

4:30 Whoever commits that through aggression and injustice, Allah will burn that person in fire, and that is easy for Allah.

4:31 If you avoid major sins that you are forbidden to do, Allah will admit you to a noble entrance (paradise).

4:32 You do not envy what Allah has conferred abundantly of it on some of you over (others). For men there is a share from what they earned, (and likewise) for women there is a share for what they earned. Ask Allah of Allah's bounty. Surely, Allah is All-Knower of everything.

4:33 To everyone, Allah has appointed heirs of that left by parents and relatives. With whom your right hands made covenant, give them their (by wills) share. Truly, Allah is a Witness over everything.

4:34 Men are in charge of women because Allah has conferred abundantly on one of them over others, and because they spend (to support) from their wealth. Thus the righteous women are devoutly obedient (to Allah and to their husbands) who guard in (husband's) absence what Allah has ordered them to guard (their chastity, their husbands property, etc). But those (women) whom you fear their rebellion, admonish them (first), and (then) leave them (alone) in the beds, (and last) beat them (lightly, if it is useful), then if they obey you, then you do not seek against them a way (excuse to punish). Surely, Allah is High, Great.

4:35 If you fear a breach between the two (man and his wife), then appoint an arbitrator from his family and an arbitrator from her family; if they both wish to set things right, Allah will bring reconciliation between them. Indeed Allah is All-Knower, All-Aware (of every thing).

4:36 You worship Allah and do not associate with Allah anything (in worship), and do good to parents, relatives, orphans, the needy, the neighbor (who is) relative, the neighbor (who is) a stranger, to the companion by your side, the wayfarer (you meet), and those captives possessed by your right hands. Surely, Allah does not love one who is proud and boastful;

4:37 those who are stingy and command others with stinginess and who hide the bounties which Allah has given them. Allah has prepared for the disbelievers a disgraceful punishment.

4:38 Also those who spend their wealth to be seen by people, and neither they believe in Allah nor in the last day, and those who take Satan for them as a companion; then what a bad companion (they have)!

4:39 What (harm) they would have if they had believed in Allah and the last day, and spend out of what Allah has given them for sustenance? Allah is All-Knower of them.

4:40 Surely! Allah does not do wrong (not even) weight of an atom. If there is a good (done), Allah doubles it, and gives (extra) with a great reward from Allah.

4:41 How (will it be) then when Allah brings from each community a witness and Allah brings you (O Muhammad) against these people as a witness?

4:42 On that day (of Judgment) those who disbelieved and disobeyed the messenger (Muhammad) will wish if they were leveled (buried) with the earth, for they will not (be able to) hide any matter from Allah.

4:43 O you who believe! Do not offer the prayer while you are intoxicated until you know (the meaning) of what you utter, nor (while you are) defiled (or in a state of sexual impurity) except when passing on way (traveling) until you wash yourselves. If you are ill, or on a journey, or one of you came from a toilet, or you had a sexual contact with women but did not find water, then do Tayammum with clean earth and rub with it your faces and your hands. Truly, Allah is Pardoning, Forgiving.

4:44 Have you not seen those who were given a portion of the book? They purchased error (wrong way), and they wish that you (believers) lose the right way.

4:45 Allah knows well your enemies. Sufficient is Allah as a Protector, and sufficient is Allah as a Helper.

4:46 Of those who are Jews (some of them) change words from their right places and they say: "We hear and we disobey," and "Hear us and (let you O Muhammad) hear nothing." And 'Raina' (an evil word used in Arabic in those days) with a twist of their tongues and a mockery of the religion (Islam). If they had only said: "We hear and we obey", and "Hear us and look at us (to make us understand)," it would have been better for them, and more proper. But Allah has cursed them due to their disbelief, so they do not believe except a few.

4:47 O you who have been given the scripture! Believe in what Allah has revealed (to Muhammad) confirming what is (already) with you, before Allah wipes out your faces and turns them to their backs, or Allah curses them as Allah cursed the people of Sabbath-breakers. The commandment of Allah is executed.

4:48 Surely, Allah does not forgive that a partner is ascribed to Allah, and Allah forgives other than that to whom Allah wills. Whoever associates anyone with Allah, indeed has devised a tremendous sin.

4:49 Have you not seen those who claim purity (though they believe in sharing partners with Allah) for themselves? Although it is Allah who purifies whom Allah pleases, and they will not be wronged the least (even equal to the thread of a date-stone).

4:50 See how they invent a lie against Allah, and it is sufficient to be a clear sin.

4:51 Have you not seen those who were given a portion of the book? They believe in baseless superstitions and false deities (forces of Satan) and they say to those who disbelieved that they are better guided than those who believed to the right way.

4:52 They are those whom Allah has cursed, whom Allah curses can find no helper,

4:53 or do they have a share in the dominion? Then they would not give people even a speck on the back of a date-stone.

4:54 Or do they envy people (Muhammad and his followers) on whom Allah has given from Allah's bounty? Indeed Allah had already given family of Abraham the book, the wisdom, and Allah gave them a great kingdom.

4:55 Of them who believed in him (Muhammad), and of them were some who turned away from him (Muhammad). Hell is sufficient for a blaze.

4:56 Surely! Those who rejected Allah's verses, Allah will burn them in fire. As often as their skins are burnt out, Allah will change them for other skins so that they may taste the punishment. Truly, Allah is Mighty, All-Wise.

4:57 Those who believe and do good deeds, Allah will admit them to gardens under which rivers flow (paradise), abide in it forever. For them in it will have purified spouses, Allah will admit them to a shade with plentiful shade.

4:58 Surely! Allah commands you that you should deliver the trusts to (those who are) worthy of them (rightful owners), and when you judge between people, you judge with justice. Surely, Allah excellently teaches you of it. Truly, Allah is All-Hearer, All-Seer.

4:59 O you who believe! You obey Allah and you obey the messenger (Muhammad), and those among you having authority. Then if you dispute among yourselves in anything, refer it to Allah and the messenger (Muhammad), if you believe in Allah and the last day. That is better and more suitable (for final) determination.

4:60 Have you not seen those (hypocrites) who claim that they believe in what has been sent down to you (O Muhammad), and what was sent down before you? They wish that they go for judgment (in their disputes) to fake judges though they were ordered that they reject it. But Satan wishes to mislead them misleading far astray.

4:61 When it is said to them: "Come to what Allah has sent down and to the messenger (Muhammad)," you (Muhammad) see the hypocrites turn away from you with dislike.

4:62 How then (they behave) when a calamity befalls them for what their hands have sent forth? They come to you (Muhammad) swearing by Allah: "Surely, we want only goodwill and reconciliation."

4:63 They (hypocrites) are those of whom Allah knows what is in their hearts; so turn away from them, admonish them, and speak to them about themselves with penetrating (effective) words.

4:64 Allah never sent a messenger, but who obeyed by permission of Allah. If they (hypocrites), when they wronged themselves, they could have come to you (Muhammad) and asked forgiveness of Allah, and the messenger had asked forgiveness for them, they would have found Allah Forgiving, Merciful.

4:65 But no (O Muhammad), by your Rabb, they will not believe until they accept you as a judge in their disputes between them, and they do not find in themselves any resistance on what you have decided, and accept with full submission.

4:66 If Allah had enjoined upon them (saying): "You kill yourselves (the innocent ones kill the guilty ones) or leave from your homes," they would not have done it except very few of them. If they had done what they were commanded of it, it would have been better for them, and would have added (to their faith) firmness;

4:67 and then Allah would have given them a great reward from Allah

4:68 and Allah would have guided them to the right way.

4:69 Whoever obeys Allah and the messenger (Muhammad), they will be with those upon whom Allah has bestowed (Allah's) blessings - the prophets, the truthful, the martyrs, and the righteous. How excellent these companions will be!

4:70 That is the bounty from Allah, and Allah is sufficient as All-Knower.

4:71 O you who believe! You take your precautions, and advance in groups or advance all together.

4:72 Indeed among you is one who lags behind (from fighting in Allah's cause). Then if a calamity befalls you, that person says: "Indeed Allah has bestowed (Allah's) blessings upon me that I was not present with them."

4:73 But if a bounty from Allah befalls you, that person would say as if there had not been affection between you and him: "(I wish) I had been with them; then I would have achieved a great success."

4:74 Let those (believers) who fight in the way of Allah only be (those) who sell life of this world in exchange of the hereafter. Whoever fights in the way of Allah and is killed or gets victory; Allah will grant a great reward.

4:75 What (is wrong) with you that you do not fight in the way of Allah (to help) the weak (and oppressed) among men, women, and children, who say: "Our Rabb! Bring us out of this town whose people are oppressors; and appoint for us from Allah a protector, and appoint for us from Allah a helper?"

4:76 Those who believe, fight in the way of Allah. Those who disbelieve, fight in the way of Satan. So you (believers) fight against the friends of Satan. Surely strategy of Satan is weak.

4:77 Have you not seen those when it was said to them to hold back their hands (from fighting) and establish the prayer, and pay obligatory charity? Now, when the fighting is enjoined upon them, then a group of them fear people as they should have feared Allah or even greater fear, and say: "Our Rabb! Why has Allah ordained on us the fighting? Why did not Allah defer it for us for another (short) period?" Say (to them): "Enjoyment of this world is short." The hereafter is better for whoever fears Allah, and you shall not be (treated unjustly) in the least (even equal to the thread of a date-stone).

4:78 Wherever you may be, death will overtake you even if you are in fortified towers. If a good happens to them, they say: "This is from Allah," but if an evil befalls them, they say: "This is from you (O Muhammad)." Say: "All are from Allah," so what (is wrong with) these people that they do not seem to understand any word?

4:79 Whatever reaches to you of good, is from Allah, but whatever befalls you of evil, is from yourself. Allah has sent you (Muhammad) for mankind as a messenger, and Allah is Sufficient as a Witness.

4:80 Whoever obeys the messenger (Muhammad) has indeed obeys Allah, and whoever turns away, then Allah has not sent you (O Muhammad) over them as a keeper.

4:81 They say: "We are obedient," but when they leave your (Muhammad's) presence, a section of them spend night (in planning) other than what you have said. But Allah records what they spend night (in planning). So turn from them, and put your trust in Allah. Allah is All-Sufficient as a Trustee.

4:82 Do they not ponder over the Qur'an? Had it been from other than Allah, surely they would have found many contradictions in it.

4:83 Whenever there comes to them a matter of peace, or fear, they spread it; but if they had referred it to the messenger and to those having authority among them, it would have been known by those who may infer (right conclusions) from them. If there had not been the bounty of Allah on you and Allah's Mercy, surely you would have followed Satan, except a few (of you).

4:84 Then fight (O Muhammad) in the way of Allah, you are not accountable except for yourself. Urge the believers (to fight), may be that Allah will restrain evil of those who disbelieved. Allah is Stronger in might and Stronger in punishment.

4:85 Whoever intercedes for a good cause, will have a share of it, and whoever intercedes for an evil cause, that person will have a burden of it. Allah has control over everything.

4:86 When you are greeted with a greeting, you greet better than that, or return it equally. Indeed, Allah keeps account over everything.

4:87 Allah! There is no one worthy of worship but Allah. Allah will gather you together on the day of Resurrection; there is no doubt in it. Who is more truthful than Allah in statement?

4:88 Then what is the matter with you regarding the hypocrites (that you have become) 2 parties? Allah has cast them back (to disbelief) for what they have earned. Do you want that you guide whom Allah lets go astray? Whoever Allah lets go astray, you will not find any way for them.

4:89 They wish that if you disbelieve, as they disbelieve, you become alike. So you should not take friends from them, till they emigrate in the way of Allah. But if they turn back (from Islam), seize them, kill them wherever you find them, and neither you take from them a friend nor a helper,

4:90 except those who join a group, between you and between them there is a treaty of peace, or those who come to you restraining their hearts that they fight you or they fight their own people. Had Allah willed, Allah would have given them power over you, and they would have fought you. So if they withdraw from you, do not fight against you, and offer you peace, then Allah has not made for you a way (to fight) against them.

4:91 You will find others (hypocrites) who wish that they be secure from you and they be secure from their people. Whenever they return to a mischief, they plunge into it. So if they do not withdraw from you, nor offer you peace, nor they restrain their hands, then seize them and kill them wherever you find them. Those people, Allah has made for you against them a clear sanction.

4:92 It is not (appropriate) for a believer to kill a believer except by mistake. Whoever kills a believer by mistake, then it is commanded to free a believing captive and blood-money (compensation) be paid to that person's (deceased's) family, except that they remit it as a charity. If that person is from enemy people to you and is a believer; then freedom of a believing captive (is sufficient). If that person is from people between you and between them is a covenant, then blood-money is paid to the family, and freedom of a believing captive. But whoever does not find it (means to free a captive and or blood-money), then fast for 2 consecutive months seeking repentance from Allah. Allah is All-Knower, All-Wise.

4:93 Whoever kills a believer intentionally, the punishment is to abide in the hell forever. That person will incur the wrath of Allah, Allah will lay curse on that person, and Allah has prepared a great punishment.

4:94 O you who believe! When you go forth (to fight) in the way of Allah, do not distinguish and say to whoever offers to you greetings of peace: "You are not a believer" seeking advantage of life of this world. Allah has abundant booties like this for you. (Remember what) you were before but then Allah graced upon you. So distinguish (carefully before considering anyone disbeliever). Surely Allah is Well-Aware of what you do.

4:95 Not equal are those of the believers who sit (at home), except those who are handicapped (disabled), and those who strive in the way of Allah with their wealth and their lives. Allah has exalted those who strive with their wealth and their lives over those who sit in rank (at home). To each, Allah has promised good (paradise), and Allah has graced those who strive above those who sit (at home) with a great reward;

4:96 (higher) ranks from Allah, and forgiveness and Mercy. Allah is Forgiving, Merciful.

4:97 Surely! Those whom the angels caused death while they have wronged themselves, they (angels) say to them: "In what (condition) were you?" They reply: "We were oppressed in the earth." They (angels) say: "Was not the earth of Allah spacious enough (for you) to emigrate in it?" Those people will find their abode in hell, an evil destination.

4:98 Except the oppressed ones from men, women and children who cannot devise a plan, and they cannot direct their way,

4:99 these people may be that Allah will pardon them. Allah is Pardoning, Forgiving.

4:100 Whoever emigrates in the way of Allah, will find in the earth many places of refuge and abundant resources. Whoever leaves from home as an emigrant of Allah and Allah's messenger and then death overtakes that person, surely reward is incumbent on Allah. Allah is Forgiving, Merciful.

4:101 When you travel in the earth, there is no sin on you to shorten your prayer if you fear that those who have disbelieved will harm you. Surely, the disbelievers are for you open enemies.

4:102 When you (O Muhammad) are among them, and you lead them in prayer (during war), let a group of them stand (in prayer) with you and let them take their arms (with them). When they finish prostrations, then let them (take positions) in your rear and let other group come up who has not yet prayed to pray with you, and let them take their precaution and their arms. Those who disbelieve wish, if you neglect your arms and your baggage, then they could jump upon you in a single rush. But there is no blame on you if you lay aside your arms due to inconvenience with you of rain or that you are sick, but take precaution for yourselves. Surely, Allah has prepared a humiliating torment for the disbelievers.

4:103 When you have finished the prayer, remember Allah standing, sitting, and on lying your sides, but when you are secure (from danger), establish prayer. Surely, the prayer is enjoined on the believers at fixed time.

4:104 Do not be weak in pursuit of these people (enemy); if you are suffering hardships, they too are suffering hardships as you are suffering; while you hope from Allah the reward what they do not hope, Allah is All-Knower, All-Wise.

4:105 Surely, Allah has sent down to you (O Muhammad) the book (this Qur'an) with the truth so that you may judge between the people with what Allah has shown you, and you do not be an advocate for those who are treacherous.

4:106 Seek forgiveness of Allah, indeed Allah is Forgiving, Merciful.

4:107 Do not argue for those who deceive themselves. Indeed, Allah does not like anyone who is treacherous and sinful.

4:108 They may hide (their crimes) from people, but they cannot hide from Allah. As Allah is with them even when they plot by night in words what Allah does not approve. Allah encompasses of what they do.

4:109 You may have argued for them in the life of this world, but who will argue with Allah for them on the day of Resurrection, or who will be over them their defender?

4:110 Whoever does evil or wrongs against own soul then seeks forgiveness of Allah, will find Allah Forgiving, Merciful.

4:111 Whoever commits a sin, only earns against own soul. Allah is All-Knower, All-Wise.

4:112 Whoever commits a fault or a sin and then throws it on an innocent person, indeed burdens own soul with false charge and flagrant sin.

4:113 Had it not been the grace of Allah upon you (O Muhammad) and Allah's Mercy, even if a group of them had decided that they would mislead you, but in fact they did not mislead except themselves, and they did not harm you in the least. Allah has sent down to you the book (the Qur'an), the wisdom, and taught you what you did not know. The grace of Allah upon you (Muhammad) is great.

4:114 There is no good in most of their secret talks except one who commands in charity, or good deeds, or conciliation between people, and who does this, seeking the pleasure of Allah, Allah will then give a great reward.

4:115 Whoever opposes the messenger (Muhammad) after what has become clear, and follows the guidance other than the way of the believers, Allah will keep that person to where that person has chosen, Allah will burn in hell - what an evil destination.

4:116 Surely! Allah will never forgive the one who associates with Allah. But other than that, Allah forgives whom Allah wills. Whoever associates others with Allah, has indeed misled misleading far away.

4:117 They (Pagan Arabs worship others than Allah) do not invoke besides Allah but female deities, and they do not invoke but rebellious Satan.

4:118 Allah cursed Satan, who said: "I will take an appointed portion of your (Allah's) servants.

4:119 I will mislead them, I will arouse in them false desires, I will order them, and they will cut off ears of the cattle. I will order them and they will change the creation of Allah." Whoever takes Satan as a guardian besides Allah, certainly has suffered a clear suffering.

4:120 He (Satan) makes promises to them, arouses in them false desires, and Satan does not promise them but deception.

4:121 These people will have their abode is hell, and they will not find from it an escape.

4:122 But those who believe (in the oneness of Allah) and do good deeds, Allah will admit them to the gardens under which rivers flow (paradise), they will abide in it forever. Promise of Allah is true, and whose word is truer than Allah?

4:123 (The final results will be) neither your desires nor desires of people of the scripture. Whoever does evil, will be required to pay for it, and will not find besides Allah any protector or any helper.

4:124 Whoever does good deeds, whether male or female, and is a believer, these people will enter paradise and they will not be wronged even a speck on the back of a date-stone.

4:125 Who can be better in religion than the one who submits face to Allah, is righteous, follows religion of Abraham the upright, and Allah did take Abraham as a friend?

4:126 To Allah belongs what is in the heavens and what is in the earth. Allah is encompassing of everything.

4:127 They ask you about women. Say: Allah instructs you about them, and what is recited to you in the book about orphan girls whom you do not give them what was ordained for them (marriage-gift and inheritance) and yet you desire that you marry them. (Allah reminds you concerning) weak (and helpless) children among you that you stand for orphans with justice. Whatever good you do, indeed Allah is All-Aware of it.

4:128 If a woman fears cruelty or desertion of her husband, then there is no blame on both of them that they reconcile themselves between reconciliation; and reconciliation is better. The souls are swayed by greed. But if you do good and fear Allah, then surely, Allah is Well- Acquainted with what you do.

4:129 You will never be able to do justice between wives even if you passionately desire, so do not incline the whole inclination (to one of them with more time and provision), and leave others as hanging. But if you act rightly and fear Allah, then indeed Allah is Forgiving, Merciful.

4:130 But if they separate (by divorce), Allah will make all independent (of each other and provide abundance) from Allah's bounty. Allah is All-Sufficient, All-Wise.

4:131 To Allah belongs whatever is in the heavens and whatever is in the earth. Surely, Allah has advised those who were given the scripture before you, and to you (O Muslims) that you fear Allah. But if you disbelieve (do at your own risk), then surely belongs to Allah what is in the heavens and what is in the earth, and Allah is Rich (free of all wants), Praise-Worthy.

4:132 Belongs to Allah what is in the heavens and what is in the earth. Allah is All-Sufficient as a Defender of affairs.

4:133 If Allah wills, Allah can take you away, O mankind, and bring others. Allah is All-Potent over that.

4:134 Whoever desires reward of this world, then (you should know that) with Allah alone is the reward of this world and the hereafter. Allah is All-Hearer, All-Seer.

4:135 O you who believe! You stand firm for justice as witnesses for Allah, though it is against yourselves, or parents, and relatives whether the party is rich or poor; Allah has more right than both of them. So you do not follow your desires to do injustice. If you distort (the facts) or you refrain, then (you should know that) Allah is Well-Aware of what you do.

4:136 O you who believe! Believe in Allah, and Allah's messenger (Muhammad), and the book (the Qur'an) which Allah has sent down to Allah's messenger, and the scripture which Allah has sent down before. Whoever disbelieves in Allah, Allah's angels, Allah's books, Allah's messengers, and the last day, then indeed is mislead a misleading far away.

4:137 Surely, those who believe, then disbelieve, then believe again, and again disbelieve, then increase in their disbelief; Allah will neither forgive them, nor will guide them on the right way.

4:138 Give tidings to the hypocrites that for them there is painful punishment,

4:139 those who take the disbelievers as allies instead of believers. Do they seek honor for them? Surely, the honor is for Allah all together.

4:140 Indeed Allah has sent down to you in the scripture (this Qur'an) that when you hear the verses of Allah being rejected and being mocked at, then you do not sit with them, until they engage in a talk other than that; otherwise indeed you are like them. Surely, Allah will collect the hypocrites and disbelievers in hell all together.

4:141 Those (hypocrites) are watching closely to you. If there is a victory for you from Allah, they say: "Were we not with you?" But if there is a chance (of success) for disbelievers, they say: "Did we not have mastery over you and did we not protect you from the believers (Muslims)?" Allah will judge between you and them on the day of Resurrection. Allah will never make for the disbelievers over the believers a way (to triumph).

4:142 Surely, the hypocrites (try to) deceive Allah, but it is Allah who deceives them. When they stand up to the prayer, they stand with laziness to be seen by the people, and they do not remember Allah but little;

4:143 (they are) swaying between this and that, neither to these nor to those. Whom Allah sends astray, you can never find for them a way (to Islam).

4:144 O you who believe! You do not take the disbelievers as allies instead of believers. Do you wish that you give Allah against yourselves a clear proof?

4:145 Surely, the hypocrites will be in the lowest depths of the fire; and you will not find for them any helper.

4:146 Except those who repent (from hypocrisy), mend their ways, hold fast to Allah, and purify their religion for Allah, they will be with the believers. Allah will grant to the believers a great reward.

4:147 Why should Allah punish you if you have thanked Allah and you have believed (in Allah)? Allah is All-Appreciative (of good), All-Knower.

4:148 Allah does not like that words of evil should be uttered publicly except (by someone) who has wronged. Allah is All-Hearer, All-Knower.

4:149 If you disclose a good, or keep it secret, or pardon an evil; then surely, Allah is Forgiving, All-Powerful.

4:150 Surely, those who disbelieve in Allah and Allah's messengers and they wish that they differentiate between Allah and Allah's messengers, they say: "We believe in some and we disbelieve in others," and they wish that they take between (belief and disbelief) a way,

4:151 they are those disbelievers in truth. Allah has prepared for the disbelievers a humiliating punishment.

4:152 Those who believe in Allah and Allah's messengers, and they do not differentiate between any one of them (messengers), Allah will give them their rewards. Allah is Forgiving, Merciful.

4:153 The people of the scripture ask you that you cause to descend upon them a book from heaven. Surely they have asked Moses greater than that, they said: "Show us Allah in public." So they were struck with a thunderbolt for their wickedness. Then they took (to worship) the calf even after what came to them with clear signs. (Even so) Allah forgave them and Allah gave Moses a clear authority.

4:154 Allah rose over them the mount (Tur) for their covenant, and Allah said to them: "Enter the gate prostrating with humility." Allah also said to them: "You do not violate (by doing worldly works in the) Sabbath (Saturday)." Allah took from them a firm covenant.

4:155 (Even then) they broke the covenant, rejected the verses of Allah, and killed the prophets unjustly. They say: "Our hearts are wrapped (we do not understand what the messengers say)." But Allah has set a seal upon them (their hearts) due to their disbelief. So they do not believe but a few.

4:156 They (went so far) in their disbelief that they uttered against Mary a mighty slander.

4:157 They say that: "We have killed Messiah Jesus, son of Mary, messenger of Allah." Neither did they kill him, nor did they crucify him, but (it was made) to resemble for them. Surely those who differed in it (they were) in doubt about it. They did not have any knowledge about it except following the guess and surely they did not kill him (Jesus).

4:158 Allah raised him (Jesus) up (with body and soul) to Allah (in the heavens). Allah is All-Powerful, All-Wise.

4:159 There is none of the people of the scripture who will believe in this fact before their death. On the day of Resurrection, he (Jesus) will be a witness against them.

4:160 Due to the wrong-doing of those who call themselves Jews, and for their hindering many people from the way of Allah; Allah made unlawful to them certain foods (which had been) lawful for them,

4:161 for their taking of usury though they were forbidden from taking it, and for their devouring of wealth of people wrongfully. Allah has prepared for the disbelievers among them a painful punishment.

4:162 But those among them who are firmly rooted in knowledge, and those believers who believe in what has been sent down to you (Muhammad) and what was sent down before you, and those who perform prayer, and who pay obligatory charity, and who believe in Allah and in the last day; it is they to whom Allah will give a great reward.

4:163 Surely, Allah has revealed to you (O Muhammad) just as Allah had revealed to Noah and the prophets after him. Allah also revealed to Abraham, Ishmael, Isaac, Jacob, and (his) offspring, Jesus, Job, Jonah, Aaron, Solomon, and to David Allah gave the Psalms.

4:164 The messengers Allah has mentioned to you before, and messengers Allah has not mentioned them to you, and Allah spoke to Moses (directly).

4:165 The messengers are bearers of glad tidings and warners so that there is not any plea for people against Allah after the messengers. Allah is All-Powerful, All-Wise.

4:166 Allah bears witness to that which Allah has sent down (the Qur'an) to you (Muhammad). Allah has sent it down with Allah's knowledge, and the angels bear witness too. Allah is All-Sufficient as a Witness.

4:167 Surely, those who disbelieve and prevent people from the way of Allah, surely they have strayed far away.

4:168 Surely, those who disbelieve and do wrong, Allah will neither forgive them, nor Allah will guide them to any way

4:169 except way of hell, they will abide in it forever, and that is easy for Allah.

4:170 O mankind! Surely, the messenger (Muhammad) has come to you with the truth from your Rabb. So believe in him, it is better for you. But if you disbelieve, then indeed to Allah belongs what is in the heavens and the earth. Allah is All-Knower, All-Wise.

4:171 O people of the scripture! Do not exceed the limits in your religion. Do not say of Allah but the truth only. The Messiah Jesus, son of Mary (no more than) a messenger of Allah and Allah's word "Be" which Allah conveyed to Mary and a soul from Allah (was created by Allah in her womb). So believe in Allah and Allah's messengers, you do not say: "Three (trinity)!" Give up, it is better for you. Only Allah is one Allah. Glory is to Allah far above that Allah should have a son. For Allah belongs what is in the heavens and what is in the earth. Allah is All-Sufficient as a Guardian.

4:172 The Messiah will never disregard that he be a servant to Allah, nor the angels near (to Allah). Whoever rejects from Allah's worship and shows arrogance, Allah will certainly gather them all together before Allah.

4:173 As for those who believe and do good deeds, Allah will give their due rewards, and give them more out of Allah's bounty. But as for those who refuse and show arrogance, Allah will punish them with a painful punishment. They will not find for them besides Allah any guardian or any helper.

4:174 O mankind! Surely, there has come to you proof (Muhammad) from your Rabb, and Allah has sent down to you a clear light (this Qur'an).

4:175 As for those who believed in Allah and held fast to Allah, Allah will admit them in Mercy from Allah and bounty (paradise), and guide them to a right way.

4:176 They ask you to pronounce a ruling. Say: "Allah pronounces for you a ruling about Al-Kalala (who leaves behind no heirs). If a man dies, he does not have a child and a sister, then for her is ½ (inheritance) of what he has left. He (brother) will inherit her (sister) if she does not have a child. If there are 2 (sisters), then for them are 2/3rd of what he left, and if they were (many) brothers (and sisters) male and female, then the male will have the 2 shares (twice) of females. Allah makes clear to you lest you go astray. Allah is All-Knower of everything."

5. Al-Ma'idah : The Table Spread
In the name of Allah, the Gracious, the Merciful

5:1 O you who believe! Fulfill your obligations. Lawful to you (for food) are beasts of cattle except what is hereby recited to you. You are not allowed to hunt while you are in state of Ihram (Pilgrimage). Surely, Allah commands what Allah wills.

5:2 O you who believe! Do not violate (the sanctity of the) symbols of Allah, nor of the sacred month, nor of the animals (brought for sacrifice), nor of the garlanded (animals marked for security), nor the people coming to the Sacred House (Makkah) seeking the bounty of their Rabb and good pleasure. When you finish the Ihram (Pilgrimage), you may hunt. Let not the hatred of some people, who once stopped you from the Sacred Mosque (at Makkah), lead you to transgress. You help one another in righteousness and piety; and do not help one another in sin and transgression. Fear Allah. Surely, Allah is Severe in punishment.

5:3 Forbidden to you (for food) are: dead animal's meat, blood, the flesh of swine, and what has been slaughtered as a sacrifice to other than Allah, (killed by) strangling and by a violent blow, and by a headlong fall, and by the goring of horns, and that devoured (partly eaten) by a beast except that slaughtered by you (before its death), and what slaughtered on altars (elevated places for sacrifice), and that you seek knowledge of your fate by dividing arrows. All these are sins (disobedience of Allah). This day, those who have given up all hope, disbelieved of your religion. So you do not fear them, but fear Allah. This day, Allah has perfected for you your religion, Allah has completed upon you Allah's favor, and Allah has approved for you Islam as your religion. Whoever is forced by hunger, not inclined to sin (not eaten forbidden food), then surely, Allah is Forgiving, Merciful.

5:4 They ask you (Muhammad) what is lawful for them (as food). Say: "Lawful are made to you pure good things. What you have taught to hunting animals (beasts and birds of prey) train them for hunting; you teach them what (knowledge) Allah has taught you. So you may eat what they catch for you, but invoke the name of Allah on it, and fear Allah. Surely, Allah is Swift in reckoning."

5:5 This day made lawful to you are pure good things. Food of those who have been given the scripture is lawful to you and your food is lawful to them. (Lawful to marry) chaste women from the believing women and chaste women from those who were given the scripture before you, when you have given them their bridal due (given by husband to his wife at the time of marriage) desiring chastity not lewdness (illegal sex), nor taking them as secret companions (girl friends).

Whosoever disbelieves in faith, indeed their work will go to waste, and they will be in the hereafter among the losers.

5:6 O you who believe! When you stand up for the prayer, then wash your faces and your hands up to the elbows, you wipe your heads, and wash your feet up to the ankles. If you are (in state of) Janaba (had sexual discharge), then purify yourself (take full bath). If you are ill or on a journey or one has come out from the toilet, or you have been in sexual contact (with wives), make Tayammum if you do not find water, then look for clean earth and you wipe your faces and hands with it. Allah does not want to lay upon you any hardship, but Allah wants to purify you, and to complete Allah's favor upon you so that you may be thankful.

5:7 You remember the favor of Allah upon you and Allah's covenant that Allah bound you with it when you said: "We hear and we obey." You fear Allah. Surely, Allah is All-Knower of what is in your hearts.

5:8 O you who believe! You be steadfast for Allah as witnesses in equity and let not enmity of people drive you so that you do not do justice, deal justly. That is nearer to piety, and fear Allah. Surely, Allah is Well-Aware of what you do.

5:9 Allah has promised to those who believe and do good deeds, for them is forgiveness and great reward.

5:10 Those who disbelieve and deny Allah's verses, they will be companions of hellfire.

5:11 O you who believe! Remember the favor of Allah upon you when some people decided (made a plan) that they stretch (harm) you with their hands, but Allah held back their hands from you. Fear Allah. In Allah let the believers put their trust.

5:12 Surely Allah took a covenant from the children of Israel, and Allah appointed among them 12 leaders. Allah said: "Certainly Allah is with you if you establish the prayer, you pay obligatory charity, you believe in Allah's messengers, you assist them, and you lend to Allah a good loan (spend in charity). Surely, Allah will wipe out from you your evil deeds, and will surely admit you to gardens under them the rivers flow (in paradise). But whoever disbelieved after this among you, indeed that person has gone astray from right way."

5:13 Then for their breach of their covenant, Allah cursed them, and Allah made their hearts hard. They changed the words from their right context and they forgot a part of message what they were cautioned of it. You will not cease to discover treachery from them, except a few of them. But forgive them, and overlook (their misdeeds). Surely, Allah loves those who do good deeds.

5:14 From those who said we are Christians, Allah took their covenant, but they forgot a good part of that message they were cautioned of it. So Allah aroused among them enmity and hatred till day of Resurrection, and Allah will inform them of what they used to do.

5:15 O people of the scripture! Indeed Allah's messenger (Muhammad) has come to you, he makes clear to you much of that you used to conceal from the scripture and passes over much. Surely, there has come to you from Allah a light (Muhammad) and a clear book (the Qur'an),

5:16 Allah guides with it those who seek Allah's good pleasure ways of peace, and Allah brings them out from the darkness to the light by Allah's will and Allah guides them to the right way.

5:17 Surely, those who disbelief say: "Surely Allah is the Messiah, son of Mary." Say (O Muhammad): "Who then has power against Allah, if Allah decides that Allah will destroy the Messiah, son of Mary, his mother, and those who are all on the earth? To Allah belongs the dominion of the heavens and the earth, and what is between them. Allah creates what Allah wills. Allah is Powerful over everything."

5:18 The Jews and the Christians say: "We are the children of Allah and Allah's loved ones." Say: "Why then Allah punishes you for your sins? But you are human being from those Allah has created, Allah forgives to whom Allah wills and Allah punishes whom Allah wills. To Allah belongs the dominion of the heavens and the earth and what is between them, and to Allah is the return."

5:19 O people of the scripture! Surely, has come to you Allah's messenger (Muhammad), he makes things clear to you, after an interval of the messengers, lest you say: "There has not come to us a bearer of glad tidings and not a warner." But surely now has come to you a bearer of glad tidings and a warner. Allah is Powerful over everything.

5:20 (Remember) when Moses said to his people: "O my people! You remember the favor of Allah upon you. When Allah raised prophets among you, and made you kings, and Allah gave you what Allah had not given to any one of the worlds.

5:21 O my people! Enter the holy land which Allah has ordained for you, and you do not turn on your backs, then you will turn as losers."

5:22 They said: "O Moses! Surely, in the holy land are people of great strength, and we shall never enter it until they depart from it. If they depart from it, then we will enter it."

5:23 Two frightened men on whom (Joshua and Caleb) Allah had favored (Allah's grace) said: "Enter (assault) upon them through the gate, and if you enter it, then indeed you will be victorious, and put your trust in Allah if you are believers."

5:24 They said: "O Moses! We shall not even enter it as long as they are in it. So both you and your Rabb go and you 2 fight, and we are sitting right here."

5:25 Moses said: "O my Rabb! I do not have control except on myself and my brother. So distinguish between us and between the disobedient people!"

5:26 Allah said: "Indeed it (the holy land) is forbidden to them for 40 years; they will wander (in disruption) in the earth. So you do not grieve over the disobedient people."

5:27 (O Muhammad) recite to them the story of 2 sons of Adam (Abel and Cain) in truth; when both offered a sacrifice to Allah, and it was accepted from one of them but was not accepted from the other. He (latter) said (to the former): "Surely I will kill you." He (former) said: "Surely, Allah accepts only from the pious.

5:28 If you stretch your hand against Allah so that you kill me, I shall not stretch my hand against you so that I kill you, for I fear Allah; the Rabb of the worlds.

5:29 Surely, I desire that you be laden with my sin and your sin, and you become inmate of the fire, and that is the reward of the wrongdoers."

5:30 Then his evil soul prompted him killing of his brother; and he killed him and became one of the losers.

5:31 Then Allah sent a crow scratching in the earth so that it shows him how he may hide dead body of his brother. He (the murderer) said: "Woe to me! Am I not even able that I could be like this crow and could hide dead body of my brother?" Then he became from those who regretted.

5:32 Because of that Allah ordained for children of Israel that whoever kills a person, except (as a punishment) for killing a person or for mischief in the earth, (it will be written) as if killed all mankind. Whoever saves a life, as if saves life of all mankind. Surely, Allah's messengers came to them with clear signs, yet indeed many of them after that are those who committed excesses in the earth!

5:33 The only recompense of those who wage war against Allah, Allah's messenger, and spread mischief in the earth is that they are killed or they are crucified or their hands and their feet are cut off from opposite sides, or be exiled from the land. That is disgrace for them in this world, and a great punishment in the hereafter,

5:34 except those who repent before you have power over them; so you should know that Allah is Forgiving, Merciful.

5:35 O you who believe! You fear Allah, you seek (the means of) approach to Allah, and you strive hard in Allah's way so that you may succeed.

5:36 Surely, those who disbelieve, if they have all that is in the earth, and as much as like therewith to ransom themselves from punishment on the day of Resurrection, it will not be accepted from them, and for them is a painful punishment.

5:37 They will wish that they come out of the fire, but they will not come out of it, and for them is a lasting punishment.

5:38 You cut off their hands of male and female thief, as a recompense for what they have earned, an exemplary punishment from Allah. Allah is All-Powerful, All-Wise.

5:39 But whoever repents after wrong-doing and amends (ways), then surely, Allah will turn towards that person (with forgiveness). Surely, Allah is Forgiving, Merciful.

5:40 Do you not know that to Allah alone belongs the dominion of the heavens and the earth? Allah punishes whom Allah wills and Allah forgives whom Allah wills. Allah is All-Powerful over every thing.

5:41 O messenger (Muhammad)! Let not grieve you those who race each other into disbelief, of those who say: "We believe" with their mouths but their hearts do not believe. Of those who have become Jews are listeners to falsehood, listeners to other people who have not come to you. They change the words from their context; they say: "If you are given this, you take it, but if you are not given this, then beware!" Whom Allah wills, falls into error, and you will never be able to do anything for that person against Allah. Those are the ones whom Allah does not want that Allah purifies their hearts; for them there is disgrace in this world, and for them there is a great punishment in the hereafter.

5:42 They are listeners to falsehood, devourers of forbidden earnings. If they come to you (O Muhammad), then either judge between them, or turn away from them. If you turn away from them, then they will never harm you anything. If you judge, then judge between them with justice. Surely, Allah loves the just.

5:43 How they appoint you a judge while they have with them the Torah, in which there is the decision of Allah? Even after that, they turn away. Those are not believers.

5:44 Surely, Allah has sent down the Torah (to Moses), wherein was guidance and light. The Prophets used to judge with it, whoever had submitted (to Allah) from those became Jews, so did scholars and rabbis. They were entrusted the protection of the book of Allah, and they were witnesses to it. So you do not fear the people but fear Allah, and you do not sell Allah's verses for a little price. Whoever does not judge by what Allah has sent down; those are indeed the disbelievers.

5:45 Allah ordained for them in it (Torah) that: "Life for life, eye for eye, nose for nose, ear for ear, tooth for tooth, and wounds for retribution." So whoever gives it up, it will be a compensation for that person. Whoever does not judge by what Allah has sent down; those are they who are the wrongdoers.

5:46 Allah sent in their foot steps, Jesus, son of Mary, confirming what had come before him from the Torah, and Allah gave him the Gospel in which was guidance and light, and confirming what has come before him from the Torah, guidance, and an admonition for the pious.

5:47 Let people of the Gospel judge by what Allah has sent down in it. Whoever does not judge by what Allah has sent down; those are they who are the transgressors.

5:48 Allah has sent down to you (Muhammad) the book (this Qur'an) in truth, confirming what came before it from the book and a watcher over it which has come to you from the truth. Allah has prescribed for each of you a law and a clear way. If Allah willed, Allah could have made you one nation, but to test you in what Allah has given you; so strive one with another in good deeds. To Allah is all of your return; then Allah will inform you about what you used to differ in it.

5:49 You (Muhammad) judge between them by what Allah has revealed and you do not follow their desires, and beware of them lest they seduce you away from some of what Allah has revealed to you. If they turn away, then you know that only the wish of Allah is to punish them for some of their sins. Truly, many of the people are transgressors.

5:50 Do they seek the judgment of ignorance? Who is better than Allah in judgment for a people who have firm faith?

5:51 O you who believe! You do not take the Jews and the Christians as allies, some of them are allies of others. Anyone of you takes them as allies, then that person will be counted as one of them. Surely, Allah does not guide the wrongdoers.

5:52 You see those in whose hearts there is a disease (of hypocrisy), they hurry to them, saying: "We fear that a misfortune may befall us." Perhaps that Allah brings a victory or a decision from Allah's will, then they will become regretful on what they have concealed in themselves.

5:53 Those who believe will say: "Are these the ones (hypocrites) who swore by Allah of their strongest oaths that they are with you (Muslims)?" Their deeds have gone to waste (because of hypocrisy), and they have become the losers.

5:54 O you who believe! Whoever among you turns back from religion (Islam), Allah will bring a people whom Allah will love and they will love Allah; humble towards the believers, strict towards the disbelievers, strive in the way of Allah, and will not fear blame of a critic. That is the grace of Allah, Allah grants whom Allah wills. Allah is All-Sufficient in resources, All-Knower.

5:55 Your only friend is Allah, Allah's messenger, and those who believe - those who establish the prayer, give obligatory charity, and they are those who bow down.

5:56 Whoever takes as friends: Allah, Allah's messenger, and those who have believe, then the party of Allah will be victorious.

5:57 O you who believe! You do not take as allies, those from among the people who were given the scripture before you and the disbelievers, who have take your religion for mockery and fun. Fear Allah if you are true believers.

5:58 When you call for prayer, they take it for a mockery and fun; because they are a people who do not understand.

5:59 Say: "O people of the scripture! Are you opposing us except that we believe in Allah, and what has been sent to us and what was sent before us? Indeed most of you are transgressors."

5:60 Say (O Muhammad): "Shall I inform you of those worse than that regarding recompense from Allah? They are those whom Allah has cursed, who have incurred the wrath of Allah, and Allah had transformed some of them to monkeys and swine; who worshipped false deities; those are worse in rank (on the day of Resurrection), and more astray from the right way."

5:61 When they come to you, they say: "We believe." But in fact they enter with disbelief and surely they go out with it. Allah knows what they are hiding.

5:62 You see many of them hurrying in sin and transgression, and devouring the forbidden earnings. Evil indeed is what they do.

5:63 Why do not the Rabbis and the scholars forbid them from their uttering sinful words and from their devouring forbidden things? Evil indeed is what they have been performing.

5:64 The Jews say: "Hands of Allah is tied up." Their own hands are tied up and they are cursed for what they have said. But Allah's hands are outspread. Allah spends bounty as Allah wills. Surely, the revelation that has come to you from your Rabb increases their rebellion and disbelief. Allah has cast among them enmity and hatred till the day of Resurrection. Whenever they kindled fire of war, Allah extinguished it; and they always strive on earth to spread mischief. Allah does not like the mischief-makers.

5:65 If the people of the scripture had believed and feared Allah, Allah would surely have wiped out from them their sins and would have surely admitted them to gardens of bliss (paradise).

5:66 If they had observed the Torah and the Gospel, and what has been sent to them from their Rabb (the Qur'an), they would surely have gotten provision from above them and from beneath their feet. Among them are moderate people (on right course), and many of them are evil what they are doing.

5:67 O messenger (Muhammad)! Convey what has been sent down to you from your Rabb. If you do not do it, then you have not conveyed Allah's Message. Allah will protect you from the people. Surely, Allah does not guide the disbelievers.

5:68 Say (O Muhammad): "O people of the scripture! You are not on anything (guided) till you observe the Torah and the Gospel, and what has been sent down to you from your Rabb (the Qur'an)." Certainly this revelation (the Qur'an) which has come to you from your Rabb will increase in many of them in rebellion and disbelief. So do not grieve over the disbelievers.

5:69 Surely, those who believe (Muslims) and those who became Jews and the Sabians and the Christians - whoever believed in Allah and the last day, and did good deeds, no fear shall be on them, nor they shall grieve.

5:70 Surely, Allah took covenant of children of Israel and Allah sent to them messengers. Whenever a messenger came to them with what not liked by them, some of them denied him, and some of them killed him.

5:71 They thought that there will be no trial, so they became blind and deaf; then Allah turned to them (with forgiveness); but again many of them became blind and deaf. Allah is All-Seer of what they do.

5:72 Surely, those who disbelieved, say: "Indeed Allah is the Messiah (Jesus), son of Mary." But the Messiah (Jesus) said: "O children of Israel! You worship Allah, my Rabb and your Rabb." Surely, whoever sets partners with Allah, then indeed Allah has forbidden paradise, and its abode will be the fire. There are no helpers for the wrongdoers.

5:73 Surely, those who disbelieved said: "Indeed Allah is 3rd of 3 (in Trinity)." But there is no one worthy of worship except one Allah. If they do not cease from what they say, surely a painful punishment will befall those who disbelieve among them.

5:74 Will not then they turn (in repentance) to Allah and ask for Allah's forgiveness? Allah is Forgiving, Merciful.

5:75 The Messiah (Jesus), son of Mary, is not except a messenger. Certainly the messengers have passed away before him. His mother (Mary) was a woman of truth. They both used to eat the food (as any other human). See how Allah makes the verses clear to them and see how they are deceived away (from the truth).

5:76 Say (O Muhammad): "Do you worship besides Allah something which has neither power for your harm nor for your benefit? Indeed, Allah is All-Hearer, All-Knower."

5:77 Say (O Muhammad): "O people of the scripture! You do not exceed limits in your religion other than the truth, you do not follow desires of people who certainly went astray before, they misled many, and strayed from the right way."

5:78 Those who disbelieved from the children of Israel were cursed by tongue of David and Jesus, son of Mary. That was because they disobeyed and they were transgressing.

5:79 They did not forbid each another from wrong deeds they committed. Evil indeed was what they used to do.

5:80 You see many of them; they make friends with those who disbelieved. Evil indeed is that they themselves have sent forth for them. For that reason, they have incurred the wrath of Allah, and they will abide forever in punishment.

5:81 If they believed in Allah and the prophet (Muhammad), and what has been revealed to him (the Qur'an), they would not have taken disbelievers as friends, but many of them are disobedient to Allah.

5:82 Surely, you will find most hostile among people in enmity to those who have believed (Muslims) are the Jews, and those who set partners with Allah. Surely you will find nearest of them in love to those who have believed (Muslims) are those who say: "We are Christians." That is because amongst them are priests and monks, who do not take pride.

5:83 When they (monks and priests) hear what has been sent down to the messenger (Muhammad), you see their eyes overflow with tears because they have recognized the truth. They say: "Our Rabb! We believe; so write us down with the witnesses.

5:84 Why should we not believe in Allah and in that which has come to us of the truth? We wish that our Rabb will admit us (in paradise) with the righteous people."

5:85 So Allah rewarded them for what they said with gardens under them the flowing rivers (in paradise), they will abide forever in it. Such is the reward of righteous people.

5:86 But those who disbelieved and denied Allah's verses, they shall be the inmates of the fire.

5:87 O you who believe! Do not make good things unlawful what Allah has made lawful to you, and you do not transgress. Surely, Allah does not like the transgressors.

5:88 Eat of what sustenance provided to you by Allah, lawful and good things. You fear Allah, in Allah you believe.

5:89 Allah will not call you to account for unintentional things in your oaths. But Allah will call you to account for earnestly sworn in oaths. The penalty (for a broken oath) is feeding 10 needy people of average of what you feed your families; or clothing them; or freeing a captive. But whoever can not afford, then fasting for 3 days. That is expiation of your oaths when you have sworn. But keep your oaths. Thus Allah makes clear to you Allah's verses so that you may give thanks.

5:90 O you who believe! Only intoxicants and game of chance (gambling) and sacrifices at altars (tribute to idols) and dividing arrows (lottery) are an abomination of handiworks of Satan. So avoid them so that you may attain success.

5:91 Satan only wants to excite between you enmity and hatred with intoxicants and games of chance (gambling), and hinder you from the remembrance of Allah and from the prayer. So, will you be of those who abstain?

5:92 Obey Allah and obey the messenger (Muhammad), and be aware. But if you turn away, then you should know that it is the duty only upon our messenger to convey clearly.

5:93 Those who believe and do righteous deeds, there is no sin for what they ate (in the past). When they fear Allah, believe, and do righteous deeds, then again they fear Allah and believe, and then (once again) they fear Allah and do good deeds (with perfection). Allah loves the righteous people.

5:94 O you who believe! Allah will surely try you with something of the game which can be taken by your hands and your lances, so that Allah knows who fears Allah unseen. Then whoever transgresses after that, there is a painful punishment.

5:95 O you who believe! You do not kill game when you are in a state of Ihram (for Pilgrimage). Whoever of you kills it intentionally, then penalty is like what was killed of cattle judged by 2 just men among you, an offering brought to the Ka'bah; or for expiation, feeding of needy or to that equivalent fasting so as to taste and grieve (punishment) of the deed. Allah has pardoned what is passed. But whoever repeats it, Allah will take retribution on that person. Allah is All-Mighty, Rabb of retribution.

5:96 Lawful to you is game of water and its eating as provision for you and for travelers, but is forbidden to you hunting on land while you are in (a state of Ihram). Fear Allah to whom you shall be gathered.

5:97 Allah has made the Ka'bah, the Sacred House, an establishment for mankind, and the sacred month, animals of offerings, and their collars (garlanded). All this is so that you may know that Allah knows what is in the heavens and what is in the earth, and that Allah knows everything.

5:98 Know that Allah is severe in punishment and that Allah is Forgiving, Merciful.

5:99 It is not on the messenger but to convey (the message). Allah knows what you reveal and what you conceal.

5:100 Say (O Muhammad): "Are not equal bad thing and good thing, even though abundance of bad things may fascinate you." So fear Allah, O people of understanding so that you may succeed.

5:101 O you who believe! You do not ask (questions) about things if they are made clear to you, they may trouble you. If you ask (questions) about these when the Qur'an is being revealed, they will be made clear to you. Allah has forgiven that and Allah is Forgiving, Forbearing.

5:102 Indeed, people asked such questions before you, then on that account they became disbelievers.

5:103 Allah has not instituted things like Bahira (a she-camel whose milk was spared for idols and nobody was allowed to milk it), or Saibah (a she-camel let loose for grazing for idols, and nothing was allowed to be carried on it), or a Wasilah (a she-camel set free for idols as it gave birth to a she-camel at its first delivery and then again at its second delivery) or Ham (a stallion camel freed from work for idols after it had finished a number of copulations assigned to it) (all these animals were liberated in honor of idols as practiced by pagan Arabs). But those who disbelieve invent a lie against Allah, but most of them do not understand.

5:104 When it is said to them: "Come to what Allah has revealed and to the messenger (Muhammad)," they say: "Sufficient for us what we found upon our forefathers," even though their forefathers did not know anything nor they had guidance.

5:105 O you who believe! Take care of your own selves. Whoever goes astray will not harm you when you are guided. To Allah all of you return, and then Allah will inform you of what you used to do.

5:106 O you who believe! Take witness between you when any of you approaches the death while making a will with 2 just men among you, or 2 others from among other than you if you are traveling through the land and calamity of the death befalls you. You detain them both after the prayer, they swear by Allah if you doubt them saying: "We will not sell it for a price even if he is a near relative. We shall not conceal the testimony of Allah, then indeed we will be among the sinners."

5:107 Then if it is discovered that the 2 are guilty of sin, let 2 others stand forth in their places, nearest in kin from among those who claim a lawful right. Let the 2 swear by Allah saying: "Our testimony is truer than testimony of the other 2, and we have not transgressed, then indeed we will be among the wrongdoers."

5:108 That is closer that they give evidence in its true nature or they fear that their oaths will be disproved after others' oaths. So fear Allah and listen. Allah does not guide those who are disobedient transgressors.

5:109 On the day when Allah will gather the messengers and will say: "What answer you were given?" They will say: "We have no knowledge, surely, only you (Allah) are All-Knower of hidden things."

5:110 (Remember) when Allah will say (on the day of Resurrection): "O Jesus, son of Mary! Remember my (Allah's) favor to you and to your mother when I (Allah) strengthened you with spirit of the holy (Gabriel), you spoke to the people in the cradle and in maturity; and when I (Allah) taught you the book and the wisdom, and the Torah and the Gospel; and when you made from clay like the figure of a bird by my (Allah's) permission, and you breathed into it, and it became a bird by my (Allah's) permission, you healed the born-blind, and the lepers by my (Allah's) permission, when you raised the dead by my (Allah's) permission, when I (Allah) restrained children of Israel from you when you came to them with clear proofs; and those who disbelieved among them said: This is nothing but clear magic."

5:111 When I (Allah) revealed to the disciples (of Jesus) to believe in me (Allah) and my (Allah's) messenger, they said: "We believe and bear witness that we are Muslims."

5:112 (Remember) when the disciples said: "O Jesus, son of Mary! Does your Rabb has power to send down to us table spread with food from the heaven?" Jesus said: "Fear Allah, if you are believers."

5:113 They said: "We wish that we eat of it, our hearts be satisfied, we know that you have indeed told us the truth, and we be witnesses on that."

5:114 Jesus, son of Mary, said: "O Allah, our Rabb! Send down upon us a table from the heaven which will be a festival for us - for first and the last of us and a sign from you (Allah); and provide us sustenance, and you (Allah) are best of sustainers."

5:115 Allah said: "Surely I (Allah) will send it down to you, but whoever disbelieves after that among you, then I (Allah) will punish with a punishment such that I (Allah) has not punished (like that) anyone of the worlds."

5:116 (Remember) when Allah will say (on the day of Resurrection): "O Jesus, son of Mary! Did you say to people: 'Take me and my mother as 2 who are worthy of worship besides Allah?'" Jesus will say: "Glory is to Allah! It was not for me that I say what I had no right to say. Had I said it, then surely you (Allah) would have known it. You (Allah) know what is in my soul and I do not know what is in your (Allah's); truly, you (Allah) know all of the hidden things.

5:117 I did not say to them except what Allah commanded me of it that (say): 'You worship Allah, my Rabb and your Rabb. I was over them a witness till I remained among them, but when you (Allah) recalled me, you (Allah) were the watcher over them, and you (Allah) are a witness over everything.

5:118 If you (Allah) punish them, surely they are your (Allah's) servants, and if you (Allah) forgive them, surely Allah is the All-Mighty, the All-Wise.'"

5:119 Allah will say: "This is the day the truthful will profit their truthfulness: for them are gardens with the rivers flowing under them (in paradise) - they shall abide in it forever. Allah is pleased with them and they are pleased with Allah. That is the great success."

5:120 To Allah belongs the dominion of the heavens and the earth, what is in them, and Allah has power over everything.

6. Al-An'am : The Cattle

In the name of Allah, the Gracious, the Merciful

6:1 The praise is for Allah, who has created the heavens and the earth, and made the darkness and the light; yet those who disbelieve in their Rabb, they hold others as equal.

6:2 It is Allah, who has created you from clay, then has decreed a term (for you to die) and a determined term (for you to be resurrected) with Allah, yet you doubt.

6:3 It is the same Allah in the heavens and in the earth, Allah knows your secret and your open deeds, and Allah knows what you earn.

6:4 Yet never comes to them a sign from verses of their Rabb, but they are turning away from it.

6:5 Indeed, they have rejected the truth (the Qur'an and Muhammad) when it came to them. But soon news will come to them of that (the punishment) they used to mock at it.

6:6 Have they not seen how many generations Allah has destroyed before them? Allah had established them (more powerful) on the earth such as Allah has not established for you. Allah sent rain on them abundantly, and Allah made the rivers flow under them. Then Allah destroyed them for their sins, and Allah raised after them other generations.

6:7 If Allah had sent down to you (O Muhammad) a book written on paper and they could have touched it with their hands, those who disbelieve still would have said: "This is not but obvious magic!"

6:8 They say: "Why has not an angel been sent down to him?" If Allah had sent down an angel, the matter would have been decided then, and no respite would have been granted to them,

6:9 and had Allah appointed him an angel, Allah would have made him in a human form, and Allah would have certainly caused confusion to them in what they are already confused.

6:10 Indeed messengers were mocked before you (O Muhammad), but those who ridiculed were surrounded by them the very thing what they were mocking at it.

6:11 Say (O Muhammad): "Travel in the land and see what the end of the rejecters was."

6:12 Say (O Muhammad): "To whom belongs what is in the heavens and the earth?" Say: "To Allah." Allah has prescribed the Mercy for Allah. Allah will gather you together on the day of Resurrection, there is no doubt in it. Those who have ruined themselves, they will not believe.

6:13 To Allah belongs all that exist in the night and the day, and Allah is the All-Hearer, the All-Knower.

6:14 Say (O Muhammad): "Shall I take a guardian other than Allah, the Creator of the heavens and the earth? It is Allah who feeds and Allah is not fed." Say: "Surely, I am commanded that I should be first who submit to Allah and should not be among the polytheists."

6:15 Say: "I surely fear, if I disobey my Rabb, the punishment of a mighty day."

6:16 Whoever is averted from it (punishment) that day, surely Allah has Mercy on him. That is the obvious success.

6:17 If Allah touches you with affliction, then none can relieve it but Allah, and if Allah touches you with good, then Allah has power over every thing.

6:18 Allah is Omnipotent (Supreme Authority) over Allah's servants, and Allah is the All-Wise, Well-Aware of everything.

6:19 Say (O Muhammad): "What thing is greatest in evidence?" Say: "Allah is a witness between me and between you; and this Qur'an is revealed to me so that I may warn you with it and whoever it may reach. Do you surely bear witness that besides Allah there are others worthy of worship?" Say: "I do not bear such a witness!" Say: "Allah is only the one worthy of worship. Indeed I am innocent of what you associate (with Allah)."

6:20 Those whom Allah has given the scripture recognize him as they recognize their sons. But those who lost their own selves will not believe.

6:21 Who is greater wrongdoer than a person who invents a lie against Allah or rejects Allah's verses? Surely, the wrongdoers will not attain success.

6:22 On the day when Allah will gather them all together, Allah will say to those who associated others (with Allah): "Where are your associates (false deities) to whom you used to assert?"

6:23 They will not have arguments but will say: "By Allah, our Rabb, we were not polytheists."

6:24 Look! How they lie against themselves! The lie will leave them what they invented.

6:25 Among them there are those who (pretend that they) listen to you; but Allah has cast veils over their hearts, and deafness in their ears, so they can not understand it. Even if they see every sign, they will not believe in it. So much so that when they come to you, they argue with you. The disbelievers say: "This is not but tales of the ancients."

6:26 They forbid others from him (Muhammad) and they themselves keep away from him. They destroy not but their own selves and they do not perceive it.

6:27 If you could see when they will be held over the fire! They will say: "We wish we were sent back (to the world), then we would not deny the verse of our Rabb, and we would be among the believers!"

6:28 But it has become clear to them what they used to conceal before. Even if they were sent back (to the world), they would have reverted to what they were forbidden. Indeed they are the liars.

6:29 (Today) they say: "There is no other life but our life of the world, and we will not be resurrected (on the day of Resurrection)."

6:30 If you could see when they will be held to stand before their Rabb! Allah will say: "Is this not the truth?" They will say: "Yes, our Rabb!" Allah will say: "Then taste the punishment for what you used to disbelieve."

6:31 Indeed they will suffer loss who denied meeting with Allah. When the hour (doomsday) will come to them suddenly, they will say: "Alas for us over what we neglected in it." They will carry the burden of their sins on their backs. Indeed evil is what they will bear!

6:32 The life of this world is nothing but a play and a pastime. Abode of the hereafter is better for those who fear Allah. Will you not then understand?

6:33 Indeed Allah knows that it grieves you (Muhammad) what they say: surely they do not reject you, but the wrongdoers deny in the verses (the Qur'an) of Allah.

6:34 Indeed, many messengers were rejected before you (O Muhammad), but they endured with patience that they were rejected, and they were hurt; till Allah's help reached them, and there is none who can alter the words of Allah. Surely, there has come to you news of those messengers.

6:35 If their dislike is hard on you, then see if you can seek a tunnel in the ground or a ladder to the sky, so that you can bring them a sign. (You know) if Allah willed, Allah could have gathered them all on the guidance. So do not be like the ignorant.

6:36 It is only those who listen (to Muhammad), will respond. For the dead (disbelievers), Allah will raise them (on the day of Resurrection), and then to Allah they will be returned (for their recompense).

6:37 They say: "Why not a sign has been sent down to him from his Rabb?" Say: "Indeed Allah has power to send down a sign, but most of them do not know (the wisdom behind it)."

6:38 There is no animal on earth and no bird that flies with its two wings, but are communities like you (who see the signs of Allah). Allah has not neglected anything in the book. Then to their Rabb they shall be gathered.

6:39 Those who reject Allah's verses are deaf and dumb in the darkness. Whom Allah wills lets go astray and whom Allah wills guides on the right way.

6:40 Say (O Muhammad): "What do you think if the punishment of Allah comes to you, or the last hour comes to you, do you call anyone other than Allah? Answer if you are truthful!"

6:41 But to Allah alone you will call, and Allah will remove the distress for which you have called upon Allah if Allah wills. You will forget whoever you have associated (with Allah)!

6:42 Surely, Allah did send messengers to nations before you (O Muhammad). Allah seized them with misfortune and hardship, so that they might humble themselves.

6:43 Why did they not humble themselves when Allah's punishment came to them? Because their hearts became hardened, and Satan made seem fair to them what they used to do.

6:44 When they forgot the warning what they had been reminded therewith, Allah opened to them the gates of every pleasant thing, until when they were rejoicing in what they were granted, Allah seized them suddenly, and then they were plunged into despair.

6:45 So last remnant of the people who did wrong were cut off. All praises are for Allah, Rabb of the worlds.

6:46 Say (to the disbelievers): "What do you think if Allah takes away your hearing and your sight, and seals up your hearts; who is there worthy of worship other than Allah who could restore them to you?" See how Allah presents the verses in various ways, yet they turn away.

6:47 Say: "What do you think if the punishment of Allah comes to you suddenly or openly, will anyone be destroyed except the wrongdoers?"

6:48 Allah has not sent the messengers but bearers of glad tidings and warners. So those who believe and mend their life, then no fear shall be upon them, nor shall they grieve.

6:49 But those who reject Allah's verses, the punishment will touch them for what they used to transgress.

6:50 Say (O Muhammad): "I do not say to you that I have the treasures of Allah, nor that I know the unseen; nor I say to you that I am an angel. I follow not but what is revealed to me." Say: "Is it equal the blind and the seeing? Why do you not think?"

6:51 (O Muhammad) warn with it (the Qur'an) those who fear that they will be gathered before their Rabb, when there will be neither a protector nor an intercessor for them besides Allah; so that they may fear Allah.

6:52 Do not turn away those who invoke their Rabb in the morning and the evening seeking Allah's favor. You are not accountable for their deeds and they are not accountable for yours. So if you turn them away, you shall be of the wrongdoers.

6:53 Thus Allah has tested some of them (poor believers) with others (chiefs of Quraish) so that they might say: "Are these the (poor) people whom Allah has favored from amongst us?" Does not Allah know better the thankful ones?

6:54 When those who believe in Allah's revelations come to you, say: "Peace be upon you." Your Rabb has made the Mercy incumbent upon Allah. If any one of you does evil in ignorance, then repents after that, and mends ways; then surely, Allah is Forgiving, Merciful.

6:55 Thus Allah explains in detail the verses, so that way of the sinners becomes clear.

6:56 Say (O Muhammad): "I am forbidden that I worship those whom you call upon besides Allah." Say: "I will not follow your desires, then I will go astray, and I will not be of the guided."

6:57 Say (O Muhammad): "I am on a clear proof from my Rabb, but you have rejected it. I do not have (the punishment) which you are demanding hastily. The decision is not but for Allah: Allah declares the truth, and Allah is the best of the judges."

6:58 Say: "If I had that power which you are asking for impatiently (the punishment), the matter would have been settled at once between me and you, but Allah knows the best the wrongdoers.

6:59 Allah has keys of the unseen, none knows them but Allah. Allah knows what is in the earth and the sea. There is not a leaf that falls but Allah knows it. There is neither a grain in darkness of the earth nor anything wet or dry, but is written in a clear book.

6:60 It is Allah, who recalls your souls by night (during sleep), and Allah knows what you have done during the day, then Allah raises you again in it (next day) so that the appointed term (your life) is completed. To Allah will be your return, then Allah will inform you of what you used to do."

6:61 Allah is the Omnipotent (Supreme Authority) above Allah's servants, and Allah sends over you guardians (angels), until when death approaches one of you. Allah's messengers (angels) cause you to die (take soul), and they do not neglect their duty.

6:62 Then they (souls) are returned to Allah, their Rabb, and the Just. Surely, Allah is the judge and Allah is the Swiftest in taking accounts.

6:63 Say (O Muhammad): "Who saves you from the darkness of the land and the sea? When you call upon Allah humbly and secretly (saying): 'If Allah saves us from this (danger), we shall be among the thankful.'"

6:64 Say (O Muhammad): "Allah saves you from this and from every distress, yet you associate partners with Allah."

6:65 Say: "Allah has power to sends upon you punishment from above you or from under your feet, or covers you with mutual discord, and lets some of you taste violence of one another. See how Allah explains verses in various ways, so that they may understand.

6:66 But your people have denied it (the Qur'an) and the truth." Say: "I am not a supervisor over you.

6:67 For every prophecy there is a fixed time and soon you will know it."

6:68 When you (Muhammad) see those who engage in (argument with) Allah's revelations, turn away from them until they engage in a talk other than that (topic). If Satan causes you to forget (the commandment), then after the remembrance, you do not sit with the wrongdoers.

6:69 Those who fear Allah (are not responsible) from their (wrongdoers') actions anything, but remind them so that they (wrongdoers) may fear Allah.

6:70 Leave alone those who take their religion as a play and amusement, and are deceived by the life of this world. But remind them with it (the Qur'an) lest their souls are caught for what they have earned. Neither will be for them besides Allah a protector nor an intercessor, and even if they offer ransom for every ransom, it will not be accepted from them. They are those who are caught for what they earned. For them will be a drink of boiling water and a painful punishment because they used to disbelieve.

6:71 Say (O Muhammad to the disbelievers): "Shall we invoke others besides Allah that can neither benefit us nor can harm us? Shall we turn on our heels after when Allah has guided us? Like those whom the Satan has misled in the earth confused, their companions call them to the guidance (saying): 'Come to us.'" Say: "Surely, the guidance of Allah is the only guidance, and we are commanded that we submit (become Muslims) to the Rabb of the worlds;

6:72 to offer prayer, fear Allah, and it is Allah to whom you shall be gathered."

6:73 It is Allah who has created the heavens and the earth in truth and on the day (of Resurrection) Allah will say: "Be!" and it shall become. Allah's word is the truth. The dominion will be Allah's on the day when the trumpet will be blown. Allah knows all the invisible and the visible. Allah is the Wise, aware of everything.

6:74 (Remember) when Abraham said to his father Azar: "Do you take idols as deities? Surely, I see you and your people in clear error."

6:75 Allah showed Abraham kingdom of the heavens and the earth so that he becomes one of the firm believers.

6:76 When the night outspread over him, he saw a star. He said: "This is my Rabb." But when it set, he said: "I do not love those who set."

6:77 When he saw the moon rising, he said: "This is my Rabb." But when it set, he said: "If my Rabb do not guide me, surely I shall be among the people who go astray."

6:78 When he saw the sun rising, he said: "This is my Rabb. This is the largest." But when it set, he said: "O my people! Surely I am free from what you associate (with Allah).

6:79 Surely, I have turned my face to Allah who has created the heavens and the earth, and exclusively I am not of the polytheists."

6:80 His people disputed with him. He said: "Do you dispute with me about Allah, whereas Allah has guided me? I do not fear what you associate with Allah except that whatever my Rabb wills; my Rabb comprehends every thing (in Allah's) knowledge. Then don't you remember?

6:81 Why should I fear what you associate with Allah, when you do not fear what you associate with Allah, for which Allah has not sent down any authority to you? Which of the 2 parties has more right to security? (Tell me) if you know.

6:82 Those who believe and do not confuse their belief with wrong-doings, for them there is the security and they are the guided."

6:83 That was Allah's argument which Allah gave to Abraham against his people. Allah raises in ranks whom Allah wills. Surely your Rabb is All-Wise, All-Knower of everything.

6:84 Allah bestowed upon him Isaac and Jacob (sons), Allah guided each of them, and before that, Allah guided Noah, and among his progeny David, Solomon, Job, Joseph, Moses, and Aaron. Thus Allah rewards the righteous people.

6:85 (Others include) Zachariah, John, Jesus, and Elias; all were of the righteous,

6:86 and Ishmael, Elisha, Jonah, Lot, and all Allah favored over the worlds

6:87 and from their forefathers, their progeny, and their brethren. Allah chose them and guided them to the right way.

6:88 This is the guidance of Allah with it Allah guides whom Allah wills of Allah's servants. If they had associated others with Allah, rendered vain from them what they used to do (deeds).

6:89 They were those whom Allah gave the book, sound judgment, and Prophethood. But if they disbelieve in it, then indeed Allah would entrust it to the people who are not disbelievers in it.

6:90 (O Muhammad) they are those whom Allah had guided. So you follow their guidance. Say: "I ask you no reward for it (delivery of the message). This is not but a reminder for the worlds."

6:91 They have not valued (the attributes of) Allah with a value due to Allah when they said: "Allah did not send down to any human being any thing." Ask (O Muhammad): "Who sent down the book (Torah) which Moses brought it, a light and guidance for mankind? You have put into sheets for people, you disclose some of it and you conceal most of it. Though you were taught (through the Qur'an) what neither you know nor your forefathers knew." (If they do not answer) say: "Allah (sent it)." Then leave them in their arguments they play.

6:92 This (the Qur'an) is a blessed book which Allah has sent down confirming (the revelations) which came before it, so that you may warn people of Mother of Towns (Makkah) and those around it. Those who believe in the hereafter, will believe in it (the Qur'an), and they will guard over their prayers.

6:93 Who is more unjust than the one who invents a lie against Allah, or says: "Revelation was sent down to me," while no revelation has come to that person? Or the one who says: "I will reveal like what Allah has revealed." If you could see when the wrongdoers are in agonies of the death and the angels are stretching out their hands (saying): "Deliver your souls! This day you shall be recompensed with the punishment of humiliation for what you used to utter against Allah other than the truth. You used to be arrogant concerning Allah's verses!

6:94 Surely you have come back to Allah all alone as Allah created you the first time. You have left behind what Allah had bestowed on you. Allah does not see with you your those intercessors whom you claimed that they share with Allah (as partners) in your matters. Indeed (bonds) have been severed between you and have forsaken you what you used to claim."

6:95 Surely! It is Allah who causes to split the grain and the fruit-stone. Allah brings forth the living from the dead, and brings forth the dead from the living. Such is Allah, then how are you being misled (from truth)?

6:96 Allah is the Cleaver (chopper) of the daybreak. Allah has made the night for resting, and the sun and the moon for reckoning. Such are the arrangements of the All-Mighty, the All-Knower.

6:97 It is Allah who has made for you the stars, so that you may guide yourselves by them in darkness of the land and the sea. Indeed Allah has made clear the revelations for people who know.

6:98 It is Allah who has created you from a single person (Adam), so there is a time-limit (on the earth) and a resting place (in the hereafter). Indeed, Allah has made clear the verses for people who understand.

6:99 It is Allah who sends down rain from the heaven, Allah brings thereby vegetation of every kind, Allah brings forth thereby green stalks, Allah brings forth from it thick-clustered grain and from date-palm and from its sprout clusters of dates hanging low, and gardens of grapes, olives and pomegranates resembling (in kind), and yet different. Look at its fruit when it bears fruit, and its ripeness. Surely! In all these are signs for people who believe.

6:100 Yet, they make the jinns associates with Allah, though Allah has created them, and they falsely attribute to Allah as sons and daughters without knowledge. Allah is glorified and exalted (far above) from what they attribute.

6:101 Allah is the Originator of the heavens and the earth. How Allah can have a son when Allah did not have a mate? Allah has created every thing and Allah is the All-Knower of everything.

6:102 Such is Allah, your Rabb! There is no one worthy of worship but Allah, the Creator of every thing. So worship Allah alone and Allah is the Guardian over every thing.

6:103 No vision can grasp Allah, but Allah grasps all visions. Allah is the Subtle, Well-Aware of everything.

6:104 Surely, proofs have come to you from your Rabb. So those who see will do so for their own self, and those who are blind, will do so against themselves. I (Muhammad) am not over you a keeper.

6:105 Thus Allah explains the verses in various ways, and they (the disbelievers) may say: "You have learned (from the scriptures of the people and brought this Qur'an)" and that Allah may make it clear for the people who have knowledge.

6:106 Follow what is revealed to you (O Muhammad) from your Rabb, there is no one worthy of worship but Allah and turn away from the polytheists.

6:107 If Allah willed, they would not have associated others with Allah. Allah has not made you a watcher over them nor you are a guardian over them.

6:108 Allah does not insult those who (disbelievers) invoke other than Allah, lest they insult Allah wrongfully without knowledge. Thus Allah has made their deeds seem fair to each nation. Then to their Rabb is their return and then Allah will inform them of what they used to do.

6:109 They swear by Allah their strongest oaths, that if a verse came to them, they would surely believe in it. Say: "Only the verses are with Allah." What will make you realize that when those verses come, they will still not believe?

6:110 Allah will turn their hearts and their eyes (away from guidance), as they did not believe in it for the first time, and Allah will leave them in their tyranny to wander blindly.

6:111 Even if Allah had sent down the angels to them, the dead had spoken to them, and Allah had gathered before them every thing open (before their eyes), they would not have believed, unless that Allah willed, but most of them are ignorant.

6:112 So Allah has made for every Prophet an enemy - devils of humans and jinns, inspiring some of them to others with adorned speech as a deception. If your Rabb had willed, they would not have done it, so leave them alone with what they fabricate,

6:113 so that the hearts of those who do not believe in the hereafter may incline (to such deception), and they may be pleased with it; so that they may commit what they wish to commit (sins and evil deeds).

6:114 (Say O Muhammad): "Shall I seek a judge other than Allah who has sent down to you the book (The Qur'an) in details?" Those whom Allah gave (previously) the scripture; they know that it is revealed from your Rabb in truth. So you should not be of those who doubts.

6:115 The word of your Rabb has been perfected in truth and justice. No one can change Allah's words. Allah is the All-Hearer, the All-Knower.

6:116 If you obey most of those on the earth, they will mislead you from the way of Allah. They do not follow but guess, and they do not but guess (lie).

6:117 Surely, your Rabb! It is Allah who knows best who strays from Allah's way, and Allah knows best the rightly guided ones.

6:118 So eat of that meat on which the name of Allah has been pronounced (during slaughter) if you are believers in Allah's revelations.

6:119 What happened to you that you do not eat of that (meat) on which the name of Allah has been pronounced (during slaughter) when indeed Allah has explained to you what Allah has forbidden to you, unless that you are constrained to it? Surely many lead people astray by their desires for lack of knowledge. Certainly your Rabb is Allah who knows best the transgressors.

6:120 Abandon (all kinds of) sin, open and secret. Surely, those who earn sin, they will be recompensed for what they have committed.

6:121 You do not eat of that (meat) on which the name of Allah has not been pronounced (during slaughter), it is indeed a transgression. Indeed, the devils do inspire their friends (from mankind) so that they dispute with you, and if you obey them, then you would surely be polytheists.

6:122 Can a person who was dead (by ignorance and disbelief), whom Allah gave life (by knowledge and belief), and whom Allah gave a light (belief) of likeness by it (can walk) among people, be like the one who is in the darkness (disbelief) from which can never come out? Thus it is made seem fair to the disbelievers what they used to do,

6:123 and thus Allah has set up in every town leaders of its wicked ones to plot in it. But they do not plot except against themselves though they do not perceive.

6:124 When a sign (verse of the Qur'an) comes to them, they say: "We shall not believe until we are given like what was given to the messengers of Allah." Allah knows best where to place Allah's message. Humiliation from Allah and a severe punishment will soon overtake the criminals for what they used to plot.

6:125 Whomever Allah wills to guide, Allah opens heart to Islam, and whomever Allah wills to let go astray, Allah makes heart closed, constricted, as if the soul is climbing to the sky. Thus Allah sets the wrath over those who do not believe,

6:126 whereas, this is the right way (Islam) of your Rabb. Surely, Allah has detailed Allah's verses for a people who take heed.

6:127 For them there will be home of peace (paradise) with their Rabb. Allah will be their protector for what they used to do.

6:128 On the day when Allah will gather them all together, (Allah will say): "O you assembly of jinns! Surely, you have misled a lot from humans." Their friends among the humans (will say): "Our Rabb! Some of us benefited from some, and now we have reached our term which you (Allah) had appointed for us." Allah will say: "The fire is your residing place to reside in it forever, except what Allah wills." Surely your Rabb is All-Wise, the All-knower of everything.

6:129 Thus Allah makes some of the wrongdoers friends of some for what they used to earn (in the world).

6:130 (Allah will ask): "O assembly of jinns and mankind! Did not there come to you messengers from among you, reciting to you Allah's verses and warning you of meeting of your this day?" They will say: "We bear witness against ourselves." It was the life of this world that deceived them. They will bear witness against themselves that they were disbelievers.

6:131 This is because your Rabb would not destroy the towns unjustly while their people were unaware.

6:132 For every one there will be ranks for what they did. Your Rabb is not unaware of what they do.

6:133 Your Rabb is Self-Sufficient, full of Mercy. If Allah wills, Allah can destroy you away, and replace you with others as Allah wills, just as Allah raised you from the offspring of other people.

6:134 Surely, what you are promised is bound to Allah and you can not escape (the punishment of Allah).

6:135 Say (O Muhammad): "O people! Work in your place, surely, I too am at work (in my way), soon you will know who will be happy for the reward of the house (paradise). Surely, the wrongdoers will not succeed."

6:136 They assign to Allah a share of the tilth (produce) and the cattle which Allah has created, and they say: "This is for Allah," so they presume, and "this is for our partners (of Allah)." But what is for their partners (of Allah) does not reach Allah, while what is for Allah reaches to their partners (of Allah)! Evil is what they judge!

6:137 Likewise to many of the polytheists, killing of their children for their partners (of Allah) have made seem fair so that they ruin them and so that they confuse them in their religion. If Allah had willed, they would not have done it. So leave them alone with what they fabricate.

6:138 They say that these (certain types of) cattle and crops are forbidden, none should eat them except those whom we allow. They presume (certain types of) cattle are forbidden to use their backs (for loads or any work), and they did not pronounce the name of Allah on cattle (during slaughter); made false fabrication against Allah. Allah will recompense them for what they used to fabricate.

6:139 They say: "What is in bellies of these cattle (milk or fetus) is exclusively for our males, and forbidden to our females, but if it is born dead, then they all have shares in it." Allah will punish them for their attribution (superstitions). Surely, Allah is All-Wise, All-knower of everything.

6:140 Indeed those who have killed their children foolishly without knowledge suffered loss, and they have made unlawful what sustenance Allah has provided them, inventing a lie against Allah. Surely they have gone astray and they are not guided ones.

6:141 It is Allah who has created gardens trellised and not trellised, the date-palms, the crops of different tastes, the olives, and pomegranates, are similar (in kind) but not similar (in taste). Eat of its fruit when it bears fruit (ripen), but pay its due (obligatory charity) on the day of its harvest. Do not exceed the limits. Surely, Allah does not like those who exceed limits.

6:142 Of the cattle some are for loads (like camel) and some are to be laid on ground (for slaughter like sheep, goats etc). Eat that what Allah has provided you, and you do not follow footsteps of Satan. Surely he is to you open enemy.

6:143 Eight in pairs: of the sheep 2 (male and female), and of the goats 2 (male and female). Ask: "Has Allah forbidden you the 2 males or the 2 females, or contain (fetuses) which the wombs of the 2 females (enclose)? Tell me with knowledge, if you are truthful."

6:144 Of the camels 2 (male and female), and of the cows 2 (male and female). Ask: "Has Allah forbidden you the 2 males or the 2 females or contain fetuses which the wombs of the 2 females (enclose)? Or were you present when Allah ordered you of this? Then who is more unjust than one who fabricates a lie against Allah so as to mislead the people without knowledge? Surely, Allah does not guide the wrongdoers."

6:145 Say (O Muhammad): "I do not find in what has been revealed to me anything prohibited to be eaten by one who intends to eat it, except that it be dead animal or blood poured out, or flesh of pork: for that is surely unclean or impious (unlawful meat slaughtered) by invoking name of other than Allah on it. But whoever is compelled (by necessity) neither craving nor transgressing, then certainly your Rabb is Forgiving, Merciful."

6:146 To those who are Jews, Allah forbade every animal with claws (undivided hoof), and Allah prohibited them the fat of the cows and the sheep, except what is carried to their backs or intestines, or what is mixed with bone. Thus Allah punished them for their rebellion. Surely, Allah is Truthful.

6:147 If they deny you (Muhammad) say: "Your Rabb is owner of vast Mercy, but Allah's punishment can not be averted from the guilty people."

6:148 Those who made partners with Allah will say: "If Allah had willed, we would have made neither partner with Allah, nor would our forefathers, nor we would have prohibited anything (against Allah)." Likewise those who were before them rejected until they tasted Allah's punishment. Say: "Is there any knowledge (evidence) with you which you can provide to us? You follow nothing but guess and you are not but guessing."

6:149 Say: "Allah has conclusive argument, and had Allah willed, Allah would have guided you all."

6:150 Say: "Bring your witnesses, who can testify that Allah has prohibited this." Even if they testify, you (O Muhammad) do not testify with them. You do not follow desires of those who have rejected Allah's verses, those who do not believe in the hereafter, and they set up others as equals with their Rabb.

6:151 Say (O Muhammad): "Come, I will recite what your Rabb has prohibited to you that you do not associate anything with Allah, do good with parents, do not kill your children (for fear) of poverty - Allah provides sustenance for you and for them; do not draw near those shameful deeds that are committed openly or secretly, do not kill a life which Allah has forbidden, except in a just cause. Allah has commanded you these so that you may understand.

6:152 Do not draw near the wealth of the orphan, except that which is better (to improve), until the orphan reaches maturity, and give full measure and weight with justice. Allah does not burden anyone, but to its capacity. When you speak, be just even if it affects your own relative, and you fulfill the covenant of Allah. Allah commands you these so that you may take heed.

6:153 Surely, this is the right way of Allah, so follow it, and you do not follow other ways, lest they will scatter you from Allah's way. Allah has commanded you this so that you may become pious.

6:154 Then, Allah gave Moses the book (the Torah) to complete (Allah's favor) on those who would do good, it explained every thing, and was guidance and a Mercy, so that they might believe in meeting with their Rabb."

6:155 This is a blessed book (the Qur'an) which Allah has sent down, so follow it and fear Allah so that you may be shown Mercy.

6:156 Lest you (pagan Arabs) say: "The book was sent down only to 2 groups before us, and surely, we were unaware from their study,"

6:157 or lest you (pagan Arabs) say: "Surely if the book had been sent down to us, we would have been better guided than them." Surely clear proof (the Qur'an) has come to you from your Rabb, guidance and a Mercy. Who is then more unjust than the one who rejects the verses of Allah and turns away from them? Allah will requite those who turn away from Allah's verses with severe punishment for what they used to turn away.

6:158 Are they waiting except that the angels should come to them, or your Rabb should come, or some verses of your Rabb should come! The day when some verses of your Rabb do come, a soul will not benefit its belief if it had not believed before, or earned good through its faith. Say: "You wait! We (too) are waiting."

6:159 Surely, those who divide their religion and break up into factions, you (O Muhammad) have no concern with them in the least. Surely, their case is with Allah, and then Allah will tell them what they used to do.

6:160 Whoever does a good deed, will have 10 times like thereof, and whoever does an evil deed, will not be punished but like thereof, and they will not be wronged.

6:161 Say (O Muhammad): "Surely, my Rabb has guided me to a right way, a right religion, way of Abraham, the upright and he was not of the polytheists."

6:162 Say (O Muhammad): "Surely, my prayer, my sacrifice, my living, and my dying are for Allah, the Rabb of the worlds.

6:163 Allah has no partner. Thus I am commanded, and I am the first of those who surrender (Muslims)."

6:164 Say: "Should I seek a Rabb other than Allah, and Allah is Rabb of every thing? Every soul will earn fruits of its own deeds; no bearer of burdens shall bear the burden of another. Then to your Rabb is your return and Allah will tell you that you have been differing.

6:165 It is Allah who has made you inheritors of the earth, and exalted some of you over others in ranks so that Allah may try you in what Allah has given you. Surely your Rabb is swift in retribution, and certainly Allah is Forgiving, Merciful."

7. Al-A'raf : The Heights
In the name of Allah, the Gracious, the Merciful

7:1 Alif-Lam-Mim-Sad.

7:2 This is a book (the Qur'an) sent down to you (O Muhammad), let not there be a hesitation from it in your heart, so that you may warn with it, and it is a reminder to the believers.

7:3 (Say O Muhammad): "You follow what has been sent down to you from your Rabb, and you do not follow any protectors besides Allah." Little that you remember!

7:4 How many towns Allah destroyed? Allah's punishment came to them suddenly by night or when they were sleeping at noon,

7:5 their plea was not uttered when Allah's punishment came to them but they said: "Surely, we were wrongdoers."

7:6 Surely, Allah will question those to whom (Allah's Message) was sent down, and surely, Allah will question the messengers.

7:7 Then Allah will narrate to them with knowledge, and Allah was not absent (from anywhere, anytime).

7:8 The weighing on that day (of Resurrection) will be the true (weighing). So those who will be heavy with good deeds in the scale, they will be those of the successful (enter paradise),

7:9 and those who will be light in the scale of good deeds, they will be those who will incur loss upon themselves (enter hell) for they used to be unjust with Allah's verses.

7:10 Surely, Allah has established you on the earth and Allah has made a livelihood for you in it. Yet little thanks that you give.

7:11 Surely, Allah created you, then Allah gave you shape, then Allah said to angels: "Prostrate to Adam," and they prostrated except Satan, who was not of those who prostrated.

7:12 (Allah) said: "What prevented you (O Satan) that you did not prostrate, when I (Allah) commanded you?" Satan said: "I am better than him (Adam), You (Allah) created me from fire, and you (Allah) created him from clay."

7:13 (Allah) said: "(O Satan) get down from this (paradise), it is not for you that you show arrogance in this. Get out; indeed you are of the disgraced ones."

7:14 (Satan) said: "Allow me respite till the day (of Resurrection) when they will be raised up."

7:15 (Allah) said: "Surely, you are granted respite."

7:16 (Satan) said: "Because Allah has sent me astray, I will surely sit in ambush for them (human beings) on your (Allah's) right way.

7:17 Then I will come to them from front of them and behind them, from their right and from their left, and you (Allah) will not find most of them as grateful."

7:18 (Allah) said (to Satan): "Get out from this (paradise) disgraced and expelled. Whoever of them (mankind) will follow you, surely I (Allah) will fill hell with you all."

7:19 (Allah said): "O Adam! Reside with your wife in paradise, and eat from where you wish, but do not approach this tree or you both will be of the wrongdoers."

7:20 But Satan whispered suggestions to them both to expose to them what was concealed to them from their private parts; and he said: "Your Rabb has forbidden you from this tree only to prevent you from becoming angels or become of the immortals."

7:21 He (Satan) swore to them both (saying): "Surely, I am one of the sincere advisers to you both."

7:22 So he led them both with deception. When they both tasted from the tree, both of their private parts (shame) were exposed to them and they began covering (shame) themselves with leaves of paradise. Their Rabb called out to them (saying): "Did I (Allah) not forbid you from that tree and tell you: surely, Satan is open enemy to you?"

7:23 They said: "Our Rabb! We have wronged ourselves. If you (Allah) do not forgive us, and have Mercy on us, we shall certainly be of the losers."

7:24 (Allah) said: "Get down; some of you are enemy to others. On the earth will be a residing place for you and a livelihood for a time."

7:25 (Allah) said: "In it you shall reside, and in it you shall die, and from it you shall be taken out (resurrected)."

7:26 O children of Adam! Surely, Allah has send down to you clothing which covers your private parts and as an adornment, and the garment of piety that is better. This is a verse of Allah so that they may remember.

7:27 O children of Adam! Let not Satan seduce you as he drove out your parents (Adam and Eve) from paradise, stripping them of their garments to expose (to them) their private parts. Surely, he and his host (tribe) see you from where you do not see them. Surely, Allah has made the devils guardians of those who do not believe.

7:28 When they do some lewdness, they say: "We found our fathers on it, and Allah has commanded us of it." Say: "Nay, Allah does not command of lewdness. Do you say on Allah what you do not know?"

7:29 Say (O Muhammad): "My Rabb has commanded justice, keep straight your faces (to Allah) at every prayer place, and invoke to Allah being sincere in faith as Allah created you so shall you return."

7:30 Allah has guided one group while another group deserved to be left in the error; because surely they took devils as guardians instead of Allah, yet they consider that they are guided.

7:31 O children of Adam! Take your adornment (wear clean clothes) at every Masjid (for prayer). Eat and drink, but do not waste by extravagance; indeed Allah does not like the wasters.

7:32 Say (O Muhammad): "Who has forbidden the adornment (to wear decent clothes) given by Allah, which Allah has produced for Allah's servants, and good things of the sustenance (lawful food)?" Say: "These are for those who believe in the life of this world, but these shall be exclusively for them on day of Resurrection." Thus Allah explains the verses for people who understand.

7:33 Say (O Muhammad): "Indeed my Rabb has forbidden shameful deeds which were committed openly, of them which were committed secretly, sins and transgression without the right, associate others with Allah what Allah has not sent with any authority, and say about Allah of which you do no know.

7:34 For every nation there is a fixed term; when their term is reached, neither can they delay for a moment nor they can bring it earlier."

7:35 O children of Adam! If messengers come to you from among you, recite to you Allah's verses, then those who fear Allah and mend themselves, there will not be any fear upon them, and they will not grieve,

7:36 but those who reject Allah's verses, and treat them with arrogance, those are the inmates of the fire; they will abide in it forever.

7:37 Who is more unjust than the one who invents a lie against Allah or rejects Allah's verses? They are those whose share will reach them from the book (of decrees) until when Allah's messengers (angels of death) come to them causing them to die, they (angels) will say: "Where are those whom you used to invoke other than Allah?" They will reply: "They have forsaken us." They will testify against themselves that indeed they were disbelievers.

7:38 (Allah) will say: "You enter in the fire and join among nations of jinns and human who have passed away before you." Every time a group will enter, it will curse its sister (preceding group) until they all will gather in it (fire). The last of them will say to the first of them: "Our Rabb! These have misled us, so give them double punishment of the fire." Allah will say: "For every one there will be double (punishment), though you may not know."

7:39 The first of them will say to the last of them: "You were not any better than us, so taste the punishment for what you used to earn."

7:40 Surely, those who reject Allah's revelations and show arrogance to it, the gates of heaven will not be opened to them, nor they will enter paradise until the camel passes through the eye of a needle (i.e., impossible). Thus Allah will recompense the criminals.

7:41 For them there will be bed of hell and above them it is covering (of fire). Thus Allah will recompense the wrongdoers.

7:42 As for those who believe and do righteous deeds, Allah does not burden any person more than to its capacity; they are the residents of paradise. They will abide in it forever.

7:43 Allah will remove what is in their hearts of any ill-feeling (against one another of the worldly life). Rivers will flow under them, and they will say: "All the praises be to Allah, who has guided us to this, never could we have found guidance if Allah would not have guided us! Indeed, the messengers of our Rabb did come with the truth." It will be cried out to them: "This is the paradise which you have inherited for what you used to do (good)."

7:44 The residents of paradise will call out to the inmates of the fire (saying): "Surely, we have found true what our Rabb had promised to us; have you also found true, what your Rabb promised?" They will say: "Yes." Then a herald will cry out between them: "The curse of Allah is upon the wrongdoers,

7:45 those who hindered from the way of Allah, and sought to make it crooked, and they were disbelievers in the hereafter."

7:46 Between the two, there will be a barrier and on Al-A'raf (heights) there will be people who will recognize every one by their marks (paradise by white faces and hell by black faces). They will call out to the residents of paradise: "Peace be on you." They (people on Al-A'raf) will not have yet entered it (paradise), but they will hope (to enter).

7:47 When their eyes will turn towards the inmates of the fire, they will say: "Our Rabb! Do not place us with the wrongdoers."

7:48 People of Al-A'raf (heights) will call out certain residents, whom they would recognize by their marks, saying: "What did benefit to you from your number (wealth) and your show of arrogance?"

7:49 Are they those about whom you swore that Allah will not grant them (Allah's) Mercy? (Today, it has been said to them): "Enter paradise, no fear shall be on you, nor shall you grieve."

7:50 The inmates of the fire will cry out to the residents of paradise: "Pour on us some water or anything Allah has provided you." They will say: "Surely, Allah has forbidden both (water and provision) to the disbelievers,

7:51 who took their religion as amusement and play, and the life of the world deceived them." (Allah will say): "So today Allah will forget them as they forgot their meeting of this day, and as they used to reject Allah's verses."

7:52 Surely, Allah has brought to them a book (the Qur'an) which Allah has explained with knowledge - guidance and a Mercy to a people who believe.

7:53 Are they waiting that its reality be unfolded? When the day will come, its reality will be unfolded, those who had forgotten it before, will say: "Surely, the messengers of our Rabb did come with the truth. Do we have any intercessors now, who might intercede for us? Or could we be sent back (to world) so that we would do good deeds other than those evil deeds we used to do?" Surely, they have lost themselves and whatever they used to fabricate has forsaken them.

7:54 Surely your Rabb is Allah, who created the heavens and the earth in 6 days, and then Allah ascended the Throne (to suit Allah's majesty). Allah makes the night cover the day, which seeks it rapidly (to follow the night). Allah has created the sun, the moon, the stars, and subjected to Allah's command. Blessed be Allah, Rabb of the worlds!

7:55 Call upon your Rabb humbly and in secret. Surely, Allah does not like the transgressors.

7:56 Do not do mischief in the earth after its order is set, and call Allah with fear and hope. Surely, the Mercy of Allah is close to the righteous people.

7:57 It is Allah who sends the winds as glad tidings in the presence of Allah's Mercy (rain). When they carry a heavy-laden cloud, Allah drives it to a dead land, and then Allah sends down water (rain) from it. Then Allah brings forth in it every kind of fruit. Similarly, Allah will raise the dead, so that you may take heed.

7:58 Its vegetation of the good land comes forth by the order of its Rabb, and that which is bad (land), does not produce but little. Thus Allah explains the verses in various ways for people who give thanks.

7:59 Indeed, Allah sent Noah to his people and he said: "O my people! Worship Allah! You do not have any one worthy of worship but Allah. Certainly, I fear for you the punishment of a mighty day!"

7:60 The leaders of his people said: "Surely, we see you in plain error."

7:61 (Noah) said: "O my people! There is not an error in me, but I am a messenger from the Rabb of the worlds!

7:62 I convey to you messages of my Rabb and give advice to you. I know from Allah what you do not know.

7:63 Or do you wonder that a reminder from your Rabb has come to you as a man among you to warn you, so that you may fear Allah and that you may be shown (Allah's) Mercy?"

7:64 But they denied Allah, Allah saved him and those with him in the ship, and Allah drowned those who denied Allah's verses. Indeed they were blind people.

7:65 To people of Ad (Allah sent) their brother Hud. He said: "O my people! Worship Allah! You do not have any one worthy of worship but Allah. Will you not then fear (Allah)?"

7:66 The leaders of those who disbelieved from his people said: "Surely, we see you in foolishness, and surely we consider you of the liars."

7:67 (Hud) said: "O my people! There is no foolishness in me, but I am a messenger from the Rabb of the worlds!

7:68 I convey messages of my Rabb to you, and I am a trustworthy adviser to you.

7:69 Or do you wonder that a reminder has come to you from your Rabb through a man from among you to warn you? Remember that Allah made you successors after people of Noah, and increased you in ample stature. So remember the bounties of Allah, so that you may succeed."

7:70 They said: "You have come to us that we worship Allah alone and forsake what our forefathers used to worship. So bring to us what you promise (threat) if you are of the truthful!"

7:71 (Hud) said: "Surely punishment and wrath have fallen on you from your Rabb. Do you dispute with me about mere names which you and your fathers have named for which Allah has not sent down any sanction? Then you wait (for the decision of Allah), surely I am with you of those who wait."

7:72 Then Allah saved him and those with him by a Mercy from Allah, and Allah cut the last remnant (wiped out) of those who denied Allah's verses, and they were not believers.

7:73 To the people of Thamud (Allah sent) their brother Saleh. He said: "O my people! Worship Allah! You do not have any one worthy of worship but Allah. Surely, a clear proof (coming out of a huge she-camel from the midst of a rock) has come to you from your Rabb. This she-camel of Allah is a sign to you, so leave her alone to graze on the earth of Allah, and do not touch her with harm, lest a painful punishment should seize you.

7:74 Remember when Allah made you successors after Ad and Allah gave you habitation in the land, you build palaces in its plains, and you carved out the mountains as homes. So remember the bounties of Allah, and do not go about in the land as mischief-makers."

7:75 The arrogant leaders from his people asked those who were oppressed among them, who believed: "Do you believe that Saleh is one sent from his Rabb?" They said: "Surely, we are believers in what he has been sent with."

7:76 Those who showed arrogance said: "Surely, we disbelieve in that which you believe in."

7:77 Then they hamstrung (killed) the she-camel, insolently defied the order of their Rabb, and they said: "O Saleh! Bring us what you have been promising (threat) us if you are indeed one of the messengers (of Allah)."

7:78 So the earthquake took them in the morning in their homes lying (dead) on their faces.

7:79 Then he (Saleh) turned away from them and said: "O my people! Surely, I have conveyed to you message of my Rabb, and have given good advice to you but you do not like advisers."

7:80 (Remember) Lot, when he said to his people: "Do you commit lewdness as none has committed (before) you in any one of the worlds?

7:81 Surely, you approach men lustfully instead of women. Nay, you are people who have exceeded limits."

7:82 The answer of his people was not but that they said: "Drive them out of your town; surely, they are people who want to be pure (from sins)!"

7:83 Then Allah saved him and his family, except his wife; she was among those who stayed behind.

7:84 Allah rained on them a rain (of stones). So see how the end of the evil-doers was.

7:85 To people of Midian, (Allah sent) their brother Shuaib. He said: "O my people! Worship Allah! You do not have any one worthy of worship but Allah. Surely, a clear proof has come to you from your Rabb. So give full measure and weight, and do not diminish (weigh less) to the people in their things, and do not mischief on the earth after it has been set in order, that is good for you, if you are believers.

7:86 Do not sit by every road, threatening and hindering from the way of Allah those who believe in Allah, seeking to make it crooked. Remember when you were a few, and Allah multiplied you. See how the ending of the mischief-makers was.

7:87 If there is a party of you who believes in the message which I have been sent with and a party who do not believe, then be patient until Allah judges between us, and Allah is the best of the judges."

7:88 The chiefs of those who were puffed with pride among his people said: "Surely, we shall drive you out, O Shuaib, and those who have believed with you from our town or you all shall return to our religion." He said: "Even though we hate that (to turn back)?

7:89 Surely, we would fabricate a lie against Allah if we return to your religion or your faith, after when Allah has rescued us from it. It is not for us that we return to it except that Allah, our Rabb wills. Our Rabb comprehends every thing in (Allah's) knowledge. In Allah alone we put our trust. Our Rabb! Judge between us and between our people in truth and Allah is best of the judges."

7:90 The chiefs of those who disbelieved among his people said: "If you follow Shuaib, then surely you will be the losers!"

7:91 So the earthquake seized them and they lay dead, prostrate in their homes.

7:92 Those who denied Shuaib were as if they never lived in it (their homes). Those who denied Shuaib, they were the losers.

7:93 So he (Shuaib) turned from them and said: "O my people! Indeed I have conveyed to you messages of my Rabb and I have given you good advice. Then how can I mourn for disbelieving people?"

7:94 Allah has not sent to a town any prophet, but Allah seized its people with adversity and calamity, so that they may grow humble.

7:95 Then Allah changed in place of the evil with the good, until they increased (in number and in wealth), and said: 'Surely, our forefathers were touched with calamity and affluence (prosperity)." So Allah seized them suddenly while they did not perceive it.

7:96 If the people of the towns had believed and had feared Allah, Allah would have opened to them blessings from the heaven and the earth, but they denied. So Allah seized them for what they used to earn.

7:97 Did the people of the towns feel secure from Allah's punishment coming to them by night while they were asleep?

7:98 Or, did the people of the towns feel secure from Allah's punishment coming to them by daylight while they play?

7:99 Did they then feel secure against the plan of Allah? Do not feel secure from the plan of Allah except the people who are the losers.

7:100 Does it not indicate to those who inherit the land after its people (in succession) that if Allah wills, Allah can punish them for their sins, and Allah can seal their hearts so that they would not hear?

7:101 Those towns whose stories Allah has related to you (O Muhammad) (as example). Surely their messengers came to them with clear proofs, but they did not believe in what they had denied before. Thus Allah sealed the hearts of the disbelievers.

7:102 Allah did not find true most of them to any commitment, rather Allah found most of them transgressors.

7:103 Then Allah sent Moses after them with Allah's verses to Pharaoh and his chiefs, but they dealt unjustly with them. So see how the end of the mischief-makers was.

7:104 Moses said: "O Pharaoh! Surely I am a messenger from the Rabb of the worlds.

7:105 It is incumbent upon me that I do not say about Allah but the truth. Surely I have come to you with a clear proof from your Rabb. So send with me children of Israel."

7:106 (Pharaoh) said: "If you have come with a sign, then show it if you are of the truthful."

7:107 Then (Moses) threw his staff and instantly it became a real serpent!

7:108 He drew out his hand, and instantly it was white (shining) to the beholders.

7:109 The chiefs of the people of Pharaoh said: "Surely this is a skilled sorcerer;

7:110 he wants that he drives you out from your land." (Pharaoh asked): "So what do you recommend?"

7:111 They said: "Keep him in suspense and his brother, and send collectors to cities,

7:112 they bring you every skilled sorcerer."

7:113 The sorcerers came to Pharaoh. They said: "Indeed there will be reward for us if we are the winners."

7:114 He said: "Yes, and indeed you will be of the nearest (to me)."

7:115 They said: "O Moses! Either you throw (first) or that shall we be the (first) throwers."

7:116 He (Moses) said: "You throw (first)." So when they threw, they bewitched the eyes of the people, scared them, and they displayed with a great magic.

7:117 Allah inspired Moses (saying): "Throw your staff," and then it swallowed what they had (showed).

7:118 Thus the truth was established, and proved vain what they used to do, so they were defeated.

7:119 They were defeated, and were returned low (disgraced),

7:120 and the sorcerers fell down prostrate,

7:121 they said: "We believe in the Rabb of the worlds,

7:122 the Rabb of Moses and Aaron."

7:123 Pharaoh said: "(How dare) you have believed in him (Moses) before I give permission to you? Surely, this is a plot you have plotted in the city that you drive out its people from it, but soon you will know.

7:124 Surely, I will cut off your hands and feet on opposite sides, and then I will crucify you all."

7:125 They said: "Surely, we are returning to our Rabb.

7:126 You do not take revenge on us because we believed in the verses of our Rabb when they came to us! Our Rabb! Pour out on us patience, and cause us to die as Muslims."

7:127 The chiefs of the people of Pharaoh said: "Will you leave Moses and his people to spread mischief in the land, and forsake you and your deities?" He said: "We will kill their sons, and we will spare their women, and indeed we have dominant powers over them."

7:128 Moses said to his people: "Seek help in Allah and be patient. Surely, the earth is Allah's. Allah gives it as a heritage to whom Allah wills of Allah's servants, and the blessed end is for the righteous."

7:129 They said: "We had suffered before you came to us, and after you came to us." He said: "May be that your Rabb will destroy your enemy and make you successors in the earth, so that Allah will see how you act."

7:130 Surely Allah punished people of Pharaoh with years (of drought) and shortness of fruits (crops), so that they might remember.

7:131 But when the good came to them, they said: "For us is this." If evil afflicted them, they ascribed misfortune to Moses and those with him. Behold! Surely, their misfortune is also with Allah but most of them do not know.

7:132 They said (to Moses): "Whatever verses you bring us herewith to enchant us with it (your sorcery), we shall not believe in you."

7:133 So Allah sent on them: the flood, the locusts, the lice, the frogs, and the blood as clear signs, but they showed arrogance, and they were criminal people.

7:134 When the punishment fell on them they said: "O Moses! Invoke your Rabb for us because of (Allah's) promise to you. If you remove the punishment from us, we will indeed believe in you, and we shall send with you the children of Israel."

7:135 But when Allah removed the punishment from them for a fixed term, which they had to reach, and then they broke the promise.

7:136 So Allah took retribution from them and drowned them in the sea, because they denied Allah's verses and they were heedless about them.

7:137 Allah made the people who were considered weak (oppressed) to inherit the east of the land and its west, which Allah had blessed. The fair promise of your Rabb was fulfilled for children of Israel because they endured (with patience). Allah destroyed what Pharaoh and his people used to manufacture what they used to erect.

7:138 Allah made the children of Israel across the sea. Then they came upon a people devoted to idols they had. They said: "O Moses! Make for us a deity worthy of worship as they have." He (Moses) said: "Surely, you are a people who know nothing.

7:139 Surely, these people will be destroyed for that which they are engaged in and their deeds are in vain.

7:140 Shall I seek for you a deity other than Allah, while Allah has exalted you above the worlds?

7:141 (Remember) when Allah saved you from people of Pharaoh, who afflicted you with worst punishment, killing your sons, letting your women live, and in that (condition) there was a great trial from your Rabb."

7:142 Allah appointed for Moses 30 nights (to mount Tur) and Allah completed them with 10 (more) to complete the set term of 40 nights with his Rabb. Moses said to his brother Aaron: "Take my place in my people, do right, and do not follow way of the mischief-makers."

7:143 When Moses came at Allah's appointment and his Rabb spoke to him, he said: "O my Rabb! Show me (give me power to see Allah) so that I may look upon you (Allah)." Allah said: "You cannot see Allah, but look at the mountain if it stands firm in its place then you shall see Allah." When his Rabb revealed (Allah's) glory to the mountain, Allah made it collapse as dust, and Moses fell down unconscious. Then when he recovered, he said: "Glory be to you (Allah), I return to you (Allah) (in repentance) and I am the first of the believers."

7:144 (Allah) said: "O Moses, Indeed I (Allah) have chosen you from among all people to deliver my (Allah's) messages and by my (Allah's) speaking (to you). So hold what I (Allah) have given you and be of the grateful."

7:145 Allah ordained for him in the tablets from every thing for admonition and explanation for every thing (and said): "So hold these with firmness, and enjoin your people to follow best of it. I (Allah) will show you soon abode of the transgressors.

7:146 I (Allah) shall turn away from my (Allah's) verses those who behave arrogantly in the earth without any right, and even if they see every verse, they will not believe in them. If they see way of righteousness, they will not take it as their way, but if they see way of error, they will take it as their way, that is because they have rejected my (Allah's) verses and they were heedless to them.

7:147 Those who reject my (Allah's) verses and the meeting of the hereafter, their deeds become vain. Should they be rewarded except for what they used to do?"

7:148 People of Moses after him (during absence) made the body of a calf (for worship) from their ornaments which had a sound (of mooing). Did they not see that neither it can speak to them nor guide them to the way? Yet, they took it (for worship) and they were the wrongdoers.

7:149 When they regretted and saw that they had gone astray, they (repented and) said: "If our Rabb do not have Mercy on us and forgive us, we shall certainly be among the losers."

7:150 When Moses returned to his people, became angry and grieved, he said: "What an evil thing you have done (worship the calf) after me! Did you hasten to decree (for punishment) of your Rabb?" He threw down the tablets and seized his brother by his head dragging him to himself. (Aaron) said: "O son of my mother! Indeed the people overpowered me weak and were about to kill me, so let not the enemies rejoice over me, and do not place me with the wrongdoers."

7:151 (Moses) said: "O my Rabb! Forgive me and my brother, and admit us to your (Allah's) Mercy, for you (Allah) are the Merciful of those who show Mercy."

7:152 Surely, those who took the calf (for worship), wrath from their Rabb and humiliation overtook them in the life of this world. Thus Allah does recompense those who fabricate lies.

7:153 But those who committed evil deeds, then repented after that and believed, surely your Rabb after that is Forgiving, Merciful.

7:154 When the anger of Moses was calmed, he took up the tablets in which there was writing of guidance and Mercy for those who fear their Rabb.

7:155 Moses chose 70 men out of his people to (the place of) Allah's appointment. (On the way) when a violent earthquake seized them, he said: "O my Rabb, had you (Allah) willed, you (Allah) could have destroyed them and me before. Would you (Allah) destroy us for what the fools did among us? It was not but your (Allah's) trial by which you (Allah) mislead with it whom you (Allah) willed, and you (Allah) guided whom you (Allah) willed. You (Allah) are our Guardian, so forgive us and have Mercy on us, and you (Allah) are the best of those who forgive,

7:156 and ordain for us good in this world, and in the hereafter. Surely we have turned to you (Allah)." Allah said: "I (Allah) will inflict my (Allah's) punishment upon whom I (Allah) will; yet, my (Allah's) Mercy embraces every thing. I (Allah) will ordain (Mercy) for those who do right and pay obligatory charity; and those who believe in my (Allah's) verses."

7:157 Those who follow the messenger, the unlettered prophet (Muhammad - could not read nor write) whom they will find written in the Torah and the Gospel, who commands them to good and forbids them from evil; and makes lawful to them the pure things and prohibits on them the impure things; and removes from them their burdens, and the fetters (bindings) which were upon them. So those who believe in him, support him, help him; follow the light (the Qur'an) which has been sent with him, it is they who will be successful (in this world and hereafter).

7:158 Say (O Muhammad): "O mankind! Surely, I am the messenger of Allah to all of you, to Allah belongs dominion of the heavens and the earth. There is no one worthy of worship but Allah. Allah gives life and causes death. So believe in Allah and Allah's messenger (Muhammad), the unlettered Prophet who believes in Allah and Allah's words (this Qur'an). Follow him so that you may find guidance."

7:159 From of the people of Moses, a party guided (others) with truth and thereby established justice.

7:160 Allah divided them into 12 tribes as communities. When his people asked him for water, Allah inspired to Moses (saying): "Strike the stone with your stuff," and there gushed out of it 12 springs, each group knew its drinking place. Allah provided shades of clouds on them and Allah sent down upon them Manna (sweet dish) and Salva (quail's meat) (saying): "Eat of the good things which Allah has provided you." (They rebelled and) they did not harm Allah but they were doing wrong to themselves.

7:161 (Remember) when it was said to them: "Reside in this town and eat from there whatever you wish, and say: 'O Allah forgives our sins,' and enter the gate prostrating (bowing with humility). Allah will forgive you your sins. Allah will increase (reward for) the righteous people."

7:162 But those among them who did wrong, changed the word other (than that) which was said to them. So Allah sent on them a punishment from the heaven because they used to do wrong.

7:163 Ask them (O Muhammad) about the town which was situated by the sea shore, when they transgressed in the Sabbath (Saturday). The fish came to them visibly on their Sabbath day, and they did not come to them on the days they had no Sabbath. Thus Allah tested them because they used to disobey.

7:164 When a group among them said: "Why do you admonish a people whom Allah is about to destroy them or punish them with a severe punishment?" (The preachers) replied: "To offer an excuse to your Rabb and that they may refrain from disobedience."

7:165 So when they forgot what they had been reminded with, Allah delivered those who forbade from evil, but Allah seized those who did wrong with severe punishment because of what they used to transgress.

7:166 But when they persistently did what they were forbidden from it, Allah told them: "You be detested monkeys."

7:167 (Remember) when your Rabb declared that Allah would send upon them others who would afflict them with a grievous punishment till the day of Resurrection. Surely, your Rabb is swift in persecution and Allah is Forgiving, Merciful.

7:168 Allah dispersed them in the land (as separate) groups among them in the earth: some of them are righteous and others among them are away from that. Allah tested them with good blessings and evil calamities in order that they might turn (to Allah).

7:169 Then after them evil successors succeeded who inherited the book, but they chose goods of this low life (evil pleasures of the world) saying (as excuse): "We shall be forgiven." If similar offer (evil pleasures of the world) comes to them, they would again seize them. Was not the covenant of the book taken on them that they would not say about Allah anything but the truth? They have studied what is in it. Abode of the hereafter is better for those who are righteous. Then do not you understand?

7:170 Those who hold fast to the book (act on it) and establish the prayer, Allah will not let the reward of the righteous go waste.

7:171 (Remember) when Allah raised the mountain over them as if it was a canopy, and they thought that it was going to fall on them. (Allah said): "Hold with strength firmly to what I (Allah) have given you, and remember what is in it so that you may refrain from evil."

7:172 (Remember) when your Rabb brought from the children of Adam, from their loins, their descendents and made them testify as to themselves (saying): "Is Allah not your Rabb?" They said: "Yes! We testify," lest you (mankind) should say on the day of Resurrection: "Surely, we were unaware of this."

7:173 Or you should say: "Only our forefathers associated with Allah before us, and we are their offspring after them. Will you destroy us for what the wrongdoers did?"

7:174 Thus Allah does explain the verses so that they may return (to the truth).

7:175 Recite (O Muhammad) to them the story of that person whom Allah gave Allah's verses but that person turned away from them, so Satan followed him, and he became of those who went astray.

7:176 If Allah willed, Allah would have exalted him with these signs but he clung (inclined) to the earth and followed its vain desires. So its parable is like the parable of a dog: if you attack it, it lolls out its tongue, or if you leave it alone, it still lolls out its tongue. Such is the parable of the people who reject Allah's verses. So narrate these stories to them, perhaps they may think over.

7:177 Evil is the example of the people who reject Allah's verses and they used to wrong themselves.

7:178 Whoever Allah guides is the guided one, and whoever Allah lets go astray, they are those losers.

7:179 Surely, Allah has created many jinns and mankind for hell. They have hearts, they do not understand with them; they have eyes, they do not see with them; and they have ears, they do not hear with them. They are like cattle, or even worse than them, they are those who are heedless.

7:180 Allah has the excellent names (over 99 attributes), so call Allah by them, and leave (company) of those who distort (in) Allah's names. They will be requited for what they used to do.

7:181 Of those whom Allah has created, there is a party who guides others with the truth and establishes justice with it.

7:182 Those who reject Allah's verses, Allah gradually seize them (with punishment) from where they do not know,

7:183 though I (Allah) grant them respite; but certainly my (Allah's) plan is strong.

7:184 Do they not reflect (think)? There is not any madness in their companion (Muhammad). He is not but a plain warner.

7:185 Have they not looked in the dominion of the heavens and the earth and every thing what Allah has created, and that may be their term of life is drawn near? Then in what message after this will they believe?

7:186 Whoever Allah lets go astray, then there is none to guide; and Allah leaves in their transgressions, they wander blindly.

7:187 They ask you (O Muhammad) about the hour (day of Resurrection): "When will be its appointed time?" Say: "Its knowledge is only with Allah. None can disclose its time but Allah. It will weigh heavy in the heavens and the earth. It shall not come to you but suddenly." They ask you as if you are very knowledgeable about it. Say: "Only its knowledge is with Allah alone but most people do not know."

7:188 Say (O Muhammad): "I do not possess for myself any good nor any harm except as Allah wishes. If I had the knowledge of the unseen, I would have (secured for myself) an abundance of good, and no evil would have touched me. But I am a warner and a bearer of glad tidings for people who believe."

7:189 Allah has created you from a single person (Adam), and Allah has created from him his mate (Eve), so that he might find comfort with her. When he covers (has sex with) her, she bore a light burden (pregnant) and move about with it. Then when it grows heavy, they both invoke Allah, their Rabb (saying): "If Allah gives us a good child, we shall indeed be among the grateful."

7:190 But when Allah gives them a good child, they ascribe partners to Allah in that which Allah has given them. But exalted is Allah above that which they associate (as partners with Allah).

7:191 Do they associate (partners with Allah) who can not create anything but they are created,

7:192 and they can neither give those help, nor can they help themselves?

7:193 If you call them to the guidance, they will not follow you. It is the same for you whether you call them or you are silent.

7:194 Surely, those whom you call other than Allah are servants like you. So call them and let them answer you if you are truthful.

7:195 Have they feet to walk with? Or have they hands to hold with? Or have they eyes to see with? Or have they ears to hear with? Say (O Muhammad): "Call your partners of Allah and then plot against Allah, and do not give Allah respite!"

7:196 Surely, my Protector is Allah who has revealed the book (the Qur'an), and Allah protects the righteous.

7:197 Those whom you call other than Allah, they can neither help you nor can they help themselves.

7:198 If you call them to the guidance, they do not hear and you see them looking at you, yet they do not see.

7:199 Show forgiveness, enjoin the good, and turn away from the ignorant.

7:200 If an evil incites you from Satan, then seek refuge with Allah. Surely, Allah is All-Hearer, All-Knower.

7:201 Surely, those who fear Allah, when an evil thought touches them from Satan, they remember Allah, and then they see (aright).

7:202 For their brothers (of devils), they plunge them deeper in error, and they do not relax (cease).

7:203 If you (O Muhammad) do not bring them a miracle, they say: "Why have you not invented one?" Say: "I only follow what is revealed to me from my Rabb.

This (the Qur'an) insight is from your Rabb, and guidance and Mercy for people who believe."

7:204 So when the Qur'an is recited, listen to it, and keep silent so that you are shown Mercy.

7:205 Remember your Rabb by your heart humbly, with fear without loudness of words in the mornings and in the evenings, and do not be of neglectful.

7:206 Surely, those who are with your Rabb, do not turn away in pride from Allah's worship, but they glorify Allah and they prostrate before Allah.

8. Al-Anfal : The Spoils of War
In the name of Allah, the Gracious, the Merciful

8:1 They ask you (O Muhammad) about the spoils of war. Say: "The spoils are for Allah and the messenger. So fear Allah and set right things (end differences) among you, and obey Allah and Allah's messenger (Muhammad), if you are believers."

8:2 Only the believers are those who, when Allah is mentioned, their hearts quake and when Allah's verses (this Qur'an) are recited to them, they increase in faith; and they put their trust in their Rabb (alone);

8:3 who establish prayer and they spend out of what Allah has provided them.

8:4 They are these who are the believers in truth. They have high ranks with their Rabb; Forgiveness, and a generous sustenance.

8:5 As your Rabb brought you (O Muhammad) out from your home (to struggle) for the truth, and surely, a party among the believers disliked it.

8:6 They disputed with you about the truth after it became clear, as if they were driven to the death while they were looking at it.

8:7 (Remember) when Allah promised you (Muslims) one of the 2 groups (of the enemy- army or caravan) that it should be for you, and you wished that one without having arms (the caravan) should be for you, but Allah willed to justify the truth by Allah's words and cut off the roots of the disbelievers (in the battle of Badr),

8:8 so that Allah proves true the truth and proves false the falsehood, even though the evil-doers dislike it.

8:9 (Remember) when you sought help of your Rabb and Allah answered to you (saying): "Indeed Allah will help you with 1,000 angels one after another."

8:10 Allah did not do this but as glad tidings, so that your hearts be at rest with it. There is no victory except from Allah. Surely, Allah is All-Mighty, All-Wise.

8:11 (Remember before the battle of Badr) when Allah covered you with a drowsiness as a security from Allah, Allah sent down rain on you from the sky to clean you thereby and take away from you the evil-thinking of Satan, to strengthen your hearts, and thereby make your feet firm therewith.

8:12 (Remember) when your Rabb inspired to the angels: "Allah is with you, so keep firm those who have believed. Allah will cast the terror in the hearts of those who have disbelieved, so strike above their necks, and strike over all their fingertips."

8:13 This is because they defied Allah and Allah's messenger. Whoever defies Allah and Allah's messenger, then surely, Allah is Severe in punishment,

8:14 that is (the punishment), so taste it, and that is for the disbeliever's punishment of the fire.

8:15 O you who believe! When you meet those who disbelieve in a battlefield, do not turn your backs to them,

8:16 and those who turn their back to them that day, unless as strategy of war, or retreat to a troop (of their own), they indeed have incurred the wrath of Allah. Their abode is hell, and worst indeed is that destination!

8:17 You did not kill them, but Allah killed them. You (Muhammad) did not throw sand when you did throw but Allah threw, so that Allah might test the believers by a fair trial from Allah. Surely, Allah is All-Hearer, All-Knower.

8:18 Surely this is the fact; Allah weakens evil designs of the disbelievers.

8:19 (O disbelievers) if you seek a judgment, then surely the judgment has come to you (with victory for the believers). If you desist, that will be better for you, and if you return (to the attack), Allah too will return, and your forces will not avail you anything though it be large in numbers, and that Allah is with the believers.

8:20 O you who believe! Obey Allah and Allah's messenger, and do not turn away from him (Muhammad) while you hear.

8:21 You do not be like those who say: "We have heard," but they have not heard.

8:22 Surely! Worst of living creatures to Allah are the deaf and the dumb, those who do not use their reason.

8:23 Had Allah known in them of any good, Allah would indeed have made them listen. Even if Allah had made them listen, they would have turned away while they were reluctant (to the truth).

8:24 O you who believe! Respond to Allah and to the messenger when Allah calls you to that which will give you life, and know that Allah comes in between a person and its heart (to prevent evil). It is to Allah you all shall be gathered.

8:25 Fear mischief which do not affect particularly those of you who do wrong (but may afflict good and bad people), and know that Allah is severe in punishment.

8:26 Remember when you were few and reckoned weak in the land, and you were afraid that the people might kidnap you. Allah provided you with refuge, strengthened you with Allah's help, and provided you with good things so that you may give thanks.

8:27 O you who believe! You do not betray Allah and the messenger, or betray your trusts while you know.

8:28 Know that your possessions and your children are just a trial and that with Allah is a great reward.

8:29 O you who believe! If you fear Allah, Allah will grant you a criterion (to judge between right and wrong), and will expiate for you your sins, and forgive you. Allah is the Rabb of the Great Bounty.

8:30 (Remember) when those who disbelieved, they plotted against you (O Muhammad) to imprison you, or to kill you, or to drive you away (from your home at Makkah). They planned, Allah also planned, and Allah is the best of the planners.

8:31 Whenever Allah's verses (of the Qur'an) are recited to them, they say: "We have heard. If we wished we could say like this. These are nothing but the tales of the ancient people."

8:32 (Remember) when they said: "O Allah! If this (the Qur'an) is indeed the truth from Allah, then rain down stones on us from the sky or brings us a painful punishment."

8:33 But Allah would not punish them while you (Muhammad) are among them. Or Allah will not punish them while they seek (Allah's) Forgiveness.

8:34 But what is with them that Allah should not punish them while they stop people from the Sacred Mosque (at Makkah), and they are not its guardians? None can be its guardians except the pious, but most of them do not know.

8:35 Their prayer at the House (the Ka'bah at Makkah) is nothing but whistling and hand-clapping. So taste the punishment for what you used to disbelieve.

8:36 Surely, those who disbelieve, they spend their wealth to hinder people from the way of Allah. They will keep on spending; and then it will become anguish for them. Then they will be defeated. Those who disbelieve, (in the hereafter) they will be gathered to hell,

8:37 in order that Allah may distinguish the wicked (disbelievers, evil-doers) from the good (believers with righteous deeds). Allah will put the wicked one upon another, will pile them all, and will cast them into hell. Those are they who are the losers.

8:38 Say (O Muhammad) to those who have disbelieved, if they desist (from disbelief), their past will be forgiven. But if they revert, then let them precede the examples of the ancients (as a warning).

8:39 (O believers) fight them until there is no more mischief and the religion (Islam) is established completely for Allah alone. But if they cease (worshipping others besides Allah), then surely, Allah is All-Seer of what they do.

8:40 If they turn away, then know that Allah is your protector, an excellent protector, and an Excellent Helper!

8:41 Know that whatever war-booty you may gain, surely $1/5^{th}$ of it (is assigned) to Allah, and to the messenger, and to the near relatives (of Muhammad), (and also) the orphans, the poor who do not beg, and the wayfarer, if you do believe in Allah and in that which Allah has sent down to Allah's servant (Muhammad) on the day of criterion (between right and wrong), the day when the 2 forces met (the battle of Badr). Allah has power over all things.

8:42 (Remember) when you (the Muslim army) were on the near side of the valley, and they were on the further side, and the caravan was on the ground lower than you. If you had made a mutual appointment to meet, you would surly have failed in the appointment; but Allah might accomplish a matter that was already ordained (in Allah's knowledge), so that those who were destined to perish might die with a clear evidence, and those who were destined to live (believers) might live with a clear evidence. Surely, Allah is All-Hearer, All-Knower.

8:43 (Remember) when Allah showed them to you (Muhammad) as few in numbers in your dream; if Allah had shown them to you as many in number, you would surely have been discouraged and you would surely have disputed in making a decision. But Allah saved you. Certainly, Allah is All-Knower of what is in the hearts.

8:44 (Remember) when you met (disbelievers during the battle of Badr), Allah showed them to you as few in number in your eyes and Allah made you appear as few in number in their eyes so that Allah might accomplish a matter that was already ordained, and to Allah all matters return (for decision).

8:45 O you who believe! When you meet a force (enemy), take a firm stand against them and remember (the name of) Allah much, so that you may be successful.

8:46 Obey Allah and Allah's messenger, and do not dispute (with one another) lest you lose courage and weaken your strength, and be patient. Surely, Allah is with those who are patient.

8:47 Do not be like those who come out of their homes boastfully in order to be seen by people, and hinder others from the way of Allah. Allah encompasses all of what they do.

8:48 (Remember) when Satan made their evil deeds seem fair to them and said: "No one from mankind can overcome you this day (battle of Badr), and surely, I am your neighbor (to help)." Yet, when the 2 forces came in sight of each other, he ran away on his heels and said: "Surely, I have nothing to do with you. Surely, I can see what you do not see. Surely, I fear Allah for Allah is Severe in punishment."

8:49 Then the hypocrites and those in whose hearts was a disease (of disbelief) said: "These people (Muslims) are deceived by their religion." But those who put their trust in Allah, and then surely, Allah is All-Mighty, All-Wise.

8:50 If you could only see when the angels were taking away souls (at death) of those who disbelieve! They were smiting their faces and their backs, (saying): "Taste the punishment of the blazing fire.

8:51 This (punishment) is because of what your hands have sent forth. Surely, Allah is not unjust to Allah's servants."

8:52 Their behavior is similar (to that) of the people of Pharaoh, and those before them. They also rejected the verses of Allah and Allah punished them for their sins. Surely, Allah is All-Mighty, Severe in punishment.

8:53 That is because Allah will never change a grace which Allah has bestowed on a people until they themselves change what is in their own selves. Surely, Allah is All-Hearer, All-Knower.

8:54 Their behavior is similar (to that) of the people of Pharaoh, and those before them. They denied the verses of their Rabb, so Allah destroyed them for their sins, and Allah drowned the people of Pharaoh, and they all were wrongdoers.

8:55 Surely, the worst of living creatures to Allah are those who disbelieve, so they shall not believe.

8:56 They are those with whom you made a covenant, then they break their covenant every time, and they do not fear (Allah).

8:57 If you gain the mastery over them in war, punish them severely in order to disperse those who are behind them so that they may learn a lesson.

8:58 If you (O Muhammad) fear treachery from any people, throw back (their covenant) to them on equal terms. Certainly Allah does not like the treacherous.

8:59 Let not the disbelievers think that they can outdo (escape punishment). Surely, they will never be able to save themselves (from punishment).

8:60 Make ready against them (enemy) all the power you can afford including steeds of war (all military means, cavalry, etc) to threaten them the enemy of Allah and your enemy, and others besides them whom you do not know but Allah knows. Whatever you shall spend in the way of Allah shall be repaid to you, and you shall not be treated unjustly.

8:61 If they incline towards peace, you also incline to it, and trust in Allah. Surely, Allah is All-Hearer, All-Knower.

8:62 If they intend to deceive you, then surely, Allah is Sufficient for you. Allah is the one who has supported you and the believers with Allah's help,

8:63 and Allah has united their (believers) hearts. If you had spent all that is in the earth, you could not have united their hearts, but Allah has united them. Certainly Allah is All-Mighty, All-Wise.

8:64 O Prophet (Muhammad)! Allah is sufficient for you and for the believers who follow you.

8:65 O Prophet (Muhammad)! Urge the believers on to fight. If there are 20 steadfast people amongst you, they shall overcome 200 (disbelievers), and if there are 100 (steadfast people) amongst you, they will overcome 1,000 of those who disbelieve, because they (disbelievers) are people who do not understand.

8:66 Now, Allah has lightened from you (task), for Allah knows that there is weakness in you. So, if there are 100 steadfast (people) amongst you, they shall overcome 200, and if there are 1,000 of you, they shall overcome 2,000 with the permission of Allah. Allah is with the patient.

8:67 It is not fit for a Prophet that he should have prisoners of war until he has thoroughly subdued the land. Do you (Muslims) desire the good of this world while Allah desires for you the hereafter? Allah is All-Mighty, All-Wise.

8:68 Had there not a previous ordainment from Allah (to take ransom), a severe punishment would have touched you for what you have taken.

8:69 Enjoy the booty in war which you have taken, for it is lawful and good, but be afraid of Allah. Certainly, Allah is Forgiving, Merciful.

8:70 O Prophet! Say to those who are from the captives in your hands: "If Allah knows any good in your hearts, Allah will give you something better than what has been taken from you, and Allah will forgive you. Allah is Forgiving, Merciful."

8:71 But if they intend to betray you (Muhammad), they have already betrayed Allah before. So, Allah gave you power over them. Allah All-Knower, All-Wise.

8:72 Surely, those who believed, emigrated, and strove hard and fought with their property and their lives in the way of Allah; and those who gave asylum and help; these are all allies to one another. As to those who believed but did not emigrate, you owe no duty of protection to them until they emigrate; but if they seek your help in religion, it is your duty to help them except against a people with whom you have a treaty of mutual alliance. Allah is All-Seer of what you do.

8:73 Those who disbelieve are allies to one another. If you (Muslims) do not do so (become allies), there will be oppression on earth, and a great mischief.

8:74 Those who believed, emigrated, and strove hard in the way of Allah, and those who gave them asylum and help; these are the believers in truth, for them is forgiveness and noble provisions.

8:75 Those who believed afterwards, emigrated, and strove hard along with you (in the cause of Allah), they are of you. But kindred by blood are nearer to one another in the book ordained by Allah. Surely, Allah is All-Knower of everything.

9. At-Taubah : The Repentance

9:1 Immunity from all obligations (is declared) from Allah and Allah's messenger (Muhammad) to those of the polytheists with whom you made a treaty:

9:2 "So travel freely (O polytheists) for 4 months throughout the land, but know that you cannot escape (from punishment of) Allah, and Allah will disgrace the disbelievers."

9:3 A declaration from Allah and Allah's messenger to mankind on the greatest day of pilgrimage that Allah is free from all obligations to the polytheists and so is Allah's messenger. So if you (polytheists) repent, it is better for you, but if you turn away, then know that you cannot escape (from the punishment of) Allah. Give tidings (O Muhammad) to those who disbelieve of a painful punishment.

9:4 Except those of the polytheists with whom you have a treaty, and who have not subsequently failed you in every detail, nor they have supported anyone against you. So fulfill your treaty with them to (the end of) their term. Surely Allah loves the pious.

9:5 When the forbidden (4) months of Islamic calendar have passed, then fight the polytheists wherever you find them, capture them, besiege them, and prepare for them each and every ambush. But if they repent, offer prayers perfectly, and give obligatory charity, then leave their way free. Surely, Allah is Forgiving, Merciful.

9:6 If anyone of the polytheists seeks your protection, grant protection so that the person may hear the word of Allah (the Qur'an), and then escort to where the person can be secure, that is because they are people who do not know (the truth).

9:7 How can there be a covenant for the polytheists with Allah and with Allah's messenger except those with whom you made a covenant near the sacred mosque (at Makkah)? So long as they are true to you, you stand true to them. Surely, Allah loves the pious.

9:8 How (can you trust them) that when they overpower you, they do not regard the ties, either of kinship or of covenant with you? They please you with (good words from) their mouths, but their hearts are averse to you, and most of them are disobedient.

9:9 They have purchased a little gain with the revelations of Allah, and they hindered people from Allah's way; indeed evil is that which they used to do.

9:10 With regard to a believer, they do not respect the ties, either of kinship or of covenant. It is they who are the transgressors.

9:11 But if they repent, establish prayers perfectly, and give obligatory charity, then they are your brothers in religion. Allah explains the revelations in detail for the people of understanding.

9:12 But if they violate their oaths after their covenant, and attack your religion with disapproval and criticism, then fight the leaders of disbelief. Surely their oaths are nothing to them, so that they may be stopped (their evil actions).

9:13 Will you not fight those people who have violated their oaths, conspired to expel the messenger, and they were the first to attack you? Do you fear them? Allah has more right that you should fear Allah, if you are believers.

9:14 Fight against them so that Allah will punish them by your hands and disgrace them. Allah will grant you victory over them and heal the hearts of a believing people,

9:15 and remove the anger from their (believers) hearts. Allah accepts the repentance of whom Allah wills. Allah is All-Knower, All-Wise.

9:16 Do you think that you will be left alone (without trial) while Allah has not yet tested those among you who have striven hard and fought, have not taken helpers (friends) besides Allah and Allah's messenger, and the believers? Allah is Well-Acquainted with what you do.

9:17 It is not for the polytheists to maintain the mosques of Allah while they witness against their own selves of disbelief. Their works are in vain and they shall abide in fire forever.

9:18 The mosques of Allah shall be maintained only by those who believe in Allah and the last day; establish prayers, give obligatory charity, and fear none but Allah. They are expected to be of the people of true guidance.

9:19 Do you consider those who provide drinking water to the pilgrims and maintain the sacred mosque (at Makkah) equal to those who believe in Allah, the last day, and strive hard and fight in the way of Allah? They are not equal before Allah. Allah does not guide those people who are the wrongdoers.

9:20 Those who believe, emigrate, and strive hard and fight in Allah's way with their wealth and their lives are far higher in degree with Allah. They are the successful.

9:21 Their Rabb gives them glad tidings of Mercy from Allah, (Allah's) pleasure, and gardens (paradise) for them in which there are everlasting delights.

9:22 They will reside in it forever. Surely, with Allah there is the great reward.

9:23 O you who believe! Do not take your fathers and your brothers as protectors if they prefer disbelief to belief. Whoever of you takes them, those will be the wrongdoers.

9:24 Say: If your fathers, your sons, your brothers, your wives, your kindred, the wealth that you have acquired, the business in which you fear a loss, and the homes in which you delight are dearer to you than Allah and Allah's messenger, and striving hard and fighting in Allah's way, then wait until Allah brings about Allah's decision. Allah does not guide the people who are disobedient.

9:25 Truly Allah has given you victory on many battle fields, and on the day of Hunain (battle) when you rejoiced at your great number (more than enemy), it availed you nothing. The earth, vast as it is, was straitened for you, then you turned back and fled.

9:26 Then Allah did send down Allah's peace (tranquility) on Allah's messenger (Muhammad), and on the believers, sent down forces (angels) which you did not see, and punished those disbelievers. Such was the recompense of disbelievers.

9:27 Then after that Allah accepted the repentance of whom Allah willed. Allah is Forgiving, Merciful.

9:28 O you who believe! Surely, the polytheists are impure. So let them not come near the sacred mosque (at Makkah) after this year, and if you fear poverty, Allah will enrich you out of Allah's bounty if Allah wills. Surely, Allah is All-Knower, All-Wise.

9:29 Fight against those who do not believe in Allah, nor in the last day, nor forbid that which has been forbidden by Allah and Allah's messenger, nor acknowledge the religion of truth (Islam) among the people who were given the scripture, until they pay the security tax willingly, and feel themselves subdued.

9:30 The Jews say: "Ezra is the son of Allah," and the Christians say: "Christ is the son of Allah". That is their saying with their mouths. They imitate the saying of those who disbelieve from old. Allah's curse is on them, how they are deluded away from the truth!

9:31 They took their rabbis and priests to be their Rabb besides Allah, and (also took as their Rabb) Jesus, son of Mary, while they were commanded (in the Torah and the Gospel) to worship no one but one Allah; there is no one worthy of worship but Allah. Praise and glory be to Allah above those whom they associate with Allah.

9:32 They want to extinguish Allah's light with their mouths, but Allah will not allow except that Allah perfects Allah's light even though the disbelievers hate it.

9:33 It is Allah who has sent Allah's messenger (Muhammad) with guidance and the religion of truth (Islam), to make it superior over all other religions even though the polytheists hate it.

9:34 O you who believe! Surely, there are many of the rabbis and the priests who devour the wealth of mankind in falsehood, and hinder them from the way of Allah. Those who hoard up gold and silver, and do not spend it in the way of Allah, announce to them a painful punishment.

9:35 On the day when their wealth will be heated in the fire of hell, and their foreheads, flanks, and backs will be branded with it. (They will be told): "This is the treasure which you hoarded for yourselves. Now taste what you used to hoard."

9:36 Surely, the number of months with Allah is 12 months (in a year) in the book of Allah since the day when Allah created the heavens and the earth. Of them 4 are sacred; that is the right religion. So do not wrong yourselves in it. But fight against the polytheists collectively, as they fight against you collectively. Know that Allah is with those who are pious.

9:37 Indeed the postponing (of a sacred month) is an addition to disbelief; thereby those who disbelieve are led to astray. They make it lawful one year and forbid it another year in order to adjust the number of months which Allah has forbidden, and make lawful what months Allah has forbidden. The evil of their deeds is made pleasing to them. Allah does not guide the people, who disbelieve.

9:38 O you who believe! What is the matter with you that when you are asked to march forth in the way of Allah, you cling heavily to the earth? Are you pleased with the life of this world rather than the hereafter? The enjoyment of this life is little compared to the life of the hereafter.

9:39 If you do not march forth, Allah will punish you with a painful punishment and will replace you with other people, and you cannot harm Allah at all, and Allah is Able over all things.

9:40 If you do not help him (Muhammad), (does not matter) indeed Allah did help him when those who disbelieve drove him out (of his town), the 2nd of 2, when they (Muhammad and Abu Bakr) were in the cave (the enemy came close to the opening of the cave), when he (Muhammad) said to his companion (Abu Bakr): "Do not worry, surely Allah is with us." Then Allah sent down Allah's peace upon him, and strengthened him with forces (angels) which you did not see, thus, Allah made the word of those who disbelieved the lowest, while the words of Allah remain uppermost. Allah is All-Mighty, All-Wise.

9:41 March forth whether you are light (healthy, young, and wealthy) or heavy (ill, old, and poor), strive hard with your wealth and your lives in the way of Allah. This is better for you, if you understand.

9:42 (For the hypocrites) if the gain would have been immediate and an easy journey, they would have certainly followed you, but the long journey (Tabuk expedition) was too hard for them. (For not joining you in the expedition) they would swear by Allah: "If only we could, we would certainly have come forth with you." They destroy their own selves, and Allah knows that they are liars.

9:43 May Allah forgive you (O Muhammad). Why did you grant permission to them (to stay behind), until those who told the truth become clear to you, and you had known the liars?

9:44 Those who believe in Allah and the last day will not ask your permission (to be exempted) from fighting with their wealth and their lives. Allah knows all of those who are pious.

9:45 It is only those who do not believe in Allah and the last day and whose hearts are in doubt that ask your permission (exemption from fighting). So in their doubts they waver.

9:46 If they had intended to march out, certainly they would have made some preparation for it. But Allah did not like their going forth; so Allah made them lag behind, and it was said (to them): "You sit along with those who sit (at home)."

9:47 Had they marched out with you, they would have added to you nothing except disorder, and they would have hurried about in your midst (spread corruption) and sowing sedition among you, and there are some among you who would have listened to them. Allah is All-Knower of those who are wrongdoers.

9:48 Surely, they had plotted sedition before, and had upset matters for you, until the truth (victory) came and the decree of Allah (Islam) became clear though they hated it.

9:49 Among them is he (Jad bin Qais) who said: "Grant me leave (exempt from fighting) and do not put me into trial (temptation)." Surely, they have already fallen into trial. Surely, hell is surrounding the disbelievers.

9:50 If good befalls you (Muhammad), it grieves them, but if a calamity overtakes you, they say: "Indeed we took our precaution before," and turn away rejoicing.

9:51 Say: "Nothing will ever happen to us except what Allah has ordained for us. Allah is our Protector." In Allah let the believers put their trust.

9:52 Say: "Do you expect for us anything except one of the 2 best things (martyrdom or victory)? But we are waiting for you either that Allah will afflict you with a punishment from Allah or at our hands. So wait, we too are waiting with you."

9:53 Say: "Spend (in Allah's cause) willingly or unwillingly, it will not be accepted from you. Surely, you are a disobedient people."

9:54 Nothing prevents them from being accepted from them their contributions except that they disbelieved in Allah and in Allah's messenger (Muhammad); and they do not come to the prayer except they are lazy; and that they offer no contributions but they are unwilling.

9:55 So let not their wealth or their children amaze you (O Muhammad); in reality, Allah intends to punish them with these things in the life of this world, and that their souls may depart (die) while they are disbelievers.

9:56 They swear by Allah that they are truly of you while they are not of you, but they are people (hypocrites) who are afraid of you.

9:57 If they find a refuge, or caves, or a hiding place, they would turn to it straightway with a swift rush.

9:58 Some of them are those who accuse you (O Muhammad) in the matter of the alms (donations). If they are given part from it, they are pleased, but if they are not given from it, behold! They are enraged!

9:59 If they would be contented with what Allah and Allah's messenger had given them, and had said: "Allah is sufficient for us. Allah will soon give us Allah's bounty, and so will Allah's messenger. We implore to Allah (to enrich us)."

9:60 Only Sadaqah (here it is obligatory charity), alms are for the poor (who beg), the poor (who do not beg), those employed to collect them (the funds), those whose hearts have been inclined (towards Islam), free the captives, those in debt, those (fighting) in Allah's way, and the wayfarer (a traveler who is in need). That is a duty imposed by Allah. Allah is All-Knower, All-Wise.

9:61 Among them are those who hurt the Prophet (Muhammad) by saying: "He is (lending his) ear (to everyone)." Say: "He listens to what is best for you, he believes in Allah, has faith in the believers, and is a mercy to those of you who believe." But those who hurt Allah's messenger (Muhammad) for them there is a painful punishment.

9:62 They swear by Allah to you in order to please you. But Allah and Allah's messenger (Muhammad) has more right, so they should please Allah if they are believers.

9:63 Do they not know that whoever opposes and shows hostility to Allah and Allah's messenger, certainly will be in the fire of hell to abide in it? That is extreme disgrace.

9:64 The hypocrites fear lest a chapter (of the Qur'an) should be revealed about them, showing them what is in their hearts. Say: "(Go ahead and) mock! But certainly Allah will bring to light all that you fear."

9:65 If you ask them about this, they declare: "We were only talking idly and joking." Say: "Was it at Allah and Allah's verses and Allah's messenger that you were mocking?"

9:66 Make no excuse; indeed you have disbelieved after you had believed. If Allah pardons some of you, Allah will punish others amongst you because they are criminals.

9:67 The hypocrite men and women are from one another. They enjoin evil (disbelief), forbid from good (Islam), and close their hands (not spending in Allah's cause). They have forgotten Allah, so Allah has forgotten them. Surely, the hypocrites are the disobedient.

9:68 Allah has promised the hypocrite men and women, the disbelievers, the fire of hell, they shall abide in it. It will be sufficient for them. Allah has cursed them and for them is a lasting punishment.

9:69 Like those before you, they were mightier than you in power, and more abundant in wealth and children. They had enjoyed their portion (worldly life), so enjoy your portion (a while) as those before you enjoyed their portion (a while); and you indulge in play and pastime as they indulged in play and pastime. Such are they whose deeds are in vain in this world and in the hereafter. Such are they who are the losers.

9:70 Has not the story reached them of those before them? The people of Noah, Ad, Thamud; the people of Abraham, the people of Midian and the cities were overthrown (the people of Lot). Their messengers came to them with clear proofs. So it was not Allah who wronged them, but they used to wrong themselves.

9:71 The believers, men and women, some are protectors of others, they enjoin good, and forbid from evil; and they establish prayers and give the obligatory charity, and obey Allah and Allah's messenger. Allah will have Allah's Mercy on them. Surely Allah is All-Mighty, All-Wise.

9:72 Allah has promised the believers, men and women, gardens under which rivers flow to reside in it forever, and beautiful mansions in gardens of Eden (paradise). The greatest bliss is the good pleasure of Allah. That is the supreme success.

9:73 O Prophet (Muhammad)! Strive hard against the disbelievers and the hypocrites, and be firm against them, their abode is hell, and worst indeed is the destination.

9:74 They swear by Allah that they did not say (bad), but really they said the word of disbelief, and they disbelieved after accepting Islam. They resolved (plot to murder Prophet Muhammad) which they were unable to carry out. They could not find (any cause to do so) except that Allah and Allah's messenger had enriched them of Allah's bounty. If they repent, it will be better for them, but if they turn away, Allah will punish them with a painful punishment in this world and the hereafter. There is none for them on earth as a protector or a helper.

9:75 Of them are some who made a covenant with Allah (saying): "If Allah bestowed on us Allah's bounty, we will surely give charity and will be certainly among those who are righteous."

9:76 Then when Allah gave them Allah's bounty, they became stingy with it, turned away, and they were reluctant.

9:77 So Allah punished them by putting hypocrisy into their hearts till the day when they shall meet Allah, because they broke (the covenant with) Allah which they had promised and because they used to tell lies.

9:78 Don't they know that Allah knows their secret ideas, and their secret talk, and that Allah is the All-Knower of the unseen?

9:79 Those who defame the believers who give charity voluntarily and those who could not find (to give charity) except what is available to them, so they mock at them (believers). Allah will throw back their mockery on them, and they shall have a painful punishment.

9:80 Whether you (O Muhammad) ask forgiveness for them (hypocrites) or not ask forgiveness for them, even if you ask forgiveness for them 70 times, Allah will never forgive them because they have disbelieved in Allah and Allah's messenger (Muhammad). Allah does not guide those people who are disobedient.

9:81 Those who stayed behind (from Tabuk expedition), rejoiced in their places behind the messenger of Allah; and they hated to strive and fight with their wealth and their lives in the way of Allah. They said: "Do not march forth in the heat." Say: "The fire of hell is more intense in heat." If only they could understand!

9:82 So let them laugh a little and they will cry much as a recompense of what they used to earn (by sins).

9:83 If Allah brings you back to a party of them (hypocrites), and they ask your permission to go out (to fight), say: "Never you shall go out with me, nor fight an enemy with me; you agreed to sit inactive on the first occasion, then you sit (now) with those who lag behind."

9:84 Never (O Muhammad) pray (funeral prayer) for any of them (hypocrites) who dies, nor stand at their graves. Certainly they disbelieved in Allah and Allah's messenger, and they died while they were disobedient.

9:85 Let not their wealth or their children amaze you. Allah intends to punish them only with these things in this world, and their souls shall depart while they are disbelievers.

9:86 When a Surah (chapter from the Qur'an) is revealed, (enjoining) that: "They believe in Allah, strive hard, and fight along with Allah's messenger," they ask your permission to exempt them (from fighting) those with wealth among them and say: "Leave us (behind), we would be with those who sit (at home)."

9:87 They are contented to be with those who sit behind (at home). Their hearts are sealed up, so they do not understand.

9:88 But the messenger (Muhammad) and those who believed with him, strove hard, and fought with their wealth and their lives. Such are they for whom are the good things, and it is they who will be successful.

9:89 Allah has prepared for them gardens (paradise) under them rivers flow, to reside in it forever. That is the supreme success.

9:90 Those who made excuses from the Bedouins came (to you, O Prophet) asking your permission to exempt them (from the battle) and stay at home. Those who had lied to Allah and Allah's messenger, a painful punishment will seize those of them who disbelieved.

9:91 There is no blame on those who are weak or on ill or on those who find no (resources) what they spend (in fighting), if they are sincere (in duty) to Allah and Allah's messenger. No ground (of complaint) can there be against the righteous people. Allah is Forgiving, Merciful.

9:92 Nor (there is blame) on those who when came to you, requested that you provide them with mounts (conveyances), and when you said: "I can find no mounts for you," they turned back on it, while their eyes were overflowing with tears of grief that they could not find anything to spend (for fighting).

9:93 The ground (of complaint) is only against those who are rich, and yet asked exemptions. They are content to be with who sit behind (at home) and Allah has sealed up their hearts so that they do not know (what they are missing).

9:94 They (the hypocrites) will present excuses to you when you return to them. Say (O Muhammad): "Present no excuses, we shall not believe you. Allah has already informed us of the news concerning you. Allah and Allah's messenger will observe your deeds. Then you will be brought back to the Knower (Allah) of the unseen and the seen, and then Allah will inform you of what you used to do."

9:95 They will swear by Allah to you when you return to them, so that you may turn away from them. So turn away from them. Surely, they are impure, and their living place is hell a recompense for that which they used to earn.

9:96 They (the hypocrites) will swear to you that you may be pleased with them, but if you are pleased with them, certainly Allah is not pleased with the people who are disobedient.

9:97 The Bedouins are the worst in disbelief and hypocrisy, and more likely do not know the limits which Allah has revealed to Allah's messenger. Allah is All-Knower, All-Wise.

9:98 Of the Bedouins, there are some who look upon what they spend as a penalty and watch for calamities for you. On them be the calamity of evil. Allah is All-Hearer, All-Knower.

9:99 Of the Bedouins there are some who believe in Allah and the last day, and look upon what they spend as means of nearness to Allah, (and a cause of receiving) the messenger's invocations. Indeed these are means of nearness for them. Allah will admit them to Allah's Mercy. Certainly Allah is Forgiving, Merciful.

9:100 The first and the foremost of the emigrants (migrated from Makkah to Madinah) and the helpers (the citizens of Madinah) and those who followed them in goodness (in faith), Allah is well-pleased with them and they are well-pleased with Allah. Allah has prepared for them gardens under which rivers flow (paradise), to reside in it forever. That is the great success.

9:101 From those around you of the Bedouins are hypocrites, and so are some among the people of Madinah, they persist in hypocrisy. You (Muhammad) do not know them, Allah knows them. Allah will punish them twice, and then they will be brought back to a great punishment.

9:102 There are others who have confessed their sins; they have mixed a deed that was righteous with another that was evil. Perhaps that Allah will turn in forgiveness upon them. Surely, Allah is Forgiving, Merciful.

9:103 Take alms from their wealth in order to cleanse their wealth and purify them with it, and invoke Allah for them. Surely! Your invocations are a source of security for them, and Allah is All-Hearer, All-Knower.

9:104 Do they not know that Allah accepts repentance from Allah's servants and takes the charity and that Allah alone is the Accepter of repentance, Merciful?

9:105 Say (O Muhammad): "Do deeds! Allah will see your deeds, and so will Allah's messenger and the believers. You will be brought back to the All-Knower (Allah) of the unseen and the seen. Then Allah will inform you of what you used to do."

9:106 Others await Allah's decree, whether Allah will punish them or will forgive them. Allah is All-Knower, All-Wise.

9:107 As for those who built a mosque (Masjid-e-Zirar) by way of harming, disbelief, to disunite between the believers, and as an outpost for those who made war against Allah and Allah's messenger (Muhammad) before. They will indeed swear that they want nothing but good. Allah bears witness that they are certainly liars.

9:108 You should never stand (to offer prayer) in it. Surely, the mosque whose foundation was laid from the first day on piety is more deserving that you stand (to pray) in it. In it are people who love to clean and to purify themselves. Allah loves those who make themselves clean and pure.

9:109 Who is a better person; the one who lays the foundation of a building on piety from Allah and Allah's good pleasure, or the one who lays the foundation of a building on a cliff edge ready to crumble down, so that it will crumble to pieces with the person into the fire of hell? Allah does not guide the people who are the wrongdoers.

9:110 Their building which they built will not cease to be a cause of doubt in their hearts unless their hearts are cut to pieces. Allah is All-Knower, All-Wise.

9:111 Surely, Allah has purchased from the believers their lives and their properties; for (the price) that theirs shall be the paradise. They fight in Allah's way, so they kill others and are killed. It is a true promise which is binding on Allah mentioned in the Torah, the Gospel, and the Qur'an. Who is truer to (fulfill) its covenant than Allah? Then rejoice in your bargain which you have made with it. That is the supreme success.

9:112 Those who repent to Allah, worship Allah, praise Allah, go out (in Allah's cause), bow down (in prayer), prostrate themselves (in prayer), enjoin people to the good and forbid people from evil, and observe the limits set by Allah (they make such a bargain with Allah). (O Muhammad) give glad tidings to such believers.

9:113 It is not proper for the Prophet and those who believe to ask Allah's forgiveness for the polytheists even though they are close relatives, after it has become clear to them that they are the inmates of the fire.

9:114 Abraham was not invoking (Allah's) forgiveness for his father but because he had made promise to his father. But when it became clear to him that he (his father) is an enemy to Allah, he dissociated himself from him. Surely Abraham was humble, forbearing.

9:115 Allah will never lead a people astray after Allah has guided them, until Allah makes clear to them what they should avoid. Surely, Allah is All-Knower of everything.

9:116 Surely, to Allah belongs the dominion of the heavens and the earth. Allah gives life and Allah causes death. Besides Allah you have neither any protector nor any helper.

9:117 Surely, Allah forgave the prophet, the emigrants, and the helpers who followed him (Muhammad) in time of distress (Tabuk expedition), after the hearts of a party of them had nearly deviated (from right way). Allah accepted repentance from them. Certainly, to them Allah is Kind, Merciful.

9:118 Allah also forgave the 3 (did not join the Tabuk expedition) who were left (deferred by the Prophet) till when the earth was straitened to them as it was vast and their own selves were straitened on them. They perceived that there was no refuge from Allah but to Allah. Then, Allah forgave them so that they could repent. Surely, Allah is Accepter of repentance, Merciful.

9:119 O you who believe! Be afraid of Allah, and be with those who are truthful (in words and deeds).

9:120 It is not proper for the people of Madinah and those around them of the Bedouins to remain behind from Allah's messenger or to prefer their own lives to his life. That is because they neither afflicts them any thirst nor fatigue, nor hunger in the way of Allah, nor take any step to anger the disbelievers, nor inflict any injury upon an enemy, but shall be written to their credit as a righteous deed. Surely, Allah does not waste the reward of the righteous people.

9:121 Nor do they spend anything (in Allah's cause), small or large, nor cross a valley (in struggle), but is written to their credit; so that Allah may recompense them with the best of what they used to do.

9:122 It is not proper for the believers to go out to fight all together. Of every troop of them, why not a party only should go forth, so that they (who are left behind) may get instructions in the religion (Islam), and they may warn their people when they return to them so that they may beware (of evil).

9:123 O you who believe! Fight the disbelievers who are close to you, and let them find harshness in you; and you should know that Allah is with those who are the pious.

9:124 Whenever there is a Surah (chapter of the Qur'an) sent down, some of them (hypocrites) say: "Which of you has increased faith by this?" As for those who believe, it has increased them in faith, and they rejoice.

9:125 But as for those in whose hearts have disease, it will add suspicion and doubt to their suspicion, disbelief and doubt; and they will die while they are disbelievers.

9:126 Do they not see that they are tested every year once or twice (with calamities, disease)? Yet, they neither turn in repentance, nor learn a lesson (from it).

9:127 Whenever there is a Surah (chapter from the Qur'an) sent down, they look at one another (saying): "Does any one see you?" Then they turn away. Allah has turned their hearts because they are a people who do not understand.

9:128 Surely, there has come to you a messenger (Muhammad) from amongst yourselves. It grieves him that you should receive any injury or difficulty. He (Muhammad) is anxious for you (to be rightly guided, to repent to Allah, etc); he is kind and merciful towards the believers.

9:129 But if they turn away, say (O Muhammad): "Allah is sufficient for me. There is no one worthy of worship except Allah, in Allah I put my trust and Allah is the Rabb of the Mighty Throne."

10. Yunus : Jonah

In the name of Allah, the Gracious, the Merciful

10:1 Alif-Lam-Ra. These are the verses of the book (the Qur'an), full of wisdom.

10:2 Is it strange for mankind that Allah has sent revelation to a man (Muhammad) from among themselves (saying) that: "Warn mankind and give good news to those who believe that they have footing (reward of good deeds) sure with their Rabb?" But the disbelievers say: "This is indeed an evident sorcerer!"

10:3 Surely, your Rabb is Allah who created the heavens and the earth in 6 days and then rose over the Throne (in a manner that suits Majesty), and is disposing the affair of all things. No intercessor (can plead with Allah) except after Allah's permission. This is Allah, your Rabb; so worship Allah alone. Then, will you not remember?

10:4 To Allah is the return of all of you. The promise of Allah is true. It is Allah who begins the creation and then repeats (will bring back to life) it so that Allah may reward those who believed and did righteous deeds with justice. But those who disbelieved will have a drink of boiling fluids and painful punishment because they used to disbelieve.

10:5 It is Allah who made the sun with a shining thing and the moon as a light and measured out for its stages so that you may compute the number of years and the calculation (such as days, weeks, months…). Allah did not create them but in truth. Allah has explained the verses in detail for people who have knowledge.

10:6 Surely, in the alternation of the night and the day and all that Allah has created in the heavens and the earth, there are signs for people who fear Allah.

10:7 Surely, those who do not hope for their meeting (day of Judgment) with Allah, but are pleased and satisfied with the life of the present world, and those who are heedless of Allah's revelations,

10:8 those, their abode will be the fire, because of what they used to earn.

10:9 Surely, those who believe, do righteous deeds; their Rabb will guide them through their faith, under them will flow rivers in the gardens of delight (paradise).

10:10 Their way of request in it (will be): "Glory to Allah, O Allah!" and their greetings in it (will be): "Peace!" Their last request (will be): "All the praises are to Allah, the Rabb of the worlds!"

10:11 If Allah were to hasten for mankind the evil (they earned) as they would hasten on the good, then their respite would be already settled. But Allah leaves those who do not expect their meeting with Allah, in their trespasses, wandering blindly in distraction.

10:12 When harm touches someone, one invokes Allah, lying down on side, or sitting or standing. But when Allah has removed harm from the same one, that person walks away as if never invoked Allah for that harm which had touched! Thus the deeds which they do made fair-seeming to the transgressors.

10:13 Indeed, Allah has destroyed generations before you when they did wrong while their messengers came to them with clear proofs, but they would not believe! Thus, does Allah requite the people who are sinners?

10:14 Then, Allah made you successors after them in the land so that Allah may see how you would conduct!

10:15 When Allah's clear verses are recited to them, those who do not hope for their meeting with Allah, say: "Bring us a Qur'an other than this, or change it." Say (O Muhammad): "It is not for me to change it on my own accord. I only follow that which is revealed to me. Surely, I fear if I were to disobey my Rabb, the punishment of the mighty day (of Resurrection)."

10:16 Say (O Muhammad): "If Allah had so willed, I should not have recited it to you nor would Allah have made it known to you. Surely, I have stayed amongst you a lifetime (40 years) before this. Why do not you think?"

10:17 So who does more wrong than the one who forges a lie against Allah or denies Allah's verses? Surely, the sinners will never succeed!

10:18 They worship besides Allah things that neither hurt them, nor benefit them, and they say: "These are our intercessors with Allah." Say (O Muhammad): "Do you inform Allah of that which Allah does not know in the heavens and on the earth? Glorified and exalted is Allah above all that which they associate as partners (with Allah)!"

10:19 Mankind was once one community (one religion); then they differed later (inventing different creeds). Had it not been for a word that went forth before from your Rabb, it would have been settled between them regarding what they differed in it.

10:20 They say: "How is it that not a sign is sent down on him from his Rabb?" Say: "Surely the unseen belongs to Allah alone. So wait, surely I am with you among those who wait."

10:21 When Allah let mankind taste Mercy after some adversity has afflicted them, behold! They have a plot against Allah's verses! Say: "Allah is Swifter in planning; indeed Allah's messengers (angels) record all that which you plot."

10:22 It is Allah who enables you to travel through land and sea; until when you are in the ships and they sail with them with a favorable wind, and they are glad in it; but when a stormy wind comes to it and the waves come to them from every place and they think that they are being encircled in it. Then they pray to Allah, making their faith pure for Allah alone (saying): "If Allah delivers us from this, we shall truly be of the grateful."

10:23 But when Allah delivers them, behold! They disobey in the earth wrongfully. O mankind! Your rebellion is only against your own selves, a brief enjoyment of this worldly life, then to Allah (at the end is) your return, and Allah will inform you that which you used to do.

10:24 Surely the likeness of the worldly life is as the water (rain) which Allah send down from the sky, it mingles with it (soil) and produces of the earth which people and cattle eat; until when the earth takes its adornments and is beautified, and its people think that they have all the powers of disposal over it, Allah's command reaches it by night or by day and Allah makes it like a clean-mown harvest, as if it had not flourished yesterday! Thus Allah explains in detail the verses for the people who think.

10:25 Allah invites to the home of peace (paradise) and guides whom Allah wills to the right way.

10:26 Those who have done good, will have the best reward and even more. Neither dust nor humiliating disgrace shall cover their faces. They are the residents of paradise; they will abide in it forever.

10:27 Those who have earned evil deeds, the recompense of an evil deed will be like thereof, humiliating disgrace will cover them. They will not have any defender from Allah. As if their faces will be covered with pieces from the darkness of night. They are the inmates of the fire; they will abide in it forever.

10:28 The day when Allah will gather them all together, Allah will say to those who did set partners in worship (with Allah): "Stop at your place, you and your partners (whom you had worshipped)." Allah will separate between them, and their partners will say: "It was not us you used to worship!

10:29 Allah is sufficient for a witness between us and between you that we were indeed unaware of your worship."

10:30 Thereupon, every person will know what he had earned before, and they will be brought back towards (the court of) Allah, their rightful Rabb, and what they used to invent (false deities) will vanish from them.

10:31 Say (O Muhammad): "Who provides for you from the sky and the earth? Or who owns hearing and sight? Who brings out the living from the dead and brings out the dead from the living? Who disposes the affairs?" They will say: "Allah." Say: "Will you not then be afraid (of Allah's punishment)?"

10:32 Such is Allah, your rightful Rabb. So after the truth, what else can save error? How then are you turned away?

10:33 Thus the word of your Rabb is justified against those who disobey that they do not believe.

10:34 Say: "Can any of your partners (of worship) originate the creation and then repeats it?" (If they do not answer) say: "Allah originates the creation and then Allah repeats it. Then how are you misled (from the truth)?"

10:35 Say: "Is there any of your partners (of worship) can guide to the truth?" (If they do not answer) say: "It is Allah who guides to the truth. Then, who is more worthy to be followed: Allah who can guide to the truth, or he who cannot find guidance (himself) unless he is guided? What is the matter with you? How do you judge?"

10:36 Most of them do not follow but guess. Certainly, guess can be of no avail against the truth. Surely, Allah is Well-Aware of what they do.

10:37 This Qur'an is not such as could ever be produced by other than Allah; in fact it is a confirmation of (revelation) which was before it (Torah, Psalms, Gospel) and a full explanation of the book; there is no doubt in it (that is revealed) from the Rabb of the worlds.

10:38 Or do they say: "He (Muhammad) has forged it?" Say: "So bring a chapter like it, and call upon (for aid) whoever you can besides Allah, if you are truthful!"

10:39 Nay, they deny the knowledge which they cannot comprehend and the interpretation of it has not yet fulfilled (seen). (In the same way) those before them did deny. Then see how the end of the wrongdoers was!

10:40 There are some of them who believe in it, and there are some of them who do not believe in it. Your Rabb is aware of all the evil-doers.

10:41 If they deny you, say: "I am (responsible) for my deeds and you are for your deeds! You are innocent of what I do, and I am innocent of what you do!"

10:42 Among them there are some who (pretend to) listen to you, but can you make the deaf to hear even though they do not understand?

10:43 Among them there are some who (pretend to) look at you, but can you guide the blind, even though they do not see?

10:44 Truly! Allah does not do wrong to mankind in any way; but mankind do wrong to themselves.

10:45 On the day when Allah will gather them all together, it will look as if they had not stayed (in the world) but an hour of a day. They will recognize each other. Indeed (they will realize that) those who will be ruined who denied the meeting with Allah, and they were not guided.

10:46 Whether Allah shows you (in your lifetime, O Muhammad) some of what Allah has promised them, or Allah causes you to die (before them), still their return is to Allah, moreover Allah is witness over what they used to do.

10:47 For every nation, there is a messenger. When their messenger comes, the matter will be judged between them with justice, and they will not be wronged.

10:48 They say: "When this promise (will be fulfilled), if you speak the truth?"

10:49 Say (O Muhammad): "I have no power over any harm or benefit to myself except what Allah wills. For every nation, there is a deadline; when their deadline comes, neither can they delay it even for a moment nor can they advance it."

10:50 Say: "Have you thought if Allah's punishment should come to you by night or by day, (if you can not avert then) which portion from it would the sinners hasten on?

10:51 Will you believe in it when it has actually befallen? Is it now (that you believe)? You used to (wish to) hasten it!"

10:52 Then it will be said to those who wronged themselves: "You taste the everlasting punishment! Should you not be recompensed for what you used to earn?"

10:53 They ask you (O Muhammad) to inform them (saying): "Is it true (the punishment)?" Say: "Yes! By my Rabb! Surely it is the absolutely true! You will not be able to escape it!"

10:54 If every person who has wronged possessed all that is on the earth, would be willing to offer it in ransom (to redeem oneself, but it will not be accepted). They will regret in their hearts when they see the punishment. It will be judged (between them) with justice, and no wrong will be done to them.

10:55 No doubt, surely, all that is in the heavens and the earth belongs to Allah. No doubt, surely, Allah's promise is true, yet, most of them do not know.

10:56 It is Allah who gives life, and causes death, and to Allah you all shall return.

10:57 O mankind! Surely a good advice has come to you from your Rabb, a cure for that (disease) is in your hearts, guidance, and a Mercy for the believers.

10:58 Say: "In the bounty of Allah, and in Allah's Mercy (for this Qur'an), so let them rejoice in it. That is better than what (worldly wealth) they collect."

10:59 Say (O Muhammad to these polytheists): "Have you seen what provision Allah has sent down to you! You have made (some) of it lawful and (others) unlawful." Say (O Muhammad): "Did Allah permit you, or do you invent a lie against Allah?"

10:60 What (punishment) do you think for those who invent lies against Allah, on the day of Resurrection? Truly, Allah is full of bounty to mankind, but most of them are not grateful.

10:61 Whatever you may be engaged in, whatever you may be reciting from the Qur'an, and whatever deeds you may be doing, Allah is witness over you when you are doing it. Nothing is hidden from your Rabb even the weight of an atom on the earth or in the heaven. Neither anything smaller than that nor larger, but is written in a Clear Record.

10:62 No doubt! Surely, for the friends of Allah, no fear shall come upon them nor shall they grieve.

10:63 Those who believe, and (constantly) fear Allah,

10:64 for them there are glad tidings in the life of the world, and in the hereafter. No change can be in the words of Allah, this is the supreme success.

10:65 Let not their speech grieves you (O Muhammad), surely, all power and honor belongs to Allah. Allah is All-Hearer, All-Knower.

10:66 No doubt! Surely, whatever is in the heavens and whatever is in the earth belongs to Allah. Those who do not follow and invoke the partners besides Allah, they do not follow but guess, and they do not but invent lies.

10:67 It is Allah who has appointed for you the night that you may rest in it, and the day to make things visible to you. Surely, there are verses in this for a people who listen.

10:68 They say: "Allah has begotten a son." Glory be to Allah! Allah is Rich. Allah owns all that is in the heavens and all that is in the earth! You have no proof for this. Do you say against Allah what you do not know?

10:69 Say (O Muhammad): "Surely, those who invent lie against Allah will never be successful."

10:70 (They have) a brief enjoyment in this world, then to Allah will be their return, and then Allah will make them taste the severest punishment because they used to disbelieve.

10:71 Recite to them the news of Noah. When he said to his people: "O my people, if my stay with you and my reminding you of the verses of Allah is hard on you, then I put my trust in Allah. So gather your plot, you and your partners, and let not your plot be in doubt for you. Then pass your sentence on me and give me no respite.

10:72 But if you turn away, I have not asked you any reward, my reward is not but from Allah, and I have been commanded to be of the Muslims."

10:73 They denied him. So Allah saved him and those with him in the ship, and Allah made them generations replacing one after another while Allah drowned those who denied Allah's verses. See how the end of those who were warned was!

10:74 Then Allah sent after him messengers to their people, they brought them clear proofs, but they would not believe what they had already rejected before. Thus, Allah seals up the hearts of the transgressors.

10:75 Then Allah sent after them Moses and Aaron to Pharaoh and his chiefs with Allah's verses. But they behaved arrogantly and they were sinners.

10:76 So when the truth came to them from Allah, they said: "This is indeed clear magic."

10:77 Moses said: "Is this what you say about the truth when it has come to you? Is this magic? The magicians are not successful."

10:78 They said: "Have you come to us to turn us away from the faith of our forefathers in order that you 2 (Moses and Aaron) may have greatness (become leaders) in the land? We are not going to believe in you 2!"

10:79 Pharaoh said: "Bring to me every skilled sorcerer."

10:80 When the sorcerers came, Moses said to them: "Cast down what you want to cast!"

10:81 Then when they had cast down, Moses said: "What you have brought, it is sorcery; surely Allah will make it invalid. Surely, Allah does not set right the work of the evil-doers.

10:82 Allah will establish and make apparent the truth by Allah's words, however sinners may hate it."

10:83 But none believed in Moses except the offspring of his people, because of the fear of Pharaoh and his chiefs, lest he should persecute them; and surely, Pharaoh was an arrogant tyrant on the earth, he was indeed one of the transgressors.

10:84 Moses said: "O my people! If you believe in Allah, then put your trust in Allah if you are Muslims."

10:85 They said: "In Allah we put our trust. Our Rabb! Make us not a trial for the folk who are wrongdoers,

10:86 and save us by Allah's Mercy from the disbelieving folk."

10:87 Allah revealed to Moses and his brother (saying) that: "You provide residences for your people in Egypt, and make your residences as your Qiblah (for worship), and establish prayers perfectly, and give glad tidings to the believers."

10:88 Moses said: "Our Rabb! You (Allah) have indeed bestowed on Pharaoh and his chiefs splendor and wealth in the life of this world. Our Rabb! Is it because they may lead people astray from your (Allah's) way? Our Rabb! Destroy their wealth, and harden their hearts, so that they will not believe until they see the painful punishment."

10:89 Allah said: "Surely, the prayer of you both is accepted. So you both keep to the right way, and do not follow the way of those who do not know the truth."

10:90 Allah took the children of Israel across the sea. Pharaoh followed them with his hosts in oppression and enmity, until when drowning overtook him, he said: "I believe that there is no one worthy of worship but Allah whom the children of Israel believe, and I am one of the Muslims."

10:91 (It was said): "Now (you believe)! But a little while before you refused to believe and you were one of the evil-doers.

10:92 So this day Allah will save your (dead) body (from the sea) so that you may be a sign to those who will come after you! Surely, many among mankind are heedless of Allah's verses."

10:93 Indeed, Allah settled the children of Israel in an honorable residing place and provided them with good things. They did not differ until the knowledge came to them. Surely, your Rabb will judge between them on the day of Resurrection in that (those matters) in which they used to differ.

10:94 So if you (O Muhammad) are in doubt concerning that which Allah has revealed to you (that your name is in the Torah and the Gospel), then ask those who have been reading the book (the Torah and the Gospel) before you. Surely, the truth has come to you from your Rabb. So you be not of those who doubt,

10:95 and you be not one of those who deny verses of Allah; for then you shall be one of the losers.

10:96 Truly! Those against whom the word of your Rabb has been justified, will not believe,

10:97 even if every verse should come to them, until they see the painful punishment.

10:98 Was there any town that believed (after seeing the punishment), and their faith benefited them (from the punishment) except the people of Jonah? When they believed, Allah removed from them the punishment of disgrace in the life of the world, and permitted them to enjoy for a while.

10:99 If your Rabb had willed, those on earth would have believed, all of them together. So, will you (O Muhammad) then compel mankind until they become believers?

10:100 It is not (possible) for anyone to believe except by the permission of Allah, and Allah will put the wrath on those who do not understand.

10:101 Say: "Behold what is in the heavens and the earth." But neither verses nor warnings benefit those who do not believe.

10:102 Then do they wait for (anything) except (for destruction) like the days of those who passed away before them? Say: "So wait, I too will wait with you."

10:103 Then (at the end) Allah saves Allah's messengers and those who believe! Thus it is incumbent upon Allah to save the believers.

10:104 Say (O Muhammad): "O you mankind! If you are in doubt as to my religion (Islam), then I will never worship those whom you worship besides Allah. But I worship Allah who causes you to die, and I am commanded to be one of the believers."

10:105 (It is revealed to me): "Direct entirely yourself (O Muhammad) towards the religion upright, and you never be one of the polytheists.

10:106 Do not invoke besides Allah, who can neither benefit nor harm you, but if you do so, surely you will then be of the wrongdoers.

10:107 If Allah afflicts you with hurt, there is none who can remove it but Allah; and if Allah intends for you any good, there is none who can repel Allah's favor. Allah reaches with it whoever Allah wills of Allah's servants. Allah is the Forgiving, the Merciful."

10:108 Say: "O you mankind! Surely the truth (the Qur'an and Muhammad) has come to you from your Rabb. So whoever follows guidance (right way), then only follows for its own good and whoever goes astray, they only goes strays at its own risk; and I am not a custodian over you."

10:109 (O Muhammad) follow what is revealed to you, and be patient till Allah gives judgment. Allah is the Best of judges.

11. Hud : Hud
In the name of Allah, the Gracious, the Merciful

11:1 Alif-Lam-Ra. This is a book, the verses in it are perfected, then explained in detail from one Allah, who is All-Wise and Well-Acquainted,

11:2 (saying) you to worship none but Allah. Surely, I (Muhammad) am to you from Allah a warner and a bearer of glad tidings.

11:3 You should seek forgiveness of your Rabb, and turn in repentance to Allah, Allah will grant you good enjoyment for an appointed term, and bestow Allah's grace to every owner of grace. But if you turn away, then I (Muhammad) fear for you the punishment of a great day (of Resurrection).

11:4 To Allah is your return, and Allah is Omnipotent (has power) over every thing.

11:5 No doubt! They cover up their hearts so that they may hide from Allah. Surely, even when they cover themselves with their garments, Allah knows what they conceal and what they reveal. Surely, Allah is All-Knower of everything of that (innermost secrets) which is in the hearts.

11:6 There is no moving creature on earth but its provision is due from Allah. Allah knows its residing place and its deposit (uterus or grave); all is in a clear book.

11:7 It is Allah who has created the heavens and the earth in 6 days and Allah's Throne was on the water, so that Allah may test you which of you are the best in deeds. But if you say (to them): "You shall indeed be raised up after death," those who disbelieve would be sure to say: "This is nothing but obvious magic."

11:8 If Allah delays the punishment for them till a determined time, they are sure to say: "What keeps it back?" Surely, on the day it reaches them, nothing will turn it away from them and they will be surrounded by what they used to mock at it!

11:9 If Allah gives a person taste of Mercy from Allah, and then withdraws it from the person, surely the person is despairing, ungrateful.

11:10 But if Allah let those taste good favor after evil (poverty and harm) have touched them, they are sure to say: "The ills have departed from us." Surely they are jubilant, and arrogant.

11:11 Except those who show patience and do righteous good deeds, those will have their forgiveness and a great reward.

11:12 So perhaps you (Muhammad) may omit to recite a part of what is revealed to you and your heart may feel straitened for it because they might say: "Why a treasure has not been sent down to him or an angel has come with him?" But you are only a warner! Allah is the guardian over all things.

11:13 Or they say: "He (Muhammad) has forged it (the Qur'an)." Say: "Then you bring 10 forged chapters like it, and call whoever you can other than Allah, if you speak the truth!

11:14 Then if they do not answer you, then know that it (the Qur'an) is sent down with the knowledge of Allah and that there is no one worthy of worship except Allah! Will you then be Muslims?"

11:15 Whoever desires the life of the world and its glitter; Allah will pay in full to them (the wages of) their deeds therein and they will have no reduction therein.

11:16 They are those there will be nothing for them in the hereafter but fire and whatever they did (deeds) are in vain. There is no effect of that which they used to do.

11:17 Can they (be like those) who have clear proof (the Qur'an) from their Rabb and to whom a witness (Muhammad) from Allah recites it; and before them came the book of Moses, a guidance and a Mercy? They will believe in it, but those of the sects that reject it (the Qur'an); the fire will be their promised meeting place. So do not be in doubt about it. Surely, it is the truth from your Rabb, but most of the mankind does not believe.

11:18 Who does more wrong than the one who invents a lie against Allah? Such people will be brought before their Rabb and the witnesses will say: "These are the ones who lied against their Rabb!" No doubt! The curse of Allah is on the wrongdoers,

11:19 those who hinder others from the way of Allah and seek a crookedness therein, they are disbelievers in the hereafter.

11:20 Such people will not be able to escape (from Allah's punishment) on earth, or they will have any protectors besides Allah. The punishment will be doubled for them. They could not bear to hear the truth and they used not to see the truth.

11:21 They are those who have lost their own selves and what they were inventing (false deities) will vanish from them.

11:22 Certainly, they are those who will be the greatest losers in the hereafter.

11:23 Surely, those who believe, do righteous deeds, and humble themselves before their Rabb, they will be residents of paradise, and they will reside therein forever.

11:24 The example of the 2 parties is as the (one who is) blind and the deaf, and the (other who is) seer and the hearer. Are they equal when compared? Will you not then take heed?

11:25 Indeed Allah sent Noah to his people (and he said): "Surely I have come to you as a plain warner,

11:26 that you worship none but Allah, surely I fear for you the punishment of a painful day."

11:27 So the chiefs of those who disbelieved among his people said: "We see you not but a man like ourselves, and we see anyone follow you but those who are the rejected among us without deep thinking. We do not see in you any merit above us, in fact we think you are a liar."

11:28 He said: "O my people! See if I am on a clear proof from my Rabb, and Allah has given me a Mercy from Allah, but that Mercy has been hidden from your sight. Can I compel you to accept it when you have hatred for it?

11:29 O my people! I ask you no wealth for it, my reward is from none but Allah. I am not going to drive away those who have believed. Surely, they are going to meet their Rabb, but I see you a people that are ignorant.

11:30 O my people! Who will help me against Allah, if I drove them away? Will you not then give a thought?

11:31 I do not say to you that with me are the treasures of Allah, nor that I know the unseen; nor do I say surely I am an angel, nor I say of those whom your eyes look down upon that Allah will never bestow any good on them. Allah knows best what is in their inner-selves (belief). Surely I will be in that case (if I say anything like this) indeed one of the wrongdoers."

11:32 They said: "O Noah! Surely you have disputed us and you have prolonged much the dispute with us, now bring upon us what you have threatened us with if you are of the truthful."

11:33 He said: "Only Allah will bring it (punishment) on you if Allah wills, and then you will not escape it.

11:34 My advice will not profit you even if I wish to give you good counsel, if Allah's will is to keep you astray. Allah is your Rabb and to Allah you shall return."

11:35 Or they (disbelievers of Makkah) say: "He (Muhammad) has fabricated it (the Qur'an)." Say: "If I have fabricated it, upon me be my crimes, but I am innocent of what crime you commit."

11:36 It was revealed to Noah: "None of your people will believe except those who have already believed. So do not be sad because of what they do.

11:37 Construct the ship under Allah's eyes and with Allah's revelation, and do not plead with Allah on behalf of those who do wrong; they are surely to be drowned."

11:38 He was constructing the ship, and whenever the chiefs of his people passed by him, they made a mockery of him. He said: "If you mock at us, so we mock at you as you mock.

11:39 You will know who will be covered by a humiliating punishment and who will fall on a lasting punishment."

11:40 It was till when there came Allah's command and the oven (Al-Tannur) gushed forth (water from the earth). Allah said: "Carry therein, of each kind 2 (male and female), and your family, except those against whom the word has already gone forth, and those who believe. Those who believed with him were only a few."

11:41 He (Noah) said: "Embark in it, in the name of Allah (who has) its moving course and its resting anchorage. Surely, my Rabb is Forgiving, Merciful."

11:42 So it (the ship) sailed with them amidst the waves like mountains, and Noah called out to his son and he was in apart: "O my son! Embark with us and not be with the disbelievers."

11:43 He (the son) replied: "I will take myself (refuge) to a mountain; which will save me from the water." Noah said: This day there is no savior from the decree of Allah except the one on whom Allah has Mercy." The wave came in between them, so he (the son) was among the drowned.

11:44 It was said: "O earth! Swallow up your water, and O sky! Withhold (your rain)." The water subsided and the decree of Allah was fulfilled. It (the ship) rested on mount Judi, and it was said: "Away with the people who are wrongdoers!"

11:45 Noah called his Rabb and said: "O my Rabb! Surely, my son is of my family. Certainly, your (Allah's) promise is true, and you (Allah) are the most Just of the judges."

11:46 Allah replied: "O Noah! Surely, he is not of your family; surely his work is not righteous. So do not ask Allah anything of which you have no knowledge! Indeed Allah admonishes you, lest you become one of the ignorant."

11:47 Noah said: "O my Rabb! Surely I seek refuge with you (Allah) for asking you (Allah) that of which I have no knowledge. Unless you (Allah) forgive me and have Mercy on me, I shall indeed be one of the losers."

11:48 It was said: "O Noah! Come down (from the ship) with peace from Allah and blessings on you and on the people who are with you. Other people to whom Allah will grant their pleasures (for some time), then a painful punishment will reach them from Allah."

11:49 This is the news of the unseen which Allah has revealed to you (O Muhammad). Neither you nor your people knew this before. So be patient. Surely, the (good) end is for the pious.

11:50 To Ad people (Allah sent) their brother Hud. He said: "O my people! Worship Allah! You have no other one worthy of worship but Allah. You do nothing but invent lies.

11:51 O my people! I ask you no reward for it (message). My reward is not but on Allah, who created me. Then will you not understand?

11:52 O my people! Ask forgiveness of your Rabb, and then repent to Allah. Allah will send (from the sky) abundant rain to you, and add strength to your strength. So do not turn away as sinners."

11:53 They said: "O Hud! No evidence you have brought to us. We shall not leave our deity just for your saying! We are not believers in you.

11:54 We do not say but (perhaps) some of our gods - (false deities) has seized you with evil." He said: "Surely I call Allah to witness and bear you witness that I am free from that which you ascribe as partners (in worship)

11:55 other than Allah. So plot against me, all of you, and give me no respite.

11:56 Surely I put my trust in Allah, my Rabb and your Rabb! There is not a moving creature but Allah has grasped its destiny. Surely, my Rabb is on the right way.

11:57 So if you turn away, then surely, I have conveyed the message what I was sent with to you. My Rabb will make other people succeed besides you, and you will not harm Allah in the least. Surely, my Rabb is Guardian over all things."

11:58 When Allah's commandment came, Allah saved Hud and those who believed with him by a Mercy from Allah, and Allah saved them from a severe punishment.

11:59 Such were Ad people. They rejected the verses of their Rabb and disobeyed Allah's messengers, and followed the command of every proud stubborn oppressor.

11:60 They were pursued by a curse in this world and will be on the day of Resurrection. No doubt! Surely, Ad disbelieved in their Rabb. So away with Ad, the people of Hud.

11:61 To the Thamud people, (Allah sent) their brother Saleh. He said: "O my people! Worship Allah, you have no other deity but Allah. Allah brought you forth from the earth and settled you therein. So ask the forgiveness of Allah, and then turn to Allah in repentance. Certainly, my Rabb is Near, Responsive."

11:62 They said: "O Saleh! Surely you have been among us as a figure of good hope before this message. Do you now forbid us to worship what our fathers have worshipped? Surely, we are really in grave doubt as to that which you invite us to it."

11:63 He said: "O my people! Do you see if I am on a clear proof from my Rabb, and Allah has given me Mercy from Allah, who then will help me against Allah if I disobey Allah? Then you increase me not but in loss.

11:64 O my people! This she-camel of Allah is a sign to you. So leave her to feed on Allah's earth, and do not touch her with evil, lest a near punishment should seize you."

11:65 But they killed her. So he said: "Enjoy yourselves in your homes for 3 days. This is a promise that will not be denied."

11:66 So when Allah's commandment came, Allah saved Saleh and those who believed with him by a Mercy from Allah, and from the disgrace of that day. Surely, your Rabb, Allah is the All-Strong, the All-Mighty.

11:67 The awful blast overtook those who wronged, so they lay (dead), prostrate in their homes,

11:68 as if they had never lived there. No doubt! Surely, Thamud disbelieved in their Rabb. So away the people of Thamud!

11:69 Surely, there came Allah's messengers (angels) to Abraham with glad tidings. They said: "Greetings of peace!" He answered: "Greetings of peace!" and he hastened to entertain with a roasted calf.

11:70 But when he saw their hands not reaching towards it (the meal), he felt some mistrust of them, and conceived a fear of them. They said: "Do not fear, we have been sent against the people of Lot."

11:71 His wife was standing there and she laughed. But Allah gave her glad tidings of (her son) Isaac, and after Isaac, of (grandson) Jacob.

11:72 She said: "Woe unto me! Shall I bear a child now when I am an old woman, and this is my husband, an old man? Surely! This is a strange thing!"

11:73 They said: "Do you wonder at the decree of Allah? The Mercy of Allah and Allah's blessings be on you, O the family (of Abraham) of the house. Surely, Allah is All-Praiseworthy, All-Glorious."

11:74 Then when the fear had gone away from (the mind of) Abraham, and the glad tidings had reached him, he began to plead with Allah for the people of Lot.

11:75 Surely, Abraham was, without doubt, forbearing, used to invoke Allah with humility, and was regretful to Allah.

11:76 (The angels said): "O Abraham! Forsake this (topic). Indeed, the commandment of your Rabb surely has come. Surely, a punishment will come for them which cannot be turned back."

11:77 When Allah's messengers (angels) came to Lot, he was grieved on their account and felt helpless to offer protection for them. He said: "This is a painful day."

11:78 His people came rushing towards him, and since they used to commit crimes (sodomy) before, he said: "O my people! Here are my daughters (of my nation); they are purer for you (if you marry lawfully). So fear Allah and do not disgrace me with regard to my guests! Is there not among you a single man right-minded?"

11:79 They said: "Surely you know that we do not have any desire in your daughters, and indeed you know well what we want!"

11:80 He said: "I wish if I had that strength (to overpower) you or that I could find myself some powerful support."

11:81 They (messengers) said: "O Lot! Surely, we are the messengers (angels) from your Rabb! They will not reach you! So travel with your family in a part of the night, and let not any of you look back except your wife (who should remain behind). Surely, it (punishment) will afflict her, will afflict them. Indeed, morning is their appointed time. Is not the morning near?"

11:82 So when Allah's commandment came, Allah turned (towns of Sodom) upside down, and rained on it stones of baked clay, piled up,

11:83 marked from your Rabb, and they are not far from the wrongdoers.

11:84 To the Midian people (Allah sent) their brother Shuaib. He said: "O my people! Worship Allah, you have no other one worthy of worship but Allah, and do not give short measure and weight. Surely I see you in prosperity; and surely I fear for you punishment of a day encompassing.

11:85 O my people! Give full measure and weight in justice. Do not defraud the people of their due things and do not commit mischief in the land causing corruption.

11:86 What is left by Allah is better for you if you are believers. I am not a guardian over you."

11:87 They said: "O Shuaib! Does your prayer command that we give up what our forefathers used to worship or that we give up doing what we like with our property? Surely, you are the gracious, right-minded!"

11:88 He said: "O my people! You see if I am on clear evidence from my Rabb and Allah has given me a good sustenance from Allah. I do not wish that I contradict to you what I forbid you from it. I do not desire but reform so far as I am able (within my power). My success is not except from Allah, in Allah I trust and to Allah I repent.

11:89 O my people! Let not my separation harm you to befall you similar to what befall on the people of Noah or of Hud people or of Saleh people, and the people of Lot are not far off from you!

11:90 Ask forgiveness of your Rabb, and then turn in repentance to Allah. Surely, my Rabb is Merciful, Loving."

11:91 They said: "O Shuaib! We do not understand much of what you say. We see you a weak (blind man) among us. Was it not for your family, we would certainly have stoned you, and you are not powerful against us."

11:92 He said: "O my people! Is then my family of more weight with you than Allah? You have taken Allah away behind your backs. Surely, my Rabb surrounds of what all you do.

11:93 O my people! Act according to your ability, and surely I am acting my way. You will know who it is on whom the punishment descends that will cover with disgrace, and who is a liar! Watch you! Surely, I too am watching with you."

11:94 When Allah's commandment came, Allah saved Shuaib and those who believed with him by a Mercy from Allah. The awful blast seized the wrongdoers and they lay prostrate dead in their homes,

11:95 as if they had never lived there! So away with Midian just as away with Thamud!

11:96 Indeed Allah sent Moses with Allah's verses and a clear authority;

11:97 to Pharaoh and his chiefs, but they followed the command of Pharaoh, and the command of Pharaoh was not rightly guide.

11:98 He will go ahead of his people on the day of Resurrection, and will lead them into the fire. Evil indeed is the place to which they will be brought.

11:99 They were pursued by a curse in this life and on the day of Resurrection. How bad is the given gift (curse)?

11:100 That is from the news of the towns which Allah relate to you (Muhammad); of them (some are) standing, and (some have) ceased to exist.

11:101 Allah wronged them not, but they wronged themselves. So their deity was other than Allah whom they invoked, profited them nothing when there came the command of your Rabb, nor did they add to them but destruction.

11:102 Such is the seizure of your Rabb when Allah seizes the town (population) while they are doing wrong. Surely, Allah's seizure is painful and severe.

11:103 Indeed in that there is a sure lesson for those who fear the punishment of the hereafter. That is a day when mankind will be gathered together for it, and that will be a day of witness (all will be present).

11:104 Allah do not delay it but for a fixed term.

11:105 When the day will come, no one will speak except by Allah's permission. Some among them will be wretched and others blessed.

11:106 As for those who are wretched, they will be in the fire, for them in it is sighing and inhaling.

11:107 They will reside therein as long as the heavens and the earth will last, except what your Rabb wills. Surely your Rabb is the doer of what Allah wants.

11:108 As for those who are blessed, they will be in paradise, abiding therein as long as the heavens and the earth will last, except what your Rabb wills, a gift without an end.

11:109 So do not be in doubt as to what these people worship. They worship nothing but what their forefathers used to worship before them. Surely, Allah will repay them their portion in full without any decrease.

11:110 Indeed Allah gave the book to Moses, but differences arose therein, and had it not been for a word that had gone forth before from your Rabb, the case would have been judged between them. Indeed they are in suspicious doubt about it (this Qur'an).

11:111 Surely to each of them your Rabb will repay them in full for their works. Surely, Allah is fully aware of what they do.

11:112 So you (Muhammad) stand firm and straight (on religion) as you are commanded and those who turn in repentance (to Allah) with you, and do not transgress. Surely, Allah is All-Seer of what you do.

11:113 Do not incline towards those who do wrong, lest the fire should touch you, and you will not have any protector other than Allah, nor you will be helped.

11:114 Establish prayers perfectly at the 2 ends of the day and in some hours of the night. Surely the good deeds remove the evil deeds (small sins). That is a reminder for the mindful.

11:115 Be patient; for surely, Allah does not waste the reward of the righteous people.

11:116 If there had not been among the generations before you, people having wisdom, prohibiting others from mischief in the earth, except a few of those whom Allah saved from among them. Those who did wrong, pursued what they were provided with good things in it (worldly life), and they were sinners.

11:117 Your Rabb would never destroy the towns wrongfully, while their people were right-doers.

11:118 If your Rabb had so willed, Allah could surely have made mankind one nation, but they will not cease to disagree,

11:119 except those on whom your Rabb has bestowed Allah's Mercy and for that Allah created them. The word of your Rabb shall be fulfilled (Allah's saying): "Surely, Allah will fill hell with jinns and human all together."

11:120 All that Allah relates to you (O Muhammad) of the news of the messengers is that Allah may make strong and firm your heart thereby. In this (the Qur'an) has come to you with the truth, as well as an admonition and a reminder for the believers.

11:121 Say to those who do not believe: "Act according to your ability, surely Allah is acting (in Allah's way).

11:122 You wait! Allah too is waiting."

11:123 To Allah belongs the unseen of the heavens and the earth and to Allah all affairs return. So worship Allah (O Muhammad) and put your trust in Allah. Your Rabb is not unaware of what you people do.

12. Yusuf : Joseph
In the name of Allah, the Gracious, the Merciful

12:1 Alif-Lam-Ra. These are the verses of the clear book.

12:2 Surely, Allah has sent it down as an Arabic Qur'an so that you may understand.

12:3 Allah relates to you (Muhammad) the best of the stories through this Qur'an what Allah has revealed to you. Though before this you were among those who did not know.

12:4 (Remember) when Joseph said to his father: "O my father! Surely, I saw (in a dream) 11 stars, the sun, and the moon - I saw them prostrating themselves to me."

12:5 He (the father) said: "O my son! Do not relate your vision to your brothers, lest they plot against you a plot. Surely! Satan is an open enemy to human beings!

12:6 Thus your Rabb will choose you; teach you from interpretation of dreams, perfect Allah's favor on you, and on the offspring of Jacob, just as Allah perfected it on your 2 forefathers, Abraham and Isaac previously! Surely, your Rabb is All-Knower, All-Wise."

12:7 Surely, there are signs in Joseph and his brothers for those who ask.

12:8 When they (his step brothers) said: "Truly, Joseph and his brother (Benjamin) are dearer to our father than us, but we are a strong group (of 10). Really, our father is in a plain error.

12:9 Kill Joseph or cast him out to some other land, so that the favor of our father may be given to us exclusively, and after that we will be righteous people."

12:10 One of them said: "Do not kill Joseph, but throw him down to the bottom of a well, so that some travelers of caravan may pick him if you are doing."

12:11 They said: "O our father! Why do you not trust us with Joseph, when we are indeed his well-wishers?

12:12 Send him with us tomorrow to enjoy himself and play. Surely, we will take care of him."

12:13 He (Jacob) said: "Truly, it will worry me if you take him away. I fear lest a wolf should devour him while you are careless of him."

12:14 They said: "If a wolf devours him while we are a strong group, then surely, we are the losers."

12:15 So, when they went away with him, they all agreed to put him down in the bottom of the well. Allah inspired in him (Joseph): "Indeed, you will (one day) inform them this about their affair, now they do not know you."

12:16 They came to their father in the early part of the night weeping.

12:17 They said: "O our father! Surely we went racing with one another, we left Joseph by our belongings, and a wolf devoured him! But you will never believe us even though we are truthful."

12:18 They brought (as proof) his shirt (stained with) false blood. He said: "Nay, but your own souls have made up a tale. So patience is most fitting for me. It is Allah alone who can help me against what you assert."

12:19 There came a caravan of travelers, they sent their water-drawer who let down his bucket (into the well). He said (seeing Joseph): "What a good news! This is a boy." So they concealed him like merchandise (a captive). Allah knew what they did.

12:20 They sold him for a low price, for a few dirham (silver coins). They were of those not concerned about him.

12:21 He (the man) from Egypt who bought him, said to his wife: "Make his stay comfortable, may be that he will profit us or we shall adopt him as a son." Thus Allah established Joseph in the land and arranged to teach him the interpretation of events. Allah has full power and control over Allah's affairs, but most of the people do not know.

12:22 When he (Joseph) attained his full manhood, Allah bestowed on him wisdom and knowledge (the Prophethood). Thus Allah rewards the righteous people.

12:23 She (wife of the master) sought to seduce (do evil act) him who was in her house. She closed the doors and said: "Come on, O you." He said: "I seek refuge in Allah! Truly, he (your husband) is my master! He made my stay agreeable! Surely, the wrongdoers will not be successful."

12:24 Indeed she did desire him and he would have inclined to her desire had he not seen the evidence of his Rabb. Thus it was Allah who turned away from him evil and indecent deeds. Surely, he was one of Allah's sincere devotees.

12:25 So they raced with one another to the door and she tore his shirt from the back (while trying to stop). They both found her husband at the door. She said: "What is the punishment for him who intended an evil design against your wife except imprisonment or a painful punishment?"

12:26 He (Joseph) said: "It was she who sought to seduce me." A witness of her household bore witness (saying): "If his shirt is torn from the front, then she is speaking the true and he is lying.

12:27 But if his shirt is torn from the back, then she is lying and he is speaking the truth."

12:28 So when he (her husband) saw his (Joseph's) shirt torn from the back; he said (to her): "Surely, it is your plot (O women). Certainly your plot is mighty!

12:29 O Joseph! Turn away from this, and you (O my wife) ask forgiveness for your sin. Surely, you were of the sinful."

12:30 Women in the city (heard the incident and) said: "The wife of Al-Aziz is seeking to seduce her young captive, indeed she has fallen in love madly with him. Surely, we see her in plain error."

12:31 So when she heard about their accusation, she invited them, and prepared a banquet for them; and she gave each one of them a knife (to cut fruit). (When they were ready to cut) she asked (Joseph): "Come out before them." When they saw him, they exalted him (at his beauty) and (to their surprise) cut their hands. They exclaimed: "Allah forbid! This is not a man! This is none but a noble angel!"

12:32 She said: "This is he (young man) about whom you did blame me. Indeed I sought to seduce him, but he refused. Now if he does not do what I order him, he will certainly be cast into prison, and will be one of those who are disgraced."

12:33 He (Joseph) said: "O my Rabb! Prison is dearer to me than what they invite me to it. Unless Allah turns away their plot from me, I may feel inclined towards them and be one of the ignorant."

12:34 So his Rabb answered his prayer and turned away their plot from him. Surely, Allah is the All-Hearer, the All-Knower.

12:35 Then it appeared to them after they had seen the proofs (of his innocence) to imprison him for a while.

12:36 There entered with him 2 young men in the prison. One of them said: "Surely, I saw myself (in a dream) pressing wine." The other said: "Surely, I saw myself (in a dream) carrying bread on my head and birds were eating from it." (They said): "Tell us the interpretation of these dreams. Surely, we think you (to be one) of the righteous people."

12:37 He (Joseph) replied: "No food will come to you as your provision, but I will inform you of its interpretation before it (the food) comes to you. This is what my Rabb has taught me. Surely, I have abandoned the religion of those people who do not believe in Allah and they are disbelievers in the hereafter.

12:38 I follow the religion of my forefathers - Abraham, Isaac and Jacob. It is not for us that we attribute any partners with Allah. This is the grace of Allah to us and to mankind, but most of the people do not thank.

12:39 O my 2 companions of the prison! Are many different Rabbs (worthy of worship) better or Allah, the One, the Irresistible?

12:40 You do not worship besides Allah but mere names which you and your forefathers have named (invented), for Allah has not sent down any authority. The command is not but for Allah. Allah has commanded that you worship none but Allah alone, that is the true religion, but most people do not know.

12:41 O 2 companions of the prison! (The interpretation of dream is) one of you will (be released and) serve wine to his master (the king of Egypt); and the other will be crucified, and birds will eat from his head. That is how the cases will be judged concerning which you both inquired."

12:42 He said to the one of them whom he knew to be saved (released): "Mention me to your master (king)." But Satan made him forget to mention it to his master. So he (Joseph) stayed in prison a few more years.

12:43 The king (of Egypt) said: "Surely, I saw (in a dream) 7 fat cows, whom 7 lean cows were devouring; and 7 green ears of corn, and 7 others dry. O notables! Explain to me my dream if you are able to interpret the dreams."

12:44 They said: "Mixed up false dreams and we are not skilled in interpretation of dreams."

12:45 One from the 2 of them (inmates) who was released remembered (Joseph) after a period, said: "I will tell you its interpretation, just send me (to Joseph in prison)."

12:46 (He said): "O Joseph, the truthful one! Explain to us the dream of 7 fat cows whom 7 lean cows are devouring, and of 7 green ears of corn, and 7 others dry; so that I may return to the people and let them know (the meaning of the dream)."

12:47 He (Joseph) said: "For 7 years, you will sow as usual and that (the harvest) which you reap, you should leave in ears, except a little of it which you may eat.

12:48 Then 7 hard years will come after that, which will eat away what you have stored in advance for them, except a little of that which you have guarded.

12:49 Then a year will come thereafter in which people will have abundant rain and in which they will press (wine and oil)."

12:50 The king said: "Bring him to me." But when the messenger came to him, he (Joseph) said: "Return to your master and ask him, what happened to the women who cut their hands? Surely, my Rabb is well aware of their plot."

12:51 He (king) said (to the women): "What do you say about the affair when you did seek to seduce Joseph?" The women said: "Allah forbid! We do not know evil against him!" The wife of Al-Aziz said: "Now the truth is clear, it was I who sought to seduce him. He is surely of the truthful."

12:52 (Joseph) said: "(I asked for this enquiry) in order that he (Al-Aziz) may know that I did not betray him in secret. Allah does not guide the plot of the betrayers.

12:53 I can not free myself (from the blame). Surely, the (human) soul is inclined to evil, except when my Rabb bestows Allah's Mercy. Surely, my Rabb is Forgiving, Merciful."

12:54 The king said: "Bring him to me so that I may attach him to my service." When he spoke to him (Joseph), he said: "Surely, from this day, you are with us high in rank and fully trusted."

12:55 He (Joseph) said: "Place me over the storehouses of the land. Surely I will guard them with full knowledge."

12:56 Thus Allah did give full authority to Joseph in the land to take possession from it, as when or where he likes. Allah bestows Allah's Mercy on whom Allah wills and Allah does not let the reward of the righteous people be lost.

12:57 Surely, the reward of the hereafter will be better for those who believe and fear Allah.

12:58 Joseph's brothers came (several years later when there was food shortage) and they entered to him. He recognized them but they did not recognize him.

12:59 When he had furnished them with their provisions, he said: "Bring me (next time) a brother of yours from your father (meant Benjamin). Do you not see that I give full measure, and that I am the best of the hosts?

12:60 But if you do not bring him to me, there shall be no measure (grain) for you with me, nor shall you come near me."

12:61 They replied: "We shall try to get permission for him from his father, and surely, we shall do it."

12:62 (Joseph) told his servants to put their money (of grain) into their bags, so that they might know about it when they go back to their people, in order that they might come back.

12:63 When they returned to their father, they said: "O our father! Measure of grain has been denied for us (unless we take our brother Benjamin). Send our brother with us so that we may get our measure and truly we are guardians for him."

12:64 He said: "Can I entrust him to you except as I entrusted on his brother (Joseph) to you before? But Allah is the best to guard and Allah is Merciful of those who show mercy."

12:65 When they opened their bags, they found their money had been returned to them. They said: "O our father! What more can we desire? Here is our money returned to us. We will get food for our family; we will guard our brother, and add more measure of camel's load (of grain). This quantity is easy (for the king to give)."

12:66 He (Jacob) replied: "I will not send him with you until you give a solemn oath to me in the name of Allah that you will bring him back to me unless you are yourselves surrounded (by enemies)." When they gave him their solemn oath, he said: "Allah is trustee over what we have said."

12:67 He said: "O my sons! Do not enter by one gate, but enter by different gates. I cannot avail you anything against Allah. Surely! The decision rests only with Allah. In Allah, I put my trust. In Allah let all those that trust, put their trust."

12:68 When they entered (the city) from where their father had ordered them, it did not avail them in the least against (the will of) Allah, but it was a need of Jacob's inner-self which he discharged. Surely, he was endowed with knowledge because Allah had taught him, but most people do not know.

12:69 When they went before Joseph, he called his brother (Benjamin) to himself and said: "Surely! I am your brother, so do not grieve for what they used to do."

12:70 So when he (Joseph) had furnished them with their provisions, he put the (golden) bowl into his brother's bag, then a crier cried: "O you in the caravan! Surely, you are thieves!"

12:71 They said turning towards them: "What is it that you have lost?"

12:72 They said: "We have lost the (golden) bowl of the king and for him who produces it (is the reward of) a load of camel; and I will be bound by it."

12:73 They said: "By Allah! Indeed you know that we came not to make mischief in the land, and we are not thieves!"

12:74 They (Joseph's people) said: "What then should be the penalty of him, if you are liars?"

12:75 They (Joseph's brothers) replied: "His penalty should be he, in whose bag it is found, and then it is his punishment. Thus we punish the wrongdoers!"

12:76 So he (Joseph) began to search their bags before the bag of his brother (Benjamin). Then he brought it out of his brother's bag. Thus Allah did plan for Joseph. He could not take his brother by the law of the king, except that Allah willed it. Allah raises to degrees whom Allah wills, but over all those endowed with knowledge is Allah who is the All-knower.

12:77 They (Joseph's brothers) said: "If he steals, surely, a brother of his (Joseph) did steal before him." But these things Joseph did keep in himself, not revealing (the secrets) to them. He said: "You are in worst case. Allah is the Best Knower of the truth what you assert!"

12:78 They said: "O mighty one! Surely, he (Benjamin) has a very old father (who will grieve for him); so take one of us in his place. Indeed we think you are one of the righteous people."

12:79 He (Joseph) replied: "Allah forbids that we should take anyone but him with whom we found our property. Indeed we then should be wrongdoers."

12:80 When they despaired of him, they held a conference in private. The eldest among them said: "Don't you know that your father indeed took an oath from you in Allah's name, and before this you did fail in your duty with Joseph? Therefore, I will not leave this land until my father permits me, or Allah decides my case (by releasing Benjamin) and Allah is the Best of the judges."

12:81 Return to your father and say: "O our father! Surely, your son (Benjamin) has stolen. We do not testify except according to what we know, and we could not be guardians of the unseen!

12:82 Ask (the people of) the town where we have been in it, and the caravan in which we returned, and indeed we are telling the truth."

12:83 He (Jacob) said: "Nay, you have lured your own souls into something (story). So patience is most fitting for me. May be Allah will bring them all to me. Truly Allah! Allah is the All-Knower, All- Wise."

12:84 He turned away from them and said: "Alas for Joseph!" His sight was whitened (lost) because of the sorrow that he was suppressing.

12:85 They said: "By Allah! You will never cease remembering Joseph until you become weak with old age, or until you are of the dead."

12:86 He said: "I only complain of my grief and sorrow to Allah, and I know from Allah what you do not know.

12:87 O my sons! You go and enquire about Joseph and his brother, and never give up hope of Allah's Mercy. Certainly no one despairs of Allah's Mercy, except the disbelievers."

12:88 When they entered unto him (Joseph), they said: "O ruler of the land! A hard time has hit us and our family, and we have brought little money, so pay us full measure and be charitable to us. Truly, Allah rewards the charitable."

12:89 He (Joseph) said: "Do you know what you did with Joseph and his brother, when you were ignorant?"

12:90 They said: "Are you indeed Joseph?" He said: "I am Joseph, and this is my brother (Benjamin). Allah has indeed been gracious to us. Surely, he who fears Allah and is patient, then surely, Allah does not make the reward of the righteous people to be lost."

12:91 They said: 'By Allah! Indeed Allah has preferred you above us, and certainly we have been sinners."

12:92 He (Joseph) said: "There is no blame on you this day. May Allah forgive you. Allah is the Merciful of those who show mercy!

12:93 You go with this shirt of mine, cast it over the face of my father, he will become clear-sighted, and bring to me all your family."

12:94 When the caravan departed, their father said: "I do indeed feel the smell of Joseph, even if you think me weak of mind due to old age."

12:95 They said: "By Allah! Certainly, you are in your old error."

12:96 Then when the bearer of the glad tidings arrived, he cast it (the shirt) over his face, and he became clear-sighted. He (father) said: "Did I not say to you, surely I know from Allah what you do not know?"

12:97 They said: "O our father! Ask forgiveness (from Allah) for our sins, indeed we have been sinners."

12:98 He replied: "I will ask my Rabb for forgiveness for you. Surely Allah! Only Allah is the Forgiving, the Merciful."

12:99 When they entered unto Joseph, he took his parents to himself and said: "Enter Egypt, if Allah wills in security."

12:100 He raised his parents to the throne, and they fell down before him prostrate. He said: "O my father! This is the interpretation of my dream from before! My Rabb has made it come true! Indeed Allah was good to me, when Allah took me out of the prison, and brought you out of the Bedouin-life, after Satan had sown enmity between me and between my brothers. Certainly, my Rabb is kind to whom Allah wills. Truly Allah! Only Allah is the All-Knower, the All-Wise.

12:101 My Rabb! Allah has indeed bestowed on me the sovereignty and taught me the interpretation of dreams; the Creator of the heavens and the earth! Allah is my Protector in this world and in the hereafter, causes me to die as a Muslim, and join me with the righteous."

12:102 This is of the news of the unseen which Allah reveals to you (O Muhammad). You were not present with them when they arranged their plan together, and while they were plotting.

12:103 Most of mankind will not believe even if you desire it eagerly.

12:104 You (O Muhammad) do not ask them any reward for it; it (the Qur'an) is a reminder and an advice to the worlds.

12:105 There are many signs in the heavens and the earth which they pass by, yet they are reluctant from it.

12:106 Most of them do not believe in Allah except that they attribute partners to Allah.

12:107 Do they feel secure that Allah's punishment will not come against them, or that the hour (of Judgment) will not come against them all of a sudden while they do not perceive?

12:108 Say (O Muhammad): "This is my way. I invite you to Allah with sure knowledge which I and my followers possess. Glory be to Allah. I am not one of the polytheists."

12:109 Allah did not send (as messengers) before you but human. Allah revealed to them from among the people of the towns. Have they (disbelievers) not traveled through the land and seen how was the end of those who were before them? Surely the home of the hereafter is the best for those who fear Allah. Do you not then understand?

12:110 (They were pardoned) until when the messengers gave up hope and thought that they were denied (by their people), then came to them Allah's help, and were rescued whoever Allah willed. Allah's punishment cannot be warded off from the people who are sinners.

12:111 Surely in their stories, there is a lesson for people of understanding. It (the Qur'an) is not a forged statement but a confirmation (of the existing books of Allah) - a detailed explanation of everything, a guide, and a Mercy for the people who believe.

13. Ar-Ra'd : The Thunder
In the name of Allah, the Gracious, the Merciful

13:1 Alif-Lam-Meem-Ra. These are the verses of the book (the Qur'an), and that which has been revealed to you (Muhammad) from your Rabb is the truth, but most people do not believe.

13:2 Allah is the one who raised the heavens without any pillars that you can see. Then, Allah rose above the Throne and has subjected the sun and the moon! Each is running (its course) for an appointed term. Allah manages all affairs. Allah explains in details the verses that you may believe with certainty in the meeting with your Rabb.

13:3 It is Allah who has spread out the earth, placed therein firm mountains and rivers, and made every kind of fruits 2 in pairs in it. Allah brings the night as a cover over the day. Surely, in these things, there are verses for people who reflect.

13:4 In the earth there are tracts side by side, gardens of vines, green crop fields and date-palms growing into 2 or 3 from a single stem root, or otherwise one stem root for every palm, watered with the same water, yet Allah make more excellent some of them than others in taste. Surely, in these things, there are signs for the people who understand.

13:5 If you (O Muhammad) wonder, then amazing is their saying: "When we are dust, shall we indeed be raised in a new creation?" They are those who disbelieve in their Rabb! They are those who will have iron chains in their necks. They will be inmates of the fire, they will abide in it.

13:6 They ask you to hasten the evil before the good, and surely exemplary punishments have occurred before them. But surely, your Rabb is full of forgiveness for mankind in spite of their wrong-doing. Surely, your Rabb is Severe in punishment.

13:7 Those who disbelieve say: "Why is not a sign sent down to him from his Rabb?" You are only a warner, and to every nation there is a guide.

13:8 Allah knows what every female bears (in womb), and by how much the wombs fall short (of time) and what they exceed (of time). Everything with Allah is in due proportion.

13:9 Allah knows everything of the unseen and the seen, the Great, the High.

13:10 It is the same (to Allah) whether any of you conceals speech and declares it openly, and whoever hides by night or go freely by day.

13:11 For each person, there are angels in succession, before and behind. They guard the person by the command of Allah. Surely, Allah does not change the condition of a people until they change what is in themselves. When Allah wills for a people misfortune, there can be no turning away of it, and there is no protector for them besides Allah.

13:12 It is Allah who shows you the lightning as a fear (for travelers) and as a hope (for rain). It is Allah who brings up the heavy clouds (with water).

13:13 The thunder glorifies and praises Allah, and so do the angels because of Allah's awe. Allah sends the thunderbolts and strikes with it whom Allah wills. Yet they (disbelievers) dispute about Allah. Allah is Mighty in punishment.

13:14 For Allah alone is the call of truth. Those (deities) whom they (disbelievers) invoke besides Allah, can not answer anything, except like the one who stretches forth its hands (at edge of well) for water to reach its mouth, but it does not reach it, and the invocation of the disbelievers is nothing but an error.

13:15 To Allah alone falls in prostration whoever is in the heavens and the earth, willingly or unwillingly, and so do their shadows in the mornings and in the afternoons.

13:16 Ask (O Muhammad): "Who is the Rabb of the heavens and the earth?" Say: "Allah." Ask: "Have you then taken (for worship) protectors other than Allah who have no power for themselves either for benefit or for harm?" Say: "Is the blind equal to the one who sees? Or darkness equal to light? Or do they assign to Allah partners who created the like of Allah's creation, so that the creation seemed alike to them?" Say: "Allah is the Creator of all things, and Allah is the One, the Irresistible."

13:17 Allah sends down water (rain) from the sky, and the valleys flow according to their measure, but the flood bears away the foam that mounts up to the surface, and also from that ore they heat it in the fire in order to make ornaments or utensils, rises a foam like to it. Thus Allah does set forth examples of truth and falsehood. As for the foam it passes away as scum upon the banks, while that which benefits mankind remains in the earth. Thus Allah sets forth examples.

13:18 (The reward) for those who answer their Rabb's call is paradise. But those who do not answer Allah, if that they had all that is in the earth together with its like, they would offer to save themselves (from the punishment). They are those for whom there will be the terrible reckoning. Their residing place will be hell; and worst indeed is that place for rest.

13:19 Shall the one who knows what has been revealed to you (O Muhammad) from your Rabb is the truth, be like the one who is blind? But it is only the people of understanding that pay heed.

13:20 Those who fulfill the covenant of Allah and do not break the covenant;

13:21 and those who join what Allah has commanded to be joined, fear their Rabb, and are afraid of the terrible reckoning;

13:22 and those who remain patient seeking the pleasure of their Rabb, establish prayers perfectly, and spend what Allah has bestowed on them secretly and openly, and they repel evil with good, they are those for whom there is the good home of the hereafter;

13:23 gardens of Eden (paradise), in which they will enter along with those who acted righteously from their forefathers, their wives, and their offspring. The angels will enter to welcome them from every gate,

13:24 (saying) "Peace be upon you for what you persevered in patience! Excellent indeed is the final home!"

13:25 Those who break the covenant of Allah after its approval, sever what Allah has commanded to join (bond of kinship), and work mischief in the land; they are those for them is the curse and for them is the evil home.

13:26 Allah increases the provision for whom Allah wills, straitens (it for whom Allah wills). They (disbelievers) rejoice in the life of the world; the worldly life as compared with the hereafter is nothing but a brief enjoyment.

13:27 Those who disbelieve say: "Why not a sign is sent down to him (Muhammad) from his Rabb?" Say: "Surely, Allah sends astray whom Allah wills and guides those who turn to Allah in repentance,

13:28 those who believe and whose hearts find rest in the remembrance of Allah, surely, in the remembrance of Allah hearts find rest.

13:29 Those who believe, and do good deeds, bliss is for them and a beautiful place of final return."

13:30 Thus Allah has sent you (O Muhammad) to a community surely before it other communities have passed away, in order that you might recite to them what Allah has revealed to you, and they disbelieve in the Gracious (Allah). Say: "Allah is my Rabb! There is no one worthy of worship but Allah! In Allah I trust, and to Allah will be my return with repentance."

13:31 If there had been a Qur'an with it mountains could be moved, or with it the earth could be cloven asunder, or with it the dead could be made to speak (it would be the same Qur'an). But the decision of all things is certainly with Allah. Yet those who believe have not known that had Allah willed, Allah could have guided all mankind? A disaster will not cease to strike those who disbelieve because what (evil) they did or it (disaster) settles close to their homes, until the promise of Allah comes. Certainly, Allah does not break promise.

13:32 Indeed many messengers were mocked before you (O Muhammad), but I (Allah) granted respite to those who disbelieved, then I (Allah) seized them. So how terrible was my (Allah's) punishment!

13:33 Is it Allah who takes charge of every one by what the person has earned it? Yet they ascribe partners to Allah. Say: "Name them! Or will you inform Allah of what Allah does not know in the earth or is it just a show of false words?" Nay! To those who disbelieve, their plotting is made fair-seeming, and they have been hindered from the right way, and those whom Allah sends astray, there is no guide for them.

13:34 For them there is a punishment in the life of this world, and certainly their punishment in the hereafter is harder. They have no protector against Allah.

13:35 The likeness of the paradise which the pious have been promised (is): rivers flow beneath it, its provision is eternal, and so is its shade; this is the end (final destination) of those who are pious and the end (final destination) of the disbelievers is fire.

13:36 Those whom Allah has given the book, rejoice at what has been revealed to you (the Qur'an), but there are those among the clans who reject a part thereof. Say (O Muhammad): "I am commanded only to worship Allah alone and not to join partners with Allah. To Allah alone I call and to Allah is my return."

13:37 Thus Allah has sent it (the Qur'an) down to be a judgment of authority in Arabic. Were you (O Muhammad) to follow their vain desires after the knowledge has come to you, then you will not have any protector or defender against Allah.

13:38 Indeed Allah has sent messengers before you (O Muhammad), and Allah has made for them wives and offspring. It was not for a messenger to bring a sign except by Allah's permission. For each and every matter there is a decree (from Allah).

13:39 Allah wipes out what Allah wills and confirms (what Allah wills). With Allah is the mother (master copy) of the book.

13:40 Whether Allah shows you (O Muhammad) part of what Allah has promised them or cause you to die, your duty is only to convey (the message) and on Allah is the reckoning.

13:41 Do not they see that Allah is gradually reducing the land from its outlying borders? When Allah judges, there is none to put back Allah's judgment and Allah is Swift at reckoning.

13:42 Surely, those (disbelievers) who devised plots were before them, but Allah is planning all. Allah knows what every one earns. The disbelievers will know for whom will be the good end of the home (of paradise).

13:43 Those who disbelieve, say: "You (O Muhammad) are not a messenger." Say: "Allah is sufficient for witness between me and between you and whoever has knowledge of the scripture."

14. Ibrahim : Abraham
In the name of Allah, the Gracious, the Merciful

14:1 Alif-Lam-Ra. This is a book which Allah has revealed to you (O Muhammad) in order that you bring out mankind from darkness (of disbelief) into light (of belief) by permission of their Rabb, to the way of the All-Mighty, the Praise-worthy.

14:2 Allah to whom belongs all that is in the heavens and all that is in the earth! Woe to the disbelievers from a severe punishment.

14:3 Those who prefer the worldly life to the hereafter, hinder people from the way of Allah (Islam), and seek crookedness in it, they are far astray.

14:4 Allah did not send any messenger except with the language of his people, in order that he might make (the message) clear for them. Then Allah misleads whom Allah wills and guides whom Allah wills. Allah is the All-Mighty, the All-Wise.

14:5 Indeed Allah sent Moses with Allah's verses (saying) that: "Bring out your people from darkness into light, and make them remember the days (history) of Allah. Truly, there are verses for every patient, thankful (person)."

14:6 (Remember) when Moses said to his people: "Call to remind Allah's favor to you, when Allah delivered you from Pharaoh's people who were afflicting you with horrible punishment, were slaughtering your sons and letting your women alive, and in it was a tremendous trial from your Rabb."

14:7 (Remember) when your Rabb proclaimed: "If you give thanks, I (Allah) will give you more (of Allah's blessings), but if you are ungrateful, surely! My (Allah's) punishment is indeed severe."

14:8 Moses said: "If you and all on earth together disbelieve, then surely! (know that) Allah is Rich (free from all needs), Praise-worthy."

14:9 Has not the news come to you, of those before you, the people of Noah, Ad, and Thamud? Those after them? No one knows them but Allah. Their messengers came to them with clear proofs, but they put their hands in their mouths (biting with anger) and said: "Surely, we disbelieve in what you have been sent with and we are really in strongly doubt as to what you invite us to it."

14:10 Their messengers said: "Can there be a doubt about Allah, the Creator of the heavens and the earth? Allah calls you (to Allah) so that Allah may forgive you of your sins and give you respite for a term appointed." They said: "You are not but a human being like us! You wish to turn us away from what our forefathers used to worship. Then bring us a clear authority."

14:11 Their messengers said to them: "We are not but human beings like you, but Allah bestows Allah's grace on whom Allah wills of Allah's servants. It is not for us that we bring you an authority (proof) except by the permission of Allah. In Allah let the believers put their trust.

14:12 What is the reason for us that we do not put our trust in Allah while indeed Allah has guided us our ways? We shall certainly bear with patience what hurt you may cause us, and in Allah Alone let those who trust, should put their trust."

14:13 Those who disbelieved said to their messengers: "Surely, you return to our religion or we will drive you out of our land." But their Rabb revealed to them: "Surely, Allah will destroy the wrongdoers.

14:14 Indeed, Allah will make you reside in the land after them. This is for those who fear standing before me (Allah) and also fear my (Allah's) threat."

14:15 But they (the messengers) sought help and victory (from Allah), and every stubborn, arrogant dictator (who refused to believe in Allah) was destroyed,

14:16 Hell is in front of that person (dictator) who will be made to drink boiling rotten water,

14:17 who will sip it (unwillingly) but will find hard to swallow. Death will surround that person from every side, yet will not die and in front of that person will be a great punishment.

14:18 The parable of those who disbelieve in their Rabb is that their deeds are like ashes, on which the wind blows furiously on a stormy day; they will not be able to get anything from what they have earned. That will be straying far away (from the right way).

14:19 Do you not see that Allah has created the heavens and the earth with truth? If Allah wills, Allah can remove you and bring (in your place) a new creation!

14:20 That is not difficult for Allah.

14:21 When they all will appear before Allah (on the day of Resurrection), then the weak (of the world) will say to those who were arrogant (chiefs): "Surely, we were following you. Can you avail us anything from Allah's punishment?" They will say: "If Allah had guided us, we would have guided you. It is equal on us (now) whether we rage, or bear (those punishments) with patience, there is no place of refuge for us."

14:22 When the matter has been decided, Satan will say: "Surely, Allah promised you a promise of truth. I too promised you, but I betrayed you. I had no authority over you except that I called you, and you responded to me. So do not blame me, but blame yourselves. I cannot help you, nor can you help me. Surely I deny what you associated me as a partner (with Allah) before. Surely, there is a painful punishment for them, the wrongdoers."

14:23 Those who believe and do righteous deeds will be made to enter (paradise with) gardens with river flowing under them, to reside therein forever with the permission of their Rabb. Their greeting therein will be: "Peace."

14:24 Don't you see how Allah sets forth an example of a good word as a good tree, whose roots are firm, and its branches are in the sky?

14:25 It gives its fruit at all times by the permission of its Rabb. Allah sets forth examples for mankind in order that they may remember.

14:26 The example of an evil word is that of an evil tree uprooted from the surface of the earth with no stability.

14:27 Those who believe with the word that stands firm, Allah will keep them firm in the life of this world and in the hereafter. Those who are wrongdoers, Allah will cause them to go astray. Allah does what Allah wills.

14:28 Have you not seen those who have changed the blessings of Allah into disbelief, and have caused their people to reside in the house of destruction?

14:29 Hell, in which they will burn, and what an evil place to settle in!

14:30 They set up rivals to Allah to mislead people from Allah's way! Say: "Enjoy (your brief life)! But certainly, your destination is the hell fire!"

14:31 Say (O Muhammad) to Allah's devotees who have believed, that they should establish prayer, and spend in charity from what Allah has provided them secretly and openly; before a day comes in which there will be neither mutual bargaining nor friendship.

14:32 Allah is the one who has created the heavens and the earth, sends down water (rain) from the sky, and thereby brings forth fruits as provision for you. Allah has made the ships to be of service to you, that they may sail through the sea by Allah's command; and Allah has made rivers to be of service to you.

14:33 Allah has made the sun and the moon to be of service to you, both constantly pursuing their courses; and Allah has made the night and the day to be of service to you.

14:34 Allah has given you all that you have asked for, and if you count the blessings of Allah, you will not be able to count them. Surely! Human being is unjust, ungrateful.

14:35 (Remember) when Abraham said: "O my Rabb! Make this city (Makkah) safe, and keep me and my sons away from the worship of idols.

14:36 O my Rabb! Surely they (idols) have led many people astray. So, those who follow me, surely they are of mine. Whoever disobeys me, still Allah is indeed Forgiving, Merciful.

14:37 O our Rabb! Surely I have made some of my offspring to reside in a valley not with cultivation near Allah's sacred house (the Ka'bah). O our Rabb! (I have done this) in order that they would establish prayers; so turn hearts among mankind love towards them, and (O Allah) provide them with fruits so that they may give thanks.

14:38 O our Rabb! Certainly, Allah knows what we conceal and what we reveal. Nothing on the earth or in the heaven is hidden from Allah.

14:39 All the praises and thanks are to Allah, who has given me Ishmael and Isaac in my old age. Surely! My Rabb indeed is All-Hearer of prayers.

14:40 O my Rabb! Make me one who establishes prayers perfectly, and from my offspring. Our Rabb! Accept my prayer.

14:41 Our Rabb! Forgive me, my parents, and all the believers on the day when the reckoning will be established."

14:42 You do not think that Allah is unaware of what the wrongdoers do. Only Allah gives them respite up to that day when their eyes will stare in horror,

14:43 they will be rushing forward with necks outstretched, their heads will be raised up (towards the sky), their gaze will not return towards them, and their hearts will be empty (because of fear).

14:44 Warn (O Muhammad) mankind of the day when the punishment will come to them; then those who wronged will say: "Our Rabb! Respite us for a little while, we will answer Allah's call and follow the messengers!" (It will be said): "Did you not sworn before that you would never suffer a decline?

14:45 You lived in the residences of those who wronged themselves and it was clear to you how Allah had dealt with them. Allah (even) put forth examples for you."

14:46 Indeed, they planned their plot, but their plots were within the sight of Allah, even though their plot was great, it could move the mountains.

14:47 So, do not think that Allah will fail to keep Allah's promise to Allah's messengers. Certainly, Allah is All-Mighty, All-Able of retribution.

14:48 On the day when the earth will be changed to other than earth and the heavens (as well), and all creatures will appear before Allah, the One, and the Irresistible,

14:49 and on that day you will see the sinners bound together in fetters (their hands and feet tied to their necks with chains),

14:50 their garments will be of tar, and fire will cover their faces.

14:51 Allah will requite each person according to its deeds. Truly, Allah is swift at reckoning.

14:52 This (Qur'an) is a message for mankind, in order that they may be warned thereby; and that they may know that Allah is the only one worthy of worship, and that people of understanding may take heed.

15. Al-Hijr : The Rock Tract

In the name of Allah, the Gracious, the Merciful

15:1 Alif-Lam-Ra. These are the verses of the book and a plain Qur'an.

15:2 Perhaps (the day will come when) those who disbelieve wish that they were Muslims.

15:3 Leave them (alone) to eat, let them enjoy, and be preoccupied (with false) hope. They will come to know (the truth)!

15:4 Allah did not destroy a town but there was a known decree for it.

15:5 Any nation can not advance its term (fate), nor delay it.

15:6 They say: "O you (Muhammad) to whom the reminder (the Qur'an) has been sent down! Surely, you are insane.

15:7 Why don't you bring angels to us if you are of the truthful ones?"

15:8 Allah does not send down the angels except with the truth (for punishment), and when they come, they (the disbelievers) are not given respite!

15:9 Truly, Allah has sent down the reminder (the Qur'an), and surely, Allah will guard it.

15:10 Indeed, Allah sent (messengers) before you (O Muhammad) amongst the early communities;

15:11 and any messenger came to them, they mocked at him.

15:12 Thus Allah lets it (disbelief) enter into the hearts of the sinners;

15:13 so they do not believe in it (the Qur'an), though the examples of (Allah's punishment of) the ancients have passed.

15:14 Even if Allah had opened to them a gate from the heaven and they continue to ascend through it,

15:15 surely they would have said: "Our eyes have been blocked (blurred). But nay, we have been bewitched."

15:16 Indeed, Allah has put big stars in the heaven and beautified it for the beholders;

15:17 and Allah has protected them from every outcast devil.

15:18 Except him (devil) who steals a hearing, he is pursued by a clear flaming fire.

15:19 Allah has spread the earth and placed firm mountains in it; and caused to grow therein every thing balanced (in due proportion),

15:20 and Allah has made provision for you therein means of living, and for those whom you do not provide.

15:21 There is not a thing but its (inexhaustible) treasures are with Allah. Allah has not sent it down except in a known measure.

15:22 Allah sends the fertilizing winds (fill clouds with water), then causes the water (rain) to descend from the sky, gives it to you to drink, and it is not you who is able to store.

15:23 Certainly Allah! It is Allah who gives life, causes death, and Allah is the Inheritors.

15:24 Indeed, Allah knows the first generations of you who have passed away, and indeed, Allah knows the present generations who will come afterwards.

15:25 Surely, your Rabb is Allah who will gather them. Truly, Allah is the All-Wise, the All-Knower.

15:26 Indeed, Allah created human from clay of mud altered into shape.

15:27 The jinn, Allah created it before from fire of smokeless flame.

15:28 (Remember) when your Rabb said to the angels: "Surely, I (Allah) am going to create a human (Adam) from clay mud altered into shape,

15:29 when I (Allah) have fashioned him and breathed into him (Adam) the soul (which Allah created for him), then you fall down prostrating before him."

15:30 So, the angels prostrated all of them together,

15:31 except Satan, he refused to be with those who prostrated.

15:32 (Allah) said: "O Satan! What is your reason that you are not with those who prostrated?"

15:33 Satan said: "I am not the one to prostrate to a human whom you (Allah) has created from clay of mud molded into shape."

15:34 (Allah) said: "Then, get out from here, for surely you are accursed.

15:35 Surely, the curse will be upon you till the day of recompense."

15:36 Satan said: "O my Rabb! Give me respite till the day of Resurrection."

15:37 Allah said: "Then surely, you are given the respite

15:38 till the day of appointed time."

15:39 Satan said: "O my Rabb! Since you (Allah) let me go astray, I shall indeed adorn (path of error) for them (mankind) on the earth, and I shall mislead them all

15:40 except those who are your (Allah's) sincere devotees."

15:41 (Allah) said: "This is the way straight to me (Allah).

15:42 Certainly, you will have no authority over my (Allah's) devotees, except those who follow you of the ones who go astray.

15:43 Surely, hell is the promised place for them all,

15:44 it (hell) has 7 gates, each gate will be assigned to a separate class (for sinners) from them.

15:45 Truly! The pious people will be in the midst of the gardens and water-springs (of paradise).

15:46 (It will be said to them): "Enter therein (paradise) in peace and security."

15:47 Allah will remove all hatred from their hearts, so they will be like brothers and sit on couches face to face.

15:48 No fatigue will touch them in it, nor shall they be removed from it.

15:49 Inform (O Muhammad) to my (Allah's) devotees that truly, I (Allah) am the Forgiving, the Merciful,

15:50 but Allah's punishment is also the most painful punishment.

15:51 Tell them about the guests (the angels) of Abraham.

15:52 They entered upon him and said: "Peace!" Abraham replied: "Indeed! We are afraid of you."

15:53 They (the angels) said: "Do not be afraid! We truly bring to you glad tidings of a son (possessing) knowledge."

15:54 Abraham said: "Do you give me glad tidings (of a son) when old age has overtaken me? What kind of glad tidings you are giving?"

15:55 They (the angels) said: "We give you glad tidings in truth. So do not be those who despair."

15:56 Abraham said: "Who despairs of the Mercy of his Rabb except those who are astray?"

15:57 Abraham (again) said: "Then what is your mission, O messengers?"

15:58 They (the angels) said: "We have been sent (to punish) the people who are criminals,

15:59 except the family of Lot. We truly will save them all (from destruction),

15:60 except his wife, Allah has decreed that she shall be of those who will stay behind (to be destroyed)."

15:61 When the messengers (the angels) came to the family of Lot,

15:62 he said: "Surely! You are people unknown to me."

15:63 They said: "Nay, we have come to you with that (punishment) concerning which they have doubts.

15:64 We have brought you the truth (news of destruction of your nation) and we are telling the truth.

15:65 Then travel with your family during the last part of the night, and you follow from their rear; no one of you look back, but go on where you are ordered to go."

15:66 Allah has made this decree known to him that the roots of those (sinners) will be cut off in the early morning.

15:67 The people of the city came (to Lot's house) rejoicing (at the news of the 2 young male visitors).

15:68 Lot said: "Surely! These are my guests, so do not disgrace me.

15:69 Fear Allah and do not disgrace me."

15:70 They (people of the city) said: "Did we not forbid you from (entertaining) the people?"

15:71 He (Lot) said: "These (the girls of the nation) are my daughters (to marry lawfully), if you must act."

15:72 Truly, by your life (O Muhammad), they were wandering blindly in their wild intoxication.

15:73 So the awful blast overtook them at the time of sunrise.

15:74 Allah turned it (towns of Sodom in Palestine) upside down and rained to them stones of baked clay.

15:75 Surely! In this are signs for those who see,

15:76 Surely, they (the cities) are on an established road (from Makkah to Syria i.e. the place where the Dead Sea is now).

15:77 Surely! Therein is indeed a sign for the believers.

15:78 Surely, the people in the wood (the people of Midian to whom Prophet Shuaib was sent by Allah) were also wrongdoers.

15:79 So, Allah took vengeance on them. They are both (ruined) on a clear road.

15:80 Surely, the people of Hijr (the rocky tract) denied the messengers.

15:81 Allah gave them Allah's verses, but they were averse to them.

15:82 They used to cut out secure homes in the mountains.

15:83 But the awful blast overtook them in the early morning

15:84 and all their earnings (building homes by craving the rock) did not avail.

15:85 Allah has not created the heavens, the earth, and all that is between them except with truth. Surely, the hour (of Doom) is coming, so overlook (O Muhammad) their faults with gracious forgiveness.

15:86 Surely, your Rabb is the All-Knowing Creator.

15:87 Indeed, Allah has given you 7 of the repeatedly recited verses (Al-Fatihah) and the glorious Qur'an.

15:88 Do not look with your eyes at what Allah has bestowed on certain classes of them (disbelievers), nor grieve over them. Lower your wings (be courteous) to the believers.

15:89 Say: "I am indeed the plain warner."

15:90 As Allah has sent down (this warning) on the dividers,

15:91 who have made the Qur'an into parts (believe some parts and deny others).

15:92 So, by your Rabb (O Muhammad), Allah will certainly ask them all,

15:93 about what they used to do.

15:94 Therefore proclaim that which you are commanded and turn away from the polytheists.

15:95 Truly! Allah will suffice you against the scoffers (mockers),

15:96 who set up another deity along with Allah, so they will come to know.

15:97 Indeed, Allah knows that your heart is distressed by what they say.

15:98 So, glorify the praises of your Rabb, be of those who prostrate (to Allah),

15:99 and worship your Rabb until the certainty (death) comes to you.

16. An-Nahl : The Bee

In the name of Allah, the Gracious, the Merciful

16:1 The Command of Allah has come, so do not seek to hasten it. Glorified is Allah and above all that they associate as partners with (Allah).

16:2 Allah sends down the angels with the revelation of Allah's command to whom Allah wills of Allah's servants (saying): "Warn (mankind) that there is no one worthy of worship but Allah, so fear Allah."

16:3 Allah has created the heavens and the earth with truth. Allah is exalted above all they associate as partners (with Allah).

16:4 Allah has created human from semen, yet the same person becomes an open opponent.

16:5 Allah has created the cattle for you; in them there is warmth (clothing), numerous benefits, and you eat some of them.

16:6 There is beauty in them for you when you bring them home in the evening and when you lead them to pasture in the morning.

16:7 They carry your loads to a land where you could not reach except with great trouble to yourselves. Truly, your Rabb is Kind, Merciful.

16:8 (Allah has also created) horses, mules, and donkeys so that you may ride them and as an adornment. Allah has created (others about which) you have no knowledge.

16:9 Upon Allah is (to show) the direction of the right way, but there are some of them (ways) that are crooked. Had Allah willed, Allah could have guided you all.

16:10 It is Allah who sends down water (rain) from the sky, from it you drink and from it grows vegetation therein to pasture your cattle.

16:11 With it Allah grows for you the crops, the olives, the date-palms, the grapes, and every kind of fruit. Surely, there is a sign in this for people who think.

16:12 Allah has subjected to you the night and the day, the sun and the moon; and the stars are subjected by Allah's command. Surely, there are signs in this for people who understand.

16:13 Allah has created for you on this earth of varying colors. Surely, there is a sign in this for people who remember.

16:14 It is Allah who has subjected the sea to you so that you may eat fresh tender meat (fish) from it, and that you may bring out ornaments to wear from it, and that you see the ships plough through it. (All these are done) so that you may seek Allah's bounty and so that you may give thanks (to Allah).

16:15 Allah has affixed mountains into the earth standing firm, lest it should shake with you. (Allah has made) rivers and roads so that you may be guided;

16:16 land-marks and the stars for your guidance.

16:17 Is then Allah, who has created all these, like the one who can not create? Why don't you remember?

16:18 If you want to count the graces of Allah, you can not count them. Surely, Allah is Forgiving, Merciful.

16:19 Allah knows what you conceal and what you reveal.

16:20 Those who invoke other than Allah, they have created nothing, and they themselves are created.

16:21 (They are) dead, lifeless, and they do not know when they will be resurrected.

16:22 Your deity is one Allah. As for those who do not believe in the hereafter, their hearts deny, and they are proud.

16:23 No doubt that Allah knows what they conceal and what they reveal. Surely, Allah does not like the proud.

16:24 When they are asked: "What is that your Rabb has sent down?" They say: "Tales of the ancient people!"

16:25 They will bear their own burdens in full on the day of Resurrection, and the burdens of those whom they have misguided without knowledge. Indeed it is evil that they will bear!

16:26 Indeed those before them also plotted, but Allah struck their buildings from the foundations, the roof fell upon them from above, and the punishment came to them from where they did not even perceive.

16:27 Then, on the day of Resurrection, Allah will disgrace them and say: "Where are those partners whom you used to associate with Allah, about whom you used to disagree and dispute (with the believers)?" Those who have been given the knowledge (about the punishment of Allah) will say: "Surely! Today disgrace and misery are upon the disbelievers,

16:28 those whom the angels cause to die while they wronged themselves." Then they will make false submission (saying): "We were not doing any evil." (The angels will reply): "Yes! Surely, Allah is the All-Knower of what you used to do.

16:29 So enter the gates of hell to abide in it." Indeed, what an evil abode for the arrogant.

16:30 When the pious people are asked: "What (is it that) your Rabb has sent down?" They say: "(That which is) good." There is good for those who do good in this world and the home of the hereafter will be even better. Excellent indeed will be the home (paradise) of the pious.

16:31 Gardens of Eden (paradise) which they will enter, rivers flow from beneath them, they will have all that they wish in it. Thus Allah will reward the pious,

16:32 those whom the angels cause to die while they are pious saying (to them): "Peace be on you, enter paradise because of what you used to do."

16:33 Do they (the disbelievers) wait for the angels to come to them (to take souls at death), or command of your Rabb to come? So did those before them. Allah did not wrong them, but they used to wrong themselves.

16:34 Then, the evil results of what they did overtook them, and surrounded them by that they used to mock at.

16:35 Those who join others in worship (with Allah) say: "If Allah had willed, neither we would have worshipped anything other than Allah, nor our forefathers, nor we would have forbidden anything without (command from) Allah." So did those who were before them. Then are the messengers charged with anything but to convey the clear message?

16:36 Surely, Allah has sent in every nation a messenger (saying): "You worship Allah, and avoid false deities." Then, there were some whom Allah has guided and there were some upon whom the straying was justified. So travel through the land and see what the end of those who denied (the truth) was.

16:37 If you (O Muhammad) desire for their guidance, then surely Allah does not guide whom Allah lets to go astray. They will have no helpers.

16:38 They swear their strongest oaths by Allah: "Allah will never raise the dead who dies (to life)." Yes, (Allah will raise them up), it is a promise upon Allah in truth, but most of mankind do not know.

16:39 (Allah will fulfill) in order to illustrate for them that they differ in it, and those who disbelieved may know that they were liars.

16:40 When Allah intends to do a thing which Allah wants, Allah only say to it: "Be!" and it is.

16:41 For those who migrated for the cause of Allah after persecution, Allah will certainly give them good residence in this world, and indeed the reward of the hereafter will be greater, if they but knew!

16:42 (They are) those who remained patient (in this world), and put their trust in their Rabb.

16:43 Allah has not send (messengers) before you (O Muhammad) but men, whom Allah has sent revelation. So ask those who knows the scripture (learned people of the Torah and the Gospel), if you do not know,

16:44 with clear signs and books. Allah has sent down to you (O Muhammad) the reminder (the Qur'an) so that you may explain to mankind what was sent down to them so that they may give thought.

16:45 Do those who devise evil plots feel secure that Allah will not sink them into the earth, or that the punishment will not come to them from directions that they do not perceive?

16:46 Or that Allah may not seize them in their going to and from (journey) so they will not be able to escape (from Allah's punishment)?

16:47 Or that Allah may seize them with a gradual wasting (of wealth and health)? Surely! Your Rabb is indeed Gracious, Merciful.

16:48 Do they not see how Allah has created from things, their shadows incline to the right and to the left, making prostration to Allah, and they are humble?

16:49 To Allah prostate all the living creatures that are in the heavens and in the earth, and the angels, and they are not proud,

16:50 they fear their Rabb above them, and they do what they are commanded.

16:51 Allah said (O mankind): "Do not take – 2 deities. Surely, Allah is the only one worthy of worship. Then you should fear Allah."

16:52 To Allah belongs all that are in the heavens and in the earth and Allah's religion is everlasting. Would you fear any one other than Allah?

16:53 Whatever blessings you have are from Allah. When harm touches you, you cry to Allah aloud for help.

16:54 Yet, when Allah removes the harm from you, behold! Some of you associate others in worship with their Rabb,

16:55 so they deny that which (favors) Allah has bestowed on them! So enjoy yourselves (short stay), soon you will come to know (the consequences).

16:56 They assign a portion of what Allah has provided them (for those deities) about whom they do not know. By Allah, you shall certainly be asked about what you used to fabricate.

16:57 They assign daughters to Allah! Glorified is Allah. To themselves what they desire (sons).

16:58 When the news of (birth of) a female child is brought to any of them, his face remains dark, and he is filled with inward grief!

16:59 He hides himself from the people because of the evil of what he has been informed. (He asks himself) shall he keep her with dishonor or bury her in the earth? Certainly, evil is what they decide.

16:60 Those who do not believe in the hereafter set an evil example, and for Allah is the highest example. Allah is the All-Mighty, the All-Wise.

16:61 If Allah were to seize mankind for their wrong-doing, Allah would not leave on it (the earth) a single living creature, but Allah postpones them for an appointed term. When their appointed term comes, neither they can delay it for an hour nor can they advance it.

16:62 They assign to Allah what they dislike. Their tongues describe the falsehood that the better things will be theirs. No doubt that for them is the fire, and they will be sent ahead of the others.

16:63 By Allah, indeed Allah has sent (messengers) to the nations before you (O Muhammad), but Satan made their deeds fair-seeming to them. So he (Satan) is their helper today (in this world), and they will have a painful punishment.

16:64 Allah has not sent down to you (O Muhammad) the book (the Qur'an) except that you may explain to them those things in which they differ, as guidance, and a Mercy for those who believe.

16:65 Allah sends down water (rain) from the sky, and it gives life in the earth after it has been dead. Surely, in this is a sign for people who listen.

16:66 Surely! In the cattle, there is a lesson for you. Allah gives you to drink of what is in their bellies, between bowels and blood - pure milk; pleasant to the drinkers.

16:67 (Similarly) from the fruits of date-palms and grapes, you derive strong drink from it and good provision. Surely, there is indeed a sign for people who think.

16:68 Your Rabb inspired the bees, saying: "Take your habitations in the mountains, in the trees, and in what they (people) erect,

16:69 then eat all fruits and follow the easy ways of your Rabb." There comes forth from their bellies, a drink of different colors, which is healing for people. Surely, in this there is indeed a sign for people who think.

16:70 Allah has created you, then Allah will cause you to die, and there are some of you who are sent back to the worst of old age so that they know nothing after having known. Surely! Allah is the All-Knower, All-Powerful.

16:71 Allah has preferred some of you above others in provision. Those who are preferred will not hand over their wealth to what their right hands possess so that they are equal in it. Then do they deny the grace of Allah?

16:72 Allah has given to you your kind wives, and has given to you from your wives, sons and grandsons, and has provided to you good things. Then do they believe in false deities and deny the favors of Allah?

16:73 They worship others besides Allah, which do not own anything to provide any provision for them from the heavens and the earth, nor they can.

16:74 So do not compare anything with Allah. Surely! Allah knows and you do not know.

16:75 Allah puts forward the example (of 2 men): a captive (disbeliever) under the possession of another, he has no power over anything, and (the other), a man (believer) on whom Allah has provided a good provision from Allah, and he spends from it secretly and openly. Can they be equal? All the praises are to Allah. Nay! But most of them do not know.

16:76 Allah puts forward an example of 2 men: one of them is dumb, has no power over anything, and is a burden to his master, whatever way he directs him, he brings no good. Is he equal to one who commands justice, and he is on the right way?

16:77 To Allah (belongs) the unseen of the heavens and the earth. The matter of the hour (of Judgment) is not but as a twinkling of the eye, or it is even nearer. Surely! Allah has power over everything.

16:78 Allah has brought you out of the bellies of your mothers, you do not know anything. Allah has given you hearing, sight, and intelligence so that you may give thanks (to Allah).

16:79 Do they not see the birds flying in the midst of the sky? None holds them but Allah. Surely, in this are clear signs for people who believe.

16:80 Allah has made for you in your homes an abode, and made for you out of the hides of the cattle (as tent for) homes which you find light during the day of your travel and during the day of your stay (in travel); and from their wool, fur, and hair, (Allah provides) furniture, articles of convenience (such as carpets, blankets), comfort for a while.

16:81 Allah has made shades (from sun) for you out of that which Allah has created. Allah has made for you places of refuge in the mountains, has made for you garments to protect you from the heat, and coats of armor to protect you from your mutual violence. Thus Allah perfects Allah's Grace to you so that you may submit (to Islam).

16:82 If they still turn away, then it is only on you (O Muhammad) to convey (the message) in a clear way.

16:83 They recognize the favors of Allah, yet they deny them and most of them are (ungrateful) disbelievers.

16:84 (Remember) the day when Allah will raise up a witness (their messenger) from each nation. Then those who have disbelieved will neither be permitted (to excuse), nor will they be allowed to repent.

16:85 When those who did wrong (disbelievers) will see the punishment, it will neither be lightened for them, nor will they be given respite.

16:86 When those who associated partners (with Allah) see their partners, they will say: "Our Rabb! These are our partners whom we used to invoke besides Allah." But they (partners) will throw back their word at them (and say): "Surely! You are liars!"

16:87 They will offer submission to Allah on that day and what they used to invent (false deities) will vanish from them.

16:88 Those who disbelieved and hinder people from the way of Allah, Allah will add punishment over the punishment for them because they used to spread corruption.

16:89 (Remember) the day when Allah will raise up a witness in every nation against them from amongst themselves. Allah will bring you (O Muhammad) as a witness against them. (For this reason) Allah has sent down to you the book (the Qur'an) as an explanation of everything, a guide, a Mercy, and glad tidings for the Muslims.

16:90 Surely, Allah enjoins justice, doing good (to others), giving help to kith and kin, and forbids lewdness, evil deeds, and oppression. Allah admonishes you so that you may take heed.

16:91 Fulfill the covenant of Allah when you have taken a covenant, and do not break your oaths after you have confirmed them; and indeed you have appointed Allah over you as guarantor. Surely! Allah knows what you do.

16:92 Do not be like that (woman) who had spun thread strongly and then undo it by weakening it; nor take your oaths as a means of deception among yourselves so that a nation may take undue advantage over another nation. Only Allah tests you by these (oaths). Allah will make clear to you on the day of Resurrection what you used to differ about it.

16:93 If Allah willed, Allah could have made you all one nation, but Allah sends astray whom Allah wills and guides whom Allah wills. Certainly you will be questioned for what you used to do.

16:94 Do not take your oaths as a means of deception among yourselves, lest your foot slip after being firmly fixed; and you may have to taste the punishment for hindering people from the way of Allah, and there will be a great punishment for you.

16:95 Do not purchase a small gain (at the cost of) Allah's covenant. Surely! What is with Allah is better for you if you but knew it.

16:96 Whatever is with you, will be exhausted, and whatever is with Allah, will remain. Allah will certainly pay those who are patient; their reward will be in proportion to the best of what they used to do.

16:97 Whoever does a righteous deed, whether male or female, while that person is a believer; Allah will give a good life, and Allah will pay such people their reward according to the best of what they used to do.

16:98 When you recite the Qur'an, seek refuge with Allah from Satan, the outcast.

16:99 Surely! Satan has no power over those who believe and put their trust in their Rabb.

16:100 Only he (Satan) has power over those who follow him, and those who join partners with Allah.

16:101 When Allah changes a verse (of the Qur'an) in place of another verse, and Allah knows the best of what Allah sends down, they (disbelievers) say: "You (O Muhammad) are but a forger, liar." But most of them do not know.

16:102 Say (O Muhammad): "The Holy Spirit (angel Gabriel) has brought it (the Qur'an) down from your Rabb with truth to strengthen those who believe, and as guidance, and glad tidings to the Muslims."

16:103 Indeed Allah knows what they (polytheists) say: "It is only a human being who teaches him (Muhammad)." But the language of the man whom they refer to him is foreign, while this (the Qur'an) is a clear Arabic language.

16:104 Surely! Those who do not believe in the verses of Allah, Allah will not guide them and for them will be a painful punishment.

16:105 It is only those who do not believe in the verses of Allah, fabricate falsehood, and they are liars.

16:106 Whoever is forced to deny faith after its acceptance while the heart is at rest with faith in Allah, shall be forgiven; but whoever opens its heart to disbelief (willingly after accepting the faith), shall incur the wrath from Allah, and for them will be a great punishment.

16:107 That is because they love and prefer the life of this world over that of the hereafter. Allah does not guide the disbelievers.

16:108 They are those whom Allah has set a seal upon their hearts, their hearings, and their eyes. They are those who are heedless!

16:109 No doubt, they will be the losers in the hereafter.

16:110 Then surely! Your Rabb is Forgiving, Merciful afterwards to those who emigrated after they had been put to trials (for their faith), struggled hard, and were patient.

16:111 (Remember) the day when every soul will come up pleading for itself, every soul will be paid in full for what it did, and they will not be dealt with unjustly.

16:112 Allah puts forward the example of a town (Makkah) which was enjoying security and peace, its provision was coming to it in abundance from every place; then it (its people) denied the favors of Allah. So Allah made it (its people) taste the seize of hunger and fear because of what they used to do.

16:113 Surely, a messenger (Muhammad) was sent to them from among themselves, but they denied him; so the punishment overtook them while they were wrongdoers.

16:114 So eat of the lawful and good things which Allah has provided for you; and thank Allah's bounty if you really worship Allah.

16:115 Allah has only forbidden you to eat the dead animal, blood, the flesh of swine, and (any animal) which is slaughtered as a sacrifice for others than Allah with it. But if one is forced (by necessity) without willful disobedience, and not transgressing, then surely, Allah is Forgiving, Merciful.

16:116 You do not say that which describe your tongues falsely: "This is lawful and this is unlawful," in order to invent lies against Allah. Surely, those who invent lies against Allah will never prosper.

16:117 A brief enjoyment is (in this life) for them, but they will have a painful punishment.

16:118 To those who are Jews, Allah has forbidden such things as Allah has already mentioned to you (Muhammad) before (6:146). Allah has not wronged to them, but they did wrong to themselves.

16:119 Then surely, yet, your Rabb is Forgiving and Merciful to those who do evil in ignorance, then they repent after that, and do righteous deeds.

16:120 Surely, Abraham was a nation (a leader with all the good qualities), straight obedient to Allah, and he was not of the polytheists.

16:121 He was thankful for Allah's Graces. Allah chose him and guided him to the right way.

16:122 Allah gave him good (life) in this world, and surely in the hereafter he will be of those who are righteous.

16:123 Then, Allah has sent the revelation to you (O Muhammad saying): "Follow the faith of Abraham and he was not one of the polytheists."

16:124 The Sabbath was only prescribed for those who differed in it. Surely, your Rabb will judge between them on the day of Resurrection about that over which they used to differ.

16:125 Invite (mankind, O Muhammad) to the way of your Rabb (Islam) with wisdom, kind advice, and reason with them in a way that it is better. Surely, your Rabb is Allah who knows best who has gone astray from Allah's way, and Allah knows best those who are guided.

16:126 If you (have to) punish, then let your punishment be like that which you were punished with. But if you endure patiently, surely, it is better for the patient.

16:127 Endure patiently (O Muhammad), and your patience is not but from Allah. Do not grieve over them (polytheists), and be not in distress from what they plot.

16:128 Surely, Allah is with those who fear Allah, and those who are righteous people.

17. Al-Isra' : The Night Journey
In the name of Allah, the Gracious, the Merciful

17:1 Glory be to Allah who took Allah's devotee (Muhammad) for a journey by night from the sacred mosque (at Makkah) to the farthest mosque (Al-Aqsa at Jerusalem), which Allah has blessed around it (vicinity), to show him (Muhammad) some of Allah's signs. Surely, Allah is the All-Hearer, the All-Seer.

17:2 Allah gave Moses the scripture and made it a guide for the children of Israel (saying): "Do not take other than Allah as protector.

17:3 (You are) offspring of those whom Allah carried (in the ship) with Noah. Surely, he was a grateful devotee."

17:4 Allah decreed for the children of Israel in the scripture: indeed you will do mischief in the earth twice, indeed you will become tyrants, and extremely arrogant!

17:5 When the promise for the first of the 2 came, Allah sent against you servants of Allah (the Assyrians) who gave a terrible warfare. They entered the very innermost parts of your homes and the promise was fulfilled.

17:6 Then Allah gave you a return of victory over them, helped you with wealth and children, and granted you more manpower.

17:7 If you did good, you did good for yourselves; but if you did evil, it was for your own selves. Then, when the last (2nd) promise came to pass, (Allah permitted your enemies – the Romans) to disgrace your faces and to enter the mosque (of Jerusalem) just as they had entered it 1st time, and they destroyed all that they had conquered (fell in their hands) with complete destruction.

17:8 It may be that your Rabb may show Mercy to you; but if you return (to sins), Allah will return (to Allah's punishment). Allah has made hell a prison for the disbelievers.

17:9 Surely, this Qur'an guides to the way which is just perfect and gives the glad tidings to the believers who do righteous deeds so that they shall have a great reward;

17:10 and those who do not believe in the hereafter; Allah has prepared for them a painful punishment.

17:11 Mankind invokes (Allah) for evil as mankind invokes (Allah) for good, and mankind is ever hasty.

17:12 Allah has made the night and the day as 2 signs. Then, Allah has covered the night with darkness and has given light to the day so that you may seek bounty from your Rabb, and that you may compute number of the years and the reckoning. Thus Allah has explained everything with full explanation.

17:13 Allah has fastened the deeds of every human in its neck, and on the day of Resurrection Allah will bring out for the person a book which will be wide open.

17:14 (It will be said): "Read your book. You yourself are sufficient today as a reckoner (accountant) against you."

17:15 Whoever goes right, then it goes right only for its own self. Whoever goes astray, then it goes astray only against its own self. No one shall bear the burden of another (on the Day of Judgment). Allah does not punish (in this world) until Allah has sent a messenger.

17:16 When Allah decides to destroy a town, Allah first sends commandments to its wealthy luxurious people, but they transgress in it. Thus the word (of punishment) is justified against it. Then Allah destroys it with complete destruction.

17:17 How many generations Allah has destroyed since after Noah? Your Rabb is Sufficient as an All-Knower and All-Seer of the sins of Allah's servants.

17:18 Whoever wishes for the quick-passing (enjoyment of this world), Allah quickly grants it to whoever Allah wills. Then, Allah condemns the person to hell who will burn therein disgraced and rejected.

17:19 Whoever desires the hereafter and strives for it with its striving while the person is a believer, then they are such that their striving will be appreciated.

17:20 Allah provides each of these and those from the bounties of your Rabb. The bounties of your Rabb can never be forbidden.

17:21 See how Allah prefers some of them over others and surely, the hereafter will be greater in degrees and greater in preference.

17:22 Do not set up another one worthy of worship with Allah, lest you sit down condemned, forsaken.

17:23 Your Rabb has decreed that you worship none except Allah. You shall be good (dutiful) to parents. If one of them or both of them attain old age with you, then do not say to them a word of disrespect, nor scold them but address them in terms of honor.

17:24 Lower to them the wing of submission (humility) through Mercy, and say: "My Rabb! Bestow on them your (Allah's) Mercy just as they raised me (when I was) a little child."

17:25 Your Rabb knows best what is in your hearts. If you are righteous, then surely, Allah is forgiving to those who often turn (to Allah).

17:26 Give to your relatives their due and to the poor, and to the wayfarers. But do not spend wastefully (your wealth like a spendthrift),

17:27 surely, the spendthrifts are brothers of the devils, and the devil is ever ungrateful to its Rabb.

17:28 If you (O Muhammad) turn away from them (kinsman, poor, wayfarer, etc) seeking a Mercy from your Rabb which you hope, then say kind word to them.

17:29 You shall neither tie your hands (like a miser) to your neck nor stretch them to their utmost reach, lest you sit back, blameworthy, and in severe poverty.

17:30 Surely, your Rabb extends the provision to whom Allah wills and straitens (for whom Allah wills). Surely, Allah is All-Knower, All-Seer of Allah's servants.

17:31 Do not kill your children for fear of poverty. Allah provides (sustenance) for them and for you. Surely, killing them is a great sin.

17:32 Do not approach adultery. Surely, it is a great sin, and it is the worst way.

17:33 Do not kill a soul which Allah has forbidden, except for a just cause. Whoever is killed wrongfully, and then surely Allah has made for its heir (guardian) an authority. But let that person not exceed limits in killing (should not kill except the killer only). Surely, that person is helped (by Islamic law).

17:34 Do not go near the property of the orphan except with what is best (to improve), until it attains the age of full strength. Fulfill the covenant. Surely! The covenant is a responsibility (will be questioned).

17:35 Give full measure when you measure, and weigh with a straight balance. That is good and better interpretation (in the end).

17:36 Do not follow (anyone blindly in matters) about which you do not have knowledge. Surely, the (use of) hearing, the sight, and the heart - for each of these, you will be questioned (by Allah on the Day of Judgment).

17:37 Do not walk on the earth with arrogance. Surely, you can neither penetrate the earth nor can attain the height of the mountains.

17:38 All that is evil are hateful to your Rabb.

17:39 This is part of wisdom which your Rabb has revealed to you (Muhammad). Do not set up with Allah another one worthy of worship lest you should be thrown into hell, blameworthy and rejected.

17:40 Has your Rabb preferred for you (O people of Makkah) to give sons and adapted (for Allah) from among the angels as females (daughters)? Surely! You utter awful statement.

17:41 Surely, Allah has explained in this Qur'an so that they (disbelievers) may take heed, but it has only increased their dislike.

17:42 Say (O Muhammad to polytheists): "If there were other one worthy of worship besides Allah as they say, they would have certainly sought a way to (dethrone) the Master of the Throne.

17:43 Glorified and exalted is Allah! Allah is far above (the great falsehood) that they say!

17:44 The 7 heavens, the earth, and all that is in them glorify Allah. There is not a single thing but glorifies Allah with praise. But you do not understand their glorification. Surely, Allah is Forbearing, Forgiving.

17:45 When you (Muhammad) recite the Qur'an, Allah makes an invisible veil (unseen barrier) between you and between those who do not believe in the hereafter.

17:46 Allah puts coverings over their hearts so that they do not understand it (the Qur'an), and create deafness in their ears. When you mention of your Rabb alone in the Qur'an, they turn their backs in extreme dislike.

17:47 Allah knows best what they like to listen when they listen to you. When they take secret counsel, then the wrongdoers say: "You follow none but a bewitched man."

17:48 See how they have put forward examples for you. They have gone astray, and they can not find a way.

17:49 They say: "When we are reduced to bones and fragments (ashes), shall we really be resurrected to a new creation?"

17:50 Say (O Muhammad):"(You will be brought back to life) even if you be stones or iron,

17:51 or even a creation that is greater (or harder) than you may think of." Then they will ask: "Who will return us (back to life)?" Say: "Allah who created you first time." Then they will shake their heads at you and ask: "When it will be?" Say: "Perhaps it is near (soon)!"

17:52 On the day when Allah will call you, you will answer with the praise of Allah, and you will think that you have stayed (in death) but a little while!

17:53 Say to the servants of Allah (true believers) that they should only say those words that are the best. Surely, Satan sows (disagreements) among them. Surely, Satan is a plain enemy to mankind.

17:54 Your Rabb knows you best. If Allah wills, Allah will have Mercy on you, or if Allah wills, Allah will punish you. Allah has not sent you (Muhammad) as a guardian over them.

17:55 Your Rabb knows best all those that are in the heavens and the earth. Indeed, Allah has preferred some of the prophets above others, and Allah gave the Psalms to David.

17:56 Say (O Muhammad): "Call to those whom you pretend (to be worthy of worship) besides Allah. They have neither the power to remove the hardship from you nor even to change it."

17:57 Those to whom they pray, desire the means of access to their Rabb, which of them should be the nearest, and they hope for Allah's Mercy and fear Allah's punishment. Surely, the punishment of your Rabb is (something to be) afraid of.

17:58 There is not a town but Allah will destroy it before the day of Resurrection, or punish it with severe punishment. That is written in the book (of records).

17:59 Nothing stops Allah to send the signs but that the people of old denied them. Allah sent the she-camel to Thamud as a clear sign, but they did her wrong. Allah does not send the signs except to warn.

17:60 (Remember) when Allah said to you (O Muhammad): "Surely! Your Rabb has encompassed mankind." Allah has not make the vision (Al-Isra) which Allah showed you (O Muhammad on the night of Al-Isra) but a trial for mankind, and likewise the accursed tree (Zaqqoom) in the Qur'an. Allah warns them but it does not increase (fear in) them except great disbelief, oppression and disobedience.

17:61 (Remember) when Allah said to the angels: "Prostrate unto Adam." They prostrated except Satan. He said: "Shall I prostrate to one whom you (Allah) have created (from) clay?"

17:62 (Satan) said: "Is this the one whom you (Allah) have honored above me? If you (Allah) give me respite (keep me alive) to the day of Resurrection, I will surely seize and mislead his (Adam's) offspring (by sending them astray) all but a few!"

17:63 (Allah) said: "Go, and whoever of them follows you, then surely, hell will be the recompense of all of you, an ample recompense.

17:64 Befool whom you can of them with your voice, and make assaults on them with your cavalry and your infantry, and share with them in wealth and children, and promise them. But Satan promises them nothing but deception.

17:65 Surely! Allah's servants, there is no authority for you over them. Your Rabb is All-Sufficient as a Guardian."

17:66 Your Rabb is the one who drives your ships in the sea in order that you may seek the bounty of Allah. Surely! Allah is Merciful towards you.

17:67 Whenever any harm touches you at the sea, all those to whom you call upon except Allah vanish. Yet, when Allah brings you safely to the land, you turn away (from Allah). Human is ever ungrateful.

17:68 Do you then feel secure that Allah will not cause side of the land to swallow you up, or send against you a violent sand-storm? Then, you shall not find a guardian for you.

17:69 Or do you feel secure that when you will return to it (sea) a 2nd time, Allah will not send a hurricane of wind against you and drown you because of your disbelief? (If that happens) then you will not find for you therein an avenger (to take revenge) against Allah.

17:70 Indeed, Allah has honored the children of Adam, Allah has carried them on land and sea, has provided them with good things, and Allah has preferred them over many of those whom Allah has created with a marked preference.

17:71 (Remember) the day when Allah will call all human beings with their leaders. Those who will be given their book (of records) in their right hand will read their records and they will not be dealt with unjustly in the least.

17:72 But those who are blind (acted) in this world will be blind in the hereafter and more astray from the way.

17:73 Surely, they were about to tempt you (O Muhammad) away from that which Allah has revealed (the Qur'an) to you, to fabricate something other than it against Allah, and (if successful) then they would have certainly taken you a friend!

17:74 Had Allah not made you stand firm, surely you would nearly have inclined to (compromise with) them a little bit.

17:75 Then, Allah would have made you taste a double punishment in this life and a double punishment after death. Then you would not have found anyone to help you against Allah.

17:76 Surely, they were about to frighten you so that they might drive you out from the land. But then they would not have stayed after you, except a little while.

17:77 (This was Allah's) way with whom indeed Allah sent Allah's messengers before you (O Muhammad), and you will not find any alteration in Allah's way.

17:78 Establish prayer from mid-day till the darkness of the night (Zuhr, Asr, Maghrib, and Isha prayers), and (recite the) Qur'an in the early dawn (the morning prayer- Fajr). Surely, the recitation of the Qur'an in the early dawn is witnessed (by angels).

17:79 In (some parts of) the night perform the night prayer with it (recite the Qur'an) as an additional prayer (Tahajjud) for you (O Muhammad). It may be that your Rabb will raise you to 'Maqam-e-Mahmood' (a station of praise-worthy).

17:80 Say (O Muhammad): "My Rabb! Make me enter (the city of Madinah) one entry in truth, and bring me out (from the city of Makkah) one exit in truth. Grant me from you (Allah) an authority helper,"

17:81 and say: "Truth has come and the falsehood has vanished. Surely! Falsehood is bound to vanish."

17:82 Allah has sent down the Qur'an which is a healing and a Mercy to the believers, while it increases nothing but loss to the wrongdoers.

17:83 When Allah bestows Allah's grace on mankind, it turns away and becomes far away at one side (from the right way). When evil touches, it is in great despair.

17:84 Say (O Muhammad to mankind): "Everyone acts according to its manner; but your Rabb knows best whose way (religion) is best guided."

17:85 They ask you (O Muhammad) about the soul (spirit). Say: "The soul is one of the commands of my Rabb and you have not been given the knowledge of it but a little."

17:86 If Allah willed, Allah could surely take away all that which Allah has revealed to you (this Qur'an). Then you would find no protector for you against Allah (to get it back),

17:87 except as a Mercy from your Rabb. Surely! Allah's Grace to you (O Muhammad) is great indeed.

17:88 Say: "If the mankind and the jinns together were to bring the like of this Qur'an, they could not bring the like thereof, even if some of them was helper to some others."

17:89 Indeed Allah has fully explained to mankind in this Qur'an every kind of similitude, but most people refuse but disbelief.

17:90 They say: "We shall not believe in you (O Muhammad) until you cause a spring to gush forth from the earth for us,

17:91 or there is a garden of date-palms and grapes for you and cause rivers to gush forth in their midst abundantly;

17:92 or you cause to fall the heaven upon us in pieces as you have claimed, or you bring Allah and the angels (face to face) before us,

17:93 or there is a house of adorable materials (like silver and gold) for you, or you ascend up into the sky, and we shall not believe in your ascension until you bring down for us a book that we would read." Say (O Muhammad): "Glory be to my Rabb! Have I (claimed) anything more but a human, sent as a messenger?"

17:94 Nothing prevented people from belief when the guidance came to them except that they said: "Has Allah sent a human as (Allah's) messenger?"

17:95 Say: "If there were angels walking on the earth in peace, then Allah would certainly have sent down to them an angel from the heaven as a messenger."

17:96 Say: "Allah is sufficient as a witness between me and between you. Surely! Allah is All-Knower, the All-Seer of Allah's servants."

17:97 Those whom Allah guides are rightly guided; but those whom Allah sends astray, they will never find protectors for them besides Allah. Allah will gather them on the day of Resurrection on their faces, blind, dumb and deaf. Their abode will be hell; whenever its flame abates, Allah will increase the fierceness of fire for them.

17:98 That is their recompense because they denied Allah's verses and they said: "When we are reduced to bones and fragments, shall we really be resurrected as new creation?"

17:99 They do not see that Allah, who has created the heavens and the earth, is able to create the people like them. Allah has made for them an appointed term; there is no doubt in it. But the wrongdoers refuse but disbelief.

17:100 Say (to the disbelievers): "Even if you possessed all the treasures of the Mercy of my Rabb, you would surely hold them back for fear of spending. Human is ever miserly!"

17:101 Indeed Allah gave to Moses 9 clear signs. Ask the children of Israel, when he came to them, then Pharaoh said to him: "O Moses! I think you are indeed bewitched."

17:102 (Moses) replied: "Surely, you know that no one has sent down these signs but the Rabb of the heavens and the earth as clear signs. Surely O Pharaoh, I think you are doomed to destruction."

17:103 So he (Pharaoh) wanted to turn them out of the land (of Egypt). But Allah drowned him and all who were with him.

17:104 Allah said to the children of Israel after him: "You reside in the land and then when the last promise comes, Allah will assemble you as a mixed crowd."

17:105 Allah has sent it (the Qur'an) down with truth and with truth it has descended. Allah has not sent you (O Muhammad) except as a bearer of glad-tidings and a warner.

17:106 Allah has divided the Qur'an (into parts) so that you may recite it to people at intervals. Allah has revealed it by stages (in 23 years).

17:107 Say (O Muhammad to them): "Whether you believe in it (the Qur'an) or do not believe, surely those who were given knowledge before it (Jews and Christians like Abdullah bin Salam and Salman Al-Farsi), they fall down on their faces in prostration when it is recited to them,

17:108 they say: 'Glory be to our Rabb! Surely, the promise of our Rabb must be fulfilled.'

17:109 They fall down on their faces, weeping and it increases their humility."

17:110 Say (O Muhammad): "Invoke Allah or invoke the Beneficent, by whatever name you invoke Allah, to Allah belongs the best names. Offer your prayer neither aloud nor make it in a low voice but seek a way between these,

17:111 say: "Praise be to Allah, who has not taken a son, and there is no partner for Allah in (Allah's) dominion, nor there is any protector for Allah out of dependence. Magnify Allah with all magnificence."

18. Al-Kahf : The Cave
In the name of Allah, the Gracious, the Merciful

18:1 All the praises be to Allah who has sent down to Allah's servant (Muhammad) the book (the Qur'an) and has not placed therein any crookedness.

18:2 (Allah has made it) right to give warning (to the disbelievers) of a severe punishment from Allah, and to give glad tidings to the believers who work righteous deeds so that they shall have a good reward (paradise),

18:3 (they shall) abide in it forever.

18:4 Also to warn those who say: "Allah has begotten a son."

18:5 They do not have knowledge about it, nor did their forefathers. Mighty is the word that comes out of their mouths. They say nothing but a lie.

18:6 Perhaps, you would kill yourself (O Muhammad) in grief over their footsteps, if they do not believe in this narration (the Qur'an).

18:7 Surely! Allah has made the earth with all kinds of adornments in order that Allah may test them (mankind) and to see which of them are best in deeds.

18:8 Surely Allah will reduce what is on it (the earth) to a bare dry soil.

18:9 Do you think that the people of the cave and the inscription (the news or the writing of names of the people of the cave) were a wonder among Allah's signs?

18:10 (Remember) when the young men fled (for refuge from their disbelieving folk) to the cave, they said: "Our Rabb! Bestow on us Mercy from Allah and facilitate for us in our affair to the right way!"

18:11 Therefore Allah covered on their ears (causing them into deep sleep) in the cave for a number of years,

18:12 then Allah raised them up (from sleep) so that Allah might test which of the 2 parties (believers and disbelievers) (was best at) calculating the time period for which they had stayed.

18:13 Allah narrates to you (O Muhammad) their story with truth. Surely they were young men who believed in their Rabb and Allah increased them in guidance.

18:14 Allah made their hearts firm and strong when they stood up and said: "Our Rabb is the Rabb of the heavens and the earth, we shall never call upon any deity other than Allah; for if we do, then we shall utter something improper (in disbelief).

18:15 These are our people who have taken for deities other than Allah. Why do they not bring for them a clear authority? Who does more wrong than the one who invents a lie against Allah?"

18:16 (They consulted with one another and said): "Now we have withdrawn from them and denounced those deities whom they worship except Allah, then seek refuge in the cave; our Rabb will open a way for us from Allah's Mercy and will make easy for us in our affair."

18:17 You might have seen the sun when it rose, it declines to the right from their cave; and when it set, it turns away from them towards the left while they lay in the middle of the cave. That is one of the signs of Allah. Whoever Allah guides is rightly guided; but whoever Allah sends astray, you will never find guiding friend (to lead to the right way) for that person.

18:18 You would have thought them awake, though they were asleep. Allah turned them to the right and to the left sides, while their dog stretched out its 2 forelegs at the entrance (of the cave). Had you looked at them, you would have certainly turned back from them in flight and (their sight) certainly would have filled with awe of them.

18:19 Thus, Allah awakened them (from long deep sleep) so that they could question among them. A speaker from them said: "How long have you stayed here?"

They said: "Perhaps we have stayed here for a day or part of a day." They said: "Our Rabb knows best how long we have stayed here. So send one of us with our silver coin to the city, and let him find out which is the purest food, and let him bring us some of it. Let him be careful and do not let anyone know our whereabouts.

18:20 Surely if they learn about you, they will stone you (to death), or turn you back into their religion, and in that case you will never ever be successful."

18:21 Thus Allah made their case known so that people might know that the promise of Allah is true and that there is no doubt about the hour (of Judgment). (Remember) when they (the people of the city) disputed among themselves about their case, they said: "Construct a building over them, their Rabb knows best about them." Those who won on their point said: "Surely we shall build a place of worship over them."

18:22 Some say they were 3 and their dog was the 4th of them. Others say they were 5 and their dog was the 6th of them guessing at the unseen. Yet, others say they were 7 and their dog was the 8th of them. Say (O Muhammad): "My Rabb knows best their number. None knows them but a few." So do not debate about them except with clear proof and do not consult about them with anyone.

18:23 Never say of anything: "Surely I shall do that tomorrow,"

18:24 except that (say): "If Allah wills!" Remember your Rabb when you forget and say: "I hope that my Rabb will guide me to a closer way of guidance than this."

18:25 (Some say) they stayed in their cave 360 years (solar) and add 9 (lunar years).

18:26 (O Muhammad) say: "Allah knows best how long they stayed. With Allah is (the knowledge of) the unseen of the heavens and the earth. How clearly Allah sees with it and how clearly Allah hears! They did not have any helper other than Allah, and Allah does not share in Allah's decision and rule with anyone."

18:27 Recite what has been revealed to you (O Muhammad) from the book (the Qur'an) of your Rabb. None can change Allah's words and you will never find a refuge other than Allah.

18:28 Keep yourself (O Muhammad) patiently with those who call their Rabb in the morning and the evening seeking Allah's pleasure, and do not let your eyes overlook them desiring the beauty of the life of the world; do not obey the one whose heart Allah has made heedless of Allah's remembrance, who follows own lusts and whose affair has been lost.

18:29 (O Muhammad) say: "The truth is from your Rabb. Then whoever wills let that person believe, and whoever wills, let that person disbelieve." Surely, Allah has prepared a fire for the wrongdoers; its walls will surround them (disbelievers). If they ask for help, they will be granted water like boiling oil that will burn the faces. Terrible is the drink and terrible is the resting place!

18:30 Surely! Those who believe and do righteous deeds, Allah will not lose the reward of that person who does good deeds.

18:31 Those are the ones for them there will be gardens of Eden; rivers flow beneath them; they will be decorated therein with bracelets of gold, and they will wear green garments of fine and thick silk. They will recline therein on raised thrones. How good is the reward, and how excellent is the resting place!

18:32 (O Muhammad) put forward to them the example of 2 men: Allah had given 2 gardens of grapes to one of them, Allah had surrounded them with date-palms, and Allah had made cultivated fields between them.

18:33 Both the gardens brought forth their produce and did not fail in the least. Allah (even) caused a river to gush forth in the middle of them.

18:34 There was abundant produce for him and he said to his companion while he was talking to him: "I have more wealth than you and stronger (in respect of) men."

18:35 He entered his garden while he was unjust to himself. He said: "I do not think that this garden will ever perish!

18:36 I do not think the hour (on the day of Resurrection) will ever come. Even if I am brought back to my Rabb, surely I shall find better than this at the end."

18:37 His companion said to him while he was talking to him: "Do you disbelieve in Allah who created you out of dust, then out of semen, then fashioned you into a man?

18:38 Allah is my Rabb and I shall not associate anyone with my Rabb.

18:39 When you entered your garden, why did you not say: 'It is as Allah wills! There is no power but with Allah!' If you see me, I have less wealth than you and children,

18:40 it may be that my Rabb will give me something better than your garden, and may send a punishment from the sky on it, then turn it into a slippery earth.

18:41 Or its water will become deep-sunken (dry underground) so that you will never be able to find it."

18:42 (It so happened that) his fruits were surrounded (with ruin). He began twisting his hands (with sorrow) over what he had spent on it while all (fruits) were destroyed on their nets, and he said: "I wish I had not associated anyone with my Rabb!"

18:43 He could neither find anyone to help him other than Allah, nor could he defend himself.

18:44 The real power (protection) comes from Allah, the true one worthy of worship. Allah is the best for reward and the best for the final end.

18:45 (O Muhammad) put forward for them the example of the worldly life. It is like water (rain) which Allah sends down from the sky and the vegetation of the earth mingles with it. (But later it) becomes dry stalks which the winds scatter. Allah has power over everything.

18:46 Wealth and children are the adornment of the worldly life. But the lasting righteous deeds are better with your Rabb for rewards and better hope.

18:47 (Remember) the day when Allah will cause the mountains to move, you will see the earth as a leveled plain (of waste), Allah will gather them, and will not leave anyone of them behind.

18:48 They will be set before your Rabb in rows (and Allah will say): "Now indeed you have come to Allah as Allah created you the first time. Nay, but you thought that Allah had never appointed a meeting for you."

18:49 The book (one's record) will be placed (before them), and you will see the sinners fearful of what is (recorded) in it. They will say: "Woe to us! What is the matter with this book? Neither it leaves out a small thing nor a big thing but has recorded it with numbers!" They will find all that they did and placed before them. Your Rabb will not treat anyone with injustice.

18:50 (Remember) when Allah said to the angels: "Prostrate to Adam," all prostrated except Satan. He was one of the jinns; he disobeyed the command of its Rabb. Will you then take him (Satan) and its progeny as your protectors rather than Allah while they are enemies to you? What an evil is the exchange for the wrongdoers!

18:51 Allah did not make them (Satan and its offspring) to witness the creation of the heavens and the earth, nor their own creation, nor Allah took the misleaders (of mankind) as helpers.

18:52 (Remember) the day when Allah will say: "Call those partners of Allah whom you claimed." They will cry to them but they will not answer them and Allah will put a barrier between them.

18:53 The sinners will see the fire and realize that they have to fall therein. They will not find a way of escape from it.

18:54 Indeed Allah explained every example in this Qur'an for mankind (to understand). But human is quarrelsome of most things.

18:55 Nothing prevents mankind from believing and asking forgiveness of their Rabb when the guidance (the Qur'an) has come to them, except that the way of the ancients come upon them or the punishment come upon them face to face.

18:56 Allah sent the messengers except as bearers of glad tidings and warners. But the disbelievers disputed with false argument in order to refute the truth. They took Allah's verses with which they were warned, as a joke!

18:57 Who is more unjust than the one who, when reminded of the verses of the Rabb, turns away from them and forgets what deeds its own hands have done? (For these people) surely, Allah has set veils over their hearts so they do not understand it (the Qur'an), and their ears are (covered) with deafness. If you (O Muhammad) call them to the guidance, even then they will never be guided.

18:58 Your Rabb is Forgiving, the Owner of Mercy. If Allah calls them to account for what they have earned, Allah would have hastened the punishment for them. But they have their appointed time, beyond which they will never find an escape.

18:59 Allah destroyed these towns with them (their inhabitants) when they did wrong. Allah appointed a fixed time for their destruction.

18:60 (Remember) when Moses said to his young servant: "I will not give up (traveling) until I reach the junction of the 2 seas or (until) I spend years (in traveling)."

18:61 But when they reached the junction between them, they forgot (about) their fish (they were carrying), which made its way through the sea as in a tunnel.

18:62 When they had passed further on, he (Moses) said to his young servant: "Bring us our breakfast; truly we have suffered this fatigue in our journey."

18:63 He replied: "Do you remember when we were resting ourselves beside the rock? Indeed I forgot the fish, none but Satan made me forget to remember it. It took its way into the sea in a strange way!"

18:64 (Moses) said: "That is what we have been seeking." So they went back retracing their footsteps.

18:65 Then they found one of the servant (Khidr) of Allah whom Allah had bestowed Mercy from Allah, and Allah had taught him knowledge from Allah.

18:66 Moses requested him: "May I follow you so that you may teach me something of that knowledge which you have been taught (by Allah)?"

18:67 Khidr said: "Surely! You will never be able to have patience with me,

18:68 how can you have patience about that which is beyond your knowledge?"

18:69 (Moses) said: "You will find me patient if Allah wills, and I will not disobey your command."

18:70 Khidr said: "Then, if you follow me, do not ask me about anything until I myself mention it to you."

18:71 So they both proceeded, till when they embarked in a ship, Khidr made a hole in it. Moses said: "Have you made a hole in it to drown its people? Surely, you have done a bad thing."

18:72 Khidr said: "Did I not tell you that you would never be able to have patience with me?"

18:73 Moses said: "Do not call me to account for what I forgot, and do not be hard on me for my affair with you."

18:74 Then they both proceeded till they met a boy, then Khidr killed him. Moses said: "Have you killed an innocent person who killed none? Surely, you have committed an evil thing!"

18:75 Khidr said: "Did I not tell you that you would never be able to have patience with me?"

18:76 Moses said: "If I ever ask you about anything after this, do not keep me in your company, (If I ask again then) surely you will have an excuse in my case."

18:77 Then they both proceeded, till they came to the people of a town. They asked its people for food, but they refused to entertain them. Then they found in it a wall that was about to collapse, so Khidr set it up straight. Moses said: "If you had wished, surely you could have taken some wages for it!"

18:78 Khidr said: "This is the parting (time) between me and you. (First) I will tell you the interpretation of those (acts) over which you could not have patience.

18:79 As for the ship, it belonged to poor people working in the sea. I intended to damage it as there was a king after them who was seizing every ship by force.

18:80 As for the boy, his parents were believers, and we feared lest he would oppress them by rebellion and disbelief.

18:81 So we intended that their Rabb should exchange for them one (son) better than him in righteousness and near to mercy.

18:82 As for the wall, it belonged to 2 orphan boys in the town and there was a treasure for them under it. Since their father was a righteous man, your Rabb intended that they should attain their age of full strength and then take out their treasure as a Mercy from your Rabb. I did not do them by my own will. That is the interpretation of (those actions) over which you could not hold patience."

18:83 (O Muhammad) they ask you about Dhul-Qarnain. Say: "I shall recite to you something of him."

18:84 Surely, Allah established him in the earth and gave him means of everything.

18:85 So he followed a way (towards the west)

18:86 until, when he reached the setting place of the sun, he found it setting in a spring of black muddy water. He found a people near it. Allah said: "O Dhul-Qarnain! Either you punish them, or treat them with kindness."

18:87 He said (to people): "Whoever will do wrong, we shall punish that person; then that person will be brought back to the Rabb, who will punish with a terrible punishment.

18:88 As for that person who believes and does righteous deeds, that person will have the best reward (paradise), and we (Dhul-Qarnain) shall speak to that person with mild words."

18:89 Then he followed another way (towards the east)

18:90 until, when he reached the rising place of the sun, he found it rising on a people for whom Allah had not provided any shelter against it (the sun).

18:91 (He left them) as it was! Allah knew whatever information was with him (Dhul-Qarnain).

18:92 Then he followed another way

18:93 until, when he reached between 2 mountains where he found near them a people who almost did not understood a word.

18:94 They said: "O Dhul-Qarnain! Surely! (The people of) Gog and Magog are doing mischief in the land. Shall we pay to you a tribute in order that you make a barrier between us and them?"

18:95 He said: "What my Rabb has granted me is better (than your tribute). Just help me with strength (manpower) and I will erect a barrier between you and them.

18:96 Give me pieces (blocks) of iron." Until when he leveled the gap between the 2 mountain-cliffs, he said: "Blow," until when he had made it (red iron) fire, he said: "Bring me molten copper to pour over it."

18:97 So they (Gog and Magog) could not scale it nor could they dig through it.

18:98 (Dhul-Qarnain) said: "This is a Mercy from my Rabb. But when the promise of my Rabb will come, Allah will make it flat (leveled). Promise of my Rabb is true."

18:99 That day (when Gog and Magog will come out), Allah will leave some of people to surge like waves on others. The trumpet will be blown and Allah will collect them (the creatures) all together.

18:100 On that day Allah will present hell to the disbelievers with plain view,

18:101 to those whose eyes had been under a covering from Allah's reminder (this Qur'an), and who could not bear to hear it.

18:102 Do the disbelievers then think that they can take Allah's servants as protectors besides Allah? Surely, Allah has prepared hell as an entertainment for the disbelievers.

18:103 Say (O Muhammad): "Should Allah inform you of the greatest losers in respect of deeds?

18:104 Those whose efforts have been wasted in the worldly life while they thought that they were acquiring good by their deeds;

18:105 they are those who disbelieve in the verses of their Rabb and the meeting with Allah (in the hereafter). So their deeds will be in vain, Allah will not assign any weight (reward) on the day of Resurrection for them.

18:106 Thus their recompense will be hell; because they disbelieved, took Allah's verses and Allah's messengers as a joke.

18:107 Surely! Those who believe and do righteous deeds, they will be entertained with the gardens of paradise.

18:108 They will reside in it forever. They will never desire for removal from there."

18:109 Say (O Muhammad to mankind): "If the sea were ink for (writing) the words of my Rabb, the sea would be exhausted before the words of my Rabb would be exhausted, even if we brought (another sea) like it for its aid."

18:110 Say (O Muhammad): "I am but a human like you. It has been revealed to me that your deity is one Allah. So whoever has hopes for the meeting with the Rabb, let that person do righteous deeds and do not associate anyone as a partner in the worship of the Rabb."

19. Maryam : Mary
In the name of Allah, the Gracious, the Merciful

19:1 Kaf-Ha-Ya-Ain-Sad.

19:2 (This is) a mention of the Mercy of your Rabb to Allah's servant Zachariah,

19:3 when he called out his Rabb in secret,

19:4 he said: "O my Rabb! Indeed I have grown weak bones, head of mine has turned grey, and I have never been unblessed in my invocation to you (Allah), O my Rabb!

19:5 Surely! I fear my relatives after me and my wife is barren. So give me an heir from you (Allah),

19:6 who shall inherit me and inherit from the family of Jacob. O my Rabb, make him a desirable (person to you (Allah))!"

19:7 (Allah said): "O Zachariah! Surely, Allah gives you the glad tidings of a son, his name shall be John. Allah has not given that name to anyone before."

19:8 He asked: "My Rabb! How shall I have a son when my wife is barren and I have reached the extreme old age?"

19:9 (Allah) said: "So (it will be). Your Rabb says: 'It is easy for me (Allah). Certainly I (Allah) have created you before when you were not anything!'"

19:10 (Zachariah) said: "My Rabb! Appoint for me a sign." Allah said: "Your sign is that you shall not speak to people for 3 nights together though you have no bodily defect."

19:11 So he came out to his people from the praying place, then he told them by signs to glorify (Allah) in the morning and in the afternoon.

19:12 (It was said to his son): "O John! Hold the scripture with strength." Allah gave him wisdom while he was a child,

19:13 compassion (sympathetic to people) from Allah, (made him) pure from sins, and he was righteous,

19:14 dutiful to his parents, and he was neither arrogant nor disobedient.

19:15 Peace be on him the day he was born, the day he dies, and the day he will be raised up to life (again)!

19:16 Mention in the book (the Qur'an, O Muhammad, the story of) Mary, when she withdrew in seclusion from her family to a place facing east.

19:17 Then she placed a screen (to separate herself) from them. Allah sent to her Allah's angel Gabriel and he appeared before her as a human in all respects.

19:18 She said: "Surely! I seek refuge with the Gracious (Allah) from you, if you fear (Allah)."

19:19 (The angel) said: "I am only a messenger from your Rabb (to inform) you that Allah gives to you a righteous son."

19:20 She said: "How can I have a son when no man has touched me, nor am I unchaste?"

19:21 He (the angel) said: "So (it will be), your Rabb says: 'That is easy for Allah. Allah will appoint him (son) as a sign to mankind and a Mercy from Allah and it is a matter (already) decreed (by Allah).'"

19:22 So she conceived him and she withdrew with him to a far place (Bethlehem about 4-6 miles from Jerusalem).

19:23 The labor pains drove her to the trunk of a date-palm. She cried (in her anguish): "Would that I had died before this, and I had been forgotten out of sight!"

19:24 So he (Gabriel) called to her from below her, saying: "Do not grieve! Indeed your Rabb has provided a water stream under you.

19:25 Shake the trunk of date-palm towards you; it will let fall fresh ripe-dates upon you.

19:26 So eat, drink, and cool your eyes. If you see anyone from human being, say: 'I have vowed a fast to the Gracious (Allah), so I shall not speak today to any human being.'"

19:27 Carrying the baby, she brought him to her people. They said: "O Mary! Indeed you have brought a mighty thing (hard to believe)!

19:28 O sister of Aaron (a woman from the family)! Your father was not a man of evil nor was your mother an unchaste woman."

19:29 Then she pointed to him (baby). They said: "How can we talk to one who is a child in the cradle?"

19:30 He (Jesus as the baby) said: "Surely! I am a servant of Allah. Allah has given me the scripture and made me a prophet.

19:31 Allah has made me blessed wherever I may be. Allah has enjoined on me (to establish) the prayer, give obligatory charity as long as I am live,

19:32 be dutiful to my mother, and made me not arrogant, unblessed.

19:33 Peace be upon me the day I was born, and the day I shall die, and the day I shall be raised alive!"

19:34 Such (was) Jesus, son of Mary. It is a statement of truth about which they dispute in it.

19:35 It is not for Allah that Allah should beget any son. Glorified is Allah when Allah decrees an affair, Allah only says to it: "Be!" and it becomes.

19:36 (Jesus said): "Surely Allah is my Rabb and your Rabb. So worship Allah. This is the right way.

19:37 Then the sects differed (the Christians about Jesus) from among themselves. So woe to those who disbelieve from meeting of a great day (of judgment).

19:38 How clearly will they hear and see the day when they will appear before Allah! But today the wrongdoers (who do not hear and see) are in plain error.

19:39 Warn them (O Muhammad) of the day of grief when the case will be decided, while (today) they are unaware, and do not believe.

19:40 Surely! Allah will inherit the earth (after destruction) and whatever is on it. To Allah they shall be returned.

19:41 Mention in the book (the Qur'an) about Abraham. Surely! He was a truthful prophet.

19:42 When he said to his father: "O my father! Why do you worship that which can neither hear, nor see, and cannot avail you anything?

19:43 O my father! Surely! The knowledge has come to me that which did not come to you. So follow me. I will guide you to the right way.

19:44 O my father! You do not worship Satan. Surely! Satan has been a rebel against the Gracious (Allah).

19:45 O my father! Surely! I fear lest a punishment from the Gracious (Allah) should touch you so that you become a companion of Satan."

19:46 He (father) said: "Do you reject my deity, O Abraham? If you do not stop this, I will indeed stone you (to death). So get away from me for a long time."

19:47 (Abraham) said: "Peace be on you! I will ask forgiveness of my Rabb for you. Surely! Allah is to me, ever Gracious.

19:48 I shall turn away from you and what you invoke besides Allah. I shall call on my Rabb; and may be I shall not be unblessed (in my invocation) in calling my Rabb."

19:49 So when he had turned away from them and what they worshipped besides Allah, Allah granted him Isaac and Jacob, and Allah made each one of them a prophet.

19:50 Allah gave them Allah's Mercy and made them honor tongues (being mentioned) of truth.

19:51 Mention in the book (this Qur'an) about Moses. Surely! He was chosen and he was a messenger and a prophet.

19:52 Allah called him from the right side of the Mount (Tur), and Allah made him draw near for whispering (for a talk).

19:53 Allah bestowed on him out of Allah's Mercy his brother Aaron, also a prophet.

19:54 Mention in the book (the Qur'an) about Ishmael. Surely! He was true in promise, and he was a messenger, and a prophet.

19:55 He used to command his family to establish prayer, give obligatory charity, and his Rabb was pleased (with him).

19:56 Mention in the book (the Qur'an) about Enoch. Surely! He was a truthful prophet.

19:57 Allah raised him to a high place.

19:58 These are they on whom Allah bestowed (Allah's grace) from among the prophets, from the offspring of Adam, of those whom Allah carried (in the ship) with Noah, of the offspring of Abraham and Israel, and from among those whom Allah guided and chose. When the verses of the Gracious (Allah) were recited to them, they fell down to prostrate and weep.

19:59 But the generations who succeeded them gave up the prayer and followed their lusts. So they will soon meet transgression.

19:60 Except those who repent, believe, and do righteous deeds. Such will enter the paradise and they will not be wronged in anything.

19:61 (They will enter) gardens of Eden which the Gracious (Allah) has promised to Allah's servants in the unseen. Surely! Allah's promise shall be fulfilled.

19:62 They will not hear in it (paradise) vain talk, but salutation (peace). They will have their sustenance in it, morning and afternoon.

19:63 Such is the paradise which Allah will give as an inheritance to those of Allah's servants who lead a pious life.

19:64 (The angel Gabriel said): "We (angels) do not descend except by the command of your Rabb (O Muhammad). To Allah belongs what is before us and what is behind us, and what is between them. Your Rabb is never forgetful.

19:65 (Allah is the) Rabb of the heavens and the earth, and what is between them, so worship Allah, and be patient in Allah's worship. Do you know of anyone similar to Allah?"

19:66 The person (disbeliever) says: "When I am dead, shall I then be raised up alive?"

19:67 Do not people remember that Allah created them before out of nothing?

19:68 By your Rabb, surely Allah will gather them together and the devils, then Allah will bring them round hell on knees,

19:69 then indeed Allah will drag out from every sect all those who were worst in rebellion against the Gracious (Allah).

19:70 Then, surely Allah knows best those who deserve to be burnt in it.

19:71 There is not one of you, who will not pass over it (hell); this is a decree with your Rabb,

19:72 then Allah will save those who feared (Allah) and Allah will leave the wrongdoers in it (hell) kneeling.

19:73 When Allah's clear verses are recited to them, the disbelievers say to those who believe: "Which of the 2 groups (believers and disbelievers) have best position and better place?"

19:74 How many from a generation has Allah destroyed before them, who were better in goods and outward appearance?

19:75 Say (O Muhammad): "Whoever is in the error, the Gracious (Allah) provides an extension (of opportunity) to that person, until they see about which they were warned; either it is the punishment or the hour (of Doom), then they will know who is in worst position, and who is weaker in forces.

19:76 Allah increases in guidance for those who seek guidance. The everlasting righteous deeds are better with your Rabb for reward and better for resort."

19:77 Have you seen the one who disbelieved in Allah's verses and yet says: "Indeed I will be given wealth and children?"

19:78 Has that person known the unseen or has that person taken a covenant from the Gracious (Allah)?

19:79 Nay! Allah will record what that person says, and Allah will increase the punishment for that person.

19:80 Allah will inherit from that person (at death) all that the person talks and that person shall come to Allah alone.

19:81 They have taken (for worship) deities besides Allah so that they might give honor (source of strength) for them.

19:82 Nay, but they (false deities) will deny their worship of them, and will turn against them (on the Day of Judgment).

19:83 Don't you see that Allah has sent the devils to the disbelievers to push them to do evil?

19:84 So do not make haste against them; Allah only counts out to them a (limited) number.

19:85 The day Allah will gather the pious persons to the Gracious (Allah) like a delegation,

19:86 and Allah will drive the sinners to hell in a thirsty state.

19:87 They shall not own (power of) intercession except those who have taken a covenant (permission) from the Gracious (Allah).

19:88 They say: "The Gracious (Allah) has begotten a son,"

19:89 indeed you have brought forth a terrible thing,

19:90 whereby the heavens are almost torn, the earth is split asunder, and the mountains fall in ruins -

19:91 that they ascribe a son to the Gracious (Allah),

19:92 but it is not suitable for the Gracious (Allah) that Allah should beget a son.

19:93 There is none in the heavens and the earth but comes to the Gracious (Allah) in full submission.

19:94 Surely, Allah knows each of them, and has counted them a full counting (of all the creatures of Allah),

19:95 and every one of them will come to Allah alone on the day of Resurrection.

19:96 Surely, those who believe and do righteous deeds, the Gracious (Allah) will bestow love for them.

19:97 Allah has only made this (the Qur'an) easy on your tongue (O Muhammad) so that you may give glad tidings to the pious with it and warn with it the most quarrelsome people.

19:98 How many generations before them Allah has destroyed? Can you (O Muhammad) find anyone from them or hear even a whisper of them?

20. Ta-Ha : Ta-Ha
In the name of Allah, the Gracious, the Merciful

20:1 Ta-Ha.

20:2 Allah has not sent down the Qur'an to you (O Muhammad) to cause you distress,

20:3 but only as a reminder to those who fear (Allah).

20:4 A revelation from Allah who has created the earth and high heavens,

20:5 the Gracious (Allah) rose over the Throne (to suit Majesty),

20:6 to Allah belongs all that is in the heavens, all that is on the earth, all that is between them, and all that is under the soil.

20:7 If you (O Muhammad) speak statement aloud, then surely Allah knows the secrets and what is hidden.

20:8 Allah! There is no one worthy of worship but Allah! To Allah belong the best names.

20:9 Has there come to you the story of Moses?

20:10 When he saw a fire, he said to his family: "You wait! Surely, I have seen a fire; perhaps I can bring you some burning brand from there, or find guidance (from someone) at the fire."

20:11 When he came to it (the fire), he was called (by name): "O Moses!

20:12 Surely! I am your Rabb! Take off your shoes; surely you are in the sacred valley of Tuwa.

20:13 I have chosen you. So listen to that which is being revealed to you.

20:14 Surely! I am Allah! There is no one worthy of worship but Allah, so worship Allah, and establish the prayer for Allah's remembrance.

20:15 Surely, the hour is almost coming and Allah hides it so that every soul may be rewarded for that which it strives.

20:16 Therefore, do not let you divert from it, one who does not believe in it and follows its own lusts, lest you perish.

20:17 What is that in your right hand, O Moses?"

20:18 He said: "This is my stick, I lean on it, beat down branches with it for my sheep, and for me there are other uses in it."

20:19 (Allah) said: "Cast it down, O Moses!"

20:20 So he cast it down, and behold! It was a snake, moving quickly.

20:21 (Allah) said: "Grasp it and do not fear, Allah will return it to its former state.

20:22 Press your hand to your side (armpit); it will become (shining) white without any disease (hurting) as another sign.

20:23 Thus Allah shows you some of Allah's greatest signs.

20:24 You go to Pharaoh! Surely, he has transgressed."

20:25 (Moses) said: "O my Rabb! Open for me my chest,

20:26 and ease my task for me

20:27 and loose knot (defect) from my tongue

20:28 so that they understand my speech

20:29 and appoint for me a helper from my family;

20:30 Aaron, my brother.

20:31 Increase my strength with him

20:32 and share him in my task,

20:33 so that we may glorify Allah frequently

20:34 and remember Allah often;

20:35 surely! Allah sees well all of us."

20:36 (Allah) said: "Indeed you are granted your request, O Moses!

20:37 Indeed Allah conferred a favor on you another time,

20:38 when Allah inspired to your mother that which is inspired,

20:39 saying that: 'you put him (the child) into a box and you float it into river. Then the river shall cast him up on the bank, and an enemy of mine (Allah) and an enemy of his shall take him.' I (Allah) brought you up with love from me (Allah) so that you may be brought up under my (Allah's) eye (supervision).

20:40 When your sister went to them and said: 'Shall I show you one who will nurse him?' So Allah restored you to your mother so that she might cool her eyes and not grieve. Then you did kill a man, but Allah saved you from great distress and Allah tested you with various trials. You stayed years with people of Midian. Now you came here according to fixed term, O Moses!

20:41 I (Allah) have chosen you for myself (Allah's service).

20:42 You and your brother go with my (Allah's) verses and both of you do not become weak in my (Allah's) remembrance.

20:43 Go both to Pharaoh, surely he has transgressed.

20:44 Speak both of you to him with soft words, perhaps he may accept admonition or fear (of punishment)."

20:45 They said: "Our Rabb! Surely! We fear that he may hasten to punish us or may transgress."

20:46 (Allah) said: "You do not fear, surely! I (Allah) am with you both, I (Allah) hear and see (everything).

20:47 So both of you go to him, and say: 'surely we are messengers of your Rabb, so let the children of Israel go with us and do not punish them. Indeed, we have come to you with a sign from your Rabb! Peace will be upon those who follow the guidance!

20:48 Surely, indeed it has been revealed to us that the punishment will be on those who deny and turn away.'"

20:49 Pharaoh said: "Then who is the Rabb of you 2, O Moses?"

20:50 Moses said: "Our Rabb is Allah who gave each thing its form and nature, then rightly guided it."

20:51 He (Pharaoh) said: "Then what is the state of the old generations?"

20:52 Moses said: "The knowledge is with my Rabb in a record book. My Rabb neither errs nor forgets."

20:53 Allah has made for you the earth as a bed, has opened roads for you in it, and has sent down water (rain) from the sky with which Allah has brought forth various kinds of vegetation.

20:54 You eat (from these) and pasture your cattle. Surely, there are indeed signs in it for the people of understanding.

20:55 Allah has created you from it (the earth), into it Allah will return you, and from it Allah will bring you out once again.

20:56 Indeed Allah showed him (Pharaoh) all of Allah's signs, but he denied and refused.

20:57 He (Pharaoh) said: "Have you come to us to drive us out of our land with your magic, O Moses?

20:58 Then surely, we can produce to you with magic like yours. So appoint a meeting between us and between you, neither we nor you shall fail to keep it, in an equal place (where both shall have equal chances)."

20:59 Moses said: "Your appointment is the day of the festival, and let the people assemble before noon."

20:60 So Pharaoh withdrew, he devised his plan and then came back.

20:61 Moses said to them: "Woe to you! You do not invent a lie against Allah, lest Allah destroy you by a punishment. Surely, he fails who invents a lie (against Allah)."

20:62 Then they debated with one another their matter among them, and they kept their talk secret.

20:63 They said: "Surely! These 2 magicians intend that they drive you out from your land with their magic, and take away from your superior way.

20:64 So devise your plot and then assemble in a row." (Pharaoh said): "Indeed he who overcomes today will be successful."

20:65 They said: "O Moses! Either you throw first or we are the first who will throw?"

20:66 Moses said: "Nay, you throw (first)!" Then behold! their ropes and their sticks appeared to him (Moses) as though they moved fast by their magic,

20:67 so Moses conceived a fear in himself.

20:68 Allah said: "You do not fear! Surely, you will have the upper hand.

20:69 Throw that which is in your right hand! It will swallow up all that they have made. They have made only trick of a magician, and the magician will never be successful no matter whatever (amount of skill) he may possess."

20:70 (When all were swallowed up by the serpent of Moses) the magicians fell down in prostration. They said: "We believe in the Rabb of Aaron and Moses."

20:71 Pharaoh said: "How do you believe in him (Moses) before I give permission to you? Surely, he is your chief who taught you the magic. So surely I will cut off your hands and your feet from opposite sides, surely I will crucify you on the trunks of date-palms, then surely you will know which of us (Pharaoh or the Rabb of Moses, Allah) is more severe in punishment and more lasting."

20:72 They said: "We never prefer you over what has come to us from the clear signs and to Allah who created us. So you decree whatever you wish to decree, you can only decree about this worldly life.

20:73 Surely! We have believed in our Rabb so that Allah may forgive us our faults and from the magic which you did compel on us. Allah is better and lasting."

20:74 Surely! Whoever comes to its Rabb as a sinner, then surely hell is for that person who will neither die nor live in it.

20:75 But whoever will come to Allah as a believer and has done righteous deeds, for such are the high ranks,

20:76 gardens of Eden with rivers flowing under them, they will abide in it forever, and such is the reward of those who purify themselves (from evil).

20:77 Indeed Allah revealed to Moses (saying) that: "You travel by night with the servants of Allah and strike a dry path for them in the sea, neither fear to be overtaken (by Pharaoh) nor being afraid (of drowning in the sea)."

20:78 Then Pharaoh pursued them with his hosts but the sea (water) completely overwhelmed them and covered them up.

20:79 Thus Pharaoh led his people astray and he did not guide them.

20:80 O Children of Israel! Indeed Allah delivered you from your enemy, Allah made a covenant with you on the right side of the mount (Tur to grant you Torah), and Allah sent down to you sweet dish (Manna) and quail meat (Salva),

20:81 (saying): "You eat from good lawful things which Allah has provided you, do not commit oppression in it lest my (Allah's) anger should descend on you, whoever incurs my (Allah's) anger is indeed perished.

20:82 Surely, I (Allah) am indeed forgiving the one who repents, believes, does righteous deeds, and then that person remains guided (till death)."

20:83 (Allah said): "What made you hasten from your people, O Moses?"

20:84 He (Moses) said: "They are close on my footsteps, and I hastened to you (Allah), O my Rabb so that you (Allah) may be pleased."

20:85 Allah said: "Surely! Allah has indeed tried your people after you and Samiri has led them astray."

20:86 Then Moses returned to his people with anger and sorrow. He said: "O my people! Did not your Rabb promise you a fair promise? Did then the promise to you seem long? Or did you desire that wrath from your Rabb should descend on you, so you broke your promise to me?"

20:87 They said: "We did not break the promise to you at our own will. We were made to carry the weight of the ornaments of (Pharaoh) people and cast them (into the fire) as Samiri suggested.

20:88 Then he took out (of the fire) for them (statue of) a calf body and it had a low sound. Then said: 'This is your one worthy of worship, and the deity of Moses, but (Moses) has forgotten (his deity).'"

20:89 Did they not see that it could not return to them a word (for answer), nor it had power for them to harm nor help?

20:90   Indeed Aaron had said to them before: "O my people! Only you are being tried with it, and surely, your Rabb is the Gracious, so you follow me and obey my order."

20:91   They said: "We will never stop worshipping it (the calf), until Moses returns to us."

20:92   He (Moses) said: "O Aaron! What stopped you when you saw them going astray,

20:93   that you did not follow me? Have you then disobeyed my order?"

20:94   He (Aaron) said: "O son of my mother! You do not seize me by my beard, or by my head! Surely, I feared lest you should say: 'You have caused a division between children of Israel, and you did not respect my word!'"

20:95   He (Moses) said: "Then what is the matter with you, O Samiri?"

20:96   He (Samiri) said: "I saw what they did not see, so I seized a handful (of dust) from the footprint of the messenger (angel) and then threw it (into the casting of the calf). This my inner soul suggested to me."

20:97   He (Moses) said: "Then go away! Surely, (the punishment) for you in this life is that you will say: 'Don't touch me (you will live alone in exile away from mankind)'; and surely you have a promise (of future punishment) that will not fail. Look at your deity which you have been devoted to it. Certainly we will burn it, and then certainly we will scatter its particles in the sea."

20:98   (Then Moses told his people): "Your one worthy of worship is only Allah; there is no one worthy of worship but Allah. Allah comprehends every thing in knowledge."

20:99   Thus Allah relates to you (O Muhammad) from information of what happened before. Indeed Allah has given you a reminder (this Qur'an) from Allah.

20:100   Whoever turns away from it (this Qur'an), then surely will bear a burden (of sins) on the day of Resurrection.

20:101   They will abide in that (fire of hell) and evil will be that load for them on the day of Resurrection.

20:102   The day, when the trumpet will be blown and Allah will gather the sinners that day (they will be) blue or blind eyed (by fear).

20:103   They will whisper among themselves (saying): "You did not stay longer than 10 (days on earth)."

20:104   Allah knows very well what they will say, the best among them in knowledge and wisdom will say: "You did not stay except a day!"

20:105   They ask you about the mountains. You say: "My Rabb will blast them as particles of dust.

20:106   Then Allah will leave it as a smooth level,

20:107   you will neither see in it crookedness nor curve."

20:108   On that day the people will follow the caller (of Allah); there is no crookedness for the caller. (All voices) will be humbled for the Gracious (Allah), so you shall hear nothing but a whisper (of footsteps).

20:109   On that day no intercession will be available, except the one to whom the Gracious (Allah) will give permission and Allah will approve a word for that person.

20:110   Allah knows what is before them, what is behind them, and they will never compass any knowledge (about Allah).

20:111 Faces shall be humbled before the ever-Living, the self-Sustaining (Allah). Indeed the one who carried a burden of wrong-doing will be disappointed.

20:112 One who is a believer and does righteous deeds, then that person will neither have fear of injustice, nor reduction (of reward).

20:113 Thus Allah has sent down the Qur'an in Arabic, has explained in it the details of the warnings so that they may fear Allah, or may generate lesson in them.

20:114 High above is Allah, the true King! Do not hasten (O Muhammad) with the Qur'an before its revelation is completed to you, and you say: "My Rabb! Increase my knowledge."

20:115 Indeed Allah made a covenant with Adam before, but he forgot. Allah found in him no firm will-power.

20:116 (Remember) when Allah said to the angels: "Prostrate yourselves to Adam." They prostrated except Satan, who refused.

20:117 Then Allah said: "O Adam! Surely, this is an enemy to you and to your wife. So let him not get you both out from paradise so that you will be distressed.

20:118 Surely, you have (a promise from Allah) that you will neither be hungry in it (paradise) nor you will be naked,

20:119 you will neither suffer from thirst in it nor you will suffer from the sun."

20:120 Then Satan whispered to him saying: "O Adam! Shall I lead you to the tree of Eternity and to a kingdom that will never waste away?"

20:121 Then they both ate from that tree, so their private parts appeared to them, and they began to stick on themselves from leaves of the garden (for covering). Thus Adam disobeyed his Rabb, so he went astray.

20:122 Then (after repentance) his Rabb chose him, Allah turned to him with forgiveness, and gave him guidance.

20:123 (Allah) said: "Get down you both together from here (paradise to earth); some of you are an enemy to some others. If guidance comes to you from me (Allah), then whoever follows my (Allah's) guidance neither will go astray, nor will fall into distress;

20:124 but whoever will turn away from my (Allah's) remembrance, then surely that person will have a life of hardship, and I (Allah) will raise up that person blind on the day of Resurrection."

20:125 That person will say: "O my Rabb! Why have you raised me up blind while indeed I had clear sight (before)?"

20:126 (Allah) will say: "Just as Allah's verses came to you but you disregarded them, so you are neglected today."

20:127 Thus Allah requites the one who transgresses and do not believe in the verses of its Rabb. Surely the punishment of the hereafter is more severe and more lasting.

20:128 Has not Allah guided them (to know) how many generations Allah has destroyed before them and in whose residences they walk? Surely, in these (ruins) there are signs for people of understanding.

20:129 Had it not been for a word that went forth from your Rabb and a term determined, it (judgment) would have been inevitable.

20:130 So you (O Muhammad) bear patiently on what they say. Glorify the praises of your Rabb before sunrise, before sunset, during hours of the night, and glorify at the ends of the day, so that you may become pleased (satisfied).

20:131 Do not strain your eyes (with envy) for what Allah has given for enjoyment to various groups of them (disbelievers), with the luxury of the worldly life Allah may test them in it. The (lawful) provision of your Rabb is better and more lasting.

20:132 Enjoin the prayer on your family, and be patient in it. Allah does not ask you a provision; Allah provides for you. The good end (paradise) is for the pious.

20:133 They say: "Why does he (Muhammad) not bring us a sign from his Rabb?" Has not proof (the Qur'an) came to them which is (contains teachings) of the previous scriptures?

20:134 If Allah had destroyed them with a punishment before this (the Qur'an), surely they would have said: "Our Rabb! If you (Allah) only had sent us a messenger, we would certainly have followed your (Allah's) verses before we were disgraced and humiliated."

20:135 Say (O Muhammad): "Each one (believer and disbeliever) is waiting, so you wait too. Then you shall know who are the owners of the right way and who have been rightly guided."

21. Al-Anbiya' : The Prophets

In the name of Allah, the Gracious, the Merciful

21:1 (The day of) their reckoning draws near for mankind, yet they are heedless and turn away (from warning).

21:2 (Every time) an admonition from their Rabb comes to them as a recent revelation, but they listen to it while they play.

21:3 In a light mood their hearts are occupied (with evil things), and they conceal the private counsels, those who do wrong (say): "Is this (Muhammad) but a human being like you? Will you go to (believe in) magic while you see it?"

21:4 He (Muhammad) said: "My Rabb knows every word spoken in the heavens and the earth. Allah is the All-Hearer, the All-Knower."

21:5 Nay, they say: "(These revelations of the Qur'an are) strange false dreams! Nay, he (Muhammad) has invented it! Nay, he is a poet! Let him then bring us a sign as the ancients (previous prophets) did!"

21:6 Not one town (people) before them believed (though Allah sent signs), which Allah destroyed. Will they then believe?

21:7 Allah did not send before you (O Muhammad) but human to whom Allah revealed. So you ask the people of the reminder (scripture - the Torah and the Gospel) if you do not know.

21:8 Allah did not make them (the messengers) bodies which did not eat food, nor they were immortals.

21:9 Then Allah fulfilled to them the promise. Allah saved them, and those whom Allah willed, but Allah destroyed the extravagant.

21:10 Indeed, Allah has sent down for you (O mankind) a book (the Qur'an) in which there is your reminder (to follow its orders). Will you not then understand?

21:11 How many nations has Allah destroyed who were wrongdoers and raised up (replaced) them with other nations!

21:12 When they perceived that Allah's punishment was coming, behold, they fled from it.

21:13 (They were told): "Do not flee but return to your luxurious of life and to your homes so that you may be questioned."

21:14 They said: "Woe to us! Surely we were wrongdoers."

21:15 Then their cry did not cease till Allah made them as a field that was reaped (all dead).

21:16 Allah has not created the heavens, the earth, and all that lies between them as a game.

21:17 Had Allah intended to take a pastime, surely Allah could have taken it by Allah (only), if Allah was going to do that.

21:18 Nay, Allah has sent down the truth (this Qur'an) against the falsehood so it destroys it, and then it (falsehood) is vanished. Woe to you for that (false deity) which you ascribe.

21:19 To Allah belongs whoever is in the heavens and on earth. Those who are near Allah (the angels), are neither proud from worshiping Allah, nor they are tired (of Allah's worship).

21:20 They (the angels) glorify Allah night and day, they never pause.

21:21 Or have they taken ones worthy of worship from the earth who (has the power to) raise the dead?

21:22 Had there been ones worthy of worship besides Allah in it (heavens and the earth), surely both would have been ruined (by disorder). Glory be to Allah, the Rabb of the Throne (high above all falsehood) that they attribute (to Allah)!

21:23 Allah cannot be questioned as to what Allah does, while they will be questioned.

21:24 Or have they taken other deities for worship besides Allah? Say: "Bring your proof. This (the Qur'an) is a reminder for those who are with me and reminder for those before me." But most of them do not know the truth, so they are reluctant.

21:25 Allah did not send any messenger before you (O Muhammad) but Allah revealed to him (every one saying) that: "There is no one worthy of worship but I (Allah), so worship me (Allah)."

21:26 (After receiving message still) they say: "The Gracious (Allah) has begotten a son." Glory be to Allah! They (angels) are but honored servants.

21:27 They do not speak until Allah has spoken and they act on Allah's command.

21:28 Allah knows what is before them, what is behind them, and they do not intercede except for the one with whom Allah is pleased. They stand in awe from the fear of Allah.

21:29 If anyone of them should say: "Surely I am one worthy of worship besides Allah," then Allah would recompense to hell. Thus Allah recompenses the wrongdoers.

21:30 Have not the disbelievers known that the heavens and the earth were once joined together (as one piece) and then Allah parted them? Allah has made every living thing from water. Will they still not believe?

21:31 Allah has placed firm mountains on the earth lest it should shake with them and Allah placed in them broad passages so that they may be guided.

21:32 Allah has made the heaven a roof, safe, and well guarded. Yet they turn away from its signs.

21:33 It is Allah who has created the night, the day, the sun, and the moon, each in a floating orbit (of their own).

21:34 Allah has not granted immortality to any human being before you (Muhammad), then if you die, will they (disbelievers) live forever?

21:35 Everyone is going to taste death, and Allah will test all of you with evil and with good as a temptation. To Allah you will be returned.

21:36 When you (Muhammad) see those who disbelieve, they do not take you except for mockery (saying): "Is this the one who talks against your deity?" They disbelieve at the mention of the Gracious (Allah).

21:37 Man is a creature of haste (impatient). I (Allah) will show you my (Allah's) signs, so do not ask me (Allah) to hasten.

21:38 They ask: "When will this promise (be fulfilled) if you are truthful?"

21:39 (They would not have asked) if the disbelievers knew the time when they will neither be able to protect their faces from the fire nor their backs, and they will not be helped.

21:40 Nay, it (the fire) will come to them all of a sudden and will perplex them, so they will neither be able to avert it nor they will get any respite.

21:41 Indeed messengers were mocked before you (O Muhammad), but those who mocked were surrounded by what they used to mock at.

21:42 Ask: "Who can protect you in the night and the day from the (punishment of) the Gracious (Allah)?" Nay, but they turn away from the remembrance of their Rabb.

21:43 Or do they have (ones worthy of worship) who can guard them from Allah? They have neither any power to help themselves, nor can they be protected from Allah (Allah's punishment).

21:44 Nay, Allah gave luxuries (of this life to) these people and their forefathers until the life grew long for them. Don't they then see how Allah (gradually) reduces the land (their control) from its all sides? Is it then they who will overcome (be victorious)?

21:45 Say (O Muhammad): "I warn you only by the revelation (from Allah)." But the deaf will not hear the call when they are warned.

21:46 If a breath (minor calamity) of punishment of your Rabb touches them, surely they will cry: "Woe to us! Surely, we were wrongdoers."

21:47 Allah will set up the balances of justice on the day of Resurrection so that no one will be dealt with unjustly at all. If there is (an act as small as the) weight of a mustard seed, Allah will bring it (to account). Allah is sufficient as Reckoner (accountant).

21:48 Indeed Allah granted to Moses and Aaron the criterion (of right and wrong), a shining light (Torah), and a reminder for the pious,

21:49 those who fear their Rabb with unseen while they are afraid of the hour (of Judgment).

21:50 This is a blessed reminder (the Qur'an) which Allah has sent down. Will you then deny it?

21:51 Indeed Allah gave Abraham his guidance from before and Allah was Well-Acquainted with him.

21:52 When he said to his father and his people: "What are these images which you are devoted to it?"

21:53 They said: "We found our forefathers worshipping to them."

21:54 He said: "Indeed you and your forefathers have been in clear error."

21:55 They said: "Have you brought us the truth, or are you one of those who play?"

21:56 He replied: "Nay, your Rabb is the owner of the heavens and the earth, who has created them, and I am one of the witnesses to that.

21:57 By Allah, surely I will plot a plan against your idols after you go away and turn your backs."

21:58 So he made them fragments, except the biggest of them so that they might turn to it.

21:59 (When they retuned and saw their idols) some said: "Who has done this to our deity? Surely he is among the wrongdoers."

21:60 Others said: "We heard a young man talking against them who is called Abraham."

21:61 They said: "Then bring him before the eyes of the people, so that they may witness."

21:62 They asked: "Have you done this to our deity, O Abraham?"

21:63 (Abraham) said: "Nay, this one, the biggest of them did it. Ask them, if they can speak!"

21:64 So they turned to themselves and said: "Surely you are the wrongdoers."

21:65 Then they turned to themselves (and said): "Indeed you (Abraham) know that these (idols) cannot speak!"

21:66 (Abraham) said: "Do you then worship these deities besides Allah, who can neither profit you nor harm you?

21:67 Shame on you and on those deities which you worship besides Allah! Don't you think?"

21:68 They said: "Burn him and help your deity, if you will be doing (any action)."

21:69 (When he was thrown in the fire) Allah commanded: "O fire! Be cool and safe for Abraham!"

21:70 They wanted to harm him, but Allah made them the worst losers.

21:71 Allah rescued him and (his nephew) Lot to the land which Allah has blessed for the worlds.

21:72 Allah bestowed upon him a (son) Isaac and a (grandson) Jacob as an extra. Allah made each one righteous.

21:73 Allah made them leaders to guide (mankind) by Allah's command, Allah revealed to them (how to) do good deeds, establish prayer, give obligatory charity, and they were the worshippers of Allah.

21:74 (Remember) Lot, Allah gave him right judgment, knowledge, and Allah saved him from the town (people) who were doing wicked and filthy deeds. Surely, they were people of evil, wicked.

21:75 Allah admitted him to Allah's Mercy; surely he was of the righteous.

21:76 (Remember) Noah, when he cried (to Allah) previously. Allah answered to him, then saved him, and his family from the great distress.

21:77 Allah helped him against those people who denied Allah's verses. Surely they were an evil people. So Allah drowned (in the great flood) them all.

21:78 (Remember) David and Solomon, when they gave judgment in the case of the field in which the sheep of certain people had pastured (at night) and Allah was witness to their judgment,

21:79 so Allah made Solomon to understand it, Allah gave right judgment, and knowledge. Allah subjected the mountains and the birds to glorify Allah's praises along with David. Allah was the doer (of all these things).

21:80 Allah taught him to make metal coats of mail (for battles) for you to protect you in your fighting. Yet, are you grateful?

21:81 To Solomon (Allah subjected) the strongly raging wind, running by his command towards the land which Allah had blessed. Allah knows everything.

21:82 Some of the devils dived for him (into the sea), did other work besides that, and Allah was guard over them (for him).

21:83 (Remember) Job, when he cried to his Rabb: "Surely the distress (disease) has seized me and Allah is the Merciful of all those who show mercy."

21:84 Allah answered to him, then Allah removed the distress that was with him, Allah restored his family to him (that he had lost) and many more with them as a Mercy from Allah, and as a reminder for those who worship (Allah).

21:85 (Remember) Ishmael, Enoch, and Isaiah: all were from among the patient ones.

21:86 Allah admitted them to Allah's Mercy. Surely, they were of the righteous.

21:87 (Remember) Jonah, when he departed in anger and thought that Allah will not punish him! Then he cried in the darkness that (saying): "There is no one worthy of worship but Allah, Allah is glorified. Truly, I have been from the wrongdoers."

21:88 Allah answered to him and Allah delivered him from the distress. Thus Allah delivers the believers.

21:89 (Remember) Zachariah, when he cried to his Rabb: "O My Rabb! Do not leave me single (childless) and Allah is the best of the inheritors."

21:90 So Allah answered him, Allah bestowed on him John, and Allah cured his wife (to bear a child) for him. Surely, they used to hasten to do good deeds, they used to call on Allah with hope and fear, and they were humble before Allah.

21:91 (Remember) her (Mary) who guarded her chastity, then Allah breathed into her through Allah's spirit (Gabriel), and Allah made her and her son (Jesus) a sign for the worlds.

21:92 Truly! This brotherhood of yours is one religion and Allah is your Rabb, so worship Allah (alone).

21:93 But they have broken up their religion (into sects) among all of them. They shall return to Allah.

21:94 Whoever shall do righteous deeds and is a believer, then those efforts will not be rejected. Surely Allah records all for that person.

21:95 A ban is laid on town (those people) which Allah has destroyed, they shall not return again.

21:96 Until, when Gog and Magog are let loose (from their barrier) and they swiftly swarm down from every mound,

21:97 and the true promise (day of Resurrection) shall draw near (of fulfillment). Then it will be fixed gazes (staring with horror) of the disbelievers. (They will say): "Woe to us! Indeed we were heedless from this; nay we were wrongdoers."

21:98 Certainly! You (disbelievers) and your deities whom you worship besides Allah shall be fuel for hell! You all will enter it.

21:99 If these (deities) were worthy of worship, they would not have entered it (hell), and all of them will abide in it.

21:100 They will be breathing out with deep sighs and roaring in it. They will not hear (anything else) in it.

21:101 Surely, those for whom the good (reward) has preceded from Allah, they will be removed far away from it (hell).

21:102 They shall not hear even the slightest sound of it (hell) and they will abide in the middle of what their souls desire.

21:103 The greatest terror (on the day of Resurrection) will not grieve them, and the angels will meet them (with the greeting): "This is your day which you were promised."

21:104 (Remember) the day when Allah will roll up the heavens like a rolled up scroll for books, just as Allah began the first creation, Allah will repeat it again, and it is a promise upon Allah. Truly, Allah will fulfill it.

21:105 Indeed Allah has written this in the Psalms after the book (Al-Lauh Al-Mahfuz, which is in the heaven with Allah) that Allah's righteous servants shall inherit the land.

21:106 Surely, in this (the Qur'an) indeed there is a plain message for people who worship Allah.

21:107 Allah has not sent you (O Muhammad) but as a Mercy for the worlds.

21:108 Say (O Muhammad): "It is revealed only to me that your one worthy of worship is one Allah. Will you then submit (to Allah's will and become Muslim)?"

21:109 But if they (disbelievers) turn away (from Islam), then say (to them O Muhammad): "I give you a notice (warning) all like. I do not know whether what you are promised (punishment) is near or far.

21:110 Surely, Allah knows from the spoken loud word and Allah knows that which you conceal.

21:111 I do not know, perhaps it (the delay) may be a trial for you, and an enjoyment for a while."

21:112 He (Muhammad) said: "My Rabb, judge us in truth! (O people) our Rabb is the Gracious whose help is sought against that which you attribute!"

22. Al-Hajj : The Pilgrimage
In the name of Allah, the Gracious, the Merciful

22:1 O mankind! Fear your Rabb! Surely, the earthquake of the hour (of judgment) will be a terrible thing.

22:2 On that day, you shall see that every nursing (mother) will forget whoever she was nursing, every pregnant woman will drop her load (miscarriage), and you will see people as if in a drunken state, yet they will not be drunken; but the punishment of Allah will be severe.

22:3 There are some among people who disputes about Allah without knowledge and follows every rebellious devil,

22:4 it is decreed for him (the devil) that whoever follows him; surely will be mislead, and will be guided by him to the punishment of the fire.

22:5 O mankind! If you are in doubt about the Resurrection, then remember, Allah has created you from dust, then from a mixed drops of male and female sexual discharge (sperm), then from a clot (thick coagulated blood), then from a little lump of human flesh formed and unformed (miscarriage), so that Allah may make it clear to you. Allah causes it to remain in the wombs whom Allah wills for an appointed term, then Allah brings you out as infants, then you may reach your age of full strength. Among you there are some who die (young), and among you there are some who are brought back to the miserable (old) age, so that they do not know anything after having known. You see the earth barren, but when Allah sends down water (rain) on it, it is stirred to life; it swells, and puts forth every lovely kind (of growth).

22:6 This is because Allah is the Truth, it is Allah who gives life to the dead, and it is Allah who is Able to do all things.

22:7 Surely, the hour (of Judgment) is coming, there is no doubt about it, and Allah will resurrect those who are in the graves.

22:8 Among people there are those who dispute about Allah, though they have neither knowledge nor guidance, nor a book giving light (from Allah),

22:9 bending things to mislead others from the way of Allah. For such persons, there is disgrace in this world and Allah will make them taste the punishment of burning (fire) on the day of Resurrection,

22:10 that is because of what their hands have sent forth. Surely Allah is not unjust to (Allah's) worshippers.

22:11 Among people there are those who worship Allah on the very edge (in doubt). If good befalls such person, that person is content with it; but if a trial befalls on that person, then the person turns back on its face (reverts back to disbelief after embracing Islam), thus loses both this world and the hereafter. That is a clear loss.

22:12 Then that person calls (other deities) besides Allah which neither hurt, nor profit. That is a deviation far away (from the right way).

22:13 That person calls those who are more likely to harm than profit; certainly an evil patron and certainly an evil friend (chosen for help)!

22:14 Truly, Allah will admit those who believe and do righteous deeds, to the gardens with rivers flow underneath them (paradise). Surely, Allah does what Allah wills.

22:15 Whoever thinks that Allah will not help him (Muhammad) in this world and in the hereafter, let them stretch out a rope to the ceiling (sky) and then let them strangle themselves. Then let them see whether their plan will remove what they rage!

22:16 Thus Allah has sent it (this Qur'an) down as clear verses, and that Allah guides whom Allah wills.

22:17 Surely, those who believe (Muslims), and those who are Jews, the Sabians, the Christians, the Magians, and those who worship others besides Allah, truly Allah will judge between them on the day of Resurrection. Surely! Allah is witness over everything.

22:18 Do you not see that whoever is in the heavens and whoever is on the earth prostrate to Allah, including the sun, the moon, the stars, the mountains, the trees, the animals, and many people? But there are many people on whom the punishment is justified. Those whom Allah disgraces, then there is none for them to honor. Surely! Allah does what Allah wills.

22:19 These 2 opponents (believers and disbelievers) dispute with each other about their Rabb; then those who disbelieve, garments of fire will be cut out for them, boiling water will be poured down over their heads;

22:20 which will melt what is in their bellies and skins;

22:21 and there will be hooked rods of iron (to punish them).

22:22 Whenever with their anguish, they try to get away from there, they will be driven back in it, and (it will be said to them): "Taste the punishment of burning!"

22:23 Truly, Allah will admit those who believe and do righteous good deeds, to gardens with rivers flow underneath (paradise). They will be adorned in them with bracelets of gold and pearls, and their garments will be of silk.

22:24 (Because) they were guided (in this world) to the good words (of Allah) and they were guided to the way of Allah, who is Praise-worthy.

22:25 Surely! Those who disbelieve, hinder people from the way of Allah and from the sacred mosque (at Makkah) which Allah has made open to all people, the local residents and the visitors (from other countries) as equal, and those who incline to evil actions or do wrong in it, Allah will cause them to taste from a painful punishment.

22:26 (Remember) when Allah showed Abraham the site of the sacred house (the Ka'bah at Makkah) (saying) that: "Don't associate anything with me (Allah), sanctify my (Allah's) house for those who make tawaf (go around counterclockwise), those who stand up for prayer, those who bow down, and make prostration;

22:27 and proclaim the pilgrimage to people. They will come to you on foot and on every lean (camel), they will come from every deep (and distant) mountain highway;

22:28 so that they may witness things that benefit them, and mention the name of Allah on appointed days (10-13th days of Dhul-Hijjah) over whatever Allah has provided them from the beast of cattle. Then eat and feed the poor from there who have a very hard time.

22:29 Then let them complete their prescribed duties (of Hajj such as cut hair, take bath), perform their vows, and go around the ancient house (the Ka'bah at Makkah as Tawaf-e-Ziyarah).

22:30 That (prescribed duties of Hajj is the obligation that mankind owes to Allah) is, and those who honor the sacred rites of Allah, it is better for them with their Rabb. The meat of cattle is made lawful to you, except what has already been mentioned to you. So shun the worshipping of idols and shun false statements.

22:31 Be upright to Allah and do not associate partners to Allah. Those who assign partners to Allah, it is as if they had fallen from the sky, and the birds had snatched them, or the wind had thrown them to a far off place,

22:32 and whoever honors the symbols of Allah, then it is truly from the piety of the heart.

22:33 You have in them (cattle for sacrifice) that benefit (such as milk) you for an appointed term, then (afterwards) they are brought for sacrifice to the ancient house (the Ka'bah).

22:34 For every nation Allah has appointed religious ceremonies so that they may mention the name of Allah over the beast of cattle which Allah has given them (for food). Your one worthy of worship is one Allah, to Allah you submit, and (O Prophet) give glad tidings to those who obey Allah with humility;

22:35 those when Allah is mentioned, their hearts are filled with fear; those who are patient on whatever may befall on them (of calamities); who establish prayer, and they spend (in Allah's cause) out of what Allah has provided them.

22:36 The cows, oxen, or camels (offered as sacrifices by the pilgrims), Allah has made them for you as among the symbols of Allah; you have much good in them. So mention the name of Allah over them when they are drawn up in lines (for sacrifice). Then when they are down on their sides (after slaughter), eat from them, and feed the poor people (who does not ask), and the beggar (who asks). Thus Allah has made these animals to you so that you may be grateful.

22:37 Neither their meat nor their blood reaches Allah, but the piety from you reaches Allah. Thus Allah has made these animals to you so that you may magnify Allah for what Allah has guided you. (O Muhammad) give glad tidings to the doers of good.

22:38 Truly, Allah defends those who believe. Surely! Allah does not like any treacherous, ungrateful.

22:39 Permission to fight (against disbelievers) is given to those (believers) against whom fighting is waged because they (believers) are oppressed, and surely, Allah is able to give them (believers) victory-

22:40 those who have been expelled from their homes without just cause only because they said: "Our Rabb is Allah." Had it not been that Allah checked one set of people by another; monasteries, churches, synagogues, and mosques in which the name of Allah is mentioned, much would surely have been pulled down. Surely, Allah will help those who help (Allah's cause). Truly, Allah is All-Powerful, All-Mighty.

22:41 Those who, if Allah gives them power in the land, will establish prayer, pay the obligatory charity, enjoin good, and forbid evil. With Allah rests the final decision of all matters.

22:42 If they deny you (O Muhammad), surely did deny before them, by the people of Noah, Ad, and Thamud;

22:43 and the people of Abraham and the people of Lot;

22:44 and the residents of Midian; and Moses were denied. But Allah granted respite to the disbelievers, then Allah seized them, and how terrible was Allah's punishment.

22:45 Many townships Allah has destroyed while they were wrong-doing. (Even today) they lie with their roofs in ruins, many deserted wells, and lofty (deserted) castles!

22:46 Have they not traveled through the land, and have they no hearts with them to understand or ears to hear (the truth)? Surely, it is not the eyes that grow blind, but it is the hearts which are in the breasts that grow blind.

22:47 They ask you to hasten on the punishment! Allah never fails on Allah's promise. Surely, a day with your Rabb is as a 1,000 years of what you count.

22:48 To many townships I (Allah) gave respite while they were wrong-doing. Then (in the end) I (Allah) seized them. To me (Allah) is the final return (of all).

22:49 Say (O Muhammad): "O mankind! Surely I am a plain warner to you."

22:50 So those who believe and do righteous deeds, for them is forgiveness and generous provision.

22:51 But those who strive against Allah's verses to frustrate people, those will be inmates of the fire of hell.

22:52 Allah did not send a messenger or a prophet before you (O Muhammad), but when he (prophet) did recite the revelation, Satan threw (some falsehood) in his recitation. But Allah abolishes what Satan throws in and then Allah establishes Allah's revelations. Allah is All-Knower, All-Wise.

22:53 Whatever Satan throws in, Allah may make as a trial for those in whose hearts there is a disease (of hypocrisy and disbelief) and whose hearts are hardened. Certainly, the wrongdoers are in an opposition far-off (from the truth),

22:54 so that those who have been given knowledge (may know) that it (this Qur'an) is the truth from your Rabb and thus they may believe in it, and may submit their hearts to it. Surely, Allah is the guide of those who believe to the right way.

22:55 Those who disbelieve will not cease to be in doubt about it (this Qur'an) until the hour comes suddenly upon them, or there comes to them the punishment of the day of disaster.

22:56 The sovereignty on that day will be for Allah. Allah will judge between them. So those who have believed and did righteous deeds will be in the gardens of delight;

22:57 but those who disbelieved and denied Allah's verses, for them will be a humiliating punishment.

22:58 Those who emigrated for the cause of Allah and afterwards were killed or died, surely, Allah will provide a good provision for them. Surely, it is Allah who indeed is the Best of those who provide sustenance.

22:59 Truly, Allah will make them enter an entrance with which they shall be well-pleased, and surely, Allah indeed is All-Knower, All-Forbearing.

22:60 That is so! Whoever retaliates which is equal to the suffering one received and then (again) one is wronged, Allah will surely help that person. Surely! Allah indeed is Lenient, Forgiving.

22:61 That is because Allah merges the night into the day, and merges the day into the night. Surely, Allah is All-Hearer, All-Seer.

22:62 That is because Allah is the truth, and whatever they (polytheists) invoke besides Allah, it is falsehood and that Allah is the Supreme, the Great.

22:63 Don't you see that Allah sends down water (rain) from the sky, and then the earth becomes green? Surely, Allah is Kind and Well-Acquainted with all things.

22:64 To Allah belongs what is in the heavens and all that is on the earth. Surely, Allah is Rich (free of all wants), Praise-worthy.

22:65 Don't you see that Allah has subjected to you (people) what is on the earth, and the ships that sail through the sea by Allah's command? Allah withholds the heaven lest it fall on the earth except by Allah's permission. Surely, Allah is full of Kindness, Merciful for mankind.

22:66 It is Allah, who has given you life, then Allah will cause you to die, and then Allah will again give you life (on the day of Resurrection). Surely! People are ungrateful.

22:67 For every nation Allah has ordained religious ceremonies that they follow it; so let them (the Pagans) not dispute with you in this matter, and invite them to your Rabb. Surely! You (O Muhammad) indeed are on right guidance.

22:68 If they argue with you, then say: "Allah knows best of what you do."

22:69 Allah will judge between you on the day of Resurrection about which you used to differ.

22:70 Don't you know that Allah knows what is in heaven and the earth? Surely, all are (recorded) in a book. Surely! That is easy for Allah.

22:71 Yet, they worship besides Allah what Allah has not sent down with any authority, they have no knowledge about them, and there is no helper for the wrongdoers.

22:72 When Allah's clear verses are recited to them, you will notice denial on the faces of those who disbelieve! They are nearly ready to attack with violence those who recite Allah's verses to them. Say: "Shall I tell you something worse than that? It is the fire (of hell) which Allah has promised to those who disbelieve, and worst indeed will be that destination!"

22:73 O mankind! An example has been coined, so listen to it (carefully). Surely! Those whom you call on besides Allah, can not create a fly even if they combine together for it. If a fly snatches away a thing from them, they will have no power to release it from the fly. So weak are both the seeker and the sought.

22:74 They have not estimated Allah's rightful estimate. Surely, Allah is All-Strong, All-Mighty.

22:75 Allah chooses messengers from angels and from human. Surely, Allah is All-Hearer, All-Seer.

22:76 Allah knows what is before them and what is behind them. To Allah all matters return (for decision).

22:77 O you who believe! Bow down, prostrate yourselves, worship your Rabb, and do good so that you may be successful.

22:78 Strive hard in Allah's cause truthfully. Allah has chosen you (to convey Allah's Message), and has not laid upon you any hardship in religion, it is the religion of your father Abraham. It is Allah who has named you Muslims before and in this (the Qur'an), so that the messenger (Muhammad) may be a witness over you and you be witnesses over mankind! So establish prayer, give obligatory charity, and hold fast to Allah, Allah is your Rabb, what an excellent Rabb and what an Excellent Helper!

23. Al-Muminun : The Believers
In the name of Allah, the Gracious, the Merciful

23:1 Indeed successful are the believers;

23:2 those who are submissive in their prayers;

23:3 and those who turn away from evil vain talk;

23:4 and those who are doers of obligatory charity;

23:5 and those who guard their chastity;

23:6 except from their wives or what their right hands (legally) possess, verily they are free from blame.

23:7 But whoever seeks beyond that, and then those are the transgressors.

23:8 Those who are true to their trusts and to their covenants,

23:9 and those who strictly guard over their prayers.

23:10 These are the inheritors

23:11 who will inherit the paradise. They shall reside in it forever.

23:12 Indeed Allah created human out of extract of clay,

23:13 then Allah made it semen drop in a safe (womb of woman) lodging,

23:14 then Allah created the drop into a clot, then Allah created the clot into a little lump of flesh, then Allah created the little lump of flesh into bones, then Allah clothed the bones with flesh, and then Allah brought it forth as another creation. So blessed be Allah, the Best of creators.

23:15 Then after that, surely you will die;

23:16 then again, surely you will be resurrected on the day of Resurrection.

23:17 Indeed Allah has created above you 7 heavens, and Allah is not unaware from the creation.

23:18 Allah sends down water (rain) from the sky in due measure, and Allah gives it lodging in the earth, and surely Allah is able to take it away,

23:19 then Allah brings forth for you by it gardens of date-palms and grapes, in it is much fruit, and from it you eat,

23:20 and a tree (olive) that springs forth from Mount Sinai that grows oil, and it is seasoning for the eaters.

23:21 Surely! In the cattle there is indeed a lesson for you. Allah gives you to drink (milk) of that which is in their bellies. There are numerous benefits for you in them, and of them you eat,

23:22 and on them and on ships you are carried.

23:23 Indeed Allah sent Noah to his people, and he said: "O my people! You worship Allah! You have no other one worthy of worship but Allah. Will you not then be afraid?"

23:24 But the chiefs of those who disbelieved among his people said: "This is no more but a human being like you, he seeks to make himself superior to you. If Allah willed, Allah surely could have sent down angels; we did not hear such a thing among our forefathers."

23:25 (Some of them said): "He is not but a human in whom there is madness, so wait for him until a while."

23:26 He (Noah) said: "O my Rabb! Help me because they deny me."

23:27 So Allah revealed to him (saying) that: "Construct the ship under Allah's eyes and under Allah's revelation. Then, when Allah's command comes and the water gushes forth from the oven, then take on board of each kind 2 spouses (male and female), and your family, except those of them against whom the word has already gone forth. Do not address Allah in favor of those who have done wrong. Surely, they are to be drowned."

23:28 When you have embarked on the ship, you and whoever is with you, say: "All the praises are due to Allah, who has saved us from the people who are oppressors."

23:29 Say: "My Rabb! Cause me to land at a blessed landing place, for Allah is the best of those who bring to land (safe)."

23:30 Surely, in this there are indeed verses (lessons); truly Allah is putting people to test.

23:31 Then after them, Allah created another generation (people of Ad).

23:32 Allah sent to them a messenger from among them (saying): "You worship Allah! You have no other one worthy of worship but Allah. Will you not then be afraid?"

23:33 The chiefs of his people, who disbelieved and denied the meeting in the hereafter, and Allah had given them luxuries and comforts of this worldly life, said: "This is not but a human being like you, he eats of that which you eat, and he drinks of what you drink.

23:34 If you obey a human being like yourself, then surely, you will be losers.

23:35 Does he promise you that when you will die and become dust and bones; you shall come out alive (resurrected)?

23:36 Far, very far is that which you are promised.

23:37 It is not but our life of this world! We die and we live! We will not be resurrected!

23:38 He is not but a man who has invented a lie against Allah, and we are not going to believe in him."

23:39 He said: "O my Rabb! Help me because they deny me."

23:40 Allah said: "In a little while, they are sure to be regretful."

23:41 So an awful cry overtook them in justice, and Allah made them as rubbish of dead plants. So gone is the people who are wrongdoers.

23:42 Then, Allah created other generations after them,

23:43 no nation can precede their term nor can they delay it,

23:44 then Allah sent Allah's messengers in succession, whenever their messenger came to a nation, they denied him, so Allah made some of them follow others (to destruction), and Allah made them as true stories (for mankind). So gone is the people who do not believe.

23:45 Then Allah sent Moses and his brother Aaron with Allah's verses and clear authority,

23:46 to Pharaoh and his chiefs, but they behaved arrogantly and they were self-exalting people.

23:47 Then they said: "Shall we believe in 2 human beings like ourselves and whose people are our captives?"

23:48 So they denied them (Moses and Aaron) and became of those who were destroyed.

23:49 Indeed Allah gave Moses the scripture, so that they may be guided.

23:50 Allah made the son of Mary (Jesus) and his mother as a sign, and Allah gave them refuge to a high ground, a place of rest, and flowing streams.

23:51 O messengers! Eat of lawful foods and do righteous deeds. Surely! I (Allah) am Well-Acquainted with what you do.

23:52 Surely! This religion is one religion, and I (Allah) am your Rabb, so fear me (Allah).

23:53 But they have broken their religion among them into sects, each group rejoices in what is with them.

23:54 So leave them in their error for a time.

23:55 Do they think what Allah gives them with wealth and children,

23:56 Allah hastens to them with good things? But they do not perceive.

23:57 Surely! Those who live in awe for fear of their Rabb;

23:58 and those who believe in the verses of their Rabb,

23:59 and those who do not join anyone in worship (as partners) with their Rabb;

23:60 and those who give charity from whatever they give and their hearts are full of fear, because they are sure to return to their Rabb.

23:61 It is these who hasten in the good deeds and they are first in (attaining) them.

23:62 Allah does not burden any person except according to its capacity, with Allah is a record which speaks the truth, and they will not be wronged.

23:63 But their hearts are covered from this (the Qur'an) and for them are other evil deeds besides what they are doing

23:64 until, when Allah grasps those of them who lead a luxurious life with punishment, behold! They make humble invocation with a loud voice.

23:65 (Allah will say): "Do not invoke loudly this day! Certainly, you shall not be helped by Allah."

23:66 Indeed my (Allah's) verses used to be recited to you, but you used to turn back on your heels (denying them)

23:67 in pride, talking evil about it (the Qur'an) by night.

23:68 Do they not ponder the word, or has there come to them what had not come to their forefathers?

23:69 Or is it that they do not recognize their messenger (Muhammad) so they deny him?

23:70 Or they say: "There is madness in him?" But he brought them the truth but most of them are reluctant to the truth.

23:71 If the truth had been in accordance with their desires, surely, the heavens and the earth, and whoever is therein would have been corrupted! But Allah has brought them their reminder, but they turn away from their reminder.

23:72 Or is it that you (O Muhammad) ask them for wages? But the recompense of your Rabb is better, and Allah is the Best of the sustainers.

23:73 Certainly, you (O Muhammad) call them to the right way.

23:74 Surely, those who do not believe in the hereafter are indeed deviating from the way.

23:75 Though Allah had Mercy on them and removed what distress is on them, still they would stubbornly persist in their transgression, wandering blindly.

23:76 Indeed Allah seized them with punishment, but neither did they humble themselves to their Rabb, nor did they invoke with submission to Allah.

23:77 Until, when Allah opens for them a gate of severe punishment, then lo! They will be plunged into it.

23:78 It is Allah, who has created for you hearing, sight, and hearts; you give little thanks!

23:79 It is Allah who has created you on the earth, and to Allah, you shall be gathered back.

23:80 It is Allah who gives life and causes death, and in Allah's control is the alternation of night and day. Will you not then understand?

23:81 But they say just like what their forefathers said.

23:82 They said: "When we are dead and have become dust and bones, shall we be resurrected indeed?

23:83 Surely, we have been promised this, we and our forefathers before us! This is not but the tales of the ancients!"

23:84 Say: "To whom belongs the earth and whatever is in it? If you know!"

23:85 They will say: "(It is) Allah's!" Say: "Will you not then remember?"

23:86 Say: "Who is the Rabb of the 7 heavens and Rabb of the great Throne?"

23:87 They will say: "(It is) for Allah." Say: "Then will you not fear Allah?"

23:88 Say: "In whose hand is the sovereignty of everything? Allah protects all, and is there any protector against Allah, if you know?"

23:89 They will say: "(It is) for Allah." Say: "How then are you deceived (from the truth)?"

23:90 But nay, Allah has brought them the truth, and surely, they (disbelievers) are liars.

23:91 Allah did not beget any son, nor is there anyone worthy of worship along with Allah. Behold, (if there had been many deities) each would have taken away what each had created, and some of them would have tried to overcome others! Glorified is Allah above all that they attribute to Allah!

23:92 Allah knows all of the unseen and the seen! Exalted is Allah over all that they associate as partners to Allah!

23:93 Say (O Muhammad): "My Rabb! If Allah would show me that with which they are being threatened,

23:94 my Rabb! Then do not put me amongst the people who are the wrongdoers."

23:95 Indeed Allah is able to show you (O Muhammad) that with which Allah has threatened them.

23:96 Repel evil with that which is better. Allah is Best-Acquainted with what they utter.

23:97 Say: "My Rabb! I seek refuge with Allah from the whisperings of the devils.

23:98 I seek refuge with Allah, My Rabb! lest they come near me,

23:99 until, when death comes to one of them who says: "My Rabb! Send me back,

23:100 so that I may do good in that which I have left behind!" No! It is but a word that one speaks it, and behind them is a barrier until the day when they will be resurrected.

23:101 Then, when the trumpet is blown in, there will be no kinship among them that day, nor will they ask of one another.

23:102 Then those who are heavy in their scales (of good deeds), they are the successful.

23:103 Those who are light in their scales, they are those who lost their own selves in hell, they will abide.

23:104 The fire will burn their faces, and they will grin (smile broadly) in it with displaced lips (disfigured).

23:105 (Allah will remind): "Were not my (Allah's) verses (this Qur'an) recited to you, and then you used to deny them?"

23:106 They will say: "Our Rabb! Our misfortune overwhelmed us, and we became erring people.

23:107 Our Rabb! Bring us out of this; then if we ever return to evil, then indeed we shall be wrongdoers."

23:108 (Allah) will say: "You stay in it with shame! Don't speak to me (Allah)!

23:109 Surely! There was a party of my (Allah's) servants who used to say: 'Our Rabb! We believe, so forgive us, and have Mercy on us, for Allah is the best of those who show mercy!'

23:110 But you took them for a laughing stock, until they made you forget my (Allah's) remembrance while you used to laugh at them!

23:111 Surely! Allah has rewarded them this day for what they kept patience, they are indeed the successful."

23:112 (Allah) will say: "How many years did you stay on the earth?"

23:113 They will say: "We stayed a day or part of a day. So ask of those who keep account (angels)."

23:114 (Allah) will say: "You stayed not but a little, if that you had known!

23:115 Did you think that Allah had created you in play (without purpose), and that you would not be returned to Allah?"

23:116 So Exalted is Allah, the true King, there is no one worthy of worship but Allah, the Rabb of the Supreme Throne!

23:117 Those who invoke any other one worthy of worship besides Allah, of which there is no proof, and then surely their reckoning is with their Rabb. Surely! The disbelievers will not be successful.

23:118 Say (O Muhammad): "My Rabb! Forgive and have Mercy, and you (Allah) are the best of those who show Mercy!"

24. An-Nur : The Light

In the name of Allah, the Gracious, the Merciful

24:1 This is a chapter (of the Qur'an) which Allah has sent down, which Allah has enjoined, and Allah has revealed in it clear verses that you may remember.

24:2 The woman and the man, who are guilty of illegal sexual intercourse, flog each of them with 100 lashes. Let not pity with them withhold you in the religion of Allah, if you believe in Allah and the last day. Let a party of the believers witness their punishment.

24:3 The adulterer shall not marry any but an adulteress or an idolatress and an adulteress shall not marry but an adulterer or an idolater. Such a thing is forbidden to the believers.

24:4 Those who accuse chaste women (of adultery), and can not produce 4 witnesses (to support allegation), then flog them with 80 lashes, and do not accept their testimony forever, they are indeed the disobedient (to Allah)

24:5 except those who repent thereafter and do righteous deeds; so surely, Allah is Forgiving, Merciful.

24:6 Those who accuse their own wives but have no witnesses for them except themselves, then the testimony of each of them is made to swear 4 testimonies by Allah that he is one of those who speaks the truth,

24:7 and the 5th (testimony) is that the curse of Allah is on him, if he is of those who tells a lie (against her).

24:8 But the punishment (of stoning to death) shall avert from her, if she testifies 4 testimonies by Allah that he (her husband) is one of those who tells a lie,

24:9 and the 5th (testimony) is that the anger of Allah be upon her if he (her husband) is one of those who speaks the truth.

24:10 Had it not been for the grace of Allah and Allah's Mercy on you (that you have a solution of this situation), and that Allah is the one who accepts repentance, the All-Wise.

24:11 Surely! Those who brought forth the slander (against Aisha, the wife of the Prophet) are a group among you. Consider it is not a bad thing for you but it is a good (lesson) for you. Every person among them (who took part) has earned its sin, and as for the one among them who had the greater share (leading part) in it, shall have a great punishment.

24:12 Why then, when you heard it (the slander), did not the believing men and believing women of their own people think good and say: "This (charge) is an obvious lie?"

24:13 Why did they not produce 4 witnesses for it? Since they (the slanderers) have not produced the witnesses, then they are the liars with Allah.

24:14 Had it not been for the grace of Allah and Allah's Mercy to you in this world and in the hereafter, a great punishment would have touched you for what you had spoken,

24:15 when you propagated it with your tongues, and uttered with your mouths about which there was no knowledge for you. You took it as a little thing while it was very great (serious offence) with Allah.

24:16 Why did you not, when you heard it, say: "It is not right for us to speak of this, glory be to you (Allah)! This is a great lie."

24:17 Allah warns you that you never ever repeat (mistake) like this, if you are believers.

24:18 Allah has made the verses clear for you, and Allah is the All-Knower, the All-Wise.

24:19 Surely, those who like that (the crime of) slander should be propagated among those who believe, they will have a painful punishment in this world and in the hereafter. Allah knows and you do not know.

24:20 Had it not been for the grace of Allah and Allah's Mercy on you (this slander would have very bad impact). Allah is full of Kindness, Merciful.

24:21 O you who believe! Do not follow the footsteps of Satan. Whoever follows the footsteps of Satan, then surely he commands to commit indecency, and evil deeds. Had it not been for the grace of Allah and Allah's Mercy on you, no one of you would ever have been purified from sins. But Allah purifies whom Allah wills, and Allah is All-Hearer, All-Knower.

24:22 Let not those among you with blessings and wealth swear to withhold help to their kinsmen, the poor, and the emigrants in the way of Allah. Let them pardon and forgive. Don't you love that Allah should forgive you? Allah is Forgiving, Merciful.

24:23 Surely, those who accuse chaste but careless believing (women), are cursed in this world and in the hereafter, and there will be a great punishment for them.

24:24 On the day when their tongues, their hands, and their legs will bear witness against them as to what they used to do.

24:25 On that day, Allah will pay them their recompense in full, and they will know that Allah is the one who manifests the Truth.

24:26 Bad women are for bad men and bad men are for bad women. Good women are for good men and good men are for good women. Those good people are innocent of what they (slanderers) say; there is forgiveness, and generous provision for them.

24:27 O you who believe! Do not enter houses other than your houses until you have asked permission and greeted by their people in it; that is better for you so that you may remember.

24:28 If you do not find anyone in it, then do not enter them (houses) until permission has been given to you. If you are asked to return (go back), then go back; for it is purer for you. Allah is All-Knower of what you do.

24:29 There is no sin on you if you enter (without permission) houses not inhabited, in which there is some usefulness for you. Allah knows what you reveal and what you conceal.

24:30 Tell the believing men to lower their gaze and protect their private parts. That is purer for them. Surely, Allah is All-Aware of what they do.

24:31 Tell the believing women to lower their gazes, protect their private parts, not expose their beauty except what is apparent (like hands or eyes) of it; let them draw their veils over their hearts and not reveal their beauty except to their husbands, their fathers, their husband's fathers, their sons, their husband's sons, their brothers or their brother's sons, or their sister's sons, or their Muslim women, or the female captives whom their right hands possess, or old male servants who lack vigor of men (sexual desire), or children who have no sense of the sexual parts of women. Do not let them strike their feet so as to reveal what they hide of their beauty. All of you repent to Allah, O you believers so that you may become successful.

24:32 Marry the single (man who has no wife and woman who has no husband) among you and the pious of your male captives and female captives. If they are poor, Allah will enrich them out of Allah's bounty. Allah is All-Sufficient, All-Knower.

24:33 Let those who do not find (financial means to) marry be chaste until Allah enriches them out of Allah's bounty. Those captives who seek a writing (of setting free) whom you possesses, give them in writing, if you find good in them, and give them from Allah's wealth which Allah has bestowed upon you. Do not force your maid captives into prostitution in order that you may seek gain of the worldly life, if they desire chastity. If anyone compels them (to prostitution), then surely after their compulsion, Allah will be Forgiving, Merciful (to those who are forced).

24:34 Indeed Allah has sent down clear verses to you, examples of those who passed away before you, and an admonition for the pious.

24:35 Allah is the light of the heavens and the earth. The parable of Allah's light is as a niche within it is a lamp, the lamp (is enclosed) in a glass, the glass as if it were a brilliant star, it is lit from oil of a blessed olive tree which is neither of the east nor of the west, its oil would almost glow forth, though no fire touched it. Light upon light! Allah guides to Allah's light whom Allah wills. Allah sets forth such parables for mankind, and Allah is All-Knower of everything.

24:36 (This light is found) in houses which Allah has permitted that they be built, and Allah's name is remembered in them; glorify Allah in them in the mornings and in the evenings,

24:37 by such people whom neither trade nor sale diverts them from the remembrance of Allah, nor from establishing the prayer, nor from giving the obligatory charity. They fear the day when the hearts and the eyes will be overturned,

24:38 so that Allah may reward them according to the best of what they have done, and add for them even more out of Allah's grace. Allah provides without measure to whom Allah wills.

24:39 As for those who disbelieve, their deeds are like a mirage in a desert. The thirsty one thinks it to be water, until when the person comes near it, finds it to be nothing, but finds Allah who pays (disbeliever's) due (punishment). Allah is swift in taking account.

24:40 Or (another parable for a disbeliever) is like the darkness in a vast deep sea, overwhelmed with waves topped by waves, topped by dark clouds, (layers of) darkness upon darkness, if a person stretches out one's hand, one can hardly see it! The one for whom Allah has not made light, there is no light for that person.

24:41 Don't you (O Muhammad) see that it is Allah who is glorified by whoever is in the heavens and the earth, and the birds with wings outspread (in flight)?

Each one knows its prayer and glorification, and Allah is All-Aware of what they do.

24:42 To Allah belongs the sovereignty of the heavens and the earth, and to Allah is the return of all.

24:43 Don't you see that Allah drives the clouds, then joins them together, then makes them into a heap of layers, and you see the rain comes forth from between them? Allah sends down hail like mountains from the sky, and strikes with them whom Allah wills, and averts from them whom Allah wills. The flash of its lightning nearly takes away the sight.

24:44 Allah causes to alternate the night and the day. Truly, there is indeed a lesson in this for those who have insight.

24:45 Allah has created every moving living creature from water. Of them there are some who creep on their bellies, of them some who walk on 2 legs, and of them some who walk on 4. Allah creates what Allah wills. Surely! Allah is powerful over everything.

24:46 Indeed Allah has sent down clarifying verses (the Qur'an). Allah guides whom Allah wills to the right way.

24:47 They (hypocrites) say: "We believe in Allah and the messenger (Muhammad) and we obey," then some of them turn away thereafter, and those are not believers.

24:48 When they are called to Allah and Allah's messenger (Muhammad) to judge between them, then some of them turn away.

24:49 But if the truth is with them, they come to him (Muhammad) with submission.

24:50 Is there a disease in their hearts? Or do they doubt or fear lest Allah and Allah's messenger (Muhammad) should wrong them in judgment? Nay, it is they who are the wrongdoers.

24:51 The only saying of the believers, when they are called to Allah and Allah's messenger (Muhammad) to judge between them is that they say: "We hear and we obey." Such are the successful.

24:52 Whoever obeys Allah and Allah's messenger (Muhammad), fears Allah, and keeps its duty to Allah, such are the successful.

24:53 They swear by Allah their strong oaths if you would order them, they would leave (homes to fight in Allah's cause). Say (O Muhammad): "Do not swear; this obedience is better known. Surely, Allah knows well what you do."

24:54 Say: "Obey Allah and obey the messenger. But if you turn away, then only on him (Muhammad) is what is placed on him (to convey Allah's message), and on you what is placed on you. If you obey him, you shall be guided. It is not on the messenger except clear conveying."

24:55 Allah has promised those among you who believe and do righteous deeds that Allah will certainly make them vicegerent in the earth as Allah made vicegerent to those before them, and that Allah will establish for them their religion which Allah has chosen for them (Islam), and that Allah will surely give them a safe security in exchange of their fear provided they worship Allah and do not associate anything with Allah. Those who disbelieve after that, they are the disobedient.

24:56 Establish prayers, pay obligatory charity, and obey the messenger (Muhammad) so that you may be treated with Mercy (from Allah).

24:57 Do not consider those who disbelieve that they can escape in the land. Their abode shall be the fire and worst indeed is that destination.

24:58 O you who believe! Let your servants and those among you who have not come to the age of puberty, should ask your permission (before they come to your presence) on 3 occasions: before Fajr (morning) prayer, while you put off your clothes for the noonday (rest) and after the Isha (late-night) prayer. These 3 times are for your privacy. There is no sin on you or on them afterwards to go around visiting one another. Thus Allah makes the verses clear to you. Allah is All-Knower, All-Wise.

24:59 When the children among you attain the age of puberty, let them seek permission as those elders who seek permission. Thus Allah makes clear for you Allah's verses. Allah is All-Knower, All-Wise.

24:60 For the past child-bearing (elderly) women who do not expect marriage, it is no sin on them if they discard their clothes without showing their beauty. But it is better for them that they refrain (do not discard their outer clothing). Allah is All-Hearer, All-Knower.

24:61 There is no restriction on the blind, nor restriction on the lame, nor restriction on the sick, nor on yourselves, to eat from your houses, or houses of your fathers, or houses of your mothers, or houses of your brothers, or houses of your sisters, or houses of your paternal uncles, or houses of your paternal aunts, or houses of your maternal uncles, or houses of your maternal aunts, or that house you hold its keys, or your friend. There is no sin on you that you eat together or apart. But when you enter the houses, then greet one another with a greeting (of peace) from Allah, blessed and good. Thus Allah makes clear the verses for you so that you may understand.

24:62 Only the true believers are those who believe in Allah and Allah's messenger (Muhammad), and when they are with him on collective matter, they do not go until they have asked his permission. Surely! Those who ask your permission, they are those who believe in Allah and Allah's messenger. So if they ask your permission for some of their affairs, give permission to whom you wish from them, and ask Allah for their forgiveness. Truly, Allah is Forgiving, Merciful.

24:63 Do not make the calling of the messenger (Muhammad) among you as your calling of one another. Truly, Allah knows those of you who slip away (hide) under shelter (behind others). Let those be beware who oppose his (Muhammad's) orders, should an affliction befall them or a painful punishment befall them.

24:64 Certainly, all that are in the heavens and the earth belong to Allah. Surely, Allah knows what you are on it (condition) and the day when they will be brought back to Allah, and then Allah will inform them of what they did. Allah is All-Knower of everything.

25. Al-Furqan : The Criterion

In the name of Allah, the Gracious, the Merciful

25:1 Blessed is Allah who has sent down the criterion (of right and wrong, i.e. this Qur'an) to Allah's servant (Muhammad), so that he may be a warner to the worlds.

25:2 Allah is the one to whom belongs the dominion of the heavens and the earth, and Allah has not begotten a son and has no partner in the dominion. Allah has created everything, and has measured it exactly according to its due measurements.

25:3 Yet they (disbelievers) have taken besides Allah ones worthy of worship, who created nothing but are themselves created, and neither they possess harm nor benefit for themselves, nor they possess power to cause death, nor can give life, nor able to raise the dead to life.

25:4 Those who disbelieve say: "This (the Qur'an) is nothing but a lie that he (Muhammad) has invented it and other have helped him at it, in fact they have produced a wrong thing and a lie."

25:5 They say: "These are the tales of the ancients which he has written down, and they are dictated to him morning and afternoon."

25:6 Say: "Allah has sent it (the Qur'an) down who knows the secrets of the heavens and the earth. Truly, Allah is Forgiving, Merciful."

25:7 They say: "Why does this messenger (Muhammad) eat food, and walk about in the markets (like ourselves)? Why not an angel is sent down to him to be a warner with him?

25:8 Or why has not a treasure been granted to him, or why has he not a garden from where he could eat?" The wrongdoers say: "You follow none but a man bewitched."

25:9 See how they apply examples to you! As they have gone astray and they cannot find a right way.

25:10 Blessed is Allah who, if wishes, will assign you better than that: gardens under which rivers flow (paradise) and will assign you palaces (in paradise).

25:11 Nay, they deny the hour (the day of Resurrection), and Allah has prepared for those who deny the hour, a flaming fire (hell).

25:12 When it (hell) shall come in their sight from a far place, they will hear it's raging and roaring.

25:13 When chained together, they will be thrown into a narrow place thereof; they will call in it for destruction (death).

25:14 (They will be told): "You do not call today for one destruction, but call for many destructions."

25:15 Ask (them O Muhammad): "Is this (punishment in hell) better or the paradise of Eternity which has been promised to the pious people? It will be for them as a reward and as a final destination,

25:16 for them there will be all that they desire in it and they will abide there forever. It is a promise upon your Rabb that must be fulfilled."

25:17 On the day Allah will gather them and those whom they worshipped besides Allah. Allah will ask: "Was it you who misled my (Allah's) servants or did they astray (themselves from) the right way?"

25:18 They (believing partners) will say: "Glory be to Allah! It was not proper for us to take any protectors besides Allah, but Allah gave them and their forefathers comfort (of the world) until they forgot the warning, and became a lost people."

25:19 Thus surely, they (believing partners) will deny you (polytheists) regarding what you say today. Then you shall neither avert (the punishment), nor get help. Those among you did wrong; Allah will make them taste the great punishment.

25:20 Allah has never sent before you (O Muhammad) any of the messengers but surely, they ate food and walked in the markets. Allah has made some of you as a trial for others. Now, will you have patience? Your Rabb is All-Seer of everything.

25:21 Those who do not expect a meeting with Allah (who deny the day of Resurrection), say: "Why are not the angels sent down to us, or why do we not see our Rabb?" Indeed they think arrogantly of themselves and are scornful with great pride.

25:22 On the day they will see the angels; no glad tidings will be for the criminals that day. Angels will say: "(All glad tidings) are strictly forbidden (for you)."

25:23 Allah will turn to whatever deeds they (disbelievers) did, and Allah will make them (deeds) as scattered floating particles of dust for them.

25:24 The residents of paradise on that day will have the best abode and the finest place for relax.

25:25 (Remember) the day when the heaven shall be rent asunder with clouds, and the angels will be sent down with a grand descending.

25:26 The sovereignty on that day will be the true (sovereignty), belongs to the Gracious (Allah), and it will be a hard day for the disbelievers.

25:27 (Remember) the day when the wrongdoer will bite on its hands saying: "Oh! Would that I had taken a way with the messenger (Muhammad)!

25:28 Oh! Woe to me! Would that I had never taken so-and-so as a friend!

25:29 Indeed they led me astray from the reminder (this Qur'an) after when it had come to me." Satan is ever a deserter to human in the hour of need.

25:30 The messenger (Muhammad) will say: "O my Rabb! Surely, my people took this Qur'an as deserted (neither learned nor acted upon it)."

25:31 Thus Allah has made for every Prophet an enemy among the criminals. But your Rabb is sufficient as a Guide and Helper.

25:32 Those who disbelieve say: "Why is not the Qur'an revealed to him all at once?" Thus (it was sent down in parts) so that Allah may strengthen your hearts thereby. Allah has recited it in recitation (gradually in stages). (It was revealed to Muhammad in 23 years).

25:33 They do not bring to you example (to oppose or find fault in you or in this Qur'an), but Allah reveals to you the truth, and better explanation.

25:34 Those who will be gathered on their faces to hell, they will be in an evil state, for they had lost the right way.

25:35 Indeed Allah gave Moses the scripture (the Torah), and placed his brother Aaron with him as a helper;

25:36 and Allah said: "Go you both to the people who have denied Allah's verses." Then Allah destroyed them with complete destruction.

25:37 The people of Noah, when they denied the messengers, Allah drowned them, and Allah made them an example for mankind. Allah has prepared a painful punishment for the wrongdoers.

25:38 (Also) Ad and Thamud, and the residents of Ar-Rass, and many generations in between (were destroyed).

25:39 For each of them, Allah has put forward examples, and each of them Allah has brought to ruin destruction.

25:40 Indeed they (disbelievers) have passed by the town (of Prophet Lot) on which the evil rain was rained. Did they not see it (with their own eyes)? But they were not used to expect (believed) any Resurrection.

25:41 When they see you (O Muhammad), they treat you not but in mockery (saying): "Is this the one whom Allah has sent as a messenger?

25:42 He (Muhammad) would have nearly misled us from our deities, had it not been that we were patient and constant in our (worship)!" They will know when they see the punishment; they will realize who actually is most astray from the right way!

25:43 Have you (O Muhammad) seen one who has taken its own desire as worthy of worship? Would you then be a Guide to that person?

25:44 Or do you think that most of them hear or understand? They are nothing but like cattle; nay they are even farther astray from the way.

25:45 Have you not seen how your Rabb spread the shadow? If Allah willed, Allah could have made it still. Then Allah has made the sun a guide over it,

25:46 then Allah withdraws it to Allah with a gradual withdrawal.

25:47 It is Allah who makes the night a covering for you, and the sleep as rest, and makes the day to get up.

25:48 It is Allah who sends the winds as heralds of glad tidings before Allah's Mercy, and Allah send down pure water (rain) from the sky,

25:49 so that Allah may give life thereby to a dead land, and Allah gives to drink thereof many cattle and men that Allah has created.

25:50 Indeed Allah has distributed it (water) amongst them in order that they may remember (the grace of Allah), yet most people refuse except disbelief (ingratitude).

25:51 Had Allah willed, Allah could have raised a warner in every town,

25:52 so do not obey the disbelievers, but strive against them with it (the Qur'an), with utmost endeavor.

25:53 It is Allah who has let the 2 seas merge, one palatable and sweet, and the other salt and bitter; and Allah has set a barrier and a suppressed partition between them.

25:54 It is Allah who has created human from water, and has appointed for them blood relationships and marriage relationships. Your Rabb is All-Powerful.

25:55 Yet they (disbelievers) worship besides Allah which can neither benefit them nor harm them, and the disbelievers are helpers (of the Satan) against their Rabb.

25:56 Allah has not sent you (O Muhammad) but as a bearer of glad tidings and a warner.

25:57 Say: "I do not ask you any reward for this (that I have brought the Qur'an from my Rabb and its preaching, etc) except that whoever wills, may take a way to its Rabb."

25:58 Put your trust (O Muhammad) in the ever-Living (Allah) who does not die, glorify Allah's praises, and Allah alone is the All-Knower of the sins of Allah's servants,

25:59 who created the heavens and the earth and all that is between them in 6 days. Then Allah rose over the Throne (that suits Allah's majesty). The Gracious (Allah)! Ask Allah (O Muhammad), as Allah is All-Knower of everything.

25:60 When it is said to them: "Prostrate yourself to the Gracious (Allah)," they ask: "What is the Gracious? Shall we fall down in prostration because you (O Muhammad) command us?" It increases dislike in them.

25:61 Blessed is Allah who has placed big stars in the sky, has placed therein a great lamp (sun) and a moon giving light.

25:62 It is Allah who has put the night and the day in succession, for those who desire to remember or desire to show their gratitude.

25:63 The servants of the Gracious (Allah) are those who walk on the earth in humility, and when the foolish address them, they say: "peace,"

25:64 and those who spend the night before their Rabb, prostrating and standing;

25:65 and those who say: "Our Rabb! Avert from us the punishment of hell. Surely! Its punishment is an inseparable, permanent punishment,

25:66 indeed it (hell) is evil as an abode and as a place to reside,"

25:67 and those who, when they spend, neither are extravagant nor stingy, but there is a medium (way) between those (extremes);

25:68 and those who neither invoke with Allah another one worthy of worship, nor kill the soul which Allah has forbidden, except for just cause, nor commit illegal sexual intercourse. Those who do this shall receive the punishment;

25:69 the punishment will be doubled for them (on the) day of Resurrection, and they will abide in it in disgrace;

25:70 except those who repent, believe, and do righteous deeds; for them Allah will change their sins into good deeds, and Allah is Forgiving, Merciful.

25:71 Those who repent and do righteous deeds, then surely they repent to Allah (with true) repentance.

25:72 Those who do not bear witness to falsehood, and if they pass by some evil play or evil talk, they pass by with dignity.

25:73 Those who, when they are reminded of the verses of their Rabb, they do not fall deaf and blind upon them.

25:74 Those who say: "Our Rabb! Bestow on us from our wives and our offspring comfort of our eyes, and make us leaders for the pious."

25:75 Those will be rewarded with the highest place (in paradise) because they kept patience. They shall meet with greetings in it and the word of peace.

25:76 (They shall) abide therein; excellent it is as an abode, and as a place to reside.

25:77 Say (O Muhammad to the disbelievers): "My Rabb pays no attention to you except for your invocation (to Allah). But indeed you have denied (Allah), so the punishment will be necessary."

26. Ash-Shuara' : The Poets
In the name of Allah, the Gracious, the Merciful

26:1 Ta-Seen-Mim.

26:2 These are the verses of the clear book (the Qur'an).

26:3 It may be that you (O Muhammad) are going to kill yourself (with grief) because they do not become believers.

26:4 If Allah wills, Allah could send down a verse to them from the heaven so their necks would bend to it in humility.

26:5 Never comes to them any reminder from the Gracious (Allah) as a recent revelation, but they have been turning away from it.

26:6 So they have denied (this Qur'an), then the news will come to them of what they were mocking at.

26:7 Don't they observe to the earth to see how much Allah has caused every good pair to grow in it?

26:8 Surely, in this is a sign, yet most of them are not believers.

26:9 Surely, your Rabb! Allah is truly the All-Mighty, the Merciful.

26:10 (Remember) when your Rabb called Moses (saying): "You go to the people who are wrongdoers,

26:11 the people of Pharaoh. Will they not fear Allah?"

26:12 Moses said: "My Rabb! Surely, I fear that they will deny me,

26:13 my breast straitens, and my tongue does not express well. So send Aaron.

26:14 They have a charge of crime (man-slaughter) against me, and I fear they will kill me."

26:15 (Allah) said: "Nay! Go, you both with Allah's signs. Surely! Allah will be with you, listening.

26:16 Go to Pharaoh both of you and say: We are the messengers of the Rabb of the worlds.

26:17 So (send to go) with us the children of Israel."

26:18 Pharaoh said to Moses: "Did we not bring you up among us as a child? You stayed with us many years of your life.

26:19 You did what you did (crime of killing a man). You are one of the ungrateful."

26:20 Moses said: "I did it then when I was from the misguided.

26:21 So I fled from you when I feared you. But my Rabb has granted me right judgment, and made me one of the messengers.

26:22 This is a favor with which you admonish me, that you have enslaved the children of Israel."

26:23 Pharaoh said: "Who is the Rabb of the worlds?"

26:24 Moses said: "Rabb of the heavens and the earth, and all that is between them, if you are seeking to be convinced with certainty."

26:25 Pharaoh said to those around him: "Don't you hear (what he says)?"

26:26 Moses said: "(Allah is) your Rabb and the Rabb of your forefathers!"

26:27 Pharaoh said: "Surely, your messenger who has been sent to you is a madman!"

26:28 Moses said: "Rabb of the east and the west, and all that is between them, if you did but understand!"

26:29 Pharaoh said: "If you choose one worthy of worship other than me, I will certainly put you among the prisoners."

26:30 Moses said: "Even if I bring you something clear?"

26:31 Pharaoh said: "Bring it forth, if you are from the truthful!"

26:32 So (Moses) threw his stick, and behold, it was a clear serpent.

26:33 Then he drew out his hand, and behold, it became white (bright) to all beholders!

26:34 Pharaoh said to the chiefs around him: "Surely! This is indeed a well-versed sorcerer,

26:35 he wants to drive you out of your land by his sorcery. Now what is it that you advice?"

26:36 They said: "Put him off and his brother (for a while), and send callers to the cities;

26:37 they will bring to you every well-versed sorcerer."

26:38 So the sorcerers were assembled at a fixed time on an appointed day.

26:39 It was said to the people: "Will you assemble?

26:40 So that we may follow the sorcerers if they are the winners."

26:41 When the sorcerers arrived, they said Pharaoh: "Is there a reward for us if we are the winners?"

26:42 Pharaoh said: "Yes, and surely then you will be of those brought near (to me)."

26:43 Moses said to them: "Throw what you are going to throw!"

26:44 So they threw their ropes and their sticks, and said: "By the might of Pharaoh, it is we who will be the winners!"

26:45 Then Moses threw his stick, and behold, it swallowed up all that they falsely showed!

26:46 The sorcerers fell down prostrate,

26:47 saying: "We believe in the Rabb of the worlds,

26:48 the Rabb of Moses and Aaron."

26:49 (Pharaoh) said: "You have believed in him before I give permission to you. Surely, he is your chief who has taught you magic! So surely, you shall come to know. I will cut off your hands and your legs on opposite sides, and I will crucify you all."

26:50 They said: "No harm (don't care)! Surely, we are going to return to our Rabb (anyway).

26:51 Surely! We hope that our Rabb will forgive us our sins, as we are the first of the believers (in Moses)."

26:52 Allah revealed to Moses saying: "Depart by night with my (Allah's) servants, surely, you will be pursued."

26:53 Then Pharaoh sent callers to the cities,

26:54 (saying): "Surely! These are (indeed but) a small band,

26:55 surely, they have enraged us;

26:56 and surely we are all assembled, well prepared."

26:57 So, Allah made them leave from their gardens, water springs,

26:58 treasures, and honorable places.

26:59 Thus Allah caused the children of Israel to inherit such things.

26:60 So they (people of Pharaoh) pursued them at sunrise.

26:61 When the 2 hosts saw (each other), the companions of Moses said: "Surely we are to be overtaken."

26:62 Moses said: "Nay, surely! With me is my Rabb, Allah will guide me."

26:63 Then Allah revealed to Moses (saying): "Strike the sea with your stick." It parted, and each part (of the sea water) became like the huge mountain.

26:64 Then Allah brought near (to that sea) the others (Pharaoh and his army).

26:65 Allah saved Moses and all those with him,

26:66 then Allah drowned the others.

26:67 Surely! In this is indeed a sign, yet most of them are not believers.

26:68 Surely, your Rabb! Allah is truly the All-Mighty, the Merciful.

26:69 Recite to them the story of Abraham,

26:70 when he (Abraham) said his father and his people: "What do you worship?"

26:71 They said: "We worship idols, and we remain devoted to them."

26:72 He said: "Do they hear you when you call (on them)?

26:73 Or do they benefit you or do they harm you?"

26:74 They said: "Nay, but we found our forefathers doing so."

26:75 He said: "Do you observe which you have been worshipping,

26:76 you and your forefathers?

26:77 Surely! They are enemies to me, except the Rabb of the worlds;

26:78 who has created me, and it is Allah who guides me.

26:79 It is Allah who feeds me and gives me to drink,

26:80 when I am ill, it is Allah who cures me;

26:81 who will cause me to die, then will bring me to life (again);

26:82 who, I hope that Allah will forgive me my faults on the day of recompense."

26:83 Abraham prayed: "My Rabb! Bestow wisdom on me, join me with the righteous,

26:84 grant me an honorable mention in later generations,

26:85 make me one of the inheritors of the paradise of delight,

26:86 forgive my father, surely he is of the erring,

26:87 do not disgrace me on the day when all creatures will be resurrected,

26:88 the day when neither wealth nor sons will avail,

26:89 except the one who will bring a clean heart to Allah,

26:90 paradise will be brought near to the pious,

26:91 the hellfire will be placed in full view for the erring,

26:92 and it will be said to them: "Where are those (false deities) that you used to worship,

26:93 instead of Allah? Can they help you or help themselves?"

26:94 Then they will be thrown on their faces into it (fire), they are those who were in error,

26:95 the hosts (soldiers) of Satan together,

26:96 they will say while they argue in it,

26:97 (saying): "by Allah, we were truly in a clear error,

26:98 when we held you (false deities) as equals (in worship) with the Rabb of the worlds.

26:99 None has brought us into error except the criminals.

26:100 Now we have no intercessors,

26:101 nor a close friend (to help us).

26:102 If we had a chance (to return to the world), we would be among the believers!"

26:103 Surely! In this narration there is indeed a sign, yet most of them are not believers.

26:104 Surely, your Rabb, Allah is truly the All-Mighty, the Merciful.

26:105 The people of Noah denied the messengers.

26:106 When their brother Noah said to them: "Will you not fear (Allah)?

26:107 Surely I am a trustworthy messenger to you,

26:108 so fear Allah, and obey me.

26:109 I do not ask you any reward for it (my message), my reward is not but from the Rabb of the worlds,

26:110 so fear Allah and obey me."

26:111 They said: "Shall we believe in you, when the lowest (of the people) follow you?"

26:112 He said: "What knowledge I have of what they used to do?

26:113 Their account is with my Rabb, if you could know.

26:114 I am not going to drive away the believers.

26:115 I am not but a plain warner."

26:116 They said: "If you do not cease, O Noah! You will surely be among those stoned (to death)."

26:117 He said: "My Rabb! Surely, my people have denied me.

26:118 Therefore judge between me and them with fair judgment, and save me and those of the believers who are with me."

26:119 So Allah saved him and those with him in the laden ship,

26:120 then Allah drowned the rest (disbelievers) thereafter.

26:121 Surely, in this is indeed a sign, yet most of them are not believers.

26:122 Surely! Your Rabb, Allah is indeed the All-Mighty, the Merciful.

26:123 Ad (people) denied the messengers.

26:124 When their brother Hud said to them: "Will you not fear Allah?

26:125 Surely! I am a trustworthy messenger to you.

26:126 So fear Allah, and obey me.

26:127 I do not ask you any reward for it, my reward is from the Rabb of the worlds.

26:128 Do you build landmark on every high palace to play for fun?

26:129 Do you take for yourselves palaces (fine buildings) as if you will reside therein forever?

26:130 When you seize anyone, you seize that person as tyrants.

26:131 So fear Allah, and obey me.

26:132 Fear Allah who has aided you with all (good things) that you know.

26:133 Allah has aided you with cattle, children,

26:134 gardens, and springs.

26:135 Surely, I fear for you the punishment of a great day."

26:136 They said: "It is the same to us whether you preach or you are not of those who preach.

26:137 This is nothing but the customs of the ancients.

26:138 We are not going to be punished."

26:139 So they denied him, and Allah destroyed them. Surely! In this is indeed a sign, yet most of them are not believers.

26:140 Surely! Your Rabb, Allah is indeed the All-Mighty, the Merciful.

26:141 Thamud (people) denied the messengers.

26:142 When their brother Saleh said to them: "Will you not fear Allah?

26:143 Surely I am a trustworthy messenger to you.

26:144 So fear Allah, and obey me.

26:145 I do not ask any reward for it (my message); my reward is from the Rabb of the worlds.

26:146 Will you be left secure in that which you have here (forever)?

26:147 Gardens, springs,

26:148 cornfields, and date-palms with its soft flowering branches,

26:149 you carve houses in the mountains skillfully?

26:150 So fear Allah, and obey me.

26:151 Do not follow the command of the wasters,

26:152 who make mischief in the land, and do not reform."

26:153 They said: "Surely you are only of those bewitched!

26:154 You are not but a human being like us. Then bring us a sign if you are of the truthful."

26:155 He (Saleh) said: "This is a she-camel (Allah sent as you asked); it has a right to drink water and you have a right to drink water on a known day.

26:156 Do not touch her with harm, lest the punishment of a great day may seize you."

26:157 But they killed her, and then they became regretful,

26:158 so the punishment overtook them. Surely, in this is indeed a sign, yet most of them are not believers.

26:159 Surely! Your Rabb, Allah is indeed the All-Mighty, the Merciful.

26:160 The people of Lot denied the messengers.

26:161 When their brother Lot said to them: "Will you not fear Allah?

26:162 Surely! I am a trustworthy messenger to you.

26:163 So fear Allah, and obey me.

26:164 I do not ask of you any reward for it (my message), my reward is from the Rabb of the worlds.

26:165 Will you go into the males (to fornicate) of the mankind,

26:166 and leave those whom Allah has created for you to be your wives? Nay, you are a transgressing people!"

26:167 They said: "If you do not cease, O Lot! Surely, you will be one of those who are expelled!"

26:168 He said: "I am, indeed of those who disapprove with severe anger and fury.

26:169 My Rabb! Save me and my family from what they do."

26:170 So Allah saved him and all his family,

26:171 except an old woman (his wife) among those who remained behind.

26:172 Then afterward Allah destroyed the others.

26:173 Allah rained on them a rain (of punishment). Evil was the rain which fell on those who had been warned.

26:174 Surely, in this is indeed a sign, yet most of them are not believers.

26:175 Surely! Your Rabb, Allah is indeed the All-Mighty, the Merciful.

26:176 The residents of Al-Aiyka (a garden with thick trees near Midian) denied the messengers.

26:177 When Shuaib said to them: "Will you not fear Allah?

26:178 I am a trustworthy messenger to you.

26:179 So fear Allah, and obey me.

26:180 I do not ask of you any reward for it (my message), my reward is from the Rabb of the worlds.

26:181 Give full measure, and do not be among those who cause loss (to others by fraud).

26:182 Weigh with the just straight balance

26:183 and neither defraud people by reducing their things, nor do evil in the land making corruption.

26:184 Fear Allah who created you and the generations before you."

26:185 They said: "Surely you are one of those bewitched!

26:186 You are not but a human being like us and surely, we think that indeed you are one of the liars!

26:187 So cause a piece of the heaven to fall on us, if you are of the truthful!"

26:188 He said: "My Rabb is Best Knower of what you do."

26:189 But they denied him, so the punishment of the day of shadow (cloud carrying Allah's punishment) seized them, indeed that was the punishment of a great day.

26:190 Surely, in this is indeed a sign, yet most of them are not believers.

26:191 Surely! Your Rabb, Allah is indeed the All-Mighty, the Merciful.

26:192 Truly, this (the Qur'an) is a revelation of the Rabb of the worlds.

26:193 The trustworthy spirit (Gabriel) has brought down

26:194 upon your heart (O Muhammad) so that you may be one of the warners

26:195 in the plain Arabic language.

26:196 Surely, it (the Qur'an) has the scriptures of former people.

26:197 Is it not a sign to them that the learned scholars knew it of the children of Israel?

26:198 If Allah had revealed it (this Qur'an) to any of the non-Arabs,

26:199 who had recited it (in Arabic) to them, they would still not have believed in it.

26:200 Thus Allah has caused it (disbelief) to enter in the hearts of the criminals.

26:201 They will not believe in it until they see the painful punishment;

26:202 it will come to them suddenly while they do not perceive it.

26:203 Then they will say: "Can we be given respite?"

26:204 Do they wish to hasten on Allah's punishment?

26:205 Have you thought if Allah does let them enjoy for years,

26:206 and afterwards comes to them what (punishment) they are promised,

26:207 of what avail will their past enjoyment be to them?

26:208 Allah never destroyed a township without sending its warners,

26:209 by way of reminder (in advance), and Allah has never been unjust.

26:210 It is not the devils who have brought it (this Qur'an) down,

26:211 neither it would suit them, nor they can produce it.

26:212 Surely, they have been removed far from hearing it.

26:213 So do not invoke with Allah another one worthy of worship lest you be among those who receive punishment.

26:214 Warn your tribe (O Muhammad) of near relatives

26:215 and lower or put down your wing (be kind and humble) to those of the believers who follow you,

26:216 then if they disobey you, say: "Verily, I am not responsible for what you do."

26:217 Put your trust in the Mighty, the Merciful,

26:218 who sees you (O Muhammad) when you stand up (at night in prayers),

26:219 and see your movements among those who fall prostrate.

26:220 Surely! Allah is the All-Hearer, the All-Knower.

26:221 Shall I inform you (O people!) upon whom the devils descend?

26:222 They descend on every lying, sinner,

26:223 who gives ear (to the devils), most of them are liars,

26:224 as for the poets, the erring ones follow them.

26:225 Don't you see that they are in every valley, they roam about

26:226 and that they say what they do not do?

26:227 Except those who believe, do righteous deeds, remember Allah much, and vindicate themselves after they have wronged. Those who do wrong (will come to know) what overturning they will be overturned.

27. An-Naml : The Ant

In the name of Allah, the Gracious, the Merciful

27:1 Ta-Seen. These are verses of the Qur'an, a clear book;

27:2 a guide, and glad tidings for the believers,

27:3 those who establish the prayer, give the obligatory charity, and believe with certainty in the hereafter.

27:4 Surely, those who do not believe in the hereafter, Allah has made their deeds seem fair to them, so that they wander about blindly.

27:5 They are those for them there will be an evil punishment (in this world). They will be the greatest losers in the hereafter.

27:6 Surely, you (O Muhammad) are being taught the Qur'an from the One who is All-Wise, All-Knower.

27:7 (Remember) when Moses said to his family: "Surely! I have seen a fire, I will bring you some information from it, or I will bring you a burning brand so that you may warm yourselves."

27:8 But when he came to it, he was called (by a voice) that: "Blessed is Allah who is in the fire, and whoever is around it! Glory be to Allah, the Rabb of the worlds.

27:9 O Moses! Surely! It is Allah, the All-Mighty, the All-Wise.

27:10 Throw down your stick!" But when he saw it moving as if it were a snake, he turned in flight, and did not even look back. (It was said): "O Moses! Do not fear, surely! The messengers do not fear in front of me (Allah),

27:11 except the one who has done wrong and afterwards even if that person changes evil for good, then surely, Allah is Forgiving, Merciful.

27:12 Now put your hand into your bosom, it will come out (shining) white without any harm. These are among the 9 verses (you will take) to Pharaoh and his people, and surely, they are not pious people."

27:13 But when Allah's verses came to them, clear to see, they said: "This is a clear magic."

27:14 They rejected them (verses) wrongfully and arrogantly, though their own selves were convinced of them. So see how the end of the evil-doers was.

27:15 Indeed Allah gave knowledge to David and Solomon, and they said: "All the praises are to Allah, who has preferred us above many of Allah's believing servants!"

27:16 Solomon inherited (the knowledge of) David. He said: "O mankind! We have been taught the language of birds and on us has been bestowed from every thing. Surely, this indeed is grace evident (from Allah)."

27:17 Solomon gathered his hosts of jinns, people, birds, and they were set in battle order,

27:18 till, when they came to the valley of the ants, one ant said: "O ants! Enter your residences, lest Solomon and his hosts crush you (by their feet) while they do not perceive."

27:19 So he (Solomon) smiled laughing at its speech and said: "My Rabb! Bestow upon me power that I may thank you (Allah) for favors, which you (Allah) have bestowed on me and on my parents, so that I may do righteous deeds that will please (you) Allah, and admit me by your (Allah's) Mercy among your (Allah's) righteous servants."

27:20 He inspected the birds, and said: "What is the matter that I do not see the hoopoe (old world bird) or is he among the absentees?

27:21 I will surely punish him with severe punishment, or slaughter him, unless he brings me a clear reason (for absence)."

27:22 But he (the hoopoe) did not stay long, he (came up and) said: "I have just found (the knowledge of a thing) which you have not found. I have come to you from Sheba with true news.

27:23 Surely I found a woman ruling over them, and she has been given from every thing, and she has a great throne.

27:24 I found her and her people prostrating themselves before the sun instead of Allah, Satan has made their deeds seem fair to them, and has barred them from (Allah's) way, so they are not guided,

27:25 they do not prostrate themselves before Allah, who brings out the hidden thing in the heavens and the earth, and knows what you conceal and what you reveal.

27:26 Allah, there is no one worthy of worship but Allah, the Rabb of the Supreme Throne!"

27:27 (Solomon) said: "We shall see whether you speak the truth or you are of the liars.

27:28 Go with this letter of mine, and deliver it to them, then bring back from them, and see what answer they return."

27:29 She (the queen) said: "O chiefs! Surely! A noble letter has been delivered to me,

27:30 surely it is from Solomon, and surely it reads: In the name of Allah, the Gracious, the Merciful.

27:31 (It reads) Do not be exalted against me, but come to me as Muslims."

27:32 She said: "O chiefs! Advise me in my case. I do not decide any case till you are present."

27:33 They said: "We have power and great strength, and the matter is for you to command; so think what you will command."

27:34 She said: "Surely! When the kings enter a town, they spoil it, and make the most honorable of its people the lowest. Thus they always do.

27:35 But surely I will send to them a present, and see with what answer the messengers return."

27:36 So when (the envoys of the Queen with the present) came to Solomon, he said: "Will you help me in wealth? What Allah has given me is better than that which Allah has given you! Nay, you rejoice in your gift!

27:37 Go back to them (your people). (If your people do not submit) surely we shall come to them with army which they will never be able to resist, we shall drive them out from there (land) in disgrace, and they will be humiliated."

27:38 (When Solomon heard that the Queen of Sheba was coming in submission) he said: "O chiefs! Which of you can bring me her throne before they come to me as Muslims?"

27:39 A strong one from the jinns said: "I will bring it to you before you rise from your place (council). Surely, I am indeed strong, trustworthy for such work."

27:40 One with whom was the knowledge of the scripture said: "I will bring it to you before your eyesight returns to you (within twinkling of an eye)!" Then when he (Solomon) saw it placed before him, he said: "This is from the grace of my Rabb to test me whether I am grateful or ungrateful! Whoever is grateful, indeed is grateful for oneself, and whoever is ungrateful (should know that) certainly, my Rabb is Rich, Bountiful."

27:41 Then he said: "Disguise for her throne so that we may see whether she will be guided (able to recognize her throne), or she will be of those who are not guided."

27:42 So when she came, it was said (to her): "Is your throne like this?" She said: "It is as though it were the same. Knowledge was bestowed on us in advance of this, and we have become Muslims (submitted to Allah)."

27:43 Other deities which she used to worship besides Allah has prevented her (from Islam), indeed she was of a disbelieving people.

27:44 It was said to her: "Enter the palace." (The floor was glass surface with water underneath it). But when she saw it, she thought it was a pool, and she (pulled up her clothes) uncovering her legs. Solomon said: "Surely, it is a palace (with a glass surface and water underneath it) traced smooth with glass." She said: "My Rabb! Surely, I have wronged myself, and I submit (accept Islam) with Solomon to Allah, the Rabb of the worlds."

27:45 Indeed Allah sent to Thamud their brother Saleh, saying: "Worship Allah." Then look! They became 2 parties (believers and disbelievers) quarreling with each other.

27:46 He said: "O my people! Why do you seek to hasten the evil (Allah's punishment) before the good (Allah's Mercy)? Why don't you seek the forgiveness of Allah, so that you may be treated with mercy?"

27:47 They said: "We consider bad luck from you and those with you." He said: "Your luck is with Allah; in fact, you are a people that are being tested."

27:48 There were in the city 9 men (leaders) who made mischief in the land, and they would not reform.

27:49 They said: "Swear one to another by Allah so that we shall surely make a night attack on him and his family, and afterwards we will surely say to his near relatives: we did not witness the destruction of his family, and surely! We are truthful."

27:50 So they plotted a plot, and Allah planned a plan, while they did not perceive.

27:51 Thus see how the end of their plot was! Surely! Allah destroyed them and their nation, all together.

27:52 These are their houses in ruin, for what they did wrong. Surely, in this is indeed a sign for people who know.

27:53 Allah saved those who believed, and used to fear Allah.

27:54 (Remember) Lot! When he said to his people: "Do you commit indecency while you see?

27:55 Why do you come to men with lust instead of women? Nay, but you are a people who are ignorant."

27:56 There was no answer by his people except that they said: "Drive out the family of Lot from your city. Surely, they are a people who are clean!"

27:57 So Allah saved him and his family, except his wife. Allah destined her to be of those who remained behind.

27:58 Allah rained down on them a rain (of stones). So evil was the rain of those who were warned.

27:59 Say (O Muhammad): "All praise is to Allah, and peace be on Allah's servants whom Allah has chosen! Is Allah better, or what you ascribe as partners (to Allah)?"

27:60 Is not Allah (better than false deities) who has created the heavens and the earth, and sends down from the sky water (rain) for you and Allah causes to grow gardens with it full of beauty and delight? It is not in your ability that you cause their trees to grow. Is there any one worthy of worship besides Allah? Nay, but they are a people who ascribe equals (to Allah)!

27:61 Is not Allah who has made the earth as a fixed abode, has placed rivers in its midst, has placed firm mountains for it, and has set a barrier between the 2 seas (of salt and sweet water)? Is there any one worthy of worship besides Allah? Nay, but most of them do not know.

27:62 Is not Allah who responds to the distressed one, when one calls Allah, who removes the evil, and makes you inheritors of the earth (generations after generations)? Is there any one worthy of worship besides Allah? Little is that you remember!

27:63 Is not Allah who guides you in the darkness of the land, the sea, and who sends the winds as heralds of glad tidings before Allah's Mercy? Is there any one worthy of worship besides Allah? High exalted is Allah above all that they associate as partners (to Allah)!

27:64 Is not Allah who originates creation, then repeats it, and who provides you from heaven and earth? Is there any one worthy of worship besides Allah? Say: "Bring your proofs if you are truthful."

27:65 Say: "No one in the heavens and the earth has the knowledge of the unseen except Allah, nor can they perceive when they shall be resurrected."

27:66 Nay, their knowledge does not reach to the hereafter. Nay, they are in doubt about it. Nay, they are blind about it.

27:67 Those who disbelieve say: "When we and our forefathers have become dust, shall we really be brought forth (again from dead)?

27:68 Indeed we were promised this to us and our forefathers before. Surely, this is nothing but tales of the ancient people."

27:69 Say to them (O Muhammad): "Travel in the land and see what has been the end of the criminals (who disobeyed Allah)."

27:70 Neither grieve over them, nor be in distress because of what they plot.

27:71 They (disbelievers) say: "When will this promise (be fulfilled), if you are truthful?"

27:72 Say: "Perhaps that which you wish to hasten on, may be close behind you."

27:73 Surely, your Rabb is full of Grace for mankind, yet most of them do not give thanks.

27:74 Surely, your Rabb knows what their hearts conceal and what they reveal.

27:75 There is nothing hidden in the heaven and the earth, but is recorded in a clear book.

27:76 Surely, this Qur'an narrates to the children of Israel most of that in which they differ.

27:77 Truly, it (this Qur'an) is guidance and a Mercy for the believers.

27:78 Surely, your Rabb will decide between them (various sects) by Allah's judgment. Allah is the All-Mighty, the All-Knower.

27:79 So put your trust in Allah; surely, you (O Muhammad) are on the clear truth.

27:80 Surely, you can neither make the dead hear, nor can you make the deaf hear the call when they flee turning their backs,

27:81 nor can you lead the blind out of their error; you can not make to hear except those who believe in Allah's verses, and who have submitted as Muslims.

27:82 When the word (of punishment) is fulfilled against them, Allah will bring out for them a beast from the earth, which will speak to them because people did not believe in Allah's verses.

27:83 (Remember) the day when Allah will gather out of every nation a troop of those who denied Allah's verses, and they shall be driven (to the place of reckoning),

27:84 until when they all come (before their Rabb), Allah will say: "Did you deny Allah's verses when you did not comprehend them by knowledge? Or what you used to do?"

27:85 The word (of punishment) will be fulfilled against them, because they have done wrong, and they will not be able to speak (to defend themselves).

27:86 Don't they see that Allah has made the night for them to rest in it, and the day to give them light? Surely, in this are verses for people who believe.

27:87 (Remember) the day on which the trumpet will be blown in and all who are in the heavens and all who are on the earth, will be terrified except the one whom Allah wills. All shall come to Allah humbled.

27:88 You will see the mountains and think them solid, but they shall pass away as the passing away of the clouds. Such is the work of Allah who perfected every thing; surely, Allah is Well-Acquainted with all what you do.

27:89 Those who bring good deeds shall be rewarded with better than it, and they will be safe from the terror on that day.

27:90 Those who brings an evil deed, they will be cast down on their faces in the fire. (It will be said to them): "Are you being recompensed except what you used to do?"

27:91 Indeed I (Muhammad) have been commanded to worship the Rabb of this city (Makkah), who has made it sacred and to whom belongs everything. I have been commanded to be from among the Muslims,

27:92 and to recite the Qur'an. So whoever receives guidance then surely will receive it for one's own good, and whoever goes astray, say: "Surely, I am one of the warners."

27:93 Say (O Muhammad): "All the praises are to Allah. Allah will show you Allah's verses, and you shall recognize them. Your Rabb is not unaware of what you do."

28. Al-Qasas : The Narration
In the name of Allah, the Gracious, the Merciful

28:1 Ta-Seen-Meem.

28:2 These are the verses of the clear book.

28:3 Allah recites to you of the news of Moses and Pharaoh in truth, for the people who believe.

28:4 Surely, Pharaoh exalted himself in the land, divided its people into sects, oppressed one group among them, killed their sons, and spared their females. Surely, he was of those who committed great sins.

28:5 Allah wished to do a favor to those who were oppressed in the land, to make them rulers, to make them the inheritors,

28:6 to establish them in the land, and to let Pharaoh, Haman, and their hosts receive from them that which they feared.

28:7 Allah inspired to the mother of Moses, (saying): "Suckle him (Moses), but if you fear for him, then cast him into the river, and do not fear or grieve. Surely! Allah will bring him back to you and will make him one of the messengers."

28:8 Then the family of Pharaoh picked him up (from river), that he might become an enemy for them and (a cause of) grief. Surely! Pharaoh, Haman and their hosts were sinners.

28:9 The wife of Pharaoh said: "(This is) a comfort of the eye for me and for you. Do not kill him, perhaps that he may be of benefit to us, or we may adopt him as a son." They did not perceive (the result of that).

28:10 The heart of the mother of Moses became empty (from worry, except the thought of Moses). Surely, she was very near to disclose him (that the child was her son), had Allah not strengthened her heart with faith so that she might remain as one of the believers.

28:11 She said to his (Moses') sister: "Follow him." So she watched him from a far place, while they did not perceive.

28:12 Allah had already forbidden for him other suckling mothers, until she (sister came and) said: "Shall I direct you to the people of a family who will care for him for you, and they will look after him in a good manner?"

28:13 Thus Allah restored him to his mother so that her eye might be delighted not grieved and that she might know that the promise of Allah is true. But most of them do not know.

28:14 When he attained his full strength and became perfect (in manhood), Allah bestowed on him judgment and knowledge. Thus Allah rewards the good doers.

28:15 He entered the city at a time when its people were unaware, and he found 2 men fighting – one was of his party (from the children of Israel), and the other one was of his foes. (The man) of his party asked him for help against the one who was of his foe, so Moses struck him with his fist and killed him. He said: "This is the work of Satan; surely, he is a plain misleading enemy."

28:16 He said: "My Rabb! Surely, I have wronged myself, so forgive me." Then Allah forgave him. Surely, Allah is the Forgiving, the Merciful.

28:17 He said: "My Rabb! After this with which you (Allah) have favored me, I shall never be a helper for the criminals!"

28:18 So he became afraid in the city (waiting for his punishment) and was looking around, when suddenly the man who had sought his help yesterday, called him for his help again. Moses said to him: "Surely, you are a plain misguided person!"

28:19 Then when he decided to seize the man who was an enemy to both of them, the man said: "O Moses! Do you want to kill me as you killed a man yesterday? You only want to become a tyrant in the land, and you do not want to be of those who do right."

28:20 Then a man came running from the farthest end of the city. He said: "O Moses! Surely, the chiefs are taking counsel together about you to kill you, so escape. Truly, I am one of the good advisers to you."

28:21 So he escaped from there with fear to look around. He said: "My Rabb! Save me from the wrongdoers!"

28:22 When he went towards (the city of) Midian, he said: "It may be that my Rabb will guide me to the right way."

28:23 When he arrived at the water well of Midian, he found a group of men watering (their flocks), and he found 2 women besides them who were keeping back (their flocks). He said: "What is the matter with you?" They said: "We cannot water (our flocks) until the shepherds take away (their flocks). Our father is a very old man."

28:24 So he watered (their flocks) for them, then he turned back to shade, and said: "My Rabb! Truly, I am in need of whatever good you (Allah) bestow on me!"

28:25 Then one of the 2 women came to him walking with shy. She said: "Surely, my father is calling you so that he may reward you for that you watered for us." When he came to him and narrated the story to him, he said: "Do not fear. You have escaped from the wrongdoers."

28:26 One of them (2 women) said: "O my father! Hire him! Surely, the best that you can hire who is strong, the trustworthy."

28:27 He said (to Moses): "Surely, I intend to wed to you one of these 2 daughters of mine with the condition that you serve me for 8 years, but if you complete 10 years, then it will be a favor from you. I do not want to make it difficult for you. You will find me, if Allah wills, one of the righteous."

28:28 He (Moses) said: 'That (is settled) between me and you. Whichever of the 2 terms I fulfill, let there be no injustice on me. Allah is the surety over what we say."

28:29 When Moses fulfilled the term and was traveling with his family, he saw a fire in the direction of the mount Tur. He said to his family: "Wait, surely, I have seen a fire; perhaps I may bring from there some information to you, or a burning brand of fire that you may warm yourselves."

28:30 So when he reached there (the fire), he was called from the right side of the valley, in the blessed place from the tree, (saying): "O Moses! Surely! I am Allah, the Rabb of the worlds!

28:31 Throw your stick!" But when he saw it moving as if it were a snake, he turned in flight and did not look back. (Allah said): "O Moses! Draw near and do not fear. Surely, you are of those who are secure.

28:32 Put your hand in your bosom, it will come out (shinning) white without any harm, and draw your hand to you (whenever needed to be free) from fear. These are 2 evidences from your Rabb to Pharaoh and his chiefs. Surely, they are rebellious people.

28:33 He said: "My Rabb! Surely, I have killed a man from them and I fear that they will kill me.

28:34 My brother Aaron, he is more eloquent in speech than me, so send him with me as a helper to confirm me. Surely! I fear that they will deny me."

28:35 Allah said: "I (Allah) will strengthen your arm with your brother and give power to both of you so that they shall not reach you. (Proceed) with Allah's signs. You 2 and those who follow you will be the victors."

28:36 When Moses came to them (Pharaoh and his chiefs) with Allah's clear signs, they said: "This is nothing but invented magic. We never heard this from our forefathers."

28:37 Moses said: "My Rabb knows the one best who comes with guidance from Allah, and who will have the happy end in the hereafter. Surely, the wrongdoers will not be successful."

28:38 Pharaoh said: "O chiefs! I do not know that you have any one worthy of worship other than me. O Haman! Kindle for me (a fire) on clay (to bake bricks) and set up a lofty tower for me so that I may look at the deity of Moses; and surely, I think that he (Moses) is one of the liars."

28:39 He and his soldiers were arrogant in the land without right, and they thought that they would not return to Allah.

28:40 So Allah seized him and his soldiers, and Allah threw them in the sea (and drowned them). So behold (O Muhammad) how was the end of the wrongdoers?

28:41 Allah made them leaders who invite (people) to the fire, and on the day of Resurrection, they will not be helped.

28:42 Allah made a curse to follow them in this world, and on the day of Resurrection, they will be among the despised.

28:43 Indeed Allah gave Moses the scripture (the Torah) after Allah had destroyed the previous generations as enlightenment for people, guidance, and a mercy so that they may remember.

28:44 You (O Muhammad) were not present on the western side (of the mount) when Allah made the commandment clear to Moses and you were not among the witnesses.

28:45 Allah created many generations (after Moses) and long time has passed over them. You (O Muhammad) were not a resident among the people of Midian, reciting Allah's verses to them. But it is Allah who is sending (you the news).

28:46 You (O Muhammad) were not at the side of the Tur mount when Allah called (Moses); but (provided you with news) as a Mercy from your Rabb so that you may warn the people to whom no warner had come before you, in order that they may remember,

28:47 so that if a calamity seizes them (people of Makkah) for what their hands have sent (the deeds), they may not be able to say: "Our Rabb! Why you (Allah) did not send us a messenger? Then we would have followed your (Allah's) verses and would have been among the believers."

28:48 Now that the truth (Muhammad with his message) has come to them from Allah, they say: "Why he is not given the like of what was given to Moses? Did they not disbelieve in what was given to Moses before? They say: "Two kinds of magic (the Torah and the Qur'an) are helping each other!" They say: "Surely! We disbelieve in both."

28:49 Say (to them, O Muhammad): "Then bring a book from Allah which is better guide than these 2 (the Torah and the Qur'an), I will follow it, if you are truthful."

28:50 But if they do not answer to you, then know that they only follow their own desires. Who is more astray than the one who follows own desires without guidance from Allah? Surely! Allah does not guide the wrongdoers.

28:51 Indeed Allah has conveyed to them the word (this Qur'an) in order that they may remember.

28:52 Those to whom Allah gave scriptures before it, they believe in it (the Qur'an).

28:53 When it is recited to them, they say: "We believe in it. Surely, it is the truth from our Rabb. Indeed we were from those who submit to Allah (as Muslims) before it (like Abdullah bin Salam, Salman Al-Farsi)."

28:54 They will be given their reward twice; because they are patient, repel evil with good, and spend (in charity) out of what Allah has provided them.

28:55 When they hear evil vain talk, they withdraw from it and say: "To us are our deeds and to you are your deeds. Peace be on to you. We do not seek the (way of the) ignorant."

28:56 Surely! You (O Muhammad) cannot guide whom you like, but Allah guides whom Allah wills. Allah knows the best of those who are guided.

28:57 They say: "If we follow the guidance with you, we shall be snatched away from our land." Has Allah not established a secure sanctuary (Makkah) for them to which are brought fruits of all kinds as a provision from Allah? But most of them do not know.

28:58 How many towns Allah has destroyed which were thankless for their means of livelihood? Those residences of theirs have not been inhabited after them except a little. Surely! Allah is the Inheritor.

28:59 Your Rabb would never destroy the towns until Allah had sent a messenger to their mother town, reciting to them Allah's verses. Allah would never destroy the towns unless their people had become wrongdoers.

28:60 Whatever you have been given from things are enjoyments and adornments of the worldly life; and that which is with Allah is better and will remain forever. Don't you have sense?

28:61 Can a person to whom Allah has promised an excellent promise (paradise) which that person will find true, be like the one whom Allah has given to enjoy the luxuries of the worldly life and then on the day of Resurrection, that person will be among those who are brought up (for punishment)?

28:62 (Remember) the day when Allah will call them and say: "Where are Allah's partners whom you used to assert?"

28:63 Those about whom the word will come true (to be punished), will say: "Our Rabb! These are they whom we led astray. We led them astray, as we were astray ourselves. We declare our innocence before Allah. It was not us that they worshipped."

28:64 It will be said (to them): "Call upon your partners (of Allah)." So they will call upon them but they will not answer to them and they will see the punishment. They will wish if they had been guided!

28:65 (Remember) the day when Allah will call them and says: "How did you answer the messengers?"

28:66 The news (of good answer) will be obscured to them on that day and they will not be able to ask one another.

28:67 But as for the one who repented, believed, and did righteous deeds, then hopefully that person will be among those who are successful.

28:68 Your Rabb creates whatever Allah wills and chooses. They do not have any choice. Glory be to Allah, and exalted is Allah about all that they associate as partners with Allah.

28:69 Your Rabb knows what their hearts conceal and what they reveal.

28:70 It is Allah; there is no one worthy of worship but Allah. Praise belongs to Allah in the first (world) and in the last (hereafter). The decision is with Allah and to Allah you all shall return.

28:71 Say (O Muhammad): "Do you see if Allah makes the night continuous for you till the day of Resurrection, which deity besides Allah could bring you light? Will you not then hear?"

28:72 Say (O Muhammad): "Do you see if Allah makes the day continuous for you till the day of Resurrection, which deity besides Allah could bring you night in which you could rest? Will you not then see?"

28:73 It is out of Allah's Mercy that Allah has made for you the night that you may rest in it, and the day that you may seek Allah's bounty, so that you may be grateful.

28:74 (Remember the day) when Allah will call them (worshipped other than Allah) and say: "Where are Allah's partners whom you used to assert?"

28:75 Allah will take out a witness from every nation and say: "Bring your proof (of other deities)." Then they shall know that the truth is with Allah and (false deities) will disappear from them which they invented.

28:76 Surely, Korah was one of the people of Moses, but he behaved arrogantly towards them. Allah gave him such treasures that indeed their keys were a burden to a group of strong men. When his people said to him: "Do not be glad. Surely! Allah does not like those who exult (jubilant).

28:77 Rather seek, with that (wealth) which Allah has given you, the home of the hereafter, and do not forget your portion of this world. Do good (to others) as Allah has been good to you and do not seek mischief in the land. Surely, Allah does not like the mischief-makers."

28:78 He said: "This has been given to me only because of the knowledge that I possess." Did he (Korah) not know that Allah had destroyed many generations before him, who were stronger in might and greater in collecting (money) than him? But the criminals will not be questioned of their sins (because Allah knows well).

28:79 So (one day) he went out before his people in his pomp (worldly glitter). Those who were desirous of the worldly life, said: "Ah, would that we had the like of what Korah has been given! Surely! He is the owner of a great fortune."

28:80 But those who had been given the knowledge (of truth) said: "Woe to you! The reward of Allah (in the hereafter) is better for those who believe and do righteous deeds; and none shall attain it except those who are patient."

28:81 Then Allah caused the earth to swallow him along with his residing place. He had no group to help him against Allah, nor was he of those who could save themselves.

28:82 Those who had desired his position (of wealth) the day before began to say: "You do not know that Allah enlarges the provision to whoever Allah pleases of Allah's servants. If Allah had not been gracious to us, Allah could have caused the earth to swallow us also! You do not know that the disbelievers will never be successful!

28:83 As for the last home (of paradise), Allah will assign it to those who neither want pride nor do mischief in the land. The good end is for the pious.

28:84 Whoever brings a good deed, shall have the better from it. Whoever brings an evil deed, then those who do evil deeds, will be punished only for what they did.

28:85 Surely, (Allah) who has enjoined on you (O Muhammad) the Qur'an, will surely bring you to the best place of return. Say (O Muhammad): "My Rabb is aware of the one who brings guidance and of the one who is in clear error."

28:86 You (O Muhammad) never expected that the book (this Qur'an) would be sent down to you, but it is a Mercy from your Rabb. So never be a supporter of the disbelievers.

28:87 Let them not turn you (O Muhammad) away from the verses of Allah after when they have been sent down to you. Invite (people) to your Rabb and be not of the polytheists.

28:88 Do not call Allah with any other one worthy of worship. There is no one worthy of worship but Allah. Everything will perish except Allah. To Allah belongs the decision and to Allah you shall be returned.

29. Al-Ankabut : The Spider
In the name of Allah, the Gracious, the Merciful

29:1 Alif-Lam-Meem.

29:2 Do the people think that they will be left alone on saying: "We believe," and that they will not be tested?

29:3 Indeed Allah tested those who were before them. Allah will certainly make it known those who are telling the truth and will certainly make it known those who are liars.

29:4 Or do those who do evil deeds think that they can escape from Allah's reach? Evil is that which they judge!

29:5 Whoever hopes for the meeting with Allah, and then surely Allah's term is coming. Allah is the All-Hearer, the All-Knower.

29:6 Whoever strives, then strives only for oneself. Surely, Allah is Rich (not in any need) from all mankind and jinns.

29:7 Those who believe and do righteous deeds, surely Allah will remit their evil deeds from them and will reward them the best according to their deeds.

29:8 Allah has enjoined on people to be good to their parents; but if they (parents) strive against you to make you join (partners in worship) with Allah of which you have no knowledge, then do not obey them. To Allah is your return and Allah will tell you what you did.

29:9 Those who believe and do righteous deeds, surely Allah will make them enter among the righteous (in paradise).

29:10 Some people are those who say: "We believe in Allah," but if they are made to suffer in the cause of Allah, they confuse the trial of people as the punishment of Allah. But if victory comes from your Rabb, they say: "Surely! We were with you." Is not Allah fully aware of what is in the hearts (of the people) of the worlds?

29:11 Surely, Allah knows those who believe, and surely, Allah knows the hypocrites.

29:12 Those who disbelieve say to those who believe: "Follow our way and we will surely bear your sins." They will not bear anything from their sins. Surely, they are liars.

29:13 Surely, they shall bear their own loads and other loads with their own loads, and surely, they shall be questioned on the day of Resurrection about their fabricated lies.

29:14 Indeed Allah sent Noah to his people and he stayed among them a 1,000 years less 50 years. The flood overtook them as they were wrongdoers.

29:15 Then Allah saved him and the people of the ship, and made it (the ship) a sign for the worlds.

29:16 (Remember) Abraham when he said to his people: "Worship Allah and fear Allah, that is better for you if you understand.

29:17 You worship only idols besides Allah and you invent falsehood. Surely, those whom you worship besides Allah, do not possess any power to give you any provision, so seek provision from Allah, worship Allah, and be grateful to Allah. To Allah you will be brought back.

29:18 If you deny, then truly nations have denied before you. The duty of the messenger is not but to convey (the message) plainly."

29:19 Don't they see how Allah originates the creation, and then repeats it? Surely, it is easy for Allah.

29:20 Say: "Travel in the land and see how Allah originated the creation, then Allah will bring forth the creation last (of the hereafter). Surely, Allah has power over everything.

29:21 Allah punishes whom Allah wills, shows Mercy to whom Allah wills, and to Allah you will be returned.

29:22 You cannot escape in the earth or in the heaven. Besides Allah you have neither any protector nor any helper.

29:23 Those who disbelieve in the verses of Allah and the meeting with Allah, they have no hope of my (Allah's) Mercy and there will be a painful punishment for them.

29:24 There was no answer of his (Abraham's) people except that they said: "Kill him or burn him." But Allah saved him from the fire. Surely, in this, there are signs for people who believe.

29:25 (Abraham) said: "You have taken (for worship) idols instead of Allah. The love between you is only in the worldly life; but on the day of Resurrection, you shall disown each other, curse each other, your abode will be the fire, and you shall have no helper."

29:26 So Lot believed in him (Abraham). (Abraham) said: "Surely, I will emigrate for the sake of my Rabb. Surely, Allah is the All-Mighty, the All-Wise."

29:27 Allah bestowed on him (Abraham), Isaac (son) and Jacob (grandson), and ordained Prophethood and the book in his offspring. Allah granted him his reward in this world, and surely in the hereafter he will be among the righteous.

29:28 (Remember) Lot, when he said to his people: "Surely you are committing the worst sin; no one has preceded you in committing it in the worlds.

29:29 Surely, do you commit (sodomy) with men, rob travelers in the road, and practice every kind of evil deed in your gatherings?" But his people gave no answer except that they said: "Bring punishment of Allah upon us if you are one of the truthful."

29:30 He (Lot) said: "My Rabb! Help me against the corrupt people."

29:31 When Allah's messengers (angels) came to Abraham with the glad tidings, they said: "Surely, we are going to destroy the people of this town, truly its people are wrongdoers."

29:32 (Abraham) said: "But Lot is in there." They (angels) said: "We know better who is in there, we will surely save him and his family, except his wife, she will be of those who remain behind."

29:33 When Allah's messengers (angels) came to Lot, he was grieved because of them, felt distressed for them, and was unable (to protect them). They said: "Do no fear and do not grieve! Truly, we shall save you and your family, except your wife, she will be of those who remain behind.

29:34 Surely, we are about to bring down a great punishment from the sky on the people of this town because of what they have been acting immorally."

29:35 Indeed Allah has left in it a sign (the Dead Sea in Palestine) evident for people who understand.

29:36 To (the people of) Midian, (Allah sent) their brother Shuaib. He said: "O my people! Worship Allah, hope (reward of good deeds) for the last day, and do not commit mischief on the earth as corrupt."

29:37 But they denied him (Shuaib), so the earthquake seized them, and they became dead in their residences.

29:38 Ad and Thamud (people)! Indeed (their destruction) is clearly apparent to you from their (ruined) residences. Satan made their deeds seem fair to them, and turned them away from the right way, though they were intelligent.

29:39 (Allah destroyed) Korah, Pharaoh, and Haman. Indeed Moses came to them with clear evidences but they were arrogant in the land, and they could not escape Allah.

29:40 So Allah seized all of them for their sins, against some of them Allah sent a violent wind with shower of stones (the people of Lot), some of them were overtaken by awful cry (Thamud or Shuaib's people), some of them Allah caused the earth to swallow (like Korah), and some of them Allah drowned (the people of Noah or Pharaoh and his people). It was not Allah who wronged them, but they were doing wrong to themselves.

29:41 The example of those who take protectors other than Allah is the example of a spider who builds (for itself) a house, but surely, the weakest of houses is the house of the spider; if they but knew.

29:42 Surely, Allah knows what things they invoke instead of Allah. Allah is the All-Mighty, the All-Wise.

29:43 These examples Allah put them forward for people, but none will grasp them except those who have knowledge.

29:44 Allah has created the heavens and the earth with truth. Surely! In that there is a sign for those who believe.

29:45 Recite (O Muhammad) what has been revealed to you of the book (the Qur'an) and establish the prayer. Surely the prayer prevents from great sins and evil wicked deed, and surely the remembrance of Allah is greater. Allah knows what you do.

29:46 Do not argue with the people of the book except (in a way it is) better, except those of them who do wrong, and say (to them): "We believe in that which has been revealed to us and revealed to you; and our one worthy of worship and your one worthy of worship is one Allah, and to Allah we have submitted (as Muslims)."

29:47 Thus Allah has sent down to you (O Muhammad) the book (this Qur'an) (in the same way as the book to Moses and Jesus). So those whom Allah gave the scripture believe in it, and some of those who believe in it, and none but the disbelievers reject Allah's verses.

29:48 Neither you (O Muhammad) have read any book before it (this Qur'an), nor have you written with your right hand. In that case, indeed, the followers of falsehood might have doubted.

29:49 Nay, but these are clear signs in the hearts of those who are given the knowledge. None but the wrongdoers deny and reject Allah's verses.

29:50 They say: "Why have the verses not sent down to him from his Rabb? Say: "The verses are only with Allah, and verily I am only a plain warner."

29:51 Is it not sufficient for them that Allah has sent the book (the Qur'an) down to you which is recited to them? Surely, in that there is a Mercy and a reminder for people who believe.

29:52 Say (to them O Muhammad): "Allah is sufficient as a witness between me and you. Allah knows what is in the heavens and on earth. Those who believe in falsehood and disbelieve in Allah, it is they who are the losers."

29:53 They ask you to hasten on the punishment for them. Had it not been for a term appointed, the punishment would certainly have come to them. Surely, it will come upon them suddenly while they do not perceive!

29:54 They ask you to hasten on the punishment. Surely! Hell will surely encompass the disbelievers.

29:55 On the day when the punishment (hellfire) shall cover them from above and from underneath their feet, and a voice shall say: "Taste what you used to do."

29:56 O my (Allah's) devotees who believe! Certainly, my (Allah's) earth is spacious (to migrate). Therefore worship me (Allah).

29:57 Every person shall taste the death. Then to Allah you shall be returned.

29:58 Those who believe and do righteous deeds, to them Allah will surely give a lofty residing place from paradise, underneath it rivers flow, to reside in it forever. Excellent is the reward of the workers,

29:59 those who are patient and put their trust in their Rabb.

29:60 So many from living creatures do not carry their own provisions! Allah provides for them and for you. Allah the All-Hearer, the All-Knower.

29:61 If you were to ask them (disbelievers): "Who has created the heavens and the earth, and subjected the sun and the moon?" They will surely reply: "Allah." How then are they deviating (from truth)?

29:62 Allah enlarges the provision for whom Allah wills of Allah's servants, and straitens it for whom (Allah wills). Surely, Allah is the All-Knower of everything.

29:63 If you were to ask them: "Who sends down water (rain) from the sky and gives life thereby to the earth after its death?" They will surely reply: "Allah." Say: "All the praises are to Allah!" But most of them have no sense.

29:64 This worldly life is nothing but amusement and play! Surely, the home of the hereafter is indeed the life (that will never end), if they but knew.

29:65 When they embark on a ship, they invoke Allah (during trouble) making their religion pure for Allah only. But when Allah brings them safely to land, behold, they join (give credit to) others in worship (besides Allah),

29:66 so that they become ungrateful for that which Allah has given them, and that they take enjoyment. But they will come to know.

29:67 Do they not see that Allah has made (Makkah) a secure sanctuary while the people from all around them are being snatched away? Then do they (still) believe in false deities, and deny the graces of Allah?

29:68 Who does more wrong than the one who invents a lie against Allah or denies the truth when it comes to oneself? Is there not a residence in hell for the disbelievers?

29:69 As for those who strive hard in Allah's cause, Allah will surely guide them to Allah's ways. Surely, Allah is with the good doers.

30. Ar-Rum : The Romans
In the name of Allah, the Gracious, the Merciful

30:1 Alif-Lam-Meem.

30:2 The Romans (Christians) have been defeated (by the Persians - idol worshippers)

30:3 in the nearest land (of Syria), but after their defeat, they (Allah revealed to Muhammad that Romans) will be victorious

30:4 within a few years. Allah is in command with the matter before (the defeat of the Romans by Persians in 615 CE) and after (the defeat of Persians by Romans in 625 CE). On that day, the believers will rejoice (for the victory)

30:5 with the help of Allah. Allah helps whom Allah wills, and Allah is the Mighty, the Merciful.

30:6 It is the promise of Allah and Allah does not fail in Allah's promise, but most people do not know.

30:7 They only know the outside appearance of the life of the world, and they are heedless of the hereafter.

30:8 Don't they think in their own minds that Allah has created the heavens and the earth, and all that is between them with truth and for an appointed term? Indeed many of mankind denies the meeting with their Rabb (on the day of Resurrection).

30:9 Don't they travel in the land and see how the end of those before them was? They were superior to them in strength, they tilled the earth and populated it in greater numbers than what these (pagans) have populated, and there came to them their messengers with clear signs. Surely, Allah did not wrong them, but they wronged themselves.

30:10 Then evil was the end of those who did evil because they denied the verses of Allah and made a mockery of them.

30:11 Allah (alone) originates the creation, then Allah repeats it, then to Allah you will be returned.

30:12 On the day when the hour (of Judgment) will be established, the criminals will be plunged into destruction with deep regret.

30:13 No intercessor they will have from their partners (whom they made equal with Allah) and they themselves will reject their partners.

30:14 On the day when the hour (of Judgment) will be established, people will be separated that day (believers will be separated from the disbelievers).

30:15 As for those who believed and did righteous deeds, they shall be honored and made to enjoy luxurious life forever in a garden of delight (paradise).

30:16 As for those who disbelieved, denied Allah's verses, and the meeting of the hereafter, they will be brought forth for punishment (of hell fire).

30:17 So glorify Allah when you come up to the evening and when you enter the morning.

30:18 All praises and thanks are to Allah in the heavens and the earth, so glorify Allah in the afternoon and when you come up to the time, when the day begins to decline.

30:19 Allah brings out the living from the dead and brings out the dead from the living. Allah revives the earth after its death. Thus you shall be brought out (resurrected).

30:20 Among Allah's signs, one is that Allah created you from dust, then behold you are human beings scattered (in the world)!

30:21 Among Allah's signs, another one is that Allah created for you wives from among yourselves so that you may find comfort with them and Allah has put affection and mercy between you. Surely, there are signs for a people who think.

30:22 Among Allah's signs are the creation of the heavens and the earth, and the difference of your languages and colors. Surely, there are signs for people of sound knowledge.

30:23 Among Allah's signs is the sleep (you take) by night and your seeking of Allah's bounty by day. Surely, there are signs for a people who listen.

30:24 Among Allah's signs is that Allah shows you the lightning by way of fear and hope, Allah sends down water (rain) from the sky, and with it revives (gives life) the earth after its death. Surely, there are signs for a people who understand.

30:25 Among Allah's signs are that the heaven and the earth stand by Allah's command, then when Allah will call you by single call, behold, you will come out from the earth (from your graves for reckoning).

30:26 To Allah belongs whatever is in the heavens and the earth. All are obedient to Allah.

30:27 It is Allah who originates the creation, then repeats it, and this is easy for Allah. To Allah belongs the highest example in the heavens and in the earth. Allah is the Mighty, the Wise.

30:28 Allah sets forth an example for you from your own lives. Do you let those whom your right hands possess (your captives) be as partners in (to share your wealth equally) what Allah has bestowed on you? Then do you fear them in it (possession) as you fear each other? Thus Allah explains the verses in details to a people who have sense.

30:29 Nay, but those who do wrong follow their own lusts without knowledge. Then who will guide them whom Allah has sent astray? They will have no helpers.

30:30 So set (O Muhammad) your face towards the religion being upright nature of Allah with which Allah has created mankind, there is no change in the creation (of laws) of Allah. That is the right religion, but most of mankind do not know.

30:31 Turn (in repentance) to Allah, fear Allah, establish the prayer, and do not be of the polytheists,

30:32 those who split up their religion and become sects, each party rejoicing in its own circle.

30:33 When a harm touches people, they cry to their Rabb, turning to Allah in repentance. But when Allah gives them a taste of Allah's Mercy, behold! a party of them associate (partners in worship) with their Rabb,

30:34 be ungrateful for what Allah has bestowed on them. Then enjoy (your short life); soon you will come to know.

30:35 Or has Allah revealed to them a scripture, which speaks of that which they have been associating with Allah?

30:36 When Allah causes mankind to taste of Mercy, they rejoice in it, but when an evil afflicts them because of (evil deeds) what their hands have sent forth, then they are in despair!

30:37 Don't they see that Allah enlarges the provision for whom Allah wills and straitens it (for whom Allah wills). Surely, there are signs for a people who believe.

30:38 (O believers) give what is due to your relative, the poor, and the wayfarer. That is best for those who seek the pleasure of Allah and it is they who will be successful.

30:39 That interest which you give in order that it may increase in wealth of other people, does not increase with Allah; but that which you give as obligatory charity seeking the pleasure of Allah, shall have manifold increase.

30:40 It is Allah who has created you, then provides (sustenance) for you, then will cause you to die, then Allah will give you life (on the day of Resurrection). Is there any of your partners (of Allah) who can do any of these things? Glory be to Allah! Exalted is Allah above all that evil they associate (with Allah).

30:41 Evil (sins and disobedience of Allah) has appeared in the land and the sea because of what the hands of people (have earned). Allah may make them taste a part of that which they have done in order that they may return (from evil).

30:42 Say (O Muhammad): "Travel in the land and see how was the end of those before you! Most of them were polytheists."

30:43 So you (O Muhammad) set your face to the right religion before there comes a day from Allah which none can avert it. On that day they (people) shall be divided (in 2 groups - a group in paradise and a group in hell).

30:44 Those who disbelieved will suffer from their disbelief, and those who have done righteous deeds will prepare a good place (in paradise) for themselves,

30:45 so that Allah may reward those who believe and do righteous deeds, out of Allah's bounty. Surely, Allah does not like the disbelievers.

30:46 Among Allah's signs is that Allah sends the winds as glad tidings, give you a taste of Allah's Mercy, the ships may sail at Allah's command, and that you may seek of Allah's bounty, in order that you may be thankful.

30:47 Indeed Allah did send messengers before you (O Muhammad) to their own people. They came to them with clear proofs. Then Allah took revenge on those who committed crimes and it was incumbent upon Allah to help the believers.

30:48 It is Allah who sends the winds to raise the clouds, then spreads them in the sky as Allah wills, then breaks them into fragments, until you see (rain) drops come forth from their midst! When Allah makes them fall with it on whom Allah wills of Allah's servants, lo! They rejoice,

30:49 and surely before that (rain) is sent down upon them, they were in despair.

30:50 Look at the effects of Mercy of Allah, how Allah revives (gives life) the earth after its death. Surely! That is Allah who will raise the dead (on the day of Resurrection), and Allah is Able (has power) on every thing.

30:51 If Allah sends a wind and they see (their crops) turn yellow, behold, then they disbelieve (more) after it.

30:52 So surely you (O Muhammad) can neither make the dead to hear, nor can you make the deaf hear the call when they (disbelievers) turn their backs and turn away,

30:53 nor you can guide the blind from their straying. None will hear you except those who believe in Allah's signs and submit to Allah in Islam (as Muslims).

30:54 It is Allah who has created you in weakness (as a baby), then gave you strength after weakness (in youth), then gave after strength weakness and grey hair (in old age). Allah creates what Allah wills. Allah is All-Knower, the All-Mighty.

30:55 On the day when the hour (of Judgment) will be established, the criminals will swear that they did not stay (in the world) but an hour, thus they are ever deluded (away from truth).

30:56 Those who are bestowed with knowledge and faith will say: "Indeed you have stayed in the decree of Allah, until the day of Resurrection, so this is the day of Resurrection, but you did not know."

30:57 So on that day, no excuse of theirs will benefit those who did wrong nor will they be allowed to return to seek Allah's pleasure.

30:58 Indeed Allah has set forth every example for mankind in this Qur'an. But if you (O Muhammad) bring any sign to them, those who disbelieve will say (to the believers): "Surely you are nothing but preaching falsehood."

30:59 Thus Allah has set a seal on the hearts of those who do not know.

30:60 So be patient (O Muhammad). Surely, the promise of Allah is true, and let not those who have no certainty of faith discourage you (from conveying Allah's message).

31. Luqman : Luqman
In the name of Allah, the Gracious, the Merciful

31:1 Alif-Lam-Meem.

31:2 These are the verses of the wise book (the Qur'an),

31:3 a guide and a Mercy for the righteous;

31:4 those who establish the prayer, give obligatory charity, and have firm faith in the hereafter.

31:5 These are on guidance from their Rabb, and such are they who will the successful.

31:6 Of mankind there are some who purchase idle talks to mislead from the way of Allah without knowledge, and takes it (the way of Allah) as a mockery. For such people there will be a humiliating punishment.

31:7 When Allah's verses (of the Qur'an) are recited to such people, they turn away in pride, as if they did not hear them, as if there is deafness in their ear. So announce to them a painful punishment.

31:8 Surely, those who believe and do righteous deeds, for them are gardens of delight (paradise)

31:9 to abide forever in it. It is a promise of Allah in truth. Allah is the Mighty, the Wise.

31:10 Allah has created the heavens without any pillars that you see and has set firm mountains on the earth, lest it should shake with you. Allah has scattered in it all kinds of animals. Allah has sent down water (rain) from the sky and Allah has caused plants of every noble kind to grow in it.

31:11 This is the creation of Allah. So show Allah what is there that others (false deities) besides Allah have created? Nay, the wrongdoers are in plain error.

31:12 Indeed Allah bestowed upon Luqman the wisdom (saying): "Give thanks to Allah," and those who give thanks, they only give thanks for their own self. Whoever is ungrateful (should know that) surely Allah is Rich, Praise-worthy.

31:13 (Remember) when Luqman was advising his son, said to him: "O my son! Do not join in worship others with Allah. Surely! Joining others in worship with Allah is a great wrong indeed."

31:14 Allah has enjoined on people (to be dutiful) to their parents. Each mother carries her child in her womb while suffering in weakness and hardship upon weakness and hardship and then weans the child in 2 years that: "You give thanks to Allah and to your parents, to Allah is the final destination.

31:15 If they both strive against you to make you join in worship others with Allah of which you have no knowledge, then do not obey them; but behave with them kindly in this world, and follow the way of that person who turns to Allah in repentance and in obedience. To Allah will be your return, and Allah will tell you what you have done."

31:16 (Luqman said): "O my son! Indeed if it (anything) is equal to the weight of a grain of mustard seed, and though it is in a rock, or in the heavens or in the earth, Allah will bring it out. Surely, Allah is subtle (able to make fine distinction), Well-Aware (of all things).

31:17 O my son! Establish the prayer, enjoin good, forbid evil, and bear with patience whatever befalls you. Surely! These are some of the important commandments.

31:18 Do not turn your face away (with pride) from people, nor walk in pride on the earth. Surely, Allah does not like each arrogant boaster.

31:19 Be moderate (no pride) in your walking and lower your voice. Surely, the harshest of all voices is indeed the voice of the donkey."

31:20 Don't you see that Allah has subjected for you whatever is in the heavens and in the earth, and has completed Allah's graces upon you, both apparent (seen) and hidden (unseen)? Yet, there are some people who dispute about Allah without knowledge or guidance or a book giving light!

31:21 When it is said to them: "Follow that which Allah has sent down," they say: "Nay, we shall follow that which we found our forefathers following." (They will follow) even if Satan invites them to punishment of the fire.

31:22 Those who submit their faces to Allah while they are righteous people, then indeed they have grasped the most trustworthy hand-hold. To Allah all matters return.

31:23 Those who disbelieve, let their disbelief not grieve you (O Muhammad). To Allah is their return and Allah will inform them what they have done. Surely, Allah is the All-Knower what are in the hearts (of people).

31:24 Allah lets them enjoy for a little while (in this world), then Allah will oblige them to enter a great punishment (in the hereafter).

31:25 If you (O Muhammad) ask them: "Who has created the heavens and the earth?" They will certainly say: "Allah." Say: "All the praises and thanks are to Allah!" But most of them do not know.

31:26 To Allah belongs whatever is in the heavens and the earth. Surely, Allah is the one who is Rich (free of all wants), Praise-worthy.

31:27 If all the trees on the earth were pens and the sea (were ink to write) with 7 more seas behind it (supply), yet (the writing of the) words of Allah would not be exhausted. Surely, Allah is All-Mighty, All-Wise.

31:28 Neither your creation nor your Resurrection is anything but as that of a single person. Surely, Allah is All-Hearer, All-Seer.

31:29 Don't you (O Muhammad) see that Allah merges the night into the day and merges the day into the night, and has subjected the sun and the moon (to follow the commandment of Allah), each running (its course) for an appointed term; and that Allah is All-Aware of all that you do?

31:30 That is because Allah is the truth and all those which they invoke besides Allah are false, and because Allah is the High, the Great.

31:31 Don't you see how the ships sail through the sea by the grace of Allah so that Allah may show you Allah's signs? Surely, there are signs for every patient, grateful person.

31:32 When a wave covers them like a shade, they invoke Allah with sincerity in faith to Allah only. But when Allah brings them safe to land, there are some among them who stop in the middle (between belief and disbelief). But none denies Allah's Signs except every ungrateful traitor.

31:33 O mankind! Be afraid and dutiful to your Rabb and fear a day when no father shall avail for his son or a son shall avail for his father anything. Surely, the promise of Allah is true. Let not the worldly life deceives you, nor let the chief deceiver (Satan) deceive you about Allah.

31:34 Surely, with Allah is the knowledge of the hour, Allah sends down the rain, and knows what is in the wombs. No one knows what a person will earn tomorrow, and no one knows in what land the person will die. Surely, Allah is All-Knower, All-Aware of everything.

32. As-Sajdah : The Prostration
In the name of Allah, the Gracious, the Merciful

32:1 Alif-Lam-Meem.

32:2 The book (the Qur'an) in which there is no doubt, is revealed from the Rabb of the worlds.

32:3 Or do they say: "He (Muhammad) has fabricated it?" Nay, it is the truth from your Rabb so that you (O Muhammad) may warn a people to whom no warner has come before you, in order that they may be guided.

32:4 It is Allah who has created the heavens and the earth, and all that is between them in 6 days. Then Allah rose over the Throne (to suit Majesty). You (people) have no protector or intercessor besides Allah. Will you not then remember?

32:5 Allah manages every affair from the heavens to the earth; then each affair goes up to Allah in one day, the period of which is 1,000 years of what you count (as worldly time).

32:6 That is Allah, the All-Knower of all the unseen and the seen, the All-Mighty, the Merciful.

32:7 It is Allah who has made everything good that Allah has created. Allah began the creation of human from clay,

32:8 then Allah made human's offspring from semen of worthless water,

32:9 then Allah fashioned human in due proportion, and breathed into human from Allah's soul (created by Allah). Allah gave you hearing (ears), sight (eyes) and hearts. Little is what thanks you give!

32:10 They say: "When we are (dead and become) lost in the earth, shall we be in a new creation?" Nay, but they deny the meeting with their Rabb!

32:11 Say: "The angel of death (Izra'il) who is set over you, will take your souls and then you will be returned to your Rabb."

32:12 If only you could see when the criminals will hang their heads before their Rabb (saying): "Our Rabb! We have now seen and heard, so send us back (to the world) and we will do righteous deeds. Surely! We now believe with certainty."

32:13 It will be said: "If Allah had willed, surely! Allah could have given every one its guidance. But the word from Allah took effect (about evil-doers) that Allah will fill hell with jinn and mankind together.

32:14 Now you taste (the punishment of the fire) because of your forgetting the meeting of this day, surely! Allah too has forgotten you; you taste the continuous punishment for what you did."

32:15 Only those who believe in Allah's signs, when they are reminded of them, fall down prostrate, glorify the praises of their Rabb, and they are not proud.

32:16 Their sides forsake their beds, they invoke their Rabb in fear and hope, and they spend (in Allah's cause) out of what Allah has bestowed on them.

32:17 No one knows what is kept hidden for them of the joy of their eyes as a reward for what (good) they did.

32:18 Can the one who is a believer be like the one who is a sinner? They are not equal.

32:19 As for those who believe and do righteous deeds, for them are gardens (paradise) as shelter to reside for what they did.

32:20 But those who have sinned, their abode will be the fire. Every time they wish to get away from it, they will be put back in it, and it will be said to them: "You taste the punishment of the fire which you used to deny."

32:21 Surely, Allah will make them taste the lighter punishment (in this life) before the greater punishment (in the hereafter), so that they may return (to the right way).

32:22 Who does more wrong than the one who is reminded of the verses of its Rabb and then that person turns aside from them? Surely, Allah will take retribution from the criminals.

32:23 Indeed, Allah gave Moses the scripture (the Torah). So do not be in doubt of his reaching it. Allah made it (the Torah) a guide for the children of Israel.

32:24 Allah made leaders from among them (children of Israel) giving guidance under Allah's command as long as they were patient and used to believe with certainty in Allah's verses.

32:25 Surely, your Rabb is Allah who will judge between them on the day of Resurrection concerning what they differed.

32:26 Is it not guidance for them of how many previous generations Allah has destroyed before them in whose residences they walk about? Surely, there are signs. Would they not listen?

32:27 Don't they see how Allah drive water (rain) to the dry land without any vegetation and bring forth crops with it which they and their cattle eat? Will they not see?

32:28 They say: "When will this decision (Judgment) happen if you are telling the truth?"

32:29 Say (O Muhammad): "On the day of decision, no benefit will be to the disbelievers, nor they will be granted respite."

32:30 So turn aside from them (O Muhammad) and await, surely they are waiting.

33. Al-Ahzab : The Confederates
In the name of Allah, the Gracious, the Merciful

33:1 O Prophet (Muhammad)! Fear Allah; do not obey the disbelievers and the hypocrites. Surely! Allah is All-Knower, All-Wise.

33:2 Follow that which is revealed to you from your Rabb. Surely, Allah is well acquainted with what you do.

33:3 Put your trust in Allah, and Allah is sufficient as a trustee.

33:4 Allah has not put 2 hearts in one person's body. Neither has Allah made your wives whom you declare (divorce) through Zihar to be like your mother's backs, (Zihar is the saying of a husband to his wife: "you are to me like the back of my mother" i.e. you are unlawful for me to approach, deprive her rights and keep her like a captive and do not let her marry anyone else) as your real mothers, nor has Allah made your adopted sons your real sons. That is your saying with your mouths. But Allah says the truth, and Allah guides to the right way.

33:5 Call them (adopted sons) by (the names of) their fathers, that is more just with Allah. But if you do not know their fathers, (call them) your brothers in the religion and your friends. There is no sin on you if you make a mistake in it, except what your hearts deliberately intend. Allah is Forgiving, Merciful.

33:6 The Prophet is closer to the believers than their own selves, and his wives are their (believers') mothers. Those who are blood relations, some of them are closer to each other in the decree of Allah (regarding inheritance) than (the brotherhood of) the believers and the emigrants (from Makkah to Madinah), except that you do kindness to your brothers. This has been written in the book (of divine decrees).

33:7 (Remember) when Allah took the covenant from the prophets, from you (O Muhammad), from Noah, Abraham, Moses, and Jesus, son of Mary. Allah took from them a strong covenant,

33:8 so that Allah may ask the truthful (messengers) about their truth. Allah has prepared a painful punishment for the disbelievers.

33:9 O you who believe! Remember the favor of Allah to you, when hosts (enemy) came against you and Allah sent winds and forces (invisible angels) against them that you did not see (during the battle of Trench). Allah sees all of what you do.

33:10 When they (enemy) came upon you from above and from below; when the eyes grew wild and the hearts reached the throats, and you were entertaining all doubts about Allah,

33:11 there, the believers were tested and shaken with a mighty shake.

33:12 When the hypocrites and those in whose hearts there was a disease (doubt) said: "Allah and Allah's messenger promised us nothing but delusion (deception)!"

33:13 A party of them said: "O people of Madinah! There is no stand for you (against the enemy attack!). Therefore go back!" Another band of them asked permission of the prophet saying: "Truly, our homes lie open (to the enemy)," they were not secure. They wished nothing but to flee (from battle).

33:14 If (the enemy) had entered on them from all its (the city) sides and they had been exhorted to trial (renegade from Islam to polytheism), they would have committed it and would not have little hesitation in it.

33:15 Indeed they had already made a covenant with Allah not to turn their backs, and a covenant with Allah must be answered for.

33:16 Say (O Muhammad to these hypocrites who ask your permission to run away from you): "Flight (run away) will not avail you if you flee from death or killing, and you will enjoy a little (while in this world)!"

33:17 Say: "Who can protect you from Allah if Allah intends to harm you, or intends to show you Mercy?" They will not find for themselves other than Allah a protector or a helper.

33:18 Surely, Allah knows those from among you who keep back (people) from fighting (in Allah's cause), and those who say to their brothers: "Come here towards us," while they (themselves) do not come to the battle except a few,

33:19 they are miserly towards you (to help in Allah's cause). When fear comes (to them), you will see them looking to you, revolving their eyes as if their deaths hover over them, but when the fear departs, they will smite you with sharp tongues, become miserly towards (spending on) good. Such people have not believed. Therefore Allah makes their deeds fruitless, and that is very easy for Allah.

33:20 They thought that the confederates would not withdraw. If the confederates should come again, they would wish if they were in the deserts (wandering) among the Bedouins and ask about your news (from a safe distance); and if they happen to be among you, they would not fight but a little.

33:21 Indeed, you have in the messenger of Allah (Muhammad) the 'best example' (to follow) for those who hope to (meet with) Allah, the last day, and remember Allah much.

33:22 When the believers saw the confederates, they said: "This is what Allah and Allah's messenger (Muhammad) had promised us, and Allah and Allah's messenger (Muhammad) had spoken the truth." It increased them in faith and obedience (to Allah).

33:23 Among the believers there are people who have been true to their covenant with Allah, some of them have fulfilled their obligations (sacrificed their lives), and some of them are still waiting, but they have never changed (their covenant) in the least.

33:24 Allah may reward the people of truth for their truth, and punish the hypocrites if Allah wills or forgive them. Surely, Allah is Forgiving, Merciful.

33:25 Allah drove back those who disbelieved in their rage; they did not gain any advantage. Allah is sufficient for the believers in the fighting. Allah is Strong, Mighty.

33:26 Those people of the scripture (Jews of Bani Quraizah) who backed them (the invaders); Allah brought them down from their forts and cast fear into their hearts. So a group you killed and a group you made captives.

33:27 Thus Allah made you to inherit their lands, their houses, their riches, and the land (Khaibar) which you had not frequented (before). Allah is Able to do all things.

33:28 O Prophet (Muhammad)! Say to your wives: "If you desire the worldly life and its glitter, then come, I shall make you a provision and set you free (divorce) in an honorable way."

33:29 But if you desire Allah and Allah's messenger, and the home of the hereafter; then surely, Allah has prepared a great reward for the righteous people amongst you.

33:30 O wives of the prophet! Whoever of you commits an open illegal sexual intercourse, her punishment will be doubled and that is easy for Allah.

33:31 Whoever of you (wives of the Prophet) is obedient to Allah and Allah's messenger, and does righteous deeds, Allah will grant her double reward, and Allah has prepared a noble provision for her.

33:32 O wives of the prophet! You are not like any other women. If you fear Allah, then do not be soft in speech (to men not related), lest the one in whose heart there is a disease (of hypocrisy, or evil desire) may be moved with desire in his heart, but speak good words.

33:33 Stay in your homes and do not display yourselves like that of the times of the first ignorance (pre-Islamic days); establish prayer, give obligatory charity, and obey Allah and Allah's messenger. O members of the family (of the prophet), Allah only wishes to remove evil deeds from you and to purify you perfectly.

33:34 Remember the verses of Allah and the wisdom (Prophet's sayings) which are recited in your houses, surely, Allah is Courteous, Well-Acquainted.

33:35 Surely, the Muslim men and the Muslim women, the believing men and the believing women, the obedient men and the obedient women, the truthful men and the truthful women, the patient men and the patient women, the humble men and the humble women, the charitable men and the charitable women, the fasting men and the fasting women, the men who guard their chastity and the women who guard it, the men who remember Allah much and the women who remember Allah - for all of them, Allah has prepared forgiveness and a great reward (paradise).

33:36 It is not proper for a believing man or a believing woman to have any option for them in their decision when Allah and Allah's messenger have decreed a matter. Whoever disobeys Allah and Allah's messenger, has indeed strayed into clear error.

33:37 (Remember) when you (Muhammad) said to him (Zaid, prophet's adopted son) on whom Allah has bestowed grace (by guiding to Islam) and you too have done favor (by freeing from captivity): "Keep your wife to yourself and fear Allah." But you did hide in yourself what (Allah has already made known to you that Allah will give her (Zaid's wife) to you in marriage) Allah will make it clear and you did fear the people (that Muhammad married the divorced wife of his captive) whereas Allah had a better right that you should fear Allah. So when Zaid had performed the necessary formality (divorced her), Allah gave her to you in marriage, so that (in future) there may be no blame on the believers in respect of the wives of their adopted sons, when the latter have performed the necessary formality (divorced) from them. Command of Allah must be fulfilled.

33:38 There is no blame on the prophet in that which Allah has made legal for him. That is the way of Allah with those who have passed away before. The command of Allah is a decree preordained.

33:39 Those who convey the message of Allah and fear Allah, do not fear anyone except Allah. Allah is sufficient as a Reckoner (to take account).

33:40 Muhammad is not the father of any of your men (he will not leave any son), but he is the messenger of Allah and the last of the prophets. Allah is All-Aware of everything.

33:41 O you who believe! Remember Allah with much remembrance,

33:42 glorify Allah's praises morning and afternoon.

33:43 It is Allah who sends blessings on you (believers), and (also) Allah's angels, so that Allah may bring you out from darkness into light. Allah is Merciful to the believers.

33:44 Their greeting on the day they shall meet Allah will be: "Peace!" Allah has prepared for them a generous reward (paradise).

33:45 O Prophet (Muhammad)! Surely, Allah has sent you as a witness and a bearer of good news and a warner,

33:46 and a caller to Allah by Allah's permission and as a lamp spreading light (guidance).

33:47 Give glad tidings to the believers that there is a great bounty for them from Allah.

33:48 Do not obey the disbelievers and the hypocrites and disregard their harm. Put your trust in Allah and Allah is sufficient as a Trustee.

33:49 O you who believe! When you marry believing women and then divorce them before you have sexual intercourse with them, you do not count on them Iddah (waiting period after divorce) in respect of them. So give them a present and set them free (divorce) in an honorable way.

33:50 O Prophet (Muhammad)! Surely, Allah has made lawful to you: your wives to whom you have paid their bridal money (given by husband to wife at the time of marriage); those (captives) whom your right hand possesses - whom Allah has given to you; the daughters of your paternal uncles and aunts, the daughters of your maternal uncles and aunts who have migrated (from Makkah) with you; a believing woman if she offers herself to the prophet and if the Prophet wishes to marry her - a privilege for you (only) other than the believers. Indeed Allah knows what Allah has enjoined upon them (believers) about their wives and those (captives) whom their right hands possess, in order that there should be no difficulty on you. Allah is Forgiving, Merciful.

33:51 You (O Muhammad) can postpone (the turn for your company) whom you will of them (your wives), and you may receive to you whom you will. There is no sin on you if you desire any of those whom you have set aside (temporarily). It is better that their eyes may be cooled and they do not grieve, and may be pleased with what you give all of them. Allah knows what is in your hearts. Allah is All-Knowing, Forbearing.

33:52 It is not lawful for you (O Muhammad) to marry more women after this, or to change them (present wives) for other wives even though their beauty attracts you, except those (captives) whom your right hand possesses. Allah is a Watcher over all things.

33:53 O you who believe! Do not enter the houses of the prophet, except when permission is given to you for a meal, and then do not wait for its preparation. But when you are invited, then enter and when you have taken your meal, then disperse, without sitting for a talk. Surely, such behavior annoys the prophet, he is shy in asking you to leave, but Allah is not shy of telling you the truth. When you ask them (his wives) for anything, ask them from behind a curtain. This is purer for your hearts and for their hearts. It is not proper for you to annoy the messenger of Allah, nor that you should ever marry his wives after him (his death). Surely! With Allah that would be a grievous offence.

33:54 Whether you reveal anything or conceal it, surely, Allah is All-Knower of everything.

33:55 There is no sin on them (your wives, if they appear unveiled) before their fathers, their sons, their brothers, their brother's sons, their sister's sons, their own (believing) women, those whom their right hand possesses (their female captives). Fear Allah. Surely, Allah is All-Witness over everything.

33:56 Surely, Allah and Allah's angels send blessings on the prophet (Muhammad). O you who believe! Send your blessings on him (Muhammad) and greet him with greetings (Assalamu Alaikum).

33:57 Surely, those who annoy Allah and Allah's messenger, Allah has cursed them in this world and in the hereafter. Allah has prepared for them a humiliating punishment.

33:58 Those who annoy believing men and believing women without any fault of theirs, then indeed they shall bear the crime of slander and plain sin.

33:59 O Prophet! Tell your wives, your daughters, and the believing women to draw their veils over them. That is better so that they will be recognized and not annoyed. Allah is Forgiving, Merciful.

33:60 If the hypocrites, those in whose hearts there is a disease (of evil desires), and those who spread false news among the people in Madinah do not desist, Allah will let you overpower them, then they will not be able to stay in the city as your neighbors but for a little while.

33:61 They shall be cursed wherever they are found; they shall be seized, and killed with a terrible slaughter.

33:62 This has been the way of Allah in the case of those who passed away before and you will never find a change in the way of Allah.

33:63 People ask you about the hour (of Judgment), say: "The knowledge of it is with Allah. What do you know? It may be that the hour is near!"

33:64 Surely, Allah has cursed the disbelievers and has prepared for them a flaming fire (hell).

33:65 They will abide in it forever. Neither will they find a protector nor a helper.

33:66 On the day when their faces will be turned over in the fire, they will say: "Oh, would that we had obeyed Allah and obeyed the messenger (Muhammad)."

33:67 They will also say: "Our Rabb! Surely, we obeyed our chiefs and our great ones, and they misled us from the right way.

33:68 Our Rabb! Give them double punishment and curse them with a mighty curse!"

33:69 O you who believe! Be not like those who annoyed Moses, but Allah cleared him of that which they alleged, and he was honorable with Allah.

33:70 O you who believe! Fear Allah and speak the truth.

33:71 Allah will bless your deeds and forgive your sins. Those who obey Allah and Allah's messenger, they have indeed won a great victory.

33:72 Truly, Allah did offer the trust (of moral responsibility, honesty, and all duties which has ordained) to the heavens, the earth, and the mountains, but they declined to undertake it and were afraid of (punishment) it. But human undertook it. Surely, human was unjust (to themselves) and ignorant (of results).

33:73 Allah will punish the hypocrites, men and women, and those men and women who associate partners with Allah. Allah will pardon the believing men and the believing women. Allah is Forgiving, Merciful.

34. Saba': Sheba

In the name of Allah, the Gracious, the Merciful

34:1 All the praises be to Allah to whom belongs all that is in the heavens and the earth. To Allah be all the praises and thanks in the hereafter. Allah is the All-Wise, the All-Aware.

34:2 Allah knows that which goes into the earth and that which comes out from it, and that which comes down from the heaven and that which goes up to it. Allah is the Merciful, the Forgiving.

34:3 Those who disbelieve say: "The hour (of Judgment) will not come to us." Say: "Yes, by my Rabb, it will surely come to you. Allah knows all the unseen, not even the weight of an atom escapes from Allah's knowledge in the heavens or in the earth; nor there is anything smaller or greater than that, but is recorded in the clear book."

34:4 Allah will reward those who believe and do righteous deeds. They are those for whom there is forgiveness and a generous provision.

34:5 But those who strive against Allah's revelations to frustrate them, there will be a severe painful punishment for them.

34:6 Those who have been given the knowledge can see that the revelations sent to you (O Muhammad) from your Rabb are the truth, and it guides to the way of the exalted in Might, owner of all praise.

34:7 Those who disbelieve say: "Shall we direct you to a man (Muhammad) who will tell you that when you will become fully disintegrated (after death into dust with) full dispersion, then surely you will be created new (again)?"

34:8 Has he (Muhammad) invented a lie against Allah, or is there madness in him? Nay, but those who disbelieve in the hereafter are in punishment, and in gross error.

34:9 Don't they see what is before them and what is behind them in the heaven and the earth? If Allah wills, Allah can sink the earth with them, or cause a piece of the heaven to fall upon them. Surely, there is a sign for every believer who turns to Allah in repentance.

34:10 Indeed Allah bestowed grace on David (saying): "O mountains! Glorify (Allah) with him!" The birds also! Allah made the iron soft for him,

34:11 (saying) that: "You make perfect coats of mail armor and balance well (the rings) of chain armor, and you do righteous deeds. Truly, I (Allah) am All-Seer of what you do."

34:12 To Solomon (Allah subjected) the wind, its morning (sunrise to mid noon) was a month's (journey), and its afternoon (midday to sunset) was a month's (journey). Allah caused a spring of (molten) brass to flow for him, the jinn worked in front of him by the permission of his Rabb, and if any of them turned aside from Allah's command; Allah caused him to taste the punishment of the blazing fire.

34:13 They worked for him what he desired of making high rooms, images, basins as large as reservoirs, and cooking fixed (in their places) vat. (Allah said): "O family of David! You work with thanks!" But few of my (Allah's) devotees are grateful.

34:14 When Allah decreed death for Solomon (he was leaning on his stick), no one informed the jinns of his death until a little termite of the earth chew away his stick and he fell down. The jinns saw clearly that if they had known the unseen, they would not have stayed in the humiliating punishment (of their task).

34:15 Indeed for the people of Sheba (a town in Yemen) there was a sign in their residing place: 2 gardens - one on the right and one on the left. (It was said to them): "Eat of the provision of your Rabb and be grateful to Allah, for a fair land and a Forgiving Rabb."

34:16 But they turned away (from Allah). So Allah sent against them a flood of Arim (released water from the dam), and Allah converted their 2 gardens into gardens which produced bitter fruits, shrubs, and some few lote-trees.

34:17 This is how Allah punished them because they were ungrateful (disbelievers). Allah never punish except those who are ungrateful (disbelievers).

34:18 Allah placed between them and between the towns which Allah had blessed, towns easy to be seen and Allah made stages of journey between them easy (saying): "Travel in them safely night and day."

34:19 But they said: "Our Rabb! Make the stages longer between our journeys." They wronged themselves, so Allah made them (in the land) as tales, and Allah dispersed them in a total scattering. Surely, there are signs for every patient, grateful person.

34:20 Indeed Satan did prove its thought true about them and they all followed him except a group of believers.

34:21 There was no authority for him (Satan) over them except that Allah might test him who believes in the hereafter from him who is in doubt about it. Your Rabb is watching over everything.

34:22 Say (O Muhammad to those polytheists): "Call upon those (deities) whom you assert besides Allah, they do not possess even the weight of an atom in the heavens or on the earth, nor they have any share in either, nor there is any supporter from among them for Allah."

34:23 No intercession with Allah profits anyone except for the one whom Allah permits. Until when the fear will be removed from their hearts, they (angels) shall say: "What your Rabb has said?" They say: "The Truth." Allah is the High, the Great.

34:24 Say (O Muhammad to these polytheists): "Who gives you provision from the heavens and the earth?" Say: "Allah, and surely, either we or you are on guidance or in a plain error."

34:25 Say (O Muhammad to these polytheists): "You will not be asked about our sins, nor we will be asked about your deeds."

34:26 Say: "Our Rabb will assemble us all together (on the day of Resurrection), then Allah will judge between us with truth. Allah is the Trust-worthy judge, All-Knower of everything."

34:27 Say (O Muhammad to these polytheists): "Show me those whom you have joined with Allah as partners. Nay! But Allah is the All-Mighty, the All-Wise."

34:28 Allah has sent you (O Muhammad) as a giver of glad tidings and a warner for all mankind, but most of people do not know.

34:29 They say: "When is this promise (the day of Resurrection will be fulfilled) if you are truthful?"

34:30 Say (O Muhammad): "The appointment day is fixed, which you can neither put back from it for an hour nor put forward."

34:31 Those who disbelieve say: "We do not believe in this Qur'an nor in that which came before it." If you could see when the wrongdoers will be made to stand before their Rabb, how they will refer the blaming word some of them to others! Those who were deemed weak will say to those who were arrogant: "Had it not been for you, we would certainly have been believers!"

34:32 Those who were arrogant will say to those who were deemed weak: "Did we keep you back from guidance after when it had come to you? Nay, but you yourself were sinners."

34:33 Those who were deemed weak will say to those who were arrogant: "Nay, but it was you who plotted night and day, when you ordered us to disbelieve in Allah and set up rivals to Allah!" They will conceal their own regret (for disobeying Allah in this world) when they will see the punishment. Allah will put iron collars round the necks of those who disbelieved. Are they rewarded exactly for what they did?

34:34 Whenever Allah has sent a warner to a town, its wealthy people said: "Surely we do not believe in (the message) what you are sent with."

34:35 They say: "We have more wealth and children (our deities are happy), and we shall not be punished."

34:36 Say (O Muhammad): "Surely, my Rabb enlarges and restricts the provision to whom Allah wills, but most people do not know."

34:37 It is neither your wealth, nor your children that bring you nearer to Allah. But those who believe, and do righteous deeds; for such, they will have double reward for what they did, and they will reside in the high residences (paradise) in peace and security.

34:38 Those who strive against Allah's verses to frustrate them, the punishment will be brought to them.

34:39 Say: "Truly, my Rabb enlarges the provision for whom Allah wills of Allah's servants, and also restricts it for some. Whatever you spend of anything (for Allah), Allah will replace it. Allah is the best of providers."

34:40 (Remember) the day when Allah will gather them all together and then will say to the angels: "Was it you that these people used to worship?"

34:41 They (angels) will say: "Glory be to Allah! Allah is our Rabb instead of them. Nay, but they used to worship the jinns; most of them were believers in them."

34:42 So today (the day of Resurrection) none of you has power to profit or harm one another. Allah will say to those who did wrong: "Taste the punishment of the fire which you denied."

34:43 When Allah's clear verses are recited to them, they say: "This man (Muhammad) wishes to hinder you from that which your forefathers used to worship." Others say: "This is nothing but an invented lie." Those who disbelieve in the truth when it has come to them say: "This is nothing but plain magic!"

34:44 Allah had neither given them scriptures to study, nor had Allah sent to them any warner (messenger) before you (O Muhammad).

34:45 Those who were before them denied; they have not received 1/10th of what Allah had granted to them, yet they denied my (Allah's) messengers, then see how was my (Allah's) punishment!

34:46 Say (O Muhammad to them): "I urge you on one thing only that you stand up for Allah's sake in pairs and individually, and then ponder (yourself the history of Muhammad), is there any madness in your companion (Muhammad)? He is only a warner to you before a severe punishment."

34:47 Say (O Muhammad): "Whatever reward I might have asked of you is for you. My reward is only from Allah and Allah is witness over every thing."

34:48 Say (O Muhammad): "Surely! My Rabb sends down the truth, the Knower of all the unseen."

34:49 Say (O Muhammad): "The truth (the Qur'an) has come, and neither falsehood can create anything nor resurrect (anything)."

34:50 Say: "Even if I go astray, surely, I shall stray only to myself. But if I remain guided, it is for what my Rabb has revealed to me. Truly, Allah is All-Hearer, Ever Near (to all)."

34:51 If you could only see when they (disbelievers on the Day of Judgment) will be terrified with no escape, and they will be seized from a nearby place.

34:52 They will say (in the hereafter): "We do believe now in it;" but how could they receive faith from a place so far off?

34:53 Indeed they did disbelieve in it before (in the world), and they used to guess about the unseen (the hereafter) from a far place.

34:54 A barrier will be placed between them and what they desired (turning to Allah in repentance), as was done before with the people of their kind. Surely, they were in grave doubt.

35. Fatir : The Originator of Creation

In the name of Allah, the Gracious, the Merciful

35:1 All the praise be to Allah, the Creator of the heavens and the earth, who has made the angels with 2, 3 or 4 (pairs of) wings as messengers. Allah adds to creation as Allah wills. Surely, Allah has power over every thing.

35:2 Whatever Mercy Allah grants to mankind, none can withhold it; and whatever Allah withholds, none can grant it thereafter. Allah is the All-Mighty, the All-Wise.

35:3 O mankind! Remember the grace of Allah upon you! Is there any creator other than Allah who provides for you from the heaven and the earth? There is no one worthy of worship but Allah. How then are you being deceived?

35:4 If they deny you (O Muhammad), so surely messengers were denied before you. To Allah all matters return (for decision).

35:5 O mankind! Surely, the promise of Allah is true. So do not let the worldly life deceive you, and do not let the chief deceiver (Satan) deceive you about Allah.

35:6 Surely, Satan is an enemy to you, so take him as an enemy. He is only inviting its followers so that they may become the inmates of the blazing fire.

35:7 Those who disbelieve, there will be a severe punishment for them; and those who believe and do righteous deeds, there will be forgiveness and a great reward for them.

35:8 Can those (be guided), to whom their evil deeds made fair seeming, so that they consider them as good? Surely, Allah sends astray whom Allah wills, and guides whom Allah wills. So do not destroy yourself (O Muhammad) for them in sorrow. Truly, Allah is the All-Knower of what they do!

35:9 It is Allah who sends the winds to raise up the clouds, then Allah drives them to a dead land, and therewith revives the earth after its death. Such will be the Resurrection (of the dead)!

35:10 Whoever desires the honor, (should know that) all honor belongs to Allah alone. Good words ascend to Allah and the righteous deeds are exalted by Allah. But those who plot evils, they will have severe punishment and their plots will perish.

35:11 Allah has created you from dust, then from a drop of semen, and then Allah made you pairs. No female conceives or gives birth without Allah's knowledge. No aged human is granted a long life or the life is cut short but is written in a book. Surely, that is easy for Allah.

35:12 The 2 seas are not alike - one is fresh sweet and pleasant to drink; and the other is salty and bitter. Yet, from each of them you eat fresh meat (fish) and get ornaments which you wear. You see the ships sailing through them, that you may seek Allah's bounty, and that you may give thanks.

35:13 Allah merges the night into the day and the day into the night. Allah has subjected the sun and the moon (to serve you), each runs (its course) for an appointed term. Such is Allah, your Rabb; Allah's is the kingdom. Those to whom you pray instead of Allah, do not even own a thin membrane of a date-stone.

35:14 If you pray to them, they do not hear your call, and even if they hear you, they can not answer you. On the day of Resurrection, they will disown your worshipping them. None can inform you (O mankind) like the one who is the All-Knower.

35:15 O mankind! It is you who stands in need of Allah, but Allah is Rich, Praise-worthy.

35:16 If Allah wills, Allah can destroy you and replace with a new creation,

35:17 and that is not difficult for Allah.

35:18 No bearer of burdens shall bear another's burden, and if one heavily laden calls another to carry it (load), nothing will be lifted from it even though that person is a close relative. You (O Muhammad) can only warn those who fear their unseen Rabb, and establish prayers. Those who purify themselves, and then they purify only for their own selves. To Allah is the final return.

35:19 The blind (disbelievers) and the seeing (believers) are not alike;

35:20 nor the darkness (disbelief) and the light (belief);

35:21 nor the shade and the sun's heat;

35:22 nor the living and the dead. Surely, Allah can make hear whom Allah wills, but you (O Muhammad) cannot make those hear who are in graves.

35:23 You (O Muhammad) are not but a warner.

35:24 Surely! Allah has sent you (O Muhammad) with the truth as a bearer of good news, and as a warner. There was not a nation which did not have a warner.

35:25 If they deny you, so surely were those who came before. Their messengers came to them with clear signs, with the scriptures, and the light-giving book.

35:26 Then Allah seized those who disbelieved, and how terrible was Allah's denial (punishment)!

35:27 Don't you see that Allah sends down rain from the sky and Allah produces therewith fruits of varying colors? Among the mountains there are streaks (paths) white and red of varying colors and intense black.

35:28 Likewise, men, beasts, and cattle have various colors. It is only those among Allah's servants who have knowledge fear Allah. Surely, Allah is All-Mighty, Forgiving.

35:29 Surely, those who recite the book of Allah (this Qur'an), establish prayer, and spend (in charity) out of what Allah has provided for them, secretly and openly, may hope for business that will never perish.

35:30 Allah may pay them their rewards in full and give them more out of Allah's grace. Surely! Allah is forgiving, ready to appreciate (good deeds).

35:31 That which Allah has revealed in you (O Muhammad) of the book (the Qur'an), it is the truth which confirms what was revealed before. Surely! Allah is indeed All-Aware and All-Seer of everything of Allah's servants.

35:32 Then Allah gave the book (the Qur'an) as an inheritance to those of Allah's servants (Muslims) whom Allah has chosen. Among them there are some who wrong their own selves, some of them follow a middle course, and some of them are foremost in good deeds by the permission of Allah. That is the great grace.

35:33 They will enter the gardens of Eden where they will be adorned with bracelets of gold and pearls and their garments will be silk therein.

35:34 They will say: "All the praise be to Allah who has removed all grief from us. Surely, our Rabb is indeed Forgiving, Ready to appreciate (good deeds),

35:35 who has admitted us in a home (in paradise) that will last forever out of Allah's grace; where no toil will touch us nor any weariness."

35:36 But those who disbelieve, there will be the fire of hell for them. Neither it (the fire) will be completed on them so that they die, nor shall its punishment be lightened for them. Thus Allah does pay back every disbeliever!

35:37 They will cry therein: "Our Rabb! Get us out, (from now) we shall do righteous deeds and shall not repeat that (evil deeds) which we used to do." (Allah will reply): "Did Allah not give you lives long enough so that whoever would, could receive warning therein? And the warner came to you. So taste (the evil of your deeds), there is no helper for the wrongdoers."

35:38 Surely, Allah is the All-Knower of the unseen of the heavens and the earth. Surely! Allah is the All-Knower of what is in the hearts.

35:39 It is Allah who has made you vicegerent in the earth. Whoever disbelieves, bears the burden of disbelief. Their disbelief of the disbelievers does not increase anything except the wrath of their Rabb. The disbelief of the disbelievers increases nothing but loss.

35:40 Say (O Muhammad): "What do you think about your partner to whom you call upon besides Allah? Show me, what they have created in the earth? Or do they have any share in the heavens? Or has Allah given them a book so that they act on clear proof from there? Nay, the wrongdoers promise one another nothing but delusions."

35:41 Surely! Allah grasps the heavens and the earth lest they move away (from their places). Even if they were to move away (from their places), there is none who could grasp them besides Allah. Truly, Allah is ever Forbearing, Forgiving.

35:42 They swore by Allah their most binding oath that if a warner ever come to them, they would be more guided than any of the nations (before them). Yet, when a warner (Muhammad) has come to them, it increased nothing in them but flight (from the truth),

35:43 (because of their) arrogance in the land and their plotting of evil. But the evil plotting encompasses only those who make it. Then can they expect anything but the way of former peoples? So you will not find any change in the way of Allah and you will not find any alternation in the way of Allah.

35:44 Have they not traveled in the land and seen how terrible was the end of those who were before them, who were greater in power than them? There is nothing in the heavens or in the earth which can escape Allah. Surely, Allah is the All-Knower, All-Powerful.

35:45 If Allah were to punish people for their evil deeds, Allah would not leave any creature on the surface (of the earth), but Allah is giving them respite for an appointed term, and when their term will come, they surely will realize that Allah is All-Seer of Allah's servants.

36. Ya-Seen : Ya-Seen

In the name of Allah, the Gracious, the Merciful

36:1 Ya-Seen.

36:2 By the Qur'an, full of wisdom,

36:3 truly, you (O Muhammad) are one of the messengers,

36:4 on a right way.

36:5 This is sent down by the Mighty, the Merciful,

36:6 to warn a people whose forefathers were not warned, so they are heedless.

36:7 Indeed the word has proved true against most of them, so they do not believe.

36:8 Surely! Allah has put on their necks iron collars up to the chins so that their heads are made raised up,

36:9 and Allah has put a barrier in front of them, and a barrier behind them, and then Allah has covered them up so they cannot see.

36:10 It is the same to them whether you warn them or you warn them not, they will not believe.

36:11 You can only warn those who follow the reminder (the Qur'an) and fear the gracious (Allah) unseen. So give them good news of forgiveness and a generous reward.

36:12 Surely, Allah will give life to the dead; Allah is recording all that which they are sending before death and their traces of deeds. Allah has recorded everything in a clear book.

36:13 Put forward to them an example; the story of the residents of the town (Antakiya, Turkey) to whom the messengers came.

36:14 When Allah sent to them 2 messengers, they denied them both, so Allah reinforced them with a 3rd, and they said: "Surely! We have been sent to you as messengers."

36:15 They (people of the town) said: "You are but humans like us. The gracious (Allah) has revealed nothing, you are telling lies."

36:16 They (messengers) said: "Our Rabb knows that we have been sent as messengers to you

36:17 and our duty is to convey the message clearly."

36:18 They (people) said: "Surely, we see an evil omen (sign) from you. If you do not stop, we will surely stone you and a painful punishment will touch you from us."

36:19 They (messengers) said: "Your evil omens be with you! (Do you call it 'evil omen' because) you are admonished? Nay, but you are a transgressing people."

36:20 There came a man running from the farthest part of the town and said: "O my people! Follow the messengers.

36:21 Follow those who do not ask of you any wages and they are rightly guided.

36:22 Why should I not worship Allah who has created me and to whom you shall be returned?

36:23 Shall I take another worthy of worship besides Allah? If the gracious (Allah) intends me no harm, their intercession will avail me nothing, nor can they save me.

36:24 Then surely, I would be in plain error.

36:25 Surely! I have believed in your Rabb, so listen to me!"

36:26 It was said (to him when the disbelievers killed him): "Enter paradise." He said: "Would that my people knew (that what I know)!

36:27 That my Rabb has forgiven me and made me among the honored ones!"

36:28 Allah did not send down against his people after him a host from heaven, nor does Allah send (such a thing).

36:29 It was only one shout and then they all were dead silent.

36:30 Alas for the mankind! Whenever a messenger came to them, they used to mock at him.

36:31 Don't they see how many generations Allah has destroyed before them who will not return to them?

36:32 Surely, all of them will be brought before Allah.

36:33 The dead land is a sign for them. Allah gives it life and brings forth grain from it so that they eat from there.

36:34 Allah produces in it gardens of date-palms and grapes, and Allah causes springs of water to gush forth from it,

36:35 so that they may eat the fruits thereof. Their hands did not make it. Should they not give thanks?

36:36 Glory be to Allah who has created all things in pairs which the earth produces, as well as their own (human) kind, and other things which they do not know.

36:37 A sign for them is the night, when Allah withdraws the daylight from it, and behold, they are in darkness.

36:38 The sun runs on its fixed course for a term (appointed) for it. That is a decree of the All-Mighty, the All-Knower.

36:39 The moon, Allah has measured its positions (phases) for it till it returns like the old dried curved date stalk.

36:40 The sun is neither permitted to overtake the moon nor does the night outstrip the day. They all each float in its own orbit.

36:41 A sign for them is that Allah carried their offspring in the laden ship (of Noah).

36:42 Allah has created for them similar (vessels) on which they ride.

36:43 If Allah wills, Allah can drown them, and there will be no helper for them, nor will they be saved,

36:44 except through the Mercy from Allah and as an enjoyment for a while.

36:45 When it is said to them: "Beware of that which is before you (worldly punishments) and that which is behind you (punishments in the hereafter) so that you may receive Mercy."

36:46 Whenever a sign of the verses of their Rabb comes to them, they turn away from it.

36:47 Whenever it is said to them: "Spend out of what Allah has provided you." Those who disbelieve say to those who believe: "Should we feed those whom, if Allah willed, Allah can feed? You are in plain error."

36:48 They say: "When will this promise (Resurrection) be fulfilled if you are truthful?"

36:49 They are waiting for a single shout, which will seize them while they are disputing (among themselves)!

36:50 Then, they will neither be able to make a will, nor they will be able to return to their family.

36:51 The trumpet will be blown in and behold! They will come out quickly from the graves to their Rabb.

36:52 They will say: "Woe to us! Who has raised us up from our place of sleep?" (It will be said to them): "This is what the beneficent (Allah) had promised and the messengers spoke the truth!"

36:53 It will only be a single shout, so behold! They all will be brought up before Allah!

36:54 This day (of Resurrection), no soul will be wronged a thing and you will be rewarded for your deeds.

36:55 Surely, on that day, the residents of the paradise will be busy in joyful things;

36:56 they and their wives will be in pleasant shade reclining on thrones.

36:57 They will have all kinds of fruits in it and they will get whatever they ask for;

36:58 (it will be said to them): "Peace," a word from the Rabb, Merciful.

36:59 (It will be said to sinners): "You get apart this day, you criminals (from the believers).

36:60 O Children of Adam! Did I (Allah) not ordain for you that you should not worship Satan? Surely, he is a plain enemy to you,

36:61 and you should worship me (Allah). That is the right way.

36:62 Indeed he (Satan) has led a great number of you astray. Didn't you understand?

36:63 This is hell which you were warned.

36:64 Now burn in it this day for what you used to disbelieve."

36:65 This day, Allah will seal up their mouths, their hands will speak to Allah, and their legs will bear witness to what they used to earn.

36:66 (If it had been) Allah's will, Allah could surely have wiped out (blinded) over their eyes so that they would struggle for the way, how then could they see?

36:67 Had it been Allah's will, Allah could have transformed them (into animals or lifeless objects) in their places. Then neither they could have been able to go forward nor they could have returned back.

36:68 Those to whom Allah grants long life, Allah reverses them in creation (weakness after strength). Will they not then understand?

36:69 Allah has not taught him (Muhammad) poetry, nor is it suitable for him. This is only a reminder and a plain Qur'an,

36:70 to warn those who are living and to establish the charge against the disbelievers.

36:71 Don't they see that it is Allah who has created for them of what Allah's orders have fashioned the cattle, which are under their dominion?

36:72 Allah has subdued them (animals) to them so that they have some of them for riding and some of them they eat,

36:73 there are other benefits in them and drinks (milk) for them. Should they not then be grateful?

36:74 Yet, they have taken others (worthy of worship) besides Allah hoping to get their help.

36:75 They cannot help them, yet, they will be brought forward as troops against those who worshipped them (at the time of reckoning).

36:76 So let not their speech grieves you (O Muhammad). Surely, Allah knows what they conceal and what they reveal.

36:77 Do not people see that Allah has created them from a sperm? Yet, they (stands up as) open opponent.

36:78 They put an example for Allah and forget their own creations. Allah says: "Who will give life to these bones when they have rotten away and became dust?"

36:79 Say (O Muhammad): "Allah, who has created them for the first time, will give life to them again! Allah is the All-Knower of every creation!"

36:80 It is Allah who produces for you fire from the green tree then behold, you kindle fire therewith.

36:81 Is not Allah who has created the heavens and the earth, able to create the like of them? Yes, indeed! Allah knows everything, supreme Creator.

36:82 Surely, when Allah intends a thing, it is only that Allah says to it: "Be!" and it is!

36:83 So glory be to Allah in whose hands (authority) is the dominion of every thing, and to Allah you shall be returned.

37. As-Saffat : Those who set the Ranks

In the name of Allah, the Gracious, the Merciful

37:1 By those (angels) arranged in rows,

37:2 by those (angels) who are strong in repelling (evil),

37:3 by those (angels) who bring the book (the Qur'an),

37:4 surely your one worthy of worship is indeed One (Allah),

37:5 the Rabb of the heavens and the earth, and all that lies between them, and Rabb of every point of the sun's risings.

37:6 Surely! Allah has adorned the lower heaven with beautiful stars

37:7 and has guarded against all rebellious devils.

37:8 They cannot even listen to the higher group (angels) for they are pelted from every side,

37:9 repulsed and they are under a constant punishment.

37:10 Except such as snatch away something by stealing and they are pursued by a flaming fire of piercing brightness.

37:11 Ask them (polytheists, O Muhammad): "Are they stronger as creation, or those whom Allah has created?" Surely, Allah has created them of sticky clay.

37:12 Nay, you (Muhammad) wonder while they mock (at you and the Qur'an).

37:13 When they are reminded, they do not pay attention,

37:14 and when they see a verse (from Allah), they mock at it

37:15 and say: "This is nothing but clear magic!

37:16 When we are dead and have become dust and bones, shall we then surely be resurrected?

37:17 Also our forefathers of old times?"

37:18 Say (O Muhammad): "Yes and you shall then be humiliated."

37:19 It will be only a single shout and they will be staring!

37:20 They will say: "Woe to us! This is the day of recompense!"

37:21 (It will be said): "This is the day of judgment which you used to deny."

37:22 (It will be said to the angels): "Assemble those who did wrong, together with their companions whom they used to worship

37:23 besides Allah, and lead them to the way of flaming fire (hell)."

37:24 (When they will be gathered, Allah will say): "Stop them, surely they are to be questioned:

37:25 What is the matter with you? Why don't you help one another (as you used to do in the world)?"

37:26 Nay, but that day they shall surrender.

37:27 Some of them will face others to question one another.

37:28 They will say (to their leaders): "Surely, you used to come to us from the right (with authority to beautify every evil, enjoin polytheism, and stop us from the truth)."

37:29 They will reply: "Nay, you were not believers.

37:30 We had no authority over you. Nay! You were transgressing people,

37:31 now the word of our Rabb has become justified against us, and indeed we shall taste (the punishment).

37:32 We led you astray because we were ourselves astray."

37:33 Then surely on that day, they will share in the punishment.

37:34 Certainly, that is how Allah will deal with sinners,

37:35 surely, when it was said to them: "There is no one worthy of worship but Allah," they used to puff themselves up with pride

37:36 and say: "Are we going to abandon our one worthy of worship for the sake of a mad poet?"

37:37 Nay! He (Muhammad) has come with the truth and he has confirmed the (previous) messengers.

37:38 (It will be said): "Surely, you (polytheists) are going to taste the painful punishment;

37:39 and you will be requited nothing except for what you had done (evil deeds)."

37:40 Except the chosen (faithful) devotees of Allah,

37:41 those for them will have known provision:

37:42 fruits, and they shall be honored

37:43 in the gardens of delight (paradise),

37:44 on the thrones facing one another,

37:45 served around (them) with a cup of pure wine,

37:46 crystal-white, delicious to the drinkers.

37:47 Neither they will have any kind of hurt, headache or sin in that, nor will they suffer intoxication from that.

37:48 With them will be chaste females restraining their glances (for husbands only) with wide and beautiful eyes,

37:49 as if they were preserved eggs.

37:50 Some of them will turn to others, questioning each others.

37:51 One of them will say: "Surely, I had a companion for me (in the world),

37:52 who used to say: 'Are you among those who believe (in Resurrection after death)?

37:53 When we die and become dust and bones, shall we indeed (be raised up) to receive reward or punishment (according to deeds)?'"

37:54 It will be said (to that person): "Will you look down (to see the friend)?"

37:55 So the person looked down and saw friend in the midst of the fire.

37:56 The person said: "By Allah! You have nearly ruined me.

37:57 Had it not been for the grace of my Rabb, I would certainly have been among those brought forth (to hell).

37:58 (The believer in the heaven will say): "Are we then not to die (any more)

37:59 after our first death and we shall not be punished?"

37:60 Truly, this is the supreme success!

37:61 For such an end, let everyone strive who wishes to strive.

37:62 Is this (paradise) a better entertainment or the tree of the Zaqqum (a horrible tree in hell)?

37:63 Truly, Allah has made it a trail for the wrongdoers.

37:64 Surely, it is a tree that grows in the bottom of hellfire,

37:65 the shoots of its fruit-stalks are like the heads of devils,

37:66 so truly, they will eat from it and fill their bellies from it.

37:67 Then surely, on top of that, they will be given a mixture of boiling water (to drink).

37:68 Then surely, their return is to the flaming fire of hell.

37:69 In fact, they found their fathers on the wrong way,

37:70 and they are too haste to follow their footsteps!

37:71 Indeed most of the ancient people went astray before them,

37:72 though Allah had sent warners (messengers) among them.

37:73 Then see how was the end of those who were warned (all perished),

37:74 except the chosen (faithful) devotees of Allah.

37:75 Indeed Noah prayed to Allah, and indeed Allah is the best to answer (the prayer).

37:76 Allah rescued him and his family from the great distress (drowning),

37:77 and made his progeny to be the only survivors,

37:78 and Allah left for him (a good name) among generations to come in later times.

37:79 Peace be upon Noah (from Allah) among the (people of) worlds!

37:80 Surely, thus Allah rewards the righteous people.

37:81 Surely, he (Noah) was one of Allah's believing devotees.

37:82 Then Allah drowned the others (disbelievers).

37:83 Surely, among those who followed his (Noah's) way was Abraham,

37:84 when he came to his Rabb with a pure heart.

37:85 When he said to his father and to his people: "What is it you worship?

37:86 Is it a falsehood worthy of worship other than Allah that you seek?

37:87 Then what do you think about the Rabb of the worlds?"

37:88 Then he looked a glance at the stars,

37:89 and said: "Surely, I am sick (he did this trick to stay in their temple of idols to destroy them and not to accompany them to the pagan's feast)."

37:90 So they turned away from him, and departed.

37:91 Then he turned to their idols and said: "Why don't you eat (from food offered)?

37:92 What is the matter with you that you do not speak?"

37:93 Then he turned upon them, striking with his right hand.

37:94 They (idol worshippers) came running towards him.

37:95 He said: "Do you worship what you carve,

37:96 while Allah has created you and what you have make?"

37:97 They said: "Build for him a building (like a furnace) and throw him into the blazing fire!"

37:98 So they plotted against him, but Allah made them the lowest (humiliated).

37:99 He said (after his rescue from fire): "Surely, I am going to my Rabb. Allah will guide me!

37:100 My Rabb! Grant me (offspring) from the righteous."

37:101 So Allah gave him the glad tidings of a gentle boy.

37:102 When he (son) was old enough to walk with him, he said: "O my son! Surely, I have seen in the sleep (a dream) that I am slaughtering you (sacrifice to Allah), so look what do you think!" He said: "O my father! Do what you are commanded, if Allah wills, you shall find me of the patient."

37:103 Then, when they had both submitted themselves (to Allah), and he laid his son prostrate on his forehead (for sacrifice);

37:104 and Allah called out to him: "O Abraham!

37:105 Surely, you have fulfilled the dream!" Surely! Thus Allah rewards the righteous people.

37:106 Surely, that was indeed a clear trial.

37:107 Allah ransomed his son for a great sacrifice

37:108 and Allah left for him (a good name) among the later generations (to come).

37:109 Peace be upon Abraham!

37:110 Thus indeed Allah rewards the righteous people.

37:111 Surely, he was one of Allah's believing devotees.

37:112 Allah gave him the glad tidings of (his son) Isaac, a prophet from the righteous.

37:113 Allah blessed him and Isaac. Of their progeny, there are some who do right, and some plainly wrong themselves.

37:114 Indeed Allah gave Allah's grace to Moses and Aaron.

37:115 Allah saved them and their people from the great distress;

37:116 and helped them, so they became victorious.

37:117 Allah gave them the clear scripture (Torah),

37:118 and guided them to the right way.

37:119 Allah left for them (a good name) among later generations (to come).

37:120 Peace be upon Moses and Aaron!

37:121 Surely, thus Allah does reward the righteous people.

37:122 Surely! They were of Allah's believing devotees.

37:123 Surely, Elias was one of the messengers.

37:124 When he said to his people: "Will you not fear (Allah)?

37:125 Will you call upon Bal (idol) and forsake the best of creators,

37:126 Allah, your Rabb and the Rabb of your forefathers?"

37:127 But they denied him (Elias), so they will certainly be brought forth (to the punishment),

37:128 except the chosen (faithful) devotees of Allah.

37:129 Allah left for him (a good name) among later generations (to come).

37:130 Peace be upon Elias!

37:131 Surely, thus Allah rewards the righteous people.

37:132 Surely, he was one of Allah's believing devotees.

37:133 Surely, Lot was one of the messengers.

37:134 When Allah saved him and all his family,

37:135 except an old woman (who was) among those who remained behind,

37:136 then Allah destroyed the rest (the towns of Sodom at the Dead Sea in Jordan).

37:137 Surely, you pass by them in the morning,

37:138 and at night; will you not then reflect (think)?

37:139 Surely, Jonah was one of the messengers.

37:140 When he ran to the laden ship,

37:141 he (agreed to) cast lots, and he was among the losers.

37:142 Then a (big) fish swallowed him while he had done an act worthy of blame.

37:143 Had it not been that he was of those who glorify (Allah),

37:144 he would have indeed remained in its belly (the fish) till the day of Resurrection.

37:145 Then Allah cast him out on the naked shore while he was sick

37:146 and Allah caused a plant of gourd (squash) to grow over him.

37:147 Then Allah had sent him to a nation of 100,000 people or even more.

37:148 They believed; so Allah gave them enjoyment for a while.

37:149 Now ask them (disbelievers, O Muhammad): (Does it make sense that) your Rabb should have only daughters while they choose to have sons?

37:150 Or did Allah create the angels as females while they were witnesses?

37:151 Surely, they invent a lie when they say:

37:152 "Allah has begotten (children). Surely, they are liars!"

37:153 Has Allah chosen daughters (rather than) sons?

37:154 What is the matter with you? How do you decide?

37:155 Will you not then remember?

37:156 Or is there any plain authority for you?

37:157 Then bring your book if you are truthful!

37:158 They have invented a kinship between Allah and the jinns, but indeed the jinns know quite well that they will be brought for account (before Allah).

37:159 Glory be to Allah! Allah is free from what they attribute to Allah

37:160 except the chosen (faithful) devotees of Allah.

37:161 So, neither you nor those whom you worship (idols)

37:162 can lead (anyone) astray over Allah

37:163 except those who are destined to burn in hell!

37:164 (The angels say): "There is one known place for us.

37:165 Surely, we stand in rows (for prayers);

37:166 surely, we are those who glorify (Allah)."

37:167 Indeed they (disbelievers) used to say:

37:168 "If we had a reminder like the people of old received (before the coming of Muhammad),

37:169 we would have indeed been the chosen devotees of Allah!"

37:170 But (since the Qur'an has come) they disbelieve in it (the Qur'an), and they will come to know (the consequence soon)!

37:171 Surely, Allah's word has gone forth for Allah's devotees, the messengers,

37:172 that surely they would be victorious,

37:173 and verily, Allah's hosts (soldiers) will be victorious.

37:174 So turn away (O Muhammad) from them for a while,

37:175 and watch them, and they shall see (your victory)!

37:176 Do they seek to hasten on Allah's punishment?

37:177 Then, when it descends into their court-yard (near them), then evil will be the morning for those who had been warned!

37:178 So turn (O Muhammad) away from them for a while,

37:179 and watch (their downfall) and they shall see (your victory)!

37:180 Glory be to your Rabb, the Rabb of honor and power, (Allah is free) from what they attribute to Allah!

37:181 Peace be upon the messengers,

37:182 and all the praise be to Allah, Rabb of the worlds.

38. Sad : Sad

In the name of Allah, the Gracious, the Merciful

38:1 Sad. By the Qur'an full of reminding.

38:2 Surely, those who disbelieve are in false pride and opposition.

38:3 How many generations has Allah destroyed before them? They cried out when there was no longer time for escape!

38:4 They wonder that a warner (Muhammad) has come to them from among themselves! The disbelievers say: "This (Muhammad) is a sorcerer, a liar.

38:5 Has he made all ones worthy of worship into one worthy of worship (Allah)? Surely, this is a strange thing!"

38:6 The leaders among them went about (saying): "Go on, and remain firm to your one worthy of worship! Surely, this is a thing designed (against you)!

38:7 We have not heard like this in the religion of the last days. This is nothing but an invention!

38:8 Has the reminder been sent down to him alone from among us?" Nay! but they are in doubt about my (Allah's) reminder (this Qur'an)! Nay, but they have not tasted (Allah's) punishment!

38:9 Or do they have the treasures of the Mercy of your Rabb, the All-Mighty, the Real Bestower?

38:10 Or is the dominion of the heavens and the earth for them and what is between them? If so, let them ascend up with their means!

38:11 They will be like a defeated army of the confederates (who were defeated).

38:12 Before them the people of Noah, Ad, Pharaoh, and the people of stakes, denied (messengers),

38:13 and Thamud, and the people of Lot, and the residents of the wood (Median); such were the confederates,

38:14 each of them denied the messengers, therefore my (Allah's) punishment was justified.

38:15 These people wait nothing but only for a single shout; it has no pause of ending.

38:16 They say: "Our Rabb! Hasten to us our account (of deeds) before the day of reckoning!"

38:17 Be patient (O Muhammad) on what they say, and remember Allah's servant David, gifted with power. Surely, he was often turning in repentance (toward Allah).

38:18 Surely, Allah made the mountains to glorify Allah's praises with him (David) in the evening and after sunrise.

38:19 All the birds too assembled with him (David) and did turn (to Allah).

38:20 Allah made his kingdom strong and gave him wisdom and sound judgment in speech (decision).

38:21 Has the news of the 2 litigants (engaged in lawsuit) reached you when they climbed over the chamber (into his praying place)?

38:22 When they entered in upon David, he was terrified of them. They said: "Do not fear! We are 2 litigants; one of us has wronged on the other, therefore judge between us with truth, and not be unjust, and guide us to the right way.

38:23 Surely, this is my brother (in religion), he has 99 ewes (female sheep), while I have only one ewe. Yet he says: 'Hand it over to me, and he overpowered me in speech.'"

38:24 (David) said (without listening to the opponent): "He indeed has wronged you in demanding your ewe to his ewes. Surely, many partners oppress one on another, except those who believe and do righteous deeds, and they are few." (While saying this) David realized that Allah has tested him, he sought forgiveness of his Rabb, he fell down prostrate, and turned to Allah in repentance.

38:25 So Allah forgave him. Surely, for him is a near access to Allah and a good place of return (paradise).

38:26 (Allah said): "O David! Surely! Allah has placed you as a vicegerent on the earth, so judge between people with justice and do not follow your desire, for it will mislead you from the way of Allah. Surely! Those who wander astray from the way of Allah, they will have a severe punishment, because they forgot the day of Reckoning.

38:27 Allah did not create the heaven and the earth and all that is between them without purpose! That is the consideration of those who disbelieve! Then woe to those who disbelieve from the fire!

38:28 Or should Allah treat those who believe and do righteous deeds like those who are mischief-makers on earth? Or should Allah treat the pious as criminals?

38:29 This is a book (the Qur'an) which Allah has sent down to you (O Muhammad), full of blessings so that they may ponder over its verses and men of understanding may learn.

38:30 Allah granted Solomon to David. How excellent a devotee! Surely, he was often turning in repentance (to Allah)!

38:31 When the well-trained horses of the highest breed (for Allah's cause) were displayed before him in one evening,

38:32 and he said: "Surely I did love the good (of these horses) instead of remembering my Rabb (in my Asr prayer)," till the time was over, and the sun had hidden in the veil (of night),

38:33 (then he said): "Bring them (horses) back to me." Then he began to pass his hand over their legs and their necks (with affection).

38:34 Indeed, Allah did test Solomon and Allah placed on his throne a body (a devil, so he lost his kingdom for a while), then he did return (to Allah with repentance, and to his throne by the grace of Allah).

38:35 He said: "My Rabb! Forgive me, and bestow upon me a kingdom such as shall not be given to anyone after me. Surely, you (Allah) are the Bestower."

38:36 So, Allah (accepted his prayer and) subjected to him the wind, it blew gently to his order wherever he willed,

38:37 and also the devils from the jinns with every kind of builder and diver

38:38 and also others bound in fetters.

38:39 (Allah said to Solomon): "This is Allah's gift, so you spend or withhold, no account will be asked."

38:40 Surely, he has a place of nearness to Allah and will have a good final return (paradise).

38:41 Remember Allah's devotee Job, when he invoked his Rabb (saying): "Surely! Satan has afflicted me with distress (by losing my health) and suffering (by losing my wealth)."

38:42 (Allah said to him): "Strike (the ground) with your foot: This is (a spring of water) to wash in, cool and drink."

38:43 Allah gave him back his family, and the like thereof along with them as a Mercy from Allah, and a reminder for those who understand.

38:44 (Allah said): "Take a bundle of branches (thin grass) in your hand and strike with it (your wife to fulfill your oath of 100 strikes which was made during sickness), and do not break your oath." Truly! Allah found him patient. How excellent is the devotee! Surely, he was often turning in repentance (to Allah)!

38:45 Remember Allah's devotees, Abraham, Isaac, and Jacob, all owners of strength (in worship) and also of religious understanding.

38:46 Surely, Allah chose them by granting them a good thing, the remembrance of the home (of hereafter).

38:47 Surely, they are to Allah, of those chosen and the best!

38:48 Remember Ishmael, Elisha, and Isaiah, and all were among the best.

38:49 This is a reminder (the Qur'an), and surely, for those pious people there is a good final return (paradise).

38:50 The everlasting (Eden) gardens whose doors will be open for them.

38:51 They will recline in it, they will call for fruits in abundance and drinks;

38:52 and with them will be chaste females (virgins) restraining their glances (only for their husbands), equal in age.

38:53 This is what you (the pious) are promised for the day of reckoning,

38:54 surely, this is Allah's provision which will never finish.

38:55 This is so! Surely for the transgressors, an evil will be return,

38:56 hell! where they will burn, and worst is that place to rest!

38:57 This is so! Then let them taste it, a boiling fluid and dirty wound discharges

38:58 and other (punishments) of similar kind, (all together) in pairs!

38:59 (The misguided leaders will be told): "This is a troop entering with you (in hell), no welcome for them! Surely, they will burn in the fire!"

38:60 (The followers of the misguided leaders will say): "Nay, you too! No welcome for you! It is you (leaders) who brought this upon us. Such an evil is this place to stay in!"

38:61 They will say: "Our Rabb! Those who brought this upon us, add to them double punishment in the fire!"

38:62 They will say (to each other): "What is the matter with us that we do not see those people whom we used to count among the bad ones?

38:63 Did we take them as an object of mockery, or our eyes failed to perceive them?"

38:64 Surely, that is the very truth: the people of the fire will have mutual dispute (common habit)!

38:65 Say (O Muhammad): "I am only a warner and there is no one worthy of worship except Allah, the One, the Irresistible,

38:66 the Rabb of the heavens and the earth and all that is between them, the Mighty, the Forgiving."

38:67 Say: "That (the Qur'an) is a great news,

38:68 from which you turn away!"

38:69 (Say): "I had no knowledge of the exalted chiefs (angels) when they disputed (about the creation of Adam).

38:70 This is inspired to me with that I am only a plain warner."

38:71 (Remember) when your Rabb said to the angels: "Surely, I (Allah) am going to create a man from clay,

38:72 so when I (Allah) have fashioned him and breathed into him (his soul) from me (Allah's spirit), then you fall down to him and prostrate."

38:73 So the angels prostrated, all of them together,

38:74 except Satan, he was proud and was one of the disbelievers.

38:75 (Allah) said: "O Satan! What prevents you from prostrating to one whom I (Allah) have created with my (Allah's) own hands? Are you too proud or are you of the high exalted?"

38:76 (Satan) said: "I am better than he, Allah created me from fire, and Allah created him from clay."

38:77 (Allah) said: "Then get out from here, for surely, you are accursed,

38:78 and surely! My (Allah's) curse shall be on you till the day of recompense."

38:79 (Satan) said: "My Rabb! Then give me respite till the day is resurrected."

38:80 (Allah) said: "Surely! You are of those allowed respite

38:81 till the day of the time appointed."

38:82 (Satan) said: "By your (Allah's) might, I will surely mislead them all,

38:83 except Allah's chosen (faithful) devotees amongst them."

38:84 (Allah) said: "Then the truth, and the truth I (Allah) say,

38:85 that I (Allah) will fill hell with you (Satan) and those of them (mankind) who follow you, all."

38:86 Say (O Muhammad): "I ask you no wage for this (the Qur'an), nor am I one of the fakers (imposters).

38:87 It (this Qur'an) is nothing but a reminder for all (worlds),

38:88 and you shall certainly know its news after a while."

39. Az-Zumar : The Groups
In the name of Allah, the Gracious, the Merciful

39:1 The revelation of this book (the Qur'an) is from Allah, the All-Mighty, the All-Wise.

39:2 Surely, Allah has sent down the book to you (O Muhammad) in truth. So worship Allah (alone) sincerely, the religion is for Allah.

39:3 Surely, the religion is completely for Allah (alone). Those who take protectors besides Allah (say): "We worship them only so that they may bring us near to Allah." Surely, Allah will judge between them concerning that in which they differ. Truly, Allah does not guide the one who is a liar, and a disbeliever.

39:4 Had Allah willed to take a son, Allah could have chosen anyone of those whom Allah has created and with whom Allah is pleased. But glory be to Allah! Allah is the One, the Irresistible.

39:5 Allah has created the heavens and the earth with the truth. Allah makes the night overtake the day and makes the day overtake the night. Allah has subjected the sun and the moon, each is running for an appointed term. Surely, Allah is the All-Mighty, the Forgiving.

39:6 Allah has created you all from a single person (Adam); then made his wife (Eve) from him. Allah has sent down for you of cattle 8 in pairs. Allah creates you in the wombs of your mothers, creation after creation in 3 layers of darkness. Such is Allah, your Rabb. The kingdom belongs to Allah; there is no one worthy of worship but Allah. How can you then turn away (from Allah)?

39:7 If you disbelieve, then surely (know that), Allah does not need you. Allah does not like disbelief from Allah's servants. If you are grateful (believer), Allah is pleased with you. No bearer of burdens shall bear the burden of another. Then your return is to your Rabb. So Allah will inform you what you did. Surely, Allah is the All-Knower of that which is in the hearts.

39:8 When some trouble touches people, they cry to their Rabb, turning to Allah in repentance. But when Allah bestows a favor upon them from Allah, they forget what they had supplicated (cried) to Allah before, and they set up rivals to Allah in order to mislead others from Allah's way. Say: "Take pleasure in your disbelief for a while. Surely, you will be one of the inmates of the fire!"

39:9 Can the one who is obedient to Allah, prostrating or standing (in prayer) during the hours of the night, fearing the hereafter and hoping for the Mercy of the Rabb (be compared with a disbeliever)? Say: "Are those who know equal to those who do not know?" It is only people of understanding who will remember.

39:10 Say (O Muhammad): "O Allah's servants who believe, be afraid of your Rabb and keep your duty (to Allah). Good reward is for those who do good in this world, and Allah's earth is spacious (if you cannot worship Allah at a place, then go to another)! Only those who are patient shall receive their rewards without reckoning."

39:11 Say (O Muhammad): "Surely, I am commanded to worship Allah sincerely doing the religious deeds for Allah

39:12 and I am commanded in order to be the first of those who submit themselves to Allah as Muslims."

39:13 Say (O Muhammad): "Surely, if I disobey my Rabb, I am afraid of the punishment of a great day."

39:14 Say (O Muhammad): "I worship Allah by doing my religion sincerely for Allah's sake."

39:15 So worship what you like besides Allah. Say (O Muhammad): "Surely, the losers are those who will lose themselves and their families on the day of Resurrection. Surely, that will be a clear loss!"

39:16 They shall have coverings of fire from above them and coverings (of fire) beneath them; so that with this Allah frightens Allah's servants: "O my (Allah's) servants, therefore, fear me (Allah)!"

39:17 Those who avoid false deities by not worshipping them and turn to Allah in repentance, there are glad tidings for them. So announce (O Muhammad) the good news to my (Allah's) servants,

39:18 those who listen to the word (to worship Allah) and follow the best thereof. Such are the ones whom Allah has guided and such are the people of understanding.

39:19 Is the one against whom the word of punishment is justified (equal to the one who avoids evil)? Can you rescue the one who is in the fire?

39:20 But those who fear their Rabb, for them lofty rooms are built one above another, with flowing rivers under them (paradise). This is the promise of Allah and Allah does not fail in Allah's promise.

39:21 Don't you see that Allah sends down water (rain) from the sky, and it penetrates in the earth and comes out as water-springs? Afterwards (Allah) produces crops of different colors, then they wither and you see them turn yellow, and then Allah makes them dry and broken pieces. Surely, in this, there is a reminder for people of understanding.

39:22 Is the one whose heart Allah has opened to Islam and is in light from its Rabb (same as one who disbelieves)? So woe to those whose hearts are hardened against remembrance of Allah! They are in plain error!

39:23 Allah has sent down the best statement, a book (this Qur'an), its parts resemble each other, often repeated. The skins of those who fear their Rabb shiver from it. Then their skins and their hearts soften to the remembrance of Allah. Such is the guidance of Allah. Allah guides with it whom Allah pleases and whomever Allah sends astray, there is no guide for that person.

39:24 Is the one who will confront with the awful punishment on the day of Resurrection (same as one who enters peacefully into paradise)? It will be said to the wrongdoers: "Taste what you earned!"

39:25 Those who also denied before them, the punishment came on them from where they did not perceive.

39:26 So Allah made them to taste the disgrace in the present life, but the punishment of the hereafter is greater if they only knew!

39:27 Indeed Allah has put forth every kind of example for mankind in this Qur'an in order that they may remember.

39:28 It is an Arabic Qur'an without any crookedness (flaw) in it in order that they may avoid all evil.

39:29 Allah puts forth an example: a captive belongs to many partners disputing with one another (like one who believes in many false deities), and a captive belongs entirely to one master (like one believes in one Allah). Are these 2 equal in comparison? All the praise be to Allah! But most of them do not know.

39:30 Surely, you (O Muhammad) will die and surely, they too will die.

39:31 Then surely on the day of Resurrection, you will dispute (to settle) before your Rabb.

39:32 Who is worse than one who utters a lie against Allah, and denies the truth when it comes to that person? Is there not an abode in hell for the disbelievers?

39:33 The one who brings the truth and believes in it - they are those who are the pious people.

39:34 They shall have all that they will desire from their Rabb. That is the reward of the righteous people.

39:35 Allah will expiate their evil deeds from them and give them the reward according to their best deeds.

39:36 Is Allah not sufficient for Allah's servants? Yet they try to frighten you with those besides Allah! The one whom Allah sends astray, there is no guide for that person.

39:37 The one whom Allah guides, there is none to mislead that person. Is not Allah the mighty, the possessor of retribution?

39:38 Surely, if you ask them: "Who created the heavens and the earth?" Surely, they will say: "Allah." Say: "Do you see the things that you invoke besides Allah, if Allah intends some harm for me, could they remove Allah's harm, or if Allah intends some Mercy for me, could they withhold Allah's Mercy?" Say: "Allah is sufficient for me. Those who trust in Allah, must put their trust."

39:39 Say: (O Muhammad): "O my people! Work according to your way, surely I am working (according to my way). Then you will come to know,

39:40 to whom a disgracing punishment will come, and on whom an everlasting punishment will descend."

39:41 Surely, Allah has sent down to you (O Muhammad) the book (this Qur'an) for mankind in truth. So those who accept the guidance, it is only for their own self, and those who go astray, they go astray only to their own loss. You (O Muhammad) are not a trustee over them.

39:42 It is Allah who takes away the souls at the time of their death, and those that do not die during their sleep. Allah keeps those souls for which Allah has ordained death and sends the rest for an appointed term. Surely, in that there are signs for people who think deeply.

39:43 Have they taken others besides Allah as intercessors? Ask: "(How can they intercede) if they do not possess anything and have no intelligence?"

39:44 Say: "All intercession belongs to Allah. The sovereignty of the heavens and the earth is with Allah, and then to Allah you all shall be brought back."

39:45 When Allah alone is mentioned, the hearts of those who do not believe in the hereafter are filled with disgust and when those (whom they worship) besides Allah are mentioned, behold, they rejoice!

39:46 Say (O Muhammad): "O Allah! Creator of the heavens and the earth, All-Knower of the unseen and the seen! Allah will judge between your servants about which they differed."

39:47 If those who did wrong (disbelievers) possessed all that is in earth and as much again with it, they surely would offer it to ransom with it (to save) from the evil punishment on the day of Resurrection. It will become apparent to them from Allah what they would never have imagined.

39:48 The evils of their deeds will become apparent to them and they will be encircled with them by that which they used to mock at!

39:49 When harm touches people, they call to Allah (for help), then when Allah grants them a favor from Allah, they say: "Only because we were given this knowledge." Nay, it is only a trial, but most of them do not know!

39:50 Surely, those before them said it, yet all that they had earned did not avail them.

39:51 So, the evil of that which they earned overtook them. Those who did wrong, will be overtaken by the evil results (punishment) of that which they earned, and they will never be able to escape.

39:52 Don't they know that Allah enlarges the provision for whom Allah wills, and straitens it (for whom Allah wills)? Surely, there are signs in this for those who believe!

39:53 (Allah) says: "O my (Allah's) servants who have transgressed against themselves (by evil deeds)! Do not despair of the Mercy of Allah, surely Allah forgives all sins. Truly, Allah is Forgiving, Merciful.

39:54 Turn in repentance to your Rabb and submit to Allah before the punishment comes upon you, then you will not be helped.

39:55 Follow the best way which is sent down (the Qur'an) to you from your Rabb before the punishment comes on you suddenly while you do not perceive!

39:56 Lest a person should say: 'Alas, my grief is that I neglected my duty to Allah, and I was indeed among those who mocked (the truth).'

39:57 Or lest a person should say: 'If only Allah had guided me, indeed I would have been among the righteous.'

39:58 Or lest a person should say when sees the punishment: 'If I had only another chance (to return to the world) then I would be among the righteous people.'"

39:59 (Allah will say): "Yes! Surely, Allah's verses did come to you, you denied them, and you were proud and were among the disbelievers."

39:60 On the day of Resurrection you will see those who lied against Allah, their faces will be black. Is there not an abode for the arrogant in hell?

39:61 Allah will deliver those who are the pious to their places of success (paradise). Evil shall not touch them, nor shall they grieve.

39:62 Allah is the Creator of all things, and Allah is the Trustee over all things.

39:63 To Allah belong the keys of the heavens and the earth. Those who disbelieve in the verses of Allah, those are they who will be the losers.

39:64 Say (O Muhammad to the polytheists): "Do you order me to worship other than Allah? O you fools!"

39:65 Indeed it has been revealed to you (O Muhammad), and to those before you: "If you join others with Allah, then surely your deeds will be in vain, and you will certainly be among the losers."

39:66 So worship Allah, and be among the grateful.

39:67 They have not made a just estimate (worth) of Allah such as is due to Allah. On the day of Resurrection, the whole earth will be grasped by Allah's authority and the heavens will be rolled up in Allah's right hand (authority). Glory be to Allah, and high is Allah above all that they associate as partners with Allah!

39:68 The trumpet will be blown in, and all who are in the heavens and the earth will fall dead, except those whom Allah wills. Then the trumpet will blow for a 2nd time and then they all will be standing, looking on (waiting).

39:69 The earth will shine with the light of its Rabb, the book (of records) will be placed open, the prophets and the witnesses will be brought forward, it will be judged between people with truth, and they will not be wronged.

39:70 Each person will be rewarded in full of what it did; and Allah is Best Aware of what they did.

39:71 Those who disbelieved will be driven to hell in groups. When they reach it, the gates will be opened. Its keepers will say to them: "Did not the messengers come to you from yourselves, reciting to you the verses of your Rabb, and warning you of the meeting of this day of yours?" They will say: "Yes." But the word of punishment has already been justified against the disbelievers!

39:72 It will be said (to them): "Enter the gates of hell to abide in it, and an evil abode of the arrogant!"

39:73 Those who kept their duty to their Rabb, will be driven to paradise in groups. When they reach it, its gates will be opened to them, and its keepers will say: "Peace be upon you! You have done well, so enter it to abide in it."

39:74 They (believers) will say: "All the praises are due to Allah who has fulfilled Allah's promise and has made us inherit the land. We can reside in paradise wherever we will." How excellent a reward for the pious!

39:75 You will see the angels surrounding the Throne (of Allah) from all round, glorifying the praise of their Rabb. They (people) will be judged with truth, and it will be said: "All praises are due to Allah, the Rabb of the worlds!"

40. Ghafir : The Forgiver
In the name of Allah, the Gracious, the Merciful

40:1 Ha-Mim.

40:2 The revelation of this book (this Qur'an) is from Allah, the All-Mighty, the All-Knower,

40:3 the Forgiver of sin, and the Acceptor of repentance, the Severe in punishment, the Bestower (of favors), no one worthy of worship except Allah, to Allah is the final return.

40:4 None disputes in the verses of Allah but those who disbelieve, so let not their ability of going about here and there through the land deceive you (O Muhammad)!

40:5 Before them the people of Noah and the confederates after them denied (their messengers). Every (disbelieving) nation plotted against their messenger to seize him, and disputed by means of falsehood to refute therewith the truth. So Allah seized them (with punishment), and how terrible was Allah's punishment!

40:6 Thus the word of your Rabb has been justified against those who disbelieved; they will be the inmates of the fire.

40:7 Those (angels) who bear the Throne (of Allah) and those who are around it glorify the praises of their Rabb, and believe in Allah, and ask forgiveness for those who believe (saying): "Our Rabb! Allah comprehends all things in Mercy and knowledge, so forgive those who repent and follow Allah's way, and save them from the punishment of the blazing fire!

40:8 Our Rabb! Make them enter the gardens of (everlasting) Eden (paradise) which you (Allah) have promised them, and who was righteous among their fathers, their wives, and their offspring! Surely, you (Allah) are the All-Mighty, the All-Wise.

40:9 Save them from (the punishment) of the sins, and whomever you (Allah) save from (the punishment of) the sins (excuse them) that day, surely, you (Allah) gave them Mercy." That is the supreme success.

40:10 Truly those who disbelieve will be addressed (at the entry time to the fire): "Allah's dislike towards you was greater (in the world when you used to reject the faith) than your dislike towards one another (now you are enemies to one another in the hellfire), when you were called to the faith but you used to refuse."

40:11 They will say: "Our Rabb! You (Allah) have made us die twice (dead in the loins of our fathers and dead in this world), and you (Allah) have given us life twice (when born and when resurrected)! Now we confess our sins, then is there any way to get out (of the fire)?"

40:12 (It will be replied): "This is because, when Allah alone was invoked (in worship) you disbelieved, but when partners were joined to Allah, you believed! So the judgment is only with Allah, the High, the Great!"

40:13 It is Allah who shows you Allah's verses and sends down provision for you from the sky. None remembers but those who turn to Allah.

40:14 So you (O Muhammad and the believers) call upon Allah making your worship pure to Allah. However much the disbelievers may hate the religion.

40:15 Allah is the owner of High Ranks and Degrees, the Owner of the Throne. Allah sends the inspiration by Allah's command to any of Allah's servants whom Allah wills, that he (the prophet who receives inspiration) warns people of the day of mutual meeting (Resurrection).

40:16 The day when they all will come out, nothing of them will be hidden from Allah. (It will be asked): "Whose kingdom is this day?" (Allah will reply to Allah's question): "It is to Allah, the One, the Irresistible!

40:17 This day every person shall be recompensed for what it has earned. Today no injustice (shall be done to anybody). Truly, Allah is Swift in reckoning."

40:18 Warn them (O Muhammad) of the day that is drawing near (the day of Resurrection), when the hearts will be choking the throats (with grief), and they can neither return them (hearts) to their chests nor they can throw them out. The wrongdoers will have neither friend nor intercessor who could be given attention.

40:19 Allah knows the fraud of the eyes, and all that the hearts conceal.

40:20 Allah will judge the truth, while those whom they invoke besides Allah, cannot judge anything. Certainly, Allah is the All-Hearer, the All-Seer.

40:21 Have they not traveled in the land and seen what was the end of those who were before them? They were superior to them in strength and in traces (they left) in the land. But Allah seized them for their sins. They had none to protect them from Allah.

40:22 That was because there came to them their messengers with clear evidences. But they disbelieved. So Allah seized them. Surely, Allah is Strong, Severe in punishment.

40:23 Indeed Allah sent Moses with Allah's verses, and a clear authority,

40:24 to Pharaoh, Haman, and Korah; but they called (Moses): "A sorcerer, a liar!"

40:25 Then, when he brought the truth from Allah to them, they said: "Kill the sons of those who believe with him and let their women live." But the plots of disbelievers (were nothing) but in errors!

40:26 Pharaoh said: "Let me kill Moses, and let him call his Rabb (to stop me)! Surely, I fear that he may change your religion or that he may cause mischief to appear in the land!"

40:27 Moses said: "Surely, I seek refuge in my Rabb and your Rabb from every arrogant who do not believe in the day of reckoning!"

40:28 A believer from Pharaoh's family, who hid his faith, said: "Will you kill a man because he says: 'My Rabb is Allah,' especially when Moses has come to you with clear signs from your Rabb? If he is a liar, his sin will lie upon him; but if he is telling the truth, then some of that (calamity) which he threatens you will befall on you. Surely, Allah does not guide the one who is a polytheist, a liar!

40:29 O my people! You are the ruler today and you are uppermost in the land. But who will save us from the punishment of Allah, if it comes to us?" Pharaoh said: "I show you what I see correct and I guide you to the way of right policy!"

40:30 He (who believed) said: "O my people! Surely, I fear for you a fate like that day (disaster) of the confederates,

40:31 like the fate of the people of Noah, Ad, Thamud, and those who came after them. Allah wants no injustice for Allah's servants.

40:32 O my people! Surely! I fear for you the day when there will be mutual calling (between the people of hell and paradise),

40:33 a day when you will turn your backs and you have no protector from Allah. Whomever Allah sends astray, there is no guide for that person.

40:34 Indeed Joseph did come to you before with clear signs, but you were always in doubt concerning what he did bring to you, till when he died with it, you said: 'Allah will never send a messenger after him.' Thus Allah leaves those astray who are the doubtful polytheists,

40:35 who dispute in Allah's verses without any authority that has come to them. It is greatly hateful to Allah and to those who believe. Thus Allah seals up every heart of arrogant, tyrant."

40:36 Pharaoh said: "O Haman! Build a tower for me so that I may arrive at the ways,

40:37 the ways to the heavens, and I may look upon the one worthy of worship of Moses but surely, I think him to be a liar." Thus it was made seem fair in Pharaoh's eyes, the evil of his deeds, and he was hindered from the right way. The plot of Pharaoh led to nothing but in loss.

40:38 The man who believed, said: "O my people! Follow me; I will guide you to the way of right conduct.

40:39 O my people! Truly, this life of the world is nothing but an enjoyment, and surely, the hereafter is the home that will remain forever.

40:40 Whoever does an evil deed, will be requited the like thereof; and whoever is a true believer and does a righteous deed, whether male or female, such one will enter paradise where they will be provided in it (all things) without limit.

40:41 O my people! How is it that I call you to salvation and you call me to the fire?

40:42 You invite me to disbelieve in Allah and to join (partners) with Allah about which I have no knowledge; while I invite you to the All-Mighty, the Forgiving!

40:43 No doubt that you call me to worship it which can neither grant a claim (request) in this world nor in the hereafter. Our return will be to Allah; and the polytheists will be the inmates of the fire!

40:44 You will remember what I am telling you and I leave all my matters to Allah. Surely, Allah is the All-Seer of everything of the servants."

40:45 So Allah saved him (that believer) from the evils what they plotted (against him), and encompassed Pharaoh's people with an evil punishment.

40:46 They are exposed to the fire morning and afternoon, and on the day when the hour will be established (angels will be told): "Cause Pharaoh's people to enter the severest punishment!"

40:47 When they will dispute in the fire, the weak will say to those who were arrogant: "Surely! We were your followers, so can you save us from a portion of the fire?"

40:48 Those who were arrogant will say: "Surely we are all together in it (fire)! Verily, Allah has judged between Allah's servants!"

40:49 Those in the fire will say to the keepers (angels) of hell: "Call upon your Rabb to lighten the punishment for us for a day!"

40:50 They (keepers) will say: "Did there not come to you messengers with clear evidences? They will say: "Yes." They will reply: "Then pray (as you like)!" But the invocation of the disbelievers is nothing but in error!

40:51 Surely, Allah will make Allah's messengers victorious and those who believe in worldly life and on the day when the witnesses will stand.

40:52 The day when their excuses will not benefit the wrongdoers. The curse will be for them and for them will be evil abode (painful punishment).

40:53 Indeed Allah gave Moses the guidance, and Allah caused the children of Israel to inherit the scripture (the Torah),

40:54 a guide and a reminder for people of understanding.

40:55 So be patient (O Muhammad). Surely, the promise of Allah is true, ask forgiveness for your fault, and glorify the praises of your Rabb in the early evening hours and in the early morning hours.

40:56 Surely, those who dispute about Allah's verses without any authority bestowed to them, there is nothing else in their hearts except arrogance. They will never have it (Prophethood which Allah has bestowed upon you). So seek refuge with Allah. Surely, Allah is the All-Hearer, All-Seer.

40:57 The creation of the heavens and the earth is indeed a greater task than the creation of mankind, yet most of mankind does not know.

40:58 Not equal are the blind and those who see; nor are equal those who believe and do righteous deeds, and those who do evil. Little do you think!

40:59 Surely, the hour (Day of Judgment) is coming and there is no doubt about it, yet most people do not believe.

40:60 Your Rabb said: "Invoke Allah, Allah will respond to you. Surely! Those who are arrogant about Allah's worship, they will surely enter hell in humiliation!"

40:61 It is Allah who has made the night for you so that you may rest in it and the day for you to see. Truly, Allah is bountiful to mankind, yet most people do not give thanks.

40:62 That is Allah, your Rabb, the Creator of all things, there is no one worthy of worship but Allah, how then you are turned away (from Allah)?

40:63 Thus those who were turned away were denying in the verses of Allah.

40:64 It is Allah who has made for you the earth as a residing place and the sky as a canopy. Allah has given you shape and made your shapes good looking and has provided you with good things. That is Allah, your Rabb, then blessed be Allah, the Rabb of the worlds.

40:65 Allah is the Ever-living; there is no one worthy of worship but Allah, so invoke Allah making your worship pure (alone) to Allah. All the praise be to Allah, the Rabb of the worlds.

40:66 Say (O Muhammad): "Surely I have been forbidden to worship those whom you worship besides Allah, since there have come to me evidences from my Rabb, and I am commanded to submit (in Islam) to the Rabb of the worlds.

40:67 It is Allah who has created you from dust, then from a sperm, then from a clot, then brings you forth as children, then (make you grow) to reach the age of full strength, then afterwards to be old among you who die before, and you reach an appointed term in order that you may understand.

40:68 It is Allah who gives life and causes death. When Allah decides upon a thing, only Allah says to it: "Be!" and it is.

40:69 Don't you see those who dispute about the evidences of Allah? How are they turning away (from the truth)?

40:70 Those who deny the book (this Qur'an), and Allah's messengers with whom Allah has sent with, then they will come to know (in the fire),

40:71 when iron collars and the chains will be rounded over their necks, they shall be dragged along

40:72 in the boiling water, then they will be burned in the fire.

40:73 Then it will be said to them: "Where are those whom you used to join in worship as partners

40:74 besides Allah?" They will say: "They have vanished from us. (Now we know that) we did not invoke (worship) anything before." Thus Allah leads the disbelievers go astray.

40:75 (It will be said): "That was because you used to be delighted in the earth without the right (worship others instead of Allah), and you used to rejoice extremely.

40:76 Enter the gates of hell to abide forever in it, what an evil abode of the arrogant!"

40:77 So be patient (O Muhammad), surely, Allah's promise is true. Whether Allah shows you (O Muhammad in this world) some part of that which Allah has promised them, or Allah causes you to die, then it is to Allah, they all shall be returned.

40:78 Indeed Allah has sent messengers before you (O Muhammad); some of them Allah has related their story to you and some of them whom Allah has not related their story to you, and it was not given to any messenger so that he may bring a verse except by the permission of Allah. So when the commandment of Allah came, the matter was decided with truth, and the followers of falsehood suffered the loss.

40:79 It is Allah who has made cattle for you so that you may ride on some of them and eat some of them.

40:80 You have many benefits in them; they carry you where you wish to reach that are in your hearts and on them as ships carry you (by sea).

40:81 Thus Allah shows you Allah's signs. So which of the signs of Allah do you deny?

40:82 Have they not traveled through the earth and seen how was the end of those from before them? They were more in numbers than them and mightier in strength, and (left behind them) the traces in the land, yet all that they used to earn did not avail them.

40:83 When their messengers came to them with clear proofs, they were glad with the (worldly) knowledge which they had; (the punishment) surrounded them at which they mocked.

40:84 So when they saw Allah's punishment, they said: "We believe in Allah alone and reject all what we associated as partners with Allah."

40:85 But their faith (in Islam) could not avail them when they saw Allah's punishment. Such was the way of Allah which were established in (dealing with) Allah's servants. Thus the disbelievers were lost.

41. Fussilat : The Detailed Explanation
In the name of Allah, the Gracious, the Merciful

41:1 Ha-Mim.

41:2 A revelation from (Allah), the Beneficent, the Merciful,

41:3 a book with its verses are explained; Qur'an in Arabic language for people who understand,

41:4 giving glad tidings and warning, but most of them turn away, so they do not listen.

41:5 They say: "Our hearts are covered (screened) from that to which you invite us, there is deafness in our ears and there is a screen between us and you; so you work (your way) and surely we are working (our way)."

41:6 Say (O Muhammad): "I am only a human being like you. It is revealed to me that your one worthy of worship is one Allah, therefore take right way to Allah and seek forgiveness from Allah. Woe to polytheists;

41:7 those who do not give the obligatory charity and they are disbelievers in the hereafter.

41:8 Surely, those who believe and do righteous deeds, they will have a reward without end."

41:9 Say (O Muhammad): "Do you really disbelieve in Allah who created the earth in 2 days and do you set up rivals (in worship) with Allah? That is the Rabb of the worlds.

41:10 Allah has placed in it (the earth) firm mountains from above it, and Allah blessed in it, and measured in it its sustenance in 4 days equal for all those who (live in and) ask for it.

41:11 Then Allah rose over towards the heaven while it was smoke, and said to it and to the earth: 'Come forward both of you willingly or unwillingly.' They both said: 'We shall come willingly.'

41:12 Then Allah completed and finished their creation of 7 heavens in 2 days and Allah made its laws in each heaven. Allah adorned the nearest (lowest) heaven with lamps (stars) and made it secure. Such is the decree of the All-Mighty, the All-Knower."

41:13 But if they turn away, then say (O Muhammad): "I have warned you of a destructive awful cry thunderbolt like the thunderbolt of Ad and Thamud (people)."

41:14 When the messengers came to them from before them and behind them (saying): "Do not worship but Allah," They said: "If our Rabb had so willed, Allah would surely have sent down the angels. So indeed! We disbelieve in what with which you have been sent."

41:15 As for Ad, they were arrogant in the land without right and said: "Who is mightier than us in strength?" Don't they see that Allah, who created them, was mightier in strength than them? They used to deny Allah's verses!

41:16 So Allah sent upon them furious wind in days of evil sign so that Allah might give them a taste of the disgracing punishment in this worldly life, but surely the punishment of the hereafter will be more disgracing, and they will never be helped.

41:17 As for Thamud, Allah guided them but they preferred blindness to guidance, the destructive awful cry of disgracing punishment seized them because of their misdeeds,

41:18 but Allah saved those who believed and feared Allah.

41:19 (Remember) the day that the enemies of Allah will be gathered to the fire, so they will be collected there,

41:20 till, when they will reach it (hellfire), their ears, their eyes, and their skins will testify against them as to what they used to do.

41:21 They will say to their skins: "Why do you testify against us?" They will say: "Allah has caused us to speak as Allah causes all things to speak. Allah has created you the first time, and to Allah you are made to return."

41:22 You used to hide (in the worldly life with your sins and never thought that) your ears, your eyes, and your skins will testify against you. Rather you thought that even Allah does not know much of what you were doing.

41:23 That thought of yours which you thought about your Rabb, has brought you to destruction, and you have become of those utterly lost!

41:24 Then, whether they have patience (or not), the fire will be a home for them, and if they beg to be excused, they are not those who will ever be excused.

41:25 Allah has assigned intimate companions (of like nature in the world) for them who have made their past and present seem fair to them. The word (of punishment) is justified against them which has passed away (generations) of jinns and men before them. Indeed they are losers.

41:26 Those who disbelieve say: "Do not listen to this Qur'an and make noise in it (during recitation) so that you may gain the upper hand."

41:27 But surely, Allah will cause the disbelievers to taste a severe punishment and Allah will requite them the worst of what they used to do.

41:28 Such is the recompense of the enemies of Allah: the fire will be their eternal home, a recompense for their denying Allah's revelations.

41:29 Those who disbelieve will say: "Our Rabb! Show us those from jinns and men who led us astray, we shall crush them under our feet so that they become the lowest."

41:30 Surely, those who say: "Our Rabb is Allah," then stick to the right way, the angels will descend (at death) on them (saying): "Do not fear or grieve, and receive the glad tidings of paradise which you have been promised!

41:31 Allah is your friend in the life of this world and in the hereafter. You will find in it what your souls desire and you will find in it what you ask for:

41:32 a hospitable gift from (Allah), the Forgiving, Merciful."

41:33 Who is better in speech than the one who invites (people) to Allah, does righteous deeds, and says: "I am one of the Muslims?"

41:34 The good deed and the evil deed are not equal. Repel (evil) with one which is better. Then surely, one with whom you had enmity, will become your close friend.

41:35 But none will be granted it (this quality) except those who are patient and none will be granted it except those who own the great portion of the happiness (with high moral character).

41:36 If an evil whisper from Satan comes to you (O Muhammad), seek refuge in Allah. Surely, Allah is the All-Hearer, the All-Knower.

41:37 From among Allah's signs are the night and the day, and the sun and the moon. Do not prostrate to the sun or the moon, but prostrate to Allah who created them, if you really worship Allah.

41:38 But if they are too proud (to do so), then those (angels) who are with your Rabb, glorify Allah night and day, and they never get tired.

41:39 Among Allah's signs, you see the earth barren; but when Allah sends down water (rain) to it, it stirs to life and growth (of vegetations). Surely, Allah who gives it life, surely, will be Able give life to the dead (on the day of Resurrection). Indeed! Allah has power over all things.

41:40 Surely, those who deviate concerning Allah's verses are not hidden from Allah. Is the one who is cast into the fire better or the one who emerges safe on the Day of Judgment? Do what you will. Surely! Allah sees all of what you do.

41:41 Surely, those who disbelieve in the reminder (the Qur'an) when it comes to them (should know that) surely, it is an honorable respected book.

41:42 No falsehood can come to it from before or from behind. It is sent down from the All-Wise, Praise-worthy (Allah).

41:43 Nothing is said to you (O Muhammad) except surely what was said to the messengers before you. Surely, your Rabb is indeed the Possessor of Forgiveness, and (at the same time) the Possessor of painful punishment.

41:44 If Allah had sent this Qur'an in a foreign language other than Arabic, they would have said: "Why its verses are not explained in details (in our language)? What (a book if) not in Arabic and (the messenger) an Arab?" Say: "It is for those who believe, a guide and a healing. As for those who disbelieve, there is deafness in their ears, and it (the Qur'an) is blindness for them. They are those who are (as if) called from a place far away (so they neither hear nor understand).

41:45 Indeed Allah gave Moses the scripture, but dispute arose in it. Had it not been for the word that went forth from your Rabb, the matter would have been settled between them. But truly, they are in suspicious doubt about it (the Qur'an).

41:46 Whoever does righteous deed, it is for its own self; and whoever does evil, it is against it (own self); and your Rabb is not unjust to Allah's servants.

41:47 To Allah (alone) is referred the knowledge of the hour (of Judgment). No fruit comes out of its sheath, nor does a female conceive, nor does she give birth except with Allah's knowledge. On the day (of Judgment) when Allah will ask them (polytheists): "Where are my (Allah's) partners (whom you associated)?" They will say: "We confess to you (Allah) that none of us bear witness to it!"

41:48 Those (deities) whom they used to invoke will vanish from them and they will realize that there is no place of refuge (to avoid punishment).

41:49 People (disbelievers) do not get tired of asking good (things from Allah), but if an evil touches them, they give up all hope and are lost in despair.

41:50 Truly, if Allah favors one with the taste of Mercy from Allah after some adversity (poverty or disease) has touched that person, one is sure to say: "This is for me (I deserve); I do not think the hour will be established. Even if I am brought back to my Rabb, surely, there will be the best (treatment) from Allah for me." Surely, Allah will inform those who disbelieve with what they have done and Allah will make them taste a severe punishment.

41:51 When Allah shows favor on a person, it withdraws and turns away; but when evil touches the (same) person, then it has long supplications.

41:52 (O Muhammad) ask: "Tell me, if it (the Qur'an) is really from Allah and you disbelieve in it, who is more astray than you who has gone far away in opposition (from truth)?"

41:53 Allah will show them Allah's signs in the universe and in their own selves, until it becomes clear to them that this (the Qur'an) is the truth. Is it not sufficient that your Rabb is a witness over all things?

41:54 Surely! They are in doubt concerning the meeting with their Rabb (day of Resurrection). Surely! It is Allah who surrounds all things!

42. Ash-Shura : The Consultation
In the name of Allah, the Gracious, the Merciful

42:1 Ha-Meem.

42:2 Ain-Sinn-Qaf.

42:3 Thus Allah, the All-Mighty, the All-Wise inspires you (O Muhammad) and to those sent before you.

42:4 To Allah belongs all that is in the heavens and all that is in the earth. Allah is the High, the Great.

42:5 The heavens might have almost broken apart from above them (by Allah's glory) while the angels glorify the praises of their Rabb and are asking forgiveness for those on the earth. Surely, Allah is indeed the Forgiving, the Merciful.

42:6 As for those who take others as protectors besides Allah, Allah is the protector over them and you (O Muhammad) are not a guardian over them.

42:7 Thus Allah has revealed to you (O Muhammad) this Qur'an in Arabic so that you may warn the residents of the mother town (Makkah) and whoever is around it. Warn them of the day of assembling; there is no doubt about it; when a group (believers) will go to paradise and a group (disbelievers) in the blazing fire.

42:8 If Allah had willed, Allah could have made them one nation, but Allah admits whom Allah wills to Allah's Mercy. The wrongdoers will not have any protector or a helper.

42:9 Or have they taken guardians besides Allah? But Allah alone is the Protector. Allah is the one who gives life to the dead and it is Allah who has power over all things.

42:10 In whatever matter you differ, its decision is with Allah. (Say O Muhammad to the polytheists): Such is Allah, my Rabb in whom I have put my trust, and to Allah I turn in repentance,

42:11 the creator of the heavens and the earth. Allah has made for you mates from among yourselves and also mates among the cattle. Allah creates you (in the womb) by this means. There is no one like Allah, and Allah is the All-Knower, the All-Seer.

42:12 To Allah belong the keys of the heavens and the earth. Allah enlarges provision for whom Allah wills, and straitens (it for whom Allah wills). Surely! Allah is the All-Knower of everything.

42:13 Allah has ordained for you the same religion (Islam) which Allah ordained for Noah, and which Allah has revealed to you (O Muhammad), and which Allah ordained for Abraham, Moses and Jesus (saying): "You should establish religion, and not be divided in it (various sects)." Intolerable is for the polytheists to which you (O Muhammad) call them to it. Allah chooses whom Allah wills, and guides to Allah who turns to Allah in repentance and obedience.

42:14 They were not divided till after knowledge had come to them through selfish transgressions between themselves. Had it not been for a word (to defer punishment) that went forth before from your Rabb for an appointed term, the matter would have been settled between them. Surely, those who were made to inherit the scripture after them are in serious doubt concerning it (the Qur'an).

42:15 So (O Muhammad) invite people to this (Islam), stand firm as you are commanded, and do not follow their desires but say: "I believe in what Allah has revealed of the book (all revealed books), and I am commanded to do justice among you. Allah is our Rabb and your Rabb. We are (responsible) for our deeds and you are for your deeds. There is no dispute between us and between you. Allah will assemble us (on the Day of Judgment) and to Allah is the final return.

42:16 Those who dispute concerning Allah after accepting (obedience) to Allah, their dispute is futile in the sight of their Rabb, on them is the wrath (of Allah), and for them there will be a severe punishment.

42:17 It is Allah who has revealed the book (the Qur'an) in truth and the balance (to distinguish between right and wrong). What will make you realize that perhaps the hour (of Judgment) is near at hand?

42:18 Those who do not believe in it, seek to hasten it. But those who believe are fearful of it, and they know that it is the very truth. Surely, indeed those who dispute concerning the hour (of judgment) are certainly in error far away.

42:19 Allah is very gracious and kind to Allah's servants. Allah gives provisions to whom Allah wills. Allah is the All-Strong, the All-Mighty."

42:20 Whoever desires (for good deeds) the reward of the hereafter, Allah increases (many fold) in its reward, and whoever desires the reward of this world (for good deeds), Allah gives it thereof (what is meant for), but will have no portion in the hereafter.

42:21 Or do they have partners (false deities), who have instituted for them from religion what Allah has not allowed? Had it not been a decisive word (already decided on the Day of Judgment), the matter would have been judged between them? Surely, for the wrongdoers, there is a painful punishment.

42:22 You will see (on the day of Resurrection) that the wrongdoers will fear for what they have earned, and it (Allah's punishment) will befall them. While those who believe and do righteous deeds will be in the flowering meadows of the gardens (paradise) and will receive for them what they wish from their Rabb. That will be the supreme grace.

42:23 That is (the grace) of glad tidings which Allah gives to Allah's servants who believe and do righteous deeds. Say (O Muhammad): "I do not ask any reward for it except to be kind to me for kinship with you." Whoever does a righteous deed, Allah will increase (many fold) for that person in it. Surely, Allah is Forgiving, Ready to appreciate (good deeds).

42:24 Or do they say: "He has invented a lie against Allah?" But if Allah willed, Allah could have sealed your heart. Allah wipes out falsehood, and establishes the truth (Islam) by Allah's word (this Qur'an). Surely, Allah knows well what is in the hearts (of people).

42:25 Allah is one who accepts repentance from Allah's servants, forgives their sins, and Allah knows what you do.

42:26 Allah answers those who believe, do righteous deeds, and gives them increase of Allah's bounty. As for the disbelievers, there will be a severe punishment.

42:27 If Allah were to enlarge the provision for Allah's servants, they would surely rebel in the earth; but Allah sends down by measure what Allah wills. Surely! Allah is Well-Aware, the All-Seer of everything of Allah's servants.

42:28 It is Allah who sends down the rain after they have lost hope, and spreads Allah's Mercy. Allah is the Protector, Praise-worthy.

42:29 Among Allah's signs is the creation of the heavens and the earth, and the moving creatures that Allah has spread in both of them. Allah is potent over their assembly (on the day of Resurrection) whenever Allah wills.

42:30 Whatever misfortune befalls you, it is because of what your hands have earned. Allah pardons from much (of your misdeeds).

42:31 You cannot escape from Allah (Allah's punishment) in the earth, and besides Allah you have neither any protector nor any helper.

42:32 Among Allah's signs are the ships like mountains in the sea.

42:33 If Allah wills, Allah can cause the wind to settle and then they would become motionless on the back (of the sea). Surely, in this example there are signs for everyone (who is) patient and grateful.

42:34 Or Allah may destroy them (by drowning) because of that which their people have earned. Allah pardons much (of their evil deeds).

42:35 Those who (polytheists) dispute about Allah's revelations should know that there is no place of refuge (from Allah's punishment) for them.

42:36 Whatever you are given is nothing but a passing enjoyment for this worldly life. What is with Allah (paradise) is better and more lasting for those who believe, put their trust in their Rabb,

42:37 avoid major sins and shameful deeds, forgive even when they are angry;

42:38 answer the call of their Rabb, establish their prayers, conduct their affairs by mutual consultation, spend of what Allah has bestowed on them,

42:39 and when they are oppressed, take defense.

42:40 The recompense for an injury is an injury like thereof; but whoever forgives and makes reconciliation, it shall be rewarded by Allah. Surely, Allah does not like the wrongdoers.

42:41 Those who take revenge after they have suffered wrong, for such there is no way (of blame) against them.

42:42 The way (of blame) is only against those who oppress people and rebel in the earth without right. It is they who will have a painful punishment.

42:43 Surely, those who show patience and forgive, surely would be from the steadfast things.

42:44 Those whom Allah sends astray, there is no protector for them after Allah. When they will face the punishment, you will see the wrongdoers say: "Is there any way for return (to the world)?"

42:45 You will see them brought forward to it (hell) made humble by disgrace, looking with stealthy glance. Those who believe will say: "Surely, the losers are they who have lost themselves and their families on the day of Resurrection. Surely, indeed the wrongdoers will be in a lasting punishment."

42:46 They will not have any protector in it to help them other than Allah. The one whom Allah sends astray, there is no way of escape.

42:47 Answer the call of your Rabb before there comes from Allah a day which cannot be averted. You will not have any refuge on that day nor will you be able to deny (your misdeeds).

42:48 But if they turn away, (they should know that) Allah has not sent you (O Muhammad) over them as a guardian. Your duty is to convey (the message). Surely, when Allah causes people to taste the Mercy from Allah, they rejoice in it; but when some ill befalls them because of (misdeeds) which their hands have sent forth, then surely, the people become ungrateful!

42:49 To Allah belongs the kingdom of the heavens and the earth. Allah creates what Allah wills. Allah bestows female (daughter) to whom Allah wills and bestows male (son) to whom Allah wills.

42:50 Or Allah combines them both males and females, and Allah renders barren whom Allah wills. Surely, Allah is the All-Knower of everything and is Able to do all things.

42:51 It is not given to any human being that Allah should speak (directly) unless (it be) by inspiration, or from behind a veil, or by sending a messenger to reveal by Allah's permission what Allah wills. Surely, Allah is High, Wise.

42:52 Thus Allah has sent to you (O Muhammad) a revelation (Qur'an) of Allah's command. You did not know what the book is or what the faith is! But Allah has made it (this Qur'an) a light, Allah guides by it whoever Allah wills of Allah's servants. Surely, you (O Muhammad) are indeed guiding mankind to the right way,

42:53 the way of Allah, to whom belongs all that is in the heavens and in the earth. Surely, all the matters return to Allah (for decision).

43. Az-Zukhruf : The Gold Adornments
In the name of Allah, the Gracious, the Merciful

43:1 Ha-Mim.

43:2 By the clear book (the Qur'an).

43:3 Allah surely has revealed it a Qur'an in Arabic so that you may be able to understand.

43:4 Surely, it (this Qur'an) is in the mother of the book (Al-Lauh Al-Mahfooz) before Allah, indeed exalted, full of wisdom.

43:5 Should Allah then take away the reminder (this Qur'an) from you in your rejection because you are a transgressing people?

43:6 How many prophets has Allah sent amongst the previous people?

43:7 Never came to them a prophet and they did not mock at him.

43:8 So Allah destroyed people stronger than them in power, and the example of the ancient people has passed away (before them).

43:9 Indeed if you (O Muhammad) ask them: "Who has created the heavens and the earth?" They will surely say: "The All-Mighty, the All-Knower of everything created them."

43:10 (Allah) who has made the earth like a bed for you and has made roads for you in it in order that you may find your way,

43:11 and who sends down water (rain) from the sky in due measure. Then Allah revives a dead land from it, and even so you will be brought out (from the dead again),

43:12 and who has created all the pairs and has appointed for you from ships and cattle on which you ride,

43:13 in order that you may mount firmly on their backs, and then may remember the favor of your Rabb when you mount on them, and say: "Glory to Allah who has subjected this to us, and we could never have ability for it (by our efforts),

43:14 and surely, to our Rabb we all shall return."

43:15 Yet they assign to some of Allah's servants a share with Allah (as partners). Surely, mankind is clearly ungrateful!

43:16 Or has Allah taken daughters (pagan Arabs used to believe that angels were daughters of Allah) out of what Allah has created, and has Allah selected for you sons?

43:17 Yet, if the news of one (the birth of a girl) of them is informed which it sets forth as a parable to the Beneficent (Allah), its face becomes dark, gloomy, and is filled with grief!

43:18 (Do they then like for Allah) a creature who is brought up in ornaments (women) and is unable to make itself clear in dispute?

43:19 They regard the angels as females who themselves are servants of the beneficent (Allah). Did they witness their creation? Their witness will be recorded and they will be questioned!

43:20 They say: "If it had been the will of the beneficent (Allah), we would not have worshipped them (false deities)." They do not have any knowledge of that. They do nothing but lie!

43:21 Or has Allah given them any book before this (the Qur'an) which they hold fast to it?

43:22 Nay! They said: "We found our forefathers following on a certain way and religion, and we guide ourselves on their footsteps."

43:23 Similarly, whenever Allah sent a warner before you (O Muhammad) to any town (people), its luxurious people among them said: "We found our forefathers following on a certain way and religion, and we are indeed following their footsteps."

43:24 (The warner) said: "What if I bring you better guidance than that which you found your forefathers on it?" They said: "Surely, We disbelieve in it with which you have been sent."

43:25 So Allah took retribution on them; and then see how the end of those who denied was?

43:26 (Remember) when Abraham said to his father and his people: "Surely, I renounce (deities) that you worship,

43:27 except Allah (alone) who created me, and surely, Allah will guide me."

43:28 He made it a word lasting among his offspring so that they may turn back (to repent to Allah).

43:29 Nay, but I (Allah) gave (good things) to these (polytheists) and their forefathers to enjoy (this life), till there came to them the truth (the Qur'an) and a messenger (Muhammad) making things clear.

43:30 But when the truth (this Qur'an) came to them, they (disbelievers) said: "This is magic, and we do not believe in it."

43:31 They said: "Why is this Qur'an not sent down to some great man of the 2 towns (Makkah and Taif)?"

43:32 Is it they who would distribute the Mercy of your Rabb? It is Allah who distributes between them their livelihood in the life of this world, and Allah raises some of them above others in ranks, so that some may employ others in their work. The Mercy of your (O Muhammad) Rabb is better than the (wealth of this world) which they accumulate.

43:33 Were it not that all mankind would become one community (of disbelievers), Allah would have provided for those who disbelieve in the beneficent (Allah), silver roofs for their houses, and elevators on which they mount,

43:34 and doors (of silver) for their houses and thrones (of silver) on which they recline,

43:35 and adornments of gold. Yet all these are nothing but an enjoyment of the life of this world. The hereafter is only for the pious which is with your Rabb.

43:36 Whoever turns away from the remembrance of the Beneficent (Allah), Allah appoints a Satan for it who becomes a companion for that person,

43:37 and surely, they (Satans) hinder them from the way (of Allah) but they think that they are guided aright!

43:38 Till, when such one comes to Allah (on the Day of Judgment), it says (to its Satan): "I wish that between me and you were the distance of the 2 easts (or the east and west), you were an evil companion!"

43:39 (It will be said to them): "It will not profit you this day as you already did wrong, and both of you will be sharing the punishment."

43:40 Can you (O Muhammad) make the deaf to hear, or guide the blind or those who are in clear error?

43:41 Even if Allah takes you (O Muhammad) away, Allah will indeed take retribution on them,

43:42 or if Allah shows you (the end of) what Allah has threatened them, then surely, Allah has perfect command over them.

43:43 So you (O Muhammad) hold fast to that (the Qur'an) which is revealed to you. Surely, you are on a right way.

43:44 Surely, this (the Qur'an) is indeed a reminder for you (O Muhammad), your people, and you will be questioned about it.

43:45 Ask (O Muhammad) those of Allah's messengers whom Allah sent before you: "Did Allah ever appoint any other one worthy of worship to be worshipped besides the beneficent (Allah)?"

43:46 Indeed Allah sent Moses with Allah's signs to Pharaoh and his chiefs (inviting them to Allah). He said: "Surely, I am a messenger of the Rabb of the worlds."

43:47 When he came to them with Allah's signs, behold! They laughed at them.

43:48 Yet, Allah showed them sign after sign each greater than its preceding and Allah seized them with punishment in order that they might turn (to right way).

43:49 Then they said (to Moses): "O you sorcerer! Invoke your Rabb for us according to what Allah has entrusted with you. Surely, Allah will guide."

43:50 But when Allah removed the punishment from them, behold! They broke their covenant.

43:51 Then Pharaoh proclaimed amongst his people, saying: "O my people! Is not the dominion of Egypt mine? Are not these rivers flowing underneath me? Then don't you see?

43:52 Or am I not better than this one (Moses), who is despicable and can hardly express himself clearly?

43:53 (If he is true messenger) why then bracelets of gold are not bestowed on him, or angels sent along with him?"

43:54 Thus he (Pharaoh) befooled and misled his people, and they obeyed him. Surely, they were a people who were sinners.

43:55 So when they angered Allah, Allah punished them, and drowned them all,

43:56 and Allah made them a precedent (a lesson for future), and an example to later generations.

43:57 When the son of Mary (Jesus) is quoted as an example (Jesus is worshipped like their idols), behold! Your people cry aloud about it,

43:58 and say: "Are our deities better or is he (Jesus)?" They did not quote the above example for you except for argument. But they are a quarrelsome people.

43:59 He (Jesus) was not more than a servant (of Allah). Allah granted Allah's favor to him, and Allah made him an example to the children of Israel (created without a father).

43:60 If it were Allah's will, Allah would have (destroyed mankind and) made angels to replace you on the earth.

43:61 He (Jesus) is a known sign for the (coming of the) hour (day of Resurrection). Therefore, do not have doubt concerning it (the day of Resurrection). Follow (the commandments of) Allah! This is the right way.

43:62 Let not Satan hinders you (from the right religion). Surely, he is your open enemy.

43:63 When Jesus came with (Allah's) clear signs, he said: "Surely I have come to you with wisdom (Prophethood), and to clarify to you some of the points in which you differ, therefore fear Allah and obey me.

43:64 Surely, it is Allah who is my Rabb and your Rabb. So worship Allah (alone). This is the right way."

43:65 But the sects differed among themselves. So woe to the wrongdoers (who ascribe things to Jesus that are not true) from the punishment of the painful day (of Resurrection)!

43:66 Are they only waiting for the hour that it will come on them suddenly, while they do not perceive?

43:67 On that day, even friends will be enemies to one another accept the pious.

43:68 (It will be said to the believers): "My worshippers! Today you have nothing to fear or to grieve,

43:69 you are those who believed in Allah's revelations and were Muslims:

43:70 'Enter paradise, you and your wives in happiness.'"

43:71 Trays of gold and cups will be (used to) serve round them, there will be everything that the souls could desire, and all that their eyes can delight in, and (it will be said to them): "You will abide in it forever.

43:72 This is the paradise which you have made to inherit because of your good deeds which you used to do (in the world),

43:73 in it you will have plenty of fruits to eat."

43:74 But the criminals will abide in the punishment of hell forever.

43:75 (Their punishment) will not be lightened for them and they will be plunged into destruction with despair in it.

43:76 Allah did not wrong them, but they were the wrongdoers.

43:77 They will cry: "O Malik (keeper of hell)! Let your Rabb put an end to us." It will say: "Surely you shall abide forever."

43:78 Indeed Allah has brought the truth (the Qur'an) to you, but most of you hate the truth.

43:79 Or have they plotted some plan (against you O Muhammad)? Then Allah too is planning (to destroy them).

43:80 Or do they think that Allah does not hear their secrets and their private counsel? Of course Allah's messengers (angels) are recording by them.

43:81 Say (O Muhammad): "If the beneficent (Allah) (suppose) had a son, then I would be the first of worshippers."

43:82 Glory be to the Rabb of the heavens and the earth, the Rabb of the Throne! (Exalted be Allah) above all that they ascribe (to Allah).

43:83 So leave them alone to speak nonsense and play until they meet their day, which they have been promised.

43:84 It is Allah who is to be worshipped in the heaven and to be worshipped on the earth. Allah is the All-Wise, the All-Knower.

43:85 Blessed be Allah to whom belongs the kingdom of the heavens and the earth and all that is between them. Allah (alone) has the knowledge of the hour (of judgment), and to whom you all will be returned.

43:86 Those whom they invoke besides Allah, has no power of intercession; except those who bear witness to the truth (believers), and they know (the facts about the oneness of Allah).

43:87 If you ask them who created them, they will surely say: "Allah." How then are they turned away (from Allah)?

43:88 (Allah has knowledge) of his (Muhammad's) saying: "O my Rabb! Surely, these are a people who do not believe!"

43:89 So turn away from them (O Muhammad), and say: Salam (peace)! They will come to know (the truth).

44. Ad-Dukhan : The Smoke

In the name of Allah, the Gracious, the Merciful

44:1 Ha-Mim.

44:2 By the clear book (the Qur'an).

44:3 Surely Allah sent it (this Qur'an) down in a blessed night (of Qadr in the month of Ramadan). Surely, Allah is ever warning (mankind).

44:4 In it (that night) every matter is decided wisely,

44:5 by a command from Allah. Surely, Allah is ever sending (the messengers),

44:6 as Mercy from your Rabb. Surely! Allah is the All-Hearer, the All-Knower.

44:7 The Rabb of the heavens and the earth and all that is between them, if you have faith with certainty.

44:8 There is no true one worthy of worship but Allah. It is Allah who gives life and causes death, your Rabb and the Rabb of your forefathers.

44:9 Nay! They play in doubt.

44:10 Then you wait for the day when the sky will bring forth a visible smoke,

44:11 covering the people, this will be a painful punishment.

44:12 (People will say): "Our Rabb! Remove the punishment from us, really we have become believers!"

44:13 How can there be an admonition (at the time when the punishment has reached) for them when a messenger explaining things clearly has already come to them?

44:14 Yet, they turn away from him (Muhammad) and said: "He (Muhammad) is a madman, taught (by others)!"

44:15 Surely, Allah will remove the punishment (famine) for a while. But you will return (to disbelief).

44:16 On the day Allah will seize you with the greatest grasp. Surely, Allah will take retribution.

44:17 Indeed Allah tried Pharaoh's people before them, when a noble messenger (Moses) came to them,

44:18 saying: "Deliver the servants of Allah (the children of Israel) to me. Surely! I am a messenger to you worthy of all trust.

44:19 Do not exalt (yourselves) against Allah. Truly, I have come to you with a clear authority.

44:20 Truly, I seek refuge in my Rabb and your Rabb, lest you stone me.

44:21 If you do not believe me, then keep away from me and leave me alone."

44:22 So he (Moses) called upon (when they were aggressive) his Rabb (saying) indeed: "These are criminal people."

44:23 (Allah said): "You depart with Allah's servants by night. Surely, you will be pursued.

44:24 (When you have crossed the sea with your people), then leave the sea as it is (quiet and divided). Surely, they are a host to be drowned."

44:25 How many gardens and springs did they (Pharaoh's people) leave behind,

44:26 and corn-fields and goodly places,

44:27 and comforts (of life) they used to take delight in it!

44:28 Thus Allah made other people inherit them (the children of Israel inherit the kingdom of Egypt).

44:29 Neither the heavens and the earth did weep for them, nor were they given a respite.

44:30 Indeed Allah saved the children of Israel from the humiliating punishment

44:31 from Pharaoh. Surely! He was arrogant and was one of the transgressors,

44:32 and surely, Allah chose them (the children of Israel) above the worlds (during the time of Moses) with knowledge.

44:33 Allah granted them signs in which there was a plain trial.

44:34 Surely, these (people of Quraish) say:

44:35 "There is nothing after our first death and we shall not be resurrected.

44:36 Bring back our forefathers if you speak the truth!"

44:37 Are they better than the people of Tubba and those who were before them? Allah destroyed them because they were indeed criminals.

44:38 Allah did not create the heavens and the earth, and all that is between them, for merely a play.

44:39 Allah has not created them but (to reveal) the truth, but most of them do not know.

44:40 Surely, the day of judgment is the time appointed for all of them,

44:41 the day when a near relative cannot avail a relative in anything, nor they can receive help

44:42 except those on whom Allah will show Mercy. Surely, Allah is the Mighty, the Merciful.

44:43 Surely, the tree of Zaqqum (very bitter taste),

44:44 will be the food of the sinners,

44:45 like boiling oil, it will boil in the bellies,

44:46 like the boiling of scalding water.

44:47 (It will be said): "Seize and drag that person into the midst of blazing fire,

44:48 then pour from the punishment of boiling water over its head,

44:49 taste you (this)! Surely, you were (pretending to be) the mighty, the noble!

44:50 Surely! This is what you used to doubt about it!"

44:51 Surely! The pious will be in place of security (paradise),

44:52 among gardens and springs;

44:53 dressed in fine silk and also in thick silk, facing each other.

44:54 So (it will be), and Allah will marry them to Houris (fair females) with wide lovely eyes.

44:55 They will call in it for every kind of fruit in peace and security;

44:56 they will never taste death in it except the first death (of this world), and Allah will save them from the punishment of the blazing fire

44:57 as a bounty from your Rabb! That will be the supreme success!

44:58 Certainly, Allah has made this (Qur'an) easy in your tongue in order that they may remember.

44:59 Wait then (O Muhammad); surely, they too are waiting.

45. Al-Jathiyah : The Kneeling
In the name of Allah, the Gracious, the Merciful

45:1 Ha-Mim.

45:2 The revelation of the book (this Qur'an) is from Allah, the All-Mighty, the All-Wise.

45:3 Surely, in the heavens and the earth there are signs for the believers,

45:4 in your own creation and that of moving creatures which Allah has scattered (through the earth), there are signs for people who have firm faith,

45:5 in the alternation of the night and the day, in the provision that Allah sends down from the sky and revives with it the earth after its death and in the turning of the winds, there are signs for those people who understand.

45:6 These are the revelations of Allah, which Allah recites to you (O Muhammad) with truth. Then in which report after Allah and Allah's revelations, will they believe?

45:7 Woe to every sinful liar

45:8 before whom the revelations of Allah are recited, yet persists with pride as if it did not hear them. So announce a painful punishment to them!

45:9 When one learns something of Allah's revelations (this Qur'an), it takes them as a joke. For such people, there will be a humiliating punishment.

45:10 Behind them there is hell, and nothing of what they have earned (in this world) will be of any benefit to them, nor those whom they have taken as protectors besides Allah. They will have a great punishment.

45:11 This (Qur'an) is guidance. Those who disbelieve in the revelations of their Rabb, there will be a terrible painful punishment for them.

45:12 It is Allah who has subjected the sea to you, so that the ships may sail through it by Allah's command, and that you may seek Allah's bounty and you may be thankful,

45:13 and has subjected to you all that is in the heavens and all that is in the earth; all from Allah. Surely, there are signs for those people who think deeply in it.

45:14 Say (O Muhammad) to those who have believed, to forgive those who do not hope for the (bad) days from Allah, so that Allah may recompense those people according to what they have earned.

45:15 Whoever does a good deed, it is for its own self; and whoever does evil, it is against it (own self). Then you will be made to return to your Rabb.

45:16 Indeed Allah gave the scripture to the children of Israel, the understanding of the scripture, and the Prophethood. Allah provided them with good things of life, and Allah preferred them above all the worlds (during that time),

45:17 and gave them clear proofs of matters (revealed in the Torah). They did not differ until after the knowledge had come to them, through transgression among themselves. Surely, Your Rabb will judge between them on the day of Resurrection about which they used to differ.

45:18 Then Allah has put you (O Muhammad) on the plain way of (Allah's) commandment. So follow it (Islam) and do not follow the desires of those who do not know;

45:19 surely, they can avail you nothing against Allah. Surely, the wrongdoers are friends of one another, while Allah is the protector of the pious people.

45:20 This (Qur'an) is a clear insight and evidence for mankind; guidance and a Mercy for those who have firm faith.

45:21 Or do those evil doers think that Allah will make them equal with those who believe and do righteous deeds, in their present life and after their death? Worst is the judgment that they make!

45:22 Allah has created the heavens and the earth with truth, in order that each person may be recompensed what it has earned, and none of them will be wronged.

45:23 Have you seen the one who has taken its own desires as worthy of worship? Allah lets it astray upon knowing, and sealed over its hearing and its heart, and put a cover on its sight. Who then will guide it after Allah (has withdrawn)? Will you not then remember?

45:24 They (disbelievers) say: "There is nothing but our life of this world. We die and we live, nothing but time destroys us." They have no knowledge of it, verily they are only guessing.

45:25 When Allah's clear revelations are recited to them, their argument is not except that they say: "Bring back our dead forefathers if you are truthful!"

45:26 (O Muhammad) say (to them): "Allah gives you life and then causes you to die; then Allah will assemble you to the day of Resurrection. There is no doubt about it. But most people do not know."

45:27 To Allah belongs the kingdom of the heavens and the earth. On the day when the hour (of judgment) will be established, the followers of falsehood shall lose on that day.

45:28 You will see every nation humbled to its knees. Each nation will be called to its record (of deeds). (It will be said): "This day you shall be recompensed for what you used to do.

45:29 This record of Allah speaks about you with truth. Surely, Allah was recording (by angels) what you used to do."

45:30 As for those who believed and did righteous deeds, their Rabb will admit them into Allah's Mercy. That will be the clear success.

45:31 But as for those who disbelieved (it will be said to them): "Were not Allah's revelations recited to you? But you were proud and became a nation of criminals."

45:32 When it was said: "Surely! Allah's promise is true and there is no doubt about the hour (of judgment)." You used to say: 'We do not know what is the hour (of Judgment); we think it only as a guess, and we have no firm convincing belief.'"

45:33 The evil of their deeds will appear to them and they will be completely encircled by that which they used to mock at!

45:34 It will be said: "This day Allah will forget you as you forgot the meeting of this day of yours. Your abode will be the fire, and there will be no helper for you.

45:35 This is because you used to take the revelations of Allah (this Qur'an) as a joke and the life of the world deceived you." So this day neither they shall be taken out from there (hell), nor shall they be allowed excuses (to amend their ways to please Allah).

45:36 So all the praises and thanks are to Allah, the Rabb of the heavens, the Rabb of the earth, and the Rabb of the worlds.

45:37 To Allah belongs the majesty in the heavens and the earth, and Allah is the All-Mighty, the All-Wise.

46. Al-Ahqaf : The Curved Sand-Hills
In the name of Allah, the Gracious, the Merciful

46:1 Ha-Mim.

46:2 The revelation of the book (this Qur'an) is from Allah, the All-Mighty, the All-Wise.

46:3 Allah has not created the heavens and the earth and all that is between them except with truth, and for an appointed term. Those who disbelieve turn away from that where they are warned.

46:4 Say (O Muhammad): "Do you see what you invoke besides Allah? Show me what have they created of the earth? Or do they have any share in (the creation of) the heavens? Bring me any book (revealed) before this or some trace of knowledge (to support your claims), if you are truthful!"

46:5 Who is more astray than one who calls (deities) besides Allah, one who will not answer till the day of Resurrection, and who are not even aware of their calls to them?

46:6 When mankind shall be gathered (on the day of Resurrection), they (false deities) will become enemies for them and will deny their worshipping.

46:7 When Allah's clear revelations are recited to them, and the truth (this Qur'an) reaches them, the disbelievers say: "This is plain magic!"

46:8 Or they say: "He (Muhammad) has fabricated it." Say: "If I have fabricated it, then you have no power to support me in anything against (the wrath of) Allah. Allah knows better of what you say among yourselves concerning it (this Qur'an)! Allah is sufficient as a witness between me and between you! Allah is the Forgiving, the Merciful."

46:9 Say (O Muhammad): "I am not a new thing among the messengers (of Allah) and I do not know what will be done with me or with you. I only follow what is revealed to me, and I am not but a plain warner."

46:10 Say: "Do you see, if this (Qur'an) is from Allah and you deny it, and a witness from the children of Israel (Abdullah bin Salam) has testified to its similarity (that this Qur'an is from Allah like the Torah), and he has believed (embraced Islam), while you are too proud (to believe). Surely! Allah does not guide the wrongdoers."

46:11 Those who disbelieve (strong and wealthy) say to those who believe (weak and poor): "Had it (the Qur'an) been a good thing, they (believers) would not have believed in it before us!" Since they did not accept its guidance (this Qur'an), they say: "This is an ancient lie!"

46:12 From before, this was the scripture of Moses as a guide and a Mercy. This book (the Qur'an) confirms it. It is revealed in the Arabic language to warn those who do wrong, and as glad tidings to the righteous people.

46:13 Surely, those who say: "Our Rabb is (only) Allah," and thereafter stand firm, there shall be no fear on them, nor they shall grieve.

46:14 They shall be the residents of paradise, abide in it forever, a reward for what they used to do.

46:15 Allah has enjoined on people to be dutiful and kind to their parents. Its mother bears it with hardships and she brings it forth with hardships, and the bearing of it, and the weaning of it is 30 months. Till when it attains full strength and reaches 40 years, it says: "My Rabb! Grant me the power and ability so that I may be grateful for your (Allah's) favor which you (Allah) has bestowed upon me and upon my parents, and that I may do righteous deeds such as to please you (Allah), and make my offspring good for me. Truly, I have turned to you (Allah) in repentance, and truly, I am one of the Muslims."

46:16 They are those from whom Allah will accept the best of their deeds and overlook their evil deeds. They will be among the residents of paradise, a promise of truth which they have been promised.

46:17 But one who says to its parents: "Uff upon you both! Do you hold out the promise to me that I shall be raised up again and surely generations before me have passed away (without rising)?" While they (father and mother) invoke Allah (for help and rebuke their son): "Woe to you! Believe! Surely, the promise of Allah is true." But it says: "This is nothing but the tales of the ancient."

46:18 They are those against whom the word (of punishment) is justified and they will be among the previous generations of jinns and mankind that surely have passed away. Surely! They will be the losers.

46:19 For all, there will be ranks according to their deed, so that Allah may recompense them fully for their deeds. They will not be wronged.

46:20 On the day when those who disbelieved will be exposed to the fire (it will be said): "You received your good things in the life of the world, and you took your pleasure in it. Now this day you shall be recompensed with a punishment of humiliation because you were arrogant in the land without a right, and because you used to rebel and disobey (Allah)."

46:21 Remember (Hud) the brother of Ad, when he warned his people in the curved sand-hills (located in the southern part of Arabian Peninsula). Surely, warners have passed before him and after him (saying): "Worship none but Allah. Truly, I fear for you the punishment of a mighty day."

46:22 They said: "Have you come to us to turn us away from our deity? Then bring us that (punishment) with which you threaten us, if you are one of the truthful!"

46:23 He said: "The knowledge (of the time of its coming) is only with Allah. I convey to you what I have been sent herewith, but I see that you are ignorant people."

46:24 Then, when they saw it (punishment) as a dense cloud coming towards their valleys, they said: "This cloud will bring us rain." Nay, but it is that (punishment) which you were asking to be hastened! It is a wind in it is a painful punishment!

46:25 It will destroy everything by the command of its Rabb. So they became such that nothing could be seen except their (ruined) residences! Thus Allah did recompense the people who were criminals!

46:26 Indeed Allah had firmly established them much better than Allah has established you (O Quraish of Makkah)! Allah had assigned for them hearing, seeing, and hearts. But their hearing, seeing and their hearts availed them nothing since they used to deny the revelations of Allah, and they were completely encircled by that which they used to mock at.

46:27 Indeed Allah has destroyed towns (populations) around you, and Allah has shown them in various ways the revelations so that they may return (to the truth).

46:28 Then why did those whom they had taken as deities besides Allah, as a way of approach (to Allah) not help them? Nay, but they (deities) vanished completely from them (where punishment came). Those were their lies and false inventions (before their destruction).

46:29 (Remember) when Allah has sent towards you (Muhammad) a party of the jinns, quietly listening to the Qur'an when they stood in the presence thereof, they said: "Listen in silence!" When it was finished, they returned to their people, as warners.

46:30 They said: "O our people! Surely! We have listened to a book (this Qur'an) sent down after Moses, confirming what came before it, and it guides to the truth and to the right way (Islam).

46:31 O our people! Respond to Allah's caller (Muhammad), and believe in him. Allah will forgive you from your sins and will save you from a painful punishment (hellfire).

46:32 Whoever does not respond to Allah's caller, it cannot escape on earth, and there will not be protectors for it besides Allah (from Allah's punishment). Those people are in clear error."

46:33 Don't they see that Allah, who created the heavens and the earth and was not tired by their creation, is Able to give life to the dead? Yes, surely Allah has power over all things.

46:34 On the day when those who disbelieve will be exposed to the fire, (it will be said to them): "Is this not the truth?" They will say: "Yes, by our Rabb!" Allah will say: "Then taste the punishment, because you used to disbelieve!"

46:35 Therefore be patient (O Muhammad) as endured by those messengers of strong will and do not haste about them (disbelievers). On the day when they will see that (punishment) with which they are being threatened as if they had not stayed more than an hour in a single day. (This Qur'an is sufficient as) a clear message. But shall anyone be destroyed except the people who are sinners?

47. Muhammad : Muhammad
In the name of Allah, the Gracious, the Merciful

47:1 Those who disbelieve and hinder people from the way of Allah, Allah will render their deeds vain.

47:2 But those who believe, do righteous deeds, and believe in what is sent down to Muhammad, for it is the truth from their Rabb, Allah will remove their sins from them, and will make their condition good.

47:3 That is because those who disbelieve follow falsehood, while those who believe follow the truth from their Rabb. Thus Allah does set forth their examples for mankind.

47:4 So, when you meet (in fight with) those who disbelieve, strike at their necks till you have killed and wounded many of them, then bind a bond firmly (and take them as captives). After the war lays down its burden, then either show generosity (free them without ransom), or ransom (to benefit Islam). But if Allah had willed, Allah could certainly have won over them. But (Allah adapted this way) in order to test some of you with others. Those who are killed in the way of Allah, Allah will never let their deeds be lost.

47:5 Allah will guide them and set their state right

47:6 and admit them to paradise which Allah has made known to them.

47:7 O you who believe! If you help (the cause of) Allah, Allah will help you, and make your foothold firm.

47:8 But those who disbelieve, there is destruction for them, and Allah will make their deeds vain.

47:9 That is because they hate that which Allah has sent down (this Qur'an), so Allah has made their deeds fruitless.

47:10 Have they not traveled through the earth and seen how was the end of those before them? Allah destroyed them completely and its likeness (similar fate waits) for the disbelievers.

47:11 That is because Allah is the protector of those who believe and the disbelievers have no protector.

47:12 Certainly! Allah will admit those who believe and do righteous deeds, to gardens under which rivers flow (paradise). While those who disbelieve, enjoy themselves (in worldly life) and eat as cattle eat, but the fire will be abode for them.

47:13 Many towns were stronger in strength than your town (Makkah) (O Muhammad), which has driven you out, Allah has destroyed them. There was none to help them.

47:14 Is the one who is on a clear proof from its Rabb be compared to those for whom their evil deeds are beautified for them, while they follow their own lusts (evil desires)?

47:15 The description of paradise which have been promised for those who fear is that there are rivers of water not stagnant in it, rivers of milk whose taste never changes, rivers of wine delicious to those who drink, and rivers of clarified honey. In it, they will have every kind of fruit, and forgiveness from their Rabb. (Are these) like those who shall reside forever in the fire and be given to drink boiling water so that it cuts up their intestines?

47:16 Among them there are some who listen to you (O Muhammad) till, when they go out from you, they say to those who have received knowledge: "What has he said just now?" Such are those Allah has sealed on their hearts and they follow their lusts (evil desires).

47:17 Those who accept guidance, Allah will increase their guidance and bestow on them their piety.

47:18 Are they waiting for the hour (of judgment) so that it should come upon them suddenly? But indeed some of its signs have already come and when it will actually be on them, then how can they benefit by their reminder?

47:19 So know (O Muhammad) that there is no one worthy of worship but Allah, and ask forgiveness for your sins, and also for believing men and believing women. Allah knows your activities well and your resting place (homes).

47:20 Those who believe say: "Why is not a Surah (chapter of the Qur'an) sent down (to allow us to fight)? But when a decisive Surah is sent down and fighting (in Allah's cause) is mentioned in it, you will see those in whose hearts is a disease (of hypocrisy) looking at you with a look of one fainting to death. But it was better for them.

47:21 Obedience (to Allah) and good words (are better for them). When the matter (preparation for fight) is resolved, then if they had been true to Allah, it would have been better for them.

47:22 Would you might then, if you were given the authority, do mischief in the land, and sever your ties of kinship?

47:23 Such are they whom Allah has cursed so that Allah has made them deaf and blinded their sight.

47:24 Will they not then think deeply in the Qur'an? Or are there locks in their hearts?

47:25 Surely, those who turn on their backs after the guidance has become clear, Satan has beautified for them (false hopes), and (Allah) has prolonged them (their age).

47:26 This is because they said to those who hate what Allah has sent down: "We will obey you in some matter," but Allah knows their secrets.

47:27 Then what will they do when the angels will take their souls at death, striking their faces and their backs?

47:28 That is because they followed what angered Allah and hated what pleased Allah. So Allah made their deeds wasted.

47:29 Or do those in whose hearts is a disease (of hypocrisy) think that Allah will never bring to light their hidden ill-wills?

47:30 If Allah willed, Allah could have shown them to you and you would have known them by their marks. But surely, you will know them by the tone of their speech! Allah knows all your deeds.

47:31 Surely, Allah will try you till Allah knows those who strive hard for Allah and from you the patient ones, and Allah will test your facts (whether lying or not).

47:32 Surely, those who disbelieve and hinder people from the way of Allah, and oppose the messenger after the guidance has been clearly shown to them, they will never hurt Allah in the least, but Allah will make their deeds fruitless.

47:33 O you who believe! Obey Allah, and obey the messenger (Muhammad) and do not render vain your deeds.

47:34 Surely, those who disbelieve, and hinder people from the way of Allah, then die while they are disbelievers; Allah will never forgive them.

47:35 So do not be weak and do not ask for peace while you have the upper hand. Allah is with you, and will never decrease the reward of your good deeds.

47:36 The life of this world is but play and pastime. But if you believe and fear Allah, and avoid evil, Allah will grant you your wages, and will not ask you your wealth.

47:37 If Allah were to ask you of it, and press you, you would withhold with extreme desire, and Allah will bring out all your ill-wills.

47:38 Behold! You are those who are called to spend in the cause of Allah. Yet among you are some who are stingy. Whoever is stingy, and then one is stingy only to one's own self. But Allah is Rich, and you people are poor. If you turn away (from the obedience of Allah), Allah will exchange you by some other people besides you who will not be like you.

48. Al-Fath : The Victory
In the name of Allah, the Gracious, the Merciful

48:1 Surely, Allah has given to you (O Muhammad) a clear victory (treaty of Hudaibiyah),

48:2 so that Allah may forgive your past as well as future sins, complete Allah's favor on you, and guide you to the right way;

48:3 and Allah may offer you with strong help.

48:4 It is Allah who has sent down the tranquility into the hearts of the believers so that they may add more faith to their present faith. To Allah belong the forces of the heavens and the earth. Allah is the All-Knower, the All-Wise.

48:5 (For good deeds) Allah may admit the believing men and the believing women to gardens under which rivers flow (paradise), to abide in it forever and to compensate them from their sins, and that is the supreme success with Allah;

48:6 and Allah may punish the hypocritical men and women, and also the polytheist men and women, who thought evil thoughts about Allah. For them there is a disgraceful punishment and the anger of Allah is upon them. Allah has cursed them, prepared hell for them, and worst indeed is that destination.

48:7 To Allah belong the forces of the heavens and the earth. Allah is the All-Powerful, the All-Wise.

48:8 Surely, Allah has sent you (O Muhammad) as a witness, as a bearer of glad tidings, and as a warner,

48:9 so that you people may believe in Allah and Allah's messenger, and that you may assist him, honor him, and glorify Allah's praises morning and afternoon.

48:10 Surely, those who gave allegiance to you (O Muhammad), indeed they gave allegiance to Allah. The authority of Allah was over their hands. Then whoever will break its pledge, will break only its own, and whoever will fulfill what it has pledged with Allah, Allah will bestow a great reward to it.

48:11 Those of the Bedouins who stayed behind will say to you: "Our possessions and our families occupied us, so ask forgiveness for us." They say with their tongues what is not in their hearts. Say: "Who then has any power (to intervene) on your behalf with Allah, if Allah intends to hurt you or intends to benefit you? Nay, but Allah is All-Aware of what you do.

48:12 Nay, but you thought that the messenger and the believers would never return to their families; and that was made seem fair in their hearts. You thought evil thoughts and you became a useless people for destruction."

48:13 Whoever does not believe in Allah and Allah's messenger (Muhammad), then surely, Allah has prepared a blazing fire for the disbelievers.

48:14 To Allah belongs the sovereignty of the heavens and the earth, Allah forgives whom Allah wills, and punishes whom Allah wills. Allah is ever Forgiving, Merciful.

48:15 When you set forth to take them to the spoils (of war), those who stayed behind will say: "Allow us to follow you." They want to change Allah's words. Say: "You shall not follow us. Allah has said this before." Then they will say: "Nay, you envy us." Nay, but they do not understand except a little.

48:16 Say (O Muhammad) to the Bedouins who stayed behind: "You shall be called to fight against a people with great warfare, then either you will fight them or they shall surrender. Then if you obey, Allah will give you a good reward, but if you turn away as you did turn away before, Allah will punish you with a painful punishment."

48:17 There is no blame or sin on the blind, nor there is blame or sin on the lame, nor there is blame or sin on the sick (excused not to go to war). Whoever obeys Allah and Allah's messenger (Muhammad), Allah will admit to gardens beneath which rivers flow (paradise); and whoever turns back, Allah will punish with a painful punishment.

48:18 Indeed, Allah was pleased with the believers when they gave the allegiance to you (O Muhammad) under the tree. Allah knew what was in their hearts, Allah sent down the tranquility upon them, and Allah rewarded them with a near victory,

48:19 and abundant spoils which they will capture. Allah is All-Mighty, All-Wise.

48:20 Allah has promised you abundant spoils which you will capture, and Allah has hastened these (spoils of Khaibar) for you. Allah has restrained the hands of people (enemy) from you so that it may be a sign for the believers and that Allah may guide you to the right way.

48:21 Others (victories and booty promised) which are not yet within your power over it, indeed Allah has compassed them. Allah has power over all things.

48:22 If those who disbelieve fight against you, they would have turned their backs, and then they would have found neither a protector nor a helper.

48:23 That has been the way of Allah which already passed away before. You will never find any change in the way of Allah.

48:24 It is Allah who has restrained their hands from you and your hands from them in the midst of Makkah (through the peace treaty of Hudaibiyah), after that Allah had made you victors over them. Allah is the All-Seer of what you do.

48:25 They are the ones who disbelieved and obstructed you from the sacred mosque (of Makkah) and detained the sacrificed animals from reaching their place of sacrifice. Had there not been believing men and believing women (in Makkah) whom you did not know, and you may trample (heavily burst) them under your feet and thus incurring a sin committed by you without your knowledge (but Allah held back your hands), so that Allah may admit to Allah's Mercy whom Allah wills. If they (believers and disbelievers) should have been apart, Allah would have punished those of them who disbelieved with painful punishment.

48:26 When those who disbelieve had put in their hearts pride and arrogance, the pride and arrogance of the time of ignorance, then Allah sent down Allah's tranquility upon Allah's messenger and upon the believers, and made them stick to the word of piety, and they were well entitled to it and worthy of it. Allah is the All-Knower of everything.

48:27 Indeed Allah will fulfill Allah's messenger's true vision (which Allah showed him) in all truth. Certainly, you shall enter the sacred mosque; if Allah wills, secure (to perform Umrah) having your heads shaved, and having your head hair cut short, having no fear. Allah knows what you do not know, and besides Allah granted a near victory.

48:28 It is Allah who has sent Allah's messenger (Muhammad) with guidance and the religion of truth (Islam), so that Allah may make it (Islam) superior over all other religions. Allah is All-Sufficient as a Witness.

48:29 Muhammad is the messenger of Allah, and those who are with him are strong against disbelievers, and merciful among themselves. You see them bowing and falling down prostrate (in prayer), seeking bounty from Allah and Allah's good pleasure. The mark of them (their faith) is on their faces (foreheads) from the traces of prostration. This is their description in the Torah. Their description in the Gospel is like a seed which sends forth its shoot, then makes it strong, it then becomes thick, and it stands right on its stem delighting the sowers (of the seed) so that Allah may make the disbelievers angry with them. Those among them who believe and do righteous deeds, Allah has promised forgiveness and a great reward.

49. Al-Hujurat : The Private Apartments
In the name of Allah, the Gracious, the Merciful

49:1 O you who believe! Do not put forward (your decision in advance) before Allah and Allah's messenger, and fear Allah. Surely! Allah is All-Hearer, All-Knower (of everything).

49:2 O you who believe! Do not raise your voices above the voice of the prophet, nor speak aloud when talking to him as some of you speak aloud to one another, lest your deeds should become fruitless while you do not perceive.

49:3 Surely! Those who lower their voices in the presence of Allah's messenger, they are the ones whose hearts Allah has tested for piety. They shall have forgiveness and a great reward.

49:4 Surely! Those who call you (O Muhammad) from behind the residences, most of them have no common sense.

49:5 If they had patience until you could come out to them, it would certainly be better for them. Allah is Forgiving, Merciful.

49:6 O you who believe! If a rebellious evil person comes to you with news, verify it, lest you should harm people in ignorance and afterwards you become regretful for what you have done.

49:7 Know that the messenger of Allah is among you. If he were to follow you (your opinions and desires) in most of the affairs, you would surely be in trouble. But Allah has made the faith beloved to you and beautified it in your hearts, and has made disbelief, wickedness and disobedience (to Allah and Allah's messenger) hateful to you. Such are they who are rightly guided,

49:8 (through) a grace from Allah and Allah's favor. Allah is All-Knower, All-Wise.

49:9 If two parties among the believers begin fighting, then make peace between them. But if one of them transgresses against the other, then you fight against the one who has transgressed until it complies with the command of Allah. Then if it complies, make reconciliation between them justly and be fair. Surely! Allah loves those who are just and fair.

49:10 The believers are only brothers (in Islam). So make reconciliation between your brothers and fear Allah, so that you may receive mercy.

49:11 O you who believe! Let not a group mock at another group, it may be that the latter are better than them (former). Nor let (some) women mock at other women, it may be that they (latter) are better than them (former), nor defame one another, nor insult one another by nicknames. How bad is it (to call) wicked name after having faith. Whoever does not repent, then such are indeed wrongdoers.

49:12 O you who believe! Avoid much of suspicions, indeed some suspicions are sins. Do not spy, nor backbite some of you to others. Would one of you like to eat the flesh of its dead brother? You would hate it. Fear Allah. Surely, Allah is the one who Accepts repentance, Merciful.

49:13 O mankind! Surely Allah has created you from a male and a female, and made you into nations and tribes so that you may know one another. Surely, the most honorable of you with Allah is the most pious of you. Surely, Allah is All-Knower, All-Aware.

49:14 The Bedouins say: "We believe." Say: "You do not believe but you only say, we have submitted (in Islam), for the faith has not yet entered into your hearts. But if you obey Allah and Allah's messenger, Allah will not decrease anything in reward for your deeds. Surely, Allah is Forgiving, Merciful."

49:15 Only those are the believers who believe in Allah and Allah's messenger, and afterward do not doubt but they strive with their wealth and their lives in the way of Allah. They are those who are truthful.

49:16 Say (O Muhammad): "Will you inform Allah about your religion? Allah knows all that is in the heavens and all that is in the earth, and Allah is All-Aware of everything.

49:17 They regard as favor upon you (O Muhammad) that they have embraced Islam. Say: "Do not count your Islam as a favor upon me. Nay, but Allah has conferred a favor upon you that Allah has guided you to the faith; (agree) if you indeed are truthful.

49:18 Surely, Allah knows the unseen of the heavens and the earth. Allah is the All-Seer of what you do.

50. Qaf : Qaf

In the name of Allah, the Gracious, the Merciful

50:1 Qaf. By the glorious Qur'an.

50:2 But they wonder that there has come to them a warner (Muhammad) from among themselves. So the disbelievers say: "This is a strange thing

50:3 that after we are dead and have become dust (we shall be resurrected), that is a far return."

50:4 Indeed Allah knows that the earth consumes them (their dead bodies) and with Allah there is a book preserved (with all records).

50:5 Nay, but they deny the truth (this Qur'an) when it comes to them, so they are confused (can not differentiate between right and wrong).

50:6 Have they not looked at the sky above them, (and see) how Allah has made it, adorned it, and there are no flaws in it?

50:7 The earth! Allah has spread it out, set on it mountains standing firm, and has produced every kind of lovely growth (plants) in it.

50:8 (All these are) an insight and a reminder for every servant turning to Allah.

50:9 Allah sends down blessed water (rain) from the sky, then Allah produces with it gardens and grain (crops) that are reaped,

50:10 and tall date-palms with arranged clusters (of dates);

50:11 and provision for (Allah's) servants. Thus Allah gives life to a dead land with it. That is how the Resurrection (of the dead) will be.

50:12 Denied before them (the pagans of Makkah) the people of Noah, the residents of Al-Rass, and the Thamud,

50:13 Ad, Pharaoh, and the brothers of Lot,

50:14 the residents of the Al-Aiykah (wood), and the people of Tubba; every one of them denied messengers, so Allah's threat took effect (upon them).

50:15 Was Allah tired with the first creation? Nay, they are in confused doubt about a new creation (Resurrection).

50:16 Indeed Allah has created mankind and Allah knows what one's own self whispers to it. Allah is nearer to one than rope of its jugular vein (by Allah's knowledge).

50:17 (Remember!) that the 2 receivers (recording angels) receive (for each human) sitting on the right and on the left (to record actions),

50:18 not a word does one utter but there is a watcher by it ready (to record).

50:19 When the agony of death will come in truth (they will say): "This is what you were trying to avoid from it!"

50:20 The trumpet will be blown; that will be the day of warning (Resurrection).

50:21 Every person will come forth along with an (angel) to drive, and an (angel) to bear witness.

50:22 (It will be said to the sinners): "Indeed you were heedless of this, but now Allah has removed your covering from you, and your eyesight is sharp this day!"

50:23 Its companion (angel) will say: "Here is (this record) ready with me!"

50:24 (It will be said): "Both of you (2 angels) throw every stubborn disbeliever into hell,

50:25 opponent of good, doubting transgressor

50:26 who set up another one worthy of worship with Allah. So (both of you) cast that person into the severe punishment."

50:27 Its companion (Satan) will say: "Our Rabb! I did not push the person to transgress but it itself was in error far astray."

50:28 (Allah) will say: "Do not dispute in front of me (Allah) and surely I (Allah) sent forth the threat (in advance) to you.

50:29 The words from me (Allah) cannot be changed and I (Allah) am not unjust to the servants."

50:30 On that day when Allah will ask the hell: "Are you filled?" It will say: "Are there any more (to come)?"

50:31 The paradise will be brought near to the pious, which will not be far off,

50:32 (it will be said): "This is what you were promised. It is for every one returning (to Allah) in sincere repentance and those who preserve (their covenant with Allah),

50:33 who feared the Gracious (Allah) in the unseen (in the world) and brought a heart turned in repentance (to Allah)."

50:34 (Allah will say): "You enter in it in peace and security; this is the day of eternal life!"

50:35 They will have all that they desire in it, and Allah has more (for them).

50:36 How many generations Allah has destroyed before them who were stronger in power than them? (When punishment came) they ran for a refuge in the land. Could they find any place of refuge (to save them from destruction)?

50:37 Surely, in that, there is a lesson for one who has a heart or gives ear while one is witness.

50:38 Indeed Allah created the heavens and the earth and all between them in 6 days, and no fatigue touched Allah.

50:39 So, bear with patience (O Muhammad) on all that they say, and glorify the praises of your Rabb before sunrise and before sunset.

50:40 During a part of the night, glorify Allah's praises and after the prostration (prayers).

50:41 Listen on the day when the caller will call from a near place,

50:42 the day when the people will hear the cry in truth; that will be the day of coming out (the dead will rise from the graves i.e., the day of Resurrection).

50:43 Surely, it is Allah who gives life and causes death; and to Allah is the final return,

50:44 on the day when the earth shall be split asunder and the people will be rushing out of it; that will be a gathering quite easy for Allah.

50:45 Allah knows very well what they (disbelievers) say. You (O Muhammad) are not a tyrant over them (to force them to believe). So warn by the Qur'an (everyone) who fears Allah's warning.

51. Adh-Dhariyat : The Winds that Scatter
In the name of Allah, the Gracious, the Merciful

51:1 By (the winds) that scatter dust;

51:2 and (the clouds) that bear heavy weight of water;

51:3 and (the ships) that float with ease and gentleness;

51:4 and those (angels) that distribute command (of Allah);

51:5 surely that which you are promised is true;

51:6 and surely, the recompense is sure to happen.

51:7 By the sky full of orbits,

51:8 certainly, you have different ideas,

51:9 turn aside from (Muhammad and the Qur'an) is the one who is turned aside.

51:10 Curse be to the liars,

51:11 who are under a cover of heedlessness (don't think about the hereafter).

51:12 They ask: "When will be the day of recompense?"

51:13 (It will be) a day when they will be punished over the fire,

51:14 (it will be said): "You taste your trial (burning)! This is what you used to ask to be hastened!"

51:15 Surely, the pious will be in the midst of gardens and springs (in paradise),

51:16 taking joy in the things which their Rabb has given them. Surely, they were before this (in the world) righteous people.

51:17 They used to sleep but little by the night,

51:18 and ask Allah for forgiveness in the hours before dawn,

51:19 and share their properties with the needy (who asked) for it, and the deprived (who did not ask).

51:20 In the earth, there are signs for those who have firm faith,

51:21 and also in your own selves. Can you not then see?

51:22 In the heaven is your provision, and all that which you are promised.

51:23 By the Rabb of the heaven and the earth, surely it is the truth just as what you speak!

51:24 Has the story of the honored guests (angel Gabriel with 2 more angels) of Abraham reached you?

51:25 When they came to him, and said: "Peace be upon you!" He answered: "Peace be upon you," and said: "You are people unknown to me,"

51:26 then he turned to his family, brought out a fat roasted calf,

51:27 and he put it before them (saying): "Will you not eat?"

51:28 (When they did not eat), he became afraid of them. They said: "Do not fear." They gave him glad tidings of an intelligent son.

51:29 Then his wife came forward with a loud voice, she strikes her face and said: "(A son to) a barren old woman!"

51:30 They said: "Even so says your Rabb. Surely, Allah is the All-Wise, the All-Knower."

51:31 He (Abraham) said: "Then for what purpose you have come, O messengers?"

51:32 They said: "We have been sent to a criminal people (of prophet Lot, who were homosexuals),

51:33 to send down upon them stones of baked clay,

51:34 marked by your Rabb for those who transgress Allah's limits."

51:35 So Allah brought out all those who were believers in the town,

51:36 but Allah found none in it except one household of the Muslims (Lot and his 2 daughters)

51:37 and Allah left in it a sign (the Dead sea in Palestine) for those who fear the painful punishment.

51:38 (There is sign in the story) of Moses, when Allah sent him to Pharaoh with a clear authority,

51:39 but he (Pharaoh) turned away (from belief) with his hosts and said: "A sorcerer, or a madman."

51:40 So, Allah took him and his hosts, and dumped them into the sea. Indeed he deserved to be blamed.

51:41 (There is sign in the story) of Ad, when Allah sent against them the barren wind,

51:42 which spared nothing that it reached and it blew on like something rotten (decayed).

51:43 (There is sign in the story) of Thamud, when it was said to them: "Enjoy yourselves for a while (3 days),"

51:44 but they disobeyed the command of their Rabb with arrogance; so the awful cry overtook them while they were looking.

51:45 So neither they were able to rise up nor could they help themselves.

51:46 (Allah destroyed) the people of Noah before them. Surely, they were people who were rebellious, disobedient (to Allah).

51:47 Allah has built the heaven with power. Surely, Allah is Able to extend the vastness of space in it.

51:48 Allah has spread out the earth, how Excellent Spreader is Allah!

51:49 Allah has created everything in pairs, so that you may remember (Allah).

51:50 (Say to mankind, O Muhammad):"Rush towards Allah, surely, I (Muhammad) am from Allah a plain warner to you.

51:51 Do not set up any other one worthy of worship with Allah. Surely, I (Muhammad) am from Allah a plain warner to you."

51:52 Likewise, whenever a messenger came to those before them, they said: "A sorcerer or a madman!"

51:53 Have they (past people) transmitted this saying (to these pagans)? Nay, but they are a people transgressing beyond bounds!

51:54 So, turn away (O Muhammad) from them (pagans), you are not to be blamed (you have conveyed message).

51:55 But remind (by preaching the Qur'an, O Muhammad), for surely, the reminding benefits the believers.

51:56 I (Allah) have not created the jinns and mankind except to worship me (Allah alone).

51:57 I (Allah) do not want any provision from them nor do I (Allah) want that they should feed me (Allah).

51:58 Surely, Allah is the All-Provider, Owner of Power, the Strong.

51:59 Surely, for those who do wrong, there is a portion of punishment similar to the portion of the punishment of their friends (predecessors), so ask Allah not to hasten on!

51:60 Then, woe to those who disbelieve from their day which they have been promised (for punishment).

52. At-Tur : The Mount Tur

In the name of Allah, the Gracious, the Merciful

52:1 By the (mount) Tur (where Moses received Torah);

52:2 and by the book inscribed

52:3 in parchment (written sheep skin) unrolled,

52:4 and by the house (Bait-ul-Mamoor, the house over the heavens parallel to the Ka'bah at Makkah), frequented (by the angels),

52:5 and by the roof raised high (sky),

52:6 and by the sea boiling blaze,

52:7 surely, the punishment of your Rabb will surely come to pass.

52:8 There is none that can avert it.

52:9 On the day when the heaven will shake with a dreadful shaking

52:10 and the mountains will move away with a horrible movement.

52:11 On that day, woe be to the rejecters (of truth),

52:12 who are engaged in falsehood.

52:13 That day they will be pushed down by force to the fire of hell with a forceful pushing,

52:14 (it will be said to them): "This is the fire which you used to deny.

52:15 Is this a magic, or do you not see?

52:16 You burn in its heat; it will be the same for you whether you be patient or not be patient. You are only being requited for what you used to do."

52:17 Surely, the pious will be in gardens (paradise), and delight,

52:18 enjoying in that which their Rabb has bestowed on them and their Rabb saved them from the punishment of the blazing fire.

52:19 (It will be said to them): "Eat and drink with happiness because of what you used to do (good deeds)."

52:20 They will recline (with ease) on thrones arranged in ranks. Allah will marry them to lovely maidens with wide lovely eyes.

52:21 Those who believe and their offspring follow them in faith, Allah will join their offspring to them, and Allah will not decrease any reward for their deeds. Every person has a pledge for that which it has earned.

52:22 Allah will provide them with fruit and meat as they desire.

52:23 They shall pass from hand to hand a wine cup in it which shall cause no dirty, false talk in it (between them), and no sin will go around,

52:24 and boy-servants will go round for them to serve them as if they were preserved pearls.

52:25 Some of them will come near to others, questioning (about worldly life)

52:26 and they will say: "Surely, we were previously afraid with our families (from the punishment of Allah).

52:27 But Allah has been gracious to us, and has saved us from the punishment of the fire.

52:28 Surely, we used to invoke Allah before. Surely, Allah is the Kind, the Merciful."

52:29 Therefore, remind and preach (mankind, O Muhammad). By the grace of Allah, you are neither a fortune-teller, nor a madman.

52:30 Or do they say: "(Muhammad is) a poet! We are waiting for him some calamity (by time)!"

52:31 Say (O Muhammad to them): "Wait! I am with you among the waiters!"

52:32 Or do their minds command them this (to tell a lie against you)? Or are they people exceeding all bounds (from belief to disbelief)?

52:33 Or do they say: "He (Muhammad) has forged it (this Qur'an)?" Nay! They do not believe!

52:34 Then let them produce a scripture like it (the Qur'an) if they are truthful.

52:35 Or were they created by no one? Or were they (themselves) the creators?

52:36 Or have they created the heavens and the earth? Nay, but they have no firm belief.

52:37 Or are the treasures of your Rabb with them? Or are they the tyrants with the authority to do as they like?

52:38 Or do they have a stairway (to heaven), by means of which they listen (to the talks of the angels)? Then let their listener produce some clear proof.

52:39 Or has Allah only daughters and you have sons?

52:40 Or is it that you (O Muhammad) ask a wage from them (for your preaching) so that they are burdened from a load of debt?

52:41 Or is the (knowledge of) unseen with them and they write it down?

52:42 Or do they intend a plot (against you)? If so, those who disbelieve are themselves (trapped) in a plot!

52:43 Or do they have one worthy of worship other than Allah? Glorified is Allah from all that they ascribe as partners (to Allah).

52:44 Even if they were to see a piece of the heaven falling down, they would say: "Clouds gathered in heaps!"

52:45 So leave them alone till they meet their day, in which they will sink into a fainting (with horror).

52:46 The day when their plotting will avail them nothing nor they will be helped.

52:47 Surely, for those who do wrong, there is punishment (in this world and in graves) before this, but most of them do not know.

52:48 So wait patiently (O Muhammad) for the decision of your Rabb, for surely Allah is watching you. Glorify the praises of your Rabb when you get up from sleep,

52:49 and also glorify Allah's praises in the night-time, and at the setting of the stars.

53. An-Najm : The Star
In the name of Allah, the Gracious, the Merciful

53:1 By the star when it goes down (vanishes),

53:2 your companion (Muhammad) has neither gone astray nor misguided,

53:3 nor does he speak of (his own) desire.

53:4 It is only a revelation that is revealed.

53:5 He (Muhammad) has been taught (this Qur'an) by one mighty in power (angel Gabriel);

53:6 the one free from any defect who rose and became stable (in view).

53:7 While he (Gabriel) was in the highest part of the horizon,

53:8 then he (Gabriel) approached and came closer

53:9 and was at a distance of 2 bow's length or even closer,

53:10 so he (Gabriel) conveyed the revelation to Allah's servant (Muhammad) what he was supposed to reveal.

53:11 (The prophet's) heart did not deny what he (Muhammad) saw.

53:12 Will you (disbelievers) then dispute with him (Muhammad) about what he saw (during his ascent journey over the 7 heavens)?

53:13 Indeed he (Muhammad) saw him (Gabriel) another descent time

53:14 near Sidra-tul-Muntaha (the lote-tree at the farthest end of the 7th heavens, beyond which none can cross).

53:15 Near it is Jannatul-M'awa (the rest-house of paradise).

53:16 When that lote-tree was covered with what covered it,

53:17 the sight (of Muhammad) did not turn aside (right or left), nor it transgressed beyond limit.

53:18 Indeed he (Muhammad) did see some of the greatest signs of his Rabb.

53:19 Have you then considered Lat, Uzza (2 idols of the pagan Arabs)

53:20 and another idol (Manat of the pagan Arabs), the other 3rd (as the daughters of Allah)?

53:21 Is it for you the sons and for Allah the daughters?

53:22 This indeed is a division most unfair!

53:23 They (Lat, Uzza, Manat) are nothing but names which you and your forefathers have named, for Allah has not sent down any authority in them. They (disbelievers) follow nothing but a guess which is their soul's desire, even though the guidance has come to them from their Rabb.

53:24 Or should human have whatever one wishes?

53:25 But to Allah belong the last (hereafter) and the first (the world).

53:26 How many angels are there in the heavens; yet their intercession can avail nothing except what Allah gives permission for whom Allah wills and pleases.

53:27 Surely those who do not believe in the hereafter, name the angels with female names.

53:28 But they have no knowledge of it. They follow but a guess; and surely guess does not substitute for the truth at all.

53:29 Therefore, withdraw (O Muhammad) from those who turn away from Allah's reminder (this Qur'an) and they only desire the life of this world.

53:30 This is their highest point of knowledge. Surely, your Rabb is Allah who knows those best who go astray from Allah's way, and Allah knows those best who receive guidance.

53:31 To Allah belongs all that is in the heavens and all that is in the earth, so that Allah may requite those who do evil with what they have done (punish them in hell), and reward those who do good with what is best (paradise).

53:32 Those who avoid major sins and shameful deeds except the small faults; surely, for them your Rabb will have abundant forgiveness. Allah knew you well when Allah created you from the earth and when you were fetuses in your mother's wombs. So do not scribe piety to yourselves. Allah knows best who fears (Allah).

53:33 Have you (O Muhammad) seen the one who (Waleed bin Mugheerah, who wanted to accept Islam but someone promised him to take the punishment on his behalf for certain amount of money, he) turned away (from Islam)?

53:34 He gave a little (amount of money), then he stopped (giving).

53:35 Does he has the knowledge of the unseen so that he sees (the reality)?

53:36 Or has he not been informed about what was in the pages (scripture) of Moses,

53:37 and of Abraham who fulfilled (his covenant):

53:38 "That no burdened person (with sins) shall bear the burden (sins) of another,

53:39 that a human can have nothing except what one strives for,

53:40 that one's efforts will be seen (checked),

53:41 that one will be fully recompensed and the best recompense,

53:42 that to your Rabb is the end,

53:43 that it is Allah who makes laugh and makes weep,

53:44 that it is Allah who causes death and gives life,

53:45 that it is Allah who created in pairs, the male and the female,

53:46 from a drop of semen when it is emitted,

53:47 that it is upon Allah to grant another life (Resurrection),

53:48 that it is Allah who gives much or little (of wealth and contentment),

53:49 that it is Allah the Rabb of Sirius (the star whom the pagan Arabs used to worship),

53:50 and that it is Allah who destroyed the former Ad (people),

53:51 and Thamud (people). So Allah spared none,

53:52 and the people of Noah previously, surely they were more unjust and more rebellious and transgressing.

53:53 Allah destroyed the overthrown cities (of Sodom and Gomorrah during prophet Lot),

53:54 who were covered by (the punishment with stones) that covered them."

53:55 Then which of the graces of your Rabb will you doubt?

53:56 This (Muhammad) is a warner just like the old warners.

53:57 The day of Resurrection is drawing near;

53:58 none besides Allah can avert it.

53:59 Do you then wonder at this recital (the Qur'an),

53:60 and laugh at it and do not weep?

53:61 You are wasting your precious life in pastime and amusements.

53:62 So you fall down in prostration to Allah and worship Allah.

54. Al-Qamar : The Moon

In the name of Allah, the Gracious, the Merciful

54:1 The hour (of doom) is drawing near, and the moon has split asunder (the people of Makkah requested Muhammad to show a miracle, so he showed them the splitting of the moon).

54:2 Yet, when they (disbelievers) see a sign, they turn away and say: "This is continuous magic."

54:3 They deny (the verses of this Qur'an) and follow their own lusts. Every matter will be settled (good deeds will take to paradise, and evil deeds will take to hell).

54:4 Indeed there has come to them the news (in this Qur'an about previous nations) wherein there is (enough warning) to check (from evil),

54:5 perfect wisdom (as a warning), but (preaching of) warners do not benefit them.

54:6 So you (O Muhammad) withdraw from them. The day when the caller will call them to a terrible thing.

54:7 They will come out from their graves with their humbled eyes as if they were locusts spread abroad,

54:8 rushing towards the caller and the disbelievers will say: "This is a hard day."

54:9 The people of Noah denied (their messenger) before them. They rejected Allah's servant and said: "A madman!" and he was rudely rebuked and threatened.

54:10 (After warning people for 950 years) he invoked his Rabb (saying): "I have been overcome, so help me!"

54:11 So Allah opened the gates of heaven with water (rain) pouring out,

54:12 and Allah caused the earth to gush out with springs. So the waters met for a matter predestined.

54:13 Allah carried him on (a ship) built with planks and nails,

54:14 floating under Allah's care, a reward for him (Noah) who was rejected (by disbelievers)!

54:15 Indeed, Allah has left this (ship) as a sign, so is there any who will remember (or take admonition)?

54:16 How terrible was my (Allah's) punishment and my (Allah's) warnings?

54:17 Allah has indeed made the Qur'an easy to understand and remember, and is there any who will remember (or take admonition)?

54:18 Ad (people) denied (their Prophet Hud), then how terrible was my (Allah's) punishment and my (Allah's) warnings?

54:19 Surely, Allah sent against them a furious wind of harsh voice on a day of evil sign and continuous calamity,

54:20 snatching out the people as if they were uprooted stems of date-palms.

54:21 How terrible was my (Allah's) punishment and my (Allah's) warnings?

54:22 Indeed Allah has made the Qur'an easy to understand and remember, then is there anyone who will remember (or take admonition)?

54:23 Thamud (people) denied the warnings,

54:24 they said: "A human alone from among us whom we are to follow? Truly, then we should be in error and madness!

54:25 Is it that the reminder is sent only to him (prophet Saleh) from among us? Nay, he is an insolent liar!"

54:26 (Allah said to Saleh): "Tomorrow they will come to know, who the insolent liar is!

54:27 Surely, Allah is sending the she-camel as a test for them. So watch them (O Saleh) and be patient!

54:28 Inform them that the water is to be shared between them (and she-camel). Each (one's right) to drink is being established (by turns).

54:29 But they (people of Thamud) called one of their comrades who took (responsibility) and killed (she-camel).

54:30 Then how terrible was my (Allah's) punishment and my (Allah's) warnings?

54:31 Surely, Allah sent against them a single punishment (awful cry) and they became like the dry stubble (crushed twigs) of a fence-builder.

54:32 Indeed, Allah has made the Qur'an easy to understand and remember, and is there any who will remember (or take admonition)?

54:33 The people of Lot denied the warnings.

54:34 Surely, Allah sent against them a violent storm of stones (which destroyed them), except the family of Lot, whom Allah saved in the last hour of the night

54:35 as a favor from Allah. Thus Allah does reward those who give thanks (by obeying Allah).

54:36 Indeed he (Lot) had warned them of Allah's grasp but they doubted the warnings!

54:37 Indeed they even sought to lure him about his guest (by asking to commit sodomy with them). So Allah blinded their eyes and said: "Now you taste my (Allah's) punishment and my (Allah's) warnings."

54:38 Surely, a lasting punishment seized them early in the morning

54:39 (as if to say): "Now you taste my (Allah's) punishment and my (Allah's) warnings."

54:40 Indeed, Allah has made the Qur'an easy to understand and remember, and is there any who will remember (or take admonition)?

54:41 Indeed, the warnings came to the people of Pharaoh (through Moses and Aaron).

54:42 They denied Allah's all signs. So Allah seized them with a seizure of the All-Mighty, All-Capable.

54:43 Are your disbelievers (O Quraish!) better than these (nations of Noah, Lot, Saleh, and the people of Pharaoh who were destroyed)? Or have you been granted immunity (against Allah's punishment) in the divine scriptures?

54:44 Or do they say: "We are great in numbers, and we shall be victorious?"

54:45 Their huge number will be put to flight, and they will show their backs.

54:46 Nay, but the hour (of judgment) is their appointed time (for recompense), and the hour will be more grievous and more bitter.

54:47 Surely, the criminals are in error (in this world) and will burn (in the hell in the hereafter).

54:48 The day when they will be dragged into the fire with their faces downwards, (it will be said to them): "You taste the touch of hell!"

54:49 Surely, Allah has created all things with divine ordainment.

54:50 Allah's commandment is but one as the twinkling of an eye.

54:51 Indeed, (O disbelievers) Allah has destroyed many like you, and is there any who will remember (or take admonition)?

54:52 Each and everything they have done is being noted in their records of deeds.

54:53 Everything, small and big, is being written down.

54:54 Surely, the pious will be in the midst of gardens and rivers (paradise),

54:55 in a seat of truth (paradise), near the most Powerful King (Allah).

55. Ar-Rahman : The Gracious

In the name of Allah, the Gracious, the Merciful

55:1 The Gracious (Allah)!

55:2 Who taught (mankind) the Qur'an,

55:3 created human

55:4 and taught human persuasive speech.

55:5 The sun and the moon (run on their fixed courses) for reckoning.

55:6 The stars and the trees both prostrate.

55:7 Allah has raised the heaven high, and Allah has set up the balance,

55:8 so that you may not transgress in the balance.

55:9 Establish the weight with justice and do not give less in measurement.

55:10 Allah has put the earth for the creatures,

55:11 therein are fruits, date-palms with sheathed fruit-stalks,

55:12 and corn with leaves and stalk for food and sweet-scented plants.

55:13 Then which of the favors of your Rabb will you both (jinns and human) deny?

55:14 Allah created man from sounding clay like the clay of pottery,

55:15 and Allah created the jinns from smokeless flame of fire.

55:16 Then which of the favors of your Rabb will you both (jinns and human) deny?

55:17 (Allah is) the Rabb of the 2 easts (places of sunrise during summer and winter) and the Rabb of the 2 wests (places of sunset during summer and winter).

55:18 Then which of the favors of your Rabb will you both (jinns and human) deny?

55:19 Allah has let loose the 2 seas (salt water and sweet water) meeting together,

55:20 Yet, between them is a barrier which none of them can transgress.

55:21 Then which of the favors of your Rabb will you both (jinns and human) deny?

55:22 Both pearl and coral come out of them.

55:23 Then which of the favors of your Rabb will you both (jinns and human) deny?

55:24 The ships are Allah's going and coming in the seas like mountains.

55:25 Then which of the favors of your Rabb will you both (jinns and human) deny?

55:26 Everyone who is on it (earth) will perish,

55:27 and the face (authority) of your Rabb will remain full of Majesty and Honor forever.

55:28 Then which of the favors of your Rabb will you both (jinns and human) deny?

55:29 Whoever is in the heavens and on earth begs of Allah (for needs). Every day Allah is engaged in some matter (task).

55:30 Then which of the favors of your Rabb will you both (jinns and human) deny?

55:31 Allah will attend to you (to give account), O you 2 classes (jinns and mankind).

55:32 Then which of the favors of your Rabb will you both (jinns and human) deny?

55:33 O assembly of jinns and mankind! If you have the power to pass beyond the zones of the heavens and the earth (to escape punishment), then pass them! But you will never be able to pass them, except with authority (from Allah)!

55:34 Then which of the favors of your Rabb will you both (jinns and human) deny?

55:35 The smokeless flames of fire and molten brass will be sent against you both (jinns and mankind), and you will not be able to defend yourselves.

55:36 Then which of the favors of your Rabb will you both (jinns and human) deny?

55:37 When the heaven will burst and it becomes rosy (or red) like red hide.

55:38 Then which of the favors of your Rabb will you both (jinns and human) deny?

55:39 On that day neither human nor jinn will be asked about their sins (their faces will be either white (for paradise) or black (for hell)).

55:40 Then which of the favors of your Rabb will you both (jinns and human) deny?

55:41 The sinners will be recognized by their marks (black faces) and they will be seized by their forelocks and their feet.

55:42 Then which of the favors of your Rabb will you both (jinns and human) deny?

55:43 (It will be said to them): "This is hell which the sinners had denied it."

55:44 They will go around between it (hell) and the boiling hot water.

55:45 Then which of the favors of your Rabb will you both (jinns and human) deny?

55:46 But for those who fear the standing before their Rabb, there will be 2 gardens (in paradise).

55:47 Then which of the favors of your Rabb will you both (jinns and human) deny?

55:48 With spreading branches (of shady trees).

55:49 Then which of the favors of your Rabb will you both (jinns and human) deny?

55:50 In both of them 2 springs will be flowing.

55:51 Then which of the favors of your Rabb will you both (jinns and human) deny?

55:52 In both of them there will be every kind of fruit in pairs.

55:53 Then which of the favors of your Rabb will you both (jinns and human) deny?

55:54 They will recline on couches whose inner livings will be of silk brocade and the fruits of the 2 gardens will be near at hand.

55:55 Then which of the favors of your Rabb will you both (jinns and human) deny?

55:56 Therein will be chaste virgins restraining their glances (upon their husbands only) whom no human or jinn has touched them before.

55:57 Then which of the favors of your Rabb will you both (jinns and human) deny?

55:58 They are (in beauty) like rubies and coral.

55:59 Then which of the favors of your Rabb will you both (jinns and human) deny?

55:60 Is there any reward for good other than good?

55:61 Then which of the favors of your Rabb will you both (jinns and human) deny?

55:62 Besides these 2 there shall be 2 other gardens (in paradise).

55:63 Then which of the favors of your Rabb will you both (jinns and human) deny?

55:64 (shaded with) dark green (trees).

55:65 Then which of the favors of your Rabb will you both (jinns and human) deny?

55:66 In both of them there will be 2 springs gushing out water.

55:67 Then which of the favors of your Rabb will you both (jinns and human) deny?

55:68 In each of them there will be fruits, date-palms, and pomegranates.

55:69 Then which of the favors of your Rabb will you both (jinns and human) deny?

55:70 Therein will be chaste and beautiful (virgins).

55:71 Then which of the favors of your Rabb will you both (jinns and human) deny?

55:72 Beautiful virgins (Huris) guarded in pavilions.

55:73 Then which of the favors of your Rabb will you both (jinns and human) deny?

55:74 Whom no human or jinn has touched them before.

55:75 Then which of the favors of your Rabb will you both (jinns and human) deny?

55:76 Reclining on green cushions and rich beautiful mattresses.

55:77 Then which of the favors of your Rabb will you both (jinns and human) deny?

55:78 Blessed is the name of your Rabb (Allah), the owner of Majesty and Honor.

56. Al-Waqi'ah : The Event

In the name of Allah, the Gracious, the Merciful

56:1 When the event (the day of Resurrection) will befall,

56:2 there will be no denying of its befalling,

56:3 it will bring low (to some), it will exalt (for others).

56:4 When the earth will be shaken with a terrible shake,

56:5 and the mountains will be powdered to dust,

56:6 so that they will become floating dust particles.

56:7 Then you all will be in 3 kinds (separate groups):

56:8 those on the right hand (receive their records in right hands) who will be those on the right hand (will go to paradise);

56:9 and those on the left hand (receive their records in left hands) who will be those on the left hand (will go to hell);

56:10 and those foremost (in Islamic faith) will be foremost (in paradise).

56:11 Those will be nearest (to Allah),

56:12 in the gardens of delight (paradise).

56:13 A most of them will be from the first generations (who embraced Islam)

56:14 and a few will be from the later generations.

56:15 They will be on thrones of gold and precious stones,

56:16 reclining on them face to face,

56:17 immortal youths will go round serving them

56:18 with cups, jugs, and glasses of flowing wine,

56:19 from where they will neither get any pain of the head, nor they will get any intoxication.

56:20 (They will have) fruits of their own choice

56:21 and the flesh of fowls that they may desire,

56:22 and Huris (chaste virgins) with wide lovely eyes,

56:23 like guarded pearls,

56:24 as a reward for what they used to do (good deeds).

56:25 They will neither hear any vain talk therein nor any sinful speech,

56:26 but the saying of Salam! Salam! (greetings with peace)!

56:27 Those on the right hand who will be those on the right hand.

56:28 They will be among thornless lote-trees,

56:29 among banana trees with fruits piled one above another,

56:30 and in long-extended shade,

56:31 by water flowing constantly,

56:32 and fruit in plenty

56:33 whose season is not limited and their supply will not be cut off,

56:34 and on high raised couches or thrones.

56:35 Surely, Allah has created them (maidens) of special creation

56:36 and made them virgins

56:37 loving (their husbands only), equal in age,

56:38 for those on the right hand.

56:39 A large number will be from the first generation (who embraced Islam)

56:40 and a large number will be from the later generations.

56:41 Those on the left hand - will be those on the left hand.

56:42 (They will be) in fierce hot wind and boiling water,

56:43 and in the shadow of black smoke,

56:44 (that shadow is) neither cool, nor good.

56:45 Surely, they were indulged in luxury before,

56:46 and were persisting in great sin

56:47 and they used to say: "When we die and become dust and bones, shall we then indeed be resurrected?

56:48 Also our forefathers?"

56:49 Say (O Muhammad): "Surely, those of old, and those of later times,

56:50 all will surely be gathered together to an appointed meeting of well known day.

56:51 Then surely, you the erring-ones, the deniers (of Resurrection),

56:52 surely you will eat of trees of Zaqqum,

56:53 then you will fill your bellies with it,

56:54 and drink from the boiling water on it,

56:55 yet, you will drink like thirsty camels!"

56:56 That will be their entertainment on the day of Resurrection.

56:57 Allah created you, then why do you not believe?

56:58 You see what you emit (semen).

56:59 Is it you who create it (make this semen into a human), or is Allah the creator?

56:60 Allah has decreed the death among you and Allah is not unable

56:61 to transfigure you by others like yourselves and creates you in forms that you do not know.

56:62 Indeed, you know the first form of creation (of Adam), why then do you not remember or take heed?

56:63 Do you see (the seed) that you sow (in the ground)?

56:64 Is it you who make it grow, or is Allah the grower?

56:65 If Allah willed, Allah could surely make it into dry pieces and you would be regretful:

56:66 (saying): "We are indeed ruined,

56:67 nay, but we are deprived (from the results of our work)!"

56:68 Do you see the water that you drink?

56:69 Is it you who cause it to come down from the rain clouds or is it Allah who causes it to come down?

56:70 If Allah willed, Allah could make it salty (undrinkable). Why then do you not give thanks (to Allah)?

56:71 Do you see the fire which you kindle?

56:72 Is it you who made the tree to grow, or is Allah the grower?

56:73 Allah has made it a reminder (of the hellfire in the hereafter); and an article of use for the travelers.

56:74 Then glorify the name of your Rabb, the great.

56:75 Surely I (Allah) swear by the setting of the stars,

56:76 and surely, that is a great oath, if you know,

56:77 surely, this is indeed a honorable recital (the Qur'an)

56:78 in a book well-guarded (with Allah),

56:79 which none can touch it (the Qur'an with Allah) except the purified (angels),

56:80 a revelation (this Qur'an) from the Rabb of the worlds.

56:81 Is it such a talk (this Qur'an) that you (disbelievers) deny

56:82 and (instead of thanking Allah for) your provision Allah gives you, you deny (Allah)?

56:83 Then why do you not (intervene) when (the soul of a dying person) reaches the throat

56:84 while you are looking at that moment,

56:85 but Allah is nearer to that person than you, but you do not see (Allah).

56:86 Then why do you not, if you are exempt from the reckoning and recompense,

56:87 bring back the soul (to its body) if you are truthful?

56:88 Then, if the dying person be of those brought near (to Allah),

56:89 for that person there is rest and provision, and a garden of delights (paradise).

56:90 Yet if the dying person be of those on the right hand,

56:91 then (there is greeting) 'Peace be upon you' for that person from those on the right hand.

56:92 Yet if the dying person is one of the denying (of the Resurrection), the erring,

56:93 then (for that person there) is entertainment from boiling water,

56:94 and burning in hellfire.

56:95 Surely, this is an absolute truth with certainty.

56:96 So glorify with praises the name of your Rabb, the greatest.

57. Al-Hadid : The Iron

In the name of Allah, the Gracious, the Merciful

57:1 All that is in the heavens and the earth glorifies Allah, and Allah is the All-Mighty, All-Wise.

57:2 To Allah belongs the kingdom of the heavens and the earth. Allah gives life and causes death and Allah has power over all things.

57:3 Allah is the First (nothing is before Allah) and the Last (nothing is after Allah), the Evident (everything is in front of Allah) and the Hidden (nothing is hidden from Allah). Allah is the All-Knower of every thing.

57:4 It is Allah who created the heavens and the earth in 6 days and then rose over the throne (in a manner that suits Allah's Majesty). Allah knows what goes into the earth and what comes forth from it, and what descends from the heaven and what ascends to it. Allah is with you (by Allah's knowledge) wherever you may be. Allah is the All-Seer of what you do.

57:5 To Allah belongs the kingdom of the heavens and the earth. All the matters return to Allah (for decision).

57:6 Allah causes the night to pass into the day and the day to pass into the night, and Allah has full knowledge of whatever is in the hearts.

57:7 Believe in Allah and Allah's messenger (Muhammad), and spend (in Allah's way) out of what Allah has made you trustees. Those of you who believe and spend (in Allah's way), they will be greatly rewarded.

57:8 What is the matter with you that you do not believe in Allah? The messenger (Muhammad) invites you to believe in your Rabb, and indeed Allah has taken your covenant if you are real believers.

57:9 It is Allah who sends down clear revelations to Allah's servant (Muhammad), so that Allah may bring you out from the darkness into the light. Surely, Allah is full of Kindness and Merciful to you.

57:10 What is the matter with you that you do not spend in the cause of Allah? To Allah belongs the heritage of the heavens and the earth. Not equal among you are those who spent and fought before the conquering (of Makkah) (with those among you who did later). Such are higher in degree than those who spent and fought afterwards. Yet, Allah has promised all of you the best (reward). Allah is All-Aware of all of what you do.

57:11 Who is the one who will lend to Allah a goodly loan, so that (Allah) will increase it manifold to its credit (by repaying), and (besides) it will have a good reward (paradise)?

57:12 On the day (of judgment) you shall see the believing men and the believing women, with their light shining before them and by their right hands. (It will be said to them): "Glad tidings for you this day! (You shall enter the) gardens under which rivers flow (paradise), to reside in it forever! Truly, this is the greatest success!"

57:13 On the day the hypocrite men and hypocrite women will say to those who believe: "Wait for us! Let us get something from your light!" It will be said: "Go back to your rear! Then seek a light!" So a wall will be put up between them with a gate in it. Inside it will be mercy and outside it will be facing toward the punishment (of hell).

57:14 (The hypocrites) will call them (believers): "Were we not with you?" They (believers) will reply: "Yes! But you led yourselves into temptations, looked forward (for our destruction), you doubted (in faith); and you were deceived by false desires until the command of Allah came, while the chief deceiver (Satan) deceived you in respect of Allah."

57:15 (They will be told): "So this day no ransom shall be taken from you (hypocrites), or from those who disbelieved. Your abode is the fire, that is your friend (proper place), and worst is that destination."

57:16 Has not the time come for the hearts of the believers to be humble by the reminder (this Qur'an) of Allah, and to the truth which has been revealed, so that they do not become like those who received the scripture before, and the term was prolonged for them but their hearts were hardened? Many of them are rebellious.

57:17 Know that Allah gives life to the earth after its death! Indeed Allah has made clear the revelations to you so that you may understand.

57:18 Surely, the charitable men and charitable women, and those who lend a goodly loan to Allah, it shall be increased manifold for them, and (besides) there shall be honorable reward (paradise).

57:19 Those who believe in Allah and Allah's messengers, they are the truthful and the true witnesses with their Rabb; they shall have their reward and their light. But those who disbelieve and deny Allah's revelations; they shall be the inmates of the blazing fire.

57:20 Know that the life of this world is only play and amusement, show, and mutual boasting among you, and rivalry in respect of wealth and children. It is like the vegetation (that flourishes) after rain: its growth pleases the tillers; afterwards it dries up and you see it turn yellow; then it becomes straw. But in the hereafter, there will be severe punishment (for disbelievers) and forgiveness from Allah and (Allah's) good pleasure (for the believers). The life of this world is not but a deceiving enjoyment.

57:21 Race one with another in hastening towards the forgiveness from your Rabb and towards the paradise, width of which is as the width of the heaven and the earth, prepared for those who believe in Allah and Allah's messengers. Such is the grace of Allah, which Allah bestows on whom Allah pleases. Allah is the Owner of great bounty.

57:22 No calamity can befalls on the earth or in yourselves, except (that is inscribed) in a book (of decrees), before Allah brings it into existence. Surely, that is easy for Allah.

57:23 (This is done) in order that you may not grieve for the things that you fail to get, or rejoice over that which has been given to you. Allah does not like any prideful boasters,

57:24 nor those who are misers and enjoin miserliness upon people. Whoever turns away (from Allah), then (know that) surely Allah is Rich (free of all wants), Praise-worthy.

57:25 Indeed, Allah has sent Allah's messengers with clear signs and revealed the scripture with them and the balance (justice) so that mankind may keep up justice. Allah sent down iron, with its mighty power (in matters of war), and benefits for mankind, so that Allah may know those who will help Allah (Allah's religion) and Allah's messengers in the unseen. Surely, Allah is All-Strong, All-Mighty.

57:26 Indeed, Allah sent Noah and Abraham, and bestowed in their offspring Prophethood and scripture. Some of them were guided ones, but many of them were rebellious.

57:27 Then Allah sent after them, Allah's messengers, and Allah sent Jesus, son of Mary, and gave him the gospel. Allah placed compassion and Mercy in the hearts of those who followed him. But the monasticism which they invented for themselves, Allah did not prescribe it for them but they sought to please Allah, but they did not observe it with the right of its observance. Yet, Allah rewarded those among them who believed, but many of them are rebellious.

57:28 O you who believe! Fear Allah, and believe in Allah's messenger (Muhammad). Allah will grant you a double portion of Allah's Mercy, provide for you a light to walk (straight) and forgive you. Allah is Forgiving, Merciful.

57:29 (Adapt this way) so that the people of the scripture may know that they do not have power over anything from the grace of Allah, and that the grace is in Allah's authority, Allah bestows it on whomever Allah wills. Allah is the Owner of great bounty.

58. Al-Mujadilah : The Woman who Disputes
In the name of Allah, the Gracious, the Merciful

58:1 Indeed Allah has heard the statement of her (Khawlah, daughter of Tha'labah), who pleaded with you (O Muhammad) against her husband (Aus, son of As-Samit) and she complained to Allah. Allah has heard the conversation between each other. Surely, Allah is All-Hearer, All-Seer.

58:2 Those of you who divorce their wives by Zihar (by saying to them "you are like my mother's back") (should know that) they cannot be their mothers. Their mothers are only those who gave birth to them. Surely, they say an evil word and a lie. Surely, Allah is Pardoning, Forgiving.

58:3 Those who divorce their wives by Zihar, then wish to go back (free themselves) from what they said, the penalty is to free a captive before they touch each other. This is prescribed for you (so that you may not return to such an evil thing). Allah is All-Aware of what you do.

58:4 He who does not find (money for freeing a captive), then must fast for 2 successive months before they both touch each other. For him who is unable to do so (fast), he shall feed 60 poor people. This is (enjoined) in order that you may believe in Allah and Allah's messenger. These are the limits of Allah. For disbelievers, there is a painful punishment.

58:5 Surely, those who oppose Allah and Allah's messenger (Muhammad); they will be disgraced as those who were disgraced before them (among the past nation). Indeed, Allah has sent down clear revelations. For the disbelievers, there is a disgracing punishment.

58:6 On the day (of judgment) Allah will resurrect them all together and inform them about what they have done. Allah has kept account (of all deeds) while they may have forgotten. Allah is Witness over all things.

58:7 Are you not aware that Allah knows whatever is in the heavens and whatever is on the earth? There is no secret counsel of 3, but Allah is their 4th (with Allah's knowledge), nor of 5 but Allah is their 6th, nor of less than that or more, but Allah is with them wherever they may be. Then on the day of Resurrection, Allah will inform them of what they did. Surely, Allah is All-Knower of everything.

58:8 Have you not seen those who were forbidden from secret counsels, and afterwards they returned to what they were forbidden from it? They conspired together for sin, wrong doing, and disobedience to the messenger (Muhammad). Yet, when they come to you, they greet you with a greeting with which Allah does not greet you, and they say to themselves: "Why Allah does not punish us for what we say?" Hell will be sufficient for them, they will burn in it, and worst indeed is that destination!

58:9 O you who believe! When you hold secret counsel, don't hold secret council for sin, wrong-doing, and disobedience towards the messenger (Muhammad); but hold secret council for righteousness and piety; and fear Allah to whom you shall be gathered.

58:10 Secret counsels (conspiracies) are only from Satan so that he may cause grief to those who believe. But he cannot harm them in anything except with the permission of Allah. In Allah let the believers put their trust.

58:11 O you who believe! When you are asked to make room in the assemblies, (spread out and) make room. Allah will make room (from Allah's Mercy) for you (in the hereafter). When you are told to rise up (in Allah's cause), then rise up. Allah will elevate those of you who believe and those who have been granted knowledge in degrees. Allah is Well-Acquainted with what you do.

58:12 O you who believe! When you wish to consult the messenger (Muhammad) in private, spend something in charity before your private consultation. That will be better and purer for you. But if you do not find (anything), then surely, Allah is Forgiving, Merciful.

58:13 Are you afraid to spend in charity before your private consultation (with Muhammad)? If you cannot afford, Allah will forgive you; so establish prayer and give obligatory charity and obey Allah and Allah's messenger (Muhammad). Allah is Well-Aware of what you do.

58:14 Have you (O Muhammad) not seen those (hypocrites) who take as friends those people who are under the wrath of Allah? They are neither of you nor of them and they knowingly swear to a lie.

58:15 Allah has prepared for them severe punishment. Indeed evil is that which they do.

58:16 They have taken their oaths as shields (for their evil actions). Thus they hinder people from the way of Allah. They shall have a humiliating punishment.

58:17 Neither their children nor their wealth will avail them anything against Allah. They will be the inmates of the fire; they will reside in it forever.

58:18 On the day when Allah will resurrect them together (for their account), then they will swear to Allah as they now swear to you. They think that they are on something (to stand for help). Lo! Surely they are liars!

58:19 Satan has overtaken them and caused them to forget the remembrance of Allah. They are the party of Satan. Lo! Surely it is the party of Satan, they will be the losers!

58:20 Surely, those who oppose Allah and Allah's messenger (Muhammad); they will be among the lowest (most humiliated).

58:21 Allah has decreed: "Surely! Allah and Allah's messengers will overcome (be victorious)." Surely, Allah is All-Powerful, All-Mighty.

58:22 You (O Muhammad) will never find any people who believe in Allah and the last day on friendly terms with those who oppose Allah and Allah's messenger (Muhammad), even though they are their fathers, or their sons, or their brothers, or their kindred (people). For such Allah has written faith in their hearts and has strengthened them with spirit (true guidance) from Allah. Allah will admit them to gardens (paradise) under which rivers flow, to reside in it forever. Allah will be pleased with them, and they will be pleased with Allah. They are the party of Allah. Lo! Surely it is the party of Allah that will be the successful.

59. Al-Hashr : The Gathering
In the name of Allah, the Gracious, the Merciful

59:1 Glorifies Allah whatever is in the heavens and whatever is on the earth. Allah is the All-Mighty, the All-Wise.

59:2 It is Allah who drove out those who disbelieve from the people of the scripture (the Jews of Bani An-Nadheer) from their homes at the first gathering. You did not think that they would ever get out. They thought that their fortresses would defend them from Allah! But Allah's (punishment) reached them from a place where from they did not expect it, and Allah cast fear into their hearts, so that they destroyed their own homes with their own hands and by the hands of the believers. So take admonition, O you with eyes (to see).

59:3 Had it not been that Allah had decreed exile for them, Allah would certainly have punished them in this world, and in the hereafter they shall have the punishment of the fire.

59:4 That is because they opposed Allah and Allah's messenger (Muhammad). Whoever opposes Allah, then surely Allah is Severe in punishment.

59:5 Whatever palm-trees (of the enemy) you (O Muslims) cut down or left them standing on their roots, it was by the permission of Allah, so that Allah might disgrace the transgressors.

59:6 What Allah gave as booty to Allah's messenger (Muhammad) from them, you made no expedition for that with either cavalry or riding-camel. But Allah gives power to Allah's messenger over whoever Allah wills. Allah has power over all things.

59:7 Whatever Allah gave as booty to Allah's messenger (Muhammad) from the people of the townships, it is for Allah, Allah's messenger (Muhammad), the kindred (relatives of messenger), the orphans, the poor, and the wayfarer; so that it may not become a fortune between the rich among you. Whatever the messenger (Muhammad) gives you, take it and whatever he forbids you, abstain from it, and fear Allah. Surely, Allah is Severe in punishment.

59:8 (There is share in this booty) for the poor emigrants who were expelled from their homes and their property, and are seeking bounties from Allah and pleasure (of Allah). This is helping Allah (in Allah's religion) and Allah's messenger (Muhammad). They are indeed the true believers.

59:9 (Share of booty shall be given to) those who had homes (Ansars in Madinah) and had faith before (the arrival of) them (emigrants) and love those who emigrated to them and they had no jealousy in their hearts for things given (from the booty) to them, and prefer them (emigrants) over themselves, even though they themselves were in need of that. Those who are saved from their enviousness, such are they who will be the successful.

59:10 Those who came after them say: "Our Rabb! Forgive us and our brothers who have preceded us in faith and do not put any hatred in our hearts against those who have believed. Our Rabb! You are indeed full of Kindness, Merciful."

59:11 Have you (O Muhammad) not observed those who were hypocrites? They say to their fellow disbelievers among the people of the scripture: "If you are expelled, we indeed will go out with you. We will never obey anyone against you. Even if you are attacked, we will indeed help you." But Allah is witness that surely they are liars.

59:12 Surely, if they (people of the book) are expelled, they (hypocrites) will never go out with them, and if they are attacked, they will never help them. Even if they help them, they (hypocrites) will turn their backs; so they will not be victorious.

59:13 Surely, you (believers) are more fearful in their (people of An-Nadir) hearts than of Allah. That is because they are a people who do not comprehend (power of Allah).

59:14 They will never fight against you together except in fortified townships or from behind walls. Their enmity among themselves is very strong. You think them as united but their hearts are divided. This is because they are a people who do not understand.

59:15 They are like their immediate predecessors (Jews of Bani Qainuqa); they tasted the evil result of their deeds, and for them will be a painful punishment.

59:16 They are like Satan who says to human: "Disbelieve." So when human disbelieves, Satan says: "I am free of you, I fear Allah, the Rabb of the worlds!"

59:17 So the end of both will be that they will be in the fire, abiding in it forever. That is the recompense of the wrongdoers.

59:18 O you who believe! Fear Allah and let every person look to what it has sent forth for tomorrow (hereafter), and fear Allah. Surely, Allah is All-Aware of what you do.

59:19 Be not like those who forgot Allah and Allah caused them to forget their own selves. Those are the transgressors.

59:20 Not equal are the inmates of the fire and the residents of the paradise. It is the residents of paradise, they will be successful.

59:21 If Allah had sent down this Qur'an on a mountain, you would have seen it humbling itself and split asunder from the fear of Allah. Such are the examples which Allah put forward to mankind so that they may reflect (think).

59:22 It is Allah, besides whom there is no one worthy of worship but Allah, the Knower of the unseen and the seen. Allah is the Beneficent, the Merciful.

59:23 It is Allah besides whom there is no one worthy of worship but Allah, the King, the Holy, the one free from all defects, the Giver of security, the Watcher over Allah's creatures, the Mighty, the Compeller, the Supreme. Glory be to Allah above all that they associate as partners with Allah.

59:24 Allah is the creator, the Inventor of all things, and the Bestower of forms. To Allah belong the best names. All that are in the heavens and the earth glorify Allah. Allah is the All-Mighty, the All-Wise.

60. Al-Mumtahanah : The Woman to be Examined

In the name of Allah, the Gracious, the Merciful

60:1 O you who believe! Do not take Allah's enemies and your enemies (disbelievers) as friends. Would you show affection towards them, when they have disbelieved in what has come to you of the truth (Islam) and have driven out the messenger (Muhammad) and yourselves (from your homeland), simply because you believe in Allah, your Rabb? If you have come forth to strive in Allah's cause and to seek Allah's good pleasure, then how can you show friendship to them in secret? Allah is aware of what you conceal and what you reveal. Whoever of you (Muslims) does that, then indeed has gone astray from the right way.

60:2 If they gain the upper hand over you, they would behave to you as enemies and stretch out their hands and their tongues against you with evil, and they wish that you should become disbelievers.

60:3 On the day of Resurrection, neither your relatives nor your children will benefit you. Allah will judge between you. Allah sees all of what you do.

60:4 Indeed an excellent example has been set for you in Abraham and those with him. When they said to their people: "Surely, we are free from you and whatever you worship besides Allah. We reject you. Hostility and hatred shall appear between us and between you forever until you believe in Allah alone." Except the saying of Abraham to his father: "Surely, I will ask for forgiveness (from Allah) for you, but I have no power to get anything for you from Allah." (They prayed): "Our Rabb! In Allah alone we put our trust, to Allah alone we turn in repentance, and to Allah alone is the final return.

60:5 Our Rabb! Do not make us a trial for those who disbelieve, and forgive us. Our Rabb! Surely Allah is the All-Mighty, the All-Wise."

60:6 Surely, there is an excellent example for you in them to follow for those who look forward to (the meeting with) Allah and the last day. Whoever turns away, then surely, Allah is Rich (free of all wants), Praise-Worthy.

60:7 Perhaps that Allah will make friendship among them between you and between those with whom you hold as enemies. Allah has power (over all things), and Allah is Forgiving, the Merciful.

60:8 Allah does not forbid you to deal kindly and justly with those who had neither fought against you on account of religion nor drove you out of your homes. Surely, Allah loves those who deal with equity.

60:9 Allah only forbids you to befriend them as regards to those who fought against you on account of religion, drove you out of your homes, and helped to drive you out. Whoever will befriend them, such are the wrongdoers.

60:10 O you who believe! When the believing women come to you as emigrants, examine them. Allah knows best as to their faith. If you ascertain that they are true believers, do not send them back to the disbelievers. They are not lawful (wives) for them (disbelievers), nor are they (disbelievers) lawful (husbands) for them. But give them (disbelievers) that (amount of money) which they have spent (as their dowries) to them. There is no sin on you to marry them if you pay them their dowries. Likewise do not hold the disbelieving women as wives. Ask for (the return of) that which you have spent (as dowry) and let them (disbelievers) ask back for what they have spent. This is the judgment of Allah. Allah judges between you. Allah is All-Knower, All-Wise.

60:11 If any of your wives have gone from you to the disbelievers (and afterwards you have your turn (of triumph)) and you have an investment (by the coming over of a woman from the disbelief), then pay to those whose wives have gone, the equivalent of what they had spent (on their dowry). Fear Allah, in whom you believe.

60:12 O Prophet! When the believing women come to you to give you the pledge that they will not associate anything in worship with Allah, that they will not steal, that they will not commit illegal sexual intercourse, that they will not kill their children, that they will not utter slander, that they will not forge between their hands and their feet (falsehood by accusing another women of having illicit relationship with a man or making illegal children and making husband believe that it belongs to her husband), they will not disobey you in any just matter (permitted by Islam), then accept their pledge, and ask Allah to forgive them. Surely, Allah is Forgiving, Merciful.

60:13 O you who believe! Do not take as friends the people who incurred upon them the wrath of Allah. Surely, they have despaired from (any good) in the hereafter, just as the disbelievers have despaired from the people of the graves (buried).

61. As-Saff : The Rank
In the name of Allah, the Gracious, the Merciful

61:1 Glorifies Allah whatever is in the heavens and whatever is on the earth. Allah is the All-Mighty, the All-Wise.

61:2 O you who believe! Why do you say that which you do not do?

61:3 It is most hateful with Allah that you say that which you do not do.

61:4 Surely, Allah loves those who fight in Allah's cause in rows (ranks in battle) as if they were a solid structure.

61:5 (Remember) when Moses said to his people: "O my people! Why do you hurt me while certainly you know that I am the messenger of Allah to you?" So when they turned away (from Allah), Allah turned away their hearts (from the right way). Allah does not guide those who are transgressors.

61:6 (Remember) when Jesus, son of Mary, said: "O Children of Israel! I am the messenger of Allah to you, confirming the Torah which came before me, and give you glad tidings of a messenger that will come after me whose name shall be Ahmed (another name of Muhammad, meaning 'The praised one').'' But when he (Muhammad) came to them with clear proofs, they said: "This is plain magic."

61:7 Who does more wrong than the one who invents a lie against Allah while he is being invited to Islam? Allah does not guide the people of wrongdoers.

61:8 They intend to put out the light of Allah (the religion of Islam) with their mouths. But Allah will perfect Allah's Light even though the disbelievers hate it.

61:9 It is Allah who has sent Allah's messenger (Muhammad) with guidance and the religion of truth (Islam) to make it victorious over all other religions even though the polytheists hate it.

61:10 O you who believe! Shall Allah guide you to a commerce that will save you from a painful punishment?

61:11 You believe in Allah and Allah's messenger (Muhammad), and that you strive hard, and fight in the cause of Allah with your wealth and your lives. That will be better for you, if you but know!

61:12 (If you do so) Allah will forgive you your sins and admit you into gardens under which rivers flow, and pleasant residences in gardens of Eden (eternity) (paradise), that is the great success.

61:13 Also (Allah will give you) another blessing which you love, help from Allah (against your enemies) and a near victory. So give glad tidings (O Muhammad) to the believers.

61:14 O you who believe! Be the helpers (in the cause) of Allah, just as Jesus, son of Mary, said to the disciples: "Who will be my helpers (in the cause) of Allah?" The disciples said: "We are helpers of Allah." Then a group of the children of Israel believed and a group disbelieved. So Allah gave power to those who believed against their enemies, and they became the uppermost.

62. Al-Jumu'ah : The Congregation
In the name of Allah, the Gracious, the Merciful

62:1 Whatever is in the heavens and whatever is on the earth glorifies Allah, the King, the Holy, the All-Mighty, the All-Wise.

62:2 It is Allah who has sent among the unlettered people, a messenger (Muhammad) from among themselves, who recites to them Allah's revelations, purifies them (from disbelief), and teaches them the book (this Qur'an) and wisdom, even though they were in clear error before,

62:3 and also to others among them (Muslims) who have not yet joined them. Allah is the All-Mighty, the All-Wise.

62:4 That is the grace of Allah, which Allah bestows on whom Allah wills. Allah is the Owner of Mighty grace.

62:5 The likeness of those who were entrusted with the Torah (to obey its commandments), but they failed it (those obligations), is as the likeness of a donkey who carries huge burdens of books (but understands nothing). How bad is the example of people who deny the verses of Allah? Allah does not guide the wrongdoers.

62:6 Say (O Muhammad): "O you who are Jews! If you claim that you are friends of Allah to the exclusion of all other people, then wish for death if you are truthful."

62:7 But they will never wish for it (death), because of what deeds their hands have sent before them! Allah knows well the wrongdoers.

62:8 Say (to them): "Surely, the death from which you flee, will surely meet you, then you will be sent back to (Allah), the All-Knower of the unseen and the seen, and Allah will tell you what you used to do."

62:9 O you who believe! When the call is proclaimed for the prayer on Friday, then hasten to the remembrance of Allah and leave off business. That is better for you if you but know!

62:10 When the (Jumu'ah) prayer is finished, you may disperse in the land and seek the grace of Allah (by working). Remember Allah much so that you may be successful.

62:11 When they (people with weak faith) see some merchandise or some amusement, they disperse headlong to it, and leave you (Muhammad) standing (while you are delivering Jumu'ah religious talk). Say: "That which Allah has is better than any amusement or merchandise! Allah is the Best of providers."

63. Al-Munafiqun : The Hypocrites
In the name of Allah, the Gracious, the Merciful

63:1 When the hypocrites come to you (O Muhammad), they say: "We bear witness that you are indeed the messenger of Allah." Allah knows that you are indeed Allah's messenger and Allah bears witness that the hypocrites are indeed liars.

63:2 They have taken their oaths as a shield (for their hypocrisy). Thus they hinder people from the way of Allah. Surely, evil is what they do.

63:3 This is because they believed, then disbelieved. Their hearts are sealed, so they do not understand.

63:4 When you look at them, their good look pleases you; and when they speak, you listen to their words. Yet, they are as blocks of wood propped up (worthless). They think that every cry is against them. They are the enemies, so beware of them. May Allah curse them! How are they deviated!

63:5 When it is said to them: "Come, so that the messenger of Allah will ask forgiveness from Allah for you," they turn aside their heads and you see them turning away (their faces) while they are in pride.

63:6 It is equal to them whether you (Muhammad) ask forgiveness for them or do not ask forgiveness for them. Allah will not forgive them. Surely, Allah does not guide the people who are disobedient.

63:7 They are the ones who say: "Do not spend on those who are with the messenger of Allah, until they desert him." To Allah belongs the treasures of the heavens and the earth, but the hypocrites do not comprehend.

63:8 They (hypocrites) say: "When we return to Madinah, indeed the more honorable (Abdullah bin Ubai bin Salul, the chief hypocrite at Madinah) will expel from there the meaner (Allah's messenger)." But honor, power and glory belong to Allah, and to Allah's messenger (Muhammad), and to the believers, but the hypocrites do not know.

63:9 O you who believe! Let neither your properties nor your children distract you from the remembrance of Allah. Those who will do so, then they are the real losers.

63:10 Spend (in charity) of that which Allah has provided you before death comes to one of you who says: "My Rabb! If only you (Allah) would give me respite for a little while (return to the worldly life), then I would give in charity, and be among the righteous."

63:11 Allah never grants respite to a soul when its appointed time (death) comes to an end. Allah is All-Aware of what you do.

64. At-Taghabun : The Mutual Loss and Gain
In the name of Allah, the Gracious, the Merciful

64:1 Glorifies Allah whatever is in the heavens and whatever is on the earth. The dominion is Allah's, to Allah belongs all the praises and thanks, and Allah has power over all things.

64:2 It is Allah who created you; yet, some of you are disbelievers and some of you are believers. Allah is All-Seer of what you do.

64:3 Allah has created the heavens and the earth with the truth. Allah has shaped you and shaped you well, and to Allah is the final return.

64:4 Allah knows what is in the heavens and the earth. Allah knows what you conceal and what you reveal. Allah is All-Knower of what is in the hearts.

64:5 Has not the news reached you of those who disbelieved before? So they tasted the evil result of their disbelief, and there will be a painful punishment (in the hereafter) for them.

64:6 That is because, when their messengers came to them with clear proofs, they said: "Shall simple human guide us?" So they disbelieved and turned away (from truth). Allah is not in need (of them). Allah is Rich (free of all wants), Praise-worthy.

64:7 The disbelievers claim that they will never be resurrected (for the account). Say (O Muhammad): "Yes! By my Rabb, you will certainly be resurrected, then you will be informed of what you did, and that is easy for Allah."

64:8 Therefore, believe in Allah and Allah's messenger (Muhammad), and in the light (this Qur'an) which Allah has sent down. Allah is All-Aware of what you do.

64:9 (Remember) the day when Allah will gather you all on the day of gathering, that will be the day of mutual loss and gain. Those who believe in Allah and perform righteous deeds, Allah will remit from them their sins and will admit them to gardens under which rivers flow (paradise), they will reside in it forever; that will be the great success.

64:10 But those who disbelieved and denied Allah's revelations, they will be the inmates of the fire, they will reside in it forever, and worst is that destination.

64:11 No calamity can ever befall except by the permission of Allah. Whoever believes in Allah, Allah guides its heart (to the truth). Allah is All-Knower of everything.

64:12 Obey Allah and obey the messenger (Muhammad). But if you turn away, then (know that the duty) of Allah's messenger is only to convey (the message) clearly.

64:13 Allah! There is no one worthy of worship but Allah, and in Allah let the believers put their trust.

64:14 O you who believe! Surely, among your wives and your children there are enemies (who may stop you from the obedience of Allah) for you; so beware of them! But if you pardon them, overlook, and forgive (their faults), then surely, Allah is Forgiving, Merciful.

64:15 Your wealth and your children are only a trial. With Allah there is a great reward (paradise).

64:16 So, fear Allah as much as you can, listen (to Allah's message) and obey, and spend in charity, that is better for yourselves. Those who are saved from their own enviousness, it is they who are the successful ones.

64:17 If you lend to Allah a goodly loan (spend in Allah's cause), Allah will double it for you, and will forgive you. Allah is Appreciative, Forbearing,

64:18 Knows all of the unseen and seen, the All-Mighty, the All-Wise.

65. At-Talaq : The Divorce
In the name of Allah, the Gracious, the Merciful

65:1 O Prophet (Muhammad)! When you (and the believers) divorce women, divorce them at (the end of) their prescribed (waiting) periods, and count their periods (correctly). Fear Allah, your Rabb. Do not turn them out from their homes (during waiting period), nor they should leave (themselves), unless they have committed adultery openly. These are the limits of Allah. Whoever transgresses the limits of Allah, then indeed has wronged itself. You (one who divorces wife) never know, Allah may bring something new (situation) after that (reconciliation for her return back to you).

65:2 Then, when they have fulfilled their appointed term (waiting period ends), either take them back in a good manner or part with them in a good manner. Take for witness 2 honest persons among you (Muslims), and establish the witness for Allah. This advice is given to all who believe in Allah and the last day. Whoever fears Allah, Allah makes a way out for that person,

65:3 and Allah provides sustenance from (sources) where that person could never imagine. Whoever puts its trust in Allah, then Allah is sufficient for that person. Surely, Allah accomplishes what Allah pleases. Indeed Allah has set a measure for every thing.

65:4 Those of your women who have passed the monthly periods (of menstruation), if you have doubts in their prescribed period, it is 3 months (of waiting), and (same period apply) for those who do not have periods (young age or diseased). For those who are pregnant (whether they are divorced or their husbands are dead), their waiting period is until they deliver their burdens. Those who fear Allah; Allah will make their matters easy for them.

65:5 This is the command of Allah which Allah has sent down to you. Those who fear Allah, Allah will remit their sins from them and will enlarge rewards for them.

65:6 Let them (divorced women during their waiting period) live where you yourself live according to your means. You do not harm them so as to straiten them (make their life intolerable and leave your house). If they are pregnant, then spend on them till they deliver their burden. Then if they give suck (to the children) for you, then give them their due payment (compensation), and let each of you accept the advice of the other between you in a just way. But if you make difficulties for one another, then some other woman may give suck for you (father of the child).

65:7 Let the rich people spend according to their means, and the people whose resources are restricted (poor), let them spend according to what Allah has given them. Allah does not put burden on any person except what Allah has given to that person. Allah will grant ease after hardship.

65:8 Many townships revolted against the command of their Rabb and Allah's messengers. So Allah called them to a severe account (punishment in this worldly life) and Allah will punish them with a horrible punishment (in the hereafter).

65:9 So they tasted the evil result of their misdeeds and the consequence of their misdeeds was loss (destruction in this life and punishment in the hereafter).

65:10 Allah has prepared for them a severe punishment (in the hereafter). So fear Allah, O men of understanding who have believed! Indeed Allah has sent down to you a reminder (this Qur'an);

65:11 (also sent to you) a messenger (Muhammad), who recites to you the verses of Allah (the Qur'an) with clear explanations, so that Allah may take out those who believe and do righteous deeds from the darkness (of polytheism) to the light (of faith). Those who believe in Allah and perform righteous deeds, Allah will admit them into gardens under which rivers flow (paradise), they will reside in it forever. Indeed Allah has granted an excellent provision for them.

65:12 It is Allah who has created 7 heavens and of the earth like them. Allah's command descends between them (heavens and earth), so that you may know that Allah has power over all things and that Allah indeed surrounds all things in (Allah's) knowledge.

66. At-Tahrim : The Prohibition

In the name of Allah, the Gracious, the Merciful

66:1 O Prophet! Why do you make unlawful (for yourself) which Allah has made lawful to you in seeking the pleasure of your wives? Allah is Forgiving, Merciful.

66:2 Allah has already ordained for you (Muslims) absolution from your oaths. Allah is your Master and Allah is the All-Knower, the All-Wise.

66:3 (Remember) when the prophet (Muhammad) disclosed a matter (secret) to one of his wives (Hafsa), she disclosed it (to Aisha). Allah made it known to him; he informed part of it (to Aisha) and left a part. Then when he told her (Hafsa) of it, she said: "Who told you this?" He said: "The All-Knower, the All-Aware (Allah) has told me."

66:4 If you both (Aisha and Hafsa) turn in repentance to Allah (it will be better) as your hearts have indeed so inclined (to oppose what the prophet likes); but if you help one another against him (Muhammad), then surely (know that) Allah is his Protector, Gabriel, and the righteous (among) the believers, and furthermore, the angels too are his helpers.

66:5 It may well be that, if he divorces you all, his Rabb will give him wives better than you in exchange: Muslims, believers, obedient to Allah, turn to Allah in repentance, worshippers, (who are) fasting or emigrating (for Allah's sake), previously married and virgins.

66:6 O you who believe! Save yourselves and your families against a fire (hell) whose fuel is people and stones, over which angels are appointed who are stern and severe, who do not disobey Allah in what Allah commands them, and they do what they are commanded.

66:7 (It will be said in the hereafter): "O you who disbelieve! Do not make excuses this day! You are being requited only for what you used to do."

66:8 O you who believe! Turn to Allah with sincere repentance! It may well be that your Rabb will remit your sins from you and admit you into gardens under which rivers flow (paradise). On that day, Allah will not disgrace the prophet (Muhammad) and those who believe with him. Their light will run before them and (their record of deeds) in their right hands, they will say: "Our Rabb! Keep our light perfect for us and grant us forgiveness. Surely, Allah has power over all things."

66:9 O Prophet (Muhammad)! Strive hard against the disbelievers and the hypocrites and be severe against them. Their abode will be hell and worst indeed is that destination.

66:10 Allah has set forth an example for the disbelievers: the wife of Noah and the wife of Lot. They were under 2 of Allah's righteous servants, but they both betrayed them (husbands by rejecting their doctrine). So they (Noah and Lot) could not protect them (their respective wives) from Allah at all, and it was said (to them): "Enter the fire along with those who enter!"

66:11 Allah has set forth an example for those who believe, the wife of Pharaoh, who said: "My Rabb! Build for me a home from you (Allah) in paradise and save me from Pharaoh and his work, and save me from the wrongdoer people."

66:12 (Another example) Mary, the daughter of Imran, who guarded her chastity, and Allah breathed into it (the sleeve of her shirt or her garment) through Allah's spirit (Gabriel), and she believed in the words of her Rabb and Allah's scriptures, and she was among the devout obedient ones (to Allah).

67. Al-Mulk : The Sovereignty
In the name of Allah, the Gracious, the Merciful

67:1 Blessed be Allah in whose authority is the dominion (the universe), and Allah has power over all things.

67:2 The one (Allah) who has created death and life, so that Allah may test you (to find out) which of you are best in deed. Allah is the All-Mighty, the Forgiving.

67:3 The one (Allah) who has created the 7 heavens one above another, you cannot see any fault in the creations of the Gracious. So look once again, can you see any rifts?

67:4 Then repeat the look again, and yet again, your sight will return to you humbled and it is worn out.

67:5 Indeed Allah has decorated the nearest heaven with lamps, Allah has made such lamps as missiles to drive away the devils, and Allah has prepared for them the punishment of the blazing fire.

67:6 For those who disbelieve in their Rabb, there will be the punishment of hell, and worst indeed is that destination.

67:7 When they will be cast in the fire, they will hear the terrible drawing of its breath as it blazes out.

67:8 It almost bursts up with fury. Every time a group is cast in it; its keepers will ask: "Did no warner come to you?"

67:9 They will say: "Yes indeed, a warner did come to us, but we rejected him and said: Allah has never sent down anything (of revelation), you are only in great error."

67:10 They will say: "Had we only listened or used our intelligence, we would not have been among the inmates of the blazing fire!"

67:11 Then they will confess their sin. So, away (from the Mercy of Allah) will be the inmates of the blazing fire.

67:12 Surely! Those who fear their Rabb unseen, they will have forgiveness and a great reward (paradise).

67:13 Whether you keep your talk secret or disclose it, surely, Allah knows all of what is in the hearts.

67:14 Should not Allah know who has created? Allah is the Kind, and Courteous (to Allah's servants), All-Aware (of everything).

67:15 It is Allah who has made the earth submissive to you, so walk in the path thereof and eat of Allah's provision, and to Allah will be (the return) for Resurrection.

67:16 Do you feel secure from Allah who is over the heaven, that Allah will not cause the earth to sink with you when it shakes (as in an earthquake)?

67:17 Or do you feel secure from Allah, who is over the heaven, that Allah will not send against you a violent tornado? Then you shall know how terrible has been my (Allah's) Warning!

67:18 Indeed those before them denied (the messengers of Allah) and then see how terrible was my (Allah's) denial (punishment)?

67:19 Do they not see the birds above them spreading out their wings and folding them in? None upholds them except the Gracious (Allah). Surely, Allah is the All-Seer all of everything.

67:20 Who is the one that has an army to help you besides the Gracious? The disbelievers are in nothing but delusion.

67:21 Who is there that can provide you if Allah withholds Allah's provision? Nay, they continue to be in pride and they flee (from the truth).

67:22 (Think) who is more rightly guided: one who walks with his face bend down without seeing, or the one who sees and walks upright on a right way?

67:23 Say: "It is Allah who has created you, and made for you hearing, seeing, and hearts. Yet, you give little thanks."

67:24 Say: "It is Allah who has created you in the earth, and to Allah you shall be gathered (in the hereafter)."

67:25 They say: "When will this promise (the day of Resurrection) come to pass, if you say is true?"

67:26 Say (O Muhammad): "The knowledge (of its exact time) is only with Allah, and I am only a plain warner."

67:27 But, when they will see it (the punishment on the day of Resurrection) approaching, the faces of those who disbelieve will be displeased (black), and it will be said (to them): "This is the promise which you were calling for!"

67:28 Say (O Muhammad): "Even if Allah destroys me and those with me or Allah bestows Allah's Mercy on us; who will save the disbelievers from a painful punishment?"

67:29 Say: "It is the Gracious (Allah), in Allah we believe, and in Allah we put our trust. Soon you will come to know who is it that is in clear error."

67:30 Say (O Muhammad): "Have you seen that if all your water were to be sunk away (in the ground), who then can supply you with flowing water?"

68. Al-Qalam : The Pen

In the name of Allah, the Gracious, the Merciful

68:1 Nun. By the pen and what they (angels) write (records of people).

68:2 By the grace of your Rabb you (O Muhammad) are not a madman,

68:3 and surely, you (O Muhammad) will have an endless reward.

68:4 Surely, you (O Muhammad) are on an exalted standard of character.

68:5 Soon you will see and they will see

68:6 which of you is afflicted with madness.

68:7 Surely, your Rabb knows those better who have gone astray from Allah's way, and Allah is the Best Knower of those who are guided.

68:8 So (O Muhammad) do not yield to the deniers (of Islam).

68:9 They wish that you should compromise (in religion with them), so they would also compromise with you.

68:10 Do not yield to everyone who swears much and is considered worthless,

68:11 a slanderer going about with mischief,

68:12 opponent of the good, transgressor, sinful,

68:13 cruel, and moreover wicked (of illegitimate birth),

68:14 though one has wealth and children.

68:15 When Allah's verses (of the Qur'an) are recited to one, who says: "Tales of the people of old!"

68:16 Allah will brand the one over the nose!

68:17 Surely, Allah will try them as Allah tried the people of the garden when they swore to pick the fruits of the garden in the morning,

68:18 without saying: If Allah wills.

68:19 Then something (fire) from your Rabb passed by on the garden (at night and burnt it) while they were asleep,

68:20 so the garden became black by the morning, like a pitch dark night (completely ruined).

68:21 Then they called out to one another as soon as the morning broke,

68:22 saying: "Go to your tilth in the morning if you want to pick the fruits."

68:23 So they departed and whispered in secret low tones (saying):

68:24 "Let no poor person enter into the garden today."

68:25 Then they went in the morning with strong intention, thinking that they have powers (to prevent the poor from taking any of the fruits).

68:26 But when they saw the garden, they said: "Surely, we have gone astray,

68:27 (then they said): Nay! Indeed we have been deprived (of the fruits)!"

68:28 The best among them said: "Did I not tell you: why do you not glorify Allah (If Allah wills)?"

68:29 They said: "Glory to our Rabb! Surely, we have been wrongdoers."

68:30 So they started blaming one another.

68:31 (Later) they said: "Woe to us! Surely, we had become transgressors.

68:32 We hope that our Rabb will give us in exchange a better garden than this. Truly, we turn to our Rabb."

68:33 Such is the punishment (in this life) and truly, the punishment of the hereafter is greater, if they but knew it.

68:34 Surely, the pious will be rewarded with gardens of delight (paradise) by their Rabb.

68:35 Shall Allah then treat the Muslims like the criminals?

68:36 What is the matter with you? How do you judge?

68:37 Or do you have a book from which you learn,

68:38 that you shall have in it all that you choose?

68:39 Or do you have oaths from Allah reaching to the day of Resurrection that your will have whatever you judge?

68:40 Ask if anyone of them will promise for that!

68:41 Or do they have 'partners (other deities besides Allah)?' Then let them bring their 'partners' if they are truthful!

68:42 (Remember) the day (of Judgment) when the events shall be unfolded and they shall be called to prostrate (to Allah), but they shall not be able to do so.

68:43 Their eyes will be cast down, humiliation will cover them; because they used to be called to prostrate (offer prayers), and they were healthy and good (in the world, but they refused to do so).

68:44 Then (O Muhammad) leave Allah alone with those who deny this speech (Qur'an). Allah will punish them gradually from where they do not perceive.

68:45 I (Allah) will (even) grant them a respite. Surely, my (Allah's) plan is strong.

68:46 Or have you (O Muhammad) asked them a wage, so they are heavily burdened from debt?

68:47 Or do they have the (knowledge of the) unseen with them, so they can write it down?

68:48 So wait with patience for the decision of your Rabb, and do not be like the companion of the fish (reference to Prophet Jonah who was swallowed by a fish), who cried out while he was in distress.

68:49 Had not a grace from his Rabb reached him, he would indeed have been (left in the stomach of the fish, but Allah forgave him, so he was) cast off on the naked shore, while he was blamed.

68:50 But his Rabb chose him and made him of the righteous.

68:51 Surely, the disbelievers would almost make you slip with their eyes (through hatred) when they hear the reminder (the Qur'an), and they say: "Surely, he (Muhammad) is a madman!"

68:52 This (the Qur'an) is nothing but a reminder to all people of the worlds.

69. Al-Haqqah : The Inevitable
In the name of Allah, the Gracious, the Merciful

69:1 The inevitable (of the day of Resurrection)!

69:2 What is the inevitable?

69:3 What will make you understand what the inevitable is?

69:4 Thamud and Ad people denied the calamity (the striking hour of judgment)!

69:5 As for Thamud, they were destroyed by the awful cry!

69:6 As for Ad, they were destroyed by a furious violent wind,

69:7 which Allah imposed on them for 7 nights and 8 days in succession, so that you could see the people lying overthrown (destroyed) in it as if they were hollow trunks of date-palms!

69:8 Now, do you see any remnants of them?

69:9 Pharaoh and those before him, and the cities (overthrown with the people of Lot who committed) sin

69:10 and they disobeyed their Rabb's messenger, so Allah seized them with a strong seize.

69:11 Surely! When the water rose beyond limits (Noah's flood), Allah carried you people in the floating ship,

69:12 that Allah may make it an event of warning for you so that it may be understood by the retaining ears (in memory).

69:13 Then when the trumpet will be blown with one blowing (first one)

69:14 and the earth with its mountains will be removed (from their places) and crushed with a single crushing,

69:15 on that day the great event will befall,

69:16 the heaven will split asunder, and for that day it (heaven) will be frail and torn up.

69:17 The angels will be on all sides and on that day 8 angels will bear the Throne of your Rabb above them.

69:18 That day you will be brought to judgment (before your Rabb), and not a secret of you will be hidden.

69:19 Then, as for the one who will be given its record (of deeds) in its right hand, will say: "Take, read my record!

69:20 Surely, I did believe that I shall meet my account!"

69:21 So it will have a life of well-pleasing,

69:22 in a lofty paradise,

69:23 with fruits in bunches which will be low and near at hand.

69:24 (It will be said to that person): "Eat and drink at ease, (this is the reward) for what you did before in past days!"

69:25 But as for the one who will be given its record (of deeds) in its left hand, will say: "I wish that I had not been given my record (of deeds)

69:26 and that I had never known what my account was?

69:27 I wish if only it had been my end (death)!

69:28 My wealth has availed me nothing,

69:29 my power and arguments (to defend myself) have gone from me!"

69:30 (It will be said): "Seize this person and fetter (with a chain around its neck),

69:31 then burn this person in the blazing fire,

69:32 then fasten this person with a chain of 70 cubits long!

69:33 Surely, this person did not believe in Allah, the Great,

69:34 and did not urge on the feeding of the poor.

69:35 This day this person has neither a friend here,

69:36 nor any food except the filth from the washing of wounds,

69:37 which none will eat except the sinners."

69:38 So, surely Allah swears by whatever you see,

69:39 and by whatever you do not see,

69:40 that surely this is the word of an honored messenger.

69:41 It is not the word of a poet, little is that you believe,

69:42 nor it is the word of a soothsayer, little is that you remember.

69:43 This is the revelation sent down from the Rabb of the worlds.

69:44 Had he (Muhammad) forged false sayings concerning Allah,

69:45 Allah certainly would have seized him by his right hand

69:46 then certainly would have cut the life artery from him

69:47 and none of you could prevent (Allah) from punishing him.

69:48 Surely this (Qur'an) is a reminder for the pious.

69:49 Surely Allah knows that there are some among you who deny (the Qur'an),

69:50 and indeed it (this Qur'an) will be an anguish for the disbelievers.

69:51 Yet, it (this Qur'an) is an absolute truth with certainty.

69:52 So glorify the name of your Rabb, the Great.

70. Al-Ma'arij : The Way of Ascent

In the name of Allah, the Gracious, the Merciful

70:1 A questioner asked concerning a punishment about to befall.

70:2 (It is) upon the disbelievers, none can avert.

70:3 (It will come) from Allah, the Rabb of the Ways of Ascent.

70:4 The angels and the spirit (Gabriel) ascend to Allah in a day the measure of which is 50,000 years.

70:5 So be patient (O Muhammad) with a good patience.

70:6 Surely! They see it (day of judgment) to be far off;

70:7 but Allah sees it quite near.

70:8 On that day, the sky will be like molten lead

70:9 and the mountains will be like flakes of wool;

70:10 and no friend will ask of a friend,

70:11 though they will be made to see one another (no one can help including relatives). The criminal would wish to ransom itself from the punishment of that day by its children,

70:12 its wife and its brother,

70:13 its kindred who gave it shelter,

70:14 and all that is in the earth, so that it might save itself.

70:15 But no means! Surely, it will be the fire of hell

70:16 to take away (burn completely) the head skin,

70:17 it will call all those who turn their backs and turn away their faces,

70:18 who collected (wealth) and hide it (from spending in the cause of Allah).

70:19 Surely, human has been created very impatient,

70:20 when the evil touches them, they are distressed,

70:21 but when good (fortune) touches them, they are stingy;

70:22 except those who devote to prayers,

70:23 those who remain steadfast in their prayers,

70:24 those who set aside a known right in their wealth

70:25 for the beggar who asks and for the deprived (who has lost property and wealth),

70:26 those who believe in the day of recompense,

70:27 those who fear the punishment of their Rabb,

70:28 surely! The punishment of their Rabb is that before which none can feel secure,

70:29 those who guard their chastity (private parts from illegal sex),

70:30 except with their wives or those whom their right hands possess so they are not to be blamed.

70:31 But those who seek to go beyond this, then it is those who are transgressors.

70:32 Those who keep their trusts and their covenants,

70:33 those who stand firm in their testimonies

70:34 and those who guard their prayers well,

70:35 it is they who will be in the gardens (paradise) with honor.

70:36 What is the matter with the disbelievers that they hasten to listen from you (O Muhammad),

70:37 sitting in groups on the right and on the left (of you, O Muhammad)?

70:38 Does every one of them seek to enter the paradise of delight?

70:39 But nay! Surely, Allah has created them out of that which they (disbelievers) know.

70:40 So, I (Muhammad) swear by the Rabb of all points of sunrise in the east and sunset in the west that surely Allah is Able (to destroy them)

70:41 and can replace them by others better than them; and Allah is not to be outrun.

70:42 So, leave them to plunge in vain talk and play about, until they meet their day which they are promised.

70:43 The day when they will come out of the graves quickly as if they are racing towards a goal,

70:44 with their eyes lowered in fear and humility, covering them with disgrace! That is the day which they are promised!

71. Nuh : Noah

In the name of Allah, the Gracious, the Merciful

71:1 Surely, Allah sent Noah to his people (saying): "Warn your people before there comes to them a painful punishment."

71:2 He said: "O my people! Surely, I am sent to you as a plain warner.

71:3 That you should worship Allah alone, be dutiful to Allah, and obey me.

71:4 (If you do so) Allah will forgive you of your sins and give you respite for an appointed term. Surely, the term of Allah when it comes, cannot be delayed, if you but knew."

71:5 (After all his efforts were exhausted) he said: "O my Rabb! Surely, I have called my people night and day,

71:6 but all my calling added nothing but to their flight (from the truth).

71:7 Surely! Every time I called to them that Allah might forgive them, they put their fingers into their ears, covered themselves up with their garments, persisted (in their refusal), and magnified themselves in pride.

71:8 Surely, I called them openly (aloud),

71:9 then surely, I proclaimed to them in public, and I have secretly appealed to them in private,

71:10 I said (to them): 'Ask forgiveness from your Rabb; surely, Allah is Forgiving.

71:11 Allah will send the sky (rain) to you in abundance,

71:12 help you with increase in wealth and children, bestow on you gardens, and bestow on you rivers.'"

71:13 What is the matter with that you do not expect to have any respect for Allah

71:14 and surely Allah has created you in stages?

71:15 Don't you see how Allah has created the 7 heavens one above another,

71:16 and has made the moon as a light in it and made the sun as a lamp?

71:17 Allah has brought you out as a growth from the (dust of) earth.

71:18 Then Allah will return you into it (the same earth), and bring you forth (to life again on the day of Resurrection)?

71:19 Allah has made for you the earth as a wide spread

71:20 so that you may go about in it on roads of mountain trails.

71:21 Noah said: "My Rabb! Surely they have disobeyed me, and followed those whose wealth and children give them no increase but only loss.

71:22 They have plotted a mighty plot,

71:23 and they have said: 'Do not leave your deity, nor shall you leave Wadd, nor Suwa, nor Yaghuth, nor Yauq, nor Nasr (names of the idols).'

71:24 Indeed they have led many astray. (O Allah): do not increase the wrongdoers (in anything) but error."

71:25 Because of their sins they were drowned (in the flood) and were made to enter the fire. They did not find any help for them instead of Allah.

71:26 Noah said: "My Rabb! Do not leave any inhabitant of the disbelievers on the earth.

71:27 Surely if Allah leaves them, they will mislead Allah's servants and they will not beget but wicked disbelievers.

71:28 My Rabb! Forgive me, and my parents, and those who enter my home as a believer, and all the believing men and women. You do not grant increase to the wrongdoers but destruction!"

72. Al-Jinn : The Jinn
In the name of Allah, the Gracious, the Merciful

72:1 Say (O Muhammad): "It has been revealed to me that a group of jinns listened (to the Qur'an). They (returned to their folk and) said: 'Surely! We have heard a wonderful recitation (this Qur'an),

72:2 it guides to the right way. We have believed in it and we shall never join (in worship) anything with our Rabb.

72:3 Surely, the majesty of our Rabb is exalted: Allah has neither taken a wife nor a son.

72:4 The foolish among us have been uttering against Allah which was wrong and not right,

72:5 and surely, we had thought that no human or jinns could utter a lie against Allah.

72:6 Surely, there were people among mankind used to seek refuge with individuals among the jinns, so they (jinns) increased them (mankind) in sin and arrogance,

72:7 and they thought as you thought that Allah will never appoint anyone (as a messenger to mankind or jinn).

72:8 We have sought to reach the heaven but found it filled with stern guards and flaming fires.

72:9 Surely, we used to sit there at stations (in heaven) to steal a hearing, but those who listen now find flaming fire (stars) watching in ambush for them.

72:10 We did not know whether an evil was intended for those on earth, or whether their Rabb intends for them a right way.

72:11 There are some among us who are righteous, and some of us contrary to that; we are groups on different ways (religious sect).

72:12 We know that we can neither escape (punishment of) Allah in the earth nor can we escape (punishment of) Allah by flight.

72:13 Indeed, when we heard the guidance (this Qur'an), we believed in it; and those who believe in their Rabb shall have neither fear of any loss nor any oppression.

72:14 Surely, there are some among us who are Muslims and some who are deviators from the truth. Those who have embraced Islam have found the right way,

72:15 and as for the unjust deviators (from truth), they will be firewood for hell."

72:16 Say (O Muhammad): "If they (the Makkans) had stood upright on the right way (Islam), Allah would surely have bestowed on them water in abundance,

72:17 so that Allah might test them thereby. Those who turn away from the reminder of their Rabb (this Qur'an), Allah will cause them to enter in a severe punishment (hell).

72:18 The mosques are built for Allah's worship alone, so do not invoke anyone along with Allah.

72:19 Yet, when the servant of Allah (Muhammad) stood up invoking in prayer to Allah, they (the jinns) just were around him in a dense crowd (to listen to the Prophet's recitation)."

72:20 Say (O Muhammad): "I only pray to my Rabb, and I associate none as partners with Allah."

72:21 Say: "Surely I do not have power to cause you harm, nor bring you the right way."

72:22 Say (O Muhammad): "(If I were to disobey Allah) none can protect me from Allah's punishment, nor can I find refuge except in Allah.

72:23 (My mission is) only to convey the truth from Allah and Allah's Messages. Those who disobey Allah and Allah's messenger, then surely, they will be put in the fire of hell to reside in it forever."

72:24 Till, when they will see (the punishment) that which they are promised, then they will know whose helpers are weak and whose (supporters) are less in numbers.

72:25 Say (O Muhammad): "I do not know whether (the punishment) which you are promised is near or whether my Rabb has appointed for it a distant term.

72:26 (Allah alone is) the All-Knower of the unseen, and Allah does not reveal Allah's unseen to anyone

72:27 except to the messenger whom Allah has chosen. Then Allah makes a band of watching guards (angels) to march before him and behind him,

72:28 so that Allah may know that surely they (the messengers) have conveyed the messages of their Rabb. Allah surrounds all their surroundings and Allah keeps a count of all things."

73. Al-Muzzammil : The One Wrapped in Garments
In the name of Allah, the Gracious, the Merciful

73:1 O you wrapped in garments (Muhammad)!

73:2 Stand to pray all night, except a little,

73:3 half of it or a little less than that,

73:4 or add to it (little more), and recite the Qur'an in a slow, (pleasant tone) style.

73:5 Surely, Allah will soon send down to you a weighty word (obligations).

73:6 Surely, the rising by night (for Tahajjud prayer) is very hard, most potent, and most suitable (to understand) for the word (of Qur'an),

73:7 surely, during the day there is prolonged occupation for you with ordinary duties.

73:8 Remember the name of your Rabb and devote yourself to Allah with a complete devotion.

73:9 Allah is the Rabb of the east and the west: there is no one worthy of worship but Allah. So take Allah alone as your guardian.

73:10 Be patient (O Muhammad) with what they say and keep away from them, withdraw (leave) in a good way.

73:11 Leave Allah alone to deal with the deniers who are in possession of good things of life. Give them respite for a little while.

73:12 Surely, Allah has fetters (in store to bind them) and a raging fire,

73:13 a food that chokes, and a painful punishment.

73:14 On the day when the earth and the mountains will be in a violent shake, the mountains will be a heap of sand poured out and flowing.

73:15 Surely, Allah has sent to you (O mankind) a messenger (Muhammad) to be a witness over you, as Allah sent a messenger (Moses) to Pharaoh.

73:16 But Pharaoh disobeyed the messenger (Moses); so Allah seized him with a severe seize.

73:17 If you disbelieve, how will you avoid the punishment on that day (of Resurrection) which will turn the children grey-headed (old),

73:18 the heaven will split asunder by it? Allah's promise will certainly be fulfilled.

73:19 Surely, this is an admonition, so let them who will, take a way to their Rabb!

73:20 Surely, your Rabb knows that you stand (to pray at night) a little less than $2/3^{rd}$ of the night, or ½ of the night, or $1/3^{rd}$ of the night, and so do a party of those with you. Allah measures the night and the day. Allah knows that you can never calculate it (unable to pray the whole night), so Allah has turned to you (in Mercy). So, recite from the Qur'an as much as may be easy for you. Allah knows that there may be some sick among you, and some others who travel through the land to seek Allah's bounty; and yet, some others who fight in Allah's cause. So recite as much of it (Qur'an) as may be easy for you, establish prayer, pay obligatory charity, and lend to Allah a goodly loan. Whatever good you will send before you (leave the world) for yourselves, you will certainly find it with Allah, which is better and greater in reward. Seek the forgiveness of Allah. Surely, Allah is Forgiving, Merciful.

74. Al-Muddaththir : The one Enveloped

In the name of Allah, the Gracious, the Merciful

74:1 O you (Muhammad) enveloped (in garments)!

74:2 Arise and warn.

74:3 Proclaim (the greatness of) your Rabb (Allah),

74:4 purify your garments,

74:5 keep away from filth (idols),

74:6 do not give a thing in order to have more (obey Allah not as a favor to Allah),

74:7 and be patient for the sake of your Rabb!

74:8 When the trumpet will be sounded,

74:9 surely, that day will be a hard day,

74:10 not easy for the disbelievers.

74:11 Leave Allah alone to deal with whom Allah created alone (without any means, including Al-Walid bin Al-Mughirah, a bitter opponent of the prophet)!

74:12 Allah granted him abundant resources,

74:13 children by his side,

74:14 and made life smooth and comfortable for him.

74:15 Yet, he desires that Allah should give more.

74:16 Nay! Surely, he has been stubborn and opposing to Allah's revelations.

74:17 Allah will soon oblige him to face (climb a slippery mountain in the hellfire) a severe punishment,

74:18 surely, he thought and plotted.

74:19 So let him be cursed, how he plotted!

74:20 (Again) let him be cursed, how he plotted!

74:21 Then he thought,

74:22 frowned and looked in a bad tempered way,

74:23 then he turned his back and was proud

74:24 and he said: "This is nothing but a magic from the old,

74:25 this is nothing but the word of a human being."

74:26 Allah will burn him in hellfire.

74:27 What will make you know exactly what hellfire is?

74:28 It does not spare (any sinner), nor does it leave (anything not burnt)!

74:29 Fire burns the skins.

74:30 Over it are 19 (angels as guardians and keepers of hell).

74:31 Allah has set none but angels as guardians of the fire. Allah has not fixed their numbers (19) except as a trial for those who disbelieve in order that those who were given the scripture may be convinced (that Qur'an is the truth as it agrees with their books i.e. their number (19) is written in the Torah and the Gospel). Those who believe may increase in faith (in Qur'an). Those who were given the scripture and the believers may say to those in whose hearts there is a disease (of hypocrisy) and the disbelievers may say: "What Allah means by this example?" Thus Allah leads astray whom Allah wills and guides whom Allah wills. No one knows the forces of your Rabb but Allah. This Qur'an is nothing but a reminder to mankind.

74:32 Nay, by the moon,

74:33 by the night when it withdraws

74:34 and by the dawn when it brightens,

74:35 surely, it (hell) is one of the greatest signs,

74:36 a warning to mankind,

74:37 to any of you that chooses to go forward (by righteous deeds), or remain behind (by sins).

74:38 Every person is held in a pledge for what it has earned,

74:39 except those on the right (true believers),

74:40 in gardens (paradise) they will ask one another,

74:41 about the criminals. (They will say to them):

74:42 "What has caused you to enter into hell?"

74:43 They will say: "We were not of those who used to offer prayers,

74:44 nor we used to feed the poor,

74:45 we used to talk falsehood with vain talkers,

74:46 and we used to deny the day of recompense,

74:47 until there came to us the certainty (death)."

74:48 So (on that day) no intercession of intercessors will be of any use to them.

74:49 Then what is wrong with them (disbelievers) that they turn away from receiving the admonition?

74:50 As if they were frightened donkeys

74:51 fleeing from a hunter, or a lion, or a beast of prey.

74:52 Nay, every of them desires that it should be given pages spread out (writing from Allah that Islam is the right religion).

74:53 Nay! But they do not fear the hereafter (Allah's punishment).

74:54 Nay, surely, this (Qur'an) is an admonition.

74:55 So whoever wills (reads it), will reflect on it.

74:56 They will not take heed unless Allah wills. Allah is the one deserve that mankind should be afraid of Allah. Allah is the one who forgives.

75. Al-Qiyamah : The Resurrection

In the name of Allah, the Gracious, the Merciful

75:1 Allah swears by the day of Resurrection,

75:2 and Allah swears by the self-reproaching person (believer)!

75:3 Does mankind think that Allah will not assemble their bones?

75:4 Yes, Allah is Able to put together in perfect order the very tips of their fingers.

75:5 But mankind desires to continue committing sins.

75:6 He (mankind) asks: "When will be this day of Resurrection?"

75:7 So, (it will come) when the sight will be dazed,

75:8 the moon will be eclipsed,

75:9 and the sun and moon will be joined together:

75:10 on that day mankind will say: "Where (is the refuge) to flee?"

75:11 No! There will be no refuge!

75:12 On that day, the place of rest will only be to your Rabb.

75:13 On that day mankind will be informed of (their deeds) what they sent forward and what they left behind.

75:14 Nay! Mankind will be witness against themselves (body parts will speak about deeds),

75:15 though they may put forth their excuses (to cover evil deeds).

75:16 (O Muhammad) do not move your tongue with it (the Qur'an) to make haste therewith (to memorize the verses),

75:17 surely, it is upon Allah to collect it and give you (O Muhammad) the ability to recite it (the Qur'an),

75:18 and when Allah has recited it to you (O Muhammad through Gabriel), then you follow its (the Qur'an's) recitation,

75:19 then surely, it is for Allah to make it clear to you,

75:20 nay but you (mankind) love the present life of this world,

75:21 and leave the hereafter.

75:22 On that day, some faces will be radiant,

75:23 looking towards their Rabb.

75:24 On that day, other faces will be gloomy,

75:25 thinking that some calamity is about to fall on them.

75:26 Nay, when it (the soul) reaches to the collar bone (up to the throat in its exit),

75:27 and it will be said: "Who can cure (save from death)?"

75:28 He (dying person) will conclude that it was the time of departure (death);

75:29 and one leg will be joined with another leg (shrouded);

75:30 on that day, the drive will be to your Rabb!

75:31 So the disbeliever neither believed nor prayed;

75:32 but (on the contrary) the disbeliever denied (this Qur'an) and turned away!

75:33 Then the disbeliever walked to its family admiring itself!

75:34 Woe to you (disbeliever)! Then woe to you!

75:35 (Again) woe to you (disbeliever)! Then woe to you!

75:36 Does the human think that it will be left (to wander) without requital (any purpose)?

75:37 Was the human not a drop of emitted semen?

75:38 Then the human became a hanging clot; then Allah created and fashioned it in due proportion,

75:39 and made it either of the 2 sexes, male and female.

75:40 Is not Allah Able to give life to the dead?

76. Ad-Dahr : The Time

In the name of Allah, the Gracious, the Merciful

76:1 Has there not come over human, a period of time when it was not a thing worth mentioning?

76:2 Surely, Allah has created human from the sperm drop of mixed semen (containing both sexual discharge) in order to test human. So Allah gave people to hear and see.

76:3 Surely, Allah showed human the way, whether it be grateful or ungrateful.

76:4 Surely, Allah has prepared for the disbelievers iron chains, iron collars, and a blazing fire.

76:5 Surely, the righteous shall drink from a cup (of wine) mixed with water from a spring in paradise called Kafoor,

76:6 a spring from where the servants of Allah will drink, causing it to gush out abundantly.

76:7 They fulfill their vows, and fear the day whose evil will be widespread,

76:8 who feed the food to poor, the orphan, and the captive for the love of Allah,

76:9 (saying): "We feed you for the sake of Allah's pleasure only. We wish neither reward nor thanks from you.

76:10 Surely, we fear from our Rabb a hard and distressful day that will make the faces look horrible."

76:11 So Allah will save them from the evil of that day, and bestow on them a radiant light and joy,

76:12 and Allah will compensate them (paradise) and garments of silk because they were patient.

76:13 (They will) recline on raised thrones in it; they will feel neither the excessive heat of the sun nor the excessive bitter cold in it.

76:14 (The trees of paradise) will have shade close upon them, and the bunches of fruits will hang low (within their reach) in it.

76:15 They will be served with round dishes of silver, cups of crystal,

76:16 crystal-clear, made of silver. They will determine the measure there (according to their wishes).

76:17 They will also be given to drink a cup (of wine) that is mixed with ginger,

76:18 from a spring there, called Salsabil.

76:19 They will be attended by boys (servants) of everlasting youth. If you see them, you would think them like scattered pearls.

76:20 Wherever you look there (in paradise), you will see a delight and a great dominion.

76:21 Their honoring garments (of the people of paradise) will be made of fine green silk and gold embroidery. They will be adorned with bracelets of silver and their Rabb will give them pure drink to drink.

76:22 (It will be said to them): "Surely, this is a reward for you and your endeavor is appreciated and accepted."

76:23 Surely! It is Allah who have sent down this Qur'an to you (O Muhammad) in stages,

76:24 therefore be patient (O Muhammad) for the command of your Rabb and do not yield to a sinner or a disbeliever among them.

76:25 Remember the name of your Rabb every morning and afternoon;

76:26 prostrate yourself to Allah at night and glorify Allah during long night hours.

76:27 Surely! These disbelievers love the present life of this world and leave behind them a heavy day (that will come).

76:28 It is Allah who created them and made their joints strong. But if Allah wills, Allah can replace (them with others) like them with a complete replacement.

76:29 Surely! This (verses of the Qur'an) is an admonition, so those who will, let them adapt the way to their Rabb,

76:30 but you cannot will, unless Allah wills. Surely, Allah is All-Knower, All-Wise.

76:31 Allah admits to Allah's Mercy whom Allah wills, and for the wrongdoers Allah has prepared a painful punishment.

77. Al-Mursalat: Those sent Forth

In the name of Allah, the Gracious, the Merciful

77:1 By the emissary winds (sent forth) one after another,

77:2 by the raging hurricanes,

77:3 by (the winds) that scatter (the clouds) to distant places,

77:4 then separate them one from another,

77:5 by those (angels) who bring down the reminder (to the messengers),

77:6 either to (remove all) excuses or to (covey the) warning.

77:7 Surely, what you are promised must be fulfilled.

77:8 (It will be fulfilled) when the stars will lose their light,

77:9 when the heaven will cleft asunder,

77:10 when the mountains will blow away (into dust),

77:11 when the messengers will be gathered to their appointed time.

77:12 For what day are these signs deferred?

77:13 For the day of sorting out (judgment)!

77:14 What will make you know, what is the day of sorting out?

77:15 Woe on that day to the deniers (of the day of Resurrection)!

77:16 Did Allah not destroy the previous generations (for evil deeds)?

77:17 Then Allah will make later generations to follow them.

77:18 Thus Allah will deal with the criminals!

77:19 Woe on that day to the deniers (of the day of Resurrection)!

77:20 Has Allah not created you from a worthless fluid (semen),

77:21 which Allah placed in a place of safety (womb),

77:22 for a known period?

77:23 Allah has measured (its term) and Allah is the best to measure (things).

77:24 Woe on that day to the deniers (of the day of Resurrection)!

77:25 Has Allah not made the earth a home for both

77:26 the living and the dead,

77:27 placed on it firm, tall and high mountains, and given you sweet water to drink?

77:28 Woe on that day to the deniers (of the day of Resurrection)!

77:29 (It will be said to the disbelievers on the Day of Judgment): "You depart to that (hell) which you used to deny!

77:30 You depart towards the shadow (of hellfire smoke ascending) in 3 columns,

77:31 neither shady nor of any use against the fierce flame of the fire,

77:32 surely! it (hell) throws up huge sparks like a castle,

77:33 as if they were yellow camels."

77:34 Woe on that day to the deniers (of the day of Resurrection)!

77:35 That will be the day when they shall not be able to speak,

77:36 they will not be permitted to put forth any excuse for them.

77:37 Woe on that day to the deniers (of the day of Resurrection)!

77:38 Such will be the day of decision! Allah will bring you and your previous generations together!

77:39 So, if you have a plot, then plot against Allah!

77:40 Woe on that day to the deniers (of the day of Resurrection)!

77:41 Surely, the pious shall reside in shades and springs

77:42 and they will have whatever fruits they desire.

77:43 (It will be said to them): "Eat and drink comfortably for that which you used to do (good deeds)."

77:44 Surely, thus Allah will reward the righteous.

77:45 Woe on that day to the deniers (of the day of Resurrection)!

77:46 (O disbelievers)! Eat and enjoy yourselves (in this worldly life) for a little while. Surely, you are the criminals.

77:47 Woe on that day to the deniers (of the day of Resurrection)!

77:48 When it is said to them: "Bow down yourself (in prayer before Allah)!" They do not bow down.

77:49 Woe on that day to the deniers (of the day of Resurrection)!

77:50 Then in what statement after this (the Qur'an), will they believe?

78. An-Naba' : The Great News
In the name of Allah, the Gracious, the Merciful

78:1 About what are they asking (one another)?

78:2 About the great news (Islam),

78:3 about which they disagree.

78:4 Nay, they will come to know,

78:5 nay, again, they will come to know (very soon).

78:6 Has not Allah made the earth like a bed,

78:7 the mountains as pegs,

78:8 created you in pairs,

78:9 made your sleep for rest,

78:10 made the night as a covering,

78:11 made the day (to work) for livelihood,

78:12 built above you 7 strong (heavens),

78:13 placed in it a shinning lamp (sun),

78:14 sent down abundant water from the clouds,

78:15 thereby to produce corn and vegetation in it,

78:16 and gardens of thick growth?

78:17 Surely, the day of decision is a fixed time.

78:18 On that day, the trumpet will be blown in and you shall come forth in crowds.

78:19 The sky will be opened, as if there were doors.

78:20 The mountains will be moved away, as if they were a mirage.

78:21 Truly, hell is a place of ambush,

78:22 a living place for the transgressors.

78:23 They will live in it for ages,

78:24 they will neither taste cool nor any drink in it,

78:25 except boiling water and pus (dirty wound discharges):

78:26 as a fitting recompense (for their evil deeds).

78:27 Surely, they never expected a reckoning (for their deeds),

78:28 and denied Allah's revelations with strong denial.

78:29 But Allah has recorded every thing in a book.

78:30 (It will be said): "So you taste (the results of evil actions). Allah will give you nothing but increase in punishment."

78:31 Surely, there will be a success (paradise) for the righteous:

78:32 gardens and grape yards,

78:33 young mature maidens of equal age,

78:34 full cups (of wine to the brim);

78:35 they will neither hear vain talk nor any lying in it;

78:36 a reward from your Rabb and a gift beyond their account (for good deeds)

78:37 from the Rabb of the heavens and the earth, and whatever is between them; the Gracious, before Allah no one will be able to speak (on the day of Resurrection).

78:38 On that day, the spirit (Gabriel) and the angels will stand in rows; none will speak except the one to whom the Gracious (Allah) will allow to speak, and that person will speak what is right.

78:39 That is (without doubt) the true day. Let those who wish, seek a way back to their Rabb (by obeying Allah in this world).

78:40 Surely, Allah has warned you of an imminent punishment, on the day when people will see (the deeds) what their hands have sent forth, and the disbeliever will cry: "Woe to me! Would that I were dust!"

79. An-Nazi'at : Those who Pull Out
In the name of Allah, the Gracious, the Merciful

79:1 By those (angels) who violently pull out (the souls of the disbelievers),

79:2 by those (angels) who gently draw out (the souls of the believers),

79:3 by those (angels) who swim swiftly (through space),

79:4 by those (angels) who press forward in a race (to fulfill Allah's orders),

79:5 by those (angels) who arrange to execute the commands (of their Rabb).

79:6 On the day when the first blowing of the trumpet will shake (the earth, the mountains, and everybody will die),

79:7 the second blowing of the trumpet will follow it (everybody will raise up).

79:8 On that day, hearts will beat (with fear and anxiety),

79:9 their eyes will be downcast.

79:10 They (disbelievers) say: "Shall we really be returned to the former state of life,

79:11 when we will become crumbled bones?"

79:12 They say: "In that case, it would be a return with loss!"

79:13 But it will be only a single shout (the second blowing of the trumpet),

79:14 when they will be awakened (alive after death).

79:15 Have you heard the story of Moses?

79:16 When his Rabb called him in the sacred valley of Tuwa,

79:17 and said: "Go to Pharaoh, surely he has transgressed all bounds,

79:18 and say to him: 'Do you have the desire to purify yourself (from sins)?

79:19 I will guide you to your Rabb, so that you may fear (Allah).'"

79:20 Then he (Moses) showed him (Pharaoh) the great sign (miracles),

79:21 but he (Pharaoh) denied and disobeyed.

79:22 Then he turned his back and strive (against Allah),

79:23 gathered his people and cried aloud,

79:24 saying: "I am your Rabb, most high."

79:25 So Allah seized him with punishment for the hereafter and this life.

79:26 Surely, in this, there is an admonition for those who fear (Allah).

79:27 Are you (O mankind) more difficult to create or the heaven that Allah constructed?

79:28 Allah raised its canopy and perfected it,

79:29 Allah covers its night with darkness and brings out light in its forenoon.

79:30 After that, Allah spreads out the earth,

79:31 and brings out its water and its pasture from there,

79:32 fixed the mountains firmly,

79:33 made a provision and benefit for you and for your cattle.

79:34 But when the greatest catastrophe (the day of recompense) will strike,

79:35 the day when people will remember what they had striven for.

79:36 When hellfire shall be made apparent in full view for those who see,

79:37 then, those who transgressed all bounds (evil deeds)

79:38 and preferred the worldly life,

79:39 surely, will have their abode in hell.

79:40 But those who feared standing before their Rabb and restrained themselves from evil desires,

79:41 then surely, will have their homes in paradise.

79:42 They ask you (O Muhammad) about the hour: "When will be its appointed time?"

79:43 But you have no knowledge to say anything about it.

79:44 Only your Rabb (has knowledge of) the term of it.

79:45 You (O Muhammad) are only a warner for those who fear it.

79:46 On that day, when they will see it, it will be as if they had not stayed (in this world) only an afternoon or one morning.

80. 'Abasa : He Frowned
In the name of Allah, the Gracious, the Merciful

80:1 He (the prophet) frowned and turned away,

80:2 when there came to him the blind man (Abdullah bin Umme Maktoom, who came to the prophet while the prophet was preaching to the chiefs of Makkah).

80:3 How can you know? He might become pure (from sins)

80:4 or he might receive admonition, and the admonition might profit him.

80:5 As for those who think themselves indifferent,

80:6 to whom you were attending;

80:7 you will not be held responsible, if they would not purify themselves (your duty is to convey the message of Allah).

80:8 Yet, to him who came to you running (with enthusiasm)

80:9 and with fear (of Allah),

80:10 you were unmindful from him.

80:11 Nay, (you should not do so), indeed this is an admonition;

80:12 so those who want, let them pay attention to it.

80:13 It is written in honored records,

80:14 exalted (in dignity), purified,

80:15 in the hands of scribes (angels),

80:16 (who are) honorable and obedient.

80:17 Be cursed (disbelieving) people! How ungrateful they are!

80:18 Out of what Allah has created them?

80:19 From semen drop Allah has created them and then set them in due proportion,

80:20 then makes their way (of life) easy for them,

80:21 then causes them to die and puts them in their graves.

80:22 Then, Allah will surely resurrect them again when Allah wills.

80:23 Nay, but they (disbelievers) have not fulfilled what Allah has commanded them.

80:24 Then let people look at their food.

80:25 Allah pours out water (rain) in abundance

80:26 then splits the earth (soil) in clefts.

80:27 Allah causes to grow in it the grain,

80:28 grapes and clover plants,

80:29 olives and date-palms,

80:30 gardens, dense with many trees,

80:31 fruits and fodder,

80:32 as a provision and benefit for you and your cattle.

80:33 Then when there will come the deafening shout,

80:34 on that day a person will flee from its brother,

80:35 its mother and its father,

80:36 its spouse and its children.

80:37 On that day, every person will have enough concern to become careless of others.

80:38 Some faces on that day will be bright (for true believers),

80:39 laughing, rejoicing at good news (of paradise).

80:40 Other faces on that day will be dusty,

80:41 darkness will cover them.

80:42 Such will be the (faces of the) disbelieving wicked.

81. At-Takwir : The Overthrowing

In the name of Allah, the Gracious, the Merciful

81:1 When the sun will cease to shine (overthrown);

81:2 when the stars will fall;

81:3 when the mountains will be moved away;

81:4 when the pregnant she-camels will be neglected (unattended);

81:5 when the wild beasts will be gathered together;

81:6 when the seas will overflow (or set on fire);

81:7 when the souls will be joined (with their bodies);

81:8 when the infant girl buried alive (as the pagan Arabs used to do) will be questioned

81:9 for what sin she was killed;

81:10 when the written pages (record of deeds) will be laid open;

81:11 when the heaven will be stripped off (taken away from its place);

81:12 when hellfire will be kindled to blaze (fierce heat);

81:13 and when paradise will be brought near;

81:14 then every person will know what it has brought (of good and evil).

81:15 So surely, Allah swears by the planets that recede;

81:16 that move swiftly and hide themselves;

81:17 by the night as it departs;

81:18 by the dawn as it brightens;

81:19 surely, this is the word (this Qur'an) of a honorable messenger (Gabriel from Allah to Muhammad),

81:20 possessor of mighty power, established (high rank) with the Owner of the Throne (Allah),

81:21 obeyed (by the angels in the heaven), and trustworthy.

81:22 (O people of Makkah) your companion (Muhammad) is not a mad man,

81:23 indeed he (Muhammad) saw him (Gabriel) in the clear horizon

81:24 and he (Muhammad) does not withhold knowledge on the unseen.

81:25 This (Qur'an) is not the word of the outcast Satan.

81:26 Then where are you going?

81:27 This (the Qur'an) is but a reminder to the people of the worlds,

81:28 to whoever among you who wishes to follow the right way.

81:29 Yet, you will not (avail your wishes) unless that Allah wills, the Rabb of the worlds.

82. Al-Infitar : The Cleaving
In the name of Allah, the Gracious, the Merciful

82:1 When the heaven will cleft asunder;

82:2 when the stars will scatter;

82:3 when the oceans are burst out;

82:4 and when the graves will be turned upside down (bring out their contents);

82:5 then every person will know what it has sent forward and what left behind.

82:6 O people! What has made you careless about your Rabb, the Generous,

82:7 who created you, fashioned you perfectly, gave you due proportion,

82:8 and put you together in whatever form Allah willed?

82:9 Nay! But you deny the Day of Judgment!

82:10 But surely, (angels have been appointed to watch) over you,

82:11 (who are) honorable writers,

82:12 they know all of what you do.

82:13 Surely, (on that day) the righteous will be in delight (paradise);

82:14 surely, the wicked (evil-doers) will be in the fire (hell),

82:15 they will burn in it on the day of recompense,

82:16 and they will not be able to escape from it.

82:17 What will make you know what the day of the recompense is?

82:18 Again, what will make you know what the day of recompense is?

82:19 It will be the day when no one will have the power to do anything for any another: on that day, the decision will be entirely with Allah.

83. Al-Mutaffifin : Those who deal in Fraud
In the name of Allah, the Gracious, the Merciful

83:1 Woe to those who give less in measure and weight (defraud),

83:2 those who, when they receive by measure from people, demand full measure,

83:3 but when they give by measure or give by weight to others, they give less than due.

83:4 Don't they think that they will be resurrected

83:5 on a great day,

83:6 the day when all mankind will stand before the Rabb of the worlds?

83:7 Nay! Truly, the record of the deeds of the wicked is (preserved) in prison register (Sijjin),

83:8 what will make you know what Sijjin is?

83:9 A register inscribed (of hell).

83:10 Woe on that day to those who deny (disbelievers),

83:11 who deny the day of recompense!

83:12 None can deny it except every transgressor beyond bounds, the sinner!

83:13 When Allah's verses (of the Qur'an) are recited to them, they say: "Tales of the ancients!"

83:14 Nay! But their sins and evil deeds which they used to earn have caused a covering on their hearts.

83:15 Nay! Surely, on that day, they (evil-doers) will be veiled from (the vision of) their Rabb.

83:16 Then, surely they will indeed burn in the hell,

83:17 and it will be said to them: "This is what you used to deny!"

83:18 Nay! Surely, the record of the righteous deeds is indeed (preserved) in register of exalted ones (Illiyun),

83:19 and what will make you know what Illiyun is?

83:20 A register inscribed (of paradise),

83:21 bears witness of those who are nearest (to Allah, i.e. the angels).

83:22 Surely, the righteous will be in delight (paradise),

83:23 on thrones, looking (at all things),

83:24 you will recognize in their faces the brightness of delight.

83:25 They will be given to drink from pure sealed wine,

83:26 the seal of that wine will be smell of musk. Those who want to strive, let them strive.

83:27 That (wine) will be a mixture of Tasnim,

83:28 a spring where those nearest to Allah will drink.

83:29 Surely! Those who committed crimes (in this world), they used to laugh at those who believed,

83:30 and wink one to another (in mockery) whenever they passed by them.

83:31 When they returned to their own people, they would return joking.

83:32 When they saw them (believers), they used to say: "Surely! These people have indeed gone astray,"

83:33 though they (disbelievers) had not been sent over them (believers) as watchers.

83:34 On that day (the day of Resurrection) the believers will laugh at the disbelievers,

83:35 as they recline on high couches and look (at then saying):

83:36 "Are not the disbelievers rewarded for what they used to do?"

84. Al-Inshiqaq : The Splitting Asunder
In the name of Allah, the Gracious, the Merciful

84:1 When the heaven will split asunder,

84:2 listens to and obeys its Rabb and it must do so.

84:3 When the earth will stretch out

84:4 and cast out all that is in it and becomes empty,

84:5 listens and obeys to its Rabb and it must do so.

84:6 O mankind! Surely, you must strive very hard towards your Rabb; then you will meet Allah.

84:7 Then those who will be given their record (of deeds) in their right hand,

84:8 surely they will receive easy reckoning

84:9 and will return to their family in joy!

84:10 But those who will be given their record (of deeds) from behind their back,

84:11 will invoke for destruction,

84:12 and shall burn in a blazing fire;

84:13 for they used to live among their people in joy,

84:14 and thought that they would never come back (to Allah for accounts)!

84:15 Yes! Surely, their Rabb was watching (over their misdeeds)!

84:16 So Allah swears by the glow of sunset;

84:17 by the night and whatever it gathers in its darkness;

84:18 by the moon when it grows full:

84:19 that you will certainly pass from stage to stage (this life and the hereafter).

84:20 What is the matter with the people that they do not believe,

84:21 and when the Qur'an is recited to them, they do not prostrate?

84:22 Nay, the disbelievers will deny (Islam);

84:23 and Allah knows best what they are hiding (in their hearts).

84:24 So, announce to them, a painful punishment,

84:25 except those who believe and do good deeds; for them there will be a never ending reward (paradise).

85. Al-Buruj : The big Stars 'Buruj
In the name of Allah, the Gracious, the Merciful

85:1 By the heaven holding the big stars!

85:2 By the promised day (of judgment)!

85:3 By the witnesses and that which is being witnessed!

85:4 Cursed be the people of the ditch,

85:5 who lit the fire fed with fuel

85:6 and they sat by it (fire),

85:7 to watch what they were doing to the believers.

85:8 They took revenge on them for no other reason except that they believed in Allah, the All-Mighty, the Praise-worthy,

85:9 to whom belongs the dominion of the heavens and the earth! Allah is witness over everything.

85:10 Surely, those who persecute the believing men and believing women and do not repent (to Allah), then they will receive the punishment of hell and they will have the punishment of the burning fire.

85:11 Surely, those who believe and do righteous deeds, they will have gardens under which rivers flow (paradise). That is the great success.

85:12 Surely, (O Muhammad) the grip (punishment) of your Rabb is very severe.

85:13 Surely, it is Allah who originates (created everything) and will repeat it (on the day of Resurrection).

85:14 Allah is Forgiving, the Loving (to the pious),

85:15 the owner of the Throne, the Glorious

85:16 and Allah does whatever Allah intends (or wills).

85:17 Has the story reached you of the hosts

85:18 of Pharaoh and Thamud?

85:19 Nay! The disbelievers (persist) in denying (the truth),

85:20 and Allah has encompassed them from all around.

85:21 Nay! This is a glorious Qur'an,

85:22 (inscribed) in the preserved tablet (Al-Lauh Al-Mahfuz).

86. At-Tariq : The Night-Comer
In the name of Allah, the Gracious, the Merciful

86:1 By the heaven and the night-comer (the bright star),

86:2 and what will make you know what night-comer is?

86:3 It is the star of piercing brightness.

86:4 There is no human being but has a protector (angel) over that person.

86:5 So let a person see from what it is created!

86:6 It is created from an emitted fluid

86:7 that is produced from between the back-bone and the ribs.

86:8 Surely, Allah is Able to bring a person back (to life),

86:9 on the day when all the secrets will be examined,

86:10 then for that person, there will be neither power, nor any helper (to save from punishment).

86:11 By the sky (with rain clouds) with the returning rain (again and again)

86:12 and by the earth which splits (for springs or growth of trees and plants);

86:13 surely! this (Qur'an) is the word that separates (the truth from falsehood),

86:14 and it is not for amusement.

86:15 Surely, these (unbelievers) are plotting a plot (against you O Muhammad):

86:16 and I (Allah) too am plotting a plan.

86:17 So give a respite to the disbelievers. Give respite to them gently (for a while).

87. Al-A'la : The High
In the name of Allah, the Gracious, the Merciful

87:1 Glorify the name of your Rabb, the High,

87:2 who has created everything, and then proportioned them.

87:3 Who has measured (destinies) and then guided them.

87:4 Who brings out the pasture (vegetation eaten by animals),

87:5 then makes it dark rubbish.

87:6 Allah will make you recite (the Qur'an) so you (O Muhammad) shall not forget it

87:7 except what Allah wills. Surely Allah knows what is open and what is hidden.

87:8 Allah will make it easy for you (O Muhammad) to follow the easy way (to do righteous deeds).

87:9 Therefore remind, surely, reminder does benefit.

87:10 Whoever fears (Allah) will heed the reminder,

87:11 and the wretched will avoid it,

87:12 who will burn in the great fire,

87:13 where it will neither die in it nor live (a good living).

87:14 Indeed whoever purifies itself shall achieve success,

87:15 who remembers the name of its Rabb and prays.

87:16 Nay, (O people) you prefer the worldly life,

87:17 although the hereafter is better and everlasting.

87:18 Surely! This is in the former scriptures,

87:19 the scriptures of Abraham and Moses.

88. Al-Ghashiyah : The Overwhelming
In the name of Allah, the Gracious, the Merciful

88:1 Has the news of the overwhelming event (of Resurrection) reached you?

88:2 On that day some faces will be humiliated (in the hellfire),

88:3 in hard labor, worn out,

88:4 burn in the hot blazing fire,

88:5 given to drink from a boiling spring.

88:6 They will have no food except bitter thorny fruit,

88:7 that will neither nourish nor satisfy hunger.

88:8 Other faces on that day will be joyful,

88:9 pleased with their endeavors (of good deeds)

88:10 in a high garden (paradise).

88:11 They will hear no vain talk in it.

88:12 They will have a running spring in it.

88:13 They will be on thrones raised high in it,

88:14 with cups placed at hand;

88:15 cushions set in rows

88:16 and rich carpets spread out.

88:17 Don't they look at the camels, how they are created?

88:18 The sky, how it is raised?

88:19 The mountains, how they are fixed firmly?

88:20 The earth, how it is spread out?

88:21 So remind them (O Muhammad), you are only a reminder,

88:22 not a dictator over them.

88:23 Except those who turn away and disbelieve,

88:24 then Allah will punish them with the greatest punishment.

88:25 Surely, to Allah will be their return,

88:26 then surely, Allah will take their reckoning.

89. Al-Fajr : The Dawn
In the name of Allah, the Gracious, the Merciful

89:1 By the dawn,

89:2 by the 10 nights (first 10 days of the month of Dhul-Hijja),

89:3 by the even and the odd (of all the creations of Allah),

89:4 and by the night when it departs!

89:5 Are there not in them (these oaths) sufficient proofs for the people of understanding?

89:6 Have you (O Muhammad) not seen how your Rabb dealt with Ad (people)?

89:7 (Tall residents of) Iram with lofty pillars,

89:8 the like of which were not created like them in the land.

89:9 With Thamud (people), who cut out rocks in the valley (to make residences)?

89:10 With Pharaoh who had the stakes?

89:11 They all transgressed beyond bounds in the lands,

89:12 and made much mischief in it.

89:13 So your Rabb poured on them different kinds of punishment.

89:14 Surely, your Rabb is ever watchful (over them).

89:15 As for people, when their Rabb tries them and gives them honor and bounties, they say: "Our Rabb has honored us."

89:16 But when Allah tries them through restricting their means of life, then they say: "Our Rabb has humiliated us!"

89:17 Nay! But you did not treat the orphans with kindness and generosity,

89:18 nor did you encourage each other in feeding the poor!

89:19 You devour inheritance (of the weak) with greed,

89:20 and you love wealth with much love!

89:21 Nay! When the earth will be grounded to exceeding grinding (powder),

89:22 your Rabb will come with the angels standing in rows,

89:23 hell will be brought near (in sight) that day. On that day people will remember (their deeds), but how the remembrance will avail them?

89:24 One will say: "Alas! Would that I had sent forth (good deeds) for my life?"

89:25 On that day, none will punish anymore except Allah's punishment,

89:26 and none can bind anyone like Allah's binding.

89:27 (It will be said to the pious): "O you the one in satisfaction!

89:28 Come back to your Rabb, well-pleased (yourself) and well-pleasing (to Allah).

89:29 Then you enter among my (Allah's) servants,

89:30 and you enter my (Allah's) paradise!"

90. Al-Balad : The City
In the name of Allah, the Gracious, the Merciful

90:1 Allah swears by this city (Makkah, where it is prohibited to harm anyone),

90:2 you (O Muhammad) are free (from sin to punish the enemies of Islam) in this city (Makka),

90:3 and by the father (Adam) and the children which he begot (mankind),

90:4 surely, Allah has created human in toil (to work hard).

90:5 Does human think that none can overcome them?

90:6 Human says (boastfully): "I have wasted wealth in abundance!"

90:7 Does human thinks that none sees them?

90:8 Has Allah not made for them a pair of eyes (to see)?

90:9 A tongue and a pair of lips (to control)?

90:10 Shown him the 2 ways (good and evil)?

90:11 Yet, human has not attempted to pass on the steep path (Aqabah)!

90:12 What will make you know what the steep path is?

90:13 (It is) the freeing of a neck (slave from bondage);

90:14 or giving food in a day of hunger (famine)

90:15 to an orphan relative,

90:16 or to a poor clinging to dust (out of misery);

90:17 then human should be one of those who believe, recommend one another to the patience, and recommend one another to kindness and compassion.

90:18 They are the people of the right hand (people of paradise).

90:19 But those who disbelieve in Allah's revelations, they are the people of the left hand (people of hell),

90:20 with the fire all around them.

91. Ash-Shams : The Sun
In the name of Allah, the Gracious, the Merciful

91:1 By the sun and its brightness,

91:2 by the moon as it follows it (sun),

91:3 by the day as it shows up (the sun's) brightness,

91:4 by the night as it conceals it (the sun),

91:5 by the heaven and Allah who built it,

91:6 by the earth and Allah who spread it,

91:7 by the soul and Allah who perfected it in proportion;

91:8 and Allah inspired it with (knowledge of) what is wrong for it and what is right for it.

91:9 Indeed one will succeed who purifies its own self (obey Allah),

91:10 and indeed one will fail who corrupts it (disobey Allah).

91:11 Thamud (people) denied (their prophet) through their transgression (by rejecting the truth)

91:12 when the most wicked person among them went out (to kill the she-camel).

91:13 The messenger of Allah (Saleh) said to them: "That is the she-camel of Allah! (Do not harm it and do not stop it from) its drink."

91:14 They denied him and killed her. So their Rabb destroyed them because of their sin, and made them equal in destruction (leveled to ground).

91:15 Allah has no fear of its consequences.

92. Al-Lail : The Night
In the name of Allah, the Gracious, the Merciful

92:1 By the night, when it covers (with darkness),

92:2 and by the day, when it appears in brightness.

92:3 By Allah who created the male and the female,

92:4 surely, your efforts are indeed diverse (different purpose).

92:5 As for the one who gives (in charity), fears Allah,

92:6 and believes in the best (deed),

92:7 Allah will make smooth for that person (the path) of ease.

92:8 As for the one who is miser and thinks itself self-sufficient,

92:9 and denies the best (deed),

92:10 Allah will make smooth for him (the path) for evil.

92:11 Think! what its wealth will benefit when one goes down (doomed)?

92:12 Surely! (It is) on Allah to give guidance,

92:13 and surely, to Allah belongs the last (hereafter) and the first (this world).

92:14 Therefore, Allah warns you of the blazing fire (of hell),

92:15 In which none will burn except the most wretched

92:16 who denies (the truth) and turns away.

92:17 But the pious will be far removed from it (hell),

92:18 the one who spends its wealth (in charity) that may grow (for self-purification),

92:19 who has in mind no favor from anyone to be paid back,

92:20 except to seek the pleasure of its Rabb, the High.

92:21 Surely such person will be pleased (with Allah when it will enter paradise).

93. Ad-Duha : The Forenoon
In the name of Allah, the Gracious, the Merciful

93:1 By the morning day light,

93:2 and by the night when it covers (with darkens),

93:3 (O Muhammad) your Rabb has neither forsaken you nor displeased with you.

93:4 Indeed, the hereafter will be better for you than the first (worldly life).

93:5 Surely, your Rabb will give you (all good) so that you will be well-pleased.

93:6 Did Allah not find you (O Muhammad) an orphan and gave you a refuge?

93:7 Did Allah not find you (O Muhammad) lost and gave you guidance?

93:8 Did Allah not find you (O Muhammad) poor and made you rich (self-sufficient)?

93:9 So, do not treat the orphan with oppression,

93:10 and do not repulse the beggar,

93:11 and proclaim the grace of your Rabb.

94. Ash-Sharh : The Opening Forth
In the name of Allah, the Gracious, the Merciful

94:1 Has Allah not opened your heart for you (O Muhammad)

94:2 and removed your burden from you

94:3 which weighed down your back,

94:4 and raised high for you your fame?

94:5 Surely, with the hardship, there is relief.

94:6 Surely, with the hardship, there is relief.

94:7 So, when you have finished (your work), then stand up (for Allah's worship)

94:8 and turn (your attention) to your Rabb.

95. At-Tin : The Fig
In the name of Allah, the Gracious, the Merciful

95:1 By the fig and by the olive,

95:2 by the mount of Sinai,

95:3 and by this city of security (Makkah).

95:4 Surely, Allah has created people in the best stature;

95:5 then Allah will reduce it to the lowest of the low

95:6 except those who believe (in Islam) and do righteous deeds, then for them will be a reward without end (paradise).

95:7 So, what causes you (disbelievers) to deny you about the Day of Judgment?

95:8 Is not Allah the best of the judges?

96. Al-'Alaq : The Clot
In the name of Allah, the Gracious, the Merciful

96:1 Read! In the name of your Rabb, who has created (everything),

96:2 created human from a clot (thick blood).

96:3 Read! Your Rabb is the Generous,

96:4 who has taught (writing) by the pen,

96:5 taught human what it did not know.

96:6 Nay! Surely, human does transgress,

96:7 because it considers itself self-sufficient,

96:8 surely, to your Rabb is the return.

96:9 Have you seen him (Abu Jahl) who prevents

96:10 a servant (Muhammad) from offering prays?

96:11 Have you seen if he (Muhammad) is on the guidance (of Allah),

96:12 or enjoins piety?

96:13 Have you seen if he (Abu Jahl) denies (truth) and turn away?

96:14 Does he (Abu Jahl) not know that Allah sees (everything)?

96:15 Nay! If he (Abu Jahl) does not stop, Allah will catch him by the forelock,

96:16 a lying, sinful forelock.

96:17 So let him call his council (of help),

96:18 Allah will call out the guards of hell (to deal with him).

96:19 Nay! (O Muhammad)! Do not obey him (Abu Jahl). Prostrate and draw near (to Allah).

97. Al-Qadr : The Night of Decree
In the name of Allah, the Gracious, the Merciful

97:1 Surely! Allah has sent this (Qur'an) down in the night of decree (Qadr).

97:2 What will make you understand what the night of decree (Qadr) is?

97:3 The night of decree is better than 1,000 months.

97:4 The angels and the spirit (Gabriel) descend at that night by the permission of their Rabb with all decrees.

97:5 (All that night) there is peace till the appearance of dawn.

98. Al-Bayyinah : The Clear Evidence
In the name of Allah, the Gracious, the Merciful

98:1 Those who disbelieve from among the people of the scripture and from the polytheists were not going to leave (from their disbelief) until clear evidence came to them,

98:2 a messenger from Allah reciting from the purified pages,

98:3 containing correct and right laws (in scriptures).

98:4 Those who were given the scripture did not differ until after clear evidence (this Qur'an) came to them.

98:5 They were commanded nothing but to worship Allah with their sincere devotion to Allah, being upright (true in their faith); to establish prayer, to pay obligatory charity; and that is the right religion.

98:6 Surely, those who disbelieve from among the people of the scripture and the polytheists will be in the fire of hell. They will abide in it forever. They are the worst of all creatures.

98:7 Surely, those who believe and do righteous deeds, are the best of all creatures.

98:8 Their reward with their Rabb shall be the gardens of Eden (eternity), beneath which rivers flow, they will abide in it forever. Allah will be pleased with them and they will be pleased with Allah. That is for those who fear their Rabb.

99. Az-Zalzalah : The Earthquake
In the name of Allah, the Gracious, the Merciful

99:1 When the earth will be shaken with its (final) earthquake,

99:2 and when the earth will throw out its inner burdens,

99:3 people will say: "What is the matter with it?"

99:4 On that day it will declare whatever had happened (to it),

99:5 because your Rabb will command it.

99:6 On that day, mankind will proceed in sorted groups so that they may be shown their (book of) deeds.

99:7 So whoever has done good equal to the weight of an atom, shall see it there,

99:8 and whoever has done evil equal to the weight of an atom, shall see it there.

100. Al-'Adiyat : Those that Run
In the name of Allah, the Gracious, the Merciful

100:1 By the (steeds) that run with panting (breath),

100:2 striking sparks of fire (by their hoops),

100:3 making raids in the morning,

100:4 leaving a trail of dust in it,

100:5 as they penetrate directly into the middle (of the enemy).

100:6 Surely! Human is ungrateful to its Rabb,

100:7 and verily, it bears witness to it (by its deeds),

100:8 and surely, it is violent in the love of wealth.

100:9 It does not know when the contents of the graves will be brought out (resurrected),

100:10 and that what is in the hearts (of people) will be made known,

100:11 surely, on that day (of Resurrection) their Rabb will be well-acquainted with them.

101. Al-Qari'ah : The Striking Hour
In the name of Allah, the Gracious, the Merciful

101:1 The striking hour (Qari'ah, the day of calamity)!

101:2 What is the striking hour?

101:3 What will make you know what the striking hour is?

101:4 It is the day when mankind will be like scattered moths

101:5 and the mountains will be like carded wool.

101:6 then as for the one whose balance (of good deeds) will be heavy,

101:7 will reside in a pleasant life (paradise).

101:8 But as for the one whose balance (of good deeds) will be light,

101:9 will abode in hell (Hawiyah);

101:10 and what will make you know what it (Hawiyah) is?

101:11 It is a blazing fire.

102: At-Takathur : The Piling Up
In the name of Allah, the Gracious, the Merciful

102:1 (O mankind) you are distracted by the mutual rivalry (of piling up of worldly gains),

102:2 (never be satisfied) until you come to the graves (die).

102:3 Nay! You will soon come to know!

102:4 Again, Nay! You will soon come to know!

102:5 Nay! If you knew with real knowledge (from Qur'an).

102:6 Surely, You will see the blazing fire (of hell),

102:7 you will see it with certainty of sight,

102:8 then, on that day, you shall be questioned about the blessings (given in the world and how you used)!

103. Al-'Asr : The Time
In the name of Allah, the Gracious, the Merciful

103:1 By the time (through the ages)!

103:2 Surely! Mankind is in loss,

103:3 except those who believe and do righteous deeds; exhort one another to the truth and exhort one another to patience.

104. Al-Humazah : The Slanderer
In the name of Allah, the Gracious, the Merciful

104:1 Woe to every slanderer and backbiter,

104:2 who gathers wealth and counts it.

104:3 One who thinks that its wealth will make it last forever!

104:4 Nay! Surely, it will be thrown into the crushing fire.

104:5 What will make you know what the crushing fire is?

104:6 The fire kindled by Allah.

104:7 The one who will leap up over the hearts,

104:8 surely, it will close on them (from all sides),

104:9 in outstretched pillars (of fire).

105: Al-Fil : The Elephant
In the name of Allah, the Gracious, the Merciful

105:1 Have you (O Muhammad) not seen how your Rabb dealt with the owners of the elephant (The elephant army came under the command of Abraha, king of Yemen, who intended to destroy the Ka'bah at Makkah in the year of Muhammad's year of birth)?

105:2 Did Allah not make their plot go in astray?

105:3 Allah sent against them birds in flocks,

105:4 which pelted them with stones of baked clay,

105:5 and Allah made them like the chewed-up stalks.

106. Quraish : Quraish
In the name of Allah, the Gracious, the Merciful

106:1 (It is a great blessing and protection from Allah) for the safety of Quraish (caretaker of the house of Allah),

106:2 for the safe passage (of their trade caravans) in winter and summer.

106:3 So let them worship the Rabb of this house (the Ka'bah in Makkah),

106:4 who provided them food against hunger and made them safe against fear.

107. Al-Ma'un : The Small Kindness
In the name of Allah, the Gracious, the Merciful

107:1 Have you seen the one who denies the Day of Judgment?

107:2 It is the one who drives away the orphan (harshly)

107:3 and do not encourage the feeding of the poor.

107:4 So woe to those who perform prayers (hypocrites),

107:5 but are heedless of their prayer;

107:6 those who do good deeds to be seen,

107:7 and they refuge (to share) small kindnesses.

108. Al-Kauther : A River in Paradise
In the name of Allah, the Gracious, the Merciful

108:1 Surely, Allah has granted you (O Muhammad) a river in paradise (Kauther).

108:2 Therefore, offer prayer to your Rabb and sacrifice.

108:3 Surely, your enemy is the one who will be cut off (from good of both worlds).

109. Al-Kafirun : The Disbelievers

In the name of Allah, the Gracious, the Merciful

109:1 Say (O Muhammad): "O disbelievers!

109:2 'I do not worship that whom you worship,

109:3 nor will you worship that whom I worship.

109:4 I will never worship those (deities) whom you worship,

109:5 nor will you ever worship (Allah) whom I worship,

109:6 to you be your religion, and to me my religion (Islam).'"

110. An-Nasr : The Help

In the name of Allah, the Gracious, the Merciful

110:1 When there comes the help of Allah (to you, O Muhammad against your enemies) and the victory (of Makkah),

110:2 you see the people entering in Allah's religion (Islam) in crowds.

110:3 So glorify the praises of your Rabb, and ask for Allah's forgiveness. Surely, Allah is the one who accepts repentance (and forgives).

111. Al-Masad : The Palm Fiber

In the name of Allah, the Gracious, the Merciful

111:1 Perish the 2 hands of Abu Lahab (an uncle of the prophet) and perish him!

111:2 His wealth and whatever he earned did not benefit him!

111:3 He will be burnt soon in a fire of blazing flames,

111:4 and his wife, the carrier of wood (she used to put thorns on the way of the prophet),

111:5 she will have a twisted rope of palm fiber around her neck.

112. Al-Ikhlas : The Purity

In the name of Allah, the Gracious, the Merciful

112:1 Say (O Muhammad): "Allah is the One and Only;

112:2 Allah is the Self-Sufficient (Samad: independent of all, while all are dependent on Allah);

112:3 Allah begets not, nor is Allah begotten,

112:4 and there is none comparable to Allah."

the Trinity does not contradict this because these are terms used only to describe a loving experience

113: Al-Falaq : The Daybreak

In the name of Allah, the Gracious, the Merciful

113:1 Say: "I seek refuge with the Rabb of the daybreak

113:2 from the evil of what Allah has created,

113:3 and from the evil of the darkness (night) as it comes with its darkness,

113:4 and from the evil of the witches who blow in the knots (black magic),

113:5 and from the evil of the envier when one envies."

114. An-Nas : The Mankind

In the name of Allah, the Gracious, the Merciful

114:1 Say: "I seek refuge with the Rabb of mankind,

114:2 the Owner of mankind,

114:3 the real one worthy of worship of mankind,

114:4 from the evil of the sneaking whispers (Satan and its workers),

114:5 who whispers into the hearts of people,

114:6 from the jinns and mankind."

References

1. *The Noble Qur'an - English Translation of the Meaning and Commentary,* Dr. Muhammad Taqi-ud-Din Al-Hilali, Dr. Muhammad Muhsin Khan, King Fahd Complex for the Printing of the Holy Qur'an, Madinah, Saudi Arabia.
2. *The Quran Translated,* International Committee for the Support of the Final Prophet (ICSFP), Washington, DC.
3. *English Translation of the Meaning of Al-Qur'an,* Muhammad Farooq-i-Azam Malik, Houston, Texas.
4. *The Meaning of the Illustrious Qur'an;* Abdullah Yusuf Ali.
5. *The Glorious Qur'an,* Muhammad Marmaduke Pickthall.
6. *Tafheem-ul-Qur'an,* Syed Abul A'la Maududi.
7. *Tafseer ibn Katheer,* Ibn-i-Katheer, Damascus, Syria.
8. *Bayan-al-Qur'an,* Ashraf Ali Thanwi, India
9. *English Translation of the Qur'an,* M.H. Shakir.
10. *Atlas of the Qur'an,* Dr. Shauqi Abu Khalil, Darusssalam, Riyadh, Saudi Arabia.
11. *Atlas on the Prophet's Biography,* Dr. Shauqi Abu Khalil, Darusssalam, Riyadh, Saudi Arabia.
12. *The Life of Muhammad,* Muhammad Husayn Haykal, North American Trust Publications.
13. *Muhammad,* Martin Lings, The Islamic Texts Society, Cambridge, UK

Informative Websites:
www.sultan.org
www.islamiccity.com
www.isna.net
www.islamworld.net
www.islamicnetwork.com
www.islamicfinder.org
www.thetruereligion.org
www.islameasy.org
www.islamfortoday.com
www.islam-guide.com
www.jews-for-Allah.org
www.msa-natl.org
www.finalrevelation.net
www.wheredoyoustand.com

Spanish websites:
www.IslamInSpanish.org
www.Islam.com.mx